The New International Relations
Edited by Barry Buzan,
University of Warwick, and
Gerald Segal,
International Institute for Strategic Studies, London

The field of international relations has changed dramatically in recent years. This new series will cover the major issues that have emerged and reflect the latest academic thinking in this particularly dynamic area.

International Law, Rights and Politics
Developments in Eastern Europe and the CIS
Rein Mullerson

The Logic of Internationalism
Coercion and accommodation
Kjell Goldmann

Russia and the Idea of Europe
A Study in Identity and International Relations
Iver B. Neumann

The Future of International Relations

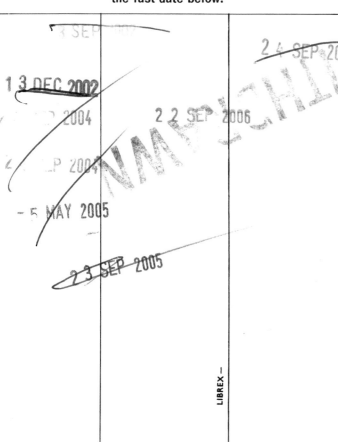
the art of inter-
rk of twelve key
edure in the field
orists with others,
it or paradigm. A
ounded character
ore representative

of international
hapter places the
v they go about
rs can learn from

bert O. Keohane,
l Alker, Nicholas
Valker and James

at the Norwegian
iet Fellow at the
Senior Research
RI). He is also
ity of California

The Future of International Relations

Masters in the Making?

Edited by Iver B. Neumann and Ole Wæver

London and New York

First published 1997
by Routledge
11 New Fetter Lane, London EC4P 4EE

Simultaneously published in the USA and Canada
by Routledge
29 West 35th Street, New York, NY 10001

Typeset in Times by
Pure Tech India Ltd, Pondicherry, India.
Printed and bound in Great Britain by Mackays of Chatham PLC,
Chatham, Kent

British Library Cataloguing in Publication Data
A catalogue record for this book is available from the British Library

Library of Congress Cataloging in Publication Data
A catalogue record for this book has been requested

ISBN 0-415-14407-8 (hbk)
     0-415-14408-6 (pbk)

Contents

Figures

Tables

Contributors

Jenny Edkins teaches in the Department of International Politics at the University of Wales, Aberystwyth where she is completing a PhD on theories of ideology and international politics, centred on a study of discourses of African famine. She also teaches for the Open University and for the Extra Mural Department in Aberystwyth. Her publications include 'Post-International Politics: An Emerging Dissident Literature' (with Véronique Pin-Fat), in Rohit Lekhi (ed.) *The State of the Academy: New Reflections on Political Studies*, London: Network, 1995. She is a convenor of the Aberystwyth PostInternational Group (APIG), and is currently working on a book (with Nalini Persram and Véronique Pin-Fat) based on APIG's recent Sovereignty and Subjectivity conference.

Stefano Guzzini, PhD, is Assistant Professor at the Central European University, Budapest College. He has recently published: 'Structural Power: the Limits of Neo-realist Power Analysis', *International Organization*, 1993; 'The "Long Night of the First Republic": Years of Clientelistic Implosion in Italy', *Review of International Political Economy* 1995, which appeared also in the *Revue Française de Science Politique* 44(6) (December 1994); and *Realism in International Relations and International Political Economy: The Continuing Story of a Death Foretold*, London, New York: Routledge, 1996.

Lene Hansen holds an MA in political science and is currently a PhD candidate at the Institute of Political Science, University of Copenhagen, writing a dissertation about the role of NATO in post-Cold War European security. She has published review essays on European security in *Co-operation and Conflict* and *Peace and Change* and with Helle Stauersböll written *International Forvaltnings Teori: En Model of dens begrænsninger – UNESCO, UNCTAD og FN's fredsbevarende styrker* [Theory on the International Civil Service: a Model and its Limitations – UNESCO, UNCTAD and UN Peacekeeping Forces], Copenhagen: Political Studies Press, 1992.

Jef Huysmans, PhD (Leuven, Belgium), is Lecturer at the London Centre of International Relations, University of Kent at Canterbury. His thesis dealt with Making/Unmaking European Disorder. He has published on international regime theory, poststructural theory in International Relations (IR), migration and securitization, and (in)security in the post-Cold War world (including OSCE and Humanitarian Intervention).

Anna Leander is Assistant Professor at the Central European University, Budapest College. She is completing her PhD at the European University Institute, Florence, on the political economy of the Turkish state. She has recently published: 'Is a Leading State an Advantage? State Management of Foreign Direct Investment in Turkey', in N. Ayubi (ed.) *Distant Neighbours. The Political Economy of Relations between Europe and the Middle East/North Africa*, Reading, Berks: Ithaca Press, 1995; 'Turkish Businessmen and the Middle East Peace Process', in L. Blin and P. Fargues (eds) *L'économie de la paix au Proche-Orient*, Vol. 2, Paris: Maisonneuve et Larose/CEDEJ, 1995; ' "Robin Hood" Politics? Turkey Missing a Chance to Adopt a New Model in the 1990s', *Review of International Political Economy*, 1996.

Hans Mouritzen is Dr Scient Pol and an associate professor at the University of Copenhagen. Since 1993 he has been a project director for 'Norden in a Transforming Europe' at the Center for Peace and Conflict Research, Copenhagen. His books include *Finlandization: Towards a General Theory of Adaptive Politics*, Aldershot, Hants: Gower, 1988; *The International Civil Service. A Study of Bureaucracy: International Organizations*, Aldershot, Hants: Dartmouth, 1990; *External Danger and Democracy: Old Nordic Lessons and New European Challenges*, Aldershot, Hants: Dartmouth, 1996; and with Ole Wæver and Håkan Wiberg, *European Integration and National Adaptations. A Theoretical Inquiry*, New York: Nova Science, 1996.

Iver B. Neumann, DPhil (Oxon.), is Jean Monnet Fellow at the European University Institute, Florence (1995–6) and heads the Centre for Russian Studies, Norwegian Institute of International Affairs, Oslo. His latest book is *Russia and the Idea of Europe: A Study in Identity and International Relations*, London: Routledge, 1995. Articles by him have appeared in journals such as *Review of International Studies* (1994/1), *East European Society and Politics* (1993/2), *Journal of Peace Research* (1992/2) and *European Journal of International Relations* (1996/2).

Heikki Patomäki, PhD, is Senior Research Fellow at the Finnish Institute of International Affairs, *Docent* at the Universities of Turku and Lappland, part-time lecturer at the Universities of Helsinki and Tampere. Books include *Facing the Change in Europe*, Helsinki: FIIA, 1989, coedited with K. Möttölä; *Critical Realism and World Politics*, Turku: University of Turku, 1992; and (ed.) *Peaceful Changes in World Politics*, Tampere: TAPRI, 1995. He has published articles in the *Journal for the Theory of Social Behaviour* (1991), *Millennium: Journal of International Studies* (1992), *Journal of Peace Research* (1994) and the *European Journal of International Relations* (1996) as well as essays in anthologies on the explanations of the end of the Cold War and meaning structures in the Gulf War.

Véronique Pin-Fat is researching a PhD on the role of language and the limits of ethics in International Relations theory. She has worked as a teaching assistant in the Department of Philosophy at Hong Kong University and is currently in the Department of International Politics, University of Wales, Aberystwyth.

Erik Ringmar received his PhD at the Department of Political Science, Yale University in 1993. He is a lecturer in Comparative Politics at the London School of Economics. His book *Identity, Interest and Action* was published by Cambridge University Press in 1996. His articles include 'The Relevance of International Law: A Hegelian Interpretation of a Peculiar Seventeenth-century Preoccupation' in *Review of International Studies* (1995), and 'On the Ontological States of the State' in the *European Journal of International Relations* (1996).

Michael Suhr is employed in the Danish Ministry of Foreign Affairs where he currently works on EU matters. He holds an MA in International Economics and Global Theories from the Johns Hopkins University, Paul H. Nitze School of International Studies, Washington DC and is currently working on his PhD at the University of Copenhagen and at the European University Institute in Florence.

Ole Wæver is a Senior Research Fellow at the Danish Centre for Peace and Conflict Research, part-time lecturer in International Relations at the University of Copenhagen, and member of the board of the Danish Commission on Security and Disarmament Affairs (since 1995, the Danish Institute of International Affairs). During 1996–7 he is at the University of California, Berkeley on a MacArthur/SSRC grant. His most recent books are *Introduktion til studiet af international politik* [Introduction to the Study of International Relations], Copenhagen: Politiske Studier, 1992 and, with Barry Buzan *et al.*, *Identity, Migration and the New Security Agenda in Europe*, London: Pinter, 1993. *Security: A Framework for Analysis* with Barry Buzan and Jaap de Wilde will be published by Lynne Riennet in 1997.

Marlene Wind, b. 1963, holds an MA in Political Science from Aarhus University and is currently finishing her PhD at the European University Institute, Florence, employing constructivist approaches to the study of European integration. Most recently she has published 'Giddens' Theory of Structuration and the Study of European Integration – or How to Explain European Integration as an Unintended Consequence of Rational State Action' (in Danish) in *Dansk Sociologi* (1994/4); and 'The Rediscovery of Institutions in IR Theory and European Community Studies? A Reflectivist Critique of Rationalist Approaches to International Institutions', in

K.E. Jørgensen (ed.) *Reflectivist Perspectives on European Governance*, London and New York: Macmillan, 1996.

Foreword

This is a book about the figures of thought of the figures of International Relations, or, to put it in a more mundane manner, about some professors of the profession. It started life in one of the youngest of the profession's organizations: first drafts for most of the chapters were presented to the inaugural conference of the Nordic International Studies Association (NISA), Oslo, August 1993. Thanks are due to NISA for their travel support on this occasion. In March 1994, Marlene Wind organized a follow-up workshop at the European University Institute in Fiesole, to which a majority of the contributors have ties. This time, the costs were shouldered by the Centre for Peace and Conflict Research, Copenhagen. One last institution which deserves a word of thanks is the Norwegian Institute of International Affairs, where Ingeborg Victoria Boe and Christian-Marius Stryken assisted in editorial matters. Finally, a word of thanks to a number of the chosen figures themselves, who kindly provided written comments as well as interview time to their portrayers. It is our hope that we may prompt our readers to expand these dialogues into a heterologue about professional figures in general, and so help to shed the unfortunate habit of discussing the discipline in terms of paradigms, debates and schools of thought only.

Series editor's preface

Part of the 'new international relations' has been the rise of a new generation of scholars, bringing with them new schools of thought (most notably critical theory and postmodernism) with which to challenge the establishment. Most of the authors of this book are younger members of that new generation. Here they present both their choice, and their evaluation, of a set of what they see as influential and/or interesting contemporary thinkers in International Relations. A few of their choices, such as Wendt, are close to their own group in age, a few others are senior figures, such as Waltz and Gilpin, but most are people now in mid-career. All of their choices are theorists, which is in itself an interesting comment on the authors and their upcoming generation of International Relations scholars. It does not seem to be possible to reach 'master' status via empirical work! Their strategy is to create a series of perspectives on the discipline not by examining its 'great debates', but by tracing and analysing a series of individual journeys through it. As they point out, this is not much done in the self-reflections of International Relations, a curiosity given its prominence in other disciplines. Yet since this is the way each active scholar actually experiences the subject, there is a wealth of useful insights to be gained from taking this approach.

Seen as a whole, the book is a thought-provoking reflection on the fragmentation of the discipline: its lack of almost any generally shared epistemological, methodological, or ontological premises. We would seem to be not only a 'divided discipline', but increasingly one with no discernible centre at all. The individual journeys traced here are notable for their distinctiveness and separateness, perhaps suggesting a trend towards ever greater conceptual decentralization. The individual chapters can be read with many purposes in mind. Some readers will want to get a grip on a difficult author. Others will have a more biographical interest, wanting to see how some of the names in the field developed, and where they came from in order to reach where they are. Still others will seek a handle on difficult theories via one of the authors who advocate them. By providing well-lit pathways into some of the more shrouded and murky areas of the discipline, and overviews of some of its more visible, but still complicated, areas, this book will be a boon to both teachers and students.

Barry Buzan
University of Westminster

1   Figures of international thought: introducing persons instead of paradigms

Ole Wæver

'Masters in the Making' was the original working title for this volume. No Europeans reacted negatively to this, but almost every American objected on grounds of political correctness – 'master' carries connotations of dominance, hierarchy, submission, control, and a whole metaphysics being negated these years, from dominance over nature to dominance of one sex over another. Even for those not troubled by such issues, the idea of crowning a dozen theorists among a dynamic multitude of the competing, and 'juridically' equal, seemed offensive. We were thinking of this book in part as a sequel to Kenneth W. Thompson's *Masters of International Thought* (1980). After the great, unchallenged masters of the early and mid-twentieth century, with whom he dealt there come the *Masters in the Making*. Or so we thought. Wrongly it seems. No more masters! America seems, however, not to be totally in the throes of political correctness. Thompson has extended the series backwards in time, while we are extending it forward. In 1994 he published a book entitled – *Fathers of International Thought*!

This book can then be seen as the one in the series dealing with the writing of International Relations (IR) in a period where the image of master (not to speak of father) has become problematic. Therefore we address *figures of thought* – an ambivalent phrase, which may refer to patterns of projects in the academic landscape, or to the individual figures who after all move around there. The resistance to our original title was not accidental. Ours is a time of crisis for images of supreme authors mastering not only their own work but also a whole discipline. That something is in crisis, however, should hardly make it uninteresting. To the extent that something like persons or authors – or persons aspiring to be authors – is still around even in IR, how do they operate?

This book aims to present the state of the art of International Relations theory through a critical reading of twelve central theorists. By focusing on theorists and their collected works, we break with the usual procedure in the field, which reserves this method for theorists long dead and rarely treats contemporary theorists as entities interesting in and of themselves. At most, aspects of their work are juxtaposed with those of other theorists and presented as a 'school of thought'. One aim of the project is to demonstrate the well-rounded character of some of the leading oeuvres in the field, and to break with the tendency to present it as consisting of a number of disembodied 'schools' or 'paradigms'.

Why should this be of interest to more than twelve readers? In addition to providing a condensed and accessible discussion of the voluminous writings of these twelve scholars, it also has a more general value: there is a certain 'existential' dimension to doing IR. Usually, someone working in IR aims at some kind of coherence at the same time as striving to make complex and novel moves across established lines. All theorists make personal choices and the ability to retain an integrated academic persona(lity) is not secured once and for all by picking a 'position'. The traditional presentation of IR in terms of 'paradigms' or 'schools' obscures this since the writings of complex authors are often cut up and treated in separate sections. Only those who fit unequivocally into one box will be treated as whole persons – and most writers do not see themselves as operating within one of the boxes. As an academic *person* one would therefore learn more from tracing other unboxable persons in their trajectories through the discipline. Newcomers will be at a loss regarding lessons at the personal/academic level with the dominant self-representations of the discipline (paradigms, schools). With the approach adopted by this book, it becomes possible to learn from how others have made their own hard choices, paying the costs and achieving their gains.

Persons – volumes of work carrying an identical signature – are points where numerous cross-pressures meet; different academic projects and discourses combine with numerous extra-academic factors. We do not claim that an oeuvre is a natural unit marked by homogeneity and coherence (cf. Foucault 1971; 1972[1969]: 23 ff.), but nor are the famed 'paradigms' or any other of those units usually chosen for introducing the discipline. Persons furthermore have the advantage of being cross-points of a special kind. However much we have learned about the decentring of the subject or the death of the author, given a mixture of academic conventions of attribution and culturally and legally enforced notions of selfhood we all probably have to operate with the fiction of a *self* making decisions and being in some sense responsible for the result. A book organized around central theorists of the day should offer a novel – or neo-traditional – entrance into the field of International Relations.

At the same time as we attempted an intervention in the debates about how to read our discipline, it was also obvious to all those involved with the project that this book could be useful in a simpler sense, as a short-cut to some difficult writers. Therefore, one of the criteria for selecting authors has been that there should be some puzzle (how can Gilpin the political economist be also Gilpin of *War and Change in World Politics*?) or some simple difficulty in understanding the project (Alker? Onuf? Walker?). Thus, each chapter offers a critical introduction to and an original interpretation of an important writer. Whether it is the development over time of this person's work or some continuing dilemma which can be seen as shaping the work, each chapter has a plot of its own, beyond the ones offered by the 'object author' *in* the writings.

THE IMPOSSIBILITY OF SELECTION

However, if focusing on theorists rather than on schools makes it easier to represent the discipline in some respects, it makes the task of picking representative theorists a crucial one. Although we have included a handful of theorists who would be on most people's lists, we admit to a certain bias in favour of people who are attacking International Relations theory from fresh angles, and who have not yet been unequivocally accepted as masters of the trade. We have tried to select the theorists with the crispest profiles in the field.

The criterion for being a 'Master in the Making' follows from the definition of a 'master'. Quite conventionally, a master can be seen as an author whose work remains in print and is still debated decades after his death. According to this criterion even Waltz is not a master; we cannot know yet. In contrast, Morgenthau and Bull are.[1] Whether our objects of study are then actually destined to become masters cannot be settled at present.[2] And since we prefer to overrepresent those that are even more 'in the making', every reader will undoubtedly be sceptical about some of our choices. This was deliberate; we want to present some of the stronger candidates from the newest approaches.

This cut-off point establishes a correlation of three different measurements. First, there is the basic definition related to the restricted notion of a 'master' (and thereby the expanded category of 'in the making'). Second, our authors are not generally treated elsewhere as authors. There are several articles and books on Morgenthau and Bull, for example, but even a much discussed author like Waltz has not been treated in this manner. There is much debate on *Theory of International Politics*, a number of critical articles, but no treatment of his whole oeuvre (except two chapters in Griffith 1992, there as part of Griffith's own project). Keohane is often quoted in introductory chapters to empirical studies, but where do you get an overview of his development and the nature of his enterprise as such? Most of the others are not dealt with at all in the literature. The third 'criterion' is that despite the existence of a related exercise, Kenneth Thompson's *Masters of International Thought*, which covers the preceding generation of IR masters, including such authors as Aron, Wight, Morgenthau, Deutsch, Mitrany, Wolfers and Herz, he describes none of our figures. Our book takes up the discipline where Thompson's left it.[3]

Still, these criteria do not produce anything close to an essential list containing exactly these twelve figures. Waltz could appropriately have been paired with Ernest Haas who has published throughout much the same period, influenced the discipline enormously and in many ways operated very differently from Waltz; for instance, he has revised his own position and fields of interest much more drastically and continuously. One could put a string of questions on the lines of 'Why NN and not MM?' Why not Kratochwil, instead of either Ruggie or Onuf, why not Ashley instead of Walker,[4] why not Enloe instead of Elshtain, why not Smouts instead of Badie? To several of these questions there are no answers other than pragmatic ones relating to the necessity of choice and the availability of authors qualified and motivated to write on these figures. We hope that each of the chapters will convince the reader of the merits of the choice.[5] Still, at the end of this process, there are regrets; the biggest is probably the absence of a neo-Marxist such as Wallerstein, Cox, Gill, or Rosenberg (depending on the point one picks out on the line from 'master' to 'in the making').[6] The difficulty of selecting only twelve, the inevitable giving of offence and the predictability of criticism – beyond optimistically suggesting that the discipline is vital enough to produce a higher number of interesting figures – all suggest there should be a second volume, although the current editors will probably be too battered from the reactions to volume 1 to dare to edit a successor. Finally, we are not claiming that these twelve are *the* Masters in the Making – they are some of the most important, but surely there are others.

All we can do for now is to repeat the principles we used to judge every candidate: any potential 'master' should present a puzzle for the author of the chapter to have something to sort out, and for the student/reader to feel a need of secondary literature purely for the purpose of *understanding* the figure. It also weighed if there was controversy around the figure; for example, if the author was read very differently by different subcultures. Furthermore, the work should be of importance in the discipline. Importance here does not mean that we pass a positive judgement on it, but that it satisfies what Vincent Descombes has called the 'noise principle' (1979): being talked about. For instance, the selection of Alexander Wendt could be questioned because he has published comparatively little, but his two main articles have sparked so much interest and have led so many others to label themselves constructivists and relate to structure–agency questions, that his relevance is established *by* academic practice.

Inconsistency is not the only criterion for inclusion! There are authors among our twelve who work quite clearly along one path, or who stay within one problematique; but then their work is either extremely complicated, and thus in need of elucidation, or may arouse questions regarding its location in the discipline. Or we simply felt that there was an interesting story to be told about this particular career, the academic choices made, and the lessons to be learned.

All of Thompson's *'Fathers'* and *'Masters' of International Thought* were male. Among the current *Figures* of the discipline, the Masters in the Making, there are eleven men and one woman, and among those who portray the figures here, the master-makers, the ratio is eight men to five women. A positive interpretation would be that this looks like an exponential curve. A negative one is certainly possible as well.

The relative dominance of Anglo-American IR might well have led us to include not only a French but also a German (yes, there are a few candidates) and especially some non-western authors. We felt, however, that this could be (read as) the token symbol of political correctness, whereas the present selection includes people who are central to the discipline as it operates today – not only our ideal of who ought to be read. Though it would have been nice to have had a chapter on Mazrui or Inoguchi.

CONTENT AND CHARACTER OF THE CHAPTERS

The main body of this book consists of twelve parallel chapters each dealing with one figure in contemporary IR. The chapters are not excessively standardized. To impose a pattern would be artificial since the different works range very widely in format. Some of the theorists have written numerous books and articles in different fields, in which case the chapter needs either to deal with the different subfields and investigate how they relate (Elshtain, Gilpin), or to do a chronological investigation of the evolving work (Badie, Ruggie, Alker and others). Others have one major book on which the presentation focuses (Walker, Onuf) with the rest of their work used to put this book in perspective. In these cases diachrony seems less interesting. In one case, Wendt, there are mainly two – very famous – articles he wrote, and the chapter on him becomes more of an essay in its own right discussing constructivism through the dilemmas with which Wendt was struggling. Because there is an established, almost ritualized debate about Waltz, the chapter, in order to keep its focus on him, not on the debate, takes an original road into Waltz's work by asking where Waltz stands in terms of philosophy of science and suggesting one reads him in parallel with Popper. The chapters on Waltz and Keohane raise the question of what their dominance says about the field in general, and about the type of theorizing that is most valued within the discipline in particular (or maybe: in the one case the kind of theorizing that makes yours a position to which everyone is forced to relate – mostly critically; and in the other case the kind that makes up the type of paradigmatic work to which most try to conform). For some of the reflectivist or critical authors, important dynamics derive from tensions between questioning International Relations as a field and simultaneously making a career in it, consequently it is natural that the respective chapters focus on such questions.

The contributors have been left relatively free in adopting a structure and an approach as long as they considered the general themes presented above and dealt with three other basic matters. First, each thinker is placed in the landscape of the discipline: *where* is he or she toiling? Second, their epistemology is considered: *how* do they go about studying IR? Third, *what* can we learn from them?

All of the chapters can be read without prior familiarity with the works dealt with, but should also be of interest to readers who are familiar with these writers. Since our task is to present comprehensively some authors that are widely seen as 'difficult', we run into what could be labelled the double bind of translation, or the blackmail of intelligibility. New and especially philosophically inclined approaches such as poststructuralism are criticized for being incomprehensible, for using strange jargon, and for not even trying to communicate. If one then tries to explain in plain words a poststructuralist work, the reaction will typically be: 'Oh, that is another matter – it is not so very problematic, except that this was already said by NN in the 1960s; it is quite sensible and not very peculiar, but then why use all these strange terms and this odd mode of expression in the first instance!'

Either it is castigated as sophisticated but incomprehensible, or as comprehensible but trivial. It is, however, quite common that an argument can only be made fully on its own terms by using a specific terminology (cf. Kantian, Hegelian, or for that matter logical positivist literature), whereas it is possible to talk *about* it in ordinary language. Thus, it should be no surprise that the new approaches in IR have developed unique concepts and styles. For instance, some peculiarities derive from modes of expression that post-structuralists find it mandatory to avoid, but that most others use unsuspectingly. If one wants fully to understand, engage with, maybe criticize these writings, one has to make an effort, has to work to get into a new language and a new problematique (as with Kantianism, Hegelianism, or logical positivism). A simplified presentation that abstains from such terms, stylistics and perspectives will always betray the enterprise to some extent, which of course has its advantages.

Our 'introductions' should not imply that our authors say nothing but what we describe them saying; there will always be immense additional benefits from actually reading their works, even the 'difficult' ones. But since we cannot all read everything, there is also a need for introductions and overviews to help us at least in judging what to invest time in reading.

This book is not written as a first introduction to the field. It will bring students who have read a standard textbook and learned the usual (and useful, but untrue) stereotypes of 'paradigms' and 'debates' closer to the complexities of contemporary theorizing. Thus it can be used as a graduate textbook for classes in International Relations theory. It may also be seen by both students and teachers as a door-opener to texts which they should have read, but have not yet come around to deciphering. (Should we after all have chosen the blunt title: 'How to save 500 hours of IR reading: books you always pretend you have read but actually never did'? No, we should not, because our purpose is not to replace the reading of primary texts by secondary ones; it is to tempt people to get started on some of the more challenging theorists and to help those who already read them to step back and reflect on complete oeuvres.)

Whereas a number of the contributors have studied with the theorists they discuss, none of them is now working in the same department or even the same country as the subject of their chapter. We have tried to combine theoretical familiarity with geographical and intellectual distance.

In addition to the twelve core chapters and this introduction, which tries to present both the project and the state of the art as a whole, the book contains a conclusion by my co-editor. It suggests how other students of International Relations can draw lessons from the theorists under discussion and tries to identify blind spots in their coverage of the theoretical landscape.

In this way, the book will, at a minimum, produce lessons on three levels:

- *substance* (i.e. theory substance): an understanding of the work of Alker, Onuf, and others.
- *life* as an IR theorist: the strategies adopted by different writers facing different kinds of dilemmas. What happens if you try to cultivate your

own school, or, conversely, if you want to integrate numerous theories, or, for instance, to work very interdisciplinarily? What kind of ironic effects do we find in the works of these known figures, and thus how can tensions and dilemmas in their ambitions explain the peculiarities in their works?

- the *landscape* of current IR theory: what is happening in the various districts, what are the trends and patterns, who is trying to do what to whom and why? (Theorizing is never a simple two-part relationship between the theorist and 'the world', it always involves an understanding of which other theories exist and how one wants to relate to them.)

The purpose of the rest of this introduction is to do the opposite from the (rest of the) book. While the book tries *not* to write about IR the usual way in terms of 'paradigms' or 'schools', this introduction will give a condensed version of the story about them. Its overview provides a common basis for the rest of the chapters. Thus, the story that follows is in part, and deliberately, traditional, because it has to present the self-images which the discipline has established and used to guide its course. In part, it ventures a novel suggestion on how to see the main patterns of debate and the definition of research programmes in recent years where no dominant metaphors or 'debates' have gained general acceptance. Finally, it reflects on the uses and abuses of debates: in relation to each period it comments on the advantages of the dominant depiction as well as its main disadvantages.

FATHERS, DEBATES AND PARADIGMS

The origins of international thought is a strangely bifurcated business. Some point to timeless wisdoms and ancient masters (Machiavelli, Thucydides, Kautilya – the older the better), others restrict themselves to treating international thought as essentially a twentieth-century matter. In between these two practices there are two cases that can be made at least as forcefully as these two extremes.

One can argue with Arnold Wolfers, for example, that our 'contemporaries' are the writers with whom we share the modern state and the modern states system, i.e. those based in the European or Europeanized international society of the last three or four hundred years (Wolfers and Martin 1956). The concepts and problematiques emerging around the sovereign territorial states have set such a specific agenda that it is difficult to apply 'wisdom' from other ages where the units were completely different. Even if Hobbes, for instance, is constantly misrepresented and 'normalized' according to twentieth-century expectations of what he probably said, to read Hobbes today still has the advantage that his writings were involved in shaping key political ideas and concepts at a constitutive moment of European political history. Thus his practice is linked to our current system – although not in exactly the way our textbooks would like it to be (Walker 1993; Williams 1996).

Second, a good case can be made for revisiting the nineteenth century. Instead of illustrating the main IR traditions through a picture of twentieth-century theories and ancient classics, it might be more relevant to look at the immediate predecessors to twentieth-century IR: nineteenth-century thinking about peace and war. Important schools which have for various reasons been downplayed in the self-understanding of the discipline were the *Machtschule* and the free trade liberals. The romantic and historicist movement among German historians (sometimes known as the 'Power School') gave to power politics and state centrism much more radical expressions than had been seen among the 'realists' of previous centuries. The state became a strong abstraction with its own drives, and at the height of historicism (with historian von Treitschke and philosopher Hegel) the result was a closed system where the state is defined as power and power as the state. This is closely akin to twentieth-century realism, which is disowned because the authors were German, and some of their ideas were continued in less fortunate ways by geopolitics, social Darwinism and (German and non-German) political practice. On the 'peace' side we moved from peace plans to a more 'sociological' thinking among free trade liberals arguing that modern capitalism, trade and public opinion, together with general enlightenment and progress, would produce peace.[7] While Kant has had a recent revival, and international political economy (IPE) might be more aware of the nineteenth-century, the predilection of the discipline of IR, especially in its most 'official' moments, is for an image of age-old classics and twentieth-century works (or, rather, postwar works), but the nineteenth-century is strangely absent despite the fact that it is actually in the late eighteenth- and nineteenth-century works that one is best able to find connecting lines, continuous ideas and real inspirations. Equipped with Ranke's essay on the great powers, Clausewitz, Bentham's works, maybe Cobden and finally Kant, it is difficult to be surprised by much in twentieth-century IR; except for the form, the scientific wrapping, of much of it.

Despite the possibility of tracing both realism and liberalism to nineteenth-century writings, it is very much a twentieth-century idea to see them as two distinct, competing schools and to hold that *the* main tradition is one connected to *Realpolitik* and that the second most important quasi-tradition consists of various mixes of 'idealism' and liberalist belief in the promises of modernity. These 'timeless' traditions are largely made up of nineteenth-century ideas in their twentieth-century political roles. These ideas unfolded in politics and in various other disciplines – only after the First World War was it possible, and only after the Second World War generally acceptable, to talk about a discipline of International Relations.

The discipline of International Relations has a convention of telling its history in terms of a number of 'great debates': idealism versus realism in the 1940s is the first; behavioralism versus traditionalism in the 1960s is the second; and the interparadigm debate in the mid-1970s between realism, interdependence theory and neo-Marxism is widely seen as the 'third debate'. In the 1980s there was a major – and often brutal – confrontation between what Keohane has labelled rationalists and reflectivists, and what others have seen as the arrival in IR of continental philosophy, postmodernism, or the humanities.[8] This debate either goes unnumbered or is referred to as – the third debate (e.g. Lapid 1989; Neufeld 1993; Holsti 1993). Neither the arena of confrontation nor the pattern of positions, however, has much in common with the 'third debate' of the 1970s. This introduction focuses on comparing this most recent debate with the previous 'great debates'. The discussion will help to situate many of the authors considered in this book as well as to clarify disagreements about how this 'fourth debate' should be presented.

One advantage of not accepting the fourth debate as a separate one is that one can stick to the general preference for the number three – there are always three approaches, three paradigms, three scenarios. But this is not a simple counting matter. It assimilates the fourth debate into the third, and thereby the interpretative schemes of the third debate are prolonged/reproduced. The third debate is the typical 'interparadigm debate', the triangle of realism, pluralism and structuralism, or realism, liberalism and Marxism, the standard textbook version of IR. It is not very helpful when applied to a discipline where this game is not driving most of the action. Self-reflection in IR of the 1990s is blocked if presented with the choice of either using the triangle as scheme or abstaining from pictures of its own development. We need new metaphors.

Pictures of specific constellations, debates, or triangles become problematic, especially when one model of schools, such as the timeless triangle, gets fixed and is projected backwards as well as forwards, as the map of all possible IR positions.[9] But, we cannot simply purge ourselves of metaphors and pictures; images of the internal battlelines do exist and they have effects. We should take seriously the question of how they function, what they are, and what could be achieved by trying to reshape them. The 'debates' operate as a dialectic between implicit pictures and articulate self-representations of the discipline. In part, they are implicit operators in (and thereby shape) actual academic practice, in part they are constructed and artificially imposed on much more diverse activities. In the second capacity they are selective readings amplifying the elements that fit into their story. But in the first, they are distinctions involved in the work of the discipline (and thus real and effective). A picture of the discipline itself as the immediate social context always guides academic work. Each of the debates first emerged as a constellation, an implicit picture. Then, the second step, this constellation was *labelled*; this reinforced it as a constellation, but also shaped the phase of moving beyond it, because that phase was defined in relation to this picture of the discipline. It makes a difference whether one tries to operate in today's IR according to an understanding of this as 'after the third debate' or 'after the fourth debate'.

The rest of this chapter will concentrate on the third and fourth debates. Since the first and second are well known, I will briefly discuss their character *as debates* and the role of the debates as images in shaping self-understanding and practice in the discipline.

The first debate – between 'realists' and 'idealists' (or 'utopians') – was not so much a discussion as a heroic *post-hoc* self-presentation by the (self-proclaimed) realists. In the 1920s and 1930s there was not much 'debating' between 'idealists' and 'realists', but after the Second World War had 'demonstrated' how wrong the idealists had been, the realists could tell a story of how right they were at a time when actually little debate took place. In the interwar period, 'idealism' was hegemonic within 'International Relations' – not within the practice of international relations, not in terms of the totality of academic reflection on international relations, but within the discipline as such. The discipline of International Relations was born after the First World War as a reaction to four years of savage conflict. Thus, contrary to the widespread idea that its history is closely linked to realism, it was born in the liberalist corner,[10] with the clear task of avoiding a repetition of world war. Normative and prescriptive, the focus of its interest lay not in studying historical experiences but in working out new models and solutions, as well as in arguments about why the future did not have to repeat the past, i.e. what social change had made war outdated.[11] One can construct positions, such as realism and idealism, and one can search the classics for corresponding arguments, but two well-defined positions did not emerge until the end of the period of IR interwar idealism, i.e. Carr 1981 [1939], Morgenthau 1946.

The idea of a debate between realists and idealists has had a powerful effect on the discipline. Positions critical of realism could be dismissed as reincarnations of interwar idealism. In addition, realism was decisively shaped by its birth in this alleged debate. As pointed out by Hedley Bull (1972), for example, postwar (or twentieth-century) realism is distinct from the more cynical *Realpolitik* of previous centuries. Much realist reasoning for power politics was presented on a battleground defined by the 'idealists' as a moral argument why idealist policies did not serve these aims, which required an understanding of reality – a line of argument quite different from Machiavellian logic, which would not accept this context of debate. Furthermore, realism's coherence is anchored in this debate. It is very difficult to come up with a list of views shared by realists, but because authors of textbooks and people debating 'paradigms' think this a necessity a string of fixed dogmas has increasingly been attributed to realism.[12] Seen in the context of its historical emergence, realism is a coherent tradition demarcated by denying (basic, qualitative) progress in international relations. The different realisms do not share premises, but they *do the same* – in different ways. They are united by their conclusion: the denial of the basic liberal argument that there is a possibility of progress.

Where most liberals assume that general societal evolution *somehow* must influence and change international relations (cf. Keohane 1990; Nye 1988; Wæver 1992: Ch. 2; and in this book Chapter 4 on Keohane and Chapter 7 on Ruggie), realists argue that progress has no place in international politics. Martin Wight claims, for instance, that 'International politics is the realm of recurrence and repetition; it is the field in which political action is most regularly necessitous'.[13] 'If this is indeed the character of international politics, it is incompatible with progressivist theory.' This 'no' unites realists. They have found different ways to argue the *no* (human nature, structure, philosophy of history, pessimism of knowledge; Wæver 1992: 33–49; Donnelly 1992). Thus, realism is unified performatively. This can be understood only when seen in the context of the *idea* of a founding debate.

'Realism' is not a 'school' because of any objective proximity of its members or any uniformity of their positions, but is unified in and by its contrast to idealism and in particular by the form of this opposition: denying progress or domestic spillover while competing to claim the moral high ground for amorality.

Where the idealist–realist debate is often criticized for the way it has served to castigate all kinds of non-realism, one should also be aware that twentieth-century realism has been deeply marked by it. Realism might be on its way to getting a second imprint from this construction. The realist/ idealist dichotomy is coming back to haunt realism. In our own time realism is cut off from its roots because most people have stopped performing the interwar exercise – castigating all non-realists as idealists – and then the realist labelling trick turns suddenly against itself. The reading of realist works and thereby the transmittence of a tradition, so essential to realism, is barred by the very label 'realist'. It has often been noticed that the labels 'realist' and 'idealist' (or 'utopian') were terribly self-serving and biased. Combined with the fact that in the first debate realism was the clear winner, this led to the situation where no one read the interwar idealists any more. They were known only through the parodies by their critics (Carr, first of all; cf. de Wilde 1991). To some extent, 'realism' seems to face the same prospects today. 'Realism' has become a predominantly negative label, which very few people are willing to attach to themselves, but which many people use in debates (cf Buzan 1996). It is easy to have an opinion on 'realism' and to mention Morgenthau in this connection, having read at most his twelve misleading pages on 'six principles of realism'; other works, such as Morgenthau's *Scientific Man vs. Power Politics*, Kissinger's *A World Restored*, or even Carr's *Twenty Years' Crisis*, which would confuse the stereotypes, remain unread. Ironically, like its old opponent, idealism, realism is becoming known only through its critics' parody.

Despite their attempt to argue – often hesitantly – for a specific discipline (a specific science) of international relations/politics, realists retained their close connections to history and the methods of the diplomatic historian (for this tension, see most clearly the bible of the period: Morgenthau 1985 [1947]). The first major attack on this mainstream therefore came from the growing social sciences. The second debate was a sustained attempt through the late 1950s and the 1960s to promote behavioural scientific approaches as superior to the traditional line of the historians. The techniques ranged from game theory, which was soon neatly absorbed into mainstream realism and strategic studies (deterrence theory), to the collection of events data in comparative foreign policy and correlates of war studies pointing towards peace research. The debates were conducted by Bull versus Kaplan in 1966 (in *World Politics*) and by Young, Singer, Vital, Jervis and others contributing to Rosenau and Knorr (1969). In contrast to the first debate, the second ended in a draw. It might be claimed that the substantial 'paradigms' as to assumptions (ontology) of international relations remained with realism, while the 'scientific' challenge had left a decisive mark within realism itself, and the second debate was to be won through delayed effect in the 1980s. In this respect, the main carrier of the 'virus' was Waltz's *Theory of International Politics*.

Labelling this the second great debate helped to 'professionalize' IR and establish it as a discipline. This was a major move in the construction of a self-referential, inner-directed debate defining a separate scientific 'sub-system'. Where the first debate was only the academic reflection of a more general exchange about foreign policy, the second was of interest primarily to the members of the profession itself.

THE INTERPARADIGMATIC TRIANGLE: A COMMANDING METAPHOR

A standard textbook presentation of International Relations explains that there are three paradigms or three dominant schools: realism, liberalism (pluralism, interdependence and world society) and Marxism (radicalism, structuralism and globalism). Some writers claim that this is the timeless pattern of International Relations – even in the classics, we find these three types of thinking (Kauppi and Viotti 1992; Viotti and Kauppi 1993 [1987]). Others are more restrictive and say that the discipline *became* like this at some specific point, e.g. in the 1970s (Holsti 1985).[14]

Here is where the disadvantage of naturalized 'paradigms' is most visible. 'The debate' is a misleading map and a bad guide by which to introduce students. This is not the pattern of debate today. The story of an 'inter-paradigm debate' does not grasp the ongoing controversies in the discipline; the debate has moved on. The next section will present some alternative maps.[15]

The debate became triangular in the mid- to late 1970s. Transnationalism and interdependence appeared as serious challengers to realism: Keohane and Nye's *Power and Interdependence* pushed Morgenthau's *Politics Among Nations* from the top of the list of textbooks. At the same time, dependence theory and Marxism were recognized as a legitimate alternative approach. First, around the mid-1970s, the transnationalist challenge to realism was established; during the second half of the decade many achieved an image of the discipline as made up of an inconclusive debate (between realists and interdependence theorists, and often also including the semi-acceptance of Marxism); and finally, towards the end of the 1970s (often not appearing in print until the early 1980s), 'paradigmatic' formulations of the new debate and the role of paradigms in international relations appeared.

In the United Kingdom this became known as the 'inter-paradigm debate' (Banks 1984, 1985). The Americans referred to the debate as a challenge to realism: 'realism v. globalism', 'the debate over interdependence', 'paradigms in IR', or, finally, 'the third debate' (Maghroori and Ramberg 1982).

In the late 1960s and throughout the 1970s, there was increasing criticism of the dominant realist paradigm. Those critiques were not primarily about methodology, but about realism's image of the world, its alleged states-centrism, its preoccupation with power, and its blindness to processes of various kinds, domestically, transnationally and beyond the political-military sphere.

The challengers not only formulated a criticism of realism but also tried to present alternative conceptions of the international system. These were phrased in terms of regional integration, transnationalism, interdependence, and a pluralist system of numerous sub-state and trans-state actors who made up a much more complicated image than the usual state-to-state one. States did not exist as such – various actors within the state interacted to produce what looked like state policy, and sometimes they even dodged the state and made their own linkages across frontiers. Not only were there other actors than the state, but also the state was not the state, it was split up into networks of bureaucracies, interest groups and individuals. Nor was the system the system, because power was no longer 'fungible' in the monetary sense, and instead of all the political arenas being connected in one great game, it was necessary to study specific issue areas, their distinctive distributions of power, maybe their specific *forms* of power, and then to work out separate theories about how issue linkages were made, how issues were politicized and de-politicized, and agendas set (cf. Keohane and Nye 1975, 1977) (realists did not need to do this because they assumed that all areas and all power deposits were always already potentially linked).

It became increasingly clear that the new theories were to win no easy victory. The realist imagery had a solid hold on decision-makers who continued to operate (as) in a world of states (Rothstein 1972). The new formulations also had difficulty consolidating into a *theory* and not just complications *of* the realist theory.[16]

There was a general understanding that an alternative image of international politics had materialized but that realism had not collapsed. The two paradigms had different strengths: realism was more successful on some issues, liberalism on others. There was no way to *prove* one or other correct. Realists and liberals *saw* different realities. If they went out to 'test' their theories, they tested them against different material. Each sorted the world according to different concepts and thus laid hold of different empirical material. This was not Keohane and Nye's conception; they tried to test the two models – and the ensuing four models of regime change – against each other. But the emerging self-perception in and of the discipline was that competing theories had emerged, each of which contained its own confirmatory stories, its own data and its own preferred issues. Some lamented this while others tried to celebrate the value of seeing the world through different lenses (Alker and Biersteker 1984; Rosenau 1984: 247 and 251; Dougherty and Pfaltzgraff 1971, who expressed this by viewing International Relations as an 'inter-discipline').

The criticism of positivism and especially Thomas Kuhn's theory of paradigms supported this understanding (Kuhn 1962; the theory gained much wider circulation in the social sciences after the publication of Lakatos and Musgrave 1970). Scholars borrowed the idea that relations among competing general theories cannot be judged in any overarching, neutral language. Each 'paradigm' constructs its own basic units (concepts) and questions – and thereby its data, its criteria and not least its stories about paradigmatic experiments or similar scientific events. Paradigms are incommensurable because each generates its own criteria of judgement and its own 'language'. Realism and its pluralist challenger appeared to be such incommensurable paradigms.[17]

Meanwhile, a third paradigm had risen: Marxism. Marxism was not new as a theory making powerful statements on international relations. It had done so at least as long as the discipline of IR had existed. (The first department of IR was established at the University of Wales, Aberystwyth in 1919; Lenin wrote his *Imperialism, the Highest Stage of Capitalism* in 1916.) Theories of imperialism had been discussed vigorously – probably more blood was spilled here than in the debates of IR. But very few had seen this as International Relations (despite the dual allegiances of one of the founding fathers, Carr). In the 1970s, however, Marxism was increasingly seen as an alternative theory of international relations. It was not as well established within IR, but to present the discipline as engaged in a triangular debate became fashionable (Marcusian 'repressive tolerance'?). Maybe the relationship was triangular, but *de facto* the debate was mainly along one side of the triangle (Figure 1.1). It is easy to see that the three schools tell different stories of international relations. Numerous 3-times-x schemes have been filled out with key actor, concept of system, main sector, etc. This will not be rehearsed here. Suffice it to point to a few of the main disagreements: what is the ultimate substance of international relations? States (realism), individuals and groups (liberals), or classes and economic structures (Marxists)? Realists focus on conflictual, political relations among states; liberals believe that these relations are imbedded in or can be transformed by non-strategic (i.e. economic and social) relations in and across societies. Radicals share with realists the focus on conflict, but see this as located not among states, but within and across them. The image is of the billiard-ball (realists), the cobweb (pluralists) and the octopus (Marxists).

The third of the four debates can be clearly singled out from the others in three ways: 1) its area for locating the differences: 'ontologically' as different conceptions of the nature, units and content of international relations;

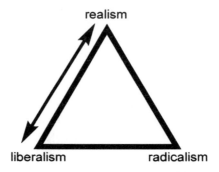

Figure 1.1 The interparadigm debate

2) its 'participants': the three schools; and 3) its self-conception as 'incommensurable paradigms'.

So, the interparadigm debate is no longer fully adequate as a representation of ongoing debates? But it is such a nice tool for teaching students, so why bother – does the interparadigm debate idea harm anyone? Yes. First, there is a tendency to produce straw men, not least of the realists (cf. Buzan 1996; Wæver 1992: Ch. 3). Second, these debates and the ideas about them are part of the discipline's self-reflection, and so its self-steering, and counting wrongly therefore has serious effects. Finally, because it presents the discipline in terms of given positions, it allots to realism and the other paradigms a quality of having established a safe ground to be defended through dogmatism (reading realism as according to 'a religious model'), whereas the 'paradigms' are probably much less stable, rather strivings for establishing platforms, for fixing solid sovereigns. This is not grasped when presenting schools in terms of families unified by shared 'assumptions'. Much more emphasis should be given to the performative praxis establishing – always with difficulty and always precariously – impressions of solidity and sovereignty (Ashley forthcoming). 'The interparadigm debate' should be retained as a very informative metaphor for telling the history of the discipline in the 1970s and the early 1980s. We need new images to grasp the later 1980s and 1990s.

MOVEMENTS IN THE 1980s AND 1990s

The fourth debate is not the third. First, it is not the same discussion: the new one is much more philosophical. Second, the fourth debate has a different pattern: the lines of controversy have shifted. And third, the fourth debate does not organize itself through the idea of incommensurability: one of its axes lacks the mutual tolerance of the interparadigm debate, the other is based on presumed commensurability.

1

This generation of critics has questioned dominant work not only with the aim of gaining another, better access to the Reality of international relations, but because the whole enterprise of the discipline is seen as just one more expression of the prevailing attitudes of modernity: a hunt for objectivity, control and security. Since the new critics are not searching for another objective truth, a difficult debate is produced: 'But what is *your* explanation?' the establishment asks when at last entering into debate; 'It is not!' the new critics reply to the bewilderment of the establishment.

These new writers try to devise new ways of writing to avoid the traps in traditional IR, and therefore end up doing things other than those normally expected of IR scholarship. Typically, they will study how meaning is constituted, how dominant ways of conceptualizing have been produced, and not least how the 'academic' writings of IR participate in the construction of what they take as their independent object: 'international relations'.

There is a general turn towards 'the problematic of subjectivity in international politics rather than the international relations of pregiven subjects'
(Campbell 1992: viii).[18]

A frenzy for words like 'epistemology' and 'ontology' often signals this
philosophical turn. Not that these words are either specific to the new
debates or especially appropriate, but they have become standardized signals to indicate that one is aware of the 'new' debates. *Epistemology* in the
sense of 'how do we know that we know what we know' raises queries
ranging from 'philosophy of science' questions (related to the debates
among such positions as inductivists, falsificationists, realists and instrumentalists) to questions close to methodology and thus to the second
debate. The quintessential second debate exchange between Kaplan (1966)
and Bull (1966) was not only about techniques (social science quantification
and modelling v. classical reflection) but largely about 'epistemology': what
kind of knowledge can be gained about international relations, by what
methods and with what degree of certainty. Today the use of the signal
word epistemology generally means an attack on the dominant view of the
scientific enterprise, call it 'positivist' or 'epistemic realist' (Campbell 1992;
George 1993). According to this view reality is 'out there' and the task of
social science is to capture it.

Ontology, if taken literally as the question of 'what is', could be read as a
reference to the third debate. It was about 'the stuff of international relations': is it made up of states, individuals, groups, classes, or structures of
some kind? When used today, the term often means a deeper – more or less
Nietzschean or Heideggerian – questioning of key categories of traditional
IR discourse, such as the state, that are treated as if they are givens. Such
units are studied by the new approaches as constituted in manifold practices
and with no ontological status deeper than these acts (Ashley 1989;
Campbell 1992: 9; Ringmar forthcoming). The ontology of mainstream
approaches narrows the horizons of imagination by making it impossible
to ask what lies behind specific elements of reality: these are things that exist
in and of and as themselves; that is ontology.

To contain the new challenge within the terms epistemology and ontology
misses, however, the abundance of projects that draw full scale on various
'continental' philosophers – so far with most effect poststructuralists like
Derrida, Foucault, Baudrillard, Kristeva, Deleuze and Virilio, but maybe in
the future (not least with the recent launch of a German theoretical journal
of IR, *Zeitschrift für internationale Beziehungen*), also a more systematic
import of Habermasian ideas. What distinguishes the new IR debates from
their precursors is that they draw on philosophies that question a general
philosophical outlook which most social science depends on – its assumptions about language, about identity, and not least about subject/object: the
subjectivity of subjects, the objectivity of objects and the subject/object
distinction as such. These challenges are difficult to deal with as separate,
technical problems – an impression one could sometimes get from the talk
of 'epistemology' and 'ontology'. Poststructuralists in particular have questioned the idea of an 'epistemology' in the sense of rules on how to produce

secure knowledge, and 'ontologies' are primarily avoided, i.e. something castigated as problematic assumptions about extra-textual pre-givens.

The debate is over deep philosophical differences. These can surface as questions of epistemology or ontology, but equally well as disagreements over the status of ghosts (Ashley forthcoming), the reading of Machiavelli (Walker 1993), the reception of maps (Krishna 1996), or the semiotics of a war memorial (Turnbull 1996).

Despite the impression often given by the 'reflectivists' themselves, the new battle-lines are not produced only, or probably even mainly, by the arrival of a new contender from outside. This is very much the story of changes within the mainstream and the opening for new critics among the derived effects hereof.

2

In the triangular third debate, the three sides were never equal. The Marxist/structuralist side did not achieve full equivalence, and for a while at least the initiative was with 'interdependence'. As often noted, Tucker's *The Inequality of Nations* (1977), Waltz's *Theory of International Politics* (1979) and Gilpin's *War and Change in World Politics* (1981) were realism's revenge, and an attempt to relaunch more 'scientific' versions of realism. Waltz's version, especially, became known under the name Richard Ashley gave to them: 'neo-realism' (Ashley 1984).[19]

What is 'neo' about it? What distinguishes the new realism from the classical one? Often the answer given is that the old realism argued from human nature, whereas neo-realism bases its realism in the anarchic nature of the international system. If that is the criterion, neo-realism dates back to the 1950s, where both Herz and Waltz emphasized that they did not include any premises about human nature, and that their arguments were based in social features peculiar to 'the international'.[20] There have always been quite different versions of how to ground realism – human nature, international structure, philosophy of history, knowledge pessimism (Wæver 1992: Ch. 3). Thus the premises, the 'basis', can hardly be the defining criterion for neo-realism. What is truly new about neo-realism is its *concept of science*. General speculation and reflection in the classical realist style are no longer sufficient. Realism has to express itself in the form of *theory*, of a system of clearly specified sentences, cf. the title of a Waltz article: 'Realist Thought and Neo-realist Theory' (1990). In this sense, the shift from realism to neo-realism can be seen as a delayed and displaced victory for the 'scientific' side of the second debate.

This change has important and interesting effects on the relationship among 'paradigms'. It opens up space for a rapprochement with neo-liberalism. (Neo-)Realism is no longer an ethico-philosophical position. Precise statements replace sweeping statements on the nature of life and politics. Compare the rhetoric of classical realists such as Morgenthau, Kissinger and Liska who generalize about the nature of human life (not necessarily human nature, but wisdom about the human condition) and

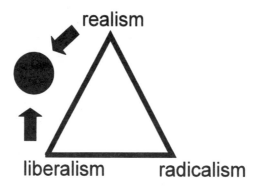

Figure 1.2 The neo-neo synthesis

tell stories about the inherently tragic nature of politics and other lessons at a level close to philosophy of history. Neo-realism consciously limits itself: it says only 'a small number of big and important things' (Waltz 1986: 329). Becoming scientific implies a certain minimalism. Plenty of space is left for developing theory and empirical studies on a number of other factors.

Liberal theory underwent a parallel development. It moved away from being a general interpretation of the nature of international relations or an idea of overall developments, and concentrated instead on asking a few precise questions. Or maybe simply one: 'How institutions affect incentives facing states' (Keohane 1989: 11). The principal thesis is

> that variations in the institutionalization of world politics exert signifi-
> cant impacts on the behaviour of governments. In particular, patterns of
> cooperation and discord can be understood only in the context of the
> institutions that help define the meaning and importance of state action.
>   (ibid.: 2)

As a basis for investigating this, the anarchy assumption of neo-realism is taken as a useful starting-point. As Keohane argues, if one smuggles on board cosmopolitan preferences it is not surprising that one reaches the conclusion that regimes are important. By instead basing the argument on (what are claimed to be) realist premises with states as egoistic, rational actors, it can be shown that institutions are possible and relevant *even* on these restricted premises. The neo-liberal institutionalists search in parallel with the neo-realists for still more limited, precise, formula-like assertions that can be reduced to simple analytical statements amenable to tests and theory. As both are extremely American, it might be appropriate to notice that neo-realism and neo-liberalism became 'leaner and meaner'.

During the 1980s, realism became neo-realism and liberalism neo-liberal institutionalism. Both underwent a self-limiting redefinition towards an anti-metaphysical, theoretical minimalism: they became increasingly com-patible. A dominant neo-neo synthesis became the research programme of the 1980s. No longer were realism and liberalism 'incommensurable' – on the contrary they shared a 'rationalist' research programme, a conception of science, a shared willingness to operate on the premise of anarchy (Waltz) and investigate the evolution of co-operation and whether institutions matter (Keohane). Inside this we saw both the emergence of direct attempts at synthesis (Ruggie 1983; Buzan, Jones and Little 1993) and a standard type of *International Organization* article operationalizing and testing realism and liberalism against each other in a specific field but with a clear idea that they could be brought back into conversation.

My term 'neo-neo' does not refer to an idea that this is newer than the new, a reformulation of neo-realism, for instance. It refers first of all to the synthesis between realism and liberalism that became possible when realism was transformed into neo-realism and liberalism into neo-liberal institutionalism. It is the synthesis of the two neo-schools that became possible by their very neo-ness.

In this cross-field produced by their rapprochement, one can find much of the empirical studies of the 1980s, especially the typical 'theory-guided' and/or 'theory-testing' article in *International Organization*. Regime theory, co-operation under anarchy, hegemonic stability, alliance theory, trade negotiations and Buzanian security analysis can all be seen as located in this field.

In this environment, the main line of controversy shifted to the opposite direction as one between rationalists and reflectivists, the postmodernism debate. As the previous line of debate 'dried up', the secondary axis leading towards the radicals came to fill the vacuum. Thus the two main poles became on the one hand a neo-realist, neo-liberal synthesis and on the other reflectivism (debate 4a).

Keohane's discussion of 'two approaches to international institutions' in his presidential address at ISA in 1988 authorized this constellation. On the one side was the rationalist approach, referring to the merged neo-realist neo-liberalist research programme of which he himself is one of the leaders, and on the other side were what Keohane united under the label 'reflectivists', which was to cover those inspired by French postmodernism and German hermeneutics as well as late-Wittgensteinian rules-perspectives and

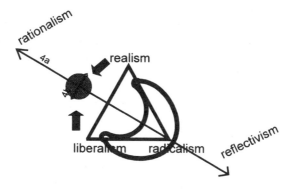

Figure 1.3 IR debate of the 1980s

social constructivism. (Sometimes, the label 'reflectivist' has – consciously or not – been changed to *reflexivists* in order to point to the self-reflective nature of the new critical approaches.[21])

Reflectivists, according to Keohane, are characterized by emphasizing interpretation, the reflections of the actors as central to institutions. Norms and regimes cannot be studied positivistically but have to be seen as inter-subjective phenomena researchable only by non-positivist methods (Kratochwil and Ruggie 1986). Institutions are not something actors rationally construct following from their interests, since they act in meta-institutions (such as the principle of sovereignty) which create the actors rather than the other way round. Institutions and actors constitute each other mutually.

That this rationalist–reflectivist axis was the main line of struggle was to be registered in many ways in the 1980s. Many younger academics who were being evaluated for tenure or applying for positions, or who wrote articles that were refereed in this period, will have stories to tell about the vehemence of resistance, especially against poststructuralism. Also, articles allegedly not dealing with this line of controversy reveal it. For instance, Keohane in a presentation of the relationship between neo-realism and neo-liberalism argues like this:

> Neo-liberal institutionalism ... shares some important intellectual com-mitments with neorealism. Like neorealists, neoliberal institutionalists seek to explain behavioral regularities by examining the nature of the decentralized international system. Neither neorealists nor neoliberal institutionalists are content with interpreting texts: both sets of theorists believe that there is an international political reality that can be partly understood, even if it will always remain to some extent veiled.
>
> (Keohane 1989: 8)

Visible here is how the unity of the neo-neo position is partly argued by reference to some unnamed academics who allegedly 'are content with interpreting texts'.

In the new set-up it could finally be noted how the reflectivists carry out a flanking operation (see Figure 1.3). In their work to reshape themselves in scientific form, both realism and liberalism had to leave behind some of their traditional fields: history and the statesman in the case of realism, and ethics in the case of liberalism. Reflectivists attempted to articulate these classical issues against the two neo- schools, which had become too scientific for such matters. Poststructuralists have argued that classical realism was in many ways superior to neo-realism (cf. e.g. Ashley 1984; Der Derian 1987). Ethics, a traditionally liberalist theme, has in recent years been articulated more often from a reflectivist basis (Brown 1992; Connolly 1991; Campbell 1993).

Why is reflectivism placed in the same corner as Marxism? Why the vague covering term 'radicalism'? Reflectivists do not share many assump-tions with Marxists. If one wants an ahistorical model of different schools, they have to have separate positions. But when the models are snapshots at a given time, they can be located in the same place: radicalism. This is because postmodernism largely replaced Marxism as the 'extreme contender', the radical challenge. Some Marxists might claim that this is an establishment plot, because postmodernism is ultimately reactionary and thus it was a nice move for the establishment to get rid of the dangerous challenge, Marxism, and be hospitable to a new challenger, postmodernism, that was ultimately not dangerous. Postmodernists will emphasize that their criticism of logo-centric, western, essentialist theories punches Marxism at least as hard as it does the establishment, and that therefore criticism has become more radical since they took over. Someone watching with the task of writing the history of the discipline may notice that the role of Marxism as a contender in great debates has waned. There is still important work done by Marxists that contributes significantly – maybe increasingly – to IPE, to foreign policy theory and not least to macro-historical reflection on the emergence and evolution of the modern state. In the debates which the discipline uses to orientate itself, the position which used to be occupied by Marxists was, in the mid- and late 1980s, taken over by postmodernists.

The rationalist–reflectivist axis was not the only axis in the 1980s, although it was the primary one. It was supplemented by a perpendicular but shorter axis: the debate over absolute and relative gains (debate 4b).[22] The remaining short distance between neo-realism and neo-liberalism is being argued out in this debate, which echoes old realist–liberalist debates, but in its form is very post-third debate: 'This is not the interparadigm debate' (as Keohane said in a panel on the relative/absolute gains debate at the APSA meeting in 1992; cf. also Keohane 1993: 291 ff.), this is not about incommensurable paradigms. We agree on 90 per cent and the remainder is essentially an empirical question. How much state action is driven by relative and how much by absolute gains, in what proportions and under what conditions? These are matters of research abundantly suited to the rationalist, neo-neo research programme. And this has become a cottage industry for the most mathematical modellers in the discipline. Not many of those who originally formulated the IR theory issues behind this can follow the Snidals and the Powells into their equations, but this is logically the apex of the neo-neo programme. One might even speculate that causality runs the opposite way: this business boomed exactly because it was so full of models – finally International Relations could make it into the *American Political Science Review* with articles full of equations. The absolute/relative gains debate is a very well-structured one among participants who have been striving to set up a joint framework. Therefore it has been possible to conduct a disciplined debate with much agreement; and lessons about how well organized it has been should not be used to tell others how to discuss (for instance: use game theory). It works only because this debate is located in a very particular place: within the neo-neo aspiration for agreement.

3

The third defining element of the third debate was incommensurability. Is the fourth debate(s) structured by a similar self-understanding of the relationship among positions? No! There is no such repressive tolerance among rationalists and reflectivists. They rather see each other as harmful, at times almost 'evil', definitely not as a legitimate parallel enterprise. According to reflectivists, the mainstream is co-responsible for upholding a repressive order,[23] while many rationalists see postmodernists as subversive, anti-scientific and generally a bad influence on students. Since most 'rationalists' perceive themselves as reformers, not defenders of the status quo, postmodernists are also seen as politically problematic because they allegedly demobilize enlightened critique and moral judgement. On the other axis, there is no incommensurability among the contenders over relative and absolute gains, because they insist on sharing basic premises, definitions and criteria of evaluating proofs. The question here is not whether the positions – for example, in the absolute/relative gains debate – actually are compatible or not, whether they are more or less commensurable than the paradigms of the 1970s that can be said to share much of which they were not aware.[24] The point is that a debate is shaped by the self-understanding about its character, and here the third debate was more or less explicitly shaped by ideas that can be expressed in the concept of incommensurability. This is not the guiding self-understanding of the fourth debate, where the sides either fight a merciless struggle over the heart of IR (similar to the second and especially maybe the first debate), or insist on being engaged in cumulative research within a joint research programme.

The fourth debate is not the third, the interparadigm debate. This move not only has taken us beyond the interparadigm debate but probably *after the fourth debate.*

In the 1990s there have been tendencies towards opening up a middle ground on the rationalist/reflectivist axis. After the polarization between rationalists and reflectivists, at times a tough struggle in the USA in the 1980s, the 1990s have witnessed increasing signs of rapprochement between the two. Among leading rationalists there have been indications of increasing boredom in relation to the quantitative/formal rational choice extremes. On the side of the reflectivists, we can see what could be called *post-radical reflectivism,* a move away from the self-marginalizing guerrilla approaches towards attempts to contribute to conceptualizations and handling of

	Debate 3 (interparadigm debate)	Debate 4a (reflectivist v. rationalist)	Debate 4b (absolute v. relative gains)
Form of relationship among debaters	incommensurability	war	differences within a research programme
Theme (or substance) of disagreement	world-view	philosophy	empirical question to be settled (ultimately: a coefficient!)
Combatants	the three paradigms	neo-neo synthesis against postmodernists	neo-realists versus liberal institutionalists

Figure 1.4 Comparing the third and fourth debates

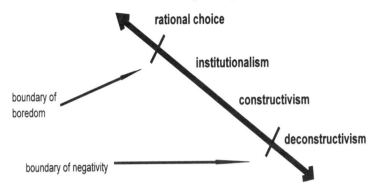

Figure 1.5 The 1990s?

various issues. Discussions on 'sovereignty' have been one meeting-point, where rationalists have admitted the existence of 'deep conventions' and thereby moved towards acknowledging the role of constitutive principles like sovereignty, very close to writings of some reflectivists (Wendt and Duvall 1989; Kratochwil 1995; compare Keohane 1988, 1995). Along the axis of debate of the 1980s – rationalist/reflectivist – we thus see an increasing marginalization of extreme rationalists (formal rational choice) and of extreme anti-IR approaches (deconstructivists), and the emergence of a middle ground where neo-institutionalists from the rationalist side meet constructivists from the reflectivist side. More 'philosophical' issues are increasingly welcome in the mainstream.

Rational choice is definitely strong as a scientific ideal, as an anchoring point for the self-understanding of the mainstream, but it is no longer self-evident as a cumulative, self-assured project; much of the work of sophisticated rat-choicers is aimed at reaching out to what it has been accused of not being able to reach, institutions or emotions (i.e. it takes up challenges from critics), and many of the leading IR figures are also trying to look in two directions, getting as much of their inspiration from constructivist challenges as from the inner logic of the rationalist programme.

Since the late 1980s, constructivism has been developing as a recognizable position. It shares many premises – and attacks on the mainstream – with deconstructivists, but can be singled out already by its tone. One of the leading constructivists (Alexander Wendt) has engaged in public flirtation with liberal institutionalists (Keohane) and cognitivists (Ned Lebow). In the first case, he told the liberal institutionalists that they are creating unnecessary difficulties for themselves in the way they are trying to handle the realist challenge. The liberal institutionalists want to show realists that co-operation is possible. But they accept a framework where state identities and interests are exogenous to the process, whereas a model where identities and interests are shaped and reshaped in interaction will be able much more convincingly to present the possibility of co-operation (Wendt 1992). The cognitivists, especially in foreign policy analysis (FPA), are told that their studies, which philosophically are rather unsophisticated, are actually a coherent constructivist approach (ISA panel 1995). Still, the constructivists have strong disagreements with the mainstream, and the constellation settles in as a general debate between rational choice approaches and social constructivists. (This pattern is reinforced by its paralleling one of the major disagreements within sociology at present.) Thus, a serious contender to mainstream rational-institutionalism has been constituted, which offers alternative explanations, not only of institutions, but also of other concepts – for instance, security issues – in a form which is still intelligible to the mainstream (Katzenstein 1996). These are, after all, attempts at competing *explanations.*[25]

Wendt can answer Keohane's 1988 call that the reflectivists come up with competing research programmes: Wendt wants to *explain* and he claims that he can explain better than Keohane. This contrasts to an Ashley or a Der Derian who would not agree that this is what we are trying to do. Therefore the Keohane move is in some sense fair *vis-à-vis* Wendt, but unfair towards Ashley and Der Derian; in the latter case it is disrespect for difference and a misrepresentation of another project (and has accordingly been ridiculed by poststructuralists as a revealing example of mainstream repression and/or naivety).[26] From a 'reflectivist' perspective, the effects of 'constructivism' are ambiguous: the rationalist mainstream is softened, opened to tolerating new kinds of questions, but the more radical impulses of the poststructuralists can now be outmanoeuvred because the mainstream can focus on the 'good guys' among the reflectivists and thereby forget about the 'bad guys' (cf. Cynthia Weber's accusation against Keohane for doing exactly this in relation to feminist IR, sorting it into 'good girls, little girls and bad girls'; Weber 1994). Some constructivists are very explicit in their distancing from poststructuralism, stressing that constructivism 'should be clearly distinguished from non-scientific poststructuralist approaches' (Adler and Barnett 1994: 19).

Poststructuralists could complain that constructivists are simultaneously exploiting 'their' opening. Constructivist 'relevance' partly stems from the attention generated by the critical work done by poststructuralists, and they directly build on the first rounds of critique of the atomism of neo-realism, the givens of rationalistic interests and the continuing positivism of the rationalists – all work done primarily by poststructuralists such as Ashley and Walker and by non-mainstream constructivists such as Kratochwil and Ruggie. All the diverse questions and destabilizations produced by these people seem to serve first of all to make room for a 'legitimate' new position in the theoretical landscape, an explanatory, constructivist social science, which we should probably start calling mainstream constructivism (Wendt, Adler, Barnett, Katzenstein *et al.*). The general silence on 'internal' differences that has paradoxically marked poststructuralists – due to their feeling of being the weak party in a tough battle – has so far been extended to constructivists as fellow 'post-positivists', but a major debate between constructivists and deconstructivists probably lies ahead.

A further reason to take constructivism seriously as a potential marker in the theoretical landscape is that it has a large, almost unlimited potential for integrating other theories within it: all kind of structures, units, or mechanisms can be tolerated as long as they are seen as 'socially constructed'. The constructivist response to almost any rationalist theory is 'You are right in substance, only your ontology is wrong!' For instance, Waltzian structure can be taken on board, though not as laws of nature, rather as socially constituted (Dessler 1989; Wæver in preparation), and constructivism thereby has an almost frightening potential as meta-theory subsuming all others. With constructivism as a socially accepted alternative to mainstream rationalism and institutionalism, there is clearly a drift towards more philosophical and meta-theoretical debates. Mainstream writers like Keohane and Krasner engage in debates on interest formation, deep conventions and generative structures.

Recent years have witnessed an increasing interest in the so-called English School. This seems to fit nicely into the 'after the fourth debate' scheme. The English School is a respectable, traditional approach which includes quasi-philosophical and historical reflection. It also cross-examines deep institutions in the system, and can relatively easily be linked to postmodernist notions, an emphasis on the cultural colouring of international systems, and especially the general 'radical' interest in thinking the basic categories of the international system instead of taking them as mechanical givens. At the same time, the classics of the English School, especially Bull's *Anarchical Society*, offer a comprehensible, seemingly straightforward discussion of the actual system with relatively clear, operational concepts. Thus, the American mainstream can find a moderate and not too dangerous way to extend its institutionalism by using Bull (and reading him almost as a regime theorist or neo-liberal institutionalist).[27] The new wave of English School enthusiasm thus ties in with the attempted rapprochement between reflectivists and rationalists, with the de-radicalization of reflectivism, and the rephilosophization of the rationalists.

What are then, finally, the advantages and disadvantages of (constructing) this 'fourth debate'? Compared with the alternative self-descriptions, it offers better strategic guidance and is a relatively up-to-date mapping of the terrain over which major battles have been fought. Among the disadvantages is that it reproduces Keohane's aggregation 'reflectivists', which hides important differences within this diverse group, and that it reduces the whole discipline to a linear debate along one axis, which tends to marginalize, for example, IPE, feminism and historical sociology, some of the most important theoretical challenges that not only squabble within IR, but challenge the boundaries of the discipline (cf. Guzzini forthcoming). It is important to have some idea of the fourth debate, because it is real as a guiding image in much IR theorizing. Still, all such maps are problematic and reductionist and, especially since it can be argued that we are now *after the fourth debate*, we should try to find other ways of reading, complementary strategies for reflecting on the discipline. One such strategy is to read its masters in the making.

LEVELS OF EXISTENCE IN IR

If one reads the pages of any major IR journal or even more strikingly the papers of an ISA conference, one gets the impression that 80 per cent of the discipline is neo-realist – therefore, most papers are prefaced with a critique of this dominant paradigm – and the rest neo-liberal institutionalist, leaving postmodernists and the like marginalized, questioned as to whether they are to be counted as legitimate members at all. If, then, one looks around an ISA conference at the actual participants, it will take hours to find anyone willing to be identified as a neo-realist, while a very high proportion of the young participants do constructivist or poststructuralist work, and the best-selling books are such as Jens Bartelson's poststructuralist genealogy of sovereignty or the Borderlines series by Campbell and Shapiro.

That neo-realism's main presence is in the form of the object of attack, that which most scholars feel a need to deal with and try to rout, means that it has a powerful position, even if there are few followers. It must have an appeal. Partly this is the Mohammed Ali effect described by Hans Mouritzen in Chapter 3: Kenneth Waltz fights with his guard down, inviting attack by the way he has constructed his theory as something simple and seemingly an easy target. Critics, however, will point to the influential position of neo-realists among the 'gatekeepers' of the discipline and therefore the need to relate to it when submitting to major journals or trying to establish a candidacy for a job at a leading university – but in these positions, one probably finds more neo-liberals and other rationalist critics of neo-realism. The power of the position must rest in the way it holds a principal claim to defining the discipline and is generally accepted as holding a corner on the map of the discipline used by most participants. One third, this is what Waltz himself claims – neo-realism is not a perfect theory, but it is the best bid so far for a theory which is really a *theory*. Another third of the explanation probably is convention: the discipline has defined neo-realism as 'the dominant position', which is actually quite comfortable for all others. Finally, in some sense realism is the prototype of what most other theories try to do: to establish sovereignty, to constitute and empower a figure of the state (Ashley forthcoming); and thus as posture and practice it is more pervasive than official realism. Others borrow rhetorical figures from realism and make novel moves while repeating, more or less frequently, core metaphors such as the domestic analogy (Bull 1977) or inside/outside (Walker 1993), now deployed on new referents – endowing new subjects with sovereignty or different spaces with order. This could be an additional reason why realism remains central to IR debates – it is still in there, within most other approaches, and direct engagement with realism also holds relevance for other parts of IR.

Despite its limited corporeal manifestation,[28] neo-realism is very real as an IR position, if one talks of one level of IR existence: that of the positions used to define the landscape, used for orientation by others. Due to the limits of strategic imagination, our picture of battle formations must be reduced to a simple pattern. The geometry of IR debates is therefore usually a duel or a triangle, or some moderate variation of either: for example, a duel with allies, or the flanking manoeuvre of radicals in a triangle where the two other corners move towards each other, or some similar figure which reduces the number of defining positions to at most a handful, and which necessarily tends towards privileging the extreme postures.

Most of the practice, however, does not take place *at* the corners – that would be a strange, repetitive, or purely combatant activity, simply consolidating the wisdom of a position while fighting the other(s). This does occur at the height of 'debates' in the discipline, but rarely. More commonly, writers engage in problematization, in alterations, in cross-overs between schools or fields. Thus, most of the interesting work is done in ways that do not fit into the boxes. This is one of the main motivations for the present book. This second level is largely the level of the Masters (in the Making). These are the works that are read and discussed, that inspire others, that appear as convincing and challenging *new* contributions. Some of these will be defined by the major metaphors and maps of the discipline – e.g. acting on the rationalist/reflectivist axis; others carve out their own problematique and become possible building-blocks for the coming definitions of what it is all about.

A third level is then the 'anonymous' mass in the discipline. The typical types here will not necessarily be the map-defining or even the master-defined ones, but various mixed positions and products of previous debates. It is impossible to sum up this complex clutter, but the book *Global Voices* (1993) offers a nice picture. Leading scholars present what they see as the contending approaches, in the form of fictitious figures debating.

James Rosenau opens by introducing two figures. One is a young rebel who is undecided about how to draw on the different new approaches – postmodernism, neo-Marxism, etc. His opponent is an old professor, a US product of the second debate: not a realist, but one of the postbehavioralists who went through what was for them a critical operation against the mainstream but what is now seen by another generation as another form of realism and positivism. Steve Smith adds two British academics. One is an old pre-realist, someone interested in case-studies and historical work, sceptical of all those modern theorists such as Morgenthau. The other is a theorist somewhat like Steve Smith himself, interested in structure-agency and in the way the discipline is an American one. Just as Rosenau and Smith in practice presented themselves as one in their pairs of figures, Christine Sylvester also introduces herself, though this time both the new characters are she: an American and a Zimbabwean feminist, the same person is some respects, different in others. At this point, one starts to notice one curious absence: realism is much talked about, much attacked, but not represented in the crowd (very realistic, probably, were this to depict actual life at an ISA conference). Der Derian then reflects on the problems associated with joining such a dialogue – very poststructuralist, to reflect on the problems of one's own enunciation – and proceeds to add a number of 'postmodern personae' through a play on texts by Ivan Turgenev and Bertolt Brecht. Finally, Jean Bethke Elshtain gives the whole story some nice twists. Her first figure is an established feminist IR scholar, her second a student who did not go into academia but became a journalist/ activist. And not least, in her story we meet finally GORP, 'the Ghost of Realism Past'.

There are many ways to tell the story of International Relations as a discipline. The social world of IR has several levels of existence. 'Positions' and 'figures' can be defined in different ways. I have here tried to sketch three levels. This book has a definite relationship to all three.

First, paradigms and dominant 'schools' are important even when few identify with them, because by defining our self-images of possible positions, of theories established with a certain argumentative foundation, they thereby define the debates *of* the discipline. (This kind of story is the usual one in textbooks, and a variation on it has been given here in this introduction). At this level, a position can be upheld even if it is hard to find a live incarnation of it because each position is partly defined by the other. At this first level positions do not exist separately, but are necessarily interconnected, because they have to form constellations in which they are defined by and in relation to each other – they have to be arranged to enable narratives that give meaning to struggles and thereby to theoretical work: who is doing what to whom? Typically patterns emerge with dichotomies, triangles, or rather more complex variations, as in my fourth debate. To present the discipline as mainly consisting of these more or less ghostly positions is, however, impoverishing. If teaching it (too rigorously), there is an especial risk of blocking students' access to much of the important work being done.

Second, the figures who write the most interesting and challenging books on IR often move away from these positions. Some relate to them, others not; some try openly to reconcile positions which are claimed to be incompatible, or to subdivide positions which are seen as one, while others try not to get caught up in these dominant definitions of choices at all. The rest of this book will present twelve such actual figures in IR who are both the bearers and negators of paradigms. We hope to break with the habit of privileging the few rare, stereotyped figures who fit into boxes, while those who try to do interesting things are cut into pieces to be distributed among different containers. This practice is paradoxical because most of us probably tend to think of ourselves as trying to move between signposts, to combine subfields, to work our way out of simple choices. Young academics trying to work out how to make their own personal choices should find it especially useful to read the stories of how others have chosen and manoeuvred and what the consequences are of adopting different academic strategies.

Third, all the other persons in the discipline, those who study, teach, research, go to conferences, are not widely seen as masters in the making. In this world, where numerous small – existential/academic – decisions are made continuously without enjoying the concentrated attention that accompanies similar decisions by the Masters in the Making, far and away the biggest quantity of IR is done. At this third level of IR, some of us had the idea of writing a collection of articles about a number of the figures of international thought.

NOTES

The author is grateful to Barry Buzan, Stefano Guzzini, Rodney Bruce Hall, Iver B. Neumann and especially Elizabeth Kier for extensive comments on various drafts of this chapter.

1 Their work is in print, with Morgenthau's *Politics Among Nations* continuously revised to keep an updated version for teaching (Morgenthau and Thompson 1985) and Bull experiencing a revival of interest in the 1990s, with the result, for example, that *The Anarchical Society* from 1977 was reissued in 1995 with a new preface. Debate on both is lively, with books like Thompson and Myers (1977) on Morgenthau, and Miller and Vincent (1990) on Bull, and with numerous articles on aspects of their work: Morgenthau and ethics, Morgenthau's concept of politics, Bull's view of justice, of intervention, etc.

2 Vincent, the only deceased theorist in our collection, qualifies as a master *in the making*, because he is probably not generally accepted as a major figure beyond the English School circle, but a case is made in Chapter 2 that he is *now* becoming one, partly for reasons internal to theory, partly because of political developments, as some of his favourite subjects (humanitarian intervention and human rights) are becoming topical.

3 Thompson's two books nicely parallel this volume because the three form a sequence, each taking over where the previous one left off, but in other ways the Thompson volumes might not be the ideal choices for accessing those older theorists. His presentations are rather brief, biographical and mainly introductory, although – especially in *Masters* – he offers thought-provoking interpretations of the inner tensions in the work of Wolfers, Morgenthau and Wight, for example. Whereas to the best of our knowledge the present book is the only one to discuss present-day theorists, many people write on 'old' authors. There are numerous articles in such journals as the *Review of International Studies, Millennium* and increasingly even *International Organization* and *International Studies Quarterly* on Morgenthau, Wight and Carr, not to speak of Hobbes, Kant, Rousseau and Grotius. Most of these figures have also been the theme of whole volumes. The early and mid-twentieth-century writers have been dealt with jointly only by Thompson, whereas the classics are also presented in, for example Kauppi and Viotti (1992) and Knutsen (1992), and Clark and Neumann (1996) focus on figures, more as the present book does, and have a penchant for the unusual classics.

4 A very specific answer here is that the Ashley chapter actually *is* written; contracted six years ago, it awaits publication in Rengger and Hoffmann (forthcoming).

5 A previous draft listed a number of authors for consideration, arguing in most cases why they were less ideal than the ones chosen. Although publication of this list might reduce criticism (and ease hurt pride), it would only add an even larger number of names to the list of those who were not even runners-up. We prefer to stand by our selection of the twelve!

6 Wallerstein has been widely written about, and Sinclair (1996) could be said to be the master-maker article on Cox, although paradoxically lacking first of all critical scrutiny.

7 Third could be mentioned the instituting of a rules/absence dichotomy through the work of such legal positivists as Austin; cf. Marlene Wind on Onuf (Chapter 9).

8 Keohane 1988 (see also Chapter 4 on Keohane). On continental philosophy and 'postmodernism' see, for example, 'Philosophical Traditions in International Relations', special issue of *Millennium* 17(2) (1988); Richard K. Ashley and R. B. J. Walker (eds) 'Speaking the Language of Exile: Dissidence in International Studies', special issue of *International Studies Quarterly* 34(3) (September), especially the overview by Jim George and David Campbell; Der Derian and Shapiro 1989. Pauline Rosenau (1990) emphasizes the import from 'the humanities', and Yosef Lapid (1989) introduced the term 'post-positivism'.

9 For a contemporary attempt to insist on 'the three images' as a valid matrix for interpreting the previous four millennia of IR thought as well as current theory, see Kauppi and Viotti (1992); and Viotti and Kauppi (1993[1987]). Knutsen presents them as the 'three paradigms of contemporary international relations' (1992: 234–9).

10 The first department of International Relations was set up in Aberystwyth in 1919; the London School of Economics followed in 1923 and the University of Oxford in 1930. Furthermore, during the years 1918–20, such institutions as the Royal Institute of International Affairs (London), and the Council on Foreign Relations (New York) were founded, while Germany in 1923 got its Institut für Auswärtige Politik. Cf. Amstrup 1989.

11 For a serious attempt to represent the work of interdependence theorists of the interwar period as interesting academic contributions, see de Wilde 1991.

12 A typical list of common assumptions attributed to realism is as follows: 1) the most important actors are nation-states, and these 2) are unitary actors, and 3) are rational; 4) within the hierarchy of international subjects, the list is topped by national security: see 'Military and Related Political Issues Dominate World Politics' (Viotti and Kauppi 1987: 6 f. and 32 f.). Most of the famous realists deviate from this stereotype on at least two of the four points; they often reflect on the end of the age of the nation-state, they regularly emphasize political, economic, or moral factors more than military ones, and, maybe most important, they argue against a belief in rationality in politics and in favour of a scepticism of knowledge.

13 Wight (1966 [1960]: 26), Wight even more provocatively writes:

> If Sir Thomas More or Henry IV, let us say, were to return to England and France in 1960, it is not beyond plausibility that they would admit that their countries had moved domestically towards goals and along paths which they could approve. But if they contemplated the international scene, it is more likely that they would be struck by resemblances to what they remembered. (...) The stage would have become much wider, the actors fewer, their weapons more alarming, but the play would be the same old melodrama.
>
> (Wight 1966: 26)

14 This section is a short version of my analysis in Wæver 1996a.

15 These maps have had a difficult time emerging, partly because of some inner, logical features of the interparadigm debate – exactly that it is an *interparadigm* debate. As a story of incommensurable paradigms, it is difficult to close, because it contains a cognitive mechanism for reinterpreting any attempt to go beyond it: 'What you say is only one perception, yet another limited view, and thus is unable to settle the debate because you too are caught in incommensurability.' Reflectivists as well as rationalists could benefit from taking a fresh and critical look at the philosophical arguments around 'incommensurability' (Wæver 1996a: 170–4).

16 Keohane and Nye, for instance, in the most famous book of the period, *Power and Interdependence*, solved the problem through what was in part a dualistic approach: realism got what was realism's (conflictual politics among not too civilized states), while an alternative model of 'complex interdependence' was deemed more relevant to politics among the developed, democratic states. The academic world did not easily absorb this complementarist approach (cf. Suhr's

Chapter 4 in this book) – it was not much reflected on, and *Power and Inter-dependence* (like other contemporary books) was taken as 'a new, alternative paradigm' (which was probably not totally against the intentions of its authors).

17 Incommensurability does not – as often wrongly suggested – imply the impossibility of dialogue. If it did, the term 'interparadigm debate' would be a contradiction in terms. It means, first of all, that no neutral language is available into which the competing theories can be translated and then compared (Kuhn 1970). It might be possible to translate one theory into the language of another, and this in a sense is what we are all asked to strive for (Kuhn 1970; Bernstein 1991: 65 ff.), but we still have to recognize that this is not the same as understanding the other theory as that which it is to itself, in its own language, nor does it supply any measure outside the competing theories by which to judge them and choose the better one.

18 Because of their analysis of the shrewd techniques of reappropriation used by western metaphysics with its ubiquitous postures, concepts and desires, the new figures will often choose writing styles and themes that appear bizarre to the mainstream. These are simply the self-imposed demands generated by another philosophy and thus equivalent to the demands of the scientific approach as construed by traditional IR (Wæver in preparation: Ch.1).

19 Robert Cox used the name 'neo-realism' in his influential 1981 article, but in his terminology 'neo-realism' was twentieth-century, or postwar, American realism – e.g. including Morgenthau – and stood in contrast to a classical realism of Machiavelli, Hobbes, Carr and Dehio. The use of 'neo-realism' as referring to the more structural and 'scientific' version that emerged in the second half of the 1970s – and thereby constructing a 'classical realism' that includes Morgenthau and the other early postwar realists – can thus be traced back to Ashley (1984) building on his earlier argument (1981) on different types of realism. Ruggie's 1983 article is subtitled 'Toward a Neo-realist Synthesis', but never spells out what 'neo-realism' means.

20 For example, John Herz wrote in 1950: 'Whether man is by nature peaceful and cooperative, or domineering and aggressive, is not the question. The condition that concerns us here is not a biological or anthropological but a social one' (1950: 157). Kenneth Waltz's book *Man, the State, and War* (1959) was organized around the argument in favour of 'third image' explanations of war, i.e. causation from the structure of the international system in contrast to first image (human nature and psychological mechanisms) and second image (the nature of the state). The distance to Niebuhrian realism was explicit in Waltz's contention with the first image.

21 Discussions on 'reflexivism' are often inspired by Anthony Giddens, see especially 1991. Mark Neufeld directly addressed the issue of 'Reflexivity and International Relations Theory' (1993) – although his article is not very reflexive. It grounds itself in a transcendental Coxianism.

22 Grieco (1988 and 1990); Keohane (1989: 10, 14 and 18). Baldwin (1993) has recently collected most of the main interventions in the debate. The neo-liberal institutionalist declares that egoistic, utility-maximizing states can achieve co-operation under anarchy through rational action without any altruistic assumptions; i.e. 'We have beaten you on your own ground.' The neo-realist replies: 'You haven't because you have misconstrued anarchy.' It is not enough to remove the idea that states are positively concerned about each other and make them egoistic maximizers of absolute gains ('How much do I gain by this?'). States are often negatively concerned about each other and therefore ask about co-operation: 'Which of us will gain most from this?' A state will not co-operate if co-operation benefits the other more than itself because ultimately it might – due to anarchy and self-help – face the other state in a contest decided by power ratios. The liberal counters that states are not concerned about relative gains all the time – if not for other reasons, then because when N is more

than 2 it will have to decide who to fear and whom to rely on. Romantic reunion: the two agree that states are concerned about absolute as well as relative gain; they agree to define a coefficient (r) determining the relative attention to the two, and to research this factor.

23 Steve Smith (1995: 26–8) has suggested another labelling pair – constitutive theory and explanatory theory – which points specifically to this argument: one side views theoretical practice as part of the reproduction or transformation of 'international relations', while the other sees our theories as separate from a reality about which they purport to speak. The memberships will be roughly similar for constitutive and reflective and for explanatory and rationalist, possibly with the exception of some constructivists around the middle.

24 It is certainly possible to argue that the absolute/relative gains debate actually is about deep disagreements – not a matter of degrees – and that the neo-neo synthesis is thus a chimera. This, however, does not invalidate my interpretation: it is not a claim that neo-realism and neo-liberalism actually *are* close or compatible. The clue is that they *want* to be, that there is an attempt to meet, to form a joint research project, to discuss *as if* rational debate were possible, i.e. to assume that the interparadigm debate is over. The self-perception of the neo-neo group as being able to reduce the absolute/relative gains debate to the size of the coefficient 'r', can be challenged by questioning whether (neo-)realists should agree to discuss 'gains' at all, or whether this is scientific form with imported utilitarian and progressivist assumptions. The relative gains argument is not about cumulative gains, in a sense suitable for models, it is about fear and negative-driven action, i.e. not cumulative gains. The counter-move made by realists to neo-liberal institutionalism should be not the relative gains formula but a *security* theory (possibly derived from Clausewitz) that spells out the logic of fear-driven speculations about hypothetical events. That the answer actually became Grieco's theory of gains shows the depth of neo'ism: it had to be something one could express in a formula and by specifying actor calculus, micro foundations.

25 Increasingly, we see articles that try to 'test' rationalist against constructivist explanations (e.g. Barnett 1995; Hurrell forthcoming; Rhodes forthcoming). It will be interesting to see how well the parties succeed in agreeing on terms of debate, and in particular on what constitutes an explanation.

26 Not all constructivists think of their own project as explanation; some emphasize that they are after understanding instead; cf. Price 1994.

27 Keohane's articles have included an increasing number of references to Bull and recently also to Wight (Keohane 1992, 1995). Buzan's English School article (1993) is in this context interesting, both because it was published in *International Organization*, and because of the explicit argument made about the usefulness of the English School for the Americans. See also the articles on regime theory and the English School: Hurrell (1993), Evans and Wilson (1992), T. Brems Knudsen (1994); for American constructivism and the English School, see Dunne (1995a, 1995b). On how to save the English School from the Americans, see Wæver (1996b and forthcoming).

28 Within the field or subdiscipline of security studies, neo-realism is much more alive and, not least through the influential journal *International Security*, has established a position as gatekeeper closer to that which it is often credited with in IR in general.

REFERENCES

Adler, Emanuel and Barnett, Michael N. (1994) 'Security Communities', presented at the annual meeting of the American Political Science Association.

Alker, Hayward R., Jr and Biersteker, Thomas J. (1984) 'The Dialectics of World Order: Notes for a Future Archeologist of International Savoir Faire', *International Studies Quarterly* 28(2): 121–42.

Amstrup, Niels (1989) 'The Study of International Relations: Old or New? A Historical Outline (1500 to 1939)', paper presented at the joint conference of ISA and BISA in London.

Ashley, Richard K. (1981) 'Political Realism and Human Interests', *International Studies Quarterly* 25(2): 204–36.

—— (1984) 'The Poverty of Neo-realism', *International Organization* 38(2): 225–86.

—— (1989) 'Imposing International Purpose: Notes on a Problematic of Governance', in E.-O. Czempiel and J. N. Rosenau (eds) *Global Changes and Theoretical Challenges*, Lexington, MA: Lexington Books, pp. 251–90.

—— (forthcoming) 'Critical Spirits/Realist Specters: Some Hypotheses on the Spectro-Poetics of International Relations', in Stephen Gill and James H. Mittelman (eds) *Innovation and Transformation in International Relations Theory*.

Baldwin, David (ed.) (1993) *Neo-realism and Neo-liberalism: The Contemporary Debate*, New York: Columbia University Press.

Banks, Michael (1984) 'The Evolution of International Relations Theory', in Michael Banks (ed.) *Conflict in World Society: A New Perspective on International Relations*, Brighton, Sx: Harvester Wheatsheaf, pp. 1–21.

—— (1985) 'The Inter-Paradigm Debate', in M. Light and A. J. R. Groom (eds) *International Relations: A Handbook of Current Theory*, London: Pinter, pp. 7–26.

Barnett, Michael N. (1995) 'Sovereignty, Nationalism and Regional Order in the Arab States System', *International Organization* 49(3): 479–510.

Bernstein, Richard J. (1991) *The New Constellation: The Ethical-Political Horizons of Modernity/Postmodernity*, Cambridge: Polity Press.

Brown, Chris (1992) *International Relations Theory: New Normative Approaches*, Hemel Hempstead, Herts: Harvester Wheatsheaf.

Bull, Hedley (1966) 'International Theory: The Case for a Classical Approach', *World Politics* 18(3): 361–77.

—— (1972) 'The Theory of International Politics, 1919–1969', in Brian Porter (ed.) *The Aberystwyth Papers: International Politics 1919–1969*, London: Oxford University Press, pp. 30–55.

—— (1977) *The Anarchical Society: A Study of Order in World Politics*, London: Macmillan.

Buzan, Barry (1993) 'From International System to International Society: Structural Realism and Regime Theory Meet the English School', *International Organization* 47(3): 327–52.

—— (1996) 'The Timeless Wisdom of Realism?', in Steve Smith, Ken Booth and Marysia Zalewski (eds) *Theorizing International Relations: Positivism and After*, Cambridge: Cambridge University Press, pp. 47–65.

—— Jones, Charles and Little, Richard (1993) *The Logic of Anarchy: Neo-realism to Structural Realism*, New York: Columbia University Press.

—— and Little, Richard (1994) 'The Idea of "International System": Theory Meets History', *International Political Science Review* 15(3): 231–55.

—— (1995) 'Reconceptualizing Anarchic Structure: Accommodating Structural and Functional Differentiation of Units', draft (12 May).

Campbell, David (1992) *Writing Security: United States Foreign Policy and the Politics of Identity*, Minneapolis, MN: University of Minnesota Press.

—— (1993) *Politics Without Principle: Sovereignty, Ethics, and the Narratives of the Gulf War*, Boulder, CO and London: Lynne Rienner.

Carr, E. H. (1981 [1939]) *The Twenty Years' Crisis 1919–1939: An Introduction to the Study of International Relations*, London and Basingstoke, Hants: Macmillan 'Papermac'.

Clark, Ian and Neumann, Iver B. (eds) (1996) *Classical Theories in International Relations*, Basingstoke, Hants: Macmillan, St Antony's series.

Connolly, William E. (1991) *Identity/Difference: Negotiations of Political Paradox*, Ithaca, NY: Cornell University Press.

Cox, Robert W. (1981) 'Social Forces, States and World Orders: Beyond International Relations Theory', *Millennium* 10(1): 126–55.

de Wilde, Jaap (1991) *Saved from Oblivion: Interdependence Theory in the First Half of the twentieth Century: a Study on the Causality between War and Complex Interdependence*, Aldershot, Harts: Dartmouth.

Der Derian, James (1987) *On Diplomacy: A Genealogy of Western Estrangement*, Oxford and Cambridge, MA: Blackwell.

——and Shapiro, Michael (eds) (1989) *International/Intertextual Relations: Postmodern Readings of World Politics*, Lexington, MA and Toronto: Lexington Books.

Descombes, Vincent (1979) *Le Même et l'Autre*, Paris: Les Editions de Minuit.

Dessler, David (1989) 'What's at Stake in the Agent–Structure Debate?', *International Organization* 43(3): 441–73.

Donnelly, Jack (1992) 'Twentieth-Century Realism', in Terry Nardin and David R. Mapel (eds) *Traditions of International Ethics*, Cambridge: Cambridge University Press, pp. 85–111.

Dougherty, James E. and Pfaltzgraff, Robert L., Jr (1971) *Contending Theories of International Relations*, Philadelphia, PA, New York and Toronto: J. B. Lippincott.

Dunne, Timothy (1995a) 'International Society: Theoretical Promises Fulfilled?', *Co-operation and Conflict* 30(2): 125–54.

——(1995b) 'The Social Construction of International Society', *European Journal of International Relations* 1(3) September: 367–90.

Evans, Tony and Wilson, Peter (1992) 'Regime Theory and the English School of International Relations: a Comparison', *Millennium* 21(3): 329–52.

Foucault, Michel (1971) 'Orders of Discourse' (translation of *L'ordre du discours*), in *Social Science Information* (April); republished as 'The Discourse on Language', an appendix in Foucault 1972 [1969].

——(1972 [1969]) *The Archeology of Knowledge*, New York: Pantheon Books.

George, Jim (1993) *Discourses of Global Politics: A Critical (Re)Introduction to International Relations*, Boulder, CO: Lynne Rienner.

Giddens, Anthony (1991) *Modernity and Self-Identity: Self and Society in the Late Modern Age*, Cambridge: Polity.

Gilpin, Robert (1981) *War and Change in World Politics*, New York: Cambridge University Press.

Grieco, Joseph M. (1988) 'Anarchy and the Limits of Co-operation: a Realist Critique of the Newest Liberal Institutionalism', *International Organization* 42(3): s. 485–508.

——(1990) *Co-operation among Nations: Europe, America, and Non-tariff Barriers to Trade*, Ithaca, NY and London: Cornell University Press.

Griffith, Martin (1992) *Realism, Idealism & International Politics – A Reinterpretation*, London and New York: Routledge.

Guzzini, Stefano (forthcoming) *Realism in International Relations/International Political Economy: The Continuing Story of Death Foretold*, London: Routledge.

Herz, John H. (1950) 'Idealist Internationalism and the Security Dilemma', *World Politics* 2(2): 157–80.

Holsti, K.J. (1985) *The Dividing Discipline: Hegemony and Diversity in International Theory*, Winchester, MA: Allen & Unwin.

——(1993) 'International Relations at the End of the Millennium', *Review of International Studies* 19(4): 401–8.

Hurrell, Andrew (1993) 'International Society and the Study of Regimes: a Reflective Approach', in Volker Rittberger (ed.) *Regime Theory and International Relations*, Oxford: Clarendon Press, pp. 49–72.

——(forthcoming) 'An Emerging Security Community in South America', in Emanuel Adler and Michael N. Barnett (eds) *Security Communities in Theory, History and Comparison*.

Kaplan, Morton A. (1966) 'The Great Debate: Traditionalism vs. Science in International Relations', *World Politics* 19(1): 1–21.

Katzenstein, Peter (ed.) (1996) *The Culture of National Security: Identity and Norms in World Politics*, New York: Columbia University Press.

Kauppi, Mark V. and Viotti, Paul R. (1992) *The Global Philosophers: World Politics in Western Thought*, New York and Toronto: Lexington/Maxwell.

Keohane, Robert O. (1988) 'International Institutions: Two Approaches', ISA presidential address, reprinted in *International Studies Quarterly* 32(4): 379–96 (and in Keohane 1989).

—— (1989) *International Institutions and State Power: Essays in International Relations Theory*, Boulder, CO: Westview.

—— (1990) 'International Liberalism Reconsidered', in John Dunn (ed.) *The Economic Limits to Modern Politics*, Cambridge: Cambridge University Press, pp. 165–94.

—— (1992) book review of Martin Wight's *International Theory*, *American Political Science Review* 86(4): 1112.

—— (1993) 'Institutionalist Theory and the Realist Challenge: After the Cold War', in David Baldwin (ed.) *Neo-realism and Neo-liberalism: the Contemporary Debate*, New York: Columbia University Press, pp. 269–300.

—— (1995) 'Hobbes' Dilemma and Institutional Change in World Politics: Sovereignty in International Society', in Hans-Henrik Holm and Georg Sørensen (eds) *Whose World Order? Uneven Globalization and the End of the Cold War*, Boulder, CO: Westview Press, pp. 165–86.

—— and Nye, Joseph S., Jr (1975) 'International Interdependence and Integration', in F. I. Greenstein and N. W. Polsby (eds) *Handbook of Political Science*, Vol. 8, *International Politics*, Reading, MA: Addison-Wesley, pp. 363–414.

—— (1977) *Power and Interdependence*, Boston, MA: Little, Brown.

Knudsen, Tonny Brems (1994) 'Det Nye Europa: Orden eller Kaos?' MA thesis, University of Aarhus.

Knutsen, Torbjörn L. (1992) *A History of International Relations Theory*, Manchester and New York: Manchester University Press.

Kratochwil, Friedrich (1995) 'Sovereignty as *Dominium*: Is there a Right of Humanitarian Intervention?', in Gene M. Lyons and Michael Mastanduno (eds) *Beyond Westphalia: State Sovereignty and International Intervention*, Baltimore, MD and London: Johns Hopkins University Press, pp. 21–42.

—— and Ruggie, John G. (1986) 'International Organization: a State of the Art on an Art of the State', *International Organization* 40(4): 753–75.

Krishna, Sankaran (1996) 'Cartographic Anxiety: Mapping the Body Politic in India', in Michael J. Shapiro and Hayward R. Alker (eds) *Challenging Boundaries: Global Flows, Territorial Identities*, Minneapolis, MN: University of Minnesota Press, pp. 193–215.

Kuhn, Thomas (1962) *The Structure of Scientific Revolutions*, Chicago: Chicago University Press.

—— (1970) 'Reflections on my Critics', in Imre Lakatos and Alan Musgrave (eds) *Criticism and the Growth of Knowledge*, Cambridge: Cambridge University Press, pp. 231–78.

Lakatos, Imre and Musgrave, Alan (eds) (1970) *Criticism and the Growth of Knowledge*, Cambridge: Cambridge University Press.

Lapid, Yosef (1989) 'The Third Debate: On the Prospects of International Theory in a Post-positivist Era', *International Studies Quarterly* 33(3): 235–54.

Lenin, V.I. (1933 [1916]) *Imperialism, the Highest Stage of Capitalism*, New York: Little Lenin Library.

Maghroori, Ray and Ramberg, Bennett (eds) (1982) *Globalism versus Realism: International Relations' Third Debate?*, Boulder, Co: Westview Press.

Miller, J. D. B., and Vincent, R. J. (1990) *Order and Violence – Hedley Bull and International Relations*, Oxford: Clarendon Press.

Morgenthau, Hans J. (1946) *Scientific Man vs. Power Politics*, Chicago: University of Chicago Press.

—— (1954[1947]) *Politics Among Nations: The Struggle for Power and Peace*, 2nd edn, New York: Knopf.

—— and Thompson, Kenneth W. (1985[1947]) *Politics Among Nations: The Struggle for Power and Peace*, 6th edn, New York: Knopf.

Neufeld, Mark (1993) 'Reflexivity and International Relations Theory', *Millennium* 22(1): 53–76.

Nye, Joseph (1988) 'Neo-realism and Neo-liberalism', *World Politics* 40(2): 235–51.

Price, Richard (1994) 'Interpretation and Disciplinary Orthodoxy in International Relations', *Review of International Studies* 20(2): 201–4.

Rengger, N. J. and Hoffmann, M. (forthcoming) *Beyond the Interparadigm Debate*, Hemel Hempstead, Herts: Harvester Wheatsheaf.

Rhodes, Edward (forthcoming) 'International Relations Theory and the 1890s: Testing Interest-Based and Cultural Cognitive Accounts of Strategic Choice', *Security Studies*.

Ringmar, Erik (1996) 'On the Ontological Status of the State', *European Journal of International Relations* 2(4) : 394–422.

Rosenau, James N. (1984) 'A Pre-Theory Revisited: World Politics in an Era of Cascading Interdependence', *International Studies Quarterly* 28(3): 245–305.

—— (ed.) (1993) *Global Voices – Dialogues in International Relations*, Boulder, CO: Westview Press.

—— and Knorr, K. (eds) (1969) *Contending Approaches to International Politics*, Princeton, NJ: Princeton University Press.

Rosenau, Pauline (1990) 'Once Again into the Fray: International Relations Confronts the Humanities', *Millennium* 19(1): 83–110.

Rothstein, Robert L. (1972) *Planning, Prediction and Policymaking in Foreign Affairs – Theory and Practice*, Boston, MA: Little, Brown.

Ruggie, John G. (1983) 'Continuity and Transformation in the World Polity: Toward a Neo-realist Synthesis', *World Politics* 35(2): 261–85.

Sinclair, Timothy J. (1996) 'Beyond International Relations Theory: Robert W. Cox and Approaches to World Order', in Robert W. Cox with Timothy J. Sinclair, *Approaches to World Order*, Cambridge: Cambridge University Press, pp. 3–18.

Smith, Steve (1995) 'The Self-Images of a Discipline: a Genealogy of International Relations Theory', in Ken Booth and Steve Smith (eds) *International Relations Theory Today*, Cambridge: Polity Press, pp. 1–37.

Thompson, Kenneth W. (1980) *Masters of International Thought: Major Twentieth-Century Theorists and the World Crisis*, Baton Rouge, LA and London: Louisiana State University Press.

—— (1994) *Fathers of International Thought – The Legacy of Political Theory*, Baton Rouge, LA and London: Louisiana State University Press.

Thompson, K. and Myers, R. J. (1977) *Truth and Tragedy – A Tribute to Hans J. Morgenthau*, New Brunswick, NY and London: Transaction Books.

Tucker, Robert W. (1977) *The Inequality of Nations*, New York: Basic Books.

Turnbull, Phyllis (1996) 'Remembering Pearl Harbor: The Semiotics of the *Arizona* Memorial', in Michael J. Shapiro and Hayward R. Alker (eds) *Challenging Boundaries: Global Flows, Territorial Identities*, Minneapolis, MN: University of Minnesota Press, pp. 407–34.

Viotti, Paul R. and Kauppi, Mark V. (1987) *International Relations Theory*, New York: Macmillan.

—— (1993[1987]) *International Relations Theory*, 2nd edn, New York: Macmillan.

Wæver, Ole (1992) *Introduktion til Studiet af International Politik*, Copenhagen: Politiske Studier.

—— (1994) 'After the Fourth Debate', unpublished draft.

—— (1996a) 'The Rise and Fall of the Inter-Paradigm Debate', in Steve Smith, Ken Booth and Marysia Zalewski (eds) *Theorizing International Relations: Positivism and After*, Cambridge: Cambridge University Press, pp. 149–85.

—— (1996b) 'Europe's Three Empires: a Watsonian Interpretation of Post-wall European Security', in Rick Fawn, Jeremy Larkins and Robert Newman (eds) *International Society: After the Cold War*, London: *Millennium* and Macmillan.

—— (forthcoming) 'Four Meanings of International Society: a Trans-atlantic Dialogue', in Barbara Allen Roberson (ed.) *The Future of International Society*, Oxford: Oxford University Press.

—— (in preparation) 'The Politics of International Structure',

Walker, R. B. J. (1993) *Intside/Outside: International Relations as Political Theory*, Cambridge: Cambridge University Press.

Waltz, Kenneth (1959) *Man, the State, and War: a Theoretical Analysis*, New York: Columbia University Press.

—— (1979) *Theory of International Politics*, New York: Random House.

—— (1986) 'Reflections on Theory of International Politics: a Response to My Critics', Robert Keohane (ed.) *Neo-realism and its Critics*, New York: Columbia University Press.

—— (1990) 'Realist Thought and Neo-realist Theory', *Journal of International Affairs* 44(1): 21–37.

Weber, Cynthia (1994) 'Good Girls, Little Girls and Bad Girls: Male Paranoia in Robert Keohane's Critique of Feminist International Relations', *Millennium* 23(2): 337–49.

Wendt, Alexander E. (1987) 'The Agent–Structure Problem in International Relations Theory', *International Organization* 41(3): 335–70.

—— (1992) 'Anarchy Is what States Make of It: the Social Construction of Power Politics', *International Organization* 46(2): 391–426.

—— and Duvall, Raymond (1989) 'Institutions and International Order', in Ernst-Otto Czempiel and James N. Rosenau (eds) *Global Changes and Theoretical Challenges: Approaches to World Politics for the 1990s*, Lexington MA: Lexington Books, pp. 51–76.

Wight, Martin (1966[1960]) 'Why Is There No International Theory?', in H. Butterfield and M. Wight (eds) *Diplomatic Investigations: Essays in the Theory of International Politics* London: Allen and Unwin, pp. 17–34.

—— (1992) *International Theory: The Three Traditions*, ed. Gabriele Wight and Brian Porter, Leicester: Leicester University Press.

Williams, Michael C. (1996) 'Hobbes and International Relations: a Reconsideration', *International Organization* 50(2): 213–36.

Wolfers, Arnold and Martin, Laurence W. (eds) (1956) *The Anglo-American Tradition in Foreign Affairs: Readings from Thomas More to Woodrow Wilson*, New Haven: CT Yale University Press.

2 John Vincent and the English School of International Relations

Iver B. Neumann

John Vincent was born in 1943 and died in 1990. He studied at Aberystwyth (BA, IR), Leicester (MA, European Studies) and the Australian National University in Canberra (PhD, IR), and taught at Keele, then Oxford and finally the London School of Economics, where he succeeded Susan Strange as Montague Burton Professor of International Relations in 1989. While on leave from Keele, he spent a year at Princeton, and another at the International Institute for Strategic Studies in London: he also paid repeated visitsto Canberra and Princeton. He was editor of the Review of International Studies, *1986–9. His work included major studies on non-intervention and human rights and, fittingly for a self-proclaimed member of 'the English School', showed his overall interest in the historical development of the modern states system and its cultures.*

Why include Vincent in a book on major figures in International Relations? There is, first, the inherent interest of his main themes, which were intervention, culture and human rights, and more specifically humanitarian intervention. These are two important test cases of the importance allocated to state sovereignty in world politics, and therefore two important indicators of the ground rules and shape of the modern international system. As the Cold War came to a halt, this issue found its way to the centre of the political and theoretical debate, and thereby also gave Vincent's work a renewed push in the direction of master status (Roberts 1993; Wheeler 1992). Furthermore, Vincent was a card-carrying member of what is often referred to as the 'English School' of International Relations. There is quite a number of people in the discipline who have received their training in, or have otherwise been inspired by, the English School (hereafter referred to simply as 'the School'). The inclusion of a member of the School thus strengthens this book's claim to representativeness, and particularly so since the School actually embodies the only fully fledged research programme in the field outside the United States.

John Vincent did his doctorate with Hedley Bull, who was a strong and lifelong influence and the outstanding exponent of the English School after the death of Martin Wight (the two other central names are C. A. W. Manning, to which Wight and Bull responded, and Adam Watson). Vincent explicitly declared himself a 'member' of the English School (1983: 69), and consciously decided to plough his academic furrow in this corner of the field of International Relations. This he did so well that, at the end of his life, he headed the largest IR department of any European university, as Montague Burton Professor at the LSE. For the hierarchically inclined, his institutional success in British and for that matter European academia may be one more reason for including him in a book on figures on International Relations. Vincent himself, however, typically played down having reached the top by quipping that he would still be the 'Anti-Pope' of British IR, with the Montague Burton Professor in Oxford, whence Vincent migrated to take up his chair, remaining the unhyphenated 'Pope'. The quip was typical of the School, and typical of the man. The drawing of a parallel between a present-day situation and the fourteenth-century wrangling between candidates for the apostolic succession to Peter based in Avignon and Rome respectively brings out the English School penchant for, some would say obsession with, putting things in historical perspective. And the partly self-deprecating, partly impish quality of the quip was a trade mark of Vincent the tutor and lecturer, roles in which his claim to mastery was also considerable, but which will not be further pursued here.

The decision to work inside the English School entailed engaging a problematique centred around five questions. I will not touch on them in the order in which they have been put forward by different members of the School or by the importance with which the School's members have inscribed them, but rather in terms of level of generality.

There is, first, the question of where systems of states – or, anachronistically, 'international' systems – are to be found in time and space. Building on Martin Wight's work (1977) and the work of the British Committee on the Theory of International Politics (see Dunne 1993b), Adam Watson (1992: esp. 14–16) has suggested that relations between human collectives at any one time may be found along a continuum ranging from independent through hegemonic and from dominion-like to imperial. Where relations are largely independent, when they are those between sovereign states, there exists a states system. Imperial relations, on the other hand, are relations graded around one centre. Watson postulates an historical pendulum swing between the two extremes, so that the case of the states system is an extreme and therefore inherently unstable one. Yet it is the traditional hunting-ground of the discipline of International Relations. The project is, then, to gain perspective on today's states system by comparing it with other historical constellations of political units. One notes that, due to its historical perspective, the School has always made a point of the legal, and so contrived rather than given a priori, nature of sovereignty (Carr 1946 [1939]: 162; Manning 1962; James 1986; Bull 1977: 112), as well as of other and related socially constructed conventions such as the equality of states (Jackson 1993).

Second, there is the distinction between a system of states on the one hand, and a society of states or international-society on the other:

A *system of states* (or international system) is formed when two or more states have sufficient contact between them, and have sufficient impact on one another's decisions, to cause them to behave – at least in some measure – as parts of a whole.... A *society of states* (or international society) exists when a group of states, conscious of certain common interests and common values, form a society in the sense that they conceive themselves to be bound by a common set of rules in their relations with one another.

(Bull 1977: 9–10, 13)

International society is seen as an imagined community with an existence in the life-worlds of statesmen. Contemporary international society, which hails historically from the modern European one and is the first to have a global reach, is also readily observable by inference back from the legal construct of international law which it has spawned. As Vincent put it in a piece on his mentor Hedley Bull:

The function of law in relation to international order, according to Bull, was not itself to produce it, as some progressivist thought asserted, but to identify the constitutive principle in the international organization of humankind – the society of states; then to state the basic rules of coexistence between them; and then to provide a language in which their formal relations could be carried on.... The interest in international law, then, was not for what it was, but for what it signified. It provided evidence for the existence of society, not the reason for its existence. It was in this regard a very useful instrument for Bull, locating society like a miner's lamp locating gas: *ubi societas ibi jus est*... [So,] the weakness of the pull of international law in a solidarist direction [is that] it is a cart, not a horse.

(1990a: 54–6)

For a system to develop into a society, certain preconditions must be met, and the English School has shown a specific preoccupation with how a common culture may alleviate this process (compare Chapter 7 on Ruggie and Chapter 9 on Onuf in this book).

Third, the English School has gone on from the question of the genesis of minimalist international society, and suggested that the stock of common rules may be expanded so as to make for a pluralist, perhaps eventually a solidarist, international society (Hurrell 1993). The School is engaged in an internal debate about the actual scope of modern international society: whether and if so to what degree it is pluralist, and so is trying to uphold order in a situation of a certain degree of consensus about procedural rules between states with a plurality of internal political orders, or is solidarist, and so is trying to go beyond pluralism in the direction of more homogenized internal political orders and substantive consensus about matters political. No clear threshold values which could keep the forms analytically apart have been established, however, and for this the School has been duly criticized (Buzan 1993). It may still be said that to a high degree this debate about the scope of modern international society hinges on the relative importance, in terms of the international society of states, of what the School refers to as a world society of sundry actors. The most important alternative actors are individuals, yet there are also international organizations and transnational firms (the School does not, however, have much to say on the latter, and more to say about institutions than about organizations).

Fourth, and again at the prompting of Martin Wight (1991), the School engages in the construction of three traditions of international theory. This question requires some clarification, which is perhaps best given by a short summary of an essay by Wight (1966[1960]) called 'Why Is There No International Theory?' Wight held that whereas political theory, which he defined as the hows and whys of ordering social life inside a *polis*, was of a cumulative nature and fairly well advanced, there was no similar body of work on the relations *between* states. He put this down to the state's role as an area of linear time, where progress was possible. The interstate ('international') sphere, on the contrary, did not allow any progress, only endless recurrence.[1] Whereas the existence of a *polis* made politics possible, only diplomacy existed as a point of reference for diplomatics. Hence the title of the volume in which the essay was published, *Diplomatic Investigations*, heralded an attempt to create international theory as the twin of political theory (Suganami 1983). Wight himself held that the eventual success of the undertaking was highly dubious, and that the lack of a communitarian object of study probably doomed the effort from the very outset (cf. also Brown 1993). None the less, Wight suggested that the works of international lawyers, historians and philosophers should be combed for clues about the working of interstate relations. In order to illuminate patterns of policy and thought, he recommended the use of a taxonomy consisting of three traditions of thought: the realist, the rationalist and the revolutionist (sometimes referred to by the School as the Hobbesian or Machiavellian, the Grotian and the Kantian). This remains the School's way of presenting the history of international theory, and of placing its own just mentioned debate about whether modern international society has become 'solidarist' or remains 'pluralist'.

Fifth, there is the question of order versus justice in international relations. One of the major books of the School is subtitled 'A Study of Order in World Politics', and its author, Hedley Bull (1977), was at work on a sequel on justice when he died in 1985 (cf. Bull 1984 for a first instalment). Bull's concern was with the moral and practical tension between the status quo of a given order and the demand for change. However, since justice may be said to be a constituent of order and the two are therefore not discrete, it is problematic to treat it as a pair of opposites. As Vincent put it, 'it [is] hard to see justice provided for except through the agency of order', thus characteristically giving anterior status to order (1978: 42).

As is the case with so many traditions of scholarship – and the international society tradition exemplifies the full sense of that term (Der Derian 1988; Kingsbury and Roberts 1990; Dunne 1993a) – the 'English School' owes its name to an opponent, Roy Jones (1981).[2] It is 'English' in the sense that most of its practitioners worked and work in England, but their background is diversely British: Hedley Bull started life as an Australian, C. A. W. Manning was South African, Ian Clark is Scottish. If nothing else, the epithet is a useful reminder that the School was and is nested in the international experiences of a European empire and great power.

The members of the School tend to concede this point and its consequence, that a vested interest in the status quo tends to tinge the thinking on international relations which takes place inside a top-dog state. Martin Wight (1978: 292) writes that 'The first thing to remember about the politics of Gladstone and Franklin Roosevelt is that Gladstone's Britain and Roosevelt's America were dominant powers. This will remind us of the great truth that morality in international politics is not simply a matter of civilized tradition, but equally the result of security.' The English School takes as its main object the political theory and practice of representatives of the most powerful states in the system. If the pursuit of knowledge cannot be fully extricated from the relations of power within which it takes place, all the members of the School can do is to be openly reflective about the sociological setting in which their thinking takes place. This they generally are.

The point has been taken further and the question asked whether the School's preoccupation with history is connected to the glorious past and, by comparison, the rather bleak present of British foreign policy (George 1978). Bearing in mind Harold Macmillan's wistful remark that Britain's role *vis-à-vis* the United States should be like the one played by the Greek slaves in the operations of the Roman Empire (Horne 1988: 160), one may speculate that one reason why the English School's realism is more 'enlightened' (Ashley 1981) or 'cuddly' (Hurrell 1993) than the American variants is to do with the nature of the power resources of the two states.

I turn now to an investigation of Vincent's work, which touches on all these questions, but which places particular emphasis on the third, the scope of modern international society and the relation between international society and world society. His publishing career falls into three phases: the doctoral work on non-intervention, a ten-year period of occasional essays on culture and international theorists and traditions, and a book on human rights.

'IF SOVEREIGNTY, THEN NON-INTERVENTION'

The book which evolved out of Vincent's doctoral work, *Nonintervention and International Order* (1974), is a major example of the kind of theory-led empirical investigation of the theory and practice of an international institution which Wight thought international scholars should produce.[3] If the text is on the one hand an epitome of the English School, however, the markers pointing beyond that tradition are barely hidden below the polished façade. What follows is an exercise in façade-climbing, an examination of the mortar which reveals a crack, and an attempt at explaining why the crack is there.

Twenty-five years later, after the end of the Cold War, it is easy to forget that the political circumstances in which Vincent wrote the book did not invite speculation on concerted great-power interest in humanitarian intervention, the possibility of which it ends up investigating. By way of introduction, however, Vincent brings in the phenomenon of intervention in terms of the nature of actors, targets and the deed itself, their classification, purpose and context, only to conclude that the core of the idea is coercive interference 'in the domestic affairs of another state' (Vincent 1974: 13). The principle of non-intervention derives from and requires respect for, it indeed protects, the principle of state sovereignty. The definition of sovereignty is Hinsley's, the standard formulation that 'there is a final and absolute political authority in the political community', and no final and absolute authority elsewhere (Hinsley 1963: 26). Thus, Vincent concludes, 'To ask what areas the principle of nonintervention protects is equivalent to asking what matters are within the domestic jurisdiction of states' (Vincent 1974: 15). Conversely, that which is not protected by the principle is the subject-matter of international society.

Vincent then embarks on a *tour de force* of the history of ideas in order to examine how the present state of affairs came about. He sees a succession of generations in the chain of thinking on non-intervention. First, there are Grotius, because he conceived of what we now call international politics and international law (*ius inter gentes* rather than *ius gentium*), and Hobbes, because he formulated the ideas of a state of nature between states and state equality, the latter of which was embellished by Pufendorff. Second, there are Wolff, because he formulated the concept of the *civitas maxima* brought about by an imagined quasi-agreement between peoples – the premise of this agreement was equality between peoples, *and therefore* it rested on a mutual acceptance of sovereignty, which ruled out meddling in the affairs of others – and also Vattel, who 'reiterates Wolff's doctrine of natural rights, but adds to it by pointing to a general law requiring respect for those rights' (Vincent 1974: 29). Third, we have the positivist lawyers of the nineteenth century, who observe that the internal order of states empirically seems to rest on internal will, and who take this to indicate that other states do not have a right to interfere in domestic concerns. Fourth, we see people like Mill (who formulated the doctrine of counter-intervention to enforce non-intervention), Cobden, Mazzini and Kant, all of whom made it their business to put forward a number of diverse arguments why, given certain conditions, it would be prudent for states to adhere to a principle of non-intervention.

The crucial epistemological twist of the School is in evidence in Vincent's insistence on covering not only what he calls the theory and principle of non-intervention, but also the role it has played in the *practice* of states. He turns to state practice in order to discuss how the principle of non-intervention has constrained the policy of the powers – that is, the importance of ideas for foreign policy outcomes. Flanked by sketches of the doctrine as interpreted by revolutionary French and pre-Second World War American statesmen, the centre-piece of this part of the book is an analysis of its place in the foreign policy of Castlereagh, Canning and Palmerston. Given their European policies and their common view of Britain as a constitutional status quo power with an interest in holding the balance in the to and fro of power politics, the three had to face the same dilemma. On the one hand, there was a perceived long-term interest in promoting the introduction of constitutionalism in continental countries as the best safeguard against revolution. This interest was predicated on Britain itself already being by institutions if not by letter constitutionalist, so seeing a regime change in this direction as a confirmation of its supreme qualities. On the other hand, there was an interest in legitimism, that is, in supporting the *ancien régime* monarchs who were actually in power in most states. Given the attitude of most continental monarchs, who tended to see constitutionalism as part and parcel of revolution, the British Foreign Secretary had delicate choices to make every time some legitimist great-power monarch intervened in another state in order to squash a constitutionalist uprising.

None of the three British ministers came down solidly on either side. They avoided promoting constitutionalism *vis-à-vis* reigning monarchs, so steered clear of the role of an interventionist crusader which aimed to ground order in the similarity of domestic regimes. Indeed, such a policy would have made only for inverted legitimism, where legitimacy did not arise directly from thrones, as in the scheme of a Metternich, but from some configuration of the bond between the rulers and the ruled. At the same time, however, they also avoided embracing legitimist interventionist practice. Of course, in 1822 Canning took Britain out of the formalized Concert system over the issue.

Vincent demonstrates how Canning steered a middle course on this issue compared with Castlereagh, who was more prone to privileging legitimism, and Palmerston, whose preference went more in the direction of constitutionalism (1974: 73). The main point, however, is that, whereas they clearly did not hold the same doctrine of non-intervention and even seemed to subscribe to different versions as prudence prescribed, foreign policy-making was always discussed, presented and defended in terms of the doctrine. To the School, including Vincent, the embellishment they and others gave the doctrine and other concerns qualified as one of the fountainheads of international theory (Wight 1966: 20).

Vincent draws the following conclusion from this material (1974: 141–2): states' lack of observation of the doctrine when it does not suit their perceived interests bears out the general point that international law does not live up to the expected standard of domestic law in this regard. However, the doctrine clearly plays a role in as much as the discourse on non-intervention is conspicuously present when foreign policy is formulated, implemented and justified. And, crucially, this discourse was transnational, so it contributed to international law as a medium through which statesmen could communicate.

Vincent then brings this material with him into an assessment of the doctrine of non-intervention in contemporary international relations.

Theory-led analyses of the role of the doctrine in Soviet and US postwar foreign policy, and of the debates about it in the forum of the United Nations, bring the narrative up to the early 1970s. The main points here are how the bipolarity of the Cold War lent a special flavour to superpower intervention in the 'Third World' outside the two alliances, how the doctrine of non-intervention was put on the defensive by the contending doctrine of socialist internationalism inside the Soviet bloc, how the USA stuck to a 'Metternichian' solidarist view rather than a 'Castlereaghian' pluralist one (1974: 242), and how the doctrine of non-intervention was strengthened where inter-bloc relations were concerned.

So far, the building-blocks of the analysis are exactly those advocated by Wight, and the presuppositions going into the mortar of the construction are ostensibly also those central to the English School. Vincent is intrigued with sovereignty and, as he announces already in the title of the work, order.

First, sovereignty. Vincent's roll-call of thinkers on non-intervention reads like one on the functioning of international relations in the modern states system generally, and that is of course the whole point. 'If sovereignty, then non-intervention' is the epigrammatical form of this text. Where the relation of sovereignty to international law is concerned, Vincent adheres to what he terms the 'dominant doctrine' of international law: that sovereignty exists within the law, so is 'limited by rules of international law binding upon it', and therefore relative. The consequences of this choice of the 'dominant doctrine' of sovereignty are wide-ranging. It was mentioned above how the School formulates the entire field of the nature of international relations as a question of what kind of international society may be said to exist. The epistemological *ordre du culte* of formulating a trilectic into the middle position of which one may then effortlessly slide is a similarly basic rule of procedure for the School, Realism, rationalism, revolutionism being the paramount example. This is the task to which Vincent now turns, and he seems to tackle it in a manner inconsistent with the one he actually professes to follow. The most pressing issue, he insists, is not whether international law is

> the common law of mankind in an early stage of its development or not, as proposed by C. Wilfred Jenks and others: It is not proposed to examine Jenks' contention that the contemporary international system presents a challenge to legal science similar to that which confronted Grotius in the seventeenth century; it is rather to ask whether the contemporary international society resembles more closely the Grotian [or Solidarist] conception of a universal society or the Positivists' conception of a primitive society of states combining for minimum purposes, for on such an analysis hangs the place of the principle of nonintervention in contemporary international law.
>
> (1974: 295–6)

In the School's own terms, he wants to discuss whether contemporary international society is 'pluralist' or 'solidarist'. This notwithstanding, and in confirmation of how gelatinous is the line drawn by the School between 'solidarism' and 'revolutionism', he then spends the remaining part of the chapter on facing down three challenges which emanate from a 'revolutionist' position. Even when he announces that he is going to concentrate on the 'realist' challenge to the middle position, he is drawn towards discussing the 'revolutionist' challenge instead. This shows up his fascination with the idea that there actually *may* be a number of signs that the transformations of world politics today *are* on the scale of those which had to be confronted by Grotius and others who lived through an early phase of the modern states system. Thus, this textual moment points to an emerging three-stranded crack in the whole edifice.

Vincent then proceeds to patch up the three strands of this crack. First is the progressivist insistence that sovereignty is basically a hindrance to the rule of international law. Vincent wards off this assault by drawing on a standard empirical argument against what is usually called the idealist position of the interwar period. At that time, he insists, it was exactly because of the progressivist insistence that the more international law constrains sovereignty the better – because one forgot that it was a cart and not a horse – that international law ran into a dead end (1974: 297). The idea of 'relative sovereignty' strikes a balance between the need to privilege sovereignty and the need to maintain the discourse on international law, and highlights the role played by the doctrine of non-intervention not only in immunizing states from interference, but also in serving as 'the frontier between international law and domestic law'. For these reasons, it fits the state of play in contemporary international relations better than the contender.

Second, is the view that the sovereignty of states is not being eroded directly, but is becoming submerged in a maze of transnational relations, which invite the practitioner and the analyst to move ever further afield from the body of international law that focuses exclusively on interstate relations. This argument is sidestepped by an insistence that the description is simply too far removed from overall practice in world politics. World politics is still dominated by a relatively autonomous interstate order, and may be expected to remain so. Vincent appeals to the authority of Aron (1966: 748), who argued that it is 'the great illusion of our time ... that economic and technological interdependence among the various factions of humanity has definitely devalued the fact of "political sovereignties", the existence of distinct states which wish to be autonomous'. Aron's (and Vincent's) point, then, is not to deny that interdependence is on the upsurge and that this makes for new challenges to states – it is and it does – but to argue that states will maintain the final say on questions of vital importance.[4]

In the same vein, Vincent denies the charge that international organizations are taking over more and more of the running in world politics. The global organization of the United Nations is written off on empirical grounds, as being simply not strong enough to be more than an arena for inter-state politics. Regional organizations like the European Community (EC), if undoubtedly important, will not for the reasons he has already given do away with sovereignty by increasing interdependence alone. And even if the EC should be turned into a state, this would simply entail a re-creation of the phenomenon of sovereignty on a larger scale, thus not changing the basic outline of the states system.

Third, Vincent takes on the view that the interstate order is being eroded as the main basis of world politics and international law by the introduction of individuals as actors and subjects in their own right. The main problems in seeing the world as a relevant arena for individuals are a lack of world-wide solidarity. The world simply does not add up to a 'justice community'. And even if it could be said to do so and individual rights were acknowledged as legitimate and relevant, Vincent insists that the lack of possibilities for enforcing such rights would still keep them from being realized.

However, Vincent acknowledges that he is not happy with the patching up of the crack in this way. His doubt springs from the ambiguous role played by the phenomenon of humanitarian intervention, an issue which, he points out, has haunted the debate about non-intervention since the time of Grotius (1974: 283). On the one hand, Vincent is dismissive of humanitarian intervention as a blanket exception to non-intervention. It would, he argues, be impossible generally to uphold human rights by intervention methods without endangering the crucial interstate order by means of side-effects and ulterior motives on behalf on the intervening state (1974: 308). On the other hand, he acknowledges that genocide constitutes a special case (1974: 347). Yet at this point he does not commit himself:

> Between a naturalism careless of state practice and a positivism that would simply render any and all state conduct as the law, international law has to find a middle way. In the present case, it is not clear that a middle course of humanitarian intervention has been traced between a virginal doctrine of non-intervention that would allow nothing to be done and a promiscuous doctrine of intervention that would make a trollop of the law. Until that course can with confidence be traced, it is perhaps nonintervention that provides the most dignified principle for international law to sanction.
>
> (1974: 348–9)

Thus, Vincent's state-centrism does not dismiss individuals as actors out of hand. Indeed, he acknowledges their obvious ontological edge as actors of a type which easily goes beyond that of modern international society: 'There is no reason to suppose that men must always choose to live together in states, and no warrant for the claim that there is some natural law suggesting the necessary conditions of existence for international society' (1974: 339; compare Bull 1977: 22). The warrant for nevertheless treating states as the main agents in world politics is mainly to do with the continued imperative of territoriality.

To Vincent, thinking in the terms of the English School, the question of the status of individuals in international society was basically conceptualized as a tug-of-war between two strands of rationalists or 'Grotians'. On the one hand are the pluralists – he has already given the example of

Castlereagh – who are happy to let politics within states remain exclusively domestic both practically and morally. On the other hand are the solidarists – for example, Metternich – who see both the type of domestic regime and the political plight of each individual as a matter of international concern. Vincent acknowledged that Grotius himself had seen international society as a universal community of mankind, where natural law applied directly to individuals as well as to states (1974: 24).

At this early point in his career Vincent is, however, unwilling to acknowledge the full destructive potential of this crack in the theoretical edifice of the English School. Only in one place does he mention the possibility that sovereignty may be a spent force as the pivot of international relations, and then the thrust is still on the continued relevance of it in a transitional period: 'In the rush to work out a new international law to meet the new political facts of the postwar world, it is worth remembering the principles established in an old sovereign-state order, which, if it is obsolescent, is taking a long time dying' (1974: 361–2). The text bears the marks of a struggle between Vincent's interest in individuals as actors on the one hand, and the tradition's insistence on keeping such preoccupations away from the heart of the research agenda on the other. No text can be entirely wrapped up into itself, and there is no such thing as a text which is 100 per cent orthodox. The reason why I nevertheless draw attention to this, is that in almost all his texts it seems to be in this area that Vincent struggles most fruitfully with the tradition he chose to work within.

Indeed, the fact is that Vincent had taken this problem with him when he went to study with Bull. He went up with the intention of writing a doctoral thesis about when military intervention would be warranted. He would himself tell the story of how he tried and tried to write up such a thesis, without success. Only when he realized that the material could more easily be ordered into a defence of the doctrine of non-intervention was he able to finish the work. And the doctrine of non-intervention, as he himself pointed out, precluded the working out of a fully fledged solidarist political programme (Vincent 1974: 341).

To sum up the discussion so far, *Nonintervention and International Order* epitomizes the English School's interest in great-power politics, the way it has evolved inside the modern states system to form an international society, and the way this development contributes to order. However, there is a subterranean theme, which is to do with the tension between seeing states or individuals as privileged actors and whether interstate relations and the dyadic legal doctrines of sovereignty/non-intervention in which they are imagined will continue to dominate world politics.

'EITHER REALPOLITIK AND WORLD COMMUNITY, OR NO WORLD COMMUNITY'

With the exception of a year in a policy analysis think-tank, which yielded an analysis of Soviet European policy (1975a), Vincent's publications over the next decade explored the cultural dimension in international relations, and continued to till classical thinking for general insights into the working of the modern states system.

Vincent's first publication ever, published while *Nonintervention and International Order* was still in the press, was a spin-off of this work, and was at the same time a harbinger of his cultural phase. It was an indictment of functionalism in the social sciences, which drew primarily on anthropological literature. Bull at this time also combed the works of social anthropologists for clues about how order is maintained in stateless societies (1977: 59–65). Vincent and Bull shared an interest in diplomatic culture which pushed them in this direction. Vincent prefaces his first important piece on culture by referring to an essay by Wight called 'Western Values in International Relations' as a pioneering work. He then goes on to assign himself the task of projecting these themes beyond international society into 'world society, and to take into moral account not only the state or the order of states, but also the individual' and other non-state actors (1978: 20). So whereas, in his first phase, Vincent set out to focus on individuals but ended up with a text where this concern gave way to considerations about the states system, in his second phase he explicitly makes it his central concern to develop the English School in the opposite direction. The focus on order remains, but states are explicitly relativized as actors in world politics.

Vincent begins his inquiry into western values by following the by now familiar grand route of the history of ideas. Due note is taken of the primacy of the *polis* and the family over individual rights in ancient Greek thinking, Augustine's obliviousness to the political, and Aquinas's natural law thinking which brought the just society back into moral purview. 'The way from natural law to natural rights passes from the demise in the Reformation of the medieval notion of a single Christian commonwealth to the eighteenth-century enlistment of Christian doctrine in the service of political principle' (1978: 25). In addition, Grotius's detachment of natural law from divine law latches back on to ancient Greek thinking, and points forward to the universalism of revolutionaries like Tom Paine, who bring natural right back to natural law. However, the advent of the nation-state made the nineteenth-century positivist lawyers treat individuals solely as citizens of states and not as men (i.e. humans). Thus, advocates of a morality of states found themselves flanked by, on the one hand, naturalists who saw no difference between the domestic and international realms and, on the other, the tradition of *raison d'état* which tended to deny the role of morality altogether.[5]

Having thus pigeonholed the development of western thinking on the rights of individuals and collectives into Wight's taxonomy of realists, rationalists and revolutionists, Vincent proceeds to examine the revolutionist camp. This is where thinking on 'world society', which Vincent compares with the medieval idea of a *communitas humani generis* that faded once the modern states system was firmly established, is to be found. Vincent's first observation is simply that what exists is not one western conception of a world society of individuals and human collectives, but many. Whereas he is most preoccupied with the possible return of a Grotian situation, where individuals join states as members of international society, he acknowledges that the main vision of a world society at the time is the one of a transnational hierarchy of classes (1978: 44). The main point, however, is that the several ideas tend to cancel each other out and thus to leave international society intact by default. His second observation is that 'in being *western* conceptions, they are inescapably a partial view of the world social whole' (1978: 31).

Vincent draws two conclusions. First, the idea of a world society 'has not yet taken a form concrete enough' to uphold it in practice (1978: 31). Second, however, individuals and non-state actors are real moral entities in world politics. And since states are contingent historic phenomena, Vincent argues, it would be rash to see their present predominance as everlasting. He then reviews the debates over idealism v. realism, the equality of states and human rights, especially the arguments for humanitarian intervention. He reaches the conclusion that the frameworks for morality drawn upon by a state-centric and a world society perspective are incompatible:

> The argument for non-intervention chooses the framework of the society of states, while the case for humanitarian intervention, asserting human rights that states have a duty to observe, derives from the framework of the individual.
>
> (1978: 44)

Whereas world society is only a place to articulate rights, international society is also a realm of implementation. Therefore, 'because of the absence of any alternative', Vincent comes down 'in defence of the conventions of diplomacy' (1978: 45). In terms of the metaphor developed in the previous section, he now acknowledges the crack not only as an inevitable architectural weakness, but as a doorway which may in principle lead to another site, another building. He is more willing to stress the importance and indeed centrality of the matters which have been sacrificed as the edifice of the School has been built. However, he also concludes that an alternative building does not yet exist, and invests this point with decisive importance.

His two other articles on culture investigate two possible contenders which pose a possible threat to the role of states as the main or even supreme actors in world politics. 'The Factor of Culture in the Global International Order' (1980) discusses cultures or 'civilizations' as possible contenders, well before Samuel Huntington's (1993) flat-footed treatment of the issue found a wide-ranging audience which craved it for all the wrong reasons. Vincent acknowledges the value of investigating thinking about international relations in cultural settings different from the western one, which is hegemonal and which he has himself explored – 'if the modern history of Europe can be written in terms of the defence of the system against revolutionaries who broke its rules', he writes, then 'it is as important to pay attention to the attack on the system as to its defence' (1980: 259). Such doctrinal studies not only have a value in themselves, but are also healthy antidotes to the views that the international system 'doles out' roles to its constituent units regardless of their internal structure, and to an undivided fascination with the interests of the strong as a universal explanatory factor.

These admissions notwithstanding, Vincent refuses to place the study of cultures at the centre of international relations for the same reason that the English School generally devotes itself to the study of the international system and international society rather than to the study of the foreign policies of particular states. Dealing specifically with two works which follow the paths of foreign policy, he charges that

> when Adda Bozeman decided that the future was not bright for law in a multicultural world, her main source material was the doctrine of the several cultures rather than their practice of co-existence. And just as [Elliot Goodman's book] *The Soviet Design for a World State* seems more alarming when put together from Marxist-Leninist texts than it does when mixed with the historical record, so might a textual approach give a harsher view of the clash of cultures in world politics than is justified by the reality of their mutual recognition.
>
> (Vincent 1980: 259)

One notes that the warning is directed against inferring too much about international relations from studies of particular cultures rather than against such studies themselves. Where the study of diplomatic culture is concerned, he is undividedly positive. He is eager to see comparative empirical work done on the extent to which international and world societies presuppose the existence of a common or third culture, the way European culture historically served as the basis for the diplomatic culture of the modern states system. However, he does not contribute substantively to the question, and his very preliminary investigation of whether there exists a 'world culture' which can match a possible 'world society' is inconclusive.

Again, in a lively piece on 'Race in International Relations' (1982b), a heavily edited form of which was later enshrined in one of the main texts of the School, Walker's *Culture, Ideology and World Order* (1984), he points out how the idea of European racial superiority clearly played a role in reinforcing the core of international society in the nineteenth century.[6] However, Japan's victory over Russia in 1905 was widely interpreted as a victory of the Mongolian people over the European. The carnage of the First World War, furthermore, demonstrated not only the precedence of nation-state over race, but also the thinness of the veneer of civilization in Europe. The use made by the warring Europeans of their various non-white colonials to assist in the butchering of other whites also went to show how race took a back-seat to other concerns. Yet, Japan's lack of success in expanding the religious equality clause into a racial one at the Paris Peace Conference showed how the racialist tinge hardly disappeared, but simply took on a more subtle form. By stressing white supremacy and the civilizing mission of the white race as reasons for imperialism, moreover, the imperial powers made certain that the struggles for national independence would also be fought with reference to race (1984b: 251). Vincent, who seems to be heavily influenced by Wight here, sees the remnants of this situation as well as the fact that the affluent and the hungry worlds still stand 'on either side of a colour line' as the two main reasons why race remains relevant. He is, however, unusually dismissive of the popular view of the early postwar period that the next war would be a race war. For this view to be correct, he argues, 'it would need to assume that race relations were either more important than national interests or had become the principal factor in them' (1982b: 670). Although, as we have seen, it was not Vincent's wont to refer to a reified national interest to end debate, in this case he obviously thought that it sufficed. In the end, he holds race to be a spurious variable in international relations.

Taken as a whole, Vincent's work on culture brings to light a cache of interesting empirical material, and it strengthens the appeal of the English School by investigating concepts which potentially overlap with international society and discussing their relationships to this master concept. Indeed, in the way he bases his theorizing on empirical material while showing sensitivity to the decisive importance of the different circumstances which surround each empirical sequence, he exhibits English School work at its finest. And by relating concepts such as culture, western values and race to that of international society, he establishes theoretical bridgeheads whose full potential seems yet to be tapped (compare Chapter 7 on Ruggie, Chapter 9 on Onuf and Chapter 10 on Wendt in this book).

The other major research interest of Vincent's second phase is classical theories of international relations themselves. Again, he very much follows Wight's bugle call to excavate what there is of international thinking. The results are two essays on the thinking of the practitioners Burke and Kissinger, two essays on 'Hobbesian' and *'Realpolitik'* traditions in international relations, and an essay on the institution of the 'Concert' in the modern states system.

The essay on Burke forms a bridge to his interest in culture by presenting the Irish politician as a major thinker on cultural solidarity in politics. 'Men are not tied to one another by papers and seals', Vincent quoted:

> They are led to associate by resemblances, by conformities, by sympathies. It is with nations as with individuals. Nothing is so strong a tie of amity between nation and nation as correspondence in laws, customs, manners and habits of life. They have more than the force of treaties in themselves. They are obligations written in the heart. They approximate men to men without their knowledge, and sometimes against their intentions.
>
> (Burke quoted in 1984a: 212)

Vincent finds contemporary traces of this kind of rhetoric in the Organization of African Unity as well as in the West. Burke, Vincent argues, is a man easy to enrol on the American side in the Cold War: less wooden than Eisenhower on the domino theory, more committed than Dulles on rollback, readier to confront what he sees as an evil enemy than the most relentless American neo-conservative. Where the specific case of the French Revolution was concerned, at least, he was a conservative crusader, who saw little reason to give state borders and regimes which had not developed the patina of a long history recognition as worthy political subjects. Indeed, his is not an interest in international society at all, but in the cultural underpinnings for politics in general. If there are echoes of this way of thinking in contemporary world politics, however, they do not make up the mainstream: 'The world in the twentieth century has, in this respect, honoured Castlereagh and Canning before Burke' (1984a: 215).

The same tension crops up in the piece on Kissinger. With reference to Kissinger's doctoral work on the restoration of the European order at the Congress of Vienna in 1815, Vincent says that in his early years, he 'resembled none of his historical figures more than Castlereagh' (1977: 16). However, Vincent argues, Kissinger was then diverted and moved decisively in the direction of Metternich's (and Burke's) weighting of the all-embracing social order rather than the procedural interstate one. First, the way ideological questions were tangled up with international reputation made it hard for him to maintain in Africa a policy based purely on the US national interest in restraint, once the Soviet Union began to interfere with local politics. Second, the fact of American hegemony and the fact that given contemporary conditions it had to be managed among other things in arenas such as the UN, called for a more 'universalist' profile than that invited by a purely interest-based vision of foreign policy. Thus, Kissinger started to veer away from the purely interest-based vision and became a conservative 'crusader *malgré lui*' (1977: 24). For example, in 1975 he said with reference to Angola that 'In a world where totalitarian governments can manipulate friendly political parties, there is a grey area between foreign policy and overt intervention which we deny ourselves only at great risk to our national security' (quoted in 1977: 10). Thus, Vincent argues, given contemporary conditions, US interests, commitments and universalism were invariably intertwined. Yet Kissinger, with his belief in personal diplomacy, 'his contempt for the bureaucracy which is characteristic of the modern State, and his pre-Marxian, indeed pre-liberal, sense of politics over economics – Kissinger is not twentieth-century man' (1977: 26). Vincent's critique, then, boils down to Kissinger's not paying attention to the way in which the interstate relations which prevailed during the earlier centuries of modern states system are now being transformed into world politics. Yet, even if Vincent points to the importance of economic and infrastructural change, that is, to the importance of the density of world-social transnational interdependence for the international society of states, he stops short of implying that interdependence has in any way overtaken international society. He would still agree with Aron that states have the final say in world politics.

In his discussion of a 'Hobbesian' tradition of thought about international relations, Vincent takes one step back. Hobbes's basic importance is located in his being the first to point out the possibility that the international anarchy is more bearable than anarchy between individual human beings, because states, in his famous phrase, 'uphold the industry of the subjects' of the sovereign. Herein lies the point of departure for his 'Hobbesian' tradition (1981: 94). The article is an attempt to enrol Hobbes among Martin Wight's 'rationalists' by drawing on his defence of the sovereign state as an agency of international order, and leaving what is traditionally seen as his 'realist account of the plurality of states leading to international disorder' to one side (1981: 95). The object of the exercise is to place Hobbes in the same 'marchlands' between these two traditions which twentieth-century British academics have occupied.

Where methodology is concerned, as he himself admits, there are problems with 'the whole enterprise of treating great thinkers like parcels at the post office' (1981: 96). Martin Wight's 'glib categories' (1981: 91) should perhaps be thought of as no more than a teaching prop for first-year courses in International Relations theory, and not as research tools. At first blush, this view seems to be a self-damning one. However, Martin Wight himself argued that 'Classification becomes valuable, in humane studies, only at the point where it breaks down' (1991: 259). The importance of taxonomies, in other words, is first and foremost to bring attention to that which is not compatible or mutually exclusive, so cannot easily be categorized. Vincent does this to good effect in the article on Burke.

A piece on '*Realpolitik*' is interesting because in it Vincent confronts the tension between a society and a community of states. First, Vincent makes the point that the *raison d'état* of the eighteenth century placed the sovereign under a certain discipline because it was reason of *state*, not of person, and the fact that there had to be *reason* in and of itself granted prudence and regularity. Second, and it is worth quoting him at length here, an idea of

> *convenance*, suggesting not merely what is convenient, but also what is conventional, was set forth in the eighteenth century as an underpinning of the European system in the absence of feudal or dynastic ties. In this doctrine, the ideas of Europe as a whole, and of a European balance, were not excluded by the sacred egotism of the state. Indeed, in the classical theory of the balance of powers, the independence of the parts of the system came to be dependent on equilibrium in the system as a whole. Thus *raison d'état* was stretched into reason of states, and each participant in the system was to recognise the limitations on its behaviour which the system itself imposed.
>
> (1982a: 77)

So far, the argument is an elegant and conventional version of the standard argument advanced by the English School – the ontological privileging of the state and of order, the implied special role of great powers in advancing it, and their success in doing so by advancing a sense of society, here encapsulated by their success in adding the plural marker 's' to the reason of state and thus increasing the intersubjectivity of international society.

This is where Vincent goes on to raise the question of whether a world community, an entity 'to which people owe their allegiance' (1982a: 30) – what he earlier called a 'justice community' – is possible. Such a community would be a world community of individuals, rather than an international society of states. Vincent points to the existence of nuclear weapons and the possibility of a global ecological crisis as challenges which invite such a community. Yet states may for their own reasons choose not to respond to them, and generally do. None the less, Vincent observes states and individuals 'granting' the citizens of other states certain favours. This small-scale granting, rather than some abstract concerted action, shows that a moral obligation already exists, so is in and of itself proof that a patchy world community also exists. The reason why the granting takes place is of no importance to this part of the argument. If world community is to develop, however, Vincent insists that a sense of common material interest must also develop. 'It seems perverse to disconnect the two', he concludes. 'Either *Realpolitik* and world community, or no world community' (1982a: 83).

Taken as a whole, the pieces of Vincent's second phase exhibit a growing dissatisfaction with the interpretation of the relationship between international society and world society set out in his first phase. His third and last phase marked a further move away from the previous formulation of that relationship.

'... A TRANSFORMATION FROM INTERNATIONAL RELATIONS TO WORLD POLITICS'

In the early 1980s, Chatham House had commissioned a book on human rights and international relations from Vincent. Although this is now a well-established subject for research within the discipline, when the work came out in 1986 it was only the second English-language, full-length theoretical study on the topic to appear (Donnelly 1994: 102).

Human rights are a challenge to the supremacy of international society in two basic respects. First, it is a direct challenge in as much as it emanates in part from a view of individuals rather than states as the privileged actors in world politics. Second, it is an indirect challenge in as much as the humanitarian arguments for intervention make up the strongest challenge to the principle of non-intervention, and thus to the principle of sovereignty which constitutes international society.

The problem appears already in the apologia for the work, where he writes that one of its aims is to make some inroads on the 'cheerful scepticism' of other member of the English School about human rights and, by implication, about the importance of world society (1986a: viii). A more concrete attack is made later, when he assails 'the suave observation of the Realists that the wheels of diplomacy turn endlessly to grind whatever grain is produced by world society' on the ground that this 'may be missing a transformation from international relations to world politics as significant as that which established the society of states, and for which the idea of human rights is a kind of midwife' (1986a: 128).[7] The interest in world society he initially justifies simply by writing that

> humankind is itself a project as well as this or that branch of it.... Natural rights, the rights of man (as a species), and human rights have a built-in push towards universal application.... The positive aspect of it is revealed in the actual spread of a global culture in virtue of the activities, attitudes and artefacts associated with modernization.
>
> (1986a: 3–4)

Following the by now familiar English School procedure, Vincent then roots the discussion of human rights as a test-case of the relationship between international society and world society in an historical excursion. The relevance of such excursions he gives elsewhere with reference to one of his favourite theorists:

> it may be helpful to compare Grotius' treatment of the emergence of the states-system with our contemporary preoccupation with its actual or potential decline... to consult Grotius not merely as a defunct publicist, someone who ran his lap long ago, but as a scholar who has thought deeply about the tension between the attachment to a local community and the more abstract obligation to world society as a whole.
>
> (1990b: 252–3)

The idea of human rights presupposes universality – which is dependent on the thinking of the ancient Greeks, on Cicero and Roman law, on Christendom and, within the purview of the modern states system, on the individualism of a Locke and the harking back to the *polis* idea of the German romantics. Vincent quotes Hegel to the effect that 'Since the state is mind objectified, it is only as one of its members that the individual himself has objectivity, genuine individuality, and an ethical life', and adds Marx's rider that man is a *zoon politicon*, 'not only a social animal, but an animal which can develop into an individual only in society' (quoted in 1986a: 29, 31). Thus Hegel, by criticizing the idea of natural rights individually held, adds to the doctrine of human rights for members of a group.

Vincent then devotes a chapter to the objections of cultural relativism to human rights, only to conclude that since relativism does not necessarily have egalitarian consequences, it can produce neither sociological nor moral arguments for universality. It simply serves as an excuse for the despotism of custom. Thus, the ultimate self-propelling nature of postulating universality is acknowledged as the normative drive of the book: 'If the single moral world were not a reality, it would be a good idea to invent it' (1986a: 56). This idea is reiterated in an even more insistent form in a later spin-off: 'to the extent that increasing attention to human rights liberates individuals and groups from sealed enclosure in what can be the stifling accommodation of the state, giving them a court of appeal beyond the state, this is a step towards the establishment of a world civil society *of which we all might approve*' (Vincent 1992a: 291).

To Vincent, the consequence of choosing – to him acknowledging – universality is, at the very least, a conception of human rights which includes the right to life. This necessitates a 'basic needs doctrine', a basic human right to an adequate supply of foodstuff. One thing leads to another, however, and Vincent is thus tempted to include the right of humans to speak up in order to avoid being obliterated. Neither is he blind to the enormous consequences the seemingly modest expansion of the idea of human rights to include subsistence would have, if the whole range of steps necessary to rearrange the international economic system were to be taken into account.

In terms of the tension between the emphasis on non-intervention in the first phase and human rights in the second, one notes how Vincent nods in the direction of the economic system and puts out economic markers in the text. One may speculate whether this is a tactical move, whether he thought that by couching the argument in what a reader inclined towards realism would presumably see as more 'substantive' than a presumably 'abstract' argument based on natural rights he expected to have a more immediate impact. Be that as it may, Vincent's next step is to trace state practice in the field of human rights, as it pertains to the wider pattern of East–West and North–South relations. Dues are freely given to the *Realpolitik* reasons why most states stick to most international law, and also most norms, most of the time: 'one of the reasons for states to be interested in the human rights record, not merely of a neighbour but of another state across the globe, is the interest it has in not suddenly being made a receiver of numbers of unmanageable refugees. An interest in human rights becomes part of the calculation of *raison d'état*' (Vincent 1986a: 106). Arguments such as these should, because of the ontological status given to states and the system of their interaction, be seen as more than simply scattered remarks. To Vincent, these confluences may be crucial, since they identify spots where international society can be bent open so that world society may seep in. To repeat an earlier quote, 'It seems perverse to disconnect the two. Either *Realpolitik* and world community, or no world community' (1982a: 83).

After the scrutiny of practice from an international society perspective, there follows a key chapter on human rights in contemporary world society. The procedure he uses to trace evidence of such a society is the same as the English School traditionally uses to excavate international society, namely to look for institutionalization in the realm of international law. To yet again repeat a quote, *ubi societas ibi jus est* – where there is society, there is also law. Two main findings are presented. First, the activity of the Economic and Social Council of the United Nations that culminated in its adopting Resolution 1503 (XLVIII), which allowed a UN organ to consider communications from individuals on situations 'which appear to reveal a consistent pattern of gross and reliably attested violations of human rights and fundamental freedoms' (quoted in Vincent 1986a: 95). 'The theme of this story', Vincent comments, 'might be taken to be the individual emerging from the shadow of the state, and the states themselves assembled at the United Nations mustering the courage to give and accept criticism of their own human rights record' (1986a: 100).[8] Vincent's second main finding to trace the advance of world society in international law is the practice of humanitarian intervention. The point here is not to juxtapose individual and state as the respective bearers of international and world society, but to trace the convergence of different bodies of state law:

> the notion of humanitarian intervention, to be both legitimate and potentially successful, presupposes a solidarist society in which it is possible to agree on the values that inform intervention, as well as on the acceptability of policing. Human rights as well established as this would indicate a situation in which what Suarez called the *ius gentium intra se* – that part of the law of nations which described all the values the nations in their domestic law have in common – had expanded almost to obliterate any significant local variation. World society would have arrived, culturally, in the sense of each local society looking like every other.
>
> (1986a: 104)

Yet, he acknowledges, the number of issues on which bodies of state law actually converge is small, and the state practice of humanitarian intervention is rare. Therefore, what there is of world society is uneven. However, we can already snatch a glimpse of what a future world society may look like.

In summing up the book, Vincent returns to a point made in an earlier work (1978), that human rights may be inimical to international society, and, by implication, world society may be the enemy of international society. Yet this time around he does not stop here, but goes on to make a crucial change in his former stance. It may be worth while to pause and listen to the master's voice at some length here:

> But there has also been a theme, adding counterpoise to this one... that has the human rights not as a challenge to the system of sovereign states, but as something which has added to its legitimacy, merely requiring that the shape taken by the internal systems of the members – what we have noted Suarez calling the *ius gentium intra se* – should be in some perhaps increasing degree similar. So, against the theme of international law of human rights as part of a progression away from the primitiveness of tribal attachment to the state and towards a situation in which individuals treat each other in their capacities as human beings rather than as members of tribes, there lies a countertheme of human rights consolidating the state rather than transcending it.... If the transnational recognition of subsistence rights improves the quality of government within states, we might extend a cautious welcome both to the penetration of the state and to its strengthening itself in response. Instead of being driven out by the *moi commun*, the *moi humain* is coopted by it....[The coming of this uneven world society] does not issue a general licence for intervention. International society is not yet as solidarist as that. But it does expose the internal regimes of all the members of international society to the legitimate appraisal of their

peers. This may turn out not to have been a negligible change in international society.

(1986a: 150–2)

Moreover, human rights may be but one of the facets of a general process,
albeit perhaps the most important one; elsewhere he remarks that quite
generally, the state 'may even be strengthened by the successful cosmopoli-
tanization of its élites, rather than weakened' (1990b: 256). In other words,
the states may feed off the coming of world society, so that the strengthening
of it will also strengthen international society. Yet, if this process is to be
qualitatively different from 'the suave observation of the Realists that the
wheels of diplomacy turn endlessly to grind whatever grain is produced by
world society', one must specify just *how* the rules and structure of international society are going to be changed. This, however, the book and the spin-
offs thereof stop short of doing (1986b; 1992a; 1992b). Yet, it is certainly a
coming into his own of an author who a decade before had despairingly told
his fellow members of the School that 'to be asked, or worse, to volunteer to
present a paper on world culture to a seminar that does not believe in world
society is to know what it is like to be an initiate at some tribal rite'
(unpublished paper quoted in Der Derian forthcoming).[9]

CONCLUSION

It remains to assess how Vincent's themes and ideas will be developed by
others. This, after all, is how a master is made in any field. Here we already
have some evidence, some of which was already mustered in the introduction to the chapter. It is one of the great consolations of working within a
School that the research programme one considers one's own is continued
after one's death. Suffice it here merely to mention the example of how
Vincent held that 'if the modern history of Europe can be written in terms
of the defence of the system against revolutionaries who broke its rules, it is
as important to pay attention to the attack on the system as to its defence'
(1980: 259), and how a major study on this topic written from within the
School has just appeared (Armstrong 1993).

The attention to history and the antidote it offers to 'chronocentrism'
remains perhaps the key lesson of Vincent's and the School's work. It is a
stock-in-trade argument against modern scholarship in general – and one
which has also been waged against the English School's interpretation of
modern international society (Neumann and Welsh 1991) – that it tells
synthesizing stories of progress which neglect contingency and differences.
It tends to restrict its celebration of difference to structurally similar and
historically isomorphic nation-states. The best antidote against this may be
not to conjure up worlds, but to ponder other historical constellations and
whether modern international society itself is being wholly transformed.
Adam Watson's (1992: 11) study of the evolution of international society
over the last four thousand years takes as its cue Polybius' injunction about
the need to derive one's judgement from practice itself – *ex auton ton*

pragmaton – and weaves from this rich material an analysis which may hardly be characterized as deterministic. John Vincent's is a fine example of this kind of scholarship, and he is justly celebrated for it inside and around the School itself: members of it are invited to the University of Keele to deliver annual Vincent memorial lectures, and the LSE has instituted a Vincent student scholarship.

Vincent, however, always showed a special interest in and concern for the scholarship which was going on in the margin of the English School. He promoted Andrew Linklater's work (e.g. 1990, blurb recommendation), notwithstanding the fact that Linklater writes off the School and Rationalism as a mere antithesis to the thesis of Realism and dissolves it in the synthesis of critical theory. This, however, was still a debate between partners who shared a number of epistemological presuppositions. Linklater still predicates his thinking on the English School's scheme of the three traditions, but instead of finding his place with the rationalists somewhere along the middle of the continuum, either with the majority among the pluralists or with Vincent among the solidarists, he self-consciously adopts what the School refers to as a revolutionist position. It could be argued, then, that he thereby becomes the official dissident of the School, that he maintains orthodoxy exactly by providing the heterodoxy which orthodoxy needs to play itself off against.[10] After all, E. H. Carr had already argued that it is not realism alone, but the tension *between* realism and utopianism, which must sustain the debate of international relations: 'If . . . it is utopian to ignore the element of power, it is an unreal kind of realism which ignores the element of morality in any world order' (Carr 1946: 235).

However, Vincent was also very interested in what was going on at the other side of the modern/postmodern divide in critical theory, by the kind of writers who would be likely to level this kind of all-out critique against what they see as the collusion between realists, the English School and modern critical theory. Richard Ashley (1987: 403), for example, defines the discursive practice of statesmen, by which he means something rather similar to what the School would call the international society of states, as the

> community-shared background understandings, skills and practical predispositions without which it would be impossible to interpret action, assign meaning, legitimate practices, empower agents, and constitute a differentiated, highly structured social reality.

In Ashley's reading, however, this community is set up *complete with smokescreen*, since it passes itself off as a 'state of nature' and thus not a community at all, yet remains a bounded field where the exclusive competence of statesmen, and this practice only, has any business:

> Together the two effects of the realist double move set up an irony of no small proportions. They constitute a community whose members will know their place only as an absence of community. More than that, they constitute a field of self-consciously 'power political' practice that refuses to entertain the question of its own power. They constitute a field of

power politics that cannot and will not speak of its own dependence upon the competing waging of an unending historical struggle to delimit the reach of rational order, pry open its own practical space, and secure recognition for its own distinctive mode of subjectivity.

(Ashley 1987: 420)

Now, Ashley's way of going about the business of IR is, both in terms of style and content, somewhat different from the English School's, and the thrust of his argument strikes at the foundations of the School. It is hardly surprising, then, that there were attempts at brushing this kind of work aside.[11] Vincent, however, declared himself 'fascinated' (1990a: 63, n. 52) by Ashley's line of argument. Another critical theorist, James Der Derian, wrote his doctoral dissertation as it were 'inside' the school, with Bull at Oxford. When his work was refused for publication by Oxford University Press, it was Vincent who quite literally took the manuscript to Blackwell's at Oxford,[12] which duly published it, complete with laudatory blurb by Vincent.

If Vincent himself refused to walk through the crack he saw leading from the School building and into a less statist construction site, then, both intellectually and practically, he worked the crack which forms the connection between the two. The point is not that this makes him a transitional figure, but that it makes him exemplary as an IR scholar who thrived on the widening differences in outlook in the field.

The similarity noted in passing between Ashley's discursive practice on the one hand and the School's central idea of an international society of states on the other seems to be crucial in this regard. From his first book onwards (1975b: 333), Vincent assailed the idea that words and deeds are opposites, and embraced the concept of what are now ubiquitously referred to as 'speech acts'. When, for example, Ole Wæver (1992: 111) criticizes the School for not specifying exactly where international society resides – is it at the level of unquestioned, given or doxic language, at the level of the clash of inherently contested concepts, or at the level of negotiating utilitarian and co-operative institutions? – this boils down to a critique of lacking formalism, not a substantive one. Similarly, when Barry Buzan (1993: 351) argues that there exists a dialectics so that 'As international society develops, substantial elements of world society become increasingly necessary to the stability and furtherance of that development', this is a fruitful formalization of Vincent's approach to the matter as it has been set out above. Perhaps it is in this direction, and particularly on the problem for international and world society of evolving and specifying rules which pertain to differentiated units spanning more than one culture, that the most spectacular challenge to the whole field of international relations is to be found (Watson 1992: 308; Buzan 1993: 336). The fact that Vincent's work has been lauded here in terms of a metaphor of opening a crack in the statist building of the English School of International Relations should not keep us from recognizing that it is the constructive work of a master builder.

NOTES

I should like to thank May Bull, Alex Danchev, James Der Derian, Tim Dunne, Christopher Hill, Andrew Hurrell, Knud-Erik Joergensen, Tonny B. Knudsen, James Mayall, Roger Morgan, Adam Roberts, Anne Julie Semb, Hidemi Suganami and Angela Vincent as well as my fellow contributors, particularly Anna Leander and Ole Wæver, for assistance and comments on earlier drafts of this chapter.

1 For this he was criticized by Morgenthau (1970), who – I think rightly – pointed out that repetitiveness caused by intellectual anarchy does not make it hard to theorize; on the contrary, repetitiveness is a presupposition for theory (i.e. the kind of objectivist, generalizing theory, of which Realism is an example).

2 Its members have reinforced the idea of a tradition by making it a habit to write pieces about the scholarship of their predecessors and co-authors; for example, Bull's and Adam Roberts's introductions to Wight 1991, Bull's editing of Wight's posthumous writings, Vincent 1990a, Watson 1990 on Bull, a forthcoming collection of Bull's writings by Andrew Hurrell.

3 In terms of method and style, Vincent is wholly representative of the qualitative essayism of the English School. Wight had no interest in the behaviourist turn of the 1960s, and perhaps the most widely known piece of English School writing is Bull's (1969) attack on it, which played a crucial role in IR's 'second debate'.

4 Bull (1977) takes on the same idea when he sees the modern international system hold out against a possible 'medievalist' order where state sovereignty is being relativized in a maze of differentiated power relations, so that different questions are decided on different levels.

5 Vincent himself acknowledges that the latter position is a target set up to be knocked down by contemporary thought: 'Even the arch-realists concede that, in international relations, it is not simply a question of morality being used to decorate interests, but of choices among moralities' (1978: 45).

6 Vincent himself insisted that these were two different works, cf. 1982b: 661, note 15. The earlier piece was reproduced in a book edited by another scholar whose work is discussed in the present book (Walker 1984).

7 The first of the other members of the English School is Bull, whose 'cheerful scepticism' did not, however, keep him from writing that individuals were somehow privileged relative to states (Bull 1977: 316). The member disseminating suave Realism is Adam Watson. When confronted with this criticism in March 1994, however, Watson pointed out that the passage criticized by Vincent appeared in a book on diplomacy, and that he would be the first to take the general point on board (personal communication, Washington, USA).

8 Vincent points to the case of *Filártiga* v. *Peña-Irala*. Filártiga brought a case against Peña, a police officer, who had tortured his son to death in Paraguay. On appeal, the court passed judgement on Peña because 'the torturer has become – like the pirate and slave trader before him – *hostis humani generis*, an enemy of all mankind' (quoted in 1986a: 104). Domestic court rulings are a potential source for international law.

9 At the time of his death, he was planning a new book on cultural relativism. Inspired by Stanley Hoffmann's *Duties beyond Borders* (1981), it was given the working title 'The diplomacy of justice' (cf. Vincent, forthcoming; personal communication, Oxford, March 1989; personal communication from Adam Watson, Washington, March 1994).

10 Walker (1993: 3), for example, explicitly states that the problem is not with realism, but with idealism, i.e. with the likes of Linklater. See Chapter 12 in this book.

11 For a particularly blunt reaction, cf. Gilpin (1986). Vincent would actually remark in his lectures on how 'Ashley' had become a by-word for non-serious

work among the British IR mainstream (private lecture notes, Oxford University, 1987 and 1988).
12 Personal communication from Der Derian, March 1994.

REFERENCES

Works by John Vincent

Vincent, R. J. (1973) 'The function of functionalism in International Relations', in *Yearbook of International Affairs*, 27, London: Institute of World Affairs, pp. 332–44.

—— (1974) *Nonintervention and International Order*, Princeton, NJ: Princeton University Press.

—— (1975a) 'The Idea of Concert and International Order', in *Yearbook of World Affairs*, 31 London: Institute of World Affairs, pp. 34–55.

—— (1975b) *Military Power and Political Influence: The Soviet Union and Western Europe*, London: International Institute of Strategic Affairs, Adelphi paper 119.

—— (1977) 'Kissinger's System of Foreign Policy', in *Yearbook of World Affairs*, 31, London: Institute of World Affairs, pp. 8–26.

—— (1978) 'Western Conceptions of a Universal Moral Order', *British Journal of International Studies* 4(1): 20–46.

—— (1980) 'The Factor of Culture in the Global International Order', in *Yearbook of World Affairs*, 34, London: Stevens & Sons, pp. 252–64.

—— (1981) 'The Hobbesian Tradition in Twentieth-Century International Thought', *Millennium: Journal of International Studies* 10(2): 91–101.

—— (1982a) '*Realpolitik* and World Community', in James Mayall (ed.) *The Community of States*, London: Allen and Unwin, pp. 73–84.

—— (1982b) 'Race in International Relations', *International Affairs* 58(4): 658–70, reprinted in Walker 1984.

—— (1983) 'Change in International Relations', *Review of International Studies*, 9(1): 63–70.

—— (1984a) 'Edmund Burke and the Theory of International Relations', *Review of International Studies* 10(3): 205–18.

—— (1984b) 'Racial Equality', in Hedley Bull and Adam Watson, *The Expansion of International Society*, Oxford: Clarendon, pp. 239–54.

—— (1986a) *Foreign Policy and Human Rights: Issues and Responses*, Cambridge: Cambridge University Press.

—— (1986b) *Human Rights and International Relations*, Cambridge: Cambridge University Press and the Royal Institute of International Affairs.

—— (1990a) 'Order in International Politics', in J. D. B. Miller and R. J. Vincent (eds) *Order and Violence. Hedley Bull and International Relations*, Oxford: Clarendon, pp. 38–64.

—— (1990b) 'Grotius, Human Rights, and Intervention', in Hedley Bull, Benedict Kingsbury and Adam Roberts (eds) *Hugo Grotius and International Relations*, Oxford: Clarendon, pp. 241–56.

—— (1990c) 'The End of the Cold War and the International System', in David Armstrong and E. Goldstein (eds) *The End of the Cold War*, London Frank Cass, pp. 196–8.

—— (1990d) 'J. D. B. Miller and International Relations', in Vincent and O'Neill, pp. 3–14.

—— (1992a) 'Modernity and Universal Human Rights', in A. McGrew, P. G. Lewis *et al.* (eds) *Global Politics*, Cambridge: Polity, pp. 269–92.

—— (1992b) 'The Idea of Rights in International Ethics', in Terry Nardin and David Mapel (eds) *Traditions of International Ethics*, Cambridge: Cambridge University Press, pp. 250–69.

—— (1994) 'The Place of Theory in the Practice of Human Rights', in Christopher Hill and Pamela Beshoff (eds) *Two Worlds of International Relations. Academics, Practitioners and the Trade in Ideas*, London: Routledge and the London School of Economics.

—— and O'Neill, R. (eds) (1990) *The West and the Third World: Essays in Honor of J. D. B. Miller*, Basingstoke: Macmillan.

—— and Wilson, Peter (forthcoming) 'Beyond Non Intervention', in Ian Forbes and Mark Hoffmann (eds) *Ethics and Intervention*

Works by other authors

Armstrong, David (1993) *Revolution and World Order: The Revolutionary State in International Society*, Oxford: Clarendon.

Aron, Raymond (1966) *Peace and War: a Theory of International Relations*, Malabar: Krieger.

Ashley, Richard (1981) 'Political Realism and Human Interest', *International Studies Quarterly* 25(2): 204–36.

—— (1987) 'The Geopolitics of Geopolitical Space: toward a Critical Social Theory of International Politics', *Alternatives* 12(4): 403–34.

Brown, Chris (1993) 'Sorry Comfort? The Case against "International Theory"', in Frank R. Pfetsch (ed.) *International Relations and Pan-Europe. Theoretical Approaches and Empirical Findings*, Hamburg: Lit, pp. 85–100.

Bull, Hedley (1969[1966]) 'International Theory: the Case for a Classical Approach', in Klaus Knorr and James Rosenau (eds) *Contending Approaches to International Politics*, Princeton, NJ: Princeton University Press.

—— (1977) *The Anarchical Society. A Study of Order in World Politics*, London: Macmillan.

—— (1984) *Justice in International Relations*, Ontario, Canada: University of Waterloo.

—— and Watson, Adam (eds) (1984) *The Expansion of International Society*, Oxford: Clarendon.

Buzan, Barry (1993) 'From International System to International Society: Structural Realism and Regime Theory Meet the English School', *International Organization* 47(3): 327–52.

Carr, E. H. (1946[1939]) *The Twenty Years' Crisis 1919–1939: An Introduction to the Study of International Relations*, 2nd edn, London: Macmillan; republished 1961.

Der Derian, James (1987) *On Diplomacy. A Genealogy of Western Estrangement*, Oxford: Basil Blackwell.

—— (1988) 'Introducing "Philosophical Traditions" in International Relations', *Millennium* 17(2): 189–93.

—— (forthcoming) 'Hedley Bull and the Idea of Diplomatic Culture', in Mary Ann Roberson (ed.) *Beyond International Society*.

Donnelly, Jack (1994) 'Post-Cold War Reflections on the Study of International Human Rights', *Ethics and International Affairs* 8(1): 97–117.

Dunne, Timothy (1993a) 'Mythology or Methodology? Traditions in International Theory', *Review of International Studies* 19(3): 305–18.

—— (1993b) 'International Relations Theory in Britain: the Invention of an International Society Tradition', DPhil. thesis, Oxford University.

George, Stephen (1978) 'Schools of Thought in International Relations', in Michael Donelan (ed.) *The Reason of States: a Study in International Political Theory*, London: Allen and Unwin, pp. 206–13.

Gilpin, Robert (1986 [1983]) 'The Richness of the Tradition of Political Realism', in Robert O. Keohane (ed.) *Neo-realism and Its Critics*, New York: Columbia University Press, pp. 287–304.

Hinsley, F. H. (1963) *Power and the Pursuit of Peace: Theory and Practice in Relations between States*, London: Cambridge University Press.

Hoffmann, Stanley (1977) 'An American Social Science: International Relations', *Daedalus* 3(106): 41–60.

—— (1981) *Duties beyond Borders: On the Limits and Possibilities of Ethical International Politics*, Syracuse, NY: Syracuse University Press.

Horne, Alistair (1988) *Macmillan 1894–1956*, Volume I of the official biography, London: Macmillan.

Huntington, Samuel (1993) 'The Clash of Civilizations?', *Foreign Affairs* 72(3): 22–42.

Hurrell, Andrew (1993) 'International Society and the Study of Regimes: a Reflective Approach', in Volker Rittberger with Peter Mayer (eds) *Regime Theory and International Relation*, Oxford: Clarendon, pp. 49–72.

Jackson, Robert (1993) *Quasi-States: Sovereignty, International Relations and the Third World*, Cambridge: Cambridge University Press.

James, Alan (1986) *Sovereign Statehood: The Basis of International Society*, London: Routledge, Chapman and Hall.

Jones, Roy E. (1981) 'The English School of International Relations: a Case for Closure', *Review of International Studies* 1(14): 29–44.

Kingsbury, Benedict and Roberts, Adam (1990) 'Introduction: Grotian Thought in International Relations', in Hedley Bull, Benedict Kingsbury and Adam Roberts (eds) *Hugo Grotius and International Relations*, Oxford: Clarendon, pp. 1–64.

Linklater, Andrew (1990) *Beyond Realism and Marxism. Critical Theory and International Relations*, London: Macmillan.

Manning, C. A. W. (1962) *The Nature of International Society*, London: Macmillan.

Morgenthau, Hans J. (1970) 'The Intellectual and Political Functions of Theory', in *Truth and Power. Essays of a Decade 1960–1970*, London: Pall Mall, pp. 248–51.

Neumann, Iver B. and Welsh, Jennifer M. (1991) 'The Other in European Self-Definition: an Addendum to the Literature on International Society', *Review of International Studies* 17(4): 327–48.

Porter, Brian (ed.) (1971) *The Aberystwyth Papers: International Politics 1919–1969*, London: Oxford University Press.

Roberts, Adam (1993) 'Humanitarian War: Military Intervention and Human Rights', *International Affairs* 3(69): 429–49.

Suganami, Hidemi (1983) 'The Structure of Institutionalism: an Anatomy of British Mainstream International Relations', *International Relations* 7(5): 2363–81.

Wæver, Ole (1992) 'International Society – Theoretical Promises Unfulfilled?', *Co-operation and Conflict* 27(1): 97–128.

Walker, R. B. J. (ed.) (1984) *Culture, Ideology and World Order*, Boulder, CO: Westview Press.

—— (1991) 'The Concept of Culture in the Theory of International Relations', in Jongsuk Chay (ed.) *Culture and International Relations*, New York, NY: Praeger, pp. 3–17.

—— (1993) *Inside/Outside: International Relations as Political Theory*, Cambridge: Cambridge University Press.

Watson, Adam (1990) 'Systems of States', *Review of International Studies* 16(2): 99–110.

—— (1992) *The Evolution of International Society. A Comparative Historical Analysis*, London: Routledge.

Wheeler, Nicholas J. (1992) 'Pluralist or Solidarist Conceptions of International Society: Bull and Vincent on Humanitarian Intervention', *Millennium* 21(3): 463–87.

Wight, Martin (1966 [1960]) 'Why Is There No International Theory?' in Herbert Butterfield and Martin Wight (eds) *Diplomatic Investigations: Essays in the Theory of International Politics* London: Allen and Unwin, pp. 17–34.

—— (1977) *Systems of States*, ed. and intro. Hedley Bull, Bristol: Leicester University Press.

—— (1978) *Power Politics*, ed. Hedley Bull, Harmondsworth, Mx: Penguin.

—— (1991) *International Theory. The Three Traditions*, ed. Gabriele Wight and Brian Porter, Leicester: Leicester University Press for the Royal Institute of International Affairs.

3 Kenneth Waltz: a critical rationalist between international politics and foreign policy

Hans Mouritzen

Kenneth N. Waltz, born in 1924, retired in 1994 from his position as a Ford Professor of Political Science at the University of California, Berkeley, which he had held since 1971. He took his MA in 1950 and his PhD in 1954 from Oberlin College, specializing in political philosophy and International Relations. Before coming to Berkeley, Waltz had held academic positions at Columbia University, Swarthmore College and Brandeis University. His article 'Nuclear Myths and Political Realities' published in the American Political Science Review in 1990 won the Heinz Eulau award.

Kenneth Waltz is the most cited author in modern IR. One major reason for that is his creation of a coherent set of provocations challenging fashionable viewpoints in significant – though shifting – segments of the IR community. He says, for instance, that systemic interdependence is low and that this has been beneficial, that states can be seen as unitary actors, that non-state actors are relatively insignificant, that nuclear weapons are beneficial, that superpower superiority was a good thing, that the USA has behaved much like the Soviet Union in the postwar period, that the domino theory is false and much of US global activism therefore redundant, that we don't 'live in a world of change', that bipolarity persists, etc.

Waltz is often identified with two books, *Theory of International Politics* (1979) and *Man, the State, and War* (1959) – in that order of preference. *Foreign Policy and Democratic Politics* from 1967 comparing British and US foreign policy-making is less well known. When references are made to 'the book' or 'the theory' by Waltz, the 1979 book is the one at stake. Its essence had appeared in 1975 in 'Theory of International Relations', Waltz's contribution to *Handbook of Political Science*. In 1986, Robert Keohane edited *Neo-realism and Its Critics*, in which Waltz was given the opportunity to respond to some of his critics (apart from the critical contributions, this volume also reprinted the essential part of the theory). In addition to discussing these works, I shall also deal in this chapter with Waltz's more recent articles addressing the post-1989 world.

My purpose is first to interpret Waltz's philosophy of science, as it underlies 'the theory' and its aftermath in particular – but also to trace vital lines of development back to his earlier works; second, to evaluate his theory. This will be an immanent evaluation: it will be based on a

sophy of science in almost all of its

clearly stated and neatly packed and
ted theory entails that I do not have
front of me as several of my fellow
e token, the very existence of a *full-
fledged* theory – whatever one's opinion of it – invites a more thorough
epistemological assessment than do looser theoretical constructs. The building is actually there; the philosophy of science equipment that one so
seldom gets the opportunity to unpack in IR can actually be used. Interpretation in terms of a philosophy of science school can be a more fruitful
undertaking than interpretation in terms of an IR school. The latter is often
justifiably met with a 'So what?' question, because the inner logic of these
schools is so weak that one is allowed to pick and choose almost freely
among them. By contrast, to interpret an author as adhering to Karl
Popper's philosophy of science, for example – as I shall do here – has
consequences in other respects. That means that the author in question
needs to come up with some good explanations/excuses, in case deviations
from these consequences can be discerned.

Karl Popper is the central philosopher of science in this century. As a
theory constructor or theory evaluator, one has somehow to relate to his
thinking, whether one agrees with it or not ('critical rationalism', a modern
version of Kant's epistemology). It is not unreasonable to structure philosophy of science debates in this century around Popper: Popper v. the
positivists (empiricists), Popper v. the Marxists and neo-Marxists, and
Popper v. relativism (idealist philosophy of language, Thomas Kuhn's
philosophy of science, and instrumentalism in various versions).

Waltz's self-interpretation is not explicitly Popperian; often, he makes
unspecified references to 'philosophy of science standards' or, at other
times, to micro-economic theory as the source of authority. Previous interpretations of his philosophy of science wrongly describe it as 'positivist'
(Ashley 1986; Cox 1986; Keohane 1986; or Griffiths 1992) or as an inconsistent blend of various traditions (Jones 1993).[1]

WALTZ'S THEORY: SURVEY AND INTERPRETATION

The object of explanation in *Man, the State, and War* (MSW) is clear and
concise: the phenomenon of war or its absence. By contrast, the object of
explanation in *Theory of International Politics* (TIP) is more vague: international politics in general (see Figure 3.1). Waltz consistently uses the
double formulation 'behaviour and outcome' about his object of explanation here. This should indicate that his theory is both one of foreign policy
(= units' behaviour) and one of international politics (= outcomes for the
international system as a whole, like peacefulness or the persistence of a
particular type of system). As we shall see, however, Waltz abstains from
the former claim. His theory is said to be one of international politics,
solely.

	Level of explanation	*Object of explanation*
MSW	Man, domestic society, or international structure (in specified ways)	War
TIP	International structure	International politics (= 'behaviour and outcome')

Key MSW = *Man, the State, and War* (1959)
TIP = *Theory of International Politics* (1979)

Figure 3.1 Level and object of explanation, respectively, in *Man, the State, and War* and in *Theory of International Politics*

Turning to the level/source of explanation, the pattern is the reverse: TIP seems to be the most specific here; it points to the structure of the international system as the proper source of explanation. By contrast, MSW operates with three 'images' for the explanation of war: the nature of man, nation-states' domestic societies, and the structure of the inter-national system. Hence, MSW is more broad-minded regarding the appro-priate source of explanation – or so it seems (cf. below). MSW is, in several ways, a natural precursor of TIP. Whereas the latter is a full-fledged nomothetic study, the former marks some initial steps in that direction. It is a history of ideas regarding the causes of war, from Thucy-dides via Machiavelli and several others to Morgenthau. But like Popper's *The Open Society and Its Enemies* (1966) dealing with Plato, Hegel and Marx, it is a *constructive* history of ideas. The main errand is not to display what thinker 'x' really thought, but whether the thinking was justified or not. Hence the aim of MSW is to examine inputs from the various thinkers regarding the causes of war in general. As with Popper, one finds little particular veneration in the face of ancient authorities – just because they are ancient.

What does Waltz make out of his inputs, then? The conclusion is, roughly, that the anarchic structure of international politics is the under-lying or 'permissive' cause of war: it *permits* the phenomenon of war to occur, because there simply is nothing to prevent war (1959a: 232–8). It explains the recurrence of war as a phenomenon, but it does not explain a specific war. In order to do that, i.e. to grasp the efficient causes of specific wars, one normally has to turn to one of the two remaining images (or both). These are the forces that determine policy, but without the third image, the framework of world politics, it is impossible to assess their importance or predict their results.

At first glance, it might seem that Waltz had made up his mind during the years between MSW and TIP, so that the number of images had narrowed down from three to one: the structural image. This is, however, hardly the case. His world-view in TIP is substantially the same as in MSW. The fundamental puzzle in both books is how to account for centuries of continuity in the outcomes of international politics, despite forceful pressures for change (from weapon-systems, technology, domestic societies, etc.). And the answer in both cases points to the international structure constraining units' behaviour and interposing itself between units' intentions and international outcomes (see Figure 3.2). Apart from the widened object of explanation, the major difference between the two books is the more pronounced nomothetic orientation in TIP. Aiming towards a simple/elegant theory, TIP consciously stakes on *one* explanatory factor only and demonstratively leaves out the rest from the domain of theory. But that does not imply that Waltz is blind to the importance of the non-selected factors for the explanation of both unit behaviour and certain systemic outcomes. The shift from MSW to TIP seems, hence, to pertain more to scientific orientation than to substance.

There are three layers of systemic structure in TIP. The lowest layer deals with the system's ordering principle; either hierarchy as in a domestic political system or anarchy as in an international system, typically. The medium layer addresses the question of the units' functional differentiation, i.e. whether they specialize functions among themselves or each unit seeks to take care of all functions for itself. These units happen presently to be nation-states, but this is no necessity.[2] Anarchy as an ordering principle entails self-help behaviour among the units; as no unit can count on others to ensure its well-being and survival, it must take care of all functions by itself, in principle. No functional differentiation will occur. Still, even if all units are similar in this sense, they are not equal in terms of power (capability). The highest layer addresses the distribution of capabilities among the system's units – i.e. whether the system is bipolar, tripolar, multipolar, etc. If a system is to qualify as an international one in Waltz's conception, the only structural variation pertains to this third layer, i.e. the number of poles (Waltz 1975: 65). Anarchy and absence of functional differentiation at the two former layers are parameters rather than variables.

In analogy to economic theory TIP then addresses what happens to 'behaviour and outcome' in the system, as its number of poles change

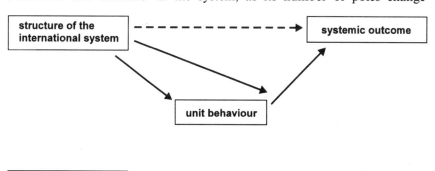

Figure 3.2 Waltz's theory of international politics: solid arrows indicate an assumed causal relationship; the dashed arrow illustrates a holistic inference avoided by Waltz (see below, p. 73)

(like the structure of a market shifting from duopoly to oligopoly to perfect competition). But as a prerequisite to this analysis, it is argued that balancing is a *universal* behavioural trait during anarchy (provided that units wish to survive and prosper). Balancing means that alliances are formed or other efforts are made that balance off the most powerful states (in contrast to bandwagoning behaviour that supports the winner). The formation of balances of power is typically the unintended consequence of behaviour motivated by other reasons. The nature of this behaviour varies with the number of poles in the system. From the viewpoint of systemic outcome/peacefulness, it is argued that a few poles are better than many, and two are better than a few. There are several reasons for this. For instance, the fewer poles there are, the less the risk of miscalculations leading to war. Internal balancing (each superpower regulating its own balancing strength; for example, through rearmament) is easier to control than balancing through alliance formation. Systemic interdependence – which may provoke conflict – is especially low during bipolarity, as the two poles are likely to be quite self-sufficient. Each of the two poles has a stake in the system and they are therefore likely to carry responsibility in the management of common global problems. Essentially, TIP saw the bipolar situation at its time of writing as the best of all worlds.[3]

One might also view Waltz's theoretical building from a different angle. If we conceive of the first layer as a variable rather than a parameter, we could say that Waltz had also built a broader theory of political systems. It says that hierarchy (a domestic political system) leads to bandwagoning behaviour, whereas anarchy (an international system) entails balancing behaviour (interpreted from TIP: 125–6). The relevance of the somewhat overlooked *Foreign Policy and Democratic Politics* to Waltz's theory should be apparent in this interpretation, as several of the relevant reasonings regarding domestic systems refer to insights from this book. Having established balancing behaviour as almost the gravitational law of international systems, the next logical step is to construct a *sub-theory*, as described above, displaying different *means* of balancing during different international polarities.

PHILOSOPHY OF SCIENCE: AN INTERPRETATION

I will now turn to an interpretation of the philosophy of science underlying Waltz's theoretical constructs as being close to that of Karl Popper. I shall briefly comment on a range of issues that any philosophy of science must address.

Metaphysical realism

The doctrine of metaphysical realism asserts that reality exists independently from our language and theories about it (contrast: idealism, relativism, instrumentalism).[4] It is labelled 'metaphysical' by Popper, since it is not refutable as a scientific theory should be. Arguments can be given in its favour, however: 'human language is always essentially descripive... and an unambiguous description is always *of* something – of some state of affairs which may be real or imaginary.... Rationality, language, description, argument, are all about some reality' (Popper 1973: 41). A corollary of realism is the *correspondence theory of truth.* 'I accept the commonsense theory... that truth is correspondence with the facts (or with reality)' (Popper 1973: 44) (contrast a coherence theory of truth, which tends to characterize idealists/relativists, and a pragmatic theory of truth, which tends to characterize instrumentalists[5]). Waltz obviously presupposes metaphysical realism, although this label is never used:

> A theory, while related to the world about which explanations are wanted, always remains distinct from that world. Theories are not descriptions of the real world; they are instruments that we design in order to apprehend some part of it.
>
> (1975: 8)

This might for a second bring doubt to one's mind about Waltz's view: Are theories mere instruments that can be more or less *useful* in virtue of their ability of produce adequate predictions and, hence, guide our practice? The answer is no. They are instruments, but instruments that can make us *apprehend* some part of the world. Therefore, they are first and foremost *about* something, an independent real world (see the first sentence). Good theories reveal the causal mechanisms in this world.[6] A further corroboration of this interpretation appears from Waltz's occasional reference to the nature of 'subject-matter' as an argument: 'The attempt to follow the general-systems model has been a misfortune, for our subject matter does not fit the model closely enough to make the model useful.... One must choose an appropriate to the subject matter' (Waltz 1975: 72). In other words, models/theories may be more or less useful, but that is *because of* some kind of relation (or lack of relation) with the segment of reality at stake.[7]

It is important to stress here that the correspondence theory of truth does not entail that truth is manifest, i.e. that it is easy to get at. Moreover, science should aim at *interesting* truth, not just truth (cf. 'The virtue of simplicity' below).

Anti-positivism/anti-inductivism

One thing is that reality exists independently from our theoretical constructs; another is that this reality – or segments of it – can be grasped only through our conceptual/theoretical lenses, according to Popper (belonging, thereby, to the Kantian philosophical tradition). That means that there is no such thing as 'facts' in and of themselves (also TIP: 12); all observation is 'theory-impregnated'. A good many of Popper's philosophical efforts have been directed against the positivist quest for certainty, i.e. that theory should be built 'from below' on a secure foundation of indisputable facts. Popper's rejection of induction has been included in this

(Popper 1973). Waltz's concept of theory is in perfect harmony with these views:

> The construction of theory is a primary task.... To believe that we can proceed otherwise is to take the profoundly unscientific view that everything that varies is a variable. To proceed by looking for associations [induction: H.M.] without at least some glimmering of a theory is like shooting a gun in the general direction of an invisible target.
>
> (1975: 15; cf. 5–12 in general)[8]

It would appear that the characterization of the Waltzian epistemology as 'positivist' (Ashley 1986; Cox 1986; Keohane 1986; Griffiths 1992) is erroneous, to say the least. The positions that Waltz holds have been established by Popper as part of a conscious *reaction* against positivism/empiricism. The characterization as 'positivist' is particularly unfair in the case of Waltz, who stood up and attacked correlationism/inductivism in political science during its behaviouralist phase.

The virtue of simplicity

Theories should preferably be simple; i.e. they should be able to explain much by little – by one or a few unifying ('simple') explanatory mechanisms (e.g. ideal types like rationality, role, or unitary actor). This view is shared by Popper (1972: 241) and Waltz (1975: 3–4). There are nuances of formulation, though. Popper has become known for his quest for *bold conjectures* in relation to our background knowledge (we should aim towards *interesting* truths). This in fact amounts to simplicity: 'what is usually called the simplicity of a theory is associated with its logical improbability' [and, hence, its boldness: H.M.] (Popper 1972: 61).

Waltz's theory is certainly simple: it has *one* independent variable that is considered able to account for behaviour and outcome in an international system. Its assumptions are simple also: states as unitary actors, states as sole actors, the system as purely anarchic, etc. And the assertion, for instance, that a bipolar system is more peaceful than a multipolar one was certainly bold at the time of its formulation, contradicting as it did the prevailing wisdom (Kaplan 1957: 22–36; Morgenthau 1961: part 4).

Anti-psychologism/anti-reductionism

The label 'anti-psychologism' refers to Popper, the label 'anti-reductionism' to Waltz, but they cover one and the same view: unit attributes should seldom or never be given the 'honour' of explaining system-wide attributes or occurrences. Popper warns repeatedly against conspiracy theories of society that seek to explain various unfortunate developments on the basis of the characteristics or motives of individual human beings or a specific group, functioning as scapegoats. In his criticism of John Stuart Mill's psychologism (*The Open Society and Its Enemies*, Ch. 14), he argues for the autonomy of sociology in relation to psychology. The preferred explanation of outcomes in the social sciences should refer to mechanisms producing consequences that were unintended by the individual actors involved. This is precisely the core type of explanation that we find in MSW and TIP. 'Structure' – albeit a non-Popperian concept – is the mechanism that intervenes between individual actions and outcomes and produces unintended results (TIP: 79, 90, 97, 102, 128, 129). For instance, balances of power may form (= outcome) without any actor in particular having pushed in this direction (TIP: 69). In fact, Waltz's emphatic criticism of 'reductionism' among alleged theories of international politics (TIP: Chs 2, 3) is actually anti-psychologism lifted up to the level of the international system, the units being nation-states instead of human beings.[9]

Anti-holism/anti-historicism

One thing is that psychologism should be avoided; but we should not, following Popper, jump to the opposite extreme and seek to explain social phenomena on the basis of emergent properties of the whole, solely (holism). Even worse, holism may easily lead to historicism, the view that the whole develops deterministically according to its own immanent law of historical development (in contrast to scientific laws of the 'if... then ...' type). In view of Waltz's crusade against 'reductionism', it is a bit odd that he does not formulate his view of holism, the opposite of reductionism. One might believe, at first impulse, that Waltz's preference for structural explanation endangered the Popperian interpretation that is being made here. This is, however, not the case. If his theory sought to account for systemic outcomes *directly* on the basis of systemic structure (cf. the dashed arrow in Figure 3.2), i.e. short-cutting units' behaviour, then holism would be at stake. But the point is that his structure is not an agent, only a primitive 'selector' (TIP: 73) that encourages certain types of behaviour and discourages others via the unit-based mechanisms of socialization and mutual competition (emulation). It may be instructive here to compare three types of economic theory: Waltz explicitly takes as his model micro-economic theory – theory that is based on the assumption of conscious actor rationality ('economic man'); it is neither macro-economic theory like that of Keynes, short-cutting the units (and, hence, being holistically committed), nor a theory of the firm like that of Cyert and March that qualifies as reductionist (Waltz 1990a).

Even though Popper and Waltz both criticize reductionism/psychologism and holism (Waltz implicitly), their preferred modes of explanation are not identical. The kind of explanation favoured by Popper is non-structural in Waltz's sense. There is no philosophical split involved here, however; it is an empirical question whether one or the other mode of explanation should be preferred. Therefore, I shall postpone this discussion until the section 'Theory Meets Reality' (p. 78).

With this non-holistic interpretation of Waltz, it should come as no surprise that there are no traces of historicism in his thinking. He can explain change in 'behaviour and outcome', in so far as the distribution of capabilities in the systems has changed. But this change, in turn, needs an extra-theoretical explanation (e.g. that the number of poles has been reduced by war or economic collapse of one of the great powers). Hence, whereas Waltz can *explain* certain types of fundamental change, he has no *theory* of change (as certain ambitious critics would like him to have; cf. Ruggie 1986). But he has never pretended to have such a theory, either; indeed, it would contradict his philosophy of science.[10]

Meeting reality: falsificationism – or what?

The bolder the conjectures, the greater the a priori likelihood that they are mistaken and, hence, the more falsifiable they are. The bolder the conjectures that spring from a theory, the more falsifiable the theory is, evidently. Popper's ideal is that science should progress (come nearer to truth) through a series of falsifications of existing theories, each time leading to the formulation of a better theory incorporating what has been learnt by previous falsifications. This ideal should explain the label 'critical rationalism': scientific progress (rationalism) is possible through criticism, i.e. learning by past mistakes. The doctrine of falsificationism was developed in opposition to the positivists' verificationism and, as the latter failed, their scepticism (Berkeley, Hume, and their modern followers). Falsificationism has faced criticism in philosophy, the natural sciences and, even more, the social sciences that I shall not report on here. Arguing in parallel with Eckstein (1975) – and other theory constructors – Waltz has advocated a more lenient course *vis-à-vis* theories than that of falsificationism. Rather than consciously seeking to kill theories at the first, the best occasion, he suggests that they be given a chance of peaceful development – at least at the outset. If theory-derived expectations fit with observations during the most unfavourable conditions ('least-likely cases'), the theory may, from a more practical point of view than Popper's, be seen as corroborated. I shall return to Waltz's strategy – and actual practice – in this regard in the section 'Theory Meets Reality'. For now, it should suffice to conclude, at the general level, that the philosophy of science tacitly underlying Waltz's theoretical endeavour is that of Karl Popper. Deviation from this pattern can be seen in one major respect only –falsificationism.[11] Supported by this conclusion, we are able subsequently to evaluate the fairness of some of Waltz's responses to his critics as well as his theory as such.

EPISTEMOLOGY MAKES A DIFFERENCE

Ever since the 'level of analysis' theme was launched in IR by Singer in 1961, there has been disagreement not only regarding which (and how many) levels should be singled out, but also as to the more fundamental question of the *relationship* among these levels: can, for instance, factors belonging to different levels be combined in one explanation – or should each level be seen as self-sufficient? According to the latter view – which I label 'complementarism' – one can explain on the basis of one level or another, but each level is seen as producing a full explanation (example: Allison 1971). According to the former view –'supplementarism' – an explanation based on one specific level can be supplemented with factors belonging to other levels, if it cannot in itself account satisfactorily for what it set out to explain (example: Wolfers 1962).[12] It seems that Waltz is oscillating between complementarism and supplementarism. Sometimes theories of international politics and foreign policy, as well as 'structural' theories and 'domestic' ones, are seen as widely different businesses that should be kept carefully apart (TIP: 71–2). A theory of international politics – like that of Waltz – should not be able to account for foreign policy. Those interested in unit behaviour are encouraged to generate their own foreign policy theories and, by implication, leave Waltz's theory alone. The fact that Waltz has written *Foreign Policy and Democratic Politics* (reprinted as recently as 1992) – and has never set at a distance those of its views that sharply contradict the assumptions of TIP[13] – also supports a complementarist interpretation. Most of the time, however, Waltz is in a supplementarist mood: a structural theory is *better* than 'reductionist' foreign policy theories; there is a competitive relation among the theories that, of course, is won by the structural theory, but in specific explanations of unit behaviour it may be necessary to supplement the structural factor with lower-level factors that are seen to be operative in the case at hand (Waltz 1986: 331, 344).[14]

Which should be preferred, then, supplementarism or complementarism? There is no straight answer to this question. It depends on one's metaphysical conviction. I shall argue here that supplementarism follows logically from metaphysical realism, whereas complementarism follows from metaphysical idealism. As a realist, one believes – as described above – in a reality existing independently from human language and its theoretical constructions. A segment of this reality corresponds to each level in our theoretical language. If factors belonging to various segments have co-produced the phenomenon for which we wish to account, then we should obviously in our explanation combine the corresponding theoretical levels. This results in supplementarism. Among the 'names' to mention in this connection are Karl Marx and Max Weber. Following an ideal-typic research strategy, they were both willing to supplement their preferred dynamics – whether class-based or rational-actor-based – with factors from outside, if reality did not correspond in full to their expectations. By contrast, the metaphysical idealist sees no reality existing independently from our language and its theoretical constructs. There is no neutral ground outside the constructs, be they Niels Bohr's complementary theories, Peter Winch's language games, or Thomas Kuhn's paradigms. The phenomenon, we wish to explain, must necessarily be described in terms of one or the other conceptual framework. Even though Allison's three models (1971) all somehow deal with 'the Cuban missile crisis', their respective ways of framing the core question lead them to exclude answers belonging to the other models and, hence, make them self-sufficient. The models provide different answers, in part because they are answers to different basic questions ('Why did the United States decide for a naval blockade against

Cuba?', 'Why was a naval blockade the outcome of interactions in the American bureaucracy?' and 'Why was a naval blockade the result of interplay between a range of individuals in cabinet and bureaucracy?'). The answers cannot meaningfully be combined in one single explanation. The complementarist must live with each model's built-in strong and weak sides; he or she cannot combine the strong sides from several models into one 'super-explanation'.

Waltz, having been classified here as a metaphysical realist, should in the name of consistency take a supplementarist position – which also happens most of the time, cf. above. But his *occasional* complementarity between 'structural theory' and 'domestic politics theory' (when under pressure by critics) is unjustified. Moreover, the distinction between a 'theory of international politics' and one of 'foreign policy' is, at best, hair-splitting. I fail to see that 'a theory about foreign policy is a theory at the national level' (TIP: 72); it is even more surprising that such a statement has been made by the constructor of a structural theory. One should not be allowed to construct a structural theory and then decline responsibility for (at least part of) units' behaviour. In that case, the structure would have no 'grip' on the units. It would simply be a bad theory. When it comes to the explanation of foreign policy behaviour, Waltz cannot evade a causal competition between his own structural factors, and environmental factors, domestic factors, bureaucratic factors, etc. Given Waltz's own epistemology, his criticism of Allison and Morgenthau at this point (TIP: 121–3) is unjustified. Morgenthau believes – erroneously according to Waltz – that 'problems of predicting foreign policy and of developing theories about it make international-political theories difficult . . . to contrive'. From the perspective of metaphysical realism, Morgenthau is certainly right, in so far as problems at the level of foreign policy are also thereby problems at the level of international politics. Waltz sees Allison's rational-actor model as one of international politics, whereas his two other models (of organizational output and bureaucratic politics, respectively) are viewed as models of foreign policy – and thereby irrelevant to theorizing on international politics. Again, granted Allison's view that organizational behaviour exerts a systematic impact on units' output, then that would certainly be a problem to be addressed also for a theory of international politics – as the units are its major actors. For the purpose of specific explanations, organizational 'disturbances' would have to be added to expectations flowing from a structural theory.

Waltz is the first to concede that his theory of international politics cannot explain much of foreign policy. From this is drawn the inference that TIP is not a theory of foreign policy. This is an illegitimate inference. Theories linking party politics or bureaucratic politics with foreign policy do likewise explain *some* of foreign policy – but far from all of it. But this does not detract from their status as theories of foreign policy. Any domain of theory claiming to have a bearing on the content of foreign policy (not its detailed implementation) is of course a theory of this phenomenon. The theories are then free to compete with each other, to create problems for each other, and to supplement each other in specific explanations of foreign policy.

I shall return to further consequences flowing from Waltz's epistemology; for now, it suffices to conclude that Waltz's structural theory must carry responsibility for (part of) units' behaviour and, therefore, be a theory of foreign policy, as well. This has consequences for the kind of tests that it can legitimately be exposed to (cf. 'Theory meets reality').

RESPONDING TO CRITICS

'For more than a decade TIP has been shot at, embellished, misunderstood, and caricatured, but never quite displaced', as rightly observed by Buzan *et al.* (1993: 6). How has Waltz's theory managed to remain at the core of IR debate ever since its publication? Its clarity and coherence are not the only explanation for this, I think. The theory also satisfies certain (conscious or unconscious) holistic impulses in the IR community, which take the form: 'Since our object of inquiry is international politics as a whole, we also ought to have a *theory* that encompasses it to its full extent'. Third, there seems to be a Mohammed Ali effect at work: Waltz fighting with his guard down. This makes it extremely tempting to try to hit him – because it appears so easy, at first glance; almost everything in the world seems to be left out from his theory. However, invoking (selected parts of) his philosophy of science, it is in fact extremely easy for Waltz to defend the theory (in fact too easy, cf. below). This means that the theory will continue to pop up in good shape, no matter how often critics feel that it has been seriously wounded.[15] Another aspect of the Ali effect is the amusement that Waltz apparently has found in challenging shifting segments of the IR – and other – communities, through his system of assertions that I mentioned initially ('nuclear weapons are beneficial', etc.). A certain tendency in the direction of 'critical overkill' has resulted, i.e. the critic punching desperately at almost anything that Waltz has allegedly asserted, in the apparent hope of landing at least one 'lucky punch'.

I shall not consider the criticism as such, only the typical dialectics between Waltz and his critics and what Waltz's ways of responding tell us about his theory and his philosophy of science.[16] Consider a construed, idealtypic conversation between a sympathetic critic (SC) and Waltz (KW):

SC: I can well understand the impact of structure on units' behaviour ('foreign policy'). However, I have spent some years studying domestic sources of foreign policy, and it strikes me how blind your theory is to these sources.

KW: So have I [*Foreign Policy and Democratic Politics* (1967)]. I do not disagree with you at all. But you should understand that my neglect of domestic politics is part of my theoretical set of *assumptions* regarding state behaviour. A scientific assumption cannot be true or false, only more or less instrumental for the purpose of theory-building. The trick is to explain much by little, not much by much. Therefore, in choosing among two theories that can explain roughly the same, I prefer the one with the most elegant/abstract assumptions.

SC: But isn't your theory a bit too elegant (or even barren)? How would you test a theory, whose independent variable may change, say, every five hundred years?

KW: That's a purely practical problem. And besides, studying continuities (in spite of pressures for change) is just as scientifically relevant as studying change.

SC: But still, you could blow some more life into your theory by adding some further structural attributes to the one you already have. What about, for instance, the state of weapon technology as an attribute of the international system? You have yourself admitted the significance of nuclear weapons to the stability and peacefulness of the bipolar international system.

KW: That is correct. But you confuse structural attributes with unit attributes. The question of weapon technology at states' disposal is a unit attribute. Likewise, some people wish me to include prevailing alliance patterns in the structure. But just like other types of inter-action patterns, they express behaviour rather than structure. Behaviour belongs to my object of explanation, not my source of explanation. Besides, all these well-intentioned would-be amendments make the theory less simple.[17]

THEORY MEETS REALITY

If only a small fraction of the IR Waltz references had represented (well-designed) case-studies, rather than more or less compulsory references, I am sure that we should know by now that Waltz's theory, in spite of all its virtues described above, is empirically false – except for some special circumstances. It cannot survive meetings with reality (note the lack of quotation marks, as we presuppose Popperian realism!). I shall briefly try to indicate this non-correspondence between theory and reality. Let us first listen to the continuation of the construed conversation above:

SC: The cases of balancing that I have seen in my empirical research have been made in response to *local* power conditions rather than systemic ones. I have also observed bandwagoning rather than bal-ancing behaviour in some of those studies that I have carried out in depth. That contradicts your theory-derived expectation.

KW: Now wait a minute. You have misunderstood what theory is all about. It cannot explain what happened last Tuesday or Wednesday – especially not a structural theory.

SC: No, but these are tendencies over several decades, and I am familiar with further cases of bandwagoning or local balancing than my own.

KW: Aha, but they are about secondary states, isn't that so?

SC: Yes, but you have actually predicted (systemic) balancing behaviour also for secondary states [TIP: 127]!

KW: Yes, but listen. Basically, my theory is one of international politics rather than foreign policy. Even if some secondary states should

SC: choose to bandwagon, that doesn't revert the overall systemic tendency in the direction of balancing behaviour.

SC: But what then about Western Europe in the wake of the Second World War? According to your theory, Western Europe should have tried to balance the US superior capability at the time by joining the Soviet camp. But in fact, the opposite happened.

(Walt 1988: 280)

As should appear, I agree with SC in this second half of the conversation. One thing is that falsificationism is probably too harsh a doctrine, at least in the social sciences (Mouritzen 1988: part VI). But Waltz is making it too easy for his theory *both* by rejecting would-be falsifications *and* by blocking a discussion of assumptions' realism. In combination – and together with a structural theory that is vague in its implications – they tend to raise the theory above empirical challenge. Waltz seems preoccupied with building grand fortifications in its defence, rather than with exposing it to constant danger in Popper's spirit (not very uncommon among theory constructors, one should add). The one fortification that is illegitimate in the case of Waltz is that pertaining to assumptions' realism. I shall briefly explain why.

Waltz's doctrine that assumptions cannot be true or false is inconsistent with his metaphysical realism; it is simply a (tactically convenient) slip of the tongue (cf. also note 6). As assumptions deal with something 'out there', it is evidently meaningful to discuss their degree of correspondence with this something (which Waltz sometimes does in his actual practice, cf. TIP: 93–5, 124).[18] The point is instead that assumptions *need not* be descriptively accurate, if this impedes their simplicity. But the fact that 'economic man', for instance, is not descriptively accurate does not entail that it is completely out of tune with reality, or – even less – that it would be meaningless to discuss its degree of correspondence with reality. The reason why 'economic man' has been a good assumption in economic theory, as I understand it, is not *only* its simplicity and, hence, manageability, but also the fact that economic actors, on the average, are not altruists and do not deviate from the idealtype in other systematic and significant ways. I agree with Koopmans' response (1968) to Friedman, saying that the sparse observation opportunities in the social sciences entail that we can hardly afford the luxury of neglecting the realism of intermediary reasonings and assumptions. This should not necessarily jeopardize their simplicity. Among two theories with equal explanatory power, we should prefer the simpler one. Among two theories of equal simplicity, we should prefer the one with the stronger explanatory power. But if the simpler theory has the weaker explanatory power (actually the typical situation), our lack of an exchange rate between simplicity and explanatory power becomes highlighted. Then, a metaphysical realist should let assumptions' realism decide. Below, I shall seek to elucidate the unrealistic nature of *one* of Waltz's (unstated) assumptions and discuss the implications of this.

As always, unstated assumptions are more interesting (and dangerous to inquiry) than those made explicitly – most Waltz critics have focused on the latter. There is actually a 'fourth layer' of structure that has not been addressed, i.e. whether a system's units are mutually mobile or non-mobile.[19] If the units are mobile, then each unit's average environment will, after a reasonable time-span, be the system as such rather than any particular segment of it. By contrast, if the units are non-mobile, each unit will face a relatively stable salient environment consisting of the major units in its geographical proximity (power waning with distance); each unit will be characterized by a specific *location* in the system's structure. In particular the combination of anarchy and non-mobility creates a system whose units are strongly affected by their salient environment at the expense of the systemic structure as a whole (Mouritzen 1980: 172, 180; Mouritzen 1996a: 17–19; Mouritzen 1996b: 262–3, 274–7). The fundamental implicit assumption in Waltz's theory seems to be that units are mobile – like molecules in a gas or firms and consumers in a market. This means that all units face one and the same system and units' respective salient environments can be neglected (as has been the tendency in much IR theorizing since Kenneth Boulding,[20] roughly speaking). This neglect is apparent already in MSW: '... the implication of the third image is, however, that the freedom of choice of any one state is limited by the actions of all others' (p. 204). Unless we conceive of systems of nomadic tribes, this is an unrealistic assumption for international politics: the freedom of choice is limited by the actions of *some* others – those in the state's salient environment. Hence, the theory is blind to the *unit/system cleavage* (see Figure 3.3) in international politics (Mouritzen 1980; Mouritzen 1996a: 17–19) – because the theory is imported from a field with no such cleavage (an economic market). The cleavage and the set of intervening variables that it represents tend to blur, or even negate, the effects of the structure (subject to modifying conditions; see below). But Waltz has overlooked the fact that between the extremes of holism and reductionism are not only his own 'structural' explanation, but also Weber's or Popper's classic 'situational explanation' of unit behaviour, stressing the unit's environment/situation and typically assuming unit rationality, but avoiding internal unit attri-

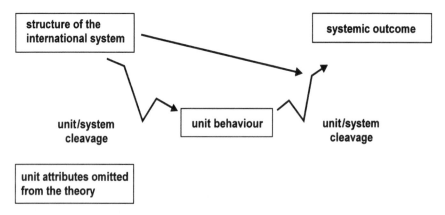

Figure 3.3 The intrusion of the unit/system cleavage into Waltz's theory

butes. The cleavage actually invites theorizing and explanation of unit behaviour on these assumptions, although neither Weber nor Popper has had international politics specifically in mind.[21]

The unit/system cleavage is most visible to those of us who have studied non-essential powers with geographically limited concerns. Even during the height of systemic bipolarity, the polarity in Cambodia's salient environment was tripolar much of the time – i.e. the USA, the Soviet Union and China were poles of roughly equal relevance to Cambodia's situation. But in principle, the unit/system cleavage should apply to all powers. Consider, for instance, a major power like China. According to balance of power theory, China should support the weaker of the two superpowers – which was the Soviet Union even as her capability culminated. But what happened? Instead we got the Sino-American rapprochement during the 1970s and 1980s. The reason was, of course, that the Soviet Union (allied with Vietnam) was the major power in China's salient environment, not least given her extensive border with that country. Given the deterioration of Sino-Soviet relations, the faraway superpower became the natural ally – analogously to the example of western Europe in the wake of the Second World War mentioned above. A consideration of the 'local balance of power' (Boulding 1962: Mouritzen 1988: part III; Mouritzen 1994) – i.e. the trend in the US/Soviet balance of power in China's salient environment – would have avoided the prediction failure of balance of power theory.

A related way of thinking is that of 'balance of threat'. Stephen Walt's (1987) balance of threat theory unknowingly pays due respect to the unit/system cleavage. States' alliance behaviour is determined by the (im)balance of threat in their salient environment – not the *one* balance of capabilities in the overall international system. This theory can account not only for the two cases of prediction failure mentioned above, but also for the cases where balance of power apparently succeeds. Stephen Walt describes his theory as a 'refinement' of that of Waltz. My point is that it amounts to nothing less than a revolution; there is no international system left in Stephen Walt's thinking with any explanatory power. A balance of threat (or a local balance of power for that matter) is meaningful in relation to a certain location, only; Waltz's balance of power, by contrast, is a systemic attribute. Admittedly, Walt's theory pays for its superior explanatory power by reduced simplicity (even though he denies this).[22] But for the reasons indicated above, I prefer the theory with the most realistic assumptions – i.e. that of Stephen Walt.

Why did it work after all?

The question now is, how much of Waltz's thinking is left, if one accepts the balance of threat theory and the significance of unit/system cleavages. I must admit that I find Waltz's theorizing on the difference between bipolarity and other polarities quite convincing, irrespective of what has just been said. The reason is simple. Focusing on the two superpowers – which not only constituted bipolarity but also formed each other's salient environments – meant that there was no unit/system cleavage to disturb the picture. The superpowers balanced each other through internal means, chiefly. By and large, they were independent of the kind of external balancing (dependent upon diplomacy in relation to other powers and, in turn, the latters' salient environments) that characterizes multipolarity. Hence, an overall systemic balance of power functioned during bipolarity. As the thrust of TIP was an analysis of bipolarity and balancing – with comparisons to multipolarity – it is no wonder that it sounded convincing (at least to some of us). But as soon as we move to a different polarity,[23] or beyond the superpowers in the bipolar system, the systemic balance of power is replaced by numerous local balance of power/threat that tend to blur – or even negate –the fragile effects, if any, of the systemic polarity. The overall structure having lost its grip on units' behaviour, TIP not only fails as a theory of foreign policy (which it did not pretend to be, either), but it likewise becomes unable to predict most systemic outcomes.[24] Its sole area of legitimate application is the special case of superpowers during bipolarity (or regional bipolarities, outside Waltz's concern, as in 'security complex analysis' (Buzan 1991); cf. note 26 below).

WALTZ AND POLARITY IN TRANSITION

The (alleged) breakdown of bipolarity should provide an excellent opportunity to test Waltz's theory, provided one still believes in it: one of the rare shifts in its independent variable seems to have taken place. This opportunity has not been exploited yet, however, since the preliminary step – the counting of poles and, hence, assessment of the independent variable – has not been completed. There seem to be two different Waltzian comments on the new situation. The first type denies the widespread view that bipolarity has broken down, referring to the continued Russian second-strike capability as safeguarding a modified bipolarity (to be followed, eventually, by multipolarity; Waltz 1993a: 71). In a nuclear world, the connection between a country's economic and technological capability, on the one hand, and its military capability, on the other, is loosened (1993a: 51–2). Even though the presence of nuclear weapons has always been a crucial element in Waltz's thinking, it has been considered secondary to the polarity structure. Now it seems to be a decisive factor in which type of polarity exists. This apparent upgrading of a unit attribute might look like the beginning of a revision of Waltz's theory (Hansen 1993).

The second type of comment (Waltz 1993b) sees the present structure as unipolar[25] (the USA being the pole) – but this is argued to represent a transitional phase before multipolarity has established itself. By the first decade of the next millennium, we can expect to have a world of five or so great powers. The emerging poles – Russia, China, Japan and Germany/EU – will eventually balance against the strongest pole; but this is not said with the usual Waltzian conviction (Waltz 1993a: 77, 79).

Post-bipolarity has made a debate on what I called the 'fourth layer of structure' just as pertinent as the 'second-layer' debate. Not that I imagine states becoming mobile – e.g. small powers moving away from their dominant neighbours, just as small boys run away from bigger bullies – but because the *implications* of non-mobility and the unit/system cleavage are particularly visible in the present international situation. It provides excellent opportunities for local incongruities – 'setting the regions free' compared with the previous situation of bipolar overlay (Buzan 1991: 219–20). In Europe, for instance, the emergence of its own regional (EU) unipolarity and various local polarities resulting from the proliferation of new states and disputed borders have entailed that the international systemic polarity (whatever its number of poles) seems more irrelevant than ever to individual salient environments, and the latter deviate significantly among each other – even among neighbouring nation-states. Paradoxically, it may be said that the structural transformation from two superpowers to one marked the last major 'Waltz effect' on international politics for a very long time: the overall structure abolished its own future influence.[26]

In relation to the fourth layer of structure, which *general* factors tend to affect the importance of the unit/system cleavage should be debated. I have previously suggested that high levels of interdependence as well as global reachability of credible weapons should improve the prospects for overall structural explanation, after all (cf. Mouritzen 1980: 173; cf. also, for example, Christensen and Snyder 1990: 168, regarding weapons). But the post-bipolar situation in Europe described above should indicate that other factors are at work as well – factors that have 'widened' the unit/system cleavage.

Will Waltz's theory remain in focus?

Balance of power theory having been superseded by balance of threat theory, the IR community should have turned to Stephen Walt and tried energetically to shoot down his theory. But that is not the way it works.[27] The factors that have brought TIP to the apex of the citation index continue to be operative, in conjunction with strong mechanisms of inertia in the IR community. Notwithstanding its non-correspondence to empirical reality in vital respects, therefore, and notwithstanding the downfall of bipolarity, I believe that the theory will remain a focus of scholarly debate. The theory has been beneficial to the discipline from a pragmatic point of view, both acting as a philosophy of science course to the IR community, and also functioning as a skeleton or structuring device for IR discussions (like the current 'second layer' debate). It has induced balancing rather than bandwagoning behaviour in the IR community – a healthy thing for the advancement of inquiry.

Only Waltz can shoot down Waltz – which may actually happen, if he settles for the first of the two interpretations of the current international polarity delineated above (the one upgrading a unit attribute like nuclear weapons). The second interpretation, however, will retain the theory intact. In that case, it will remain at the centre of IR debate.

NOTES

1 Jones's main point, as I understand it, is that inconsistencies in Waltz's mix of positivist, rationalist and pragmatist traditions make the foundation of his theory unsafe (p. 192). As I shall seek to demonstrate below, in a Popperian interpretation of Waltz all but one of these alleged inconsistencies disappear. In my view, it is wishful thinking that makes Jones in *The Logic of Anarchy* magnify the pragmatist flavour in certain Waltzian formulations, so as to make Waltz a natural precursor of his own 'thoroughgoing pragmatism' (1993: 185).

2 They could as well be city-states or empires, for instance; cf. Waltz 1979: 91.

3 This theoretical building is a natural development of previous IR realism (and in particular the work of Morgenthau), being based on assumptions about unitary actors (states), power motivations, international anarchy, etc., and balance of power thinking. The major differences are, first, that Waltz bases this thinking on a rigorous social scientific footing (a Popperian footing, as I would say), and, second, that he introduces a causally active structure that is kept apart from the unit level. This difference between Waltz ('neo-realism') and his predecessors has been extensively discussed in the 1986 volume, cf. in particular Keohane 1986: 9–12, 15, and Waltz 1986: 336–7 (cf. also Waltz 1990a). I see no real disagreement between Keohane and Waltz in this respect, and I have nothing to add to their views. Cf. also Buzan *et al.* 1993: Ch. 1.

4 It has nothing to do, of course, with the IR schools of 'realism' or 'neo-realism', under which Waltz's work also happens to be subsumed; cf. the preceding note.

5 The criterion of truth being internal logical coherence in the former case and practical usefulness in the latter case.

6 For a possibly instrumentalist view of theory, see Friedman 1968. Nagel (1973) in his assessment of Friedman's epistemology is explicitly in doubt as to Friedman's being a realist or an instrumentalist (p. 137). The only *deviation* from the pattern of metaphysical realism that I ascribe to Waltz are the formulations declaring that a theory's assumptions are neither true nor false – just more or less useful (e.g. 1979: 119). This has, of course, an instrumentalist/pragmatist flavour that Jones enjoys, cf. note 1. But Waltz nowhere asserts that theories as a whole cannot be true or false (as postulated by Jones 1993: 188); it only pertains to their assumptions. Consider, for instance, the following formulation: 'Testing theories is a difficult and subtle task, made so by the ... elusive relation between reality and theory as an instrument for its apprehension. Questions of truth and falsity are somehow involved, but so are questions of usefulness and uselessness' (1979: 123–4). Hence, there is no doubt about the existence of an independent reality in Waltz's thinking; metaphysical realism applies. None the less, his formulations about the status of assumptions amount, of course, to a deviation from this. I shall deal with its unfortunate effects below.

7 Also, realism appears indirectly from Waltz's saying that theories, unlike laws, do not strive to be 'descriptively accurate'. For this 'accuracy' to be meaningful, it must refer to some reality 'out there' that exists independently from our laws and theories. Laws must be descriptively accurate; theories can deal with accuracy in a much broader sense. Waltz's use of the history of ideas in MSW, as I emphasized above, speaks against a relativist conception of history and, hence, in favour of realism.

8 Waltz is attacked by both Griffiths (1992) and Jones (1993: 188) for not accounting for the discovery of theories: 'One cannot say how the intuition comes and how the idea is born' (TIP: 9). Given the Popperian interpretation of Waltz, however; these attacks are unfair. According to Popper, it is crucial to distinguish between theories' context of discovery and context of justification. The former should have no bearing on the latter. In other words: how a theory has been *discovered* (through reading, through a particular experience, through dreaming at night, or all three) has no implications for its scientific quality.

9 But in fact, we find anti-psychologism, proper, in the criticism of the 'first image' in MSW (pp. 4, 28, 238).

10 On explanation and theory of change from a Popperian perspective, cf. Nisbet (1972).

11 Paradoxically, the only point where Popper is mentioned by Waltz is in connection with this deviation from his thinking (TIP: 123). At the time of writing TIP, Waltz had read little of Popper's work beyond 'The Open Society'; the main philosophical influence was Kant (letter from Waltz to the present author, 20 February 1995). But as should appear, the Kantian inspiration is not inconsistent with the interpretation made here; quite to the contrary.

12 Singer (1961) might seem to be a complementarist, as his systemic and his subsystemic levels cannot be combined in one single explanation. This is, however, due to the fact that he sees the subsystemic level as the most suitable locus of explanation proper (v. description or prediction). Therefore, there is not much to combine it with, for obvious reasons.

13 For instance, 'Indecision and stalemate, zigzags in policy produced by internal struggles for power, timidity abroad because of insecurity at home, and adventures in foreign policy for the sake of impressing a domestic audience are all familiar aspects of both totalitarian and authoritarian rule' (1967a: 310). This is in diametric opposition to the neglect of domestic politics in TIP. Seen from a complementarist point of view, Waltz's theory construction becomes a game of its own, unrelated to any conception of reality. He can play according to one set of rules (assumptions), and then suddenly switch to an entirely different set. But he cannot follow two sets of rules simultaneously. Cf. also Waltz 1986: 339.

14 In certain formulations, the levels of structure and unit are actually conceived on an equal footing (TIP: 175; Waltz 1975: 47, 55, 65, 75). Waltz's reason for framing a structural theory is that this level so far has been very much overlooked in IR theory; such a theory having been established, it should be possible to assess the comparative causal weight of the structural level and the unit level. This humble attitude, as well as the not so humble attitude giving priority to structure, can be neatly subsumed under the heading of supplementarism. In the former case, Waltz is neutral as to the outcome of the causal competition; in the latter, he trusts his own theory and adds exogenous factors only at the margin. But the additive mood is the same in both cases.

15 MSW was also a citation success, but far from the level of TIP. There was simply not the same Mohammed Ali effect; after all, three images were presented, so everyone could presumably find one to their liking.

16 Parts of this criticism are included elsewhere in this volume; see Chapter 7 on Ruggie, Chapter 10 on Wendt, and Chapter 5 on Gilpin. Cf. also the volume by Buzan *et al.* (1993), critically elaborating on Waltz's theory. Since Ruggie's review of TIP in 1983 (reprinted as Ruggie 1986), there has been debate on the 'second layer of structure' dealing with units' functional differentiation or separateness. The debates on the first and third layers are, of course, much older than TIP.

17 The response of some sympathetic critics, in turn, has been to introduce explanatory notions that are non-structural, but still systemic: Ruggie's 'dynamic density' (1986), Keohane and Nye's 'process' (1987), and Buzan's 'interaction capacity' (1993a). Cf. also Chapter 7 on Ruggie. They deal with such factors as communication, institutionalization, technology and interdependence. In a comment on Waltz's Handbook chapter (Mouritzen 1980: 173–4), I sought to draw attention to explanatory factors 'between' units and structure, cf. below.

18 It seems that Waltz is willing to discuss precisely those assumptions whose basic correctness he trusts the most (e.g. states as dominant actors).

19 Units' mutual mobility is a fundamental structural property – i.e. it is nonreducible to a more basic property. In the spirit of Waltz, mobility and nonmobility should be seen as dichotomous categories – just like anarchy and hierarchy.

20 Tellingly it has required an *economist* with a comparative perspective on different types of systems to grasp one of the fundamental peculiarities of international politics: 'Yet another difference between international conflict and the competition of firms is the much greater importance of geographical boundaries in international relations. The firm competes in a market area where boundaries are shifting and ill defined and where effort is spread over the whole area rather than being concentrated at the boundary' (Boulding 1962: 264).

21 Waltz presents a dozen times or so in his works a 'list of omissions', i.e. a list of explanatory factors that have been consciously left out from the theory (e.g. TIP: 139; Waltz 1990a: 31, 34, 36) – such as governmental form, ideology, bureaucratic factors, etc., all belonging to his 'unit level'. The point is that for Waltz, the alternative to his 'structure' is always the unit level dealing with unit attributes – never situations *around* units. Likewise, in a criticism of classic realism, Waltz asserts that 'realists cannot handle causation at a level above states because they fail to conceive of structure as a force that shapes and shoves the units'. In other words, 'above states' can mean only structure; he is blind to a unit/structure cleavage as here advocated.

22 This is not a very convincing denial, cf. Walt 1987: 263, n. 3. For one thing, there are more components in a 'balance of threat' than in a balance of power (apart from the threatening parties' capabilities, their proximities, offensive capabilities and perceived intentions *vis-à-vis* the state in question). Second, and more important, Walt substitutes for one overarching international structure and balance of power as many balances of threat as there are states in the system, in principle.

23 An impression of the reduced predictive powers of Waltz's theory during multipolarity (compared to bipolarity) is provided by Christensen and Snyder 1990.

24 It should be added, of course, that overall systemic vocabulary may be useful for *descriptive/comparative* purposes. When dealing with a number of historic international systems (e.g. Buzan 1993b), it is useful from a comparative point of view to label them as unipolar, bipolar, multipolar, etc., or to use other systemic vocabulary. Moreover, as a prelude to environmental explanation of unit behaviour, it may be natural briefly to describe the properties of the overall international system. This is, of course, perfectly legitimate, as long as one does not mistake it for explanation, proper.

25 Strangely enough, Waltz avoids the term 'unipolarity'; instead, power is said to be 'severely unbalanced' in the current international system. In his previous works, unipolarity is never mentioned as a possibility; there is no middle ground between hierarchy and bipolarity (Hansen 1993: 15). This is odd, indeed, since there is no contradiction between a system having one superior power and most other powers forming an alliance that succeeds in counterbalancing it. The former is structure, the latter is behaviour.

26 'Structure' refers here to the third layer of structure, solely. Following the reasoning above, it would require a new bipolarity for the structure to regain its power. But of course, we shall face lower-level bipolar symmetries that justify (sub)systemic analyses – for the simple reason that a unit/subsystem cleavage will generally be easier to bridge than a unit/system cleavage.

27 As already indicated, Waltz himself has upheld the balance of power theory after Stephen Walt's presentation of the balance of threat theory; cf. Waltz 1993b: 74.

REFERENCES

Works by Kenneth N. Waltz

Waltz, Kenneth N. (1959a) *Man, the State, and War*, New York: Columbia University Press.

—— (1959b) 'Political Philosophy and the Study of International Relations', in W. T. R. Fox (ed.) *Theoretical Aspects of International Relations*, Notre Dame, IN: University of Notre Dame Press.

—— (1959c) 'Reason, Will and Weapons', *Political Science Quarterly* 74 (September): 412–19.

—— (1962) 'Kant, Liberalism and War', *American Political Science Review* 56(2): 331–40.

—— (1964) 'The Stability of a Bipolar World', *Daedalus* 93(3): 981–90.

—— (1965) 'Contention and Management in International Relations', *World Politics* 18 (July): 720–44.

—— (1967a) *Foreign Policy and Democratic Politics*, Boston, MA: Little, Brown.

—— (1967b) 'International Structure, National Force and the Balance of World Power', *Journal of International Affairs* 21(2): 215–32.

—— (1967c) 'The Politics of Peace', *International Studies Quarterly* 11(3) (September): 199–211.

—— (1968) 'Realities, Assumptions and Simulations', in William D. Coplin (ed.) *Simulation in the Study of Politics*, Chicago: Markham.

—— (1970) 'The Myth of National Interdependence', in Charles P. Kindleberger (ed.) *International Corporation*, Cambridge, MA: MIT Press, pp. 205–20.

—— (1974) 'America's European Policy Viewed in Global Perspective', in Wolfram Hanreider (ed.) *The United States and Western Europe in the 1970s*, Cambridge, MA: Winthrop.

—— (1975) 'Theory of International Relations', in Fred I. Greenstein and Nelson W. Polsby (eds) *International Politics, Handbook of Political Science*, vol. 8, Reading, MA: Addison-Wesley, pp. 1–85.

—— (1979) *Theory of International Politics*, New York: Random House.

—— (1981a) *The Spread of Nuclear Weapons – More May Be Better*, Adelphi Papers no. 171, London: International Institute of Strategic Affairs and Brasseys.

—— (1981b) 'A Strategy for Rapid Deployment Force', *International Security* 5 (Spring): 49–73.

—— (1982a) 'Exchange with Richard Rosecrance', *International Organization* 36(3): 679–81.

—— (1982b) 'The Central Balance and Security in North East Asia', *Asian Perspective* 6(1) (Spring/Summer): 88–107.

—— (1983) 'Toward Nuclear Peace', in D. Brito and M. Intrilligator (eds) *Strategies for Managing Nuclear Proliferation*, Lexingon, MA: Lexington Books.

—— (1985) 'Balance of Power', in J. Solomon *et al.* (eds) *Power, Principles and Interests*, Lexington, MA: Ginn.

—— (1986) 'Reflections on Theory of International Politics: a Response to my Critics', in Robert O. Keohane (ed.) *Neo-realism and Its Critics*, New York: Columbia University Press, pp. 322–47.

—— (1988) 'The Origins of War in Neo-realist Theory', *Journal of Interdisciplinary History* 18(4): 615–28.

—— (1990a) 'Realist Thought and Neo-realist Theory', *Journal of International Affairs* 44(1): 21–37. Reprinted in Robert Rothstein (ed.) *The Evolution of Theory in International Relations*, Columbia, SC: University of South Carolina Press, 1991, pp. 21–39.

—— (1990b) 'Nuclear Myths and Political Realities', *American Political Science Review* 84(3): 731–45.

—— (1991) 'America as a Model for the World? A Foreign Policy Perspective', *Political Science* 24 (December): 667–70.

—— (1993a) 'The New World Order', *Millennium* 22(2): 187–96.

—— (1993b) 'The Emerging Structure of International Politics', *International Security* 18(2): 44–79.

—— and Sagan, Scott D. (1995) *The Spread of Nuclear Weapons: A Debate*, New York: W. W. Norton.

Works by other authors

Allison, Graham T. (1971) *Essence of Decision. Explaining the Cuban Missile Crisis*, Boston, MA: Little, Brown.

Ashley, Richard K. (1986[1984]) 'The Poverty of Neo-realism', in R. Keohane (ed.) *Neo-realism and Its Critics*, New York: Columbia University Press.

Boulding, Kenneth (1962) *Conflict and Defense*, New York: Harper and Brothers.

Buzan, Barry (1991) *People, States, and Fear*, London: Harvester Wheatsheaf.

——(1993a) 'Rethinking System and Structure', in Barry Buzan, Charles Jones and Richard Little, *The Logic of Anarchy*, New York: Columbia University Press.

——(1993b) 'The Idea of International System: Theory Meets History', manuscript, 33 pp.

——Jones Charles, and Little, Richard (1993) *The Logic of Anarchy*, New York: Columbia University Press, pp. 19–80.

Christensen, Thomas J. and Snyder, Jack (1990) 'Chain Gangs and Passed Bucks: Predicting Alliance Patterns in Multipolarity', *International Organization* 44(2): 137–68.

Cox, Robert W. (1986) 'Social Forces, States, and World Orders: Beyond International Relations Theory', in Robert O. Keohane (ed.) *Neo-realism and Its Critics*, New York: Columbia University Press, pp. 204–55.

Eckstein, Harry (1975) 'Case Study and Theory in Political Science', in Fred I. Greenstein and Nelson Polsby (eds) *Handbook of Political Science*, Vol. 7, Reading, MA: Addison-Wesley, pp. 79–137.

Friedman, Milton (1968) 'The Methodology of Positive Economics', in May Brodbeck (ed.) *Readings in the Philosophy of the Social Sciences*, New York: Macmillan, pp. 508–28.

Griffiths, Martin (1992) *Realism, Idealism and International Politics*, London: Routledge.

Hansen, Birthe (1993) 'Waltz' neo-realisme – efter det sovjetiske sammenbrud', *Working Paper 1993/16*, Copenhagen: Institute of Political Studies.

Jones, Charles (1993) 'Rethinking the Methodology of Realism', in Barry Buzan, Charles Jones and Richard Little, *The Logic of Anarchy*, New York: Columbia University Press, pp. 169–231.

Kaplan, Morton A. (1957) *System and Process in International Politics*, New York: John Wiley.

Keohane, Robert O. (1986) 'Realism, Neo-realism and the Study of World Politics', in Robert O. Keohane (ed.) *Neo-realism and its Critics*, New York: Columbia University Press, pp. 1–27.

——and Nye, Joseph (1987) 'Power and Interdependence Revisited', *International Organization* 41(4): 725–53.

Koopmans, Tjalling C. (1968) 'The Construction of Economic Knowledge', in May Brodbeck (ed.) *Readings in the Philosophy of the Social Sciences*, New York: Macmillan.

Morgenthau, Hans J. (1961) *Purpose of American Politics*, New York: Knopf.

Mouritzen, Hans (1980) 'Selecting Explanatory Level in International Politics: Evaluating a Set of Criteria', *Co-operation and Conflict* 15(3): 169–82.

——(1988) *Finlandization. Towards a General Theory of Adaptive Politics*, Aldershot, Hants: Gower.

——(1994) 'Testing Weak Power Theory: Three Nordic Reactions to the Soviet Disintegration', in Walter Carlsnaes and Steve Smith (eds) *European Foreign Policy. The EC and Changing Perspectives in Europe*, London: Sage, pp. 156–77.

——(1996a) 'Polarity and Constellations', in Hans Mouritzen, Ole Wæver and Håkan Wiberg, *European Integration and National Adaptations: a Theoretical Inquiry*, New York: Nova Science.

——(1996b) 'Comparative and Theoretical Insights', Ch. 12 in Hans Mouritzen, Ole Waever and Håkan Wiberg, *European Integration and National Adaptations: a Theoretical Inquiry*, New York: Nova Science.

Nagel, Ernest (1973) 'Assumptions in Economic Theory', in Alan Ryan (ed.) *The Philosophy of Social Explanation*, London: Oxford University Press, pp. 130–9.

Nisbet, Robert (ed.) (1972) *Social Change*, New York: Harper and Row.

Popper, Karl R. (1966[1945]) *The Open Society and Its Enemies*, Vols 1 and 2, London: Routledge.

—— (1972[1963]) *Conjectures and Refutations*, London: Routledge.

—— (1973[1972]) *Objective Knowledge*, London: Oxford University Press.

Ruggie, John G. (1986) 'Continuity and Transformation in the World Polity: towards a Neo-realist Synthesis', in Robert O. Keohane (ed.) *Neo-realism and Its Critics*, New York: Columbia University Press, pp. 131–58.

Singer, David (1961) 'The Level-of-Analysis Problem in International Relations', in Klaus Knorr and Sidney Verba (eds) *The International System: Theoretical Essays*, Princeton, NJ: Princeton University Press.

Walt, Stephen (1987) *The Origins of Alliances*, Ithaca, NY: Cornell University Press.

—— (1988) 'Testing Theories of Alliance Formation: the Case of Southwest Asia', *International Organization* 42(2): 275–316.

Wolfers, Arnold (1962) *Discord and Collaboration*, Baltimore, MD: Johns Hopkins University Press.

4 Robert O. Keohane: a contemporary classic

Michael Suhr

Robert O. Keohane received a BA from Shimer College and his PhD from Harvard University in 1966 when he was only 24 years old. Advised by Stanley Hoffmann, he dealt in his dissertation with politics in the UN General Assembly. More specifically the question he addressed was, did the institutional context of the UN General Assembly significantly affect the outcomes of interstate relations taking place within the UN. After graduation he got his first assignment at Swarthmore College where Kenneth Waltz also taught. By 1973 Keohane left to set up an undergraduate degree programme at Stanford University while pursuing a successful partnership with Joseph Nye. In 1981 he left for Brandeis University where he worked until 1985 when he received a position as Professor at Harvard University, Department of Government. As of July 1996, he is James B. Duke Professor at Duke University.

From day one in most International Relations (IR) classes students are introduced to one or other of the well-known texts by Keohane. He is probably one of the most quoted IR scholars in recent years. By studying his authorship one can get an insight into the development of International Relations theory in the last two decades and thereby locate some of the general problems facing IR today. Furthermore, his work can help us understand the process of agenda-setting in the Anglo-Saxon academic world.

Broadly speaking, Keohane has been instrumental in developing two influential research programmes, and a third appears to be in the making. To a large extent he has come to symbolize these two research programmes: transnationalism/interdependence and international regimes; both have been at the very centre of our International Relations debates. The third campaign, international institutionalism, still has to be elaborated upon further before one can judge how influential it will become. Since the development of these campaigns has evolved progressively over the years the presentation of Keohane's work will follow a rather ordered chronology.

Moreover, I will argue that Keohane's creative construction of new labels – world politics paradigm, after hegemony, functional regime theory, etc. – is also interesting to study in order to understand the process of agenda-setting in IR. Thus, I will attempt to go beyond these labels in order to point out some of the continuous questions and hypotheses about international governance he has worked with over the years despite his new labels and campaigns. In doing so, this article also seeks to analyse Keohane's application of new theories from social science at large to IR. Finally, I will analyse how he draws upon and distances himself from both realism and liberalism, in order that I may present a more nuanced picture of his more fundamental assumptions.

THE FIRST CAMPAIGN: TRANSNATIONALISM AND INTERDEPENDENCE

Keohane's major breakthrough came with the literature on the politics of the modern, interdependent world. In the US foreign policy establishment of the end of the 1960s there was a growing concern with how to manage or control what was perceived to be an increasingly vulnerable economy.[1] Realization of the USA's inability to determine its own economic policy was gradually perceived as a serious problem by policy-makers and thus also by a growing number of American academics. As Bretton Woods, the oil crisis, and the defeat in Vietnam brought West–West relations to the fore, the playground for Keohane and other likeminded people was laid out. In 1971, Keohane and Nye put forward a loose paradigm termed 'world politics', which was distanced from modernism; according to this, multinational corporations (MNC), transnational social movements and international organizations had created a world without borders and thus eclipsed the territorial state (1977: 3). At the same time it also came to represent a significant challenge to the realist explanation, or rather to the 'traditionalist' explanation, as they labelled it (1971a: 729). The idea was to promote a theory with limited applicability, namely to relations among Western industrialized nations. For explaining relations among other nations in the world, i.e. in the Middle East, the traditionalist theory was more appropriate, they suggested. But not only did it become a complementary approach to realism, that is, a self-sufficient theory, the group of non-realist writers also came to substitute it for their concern with European and Central American regional integration. Out of the lack of progress in the actual integration process grew the concern with interdependence and the possibility of co-operative solutions among the industrialized countries. Despite integration theory's teleology and limited geographical concern, many of 'the insights into the politics of complex sets of interdependent entities' were reused (Keohane and Nye 1975a: 401).

What Keohane and Nye saw evolving among the industrialized nations was a more complex pattern of actors and issues than claimed by realists. Force and thereby military matters did not have the same importance as earlier due to the process of modernization. IR was no longer only a status game, but also a welfare game. Thus the prospect of transferring military might to such low politics issues as welfare was increasingly seen as impossible. The validity of Stanley Hoffmann's distinction between high and low politics was questioned. Various kinds of transnational actors – transnational corporations (TNCs), the Catholic Church, international organizations, etc. – had become important in determining the outcome of this game and should be included in any study.[2] By transmitting policy signals across nations, non-governmental organizations (NGOs) had catalysed a break-down between foreign and domestic politics, and thus expanded the foreign policy agenda. This process of transnationalization, or intersocietalism, and broadening of the substance of foreign policy promoted an equivalent process of transgovernmentalism. Bureaucratic subunits were increasingly 'competitors for influence rather than instruments of a co-ordinated strategy' of a state, Keohane and Nye argued (1975a: 392), echoing Karl Kaiser's conceptualization of multibureaucratic coalition build by transgovernmental actors. Intergovernmental relations had, in other words, become transgovernmental. It was Keohane and Nye (1974) who emphasized how coalitions grew out of these transgovernmental relations. On one hand the strengthening of these intersocietal relations helped in breaking down the hierarchy among issues, and thus the easy fungibility of power from military resources to economic issues, on the other hand it was said to increase the possibility of linking various issue areas since more issues are transsocietally linked; this way of thinking was recognized not only by Brzezinski but also by Kissinger. In contrast to neo-functional integration theorists, according to whom automatic spillover would occur based on a functional logic, Keohane and Nye suggested that this more often resulted from spurious variables such as timing for decisions, or political strategy (Keohane and Nye 1975a: 396). Consequently, the transgovernmental and transsocietal focus not only challenged the centrality of the state as the most important actor in international relations, but also represented a threat to the level-of-analysis problem as defined by Waltz (1959) and labelled by Singer (1961) due to the blurring of the distinction between explaining behaviour by factors either at the level of the international system or at the level of the state.

Yet, Keohane and Nye (1971a: 336) distanced themselves from more modernist writers by emphasizing among other things that the transnational actors were in essence often managed by a group of people from specific countries. Transnational firms were not really multinational but nationally linked and biased if one was to take the management's nationality as an indicator of loyalty.

In contrast to the positive and egalitarian overtones of other pluralist writers Keohane and Nye stressed the uneven distribution of wealth and power among nations. Therefore, they focused on the asymmetrical degree of interdependence, i.e. how states experience different degrees of sensitivity to economic events. By arguing that it was a question not of how much two states traded, but of how affected their respective policies were by price and income developments in other states, as well as by those states' policies, they echoed Richard Cooper's hypothesis (1975b: 366–77). One of Keohane and Nye's contributions to the development of theory was to combine this question of sensitivity with the realist question of who is most vulnerable to changes in the rules of the international system (Waltz 1970). That is to say, who incurs the highest costs from changes. When the costs of avoiding the consequences of interdependence are too high, 'it may seem more sensible, rather than changing its level, to alter its form, that is, to institute a joint decision-making procedure' (Keohane and Nye 1975b: 374). Thus, political integration was to be seen as a way to avoid the problems arising from interdependence. But one should not be overly optimistic about this solution: while integration might enhance some values, others might diminish; integration could have adverse distributional effects, or unwanted social and cultural effects on society; and finally it might create normative problems such as loss of national democratic control and export costs to third parties thereby creating conflict with these (Keohane and Nye 1975b: 376–7).

Yet, two aspects of liberalism were assumed to be valid. One was the idea that together with the decreased cost of transportation and communication the modernization of states accounted for some of the most important factors explaining complex interdependence (1971b: 737). The other idea was a restatement of Kaiser's earlier hypothesis that these transnational factors had created a control gap for the western welfare state. On the one hand states' areas of responsibility had increased significantly, on the other hand the means of achieving them were gradually disappearing. Because the transnational interaction was mostly beyond the ability of central governments to manage, governments' means of solving problems were disappearing. On this basis, Keohane and Nye promoted the idea of the state's autonomy as being more relevant than the state's sovereignty (1971b: 744).

The partnership between Keohane and Joseph Nye was so successful that they got to the forefront of the theoretical discussion in International Relations. They were not inventing transnationalism as a new theory. It was very much in the making when they entered the scene. Instead, their main contribution to IR was their ability to synthesize, categorize and make more precise what others had been discussing for some years. But, it seems that their perspective on international relations also grew significantly with their partnership. With the publication of one of Keohane and Nye's most quoted books, *Power and Interdependence*, a significant shift in conceptual focus towards regimes took place, although it came to stand out as one of the prime examples of transnationalism and interdependence. Yet the book was published in 1977 after the heyday of the debate. Moreover, in this book Keohane and Nye retreated from attempting to build another paradigm, or to construct an interparadigm debate. Instead, they wanted to build a new research programme, which meant giving up the idea of complementarity in favour of supplementarity. That is to say, they favoured that 'an explanation based on one specific level can be supplemented with factors belonging to other levels, if it cannot in itself account satisfactorily for what it set out to explain.'[3]

They presented four models which one should use depending on which situation one wanted to analyse (1977: Chapter 3). If the underlying sources of power could be translated at low cost into changes in international regimes one should start the analysis by using an overall power structure explanation, i.e. a kind of pure realist model. If power sources were not fungible from one issue area to another, the issue structure model should be the point of analytical departure. If power over outcome were conferred 'by organizationally dependent capabilities, such as voting power, ability to form coalitions, and control of elite networks: that is by capabilities that are affected by the norms, networks, and institutions' (1977: 55) then the international organization model should be used as the basis for analysis, i.e. Keohane and Nye's model. Finally, if the economic costs of disrupting patterns of economic interdependence were high, one should begin the analysis by using the economic process explanation.

Thus, one needs to analyse the conditions dominating the area of the international system which one wants to analyse before determining which model or combination of models to use. Obviously, the interesting contribution made by Keohane and Nye was the claim that their issue structure and international organization models are better explanations for change and inertia in international regimes when states act in complex interdependent situations. At the same time they warned us against believing that such a situation, or area of study, is stable over time. '[O]ne model may apply quite well for one period, but poorly for another' (1977: 59), they argued. Thus, with this situationology they seemed to distance themselves from the view that the international system was undergoing a gradual, but fairly linear, modernization, which was characterized by complex interdependence. Accordingly, there was no longer a basis for claiming that the international system consisted of two 'worlds' – the traditional world where one should use realism and the modernized world where one should use the world politics paradigm.

By presenting this more nuanced view of the possibility of combining or using various models depending on the situation they attempted to construct a middle position in between realism/modified realism and modernism by encouraging 'a differentiated approach that distinguishes among dimensions and areas of world politics' (1977: 29).

This modification implied de-emphasizing transsocietal relations and transgovernmental actors. Consequently, Keohane and Nye reintroduced the level-of-analysis distinction:

> In this book we try to understand world politics by developing explanations at the level of the international system. This does not mean that we regard the domestic politics or foreign policy as unimportant. Quite the contrary. Foreign policy and domestic policy, as we repeatedly emphasize, are becoming increasingly difficult to disentangle. Nevertheless, the complex relations between foreign and domestic policy make it essential to know how much one can explain purely on the basis of information about the international system.
>
> (1977: vi)

Essentially, they gave up on the task of incorporating domestic and foreign policy into the interdependence and transnationalist model which reflected the praxis of their predecessors. How nations behave remained an integrated part of their transnationalist model, which raised the classical problem of tautological reasoning, as Keohane and Nye acknowledged twelve years later in their review of the work. This is so since what they had sought to explain – how nations behave – also was one of the causal variables in their processual theory (1989: 262–3). Their remedy to the danger of tautology was to suggest specifying both the dependent variable in terms of a specific behaviour one seeks to explain, and the causal factors of the processes. Technological change, economic interdependence, issue density, and international regimes are some of the parameters at the processual level which could be separated out as causal factors. How these affect nations' behaviour is what needs to be traced. That is to say, Keohane and Nye suggest we should leave out domestic politics as an explanatory variable. How nations behave should be only the dependent variable: a theoretical reorientation which, in their 'second thoughts' twelve years later, they admitted left a gap in their work (1989: 251–60).

With this latter theoretical modification Keohane and Nye came to represent early proponents of the more moderate liberal establishment of the USA, which was inspired by the Vietnam imbroglio, the Watergate scandal, superpower *détente* and the breakdown of the fixed exchange rate regime but which showed due respect to the reality and symbolism of national security: a moderation which many liberal American writers came to adhere to as *détente* faded away.

THE SECOND CAMPAIGN: A FUNCTIONAL THEORY OF REGIMES

With the breakdown of *détente* and the questioned US hegemonic position in the world from the late 1970s onwards, Keohane turned towards discussions based on the premises of realism, and so did many others in the IR discipline. The goal for Keohane became to investigate 'the effects of changes in hegemony on co-operation among the advanced industrialised countries' (1984a: 41). Keohane's tactic, it seems, was to give in on key assumptions for the heuristic purposes of showing that with such premises one can argue favourably for persistence of regimes in the post-hegemonic world. Keohane's main theoretical concern became how to rescue the idea of international regimes being important phenomena in explaining behaviour in the international system even in a world dominated by rational, egoistic states. In other words, he wanted to build a research programme which sought to qualify how anarchy worked in the international system based on a heuristic acceptance of the realist dichotomy of hierarchy versus anarchy. In doing so, he elaborated upon earlier hypotheses of an international organization model for regime change but renamed the research programme. It was, in other words, not merely a creative adaptation of old ideas to a new political context, but also an attempt to elaborate on the old ideas by importing insights from economic theory into IR.

In reaction to the exaggerated role of international organizations in International Relations studies John Gerard Ruggie (1975: 569) had introduced the concept of regimes. He heralded a change of focus towards how collective response was to be analysed as broader, more informal patterns of interstate behaviour. Thereby he sought to conceptualize the space within which international organizations operated. Keohane and Nye favoured this change in focus, but co-opted only the concept of international regimes (1977) in their analytical framework leaving out the broader design within which these regimes were said to exist, namely the epistemic communities. Based on the work of Michel Foucault, Ruggie meant to incorporate a purely cognitive level according to which 'a dominant way of looking at social reality, a set of shared symbols and references, mutual expectations and a mutual predictability of intention' exist that fix the limits of the 'proper construction of social reality'. Therefore, international regimes originally were a second order concept to understand the transformational process of institutionalization, meaning

> sets of mutual expectations, generally agreed-to rules, regulations and plans, in accordance with which organizational energies and financial commitments are allocated [accepted by a group of states].[4]

In the following discussion the status of international regimes and the concept itself were contested. International regimes came to mean different things to different writers who therefore assigned different explanatory importance to them. Nevertheless, it has since become one of the most fashionable terms in American, Scandinavian and German studies of international relations. No consensus on what was meant by international regimes and what explanatory importance one should assign to them ever really emerged. To a large extent Keohane subscribed to the consensus-seeking definition put forward by Krasner in the early 1980s,[5] or at least to the idea that it was important to reach an agreement among the contributors to the issue of *International Organization* which Krasner edited in order to redirect the research on international relations, although this definition did put more emphasis on the explanatory power of the normative dimension in IR. But it is hard to say precisely since Keohane changed his perception of the status of international regimes in the international system over the years. He contended that in practical terms it was difficult to distinguish between principles, norms and rules, but it was precisely their linkage which gave international regimes legitimacy.

To Oran Young a regime was a social institution that emphasized recognized practice and converging expectations,[6] and to Puchala and Hopkins it meant any kind of discernible patterned behaviour.[7] To Keohane and Nye (1977: 5, 19) international regimes were governmental arrangements which were intended to regulate and control transnational and interstate relations. By the creation and acceptance of networks of rules, norms and procedures state behaviour was regularized and states' effects controlled. Yet, in his empirical analysis he loosened up on this state-centristic understanding of a regime. In the analysis of the political economy of oil he emphasized the crucial role of the firms in creating and maintaining a regime (1984a: 177). A regime need not be based on formal intergovernmental agreements (1984a: 185). Yet, in analysing the development of the oil regime, after its fundamental change in the early 1970s, Keohane changed his analytical perspective from emphasizing the economics of international political relations to emphasizing the politics of international economic relations.[8] The downside of Keohane's way of defining and identifying a regime was its disembeddedness in any larger system of ideas 'that would help to solve the definitional ambiguities... and that would offer guidance in formulating key questions and hypotheses regarding international regimes' (Young 1986: 106). According to Young, one such consequential misguidance is the one-dimensional emphasis on negotiated institutions instead of spontaneous institutions (1986: 111).

These negotiated international regimes are not epiphenomena, but neither should they be conceived of as so important as to constitute a new international order 'beyond the nation-state', as Keohane said (1984a: 53). In contrast to a Grotian view of international regimes in which once the rules to be followed have been chosen they come to dominate actors' behaviour, in Keohane's world of self-interested utility maximizers international regimes are more volatile although decisive for explaining behaviour. International regimes are, in this model, components of an international system which most fundamentally rests upon sovereignty and self-help. In other words, Keohane did subscribe to the most fundamental premise of the Waltzian realism, although he wanted to add to it a functional theory of international regimes. In this sense, it is fair to argue that he was a participant in the neo-realistic research programme for a while despite his criticism of Waltz (1986a: 1–26) and despite international regimes being a classical example of an old liberal preoccupation, namely how to explain international governance.

Like other American scholars Keohane (1980 and 1984a) was concerned with what would happen to the international order manifested in various regimes after the relative decline of the USA. In contrast to mainstream hegemonic stability theorists he questioned their prediction of an automatic decline of international regimes, and thereby of the order at large – *Pax Americana* – as a consequence of US hegemonic decline. Keohane argued that changes in power could not alone 'account for changes in patterns of co-operation' (1984a: 135). The provision of the public goods in this *Pax Americana* could be maintained through the co-operation of non-hegemonic states. This would most likely result not in changes to the regimes but only in changes within them. Moreover, Keohane argued for the possibility of new regimes emerging as a result of non-hegemonic co-operation among states with common or complementary interests (1984a: 50).

Underlying these hypotheses was a critique of the reductionistic view of regimes in the orthodox hegemonic stability theory whereby a regime was seen merely as an intervening variable between basic causal variables – structures of the international system and power-seeking actions – and the related outcome. Keohane and Nye had already pointed out in 1977 the limitations of this type of explanation and had commented on its lack of predictive power. It ignores cross-societal coalitions wanting to maintain certain regimes, is insensitive to differentiation among issue areas, and disregards transgovernmental and transsocietal multiple channels of contacts which pervert the utility of an overall hegemonic position, they argued.

The question Keohane sought to answer in the early 1980s was why the demand for regimes continued (Keohane 1983a). To focus only on how hegemons supplied regimes, Keohane argued, was too one-sided (1984a: 209). Why was the international order not destroyed, and why did international co-operation prevail in monetary and trade issues while US hegemony vanished (1984a: 183)? In order to explain this maintenance and possible creation of regimes during periods of relative decline of the USA Keohane built on rational choice theory. If states were assumed to be rational egoists co-operation among them could evolve as long as they had complementary or common interests. Rational choice directed him, in other words, to focus on the incentives facing actors. On this basis he constructed a functional explanation of regimes. Reasonable men might create or maintain international regimes in order to gain certain effects, he argued (1984a: 80). The causes which give rise to a regime should in general be explained in terms of its anticipated, or rationally expected, effects. Thus we have to demonstrate that a state which is maintaining, or creating, a specific regime does so to achieve the realized effects. But one should not forget that hegemonic stability theory provides an informative first cut for a general explanation, Keohane stressed (1984a: 184). The first cut helps one in analysing only some issue areas, not all. In the oil issue area, for example, one needs to make a second cut in order to explain emergence of a consumer regime in oil (1984a: 205). The second cut was then to be Keohane's functional theory of regimes which according to Keohane is one of his 'most important contributions to the study of world politics' (1989a: 28).

This functional theory of regimes was laid out in what was probably Keohane's most important piece of work: *After Hegemony. Co-operation and Discord in the World Political Economy* (1984a). In this book he actually constructs an original theory, which has inspired numerous students of IR to test it on a broad range of issue areas and whose insights are still part of his research programme today. World politics is, he argued, like the imperfect market, 'characterized by institutional deficiencies that inhibit mutually advantageous co-operation' (Keohane 1984a: 85). By inverting the coase theorem[9] and relying on institutional economics and industrial organization, Keohane established a regime's main functions to be:

1 creating a pattern within sets of issue areas which approximate legal liability whereby the states conform to agreed rules due to converging expectations and due to the enhancement of co-ordinated sanctions against defectors;
2 reducing uncertainty by making the provision of information more symmetrical, avoiding moral hazard, and increasing the likelihood of responsibility (which is to say, minimizing free-riding);
3 reducing transaction costs for legitimate bargains, whereby it becomes cheaper for states to co-operate since linkages and thereby side-payments

easily can be made, and increasing transaction costs for illegitimate bargains.

Due to these functions, Keohane argues that international co-operation is facilitated by regimes (1984a: 97) because negotiation on issues related to a regime's overall framework is easier to get started.

Still, a question remains: why were more regimes merely maintained, with changes only to their rules and procedures, than were created from scratch? Keohane's answer to this consists of two arguments. First, there are high sunk costs involved in existing regimes whereas it takes quite some effort to create a new regime. Thus, it is less costly to adapt an existing regime to a new environment than to destroy the old regime and construct a new one (1984a: 100). Second, the regimes themselves have over time changed states' perception of their self-interests via the earlier described functions. States' interests are not myopic. In other words, Keohane assigned regimes an autonomous status in explaining outcome in his modification of hegemonic stability theory (Keohane 1984a: 214–16). States' strategies cannot be chosen independently within issue areas where well-functioning international regimes exist because these regulate states' behaviour. Thus, the ontological assumptions in Keohane's research programme consist not simply of atomistically interacting states, but also of international regimes (for a counterargument see Chapter 9 on Onuf in this book).

The strength of such a functional explanation lies in its ability to explain a regime's persistence, even in the case of a change in the basic structural conditions which initially created the regime. Thus, one unavoidably gets the impression of a theory biased towards the status quo. But that is not the case. Not only can one explain why a regime often tends to expand in scope by arguing that the marginal costs of handling an extra issue will be lower until a certain point – marginal return to scale – but by using his theory one can also explain why changes within regimes may take place. However, in order to explain why a regime emerges in the first place, why it emerges in a specific issue area and not in others, why a regime carries out certain functions in one issue area and not in others, and why some regimes have highly developed organizational capacities while others do not, one will actually make an intentional explanation when following Keohane's theory!

If one seeks to answer these questions one should according to Keohane demonstrate, for example, that certain states have created a given regime with the intention of achieving the expected benefits or at least have recognized the prospect of their occurring. But a functional explanation requires, in contrast to Keohane's view, that the actors benefiting from the patterned behaviour – institution – are not to recognize this or to intend this to happen.[10] When one explains the emergence or maintenance of a regime in terms of the actors' intention instead, the explanation is consequently reduced to one specific to the situation, rather than being a recurrent behavioural pattern – as is required for a functional explanation. There is nothing wrong in making an intentional explanation. It is just not a theory which can be valid for regimes in general.

Keohane's importation of institutional economics and functional theory is an interesting example of how we import ideas from other studies into the study of international relations. Keohane has shown us some of the benefits IR might gain from importation, but his importation also points to the danger of doing so without a critical evaluation.[11]

Furthermore, it has been argued that such a 'functional' theory cannot explain, or rather present, a way to understand how a change of the international regimes would take place since that would presuppose an intersubjective evaluation of both the constitutive and also the regulatory aspects of international regimes (see Chapter 7 on Ruggie in this book). This is necessarily so, according to Kratochwil and Ruggie, since 'the ontology of regimes rests upon a strong element of intersubjectivity' which cannot be accounted for by the positivist epistemology (1986: 764).[12] Keohane doubts that any epistemology and methodology would be able to determine principled and shared understandings and thus the intersubjective aspect, which is how Kratochwil and Ruggie argue that we know if a regime exists or not. 'How are we to enter into the minds of human beings to determine this?... What standard of convergence would we require to determine that a regime existed?' Keohane asks (1993b: 27). Furthermore, he rejects such a 'thick' substantive definition of regimes since 'it would be circular reasoning to identify regimes on the basis of observed behaviour, and then to use them to "explain" observed behaviour' (Keohane 1993b: 27). Instead international regimes should be identified by their explicit rules and procedures which have continuing validity. It seems as if Keohane rejects the intersubjective ontology of regimes on the grounds of the epistemological impossibilities this would entail rather than that the ontology of international regimes is in fact intersubjective. That is to say, Keohane suggests the ontological status of international regimes are explicit rules and procedures because these can be 'an issue for descriptive inference, based on publicly available texts, rather than psychological insight or causal inference' (1993b: 28).

Based on a close examination of the politics of oil Keohane showed that we should not view regimes in a post-hegemonic world as quasi-governments with enforceable rules and decision-making procedures. Rather, we should be aware of the role of the general principles which help to legitimize and guide bargains via their symbolic character (1984a: 237–9). The consumers' energy regime established in the early 1970s,[13] which was treated by Keohane as an example of how regimes would behave in a post-hegemonic era since it was created within this, had been facilitating agreements by reducing 'the costs of co-ordination by providing information and by mobilizing workable coalitions around political feasible policies' (1984a: 237). Instead of implementing the more specific injunctions – rules – the energy regime made use of its principles 'to guide and to legitimate informal attempts at mutual adjustment of policies' (Keohane 1984a: 239). Regimes created in a post-hegemonic era are not to be seen as constituting a new form of order and thereby replacing the hegemonic one. Instead, they can 'sometimes tip the balance towards self-fulfilling expectations of success and away from panic and failure' (1984a: 240). But his analysis actually raises the question of how useful the international regime theory is when analysing this issue area. The unsuccessful attempt to make France join and establish rules in the International Energy Agency (IEA) in 1974–6 did not make the actors' expectations and behaviour converge, as their behaviour in 1979, when the Organization of Petroleum Exporting Countries 'OPEC' raised oil prices again, illustrated. States acted more upon the rule of self-help, than on commonly established rules in IEA.

More than ten years have passed since Keohane put forward his functional theory. According to Keohane this should provide us with a sufficiently long period of post-US hegemony to test if his theory holds or not (1984a: 219). Keohane suggested that had there been a 'continual spiral into trade and monetary wars and "beggar thy neighbour" policies', his theory would be falsified! Were one to analyse the trade area based on Keohane's functional regime theory, that is, one would analyse whether states' intentions in establishing the World Trade Organisation (WTO) were caused by the expected benefits of creating a better contractual environment for international trade. But such an evaluation should also include the search for other explanatory variables, such as domestic politics, state–firm relations, and the evolution of the production and trade structure.

This interaction between states, firms and domestic politics is not alien to Keohane. Not only did he actually emphasize it in his first campaign, but he also kept relying on aspects of it in his empirical analyses when explaining international co-operation and regime developments. When Keohane argues why an international oil regime was not created after the war as a part of *Pax Americana*, he explains it with the domestic politics of the USA (1984a: 141) and especially with the bargaining between the state and the oil companies (1984a: 150– 9). In fact, the transsocietal role of firms and the politics of transnational firms are stressed in this analysis (1982a: 159–77 and 1984a 217–40). This discrepancy between theoretical refocusing and empirical continuity has not been instrumental in further clarification of Keohane's conceptualization of the state–civil society relations and the domestic politics of interest formation into his theoretical framework; a missed opportunity Keohane and Nye regretted in their 1989 evaluation (1989a: 257).

The purpose of Keohane's work on theory during this period was to subsume realism into his framework by supplementing it with some novel hypotheses. Judged purely from his theoretical work it appears as if it turned out to be the other way around. His hypotheses were subsumed into the realist research programme. It would have taken further development of how to incorporate the state–civil society relations and transnationalism into his theoretical framework for it to be as he intended. To some extent one can argue that Keohane himself acknowledged this since he recognized that one should base the first cut on the hegemonic stability theory and the second cut on his functional theory of regimes. The irony of this result was recognized by Keohane in a review of his earlier research:

Ironically, in view of our earlier work on transnational relations, the result...has been to broaden neo-realism and provide it with new concepts rather than to articulate a coherent alternative theoretical framework for the study of world politics.

(Keohane & Nye 1989a: 251)

THE THIRD CAMPAIGN: INTERNATIONAL INSTITUTIONALISM

As the Cold War was thawing and the bipolar system breaking down, Keohane's empirical focus changed towards Europe. Theoretically, it shifted from how international regimes have an independent explanatory importance for international phenomena to how the old western institutions affect state strategies and thereby shape post-Cold War Europe. The actual research questions were not entirely new, but adapted to the new circumstances with some sharpened propositions and put together in a more ambitious way. The idea is currently to create an institutionalist research programme distinct from realism and liberalism, yet drawing on both, as indicated already in the early 1980s (i.e. 1984a: 7–10).

The institutionalism of international relations makes the distinctive claim that co-operation is possible under anarchy if mutual interests are present, if a long-term relationship among a small group of actors exists, and if reciprocity is practised (Keohane 1993a: 4). Although the realist description of anarchy is accepted, Keohane kept challenging the presupposed drastic implications for state behaviour. He predicted the consequences to be a less competitive impulse and not quite so stark a security dilemma facing states. This is so because the increased possibility for states to communicate and co-operate depends on how institutionalized is the area of the international system in which action takes place. By institutionalized behaviour in the international system Keohane (1989a: 1) means behaviour 'recognized by participants as reflecting established rules, norms, and conventions, and its meaning is interpreted in the light of these understandings'.

As an elaboration of the situationology presented in his first campaign Keohane recently (1989) presented a nuance to this idea. Which theory is appropriate to use is determined by the *degree of institutionalization* and the degree to which actors' interests are mutual within the part of reality under scrutiny. If variations in the degree of institutionalization exert substantial effects on state behaviour, and if actors have mutual interests – that is to say, act on the basis of absolute gains – then Keohane's institutionalism would be increasingly relevant. In situations which are nearly non-institutionalized although actors have mutual interests; or which are highly institutionalized although actors have antagonistic interests; or which are non-institutionalized although actors have antagonistic interests: Keohane's institutionalism is inapplicable. The first two situations are assumed to be rare and the latter the playing ground of realism. Nevertheless, when Keohane writes about a field which is only weakly institutionalized it most commonly is assumed to be a situation where actors have diverging interests, whereas in a highly institutionalized situation actors often are assumed to have common or complementary interests although the overall idea is more complex.

The first of two variables determining the relevance of this institutionalism – the degree of institutionalization within an issue area – should be judged on three dimensions, Keohane suggested (1989a: 4–5); an idea based on the insights of Samuel Huntington from 1968. These three dimensions are: to what degree do actors have common expectations (commonality); to what extent are these explicitly specified in rules (specificity); and to what extent can the institution alter its own rules (autonomy). Based on these three variables, and an analysis of how durable this institutionalization is over time, one can analyse the strength of an institution (Keohane 1989a: 2).

Likewise, one has to judge the degree to which actors have mutual interest. That is the extent to which action is based on absolute gains thinking. Action is not based either on relative or absolute gains thinking, Keohane stressed.[14] Thus, this dichotomy should not be used as a dogmatic premise for analysis. The extent to which relative or absolute gains motivate actors is conditioned by the situation (1984a: 123, n. 9 and 1993a: 9–19); that is:

> Relative gains may be important motivating forces for states and firms, but only when gains in one period alter power relations in another, when there is some likelihood that subsequent advantages in power may be used against a partner, and when small numbers of actors are involved
>
> (1993a: 10)

Depending on the degree of institutionalization, on the number of actors interacting, and on each state's evaluation of other states' capabilities and intentions, a state will be motivated by a degree of absolute or relative gains.

Naturally the very concept of an institution is at the centre of Keohane's institutionalistic theory. As he recognized, it is as widely disputed as that of a regime. In fact when one studies Keohane's proposed definitions of an institution it is difficult not to notice the similarities to that of a regime:

> I define institutions as 'persistent and connected sets of rules (formal or informal) that prescribe behavioral roles, constrain activity, and shape expectations.'
>
> (1989a: 3)[15]

In fact, one can argue that this definition of an institution is a somewhat simplified and less demanding edition of that of a regime. In contrast to Krasner's consensus definition (1983) it does not distinguish between principles, norms and rules, for which reason the earlier distinction between changes of and within a regime may be lost. At the same time expectations are no longer assumed to 'converge', but are merely 'shaped'. Nevertheless, empirical work still has to show us how the distinction makes a difference for actual analysis.

Keohane suggests (1989a: 3–4) that one should distinguish between three forms of international institutions. First, they may be *formal intergovernmental or cross-national non-governmental organizations* which are purposive organizations with a formal bureaucratic structure typically based on explicit agreements. Second, *international regimes* are based on explicit rules pertaining to a specific set of issues agreed upon by states. This reconceptualization of international regimes is quite interesting because Keohane takes the theoretical consequences of earlier assumptions made in the empirical research on international regimes, namely that they have to be based on explicit rules agreed upon by governments. The informal aspect as well as the non-governmental character, which according to his earlier definitions and Krasner's common-sense definition (1983) were part of what should be understood as a regime, has in other words been abandoned in favour of a much narrower, and more traditional, IR conceptualization. This more restricted concept of a regime covers what Oran Young earlier described as one of three types of institutional order, namely a negotiated order (Young 1983: 99) which was based on what Rawls called a 'summary view of rules'.

Third, he suggests *conventions* (i.e. reciprocity), the most informal type of international institutions, which are temporally and logically prior to regimes and formal international organizations. They are typically based on implicit rules and understandings that shape the expectations of their actors. This third type of institution is similar to the second type of institutional order introduced by Young (1983), which he termed spontaneous order. Young developed this category on the basis of Hayek to whom it was 'the product of the action of many men but...not the result of human design' (Young 1983: 98); a notion which is somewhat similar to what Rawls labelled 'the practice conception' of rules. In accordance with Keohane's use of the insights from his work on creating a functional theory of regimes, he separated out this type of institution as not being part of his conceptualization of a regime. Keohane's study of reciprocity (1986c) is one such example of a convention. Reflectivists have argued that studying conventions of international relations, or 'fundamental institutions', is not to be the ball game of the rationalistic edition of new institutionalism (Wendt and Duvall 1989: 53–4). But Keohane's recent article (1994) on sovereignty refutes this argument. Basing his argument on a rationationalistic approach, he shows how the meaning of sovereignty has changed from the seventeenth century to the present situation of high interdependence. At first, sovereignty was a doctrine to justify the sovereign rule of a state, only later, as the enlightenment project began to dominate society and the idea of internal sovereignty became pluralized and constitutionalized, did it evolve through the eighteenth and nineteenth centuries as a doctrine that legitimized 'legal authority of the nation to give and enforce the law within a certain territory' (Morgenthau in Keohane 1994: 275). Sovereignty as an exchange of legal right of self-determination was a redefinition of states' conceptualization of self-interests to favour the idea of non-intervention and thereby restrain actual intervention. As 'high interdependence' evolved in the second half of the twentieth century, sovereignty became 'less a territorially-defined barrier than a bargaining resource for a politics characterized by complex transnational networks' (1994: 283). States do not have a *de facto* grip or supremacy within a given territory, only *de jure*. This can 'either be exercised to the detriment of other states' interests, or be bargained away in return for influence over others' policies and therefore greater gains from exchange' (1994: 282). To Keohane, this change in the meaning of sovereignty was a functional necessity due to the conditions of high interdependence under which fundamental contracting problems arise which can be solved only if states are willing to bargain them away when establishing firm commitments in international institutions. Such a conceptualization of sovereignty could be seen as a constructive attempt to go beyond the transnationalists' attempt to replace the concept of sovereignty with that of autonomy as referred to in the analysis of Keohane's first campaign.

By characterizing sovereign statehood as a convention type of institution, Keohane manages to launch a severe attack on realism in that he successfully argues that the realist notion of the nature of the international society is inappropriate. As an institution, sovereignty 'significantly' modifies 'the Hobbesian notion of anarchy' (1994: 268). Anarchy 'was institutionalized by general acceptance of the norm of sovereignty' (1994: 276). Moreover, Keohane challenges Hobbes's solution to his dilemma[16] – a war of all sovereigns against all – by arguing that institutions have helped in shaping states' self-interest both domestically and internationally (1994: 271). That is to say, institutions have changed the constraints and incentives of states.

Interestingly, the development of Keohane's conceptual work is basically to substitute for what many scholars earlier understood by the concept of a regime, the concept of institution. As he indirectly shows, Young, for example, explicitly understood a regime as being a social institution which can be categorized in three types of orders covering what Keohane lately has defined as an institution. Also the compromise conceptualization of a regime by Krasner (1983) could cover all Keohane's types of institutions. In fact one can almost see in this a reintroduction of Ruggie's original conceptualization of a regime (1975) as being a phenomenon in between international organizations and epistemic communities. Although his Foucault-inspired concept of epistemic communities has quite a different meaning from that of a convention.

Keohane's conceptual exercise does not just represent a new marketing strategy, but reflects an intellectual honesty in that he thereby adjusts his theory to the way he actually has been analysing regimes, namely in this more narrow sense as based on deliberate governmental action. In accordance with his continued reliance on the insights of the functional theory of regimes – assuming that men design a regime in order to obtain certain effects – he excludes Young's spontaneous orders which presuppose unintended consequences of action.[17] With this recent introduction of international institutions Keohane has helped clarify some of the conceptual mess which has led to some confusion when reading his empirical analyses.

Despite warning students not to underestimate 'the pressure from domestic interests, and those generated by the competitiveness of the state system' (1989a: 6) Keohane continued his own main hypothesis: that institutionalization in its various degrees exerts impact on governments' behaviour in that it helps in defining the meaning and importance of state action. Based on his insight outlined in the functional theory of regimes, institutions are hypothesized to influence state action via:

- the flow of information and opportunities to negotiate;
- the ability of governments to monitor others' compliance and to implement their own commitments – hence their ability to make credible commitments in the first place; and
- prevailing expectations about the solidity of international agreements.

Lately, Keohane and Hoffmann have elaborated on this point by speaking of different roles whereby international institutions help to shape the preferences, or even the identities, of states (1993: 395–404). 'That is, institutions differentiate among actors according to the roles that they are expected to perform, and institutions can be identified by asking whether patterns of behaviour are indeed differentiated by role' (Keohane 1988: 165–6). This notion of roles in relation to institutions seems to be inspired by March and Olson (1984) and thus the new institutionalists' debate within political science and sociology in general.

Together with Hoffmann and Nye, Keohane gathered a group of young scholars to test this institutionalist research programme by analysing how international institutions affected state strategies in the post-Cold War period in Europe. The following are the roles Keohane and Hoffmann suggested institutions play:

1 Institutions are 'potential sources of leverage for ambitious governments, thus we should expect, in a period of rapid change, to see them used as arenas for the *exercise of influence*' (1993: 395).
2 If there is a conflict of interests, but a prospect of complementarity, among states when they pursue influence within international institutions, these may in turn *constrain bargaining strategies* whereby agreement is facilitated (1993: 397).
3 International institutions can 'serve as *instruments to balance against or replace other institutions*' (1993: 398) as the discussion in Europe about how to organize security has proved lately.
4 International institutions may stimulate states politically to '*signal governments' intentions*, providing others with information and making policies more predictable' (1993: 399).

Whereas the first four roles could be fitted into either the realist or the institutionalist theoretical framework and do not represent new theoretical insight, the fifth and sixth roles can be part of the institutionalist one only. The roles continue:

5 International institutions can also be said to play the role of helping to *'specify obligations* that guide state action, thereby serving as "templates" for policy choice' (1993: 400) which clearly is illustrated in the way various eastern European states adapted their policies to the rules of the EC and the Organization for Economic Co-operation and Development (OECD) after 1989 in anticipation of or hope for co-optation in the EC or more broadly the western world.

6 International institutions can *affect not only states' interests, but also their fundamental preferences*, i.e. via socialization of weak or young states, that is 'a process of learning in which norms and ideals are transmitted from one party to another' (J. Ikenberry and C. Kuphan) 'and accompanied by material inducement' (1993: 401). This last role represents a novel idea of how international institutions can affect state strategies, whereas the other hypotheses of institutional roles are borrowed from earlier work on the functional importance of regimes. This underlines the strong continuity from the second to the third campaign.[18] In another recent application of the institutional theory to the international politics of the environment Keohane together with P. Haas and M. Levy (1993b: 405–7) suggests another idea of what roles international institutions might play, namely the role of *increasing national capacity* to protect the quality of the global environment. Institutions can 'foster the transfer of informations, skills, and expertise necessary for effective domestic programs' and deliver outright aid which naturally is most relevant when speaking of less developed countries.

Closely connected to these differences in the roles or functions which international institutions perform are differences in institutional membership, that is to say, the form of institution. Keohane (1993b: 39–41) distinguishes between three such forms:

1 restricted institutions, such as the North Atlantic Treaty Organization (NATO) and the EU, which seek either to achieve relative gains or to build community bonds;
2 conditionally open institutions, such as WTO, which are designed to foster collaboration, that is, to cope with free-riding when acting collectively;
3 open institutions, such as the UN, which develop out of the need for pure co-ordination and most likely are limited to symbolic issues.

Despite Keohane's continued reliance on the insights from his second campaign – the contractual arguments – he does recognize the empirically based criticisms made by Moravcsik, for example, who argued (1989) that the effects of regimes as Keohane pointed out were insignificant, or by Smith (1987) and P. M. Haas (1990) who held that changes in states' conception of their preferences, as affected by transnational networks, were more important than assumed by Keohane (1993b: 37). Yet, this recognition of the limitations of his hypotheses made Keohane stress again that his institutionalism is not a theoretical panacea but a novel supplement to other modes of analysis. There is, in other words, a recognition of a sensible division of labour, in which Moravcsik, a former student of Keohane, covers the domestic politics side of explaining international governance.

With the elaboration of the fifth and sixth roles plus the inclusion of conventions as part of his theory of international institutions Keohane has to broaden his research programme to handle both the way in which international institutions organize the practices of state actors, and also how they structure those practices.[19] That is to say, based on Keohane's theory one is able to analyse not only how states' strategies are constrained by international institutions, but also how they define, or make possible, state strategies as well as constitute international practices. Although this distinction, which has also been seen in terms of 'regulative' versus 'constitutive' rules (see Chapter 9 on Onuf in this book for an elaboration), is far from clear-cut, and both often are aspects of the same institutionalized domain, it is still a useful line to draw.

Still being a young research programme, this theory of international institutions has already been applied to an amazing number of issue areas, while some of the hypotheses and findings are actually quite interesting. In contrast to a realist prediction, Keohane expected, on the basis of the long-standing hypothesis of institutional inertia, that NATO would adapt to the new environment or that international groups of civil servants and states would try to remake their role to fit the new circumstances. In contrast to realist writers, an institutionalist expects the EC to grow not weaker but stronger since it has provided its members with substantial gains and extensive transnational ties and coalitions which have been built up over a long period (1993a: 27). Due to the densely institutionalized European environment Keohane expected more co-operation to take place in Europe in the immediate post-Cold War period, not the outbreak of instability which some realists argued would occur in a multipolar environment. By and large, this expectation must be said to have been fulfilled despite the conflict in what used to be Yugoslavia.

In the same way Keohane and Nye explained why the internal tensions over the post-Cold War strategy in the USA during the Reagan and Bush administrations were tempered, the reason being the embeddedness of the US strategy in multilateral security and economic ties of the various post-war institutions (Keohane and Nye 1993: 106). The USA, in fact, did not try to make drastic reforms of the old cold war institutions. As Nye and Keohane put it: 'The lag in the adjustment of American policy to the new structure was caused in part by domestic politics, in part by uncertainty about Soviet intentions, and in part by the commitment to Roosevelt's global institutional design' (Keohane and Nye 1993: 108). Except for quite a strong lobby against 'any breakdown in EC–US trade and investment relations' (1993: 122) the US administration actually had a relatively free hand in remaking its economic strategy towards Europe in the post-Cold War period (Keohane and Nye 1993: 116).

Looking back on Keohane's intellectual career, so far, it is ironic that his theoretical work increasingly has been inspired by new economic theories, while the part played by economic actors in his theoretical writings has become more and more inferior. His theory of institutions is state-centred, yet still based on rationalistic institutional economics. Not all his empirical work has assigned a very modest explanatory importance to firms, transnational corporations and strategic alliances,[20] but his theorizing increasingly has done so. Furthermore, Keohane's firm belief in governmental actions furthering institutionalization, and thereby certainty in what we can expect, is quite noteworthy. He suggests that the development of a regime – based on governmental bargaining – will 'typically expand and clarify the rules governing the issues concerned' (1989a: 5). Why would this necessarily be so? Could it not be that governmental action explicating the rules in a certain issue area actually expresses the wish of how all societal actors – TNEs, NGOs, etc. – should behave? Intergovernmental institutions might merely create dreams which may or may not come true. It seems that Keohane underestimates the cynical interpretation of why international institutions are set up. The establishment of an international institution might merely be a way to sustain the myth that some are really doing something in this field; it need not necessarily reflect an increasing *de facto* institutionalization. Sometimes such myths hide the real intentions or conflicts: they show off our good intentions – while the rules that matter are perhaps only implicit. Such important implicit rules are often hidden in the practical actions of the non-governmental actors involved in a certain set of issues constituting an institution. Is not the 'true' degree of institutionalization then to be found exactly in the interplay of the formal rules, organizations, etc., and the informal ones – the conventions – which one can understand only by studying the practical actions of all the actors involved?

Thus, when Keohane deals with political economy, it becomes a study of the politics of economic relations. That is to say, the perspective remains within the domain of political science instead of being more interdisciplinary as his research agenda originally started out to be.

Keohane concludes his self-critical review of his intellectual history by saying:

> that the major step forward in understanding international co-operation will have to incorporate domestic politics fully into the analysis – not on a merely ad hoc basis, but systematically.
>
> (1989a: 30)

Despite this, a formal inclusion of domestic politics into his theoretical framework has not been carried out. Recently, he has repeated this need for an analysis of domestic politics in order to account for the formulation of interest and state strategies without which 'no theory of international relations can be fully adequate' (1993a: 33): 'We will have to examine more closely how domestic politics are linked to international institutions' (1993a: 34). By opening up for an analysis of how international institutions structure state strategies Keohane has taken the first step towards 'problematizing the co-operation problem', but the second step of creating an explicit theory of the state – how their preferences are constituted, how they vary culturally and how individual and social reflection leads to changes in preferences – is still missing, as recognized by Keohane (1989a: 170–2). This desire for a two-level explanation is a widespread one, but highly complicated. However, as seen earlier, Keohane did to some extent in his empirical analysis of the creation of the single European market attempt to incorporate domestic politics as a determinant explaining how the political strategy of the main European governments converged (Keohane and Hoffmann 1991: 23). This process of convergence of neo-liberal preferences was seen as decisive for explaining the timing of the 'Europe 1992's creation.

CONCLUDING REMARKS: KEOHANE AND THE -ISMS OF INTERNATIONAL RELATIONS

As one can see from the previous chapters Keohane cannot easily be boxed in one of the three classical schools of thought in International Relations. He started out with a group of writers trying to define an independent research programme in between modernism and realism, then he moved on with the mainstream discipline back to the hard core premises of traditionalism although putting forward a functional regime theory, and lately he has expanded this auxiliary hypothesis of regimes into an independent research programme which named international institutionalism in between liberalism and neo-realism. In itself this broad characterization of the tendencies in Keohane's authorship is of limited value. Instead, one will find the interesting subtleties and a significant degree of continuous development through the study of the actual research. It is interesting to try to specify which views Keohane shares with liberals and traditionalists, and which he does not; he has defined himself in relation to these two main research programmes of International Relations. Keohane's particular contribution to the study of International Relations has been analysed above. Thus, it would be appropriate here to summarize the similarities to each.

First of all, he shares the liberal view of history as being progressive instead of cyclical: one of the basic premises of enlightenment projects. In contrast to some liberals, he argues that progress does not take place automatically. Instead, progress is a political possibility to struggle for. Thus, in contrast to the republican or commercial liberal point of view he does not believe that trade automatically would lead to peace based on a harmony of interests. Republics do not necessarily act peacefully to non-republics, he argues (1989a: 11); a point which is accepted by the Kantian edition of perpetual peace. In fact, the increased interdependence among western societies does not necessarily lead to co-operation among them, although it is imperative that they co-operate to solve their mutual problems. But even if they do co-operate with this as their aim, their co-operation should not be mistaken for a view of the world that is developing into a more harmonious one. Keohane has clearly distinguished himself from the interwar idealist doctrine of 'harmony of interests' among states by stressing the international system's non-harmonious nature. The international society is primarily dominated by interstate rivalry, and only secondly does co-operation exist to temper this. Yet, the international society is not anarchical in a Waltzian sense since international institutions actually do constrain and enable action.

Second, this view of history rests on a view of human action which differs from the one typically found in traditionalist writings. Keohane assigns greater importance to each human being's possibility of affecting the course of history, implicitly refuting the cyclical and predetermined view of history. Each person, and each writer in particular, can affect the international development by enlightening the civic and, in particular, the business leaders and the statesmen. By being able to explain international institutionalization and how the complex processes of interdependence and transnationalism affect efficiency and wealth creation, Keohane sought to enlighten the world by showing how one can provide incentives for peaceful coexistence rather than aggressive expansion. That is, to advise policy actors how to find different ways of establishing and strengthening international co-operation during the current period of 'high interdependence' in which independent national action is an unviable path. By the first research programme of interdependence and transnationalism Keohane, among others, successfully tried to make the public realize they had a political problem affecting societal change because all states were penetrated economically and culturally. With the second research programme – state-centred regimes – he demonstrated to policy-makers which functions it was feasible to strive for in changing or creating international regimes during a period of *post Pax Americana* in order to promote international co-operation. Despite these classical liberal concerns in his policy prescriptions, Keohane warns us against the liberal doctrine. In the essay on liberal IR theory he emphasizes that liberal theory must be seen only as a partial theory. 'It is incomplete as an explanation, it can become normatively myopic, and it can backfire as a policy prescription' (1990b: 192). Increasingly, it seems that he has accepted one piece of criticism: Strange (1983) – echoing Carr (1981) – argues that mercantile liberal IR theory risks legitimizing the emergence and persistence of the strong state's normative claims. Rather it tends to forget the disadvantaged groups' position whereby it implicitly downplays the liberal value of equality. Thus, Keohane disagrees with the commercial liberal account of the necessary good in an unregulated market because it is 'biased against people disadvantaged by lack of marketable skill, mobility, or sophistication. Some regulation is needed not merely to keep markets functioning efficiently but also to counteract the inequities that they generate' (1989a: 18, n. 13).

Third, as a consequence of his view of international relations at large Keohane over time has come to share the realist assumption of the nation-state being the most powerful actor in international affairs. He has even tended to accept the state's being treated as a coherent actor, acting as a rational egoist, as seen in his work on the functional theory of regimes.

Nevertheless, he has not completely abandoned the liberal focus on a plurality of actors within the states whose action has to be analysed in order to make a complete analysis of international relations phenomena. This is most clearly illustrated in his articles on the link between US foreign economic policy and international political economy. Although these are empirical pieces of research rather than theoretical ones they witness less of a break with the traditional liberal choice of unit of analysis than is sometimes pointed out.

Nevertheless, quite a few students argue that Keohane is in fact a liberal international theorist. Keohane has now and then characterized himself as a *sophisticated liberal* (1990b) and a *liberal institutionalist* (1989a). According to Keohane one ought to distinguish between four strands of liberal IR theory: republican, commercial, regulatory and sophisticated liberalism (Keohane 1990b: 176–85). The latter, which to him then constituted an interpretative framework, was a combination of commercial and regulatory liberalism. 'Such a sophisticated liberalism emphasizes the construction of institutions that facilitate both economic exchange and broader international co-operation' (1990b: 167). Yet, the inequalities created by the international political economy cause morally questionable violations of the principle of justice. To Keohane this represents unresolved consequences of his sophisticated liberalism. It is, nevertheless, the best choice for peace and prosperity, he argued in 1990. Accordingly, one should not stress the moral evaluation of world politics based on the doctrine of liberty and rights, but 'liberalism as an approach to the analysis of social reality' (1990b: 174), which he describes as follows:

> (1) [it] begins with individuals as the relevant actors, (2) seeks to understand how aggregations of individuals make collective decisions and how organizations composed of individuals interact, and (3) embeds this analysis in a worldview that emphasizes individual rights and that adopts an ameliorative view of progress in human affairs.
>
> (1990b: 174)

Today, it seems as if he wants to distance himself altogether from the liberal label, and rather to be characterized as an institutionalist. This neo-liberal institutionalism (1989a), or institutionalism (1993a), should be conceived as a third position distinct from both liberalism and neo-realism, yet drawing on both. But as showed previously this does not represent a break with earlier research, it is merely the continuous growth and adaptation of a research programme. Whether it actually performs as an independent research programme, only the future will show. Perhaps the need for Keohane to distance himself from liberal international relations has to do with the difficulties of specifying what liberal international relations theory is about. What is actually so liberal about liberal international relations theory?

Anyway, according to Keohane institutionalism distances itself from neo-realism by not having as narrow and confining a concept of structure as neo-realism without clarifying this further. It could be argued that international institutions should be seen as a part of his concept of structure in that they, to Keohane, are important factors explaining change together with the relative distribution of state capabilities. Furthermore, institutionalism is a geographically limited theory to the western, industrialized countries governed on the basis of democracy, not a proclaimed global theory. Keohane considers neo-realism as underspecified and unable to explain the use of power among these countries because these are mediated through rules, norms, etc., not only via the threat of use of force.

With the approximation of the liberal research programme to the realist as seen reflected in Keohane's second campaign the greatest contrast in perspectives on international relations shifted to that between rationalists and reflectivists (Wæver 1994: 13–15). This also came to mark Keohane's third campaign in that he became receptive to a more critical attitude toward the rationalistic perspective and stated that 'we may hope for a synthesis' between the two approaches leaving aside 'dogmatic assertions of epistemological or ontological superiority' (1989a: 174). Since Keohane's methodology to a large extent can be said to be based on the Lakatosian thinking (1983 in 1989a: 37–8) there is nothing abnormal when more research programmes exist simultaneously. Theoretical dialogues and competition take place constantly and are expected eventually to lead to progress. Belonging to a research programme does not mean that one speaks a different language, according to Lakatos. On the contrary no research programme is so coherent that outsiders' concepts cannot be integrated into another programme since knowledge is fundamentally assumed to be commensurable. Thus different programmes might even borrow concepts and issues from each other. In essence a research programme strives to outdo others, but in many cases research programmes are preoccupied with explaining different aspects of the same phenomenon or even different phenomena. In those cases where research programmes are aiming at establishing explanations of different aspects of the same phenomenon, their work might be supplementary. This can be based on either research programmes with different hard cores, as in Keohane's first and third campaigns, or with a set of different auxiliary hypotheses, as in Keohane's second campaign.

In accordance with the Lakatosian thinking, Keohane's method of searching for the truth, his criterion of progress, is that an old theory is not abandoned until a new, more comprehensive theory emerges to replace the old no matter how many anomalies one might be able to point out. Yet, most theory develops gradually. Rarely does the development of theory have to do with a change of the research programme, it merely represents a change *within* a research programme. Auxiliary hypotheses are constantly under pressure of competitors who try to demonstrate that their hypotheses have stronger explanatory power. Just as Keohane sought to do with the functional theory of regimes. Sometimes the transferral of concepts or ideas from one research programme to another has ontological ramifications, which could then lead to a change in the hard core of the research programme. But accepting such a change of the very research programme itself requires that the ontological assumptions point towards new 'facts' and solve some of the old mysteries.

Keohane's acknowledgement of the need for a theory of the state, preference formation, etc., plus that we need more information about the premises of the situation-strategic choice (1989a), would if carried out be a change of the ontological assumption and thus of the hard core of his research programme, but in accordance with his supplementarist assumption. Furthermore, it would then be equivalent to an attempt to make a synthesis between the rationalistic and the reflectivistic research programmes.[21]

Keohane accepts that the structure of a situation – prior institutional context – matters much more than first assumed. Even knowing this rational choice 'seems to leave open the issue of what kinds of institutions will develop, to whose benefit, and how effective they will be' (1989a:390). It leaves us with many unanswered questions. Keohane's study of the convention type of institutions, i.e. sovereignty, and elaboration of the roles international institutions play might be seen as an attempt to fulfil this promise. Like Krasner (1988) Keohane also suggested the need for combining rational choice theory with a path-dependent perspective as seen from evolutionary economics, i.e. North 1981 and 1990, according to which we must explain development as influenced by exogenous shocks and particular leaders. Outcome is unpredictable, but certain possibilities are gradually excluded. Randomly accumulated variations may under certain circumstances have surprising developmental effects. Positive externalities or sunk costs, he pointed out, could explain path-dependency. Indirectly, one can argue that this concern with path-dependency was reflected in Keohane's analysis of sovereignty (1994), a research path Krasner had pointed out earlier when dealing with the same issue (1988).

EPILOGUE: HOW TO DO BUSINESS IN IR

What does Keohane's success tell us in terms of how to pursue academic careers? Three thoughts come to mind. First, it tells us to be topical. Be sensitive especially to the politicians' agenda. When Keohane entered both the first and the second campaigns the underlying topic he dealt with – interdependence and the decline of American hegemony – was on the political agenda. When one reads his advice to the reflectivists – that they are too marginal, are invisible – one can get the impression of a writer who is very much aware of how pragmatic one needs to be in order to be heard by mainstream scholars of International Relations. But with the rationalistic turn in the second campaign in the 1980s Keohane had become an agenda-setter for which reason his research orientation must be considered as more than merely adaptation to actual development in the world.

But abiding by the rule – accommodate to succeed – also has some costs. One of these is the continuously unsolved puzzle of how domestic politics can explain international institutionalization as well as the other way round. Keohane has been pointing to this problem of inside-out relations for many years – basically, since he started writing on transnationalism. He has returned to it again and again, but not yet come up with a solution that satisfies him. Perhaps one could say that it is the most crucial gap of his authorship. A gap students of his recently have tried to fill.[22]

Second, his success also tells us to be sensitive to other disciplines. Keohane has shown that it pays to be informed of fields other than IR at the same time. If you master staying on top of, say, institutional economics, as he obviously has done (1984a), you can import some of these concepts and issues into the study of international relations and thereby help shape the research agenda and add to the explanation of the international phenomena. In fact, this ability of Keohane's is important for explaining how he has become a contemporary master of the field. Being able to use these skills probably has to do with the early stage of development of our field of study. The danger of importing other social or natural science theories into the study of international relations or international political economy lies in the difficulty of seeing the fallacies of those theories. If one does not look at them from a meta-theoretical perspective, one risks not being able actually to point out the problematic parts of the theory one wants to import. Keohane's import of a functional explanation to create a theory of regimes might serve as an example of this danger in that it led him to remake an intentional explanation.

Third, one needs to find a research corner where it is possible to create a theoretical project applicable to the empirical desire of many researchers. Only by making other researchers interested in trying to test-drive one's theoretical work is it possible to master the baronial game in the study of international relations. In order to protect one's research corner and succeed in the marketing game of international relations one needs to be quite inventive in labelling the research programme. Furthermore, reciprocal communication with students has been crucial for this contemporary classic's work and way of working.

NOTES

I am grateful to the co-authors of this volume and to Barry Buzan, Jaap de Wilde and Sonia Lucarelli for their comments and criticisms.

1 The word interdependence, as Keohane points out, was popular in the US administrations in the 1960s. But it was assigned very different meanings.
2 A point made earlier by A. Wolfers in 1959, but not recognized theoretically before the late 1960s.
3 For an elaboration of this distinction see Mouritzen 1979 and Chapter 3 of this book.
4 Ruggie (1975: 569–73) argued that international regimes could be distinguished 'by the purposes they serve, the instrumentalities they use and the functions those instrumentalities actually perform'. For an elaboration of this, see Chapter 7 of this book.
5 'Regimes can be defined as sets of implicit or explicit principles, norms, rules, and decision-making procedures around which actors' expectations converge in a given area of international relations. Principles are beliefs of fact, causation, and rectitude. Norms are standards of behavior defined in terms of rights and obligations. Rules are specific prescriptions or proscriptions for action. Decision-making procedures are prevailing practices for making and implementing collective choice' (Krasner 1983: 2).

6 Young 1983: 93: 'Regimes are social institutions governing the actions of those interested in specificable activities (or accepted sets of activities). Like all social institutions, they are recognized patterns of behavior or practice around which expectations converge.' But they can be informal and lacking in organizational components as well as the opposite. See also 1980: 331–5.

7 Puchala and Hopkins 1983: 62–3: 'Regimes constrain and regularise the behavior of participants, affect which issues among protagonists move on and off agendas, determine which activities are legitimised or condemned, and influence whether, when, and how conflicts are resolved.' The authors therefore claim that an international regime exists 'in every substantive issue-area in international relations where there is discernibly patterned behavior'.

8 For an elaboration of the difference between these two ways of studying international political economy see Strange (1988: 12).

9 According to the coase theorem the presence of externalities alone does not necessarily prevent effective co-ordination among independent actors. Under certain conditions – legal framework, perfect information and zero transaction costs –bargaining among these actors could lead to solutions that are Pareto-optimal regardless of the rules of legal liability (Keohane 1984a: 85–7).

10 Elster (1983: 57) puts forward a helpful logical schematic presentation of the requirements for such a functional explanation. An institution or a behavioural pattern X is explained by its function Y for group Z if and only if:

   1 Y is an effect of X;
   2 Y is beneficial for Z;
   3 Y is unintended by the actors producing X;
   4 Y – or at least the causal relation between X and Y – is unrecognized by the actors in Z;
   5 Y maintains X by a causal feedback loop passing through Z.

Keohane's construction of the functional theory does not fulfil either the third or the fourth requirement for an explanation to be functional.

11 For another illustration of this point see Hollis and Smith 1991.

12 It is interesting to note that despite this critique, Kratochwil and Ruggie nevertheless suggested that Keohane's functional theory, complemented by their interpretive approach, could then 'push the heuristic fruitfulness of the regime research program "forward" yet another step, linking it back to the study of international organizations' (1986: 774).

13 According to Keohane the consumers' energy regime is institutionalized by the establishment of the International Energy Agency (IEA).

14 The debate of relative versus absolute gains was to a large extent triggered by Keohane's writing during the second campaign, but defined explicitly by Grieco in 1990.

15 Keohane recognizes that an institution may refer to a 'general pattern or categorization of activity or to a particular human-constructed arrangement, formally or informally organized', but he settles for a more narrowly defined one as mentioned.

16 Keohane summarizes the Hobbesian dilemma as follows: '1) *Since people are rational calculators, self-interested, seeking gain and glory, and fearful of one another, there is no security in anarchy.* Concentrated power is necessary to create order; otherwise, "the life of man [is] solitary, poor, nasty, brutish and short." 2) *But precisely since people are self-interested and power-loving, unlimited power for the ruler implies a predatory, oppressive state.*' The dilemma is then 'how can political order be created, given the nature of human beings?' (Keohane 1994: 269–71). Leviathan must, in the words of Martin Wight, 'prove a partial exception to the rule that men are bad and should be regarded with distrust'.

17 If Keohane had fulfilled the requirements of a functional explanation, as outlined earlier, then unintended action, as thus spontaneous orders, would have been an essential part of the functional theory of regimes.

18 In order to avoid connotations of sociological functionalism, Keohane has begun to use the language of 'contractualism' instead of 'functionalism'. But because this move is purely semantic, it does not have any consequences for the critique of his way of using functional explanations.

19 For an elaboration of this distinction, as well as the argument to the contrary, see Wendt and Duvall 1989: 54 and Chapter 9 of this book.

20 Notice his studies of oil and energy, namely the interactions between firms and states, and how they constitute the development and change of international institutions (1982/3).

21 Sonia Lucarelli reaches the same conclusion although from a different line of arguments.

22 See the work of Andrew Moravcsik and Beth Simmons.

REFERENCES

Works by Robert O. Keohane

Keohane, R. O. (1966) 'Political Influence in the General Assembly', *International Conciliation* 557.

—— (1967) 'The Study of Political Influence in the General Assembly', *International Organization* 21(2) (Spring): 221–37.

—— (1969a) 'Institutionalization in the United Nations General Assembly', *International Organization* 23(4) (Fall): 859–96.

—— (1969b) 'Lilliputians' Dilemmas: Small States in International Politics', *International Organization* 23(2) (Spring): 291–310.

—— (1969c) 'Who Cares about the General Assembly', *International Organization* 23(2): 141–9.

—— (1971a) 'The Big Influence of Small Allies', *Foreign Policy* 1(2) (Spring): 161–82.

—— (1971b) 'Coalition Theory and the Security Council: Some Notions about Institutional Change', in Edwin A. Fedder (ed.) *The United Nations: Problems and Prospects*, St Louis, MO: Center for International Studies, University of Missouri.

—— (1972a) 'The Multinational Enterprise and World Political Economy', *International Organization* 26(1): 84–120.

—— (1972b) 'The US Multinational Enterprise and the Nation-State', *Journal of Common Market Studies* 11(1): 61–7.

—— (1978) 'The International Energy Agency: State Influence and Transgovernmental Politics', *International Organization* 32(4) (Autumn): 929–51.

—— (1980) 'Theory of Hegemonic Stability and Changes in International Economic Regime, 1967–77', in Ole Holsti (ed.) *Change in the International System*, Boulder, Co: Westview Press, pp. 131–62.

—— (1982a) 'State Power and Industry Influence', *International Organization* 36(1) (Winter): 165–83.

—— (1982b) 'Hegemonic Leadership and U.S. Foreign Economic Policy in the "Long Decade" of the 1950s', in *America in a Changing Global Economy*, ed. W. Avery and D. P. Rapkin, New York: Longman, pp. 46–76.

—— (1983a) 'The Demand for International Regimes', in *International Regimes*, ed. Stephen Krasner, Ithaca, NY: Cornell University Press.

—— (1983b) 'Theory of World Politics: Structural Realism and Beyond', in *Political Science: The State of the Discipline*, ed. A. W. Finifter, Washington, DC: American Political Science Association, pp. 503–40.

—— (1983c) 'Associative American Development, 1776–1860: Economic Growth and Political Disintegration', in *The Antinomies of Interdependence*, ed. J. G. Ruggie, New York: Columbia University Press, pp. 43–90.

118   Michael Suhr

—— (1984a) *After Hegemony. Co-operation and Discord in the World Political Economy*, Princeton, NJ: Princeton University Press.

—— (1984b) 'The World Political Economy and the Crisis of Embedded Liberalism', in *Order and Conflict in Contemporary Capitalism*, ed. J. H. Goldthorpe, Oxford: Clarendon Press, pp. 15–38.

—— (1986a) 'Realism, Neo-realism and the Study of World Politics', in *Neo-realism and Its Critics*, ed. R. Keohane, New York: Columbia University Press.

—— (1986b) 'Theory of World Politics: Structural Realism and Beyond', in *Neorealism and Its Critics*, ed. R. Keohane, New York: Columbia University Press.

—— (1986c) 'Reciprocity in International Relations', *International Organization* 40(1) (Winter): 1–27.

—— (1988) 'International Institutions: Two Approaches', *International Studies Quarterly* 32(4) (December): 379–96.

—— (1989a) *International Institutions and State Power. Essays in International Relations Theory*, Boulder, Co: Westview Press.

—— (1989b) 'A Personal Intellectual History', in *Understanding World Politics*, ed. J. Kruzel and J. N. Rosenau, Lexington, MA: Lexington Books, pp. 403–15.

—— (1989c) 'International Relations Theory: Contributions of a Feminist Standpoint', *Millennium: Journal of International Studies* 18(2): 245–53.

—— (1990a) 'Multilateralism: an Agenda for Research', *International Journal*, 45(4): 731–64.

—— (1990b) 'International Liberalism Reconsidered', in *The Economic Limits to Modern Politics*, ed. John Dunn, Port Chester, Canada: Cambridge University Press, pp. 165–94.

—— (1993a) 'Institutionalist Theory and the Realist Challenge after the Cold War', in *Neo-realism and Neo-liberalism: the Contemporary Debate*, ed. David Baldwin, New York: Columbia University Press, pp. 269–300.

—— (1993b) 'The Analysis of International Regimes: towards a European–American Research Programme', in Volker Rittberger (ed.) *Regime Theory and International Relations*, Oxford: Clarendon Press, pp. 23–48.

—— (1994) 'Hobbes' Dilemma and Institutional Change in World Politics: Sovereignty in International Society' in *Whose World Order? Uneven Globalization and the End of the Cold War*, ed. Hans-Henrik Holm and Georg Sørensen, Boulder, CO: Westview Press.

—— Haas, P. M. and Levy, M. A. (eds) (1993a) 'The Effectiveness of International Environmental Institutions', in *Institutions for the Earth. Sources of Effective International Environmental Protection*, Cambridge, MA: MIT Press.

—— Haas, P. M. and Levy, M. A. (1993b) (eds) 'Improving the Effectiveness of International Environmental Institutions', in *Institutions for the Earth. Sources of Effective International Environmental Protection*, Cambridge, MA: MIT Press, pp. 397–426.

—— and Hoffmann, S. (1990) 'Conclusions: Community Politics and Institutional Change', in *The Dynamics of European Integration*, ed. W. Wallace, London: Frances Printer, pp. 276–300.

—— (eds) (1991) 'Institutional Change in Europe in the 1980s', in *The New European Community: Decisionmaking and Institutional Change*, Boulder, CO: Westview Press, pp. 1–84.

—— (1993) 'Conclusion: Structure, Strategy, and Institutional Roles', in *After the Cold War. State Strategies and International Institutions in Europe, 1989–1991*, ed. R. Keohane, J. Nye and S. Hoffmann, Cambridge, MA: Harvard University Press, pp. 381–406.

—— and Nye, J. (1971a) 'Transnational Relations and World Politics: an Introduction', *International Organization* 25(3) (Summer): 329–49.

—— (1971b) 'Transnational Relations and World Politics: a Conclusion', *International Organization* 25(3) (Summer): 721–48.

—— (1975a) 'International Interdependence and Integration', *Handbook of Political Science*, Vol. 8, ed. Fred Greenstein and Nelson W. Polsby, Reading, MA: Addison-Wesley, pp. 363–414.

—— (1975b) 'Transgovernmental Relations and International Organizations', *World Politics* 27(1): 39– 62.

—— (1977) *Power and Interdependence: World Politics in Transition*, New York: Little, Brown.

—— (1989) *Power and Interdependence*, 2nd edn, Glenview, IL: Scott, Foresman; two new essays appear in this edition: 'Afterword' on pp. 245–67 and 'Two cheers for multilateralism' on pp. 268–82.

—— (1993) 'The United States and International Institutions in Europe after the Cold War', in *After the Cold War. International Institutions and State Strategies in Europe, 1989–1991*, ed. R. Keohane, J. Nye and S. Hoffmann, Cambridge, MA: Harvard University Press, pp. 104–26.

Works by other authors

Carr, E. H. (1981[1939]) *The Twenty Years' Crisis 1919–1939: An Introduction to the Study of International Relations*, London: Macmillan.

Elster, Jon (1983) *Explaining Technical Change. A Case Study in the Philosophy of Science*, Cambridge: Cambridge University Press.

Haas, P. M. (1990) *Saving the Mediterranean: The Politics of International Environmental Co-operation*, New York: Columbia University Press.

Hollis, M. and Smith, S. (1991) 'Beware of Gurus: Structure and Action in International Relations', *International Studies* 17: 393–410.

Krasner, Stephen (1983) 'Introduction', in Stephen D. Krasner (ed.) *International Regimes*, Ithaca, NY: Cornell University Press.

—— (1988) 'Sovereignty: an Institutional Perspective', *Comparative Political Studies* 21(1): 66–94.

—— (1993) 'Westphalia and All That', in Judith Goldstein and Robert O. Keohane (eds) *Ideas and Foreign Policy: Beliefs, Institutions, and Political Change*, Ithaca, NY: Cornell University Press, pp. 235–64.

Kratochwil, Friedrich (1984) 'The Force of Prescriptions', *International Organization* 38: 685–708.

—— and Ruggie, John G. (1986) 'International Organization: a State of the Art on an Art of the State', *International Organization* 40(4): 753–75.

March, J. G. and Olsen, J. P. (1984) 'The New Institutionalism: Organizational Factors in Political Life', *American Political Science Review* 78: 734–75.

Moravcsik, Andrew (1989) 'Disciplining Trade Finance: the OECD Export Credit Arrangement', *International Organization* 43: 173–205.

Morse, Edward (1976) *Modernization and the Transformation of International Relations*, New York: Free Press.

Mouritzen, Hans (1979) 'Politologisk egenart – også i "case"-studier?', *Statsvetenskaplig Tidskrift* 3: 179–90.

North, Douglass C. (1981) *Structure and Change in Economic History*, New York: W. W. Norton.

—— (1990) *Institutions, Institutional Change and Economic Performance*, Cambridge: Cambridge University Press.

Puchala, D. J. and Hopkins, R. E. (1983) 'International Regimes. Lessons from Inductive Analysis', in Stephen D. Krasner (ed.) *International Regimes*, Ithaca, NY: Cornell University Press.

Ray, James L. (1989) 'The Abolition of slavery and the End of International War', *International Organization* 43(3): 405–37.

Ruggie, John G. (1975) 'International Responses to Technology: Concepts and Trends', *International Organization* 29: 557–83.

——(1983) 'Continuity and Transformation in the World Polity: toward a Neo-Realist Synthesis', *World Politics* 35(2): 261–85.

Singer, J. D. (1961) 'The Level of Analysis Problem', *World Politics* 14: 77–92.

Smith, R. K. (1987) 'Explaining the Non-Proliferation Regime: Anomalies for Contemporary International Relations Theory', *International Organization* 41: 253–82.

Strange, Susan (1983) '*Cave! hic dragones*: a Critique of Regime Analysis', in S. Krasner (ed.) *International Regimes*, Ithaca, NY: Cornell University Press.

——(1988) *States and Markets. An Introduction to International Political Economy*, New York: Basil Blackwell.

Wæver, Ole (1992) *Introduktion til Studiet af International Politik*, Copenhagen: Forlaget Politiske Studier, Institut for Statskundskab.

——(1994) 'The Rise and Fall of the Inter-paradigm Debate', *Working Papers* 13, Copenhagen: Centre for Peace and Conflict Research.

——(in preparation) 'The Politics of International Structure' (book manuscript).

Waltz, Kenneth N. (1959) *Man, the State, and War. A Theoretical Analysis*, New York: Columbia University Press.

——(1970) 'The Myth of National Interdependence', in Charles P. Kindleberger (ed.) *The International Corporation*, Cambridge, MA: MIT Press.

Wendt, A. and Duvall, R. (1989) 'Institutions and International Order', in Ernst-Otto Czempiel and James N. Rosenau (eds) *Global Changes and Theoretical Challenges: Approaches to World Politics for the 1990s*, Lexington, MA and Toronto: Lexington Books.

Young, Oran R. (1980) 'International Regimes: Problems of Concept Formation', *World Politics* 29(1): 104–22.

——(1983) 'Regime Dynamics: the Rise and Fall of International Regimes', in Stephen D. Krasner (ed.) *International Regimes*, Ithaca, NY: Cornell University Press.

——(1986) 'International Regimes: toward a New Theory of Institutions', *World Politics* 39(1): 104–22.

5 Robert Gilpin: the realist quest for the dynamics of power

Stefano Guzzini

Robert Gilpin, born in 1930, studied Philosophy at Vermont (BA) and Rural Sociology at Cornell (MS), and took a PhD in Political Science at the University of California. He taught first at Columbia University. Since 1962 he has been at Princeton University. His main research interests are International Relations and International Political Economy, as well as European and Asian affairs. Gilpin is presently Eisenhower Professor of International Affairs at Princeton.

A crucial date in recent international political economy (IPE) was 15 August 1971, when the US administration decided to suspend the Bretton Woods monetary system. Not only did this unilateral decision change the way the international monetary system was run, but the USA was perceived to have officially declared its power position as challenged. After the 1973 crisis, observers began to link the erosion of US power with the recession and the increasing protectionism. US academics began for the first time to apply analyses of the decline of power to their own country. The oil shock and the accrued influence of economic weapons moved economic issues to the level of 'high politics', i.e. to questions of diplomacy and war.

A scholar relatively well prepared to respond to these issues was Robert Gilpin. One reason was that he had *not* specialized in the core of International Relations with its emphasis on narrowly defined security, strategy and traditional diplomacy. Gilpin specialized in the role of science and technology both for domestic and foreign policies. At the time of the 1971 watershed, his most recent book was a detailed analysis of the social and political responses of one former great power (France) to the challenges of the after-war period (1968a).

In an article in which he presented some of his book's central theses, he focused on industrial and technological policies which different European countries had devised to close the so-called 'technology gap' between them and the USA (1968b). In answer to T. Levitt's critique that the 'gap was not technological', but managerial, Gilpin responded that this was true, but beside the point. The 1968 text is worth quoting at length because it spells out much of Gilpin's later research programme.

> The point is that the technology gap is much less an economic than a political problem. This is true in several senses. In the first place, what is

at issue for Europeans is their political position *vis-à-vis* the great powers and their capacity for long-term national independence. Whereas, beginning in the latter part of the nineteenth century, control over petroleum resources became essential once naval ships shifted from sail to diesel, so today an independent aerospace and electronics industry, along with the supporting sciences, is seen to be crucial for a nation to enjoy diplomatic and military freedom of action. Second, the intensity of the European reaction to the technology gap must be understood in the context of the profound economic and political developments which have engulfed western Europe since the end of World War II.... First, there has been the trauma for France, Great Britain, and several other European countries of decolonization; seldom in history have proud and ruling peoples been reduced to second-class status so fast. Second, for the first time in history the political and industrial leaders of western Europe have experienced and must come to terms with a full-employment market economy.

(1968c: 125–6)

Gilpin's research programme, as will be claimed here, is an attempt to understand the historically changing nature of 'power' and the rise and decline of great 'powers'. In other words, it is about the *dynamics of power*. Gilpin wants to understand when and which resources provide power, and why and how the hierarchy of powers changes. For him, two historical shifts are central to answering these concerns at the end of the twentieth century, namely the increasing prominence of technological and economic sources of power, and the qualitative change from states to welfare states. More particularly, his research programme can be characterized by three central puzzles:

1 *the basic driving forces of change*: on the level of the actor, the quest for power and wealth; on the system level, market mechanisms and technological change. In the modern age, technology/efficiency and power have become inextricably linked. The result is a global, i.e. national and transnational, 'struggle for efficiency';
2 *the domestic response to this struggle* in which many governments find themselves often sandwiched between international requirements and a domestic social contract whose legitimacy increasingly rests upon material well-being for the majority of the society. Gilpin's judgement on the welfare state is therefore twofold. On the one hand, he values it for its capacity to stabilize democracies. On the other hand, he is aware of the protectionist, at times also nationalist, tendency to shift the costs of resolving domestic problems abroad;
3 *the international management of power shifts*, especially great-power decline, where competition risks degenerating into technological and other wars.

When Gilpin in 1987 recalls his crucial turn in 1970 to what would later be called the discipline of IPE, he refers to his experiences in France where

the US multinational corporations would have been kicked out had General de Gaulle been able to convince the German government to follow suit. According to Gilpin's analysis the German refusal was linked to a wider bargain in which the US military guarantee to Germany was 'traded off' for the multinationals: only the *Pax Americana* made transnationalism of this kind and speed possible.

> Although I did not fully appreciate it at the time, I had returned to a realist conception of the relationship of economics and politics that had disappeared from postwar American writings, then almost completely devoted to more narrowly conceived security concerns.
>
> (1987a: xii)

This research programme about the dynamics of power makes it difficult to fit Gilpin into the boxes available in IR/IPE. He is normally referred to as a neo-realist, mainly for two reasons: his use of utilitarian (economic) methodology and his apparent ahistorical assumptions. This interpretation focuses primarily on his book *War and Change in World Politics* (1981), and in particular Chapter 6, where he develops a utilitarian theory of war, expansion, hegemony and decline. Ever since Gilpin declared that Thucydides 'would [following an appropriate course in geography, economics, and modern technology] have little trouble in understanding the power struggle in our age' (1981: 211), he has been considered one of the most ahistorical realists who put their faith in the profoundly unchanged and unchanging character of the international system. Yet, seen from the, rather simplistic, dichotomy between historical and scientific forms of Realism, he represents a curious mixture at best. Although he tries to systematize a theory of (hegemonic) action, based upon generally unchanged utilitarian assumptions, he derives the present system and its ordering principles historically.

Indeed, and this is the second major claim of this chapter, Gilpin's Realism is profoundly at odds with several central tenets of neo-realism, at least if Kenneth Waltz's *Theory of International Politics* (1979) is understood as its paradigmatic text. He does not derive conflict solely from international anarchy. His theory draws a historical and qualitative difference between international systems. His international theory necessarily requires a theory of the state. For Gilpin, Realism needs to be broadened so as to become a form of neo-mercantilism. The treatment of change might perhaps best exemplify this central difference between Gilpin's neo-mercantilism and neo-realism. Gilpin's approach sees both more and less change than neo-realism. On the one hand, he analyses at length the changes that have occurred in the international system since the Peloponnesian War – with the coming of capitalism, its globalization, the rise of the nation-state and the welfare state. On the other hand, if applied to the understanding of the end of the Cold War, Gilpin's approach would systematically relativize those changes emphasized by neo-realist analyses. Whereas neo-realist theories would identify the change in terms of shifts in the balance of power (see also Chapter 3 on Waltz in this book), Gilpin's neo-mercantilism stresses the

profound continuity of the international political economy and the increasing difficulties in managing an international liberal order – which are partly independent from the effects of strategic polarity.

The following discussion will, in more detail, deal with these two central claims of this chapter, namely first that Gilpin's research programme is best understood as a realist quest for the understanding of the dynamics of power, and second that he does not fit the neo-realist category well. Section I examines Gilpin's underlying assumptions. Although his link between human nature and group conflict is slightly unclear, his approach is certainly closer to Morgenthau than to Waltz. Second, his academic project will be identified as a plea for a necessary updating of realist IR as neo-mercantilist IPE. Section III presents Gilpin's design for rendering the realist approach more dynamic. It will be spelled out as a research strategy around three basic theoretical 'dialogues': between Clausewitz and Lenin, between Marx and Keynes, and between Lenin and Kautsky. This is followed by a short discussion of his empirical and normative assessment of the present global political economy, which according to him requires, but lacks, a hegemon. The final section indicates some limits in this neo-mercantilist approach, in particular Gilpin's state-centrism.

This chapter argues that Gilpin's main contributions lie in the updating and development of realist theory, and in the redirection of IR towards IPE. Before the detailed analysis of Gilpin's ideas begins a last preliminary remark is warranted. The following discussion is built around central tensions in Gilpin's thought, often acknowledged by Gilpin himself. His work is characterized by an attempt to do justice to a wide variety of approaches. Sometimes this results in a rather accrued sense of indecision. Gilpin once referred to himself as a 'liberal [with regard to his moral values] in a realist world and frequently also in a Marxist world of class struggle' (1986: 304). Given the established categories of our disciplines, such or similar passages can be considered as confusing, and thus a major weakness of his work. I think they should rather be read as an indicator of academic transparency. Gilpin makes no effort to hide or cover uncertainties which, to be sure, are not only his. This is another, perhaps not minor, contribution to the discipline. In our times of hasty disciplinary closures his work stands for an attempt to offer the possibility of mutual learning.

ASSUMPTIONS: ONTOLOGICAL AMBIGUITIES AND METHODOLOGICAL INDIVIDUALISM

Gilpin's assumptions represent a singular realist mix of permanence and change. His ontology posits the permanence of human drives, group organization and intergroup conflict. Yet his analysis of international systems stresses historical changes. To this, he adds a methodological individualist approach which expands the utilitarian realist tradition. The goals are threefold: security, power and wealth. They are given. The actors, however, are historically defined. Today's main social group is the nation. The changing international systems define the constraints within which these

actors can pursue their goals. This section will, in turn, take up these ontological and methodological assumptions.

Moral pessimism and the permanence of human nature

Pressed to define what he understands by Realism, Gilpin refers to Rose-crance's description of political Realism not as a systematic theory, but 'as an attitude regarding the human condition'. Gilpin bases his interpretation of political Realism on three assumptions: the essentially conflictual nature of international affairs; the essence of social reality being the group, which, in modern times, means the nation; and the primacy in all political life of power and security in human motivation (1986: 304–5).

For this last item, the unchanging human motivation, Gilpin quoted Thucydides with approval. And indeed, at many points he refers to a sceptic view of human nature as the underlying criterion to distinguish Realism from both liberalism and Marxism; because liberalism believes in the possible harmony of interests and Marxism insists that socialism will overcome the propensity to social conflicts.[1] Whereas changing contexts might make conflicts less likely, human conflictual nature remains constant.[2] The incessant attack on the realist story as a never-ending repetition and rehearsal on the stage of world politics has its core here. This ontological assumption is also consequential for Gilpin's methodology. If one can perceive a permanent basic motivation in human beings, then this is the place to start theorizing. Gilpin's turn to a utilitarian, or as he, following Brian Barry, calls it, an economic approach, is inextricably linked to this realist assumption.

The utility function of security, power and wealth

The economic approach to Realism and IR is not exactly new. In micro-economic theory, agents try to maximize their utility functions. That is, given a set of preferences and for a particular set of resources at hand, agents will choose to allocate their resources in order to maximize their return. Neo-classical economic theory cannot determine exactly what utility means for a particular agent. Yet the concept, and historical fact, of *money* allows the economists to commensurate the variety of aims on a common scale.

When applied to international relations, utility is interchangeably identified with 'security' or the 'national interest'. Once again, there is no way of knowing exactly what this means for any international agent (generally the state or government), but power is often conceived as functionally analogous to money in economic theory. Utility maximizing in IR means the maximization of security expressed in power.

This approach has been severely criticized by a few writers, either because the power–money analogy is said not to exist at all,[3] or because the analogy is only of limited use due to the incomplete transferability of power resources from one issue area to another, i.e. due to the lacking 'fungibility' of power (Baldwin 1989). Whereas an individual agent is able to 'cash in' labour in money and use money to buy something else, states cannot necessarily 'cash in' atomic weapons (strategic issue area) for lower tariffs (trade issue area).

Gilpin uses this approach in an unorthodox way. His main interest is the understanding of change. Besides his inquiry into the changing bases of power, he wants to understand the origins of power shifts and expansion. He transfers the analogy of marginal economics to the phenomenon of territorial expansion. Teritorial expansion will occur as long as the marginal return outweighs the incurred costs. When the two are equal, expansion will stop. This idea of equilibrium is, of course, an economic translation of the balance of power. Similarly, it alludes to the classical realist argument about a 'power vacuum' which inevitably will be filled. As will be discussed in more detail later, Gilpin's major variance with the traditional realist approaches is that he applies this utilitarian theory of action not to strategic theory but to the order of world political economy: from deterrence theory to the theory of hegemonic war.

This redefinition of utilitarian Realism is a consequence of Gilpin's historical situating of today's international political economy. For Gilpin, the international system has been profoundly changed by the mutual feeding dynamics of the rise of the global market economy, and the emergence of the territorial state. Its ordering principle refers not only to strategic characteristics, as, for instance, the distribution of power, but to the global political economy which, in the present historical context, is either a (liberal) hegemony or in a state of anomy. As we will see later, for Gilpin Realism today necessarily means neo-mercantilism; to be an IR scholar requires one to be an IPE scholar.

Individual or group permanence?

Gilpin does not follow those who have tried to 'rescue' Realism from Morgenthau's 'dark' assumptions of human nature and who derived international conflicts from the nature of the international system. Gilpin is here particularly at odds with Waltz's neo-realism. But nor does he adopt a Hobbesian view, which likens the international realm to a pre-societal state of nature. His starting-point is the social groups in which humans organize themselves.

> The building blocks and ultimate units of social and political life are not the individuals of liberal thought nor the classes of Marxism.... Realism, as I interpret it, holds that the foundation of political life is what Ralf Dahrendorf has called 'conflict groups'.... This is another way of saying that in a world of scarce resources, human beings confront one another ultimately as members of groups, and not as isolated individuals. ... True, the name, size, and organization of the competing groups into which our species subdivides itself do alter over time – tribes, city-states, kingdoms, empires, and nation-states – due to economic, demo-

graphic, and technological changes. Regrettably, however, the essential nature of inter-group conflict does not.

(1986: 305)

This poses a theoretical problem. Scholars like Gilpin whose Realism rests on a strong assumption about human nature, should logically start their analysis on the level of the individual. Instead, the privileged unit of analysis is the state – for Gilpin, the nation; that is, a collective actor. There exist different solutions to this old problem.

Morgenthau (1948: 17) posits three basic drives of 'all men': to live, to propagate and to dominate. In a world of scarce resources, these different drives must result in a struggle for power. Hence, domestic politics is mainly about the collective attempt to control the individual struggle for power. But this lust for power cannot be eradicated. As a result, power drives frustrated within societies are projected abroad, a phenomenon that Morgenthau calls 'nationalistic universalism' for the universalization of nationalist drives – as opposed to a foreign policy which is both primary to, and isolated from, domestic politics. Morgenthau sees a close relation between social disintegration, personal insecurity and the ferocity of modern nationalistic power in international affairs. Methodologically speaking, this also implies that the analysis of IR can start at the national level, by reapplying the arguments derived from human nature now to another political environment, the international system, where the struggle for power is not checked by an overarching authority comparable to the state.

Gilpin has a similar view on human nature. He does, however, leave unanswered exactly how the link between the individual level and the national one should be conceived. If human nature and motivation are the permanent factors (as he says in the last of three characteristics of Political Realism), and intergroup conflict a permanent (or even 'essential') feature, then this aggregation should be spelled out. It seems that Gilpin presupposes that since everyone shares the same motivation, the group in which they are embedded will just do the same. But this begs the question, and we will return later to the issue of whether there is anything like a unified national interest. The economic model Gilpin uses must actually assume this, although he himself appears to question it.

REALIST IR AS NECESSARILY NEO-MERCANTILIST IPE

On the basis of these assumptions, Gilpin proposes an academic project which tries to overcome the military emphasis of international studies and which redefines the borders of the discipline of IR. Particularly different from Waltz's form of neo-realism is his sensitivity to historical changes in the forms of intergroup conflict. For him, with the evolution of the groups' *internal* organization, the nature of conflict among groups also changes. The advent of the nation-state and market economy make a difference to realist theory: they require a neo-mercantilist conception of Realism. The welfare state in the twentieth century leads him to plead for a study of IPE around themes that synthesize neo-mercantilist and Marxist concerns.

The changed modern international political economy

Ever since his initial studies of technology and industrial policy, Gilpin believes that with the rise of the nation-state and market economy, power cannot be understood independently from the economic base. This basic insight of mercantilists and Marxists alike is the driving force of his theorizing: wealth and power, and the agent's pursuit of these, are inextricably linked. Thus, Gilpin provides a historical picture of today's IPE.

Gilpin believes that the rise of an international market economy had a major impact on state security, because it constituted a more or less autonomous sphere within and across borders, due to its independent dynamic and its aims, which were separate from the state or society at large.[4] This extraordinary development was possible for three reasons: the invention of a monetarized economy; the rise of a merchant middle class; and the avoidance (or postponement) of a unifying empire in Europe. The European balance of power allowed the merchant class to develop its strength in an environment where competition for wealth and power was pushing societies to adopt the modern state organization. Since the modern nation-state had an unchallenged fiscal and war-making capacity, it became from then on the major group organization whose expansion has lasted until today (1981: 123).

From the advent of the European state system (city-states) until the *Pax Britannica* is the phase of *mercantilism*; the first attempt of the modern world to organize a market economy on a global scale. Technological and organizational innovations in warfare bolstered the rise of mercantilism – as a form of political economy and concomitantly as a theory. Both the production of gunpowder and the rise of professional armies depended on the merchant trading system (to assure the provision of powder) and wealth (to pay the armies). In return, the sovereign guaranteed property rights.

But only Britain's victory in the Napoleonic wars, the industrial revolution, and new means of communication brought together all the conditions necessary to create an interdependent world. The nineteenth-century balance of power (balance for the continent and power for Britain) allowed the competitive leader to manage the international economy financially and commercially. Britain's comparative advantage and national security interest demanded a 'liberal' approach based on a open market strategy. In short, the *Pax Britannica* provided the political framework for the emergence of a liberal international economy and concomitantly for (economic) liberalism as a doctrine.

This doctrine was soon criticized by economic nationalists like Hamilton or List who argued for a dynamic theory of comparative advantage where endowments might be created by conscious policies and must be protected in their infant phase, and later by socialists and in Lenin's theory of imperialism.

For Gilpin, the First World War was the test for the shift in power that occurred with Britain's decline and the rise of Germany and the USA. The absence of strong leadership in the interwar period produced the break-down of the system.[5] Only with the *Pax Americana* after 1945 could a new liberal international order be established.

Gilpin generalizes from this historical account the factors that affect the incentive structure of actors and thus the stability of an international system. In his utilitarian theory of war, instability arises whenever a state calculates that it will be rewarding. This calculus is affected by changes in transport and communication, and military technology, and by demographic and economic factors that distinguish our period from the pre-mercantilist ones.[6] Thus, although neo-realist theory might refer to the eternal return of power politics, Gilpin's necessarily mercantilist approach introduces as endogenous factors many otherwise neglected features. The causal chain of his approach starts with organizational and technical technological and economic change, often induced by the international competition of states. This affects the distribution of power in the system, and the incentives for agents to change their behaviour. Actual policies finally determine the specific international system (liberal or not).

Finally, Gilpin places today's IPE in the context of an international system which does not start in 1648 with the Westphalian Treaties, but which has existed only since 1815 with the advent of a British-led international liberal order. 'First in the European system and then on a global scale, successive political and economic hegemonies have supplanted the pattern of successive empires as the *fundamental ordering principle of international relations*' (1981: 144, italics added).

If neo-realism has been criticized for not being able to differentiate the change from the medieval to the modern system, Gilpin's historic and more dynamic account cannot be attacked on this charge.[7] A neo-mercantilist realist finds the major ordering principle of IR in the hegemonic governance of the international political economy, whether liberal or not.

Definition and ideologies of IPE

The historical development of IPE in the last few centuries also informs Gilpin's (1975a) typology of approaches to IPE: economic nationalism (or neo-mercantilism), liberalism (called, with reference to Raymond Vernon, the 'Sovereignty at bay' model) and neo-Marxism (or dependency). Later the same 'models' for the understanding of Foreign Direct Investment have been expanded into three 'ideologies' of IPE in general (1987a: Chapter 2).

Since he repeats this tryptic at a time when the components have become common wisdom also in IR, Gilpin gives the impression that he wants to conceive IPE as a sister discipline of IR ('the economic approaches of Realism, Pluralism, Marxism').[8] Yet, as we will see, his view of IPE *de facto* attempts to overcome the limits of IR by a wider approach based essentially on the integration of ideas derived from neo-mercantilism and neo-Marxism. If, for historical reasons, it is impossible to preserve a purely political understanding of the state in realist theory, Realism must, according to Gilpin, be based on an approach which integrates politics and economics on the same footing. Similarly, the discipline of IR should become IPE.

Together with the threefold typology, Gilpin provides a rather succinct focus of the subject-matter that IPE is supposed to cover (and that defines its scientific research programme). His definition is often repeated in the standard literature:[9]

> political economy in this study means the reciprocal and dynamic inter-action in international relations of the pursuit of wealth and the pursuit of power. In the short run, the distribution of power and the nature of the political system are major determinants of the framework within which wealth is produced and distributed. In the long run, however, shifts in economic efficiency and in the location of economic activity tend to undermine and transform the existing political system. This political transformation in turn gives rise to changes in economic rela-tions that reflect the interests of the politically ascendant state in the system.
>
> (1975b: 40)

This definition claims to be broad enough to integrate the three 'models of the future' into one discipline. This is also what he attempts in the later textbook. Yet the three ideologies do not seem to be entirely satisfactorily integrated. The difficulty lies in the 'liberal model'. There is, at least, a tension in the solution he provides us.

In his book on multinational corporations (MNCs), the liberal model was subsumed under the interdependence literature. The essential claim of this literature was that increasing economic interdependence and technological advances in communication and transportation are making the nation-state an anachronism and shifting the control of world affairs to transnational actors and structures (e.g. the Eurodollar market). To this framework is added a world-view of voluntary and co-operative relations among inter-dependent economies, whose goal consists in accelerating economic growth and all-round welfare by means of the MNC as transmission belt of capital, ideas and growth.

This presentation superimposes insights from the interdependence litera-ture on the liberal economists' or neo-functionalist credo. In other words, Gilpin links the transnationalist framework of analysis, which privileges non-state actors and dynamics, with the old-established, and simplified, idealist creed, which says that more commerce breeds harmony. By fusing these two ideas, his category of a 'liberal' school bridges the gap between transnational politics and the idealism of economic liberalism. As a result, Gilpin runs into a problem for his general definition of IPE. For political economy, political or power-analysis is an endogenous variable of the explanation. Liberal international economics, however, treats power as *exogenous*. By the force of his definition (where power and wealth are integrated), Gilpin seems pushed to exclude liberal international economics from the body of theory.

Maybe this is why he adjusts the definition in the 1987 textbook to what seems to be the present orthodoxy for the definition of IPE, the 'state-market nexus':

> The parallel existence and mutual interaction of 'state' and 'market' in the modern world create 'political economy'.... In the absence of the state, the price mechanism and market forces would determine the outcome of economic activities; this would be the pure world of the economist. In the absence of the market, the state ... would allocate economic resources; this would be the pure world of the political scientist.... For the state, territorial boundaries are a necessary basis of national autonomy and political unity. For the market, the elimination of all political and other obstacles to the operation of the price mechanism is imperative. The tension between these two fundamentally different ways of ordering human relationships has profoundly shaped the course of modern history and constitutes the crucial problem in the study of political economy.
>
> (1987a: 8, 11)

This definition allows an integration of liberal economic theory as the model for the study of markets – even if power is treated as an exogenous variable. Nevertheless, he cannot but later admit that therefore 'liberalism lacks a true political economy' (1987a: 45). This squaring of the circle (how to integrate the liberals, even if they are, as defined here, of no use) leaves one rather perplexed. The stress on *political economy* (as in his first definition) was a reaction against the compartmentalization of the subject-matter in two different disciplines which often treat the other as exogenous to the subject. The field of economics was considered insufficient, because it did not integrate power analysis in its explanatory models. In its turn, political science often treated economics as exogenous to, or sometimes only dependent on, the political setting: the autonomy of market *forces* was missed. To alter the definition which stresses the 'organization' of the pursuit of power and wealth, rather than the 'objective' of this activity (1987a: 11), is to fall back on a conceptual and disciplinary split that political economy was supposed to overcome.

DYNAMIZING NEO-MERCANTILISM: THREE DIALOGUES

In coherence with his earlier view, Gilpin in fact tries to overcome this split by elaborating an approach which is a mix of the two 'real' theories of political economy: mercantilism and Marxism. They will be articulated here in the form of three 'dialogues'.

State dynamics: the dialogue between Lenin and Clausewitz

An economic approach whose basic unit is the state necessarily requires a 'theory of the state'. Gilpin offers one that can accommodate both Marxists and the elitist theorists of the state (thus, also realists). The state is an 'organization that provides protection and [welfare]. . . . in return for revenue' (1981: 15). This corresponds to the above-mentioned historical bargain between the political system and the rising middle class when the nation-state developed in concomitance with the (global) market economy. The primary function of states is to provide protection/security against foreign threats, establish property rights and distribute wealth domestically.

Aware of the long-lasting problem of assuming a national interest, or a state's utility function, he states that, of course, no such thing exists, and that strictly speaking only individuals have interests. This brings us back to the initial ontological question: is the individual or the state the 'essential' unit? Gilpin does not really discuss this, but refers to the national interest, in a manner not entirely unsimilar to elitist or radical theories of the state as determined 'primarily by the interests of their dominant members or ruling coalitions' (1981: 19).

Yet when he goes on discussing the so-called national or foreign policy interests, he falls back on a 'universalist' position, the interests being security and welfare, that are the logical consequence of the permanent motivation at the individual level. Thus, he remains undecided whom to side with in what Raymond Aron has called the 'dialogue between Clausewitz and Lenin':

> Le premier ne mettait pas en doute la notion du bien de la communauté (ou de l'intérêt national, dans le vocabulaire d'aujourd'hui). . . . Lénine répliquait à Clausewitz qu'il admirait, que dans un Etat de classes, il ne pouvait y avoir de bien commun. L'action extérieure des Etats exprimerait la volonté d'une classe ou d'une autre. Les événements, depuis la révolution de 1917 réfutent simultanément, me semble-t-il, les théories extrêmes. [He [Clausewitz] did not question the notion of the common good (or the national interest, in today's vocabulary). . . . Lenin answered to Clausewitz, whom he admired, that in a class society there could be no common good. The foreign action of states would express the interests of one class or another. It seems to me that the events since the 1917 revolution simultaneously refute the extreme version of both theories.]
>
> (Aron 1984b: 30; my translation)

If for the external function and motivation there has been little change, at least on the domestic side, Gilpin sees in the type of 'social formations' (the concept is taken from Samir Amin) a major source of international change. Social formations determine how the economic surplus is generated, transferred and distributed both within and among societies. The change from one social formation to another determines the change from one international system to another.

> The distinguishing features of premodern and modern international relations are in large measure due to significant differences in characteristic social formations. The displacement of empires and imperial-

command economies by nation-states and a world market economy as the principal forms of political and economic organization can be understood only as a development associated with the change from an agricultural formation to an industrial formation.

(1981: 110)

It is important to note here that for Gilpin the former socialist countries and the western liberal countries have, of course, many differences, but they share the aspect that the economic surplus is generated by industrial production and this affects their foreign behaviour. It is, however, probably not only the similar industrial social formation but its insertion into a common international market system that creates a pressure for similar behaviour. If for a Waltzian neo-realist, states in a self-help system behave similarly, inaependent of their political system, neo-mercantilism redefines both the unit and the system level, as well as their effect on the behaviour of states. The shift to welfare states implies a redefinition of the 'self' of the state; a new identity which needs to be protected and for which states do compete. The international political economy, which results *also* from the character of the political economy of individual social formations, means that the international system is not just a configuration of power, and that states have to find means to conform to the pressures of a world market economy.

Socioeconomic dynamics: the dialogue between Marx and Keynes

More recently Gilpin has come to specify a change that might in fact correspond to another major historical shift, although he does not characterize it as such. As Gilpin describes the global political economy after 1945, it is characterized by a hegemonic liberal international order, the *Pax Americana*. Yet this hegemony is different from the British one. The key to the difference lies precisely in the link between the social formations and the international system they create. The change that has occurred and that was institutionalized after the First World War is the change to mass societies in which legitimacy derives from their capacity to enrich their people and to do it on a more equal basis. The *Pax Americana* is based on a special kind of the liberal state, the welfare state, which under US leadership collaborates in an international system of 'embedded liberalism'.[10]

Gilpin analyses the Keynesian revolution as a response to the inherent problems of nineteenth-century capitalism that Marx had more or less rightly recognized (1987a: 59). For him, the welfare state has 'nullified' three Marxist laws of the internal contradictions of capitalism. The 'law of disproportionality' has been overcome by the welfare state's demand management through fiscal and monetary policy. The 'law of accumulation' could be countered through income redistribution, support for trade unions, and regional and small business policies. Government support for education and research can increase the efficiency of all factors of production so as to upset the 'law of the falling rate of profit'. Yet capitalism is intrinsically expansionist. With the end of territorial imperialism and consequently the diminished capacity to export the burden of capitalist adjustments, the contradictions of capitalism ricochet back on the leading economies. As the world has been recognized as finite since the end of the nineteenth century, capitalism becomes inherently conflictual on the international level. Whereas capitalism can be supplemented by a welfare state to overcome its contradictions on the domestic level, the question arises if it can work on the international level where no world welfare state exists. Gilpin believes that

> the logic of the market economy as an inherently expanding global system collides with the logic of the modern welfare state. While solving the problem of a closed economy, the welfare state has only transferred the fundamental problem of the market economy and its survivability to the international level.

> (1987a: 63)

The result is a system where states compete over the international division of economic activities, by using and creating comparative advantages, and by attracting production into their countries. The domestic welfare legitimacy makes states more nationalist than before. For Gilpin, only a hegemon can impose a liberal order in this competitive environment. Only the hegemon can provide the necessary public goods to allow the 'compromise of embedded liberalism', i.e. to run a multilateral system by allowing autonomous national economic policies.

IPE dynamics: the dialogue between Lenin and Kautsky

If the present international system has been the second in a series of liberal hegemonies (and not just empires), then the rise and decline of hegemons are the major research focus at the international level. The research is part of what has come to be called 'hegemonic stability theory'.[11] The latter can be characterized by three theses:

1 the emergence of a hegemon is necessary for the provision of an international public good (Hegemony thesis);
2 the necessary existence of free riders (and thus the unequal distribution of costs) and/or a loss of legitimacy will undermine the relative power position of the hegemon (Entropy thesis);
3 a declining hegemon presages the declining provision of an international public good (Decline thesis).

Such a hegemon normally arises after a rearrangement of power shifts, which is most probably violent. The reason is that power (and efficiency) shifts are quicker than the political reactions and thus produce an incentive structure for the rising powers to go to war in order to change their status in the system.[12]

The particular public goods that Gilpin finds the hegemon providing are roughly those that Kindleberger analysed as lacking in the interwar period:

1 the stabilization of monetary and trade relations via
- rediscount mechanisms for providing liquidity during international crises
- lender of last resort function
- management of the international monetary system (Kindleberger would add the maintenance of a structure of exchange rates and co-ordination of macroeconomic policies)
- openness of markets for distressed goods
- a steady, if not countercyclical flow of capital;

2 redistribution of income through foreign aid; and

3 regulation of abuses (sanction mechanisms).[13]

Thereby, Gilpin gives a two-sided account of hegemony in general, and the international liberal order in particular.

On the one hand, he follows the typical realist account that hegemony breeds order in the sense of limiting (and deterring) conflicts.[14] He does not, or at least does not want to, subscribe to the idealist turn which speaks of the US 'sacrifice' for a liberal order.[15] Quite to the contrary, he follows Carr's critique of the British ideology of a harmony of interests:

> Once industrial capitalism and the class system had become the recog-nised structure of society, the doctrine of the harmony of interests acquired a new significance, and became ... the ideology of a dominant group concerned to maintain its predominance by asserting the identity of interests with those of the community as a whole. (...) No country but Great Britain had been commercially powerful enough to believe in the international harmony of economic interests.
>
> (1946: 44, 46)

He states explicitly that the hegemon must perceive it in its own (perhaps long-term, or enlightened) interest to provide the public good. Only this is consistent with the underlying economic approach (1986: 311–12).

On the other hand, Gilpin shifts from the focus on the utilitarian cal-culation to a domestic analogy: the hegemon takes over the same functions in the international society as the government has in domestic society, namely providing the public goods of security and protection of property rights in exchange for revenue (1981: 145). This is linked to the basic assumption of the ubiquitous nature of conflict in politics *tout court*. It is in this vein that he follows Keohane's (1984) argument against the Hege-monic Stability Theory which rejects the decline thesis, that regimes (Keo-hane's public good) once established can take on a dynamic of their own and subsist, although the hegemon that issued the system may decline in power. In that respect, Gilpin translates the common norms that realists have found necessary for the functioning of a (political) concert system into IPE. The concert has to be run not just by the major powers, but, in order to allow a liberal order to function, by all the major *liberal* powers. Their common code integrates domestic political and international economic issues.

This having been said, Gilpin believes that the decline of the hegemon definitely weakens the international liberal order. It weakens the first of the three political foundations of such an order, which are a dominant liberal hegemonic power or powers able to manage and enforce the rules; a set of common economic, political and security interests that binds them together; and a shared ideological commitment to liberal values. Here, he refers to the classical socialist debate between Lenin and Kautsky (1987a: 38–40). Lenin stipulated that the 'law of uneven development', i.e. the necessarily differential growth of national capitalist economies, would undermine any attempt to establish an international multilateral order. The expansionist drive of monopoly capitalism at the imperialist stage would necessarily provoke wars. Kautsky, on the other hand, argued that the capitalist countries would not be so stupid as to go permanently to war with one another if a collaboration in international exploitation would be more lucrative. This is his doctrine of 'ultra-imperialism'. Consequently, Gilpin's empirical question has become the future of the liberal order after the decline of the *Pax Americana*.

INTERNATIONAL LIBERAL ORDER AFTER THE DECLINE OF THE *PAX AMERICANA*

The crisis of 1971/3 has been aggravated by recent developments. The first major change came when the US capacity to handle both the international political economy and its own society became visibly strained. This was, according to Gilpin, the consequence of a massive redistribution of world economic power away from the United States towards first Europe and then the Pacific around Japan and Southeast Asia. The USA has become deeply indebted and needs foreign, in particular Japanese, help to run international monetary relations. Furthermore, the monetary system's change to a flexible system has removed the former discipline and induced the phenomenon of global inflation. This risk factor heavily constrains traditional Keynesian policies. The monetary system is by now nearly out of control due to the revolution in the financial sector. The management of industrial production in a firm has become vertically integrated, and is now genuinely transnational. Finally, Gilpin speaks of a change to a third phase of the industrial revolution, with the coming of knowledge-intensive industries, which has 'undermined the basic assumption of the Bretton Woods trading system that comparative advantage was a "given" of nature and could not be altered by the policies of corporations and/or governments' (1991: 16–17).

Consequently, the present system is characterized simultaneously by the transnationalization and integration of markets *and* by increasing nationalistic impulses. At the same time, the 'struggle for the world product' (a Helmut Schmidt quote Gilpin likes to use) will be decided with the victory of one hegemon, because, for Gilpin, economic efficiency and political power have become increasingly linked. The identity of this hegemon will largely determine the character of the next international order.

The pressure has already led to many adjustment programmes, both domestically (supply-side economics, education, industrial policies, and so on) and externally (protectionism in different forms, the use of political power for markets or investments). The biggest of these adjustments was certainly the Soviet one. For Gilpin, Gorbachev's policies were induced from abroad. Aware of the increasing 'technological gap' to the G7, the Soviet Union decided on the most liberal reforms since the Bolshevik Revolution.[16] But domestic restructuring also took place in Japan and Europe started a new initiative to regain some macroeconomic instruments via an accelerated political and economic integration (Maastricht). The Third World has given up its demands for a New International Economic Order (NIEO) and competes for the attraction of Foreign Direct Investments (FDIs) (the worst is not to be exploited, but to be neglected by the international division of production). Finally, even the USA seemed to be reconsidering its policies after years of 'mask[ing] the profound developments that have occurred and the challenges they have posed. The United States has lived on borrowed time – and borrowed money – for much of the last decade' (1987b: 33). Many of Gilpin's later writings are filled with policy recommendations in which he also incorporates his studies on technological policies.[17]

But the major risk of the system is the threat not only to the liberal order inside or outside individual countries, but to the very existence of this present international system as a whole. This theme appears twice. First, the increasing transnationalization of production exposes not only industries, but entire social formations, to competitive pressures from abroad, which can disrupt existing social consensus and, in turn, spill over conflict to the international level. This partly explains Gilpin's repeated concern with Japan–US (or Western) relations. Second, the decline of the *Pax Americana* seems to be accompanied by a decline of the legitimacy of the principles on which it was built. 'Inter-civilizational conflict' (his term) looms on the international scene.

Gilpin's solutions correspond to a typically realist solution, both pragmatic and normative. On the pragmatic level, he is rather critical of the attempts to impose changes on the social structure of specific states from abroad. Hence, he does not endorse the 'cultural' turn US–Japanese mutual reproaches sometimes take. To salvage at least a partial version of embedded liberalism and reduce the impact of possible trade wars, Gilpin follows the general idea of a 'benign mercantilism' organized through the partition of the world into three hegemonic orders (USA–Europe–Japan) with respective economic spheres of influence (1987a: Chapter 10). His normative answer to forms of inter-civilizational conflict is once again separation, this time not geographically into world regions, but axiomatically between internal and external relations. Gilpin hereby reiterates a recent theme of the Rawlsian liberal political philosophy. Taking seriously the 'plurality of incommensurable conceptions of the good',[18] legitimate collective choices are possible in liberal orders only by means of a private (values)/public (space of tolerance) distinction. Incommensurable values are confined to the private sphere, as religion, for instance, to preserve a public sphere of debate and compromise, indeed of justice. Liberalism claims therefore to be neutral or to provide a 'higher order theory' compared with all other political theories or ideologies. Gilpin, who finds himself a Grotian realist in this respect, uses this liberal distinction and procedural solution as his maxim for the establishment of order at the international level. States (should) understand that the best way to avoid major conflicts lies in the sharp division between domestic value-systems and international politics and in the reciprocal acceptance and moderation of national interests. Hence, for Gilpin 'in contrast to liberalism and Marxism, realism is a universal political theory which every society can understand' (1990: 137). To state and hopefully reduce the confusion between the disciplines: Grotian *Realism* in IR relies on a public–private distinction which permits it to claim to be neutral or potentially universal, just as recent (domestic) political *liberalism* does.

It also shares the problem of political liberal theories: how to 'persuade' an actor to follow such a universal maxim, when the latter's underlying value-system cannot accept the private–public distinction. In IR the problem is more consequential. Although major conflicts are to be avoided, war in its limited form is at times a justified instrument of realist politics. Revolutionary powers who want to export their ideology are checked by force. After so many attempts to update Realism, we are back to the basic dilemmas as posed by Classical Realism. As long as neither human nature nor the conflictuality of the international system varies, neo-mercantilist IPE is certainly a valuable advance in order better to apprehend the dynamics of the system and the possible widening of the cracks in the wall of the existing order. When asked how to react, however, its instruments do not differ from those of realist normative theory.

THE LIMITS OF NEO-MERCANTILIST IPE

Gilpin's initial interest is double: it concerns both the capacity of societies to react and adapt to a changing international environment and the possible spillovers of societal dynamics on to the international order. It is guided by a liberal concern for the welfare state and for a liberal international order, which is, as we will see, not always clearly defined.

Therefore, Gilpin cannot indulge in the purely structural turn of neo-realism, because this approach neglects the societal level. As we have seen, Gilpin's approach needs the latter to historicize the international structure, as, for instance, the present link between the welfare state and the international liberal order. In fact, whereas Gilpin integrates Waltz's structure as one of the elements of the systemic level into his model, the latter does not integrate a theory of the unit-level, although Waltz (1986: 331) admits that 'international-political theory at times [*sic!*] needs a theory of the state'.

Gilpin's attempt to dynamize Realism problematizes the co-determination of the two levels. It can be understood as a way to overcome two major problems in balance of power theories. First, a focus on changing power bases and actors' power dynamics should help to prevent the risk of tautological reasoning where any outcome can be explained *ex post* by a reassessment of the initial distribution of power. To avoid tautology, balance of power theories in fact require an actor-based relational rather than a structural-positional power approach.[19] Second, this approach allows for *competing* unit and system-level explanations of international events (see also Chapter 3 of this book). To give up the mechanical view of the balance of power has more implications than is usually acknowledged. If international politics is articulated along unpredictable patterns of the actors' amity and enmity (Wolfers 1962) or of the 'homogeneous or heterogeneous' character of the international society of states (Aron 1984a: 108 f.), then no extrapolation can be done from the distribution of power. The balance of power theories are indeterminate (Wolfets 1962: 86). Or the other way round: a structural analysis based on the anarchy assumption might exclude security and behavioural options that features of amity and homogeneity create at the level of interaction.

As we have seen, Gilpin's neo-mercantilist project is a somewhat ambiguous mix, or an 'ambivalent juxtaposition'[20] of a scientific (choice-) theoretical ideal on an historical approach – at first hand a puzzle for those used to classifying him into the scientific corner of Realism. The mix should rather be read the other way round. Gilpin is a historicist realist who tries to clarify the assumptions that underlie many traditional empiricist accounts of international politics, namely utilitarian thinking and consequentialist ethics. Unfortunately, he dismisses debate about these assumptions with a single reference to an underdiscussed liberal political theory and to choice-theoretical approaches, both acceptable to the main canons of IR/IPE. His first and only reaction to meta-theoretical critique is telling in this regard.[21]

This is also the general thrust of the following critique of this neo-mercantilist project: in a sense the later writings of Gilpin restrict the interdisciplinary exchange to which his own approach had initially contributed. On the one hand his project consisted in a more general critique of how IR should be analysed (namely as IPE), i.e. in an attempt to overcome Realism by integrating some of its insights. On the other hand, the turn to a more systemic hegemonic stability theory and the state/market nexus provided no more than an update of Realism. Being one of the forerunners of IPE as a redefinition of IR, Gilpin might unwittingly have 'normalized' it to an unchallenging subcategory of international and increasingly US politics.

By insisting on the necessity of a theory of the state, he opens the door to both 'comparative political economy' and historical sociology, disciplines that have became increasingly isolated within IR. Both approaches study the articulation of the particular state–society nexus in the changing global political economy, either by in-depth studies of one case or by more macro-level comparisons.[22] In stressing both the transnationalization of production and the adaptation processes at the societal level, Gilpin should logically proceed to analyse transnational blocking groups and lobbies and integrate the study of domestic dynamics with transnational ones.[23] In short, seen from this perspective transnational actors and networks cannot be reduced to the outside environment of state action, but must be regarded as participating in a single realm of world politics.

Yet Gilpin repeatedly shifts back to a policy-making level. An example is his discussion of Third World development, where he rightly points to domestic reasons for underdevelopment, but in fact bypasses them. 'Those less developed societies that have put their houses in order and have created efficient domestic economies have succeeded in achieving very rapid rates of economic growth' (1988a: 205). This explanation begs the question: how can a country with a specific social formation, a particular position in the global political economy, and specific transnational links put its house in order? What are the systematic and what the contingent constraints and opportunities, including the domestic history of social groups and the collective memory that patterns political debate and the active understanding of issues?

Despite his own analysis of the vertical integration via firms, of the increasing globalization of political economy, it is as if politics were conducted only by states. This could be due to the central role of hegemons in the theory and thus the concentration on great power policies. Or maybe it is because the role of the (realist) writer to provide counsel to the prince (1986: 320) requires a state-policy oriented perspective.

Yet returning to a national (or state) perspective has consequences for the very identification of the problems of the present global political economy. There is first of all a reduction of liberalism to a free-trade order (1986: 311ff.). Protectionism therefore represents the main evil to be avoided. This appraisal is influenced by the historical lesson of the interwar period, with competitive 'beggar-thy-neighbour' policies, or more aggressive ways to export the burden of domestic adjustments abroad. In this reading, the welfare state is as much a liberal domestic solution as an international problem. Gilpin is, however, well aware that today's technological and economic change has brought about a system of international production where international trade is decreasingly important and the major flows either are goods exchanged within firms (also across different states) or are in the form of capital, know-how or other forms of what is called the 'New Foreign Direct Investments' (patents, licences, domestic savings used for FDIs, and so on). In other words, it seems clear that, contrary to Gilpin's opinion, the 'health' of the global market system can hardly be satisfactorily measured with the thermometer of its free trade conviction.

This signifies that the liberal international order has to cope with a transnational agenda, where national reversals to more neo-liberal policies, which Gilpin at times notes with tentative approval, only increase the fiscal crisis at the state level, not on the expense, but on the income side. Far from preparing a return to a less national (because less state-interventionist) order, neo-liberal policies, in fact, constitute a kind of nationalist strategy in the new global competition for foreign investment and market shares.

Gilpin's focus on trade might induce one to think that if only multilateral management of national trade policies were introduced, the liberal order could be saved. Yet the novelty is not hegemonic decline and rising protectionism, but the global stage of production. The difficulty is not the rising use of national economic policy means, i.e. an affirmation of national sovereignty that could be negotiated with others, but the increasing power-lessness of these very means at the disposal of individual states.[24] Even if we had a hegemon, in today's world, the hegemon could hardly enforce a liberal order as before.

It is difficult not to have the impression that Gilpin's very legitimate interest in the adaptation of his own society eventually plays a trick on his neo-mercantilist approach: it becomes increasingly not only state, but US-centred. The link to social formations, elsewhere neglected, reappears in the implicit (and sometimes explicit) US agenda. Although Gilpin has helped to open many new routes in the study of politics, widely conceived, he may thus have contributed to making IPE just a particular subfield of the 'American science' IR.

CONCLUSION

Informed by a historical analysis of different orders in the international political economy, Gilpin has challenged established realist IR and proposed to renew it as neo-mercantilist IPE. The basic questions in his research concern the dynamics of power and powers. Gilpin set out a research programme which can be divided into three sets of problems: the identifica-tion of state dynamics, socioeconomic dynamics and the tensions in global governance. As the preceding chapter attempted to show, this research programme incorporates many more historical and conceptual facets than the official version of neo-realism made the discipline believe. His intellec-tual breadth makes him a classical realist who plays with the potential of utilitarian analysis, rather than one of those rational choice scholars who want to discipline IR/IPE on the basis of economic methodology.

Maybe the development of the nation-state and of the last phase of global productive integration requires a further step outside the neo-mercantilist logic. Maybe the opening to the historical sociology of social formations demands a greater sensitivity towards meta-theoretical and theoretical cri-tiques of utilitarian approaches. Gilpin provides some hints, he openly acknowledges theoretical and normative tensions and yet he remains un-decided. Apart from his many historical, conceptual and theoretical in-sights, it is this honesty which honours his work and still provides needed thinking space for the discipline.

NOTES

I would like to thank the participants of the two meetings in Oslo and Florence for comments on the previous draft of the chapter. Moreover, I am indebted to Monika Berkman for language-editing the text.

1 To what extent it makes sense to present IR/IPE in three opposing schools will be treated later in section II.
2 So also for the advent of nuclear weapons; see Gilpin (1988b: 613).

3 For this early and trenchant critique, see in particular Raymond Aron (1984a). For a late and insufficient response to this critique, see Kenneth Waltz (1990).

4 For this and the following, see Gilpin (1977: 21 ff.).

5 Gilpin (1972) interpreted the interwar period as a period where one leader was not strong enough and the other not willing to play the leader for the establishment of a liberal international order. This thesis got its authorative formulation by Kindleberger (1987) to whom Gilpin later often refers.

6 For this and the following, see Gilpin (1981: 55–84).

7 For its classical statement, see John Gerard Ruggie (1983). For a discussion, see Chapter 7 of this book.

8 To cite just some of the innumerable triads in IR, see K. J. Holsti (1985) and Michael Banks (1985). In IPE, see R. J. Barry Jones (1981), Nazli Choucri (1980), and finally Stephen Gill and David Law (1988).

9 See, as an example, already ten years later: Martin Staniland (1985).

10 The concept and the analysis to which Gilpin refers are from John Gerard Ruggie (1982). See also Chapter 7 of this book.

11 This section owes much to Anna Leander.

12 The same logic applies to Krasner's (1982: 498–500) image of the 'two tectonic plates', which might produce an earthquake (major conflict), if the shifts in one (distribution of power) are not reflected in the other (international regimes).

13 For the original statement, see Kindleberger (1987: 288–95; and 1981: 247). For Gilpin's initial formulation, see 1972; for his more developed formulation, see 1987a: 368.

14 For instance, Kenneth Waltz (1969: 312) says: 'Extreme equality [among states] is associated with extreme instability.'

15 For this unexpected idealism in a staunch Realist, see Charles P. Kindleberger (1976: 10).

16 For Gilpin, the fundamental change in recent world politics is an inextricable link between technological and power competition. This provides the background against which the end of the Cold War must be understood.

17 For an account of the most efficient technology policies, see Gilpin (1982).

18 The formulation refers to John Rawls. See in particular his turn of the 1980s (Rawls 1985: 248–9; and 1987: 4 ff.). One of the potential differences is that realism says to accept any (national) value-system, whereas Rawlsian liberalism requires the necessary acceptance of principles of justice for a conception of the good to be admitted.

19 Since the 1970s, this point has been repeatedly advanced by David Baldwin. See his 1989.

20 For the critique of this Realist strategy to overcome its inherent tension between structuralism and historicism in general, but applied to Gilpin, see R. B. J. Walker (1987: 78f.).

21 'The Richness of the Tradition of Political Realism' is a response to Ashley's (1986) critique of neo-realism in which Gilpin does not even mention the meta-theoretical level on which Ashley's critique is pitched.

22 Representative of others, see Peter Katzenstein (1985) and Theda Skočpol (1984).

23 This is one of the tenets of more radical political economy, as, for instance, in Robert Cox (1987).

24 In her recent writings, Susan Strange (1994; and together with John Stopford, 1991) is stressing the diffusion and 'disappearance' of authority.

REFERENCES

Works by Robert Gilpin

Gilpin, Robert (1968a) *France in the Age of the Scientific State*, Princeton, NJ: Princeton University Press.

—— (1968b) 'European Disunion and the Technology Gap', *The Public Interest* 10: 43–54.

—— (1968c) 'Of Course the Gap's Not Really Technological', *The Public Interest* 12: 124–9.

—— (1972) 'The Politics of Transnational Economic Relations', in Robert Keohane and Joseph Nye, Jr (eds) *Transnational Relations and World Politics*, Cambridge, MA: Harvard University Press.

—— (1975a) 'Three Models of the Future', *International Organization* 29(1): 37–60.

—— (1975b) *U.S. Power and the Multinational Corporation: The Political Economy of Foreign Direct Investment*, New York: Basic Books.

—— (1977) 'Economic Interdependence and National Security in Historical Perspective', in Klaus Knorr and Frank N. Trager (eds) *Economic Issues and National Security*, Lawrence, KS: Regents Press of Kansas.

—— (1981) *War and Change in World Politics*, Cambridge, MA: Cambridge University Press.

—— (1982) 'Trade, Investment, and Technology Policy', in Herbert Giersch (ed.) *Emerging Technologies: Consequences for Economic Growth, Structural Change, and Employment*, Tübingen: J. C. B. Mohr.

—— (1986) 'The Richness of the Tradition of Political Realism', in Robert O. Keohane (ed.) *Neo-realism and Its Critics*, New York: Columbia University Press (originally published 1984 in *International Organization* 38(2): 287–304).

—— (1987a) with the assistance of Jean M. Gilpin, *The Political Economy of International Relations*, Princeton, NJ: Princeton University Press.

—— (1987b) 'American Policy in the Post-Reagan Era', *Daedalus* 166(3): 33–67.

—— (1988a) 'Development and Underdevelopment: Conflicting Perspectives on the Third World', in Sidney Hook, William O'Neill and Roger O'Toole (eds) *Philosophy, History and Social Action: Essays in Honor of Lewis Feuer*, Dordrecht: Kluwer Academic Publishers.

—— (1988b) 'The Theory of Hegemonic War', *Journal of Interdisciplinary History* 18(4): 591–613.

—— (1990) 'The Global Political System', in J. D. B. Miller and John Vincent (eds) *Order and Violence: Hedley Bull and International Relations*, Oxford: Clarendon Press.

—— (1991) *The Transformation of the International Political Economy*, Jean Monnet Chair Papers, Florence: the European Policy Unit at the European University Institute.

—— and Bienen, Henry, (1980) 'Economic Sanctions as a Response to Terrorism', *Journal of Strategic Studies* 3(1): 89–98.

Works by other authors

Aron, Raymond (1984a [1962]) *Paix et guerre entre les nations*, 8th edn, Paris: Calmann-Lévy.

Ashley, Richard K. (1986 [1983]) 'The Poverty of Neo-realism', in Robert O. Keohane (ed.) *Neo-realism and Its Cities* New York: Columbia University Press.

—— (1984b) *Les dernières années du siècle*, Paris: Julliard.

Baldwin, David (1989) *Paradoxes of Power*, Oxford and New York: Basil Blackwell.

Banks, Michael (1985) 'The Inter-Paradigm Debate', in Margot Light and A. J. R. Groom (eds) *International Relations. A Handbook in Current Theory*, London: Frances Pinter.

Barry Jones, R. J. (1981) 'International Political Economy: Problems and Issues – Part I', *Review of International Studies* 7: 245–60.

Carr, E. H. (1946) *The Twenty Years' Crisis 1919–1939: An Introduction to the Study of International Relations*, 2nd edn, London: Macmillan.

Choucri, Nazli (1980) 'International Political Economy: a Theoretical Perspective', in A. L. George, O. R. Holsti and R.M. Siverson (eds) *Change in the International System*, Boulder, CO: Westview Press.

Cox, Robert W. (1987) *Production, Power and World Order: Social Forces in the Making of History*, New York: Columbia University Press.

Gill, Stephen and Law, David (1988) *The Global Political Economy*, New York: Harvester.

Holsti, K. J. (1985) *The Dividing Discipline: Hegemony and Diversity in International Theory*, Boston, MA: Allen and Unwin.

Katzenstein, Peter (1985) *Small States in World Markets: Industrial Policy in Europe*, Ithaca, NY and London: Cornell University Press.

Keohane, Robert O. (1984) *After Hegemony: Co-operation and Discord in the World Political Economy*, Princeton, NJ: Princeton University Press.

Kindleberger, Charles P. (1976) 'International Public Goods without International Government', *American Economic Review* 76(1): 1–12.

——(1981) 'Dominance and Leadership in the International Economy: Exploitation, Public Goods, and Free Rides', *International Studies Quarterly* 25(2): 242–54.

——(1987 [1973]) *The World in Depression 1929–1939*, 2nd edn, Harmondsworth, Mx: Penguin Books.

Krasner, Stephen D. (1982) 'Regimes and the Limits of Realism: Regimes as Autonomous Variables', *International Organization* 36(2): 497–510.

Morgenthau, Hans J. (1948) *Politics among Nations: The Struggle for Power and Peace*, New York: Alfred A. Knopf.

Rawls, John (1985) 'Justice as Fairness: Political not Metaphysical', *Philosophy and Public Affairs* 14(3): 223–51.

——(1987) 'The Idea of an Overlapping Consensus', *Oxford Journal of Legal Studies* 7(1): 1–25.

Ruggie, John Gerard (1982) 'International Regimes, Transactions, and Change: Embedded Liberalism in the Postwar Economic Order', *International Organization* 36(2): 379–415.

——(1983) 'Continuity and Transformation in the World Polity: Toward a Neo-realist Synthesis', in Robert O. Keohane (ed.) (1986) *Neo-realism and Its Critics*, New York: Columbia University Press.

Skočpol, Theda (ed.) (1984) *Visions and Method in Historical Sociology*, Cambridge, MA: Cambridge University Press.

Staniland, Martin (1985) *What is Political Economy?*, New Haven, CT and London: Yale University Press.

Stopford, John and Strange, Susan with Henley, John S. (1991) *Rival States, Rival Firms: Competition for World Market Shares*, Cambridge: Cambridge University Press.

Strange, Susan (1994 [1988]) *States and Markets: Introduction to International Political Economy*, 2nd edn, London: Frances Pinter.

Walker, R. B. J. (1987) 'Realism, Change and International Political Theory', *International Studies Quarterly* 31(1): 65–86.

Waltz, Kenneth (1969 [1967]) 'International Structure, National Force, and the Balance of World Power', in James Rosenau (ed.) *International Politics and Foreign Policy: A Reader in Research and Theory*, New York: Free Press.

——(1986) 'Reflections on *Theory of International Politics*', in Robert O. Keohane (ed.) *Neo-realism and Its Critics*, New York: Columbia University Press.

——(1990) 'Realist Thought and Neo-realist Theory', *Journal of International Affairs* 44: 21–38.

Wolfers, Arnold (1962) *Discord and Collaboration: Essays on International Politics*, Baltimore, MD: Johns Hopkins University Press.

6 Bertrand Badie: cultural diversity changing international relations?

Anna Leander

Bertrand Badie, born in 1950, studied political science, law, contemporary history and oriental studies at the Institut d'Etudes Politiques de Paris, at Paris-I and at the Institut de Langues Orientales. He received his doctoral degree from the IEP in 1975 ('Le PCF et la Grève') and became an 'agrégé' of political science in 1982. He has taught at Paris-I, the Université de Clermont-Ferrand I and the Ecole des Hautes Etudes en Sciences Sociales and he is currently professor at the Institut d'Etudes Politiques and director of 'les collections des Presses de Sciences Po'.

Bertrand Badie is professor at the Institut d'Etudes Politiques de Paris, where he teaches International Relations. However, Badie's involvement in 'International Relations' (IR) is recent. Most of his publications deal with state-building and comparative politics where international aspects are no doubt important but not central. Badie's recent involvement in IR is the logical outcome of his earlier work. Both his critique of theories and concepts claiming universal validity and his studies of political development inside and outside western Europe lead to a recognition of the plurality of meanings and of the concrete problems that arise when several coexisting perceptions of the world interact with, dominate and change each other. In his view, the legitimacy crisis of states outside the West is the result of a contradiction between the imported/imposed practice of the state and practices organizing political life according to another logic or rationality. The legitimacy crisis of the 'imported' state in turn affects the international system. The international is therefore essential both for understanding political problems and for resolving them. 'International Relations', though of an unusual kind, take a central place in the study.

This chapter argues that IR can benefit from the work of a newcomer/outsider like Badie. Badie is concerned with one of the most central issues in the theoretical and methodological debates, namely the implications of cultural plurality for the theory and practice of IR. Rather than drawing on philosophical and meta-theoretical discussions, he draws on comparative politics and owes more to anthropology than to philosophy, more to Geertz than to Derrida. This approach may enrich the discussion in IR and perhaps open up new fields of dialogue.

Badie, who has done both theoretical and applied work, is more than a theoretician interested in applied studies or an area specialist with some concern for theory. His method reflects a central theoretical proposition: that theories and concepts with claims to universal validity cannot be used to interpret social relations. The only way to understand political and social phenomena is to treat both history and culture seriously. This chapter starts with a summary of the main theoretical claims, proceeds to discuss the treatment of one subject, the state, and finally discusses the relevance of Badie's work to current IR debates.

A CRISIS OF UNIVERSALISM?

Badie's theoretical work is part of a scholarly trend that opposes social theories which analyse and explain social phenomena with concepts valid at all times and for all societies, claiming to know the ultimate direction of history, such as Marxism or modernization theory. Such theories, Badie argues, have been disproved as political science and sociology have expanded outside western Europe (1985: 599). Time has also proved the inapplicability of overly general models. Developing countries have not followed prescribed paths. They have neither become images of western democracies nor necessarily remained in the 'periphery' of a world-system. Therefore, Badie argues, the social science are undergoing a crisis which 'stems from questioning universalism, monodeterminism and the compartmentalisation of political science and history. New paradigms are now being conceived to overcome this crisis: culturalism, social action and historical sociology' (1989a: 340). This crisis manifests itself in what Badie calls the 'three major crises of classical comparative analysis': the crises of universalism, of space and of time. In this section we will first pursue the arguments behind each crisis. Second, we will consider the use Badie makes of historical sociology to introduce the elements missing in a universalist analysis, namely history and culture. Last, we will suggest that the development of this approach is still tentative and in many ways understandable only in relation to Badie's applied research.

The expression of a crisis

Badie's first crisis is the 'crisis of universalism' or the crisis of *monocausal* explanations. A caricature of monocasual explanation that Badie often uses as an example is Robert Dahl's early claim that GNP growth determines the development of democracy. In more subtle forms the use of monocausal explanations in academia remains widespread. A main cause is sought and given a central position in an explanatory framework granted general validity. Badie sees this as the most common procedure in political science.

This type of explanation assumes that there is a specific logic underlying a system wherever and whenever that system operates. However, Badie points out that the factors most relevant to explanation vary with the context. Since societies do not function in a single way, no single theory, with its gamut of concepts, methods and categories, can adequately explain events.

A theory developed in a context different from the one under analysis may obscure more than it clarifies.

In addition, implicit in most monocausal explanations is the unidirectional assumption – if A (differentiation, economic development, strong state) then B (development of a modern state, democratization, economic development) – which disregards the evidence that similar events or developments might have not only varying but opposite effects in different contexts. In most cases it is the specific combination of construction of new structures and destruction of old ones which is important, so any deep-going sociological analysis must 'account for the totality of evolutive and devolutive factors', or, in other words, account not only for that which develops but also for that which disappears (Badie and Birnbaum 1979: 92).

This first crisis leads to a second, which Badie calls a 'crisis of explanation'. Having posited that social science can no longer apply a universal framework, Badie explains this in terms of the plurality of rationalities, linked to the cultures within which they have evolved. On Weberian lines, Badie argues that since people's motivations and behaviour are linked to their values, and their values are defined by culture, it is necessary to account for culture. Culture already gives rise to variations in behaviour among countries and regions in the western world, but when we look beyond it, its significance becomes even clearer. In this sense, the second crisis is a crisis of *space* provoked by the expansion of political science beyond the 'West', 'pointing to the fact that political processes cannot be studied without reference to cultural variables' (1989a: 343).

Finally, in addition to the difficulties caused by spatial expansion, generalizing explanations are shaken by a third crisis which Badie refers to as 'a crisis affecting the relation to history', or in other words a crisis related to *time*. Like culture, time changes the relevance of different variables. Historical change may invalidate a universal framework. The relevant factors for understanding 'state-building' in present-day developing countries are fundamentally different from those underlying the historical development of the states in western Europe. Badie refutes the all too common teleological assumption that history is governed by 'historical laws'. The 'less developed' will not necessarily evolve into the 'more developed'. On the contrary, respect for history entails recognizing that we have no means of knowing the future. What develops out of the present may be not a version of what already is, but something else. According to Badie there is, for instance, not one modernity towards which all countries evolve, but a plurality of modernities. Modernities in the Islamic world 'defy all known models, by taking new forms which in no way repeat the history of the western state-building' (1987a: 219).

To declare war on unicausal monodirectional theories may strike one as flogging a dead horse. Systemic theories as well as reductionist and ahistorical forms of Marxism seem discredited and abandoned along with Grand Social Theory in most academic camps. Yet, in many subjects, including IR, concepts are blithely transferred from one cultural and historical context to another and theories applied to widely different realities, as will be seen in greater detail below. This gives the criticism continued relevance.

The missing elements: history and culture

The causes underlying the crisis Badie discerns in the social sciences clearly indicate the elements which have to be introduced to resolve it: history and culture.

History is necessary to place social groups and institutions in their proper context. Standardized categories pave the way for misleading parallels and impede understanding. Badie argues that relations between social groups have to be looked at in context. The past of these relations, with the concomitant institutionalization and practice, indicates possible future development. It is, however, not enough to stress that concepts must be historically contextualized; a method to do so must also be developed. For this purpose Badie reverts to a specific brand of historical sociology.[1]

First Badie argues that authors who use a general model to explain historical events – Wallerstein, for instance – have made a valuable contribution by defining and refining abstract concepts in order to operationalize them. However, their concepts suffer from being based on a method designed to provide confirmation of an a priori theory. Since the model defines what the historian looks for, it is almost inevitable that myopia will lead him to observe the causal relations posited by the model from the outset. There is little check on other possible causal factors. Moreover, there is an inbuilt inclination to select and interpret material to make it 'fit' the categories defined by the theory.

Next Badie criticizes the approach of Skočpol and others, namely 'analyzing causal regularities in history' by comparing historical phenomena such as social revolutions, democracy or dictatorship, or revolutions from above. This approach aims at identifying common causes and structures underlying the events. According to Badie it assumes that the phenomena studied are essentially the same despite the underlying cultural diversity. A revolution in China is presumed to be the same as a revolution in Russia, a claim Badie challenges (1989a: 350).

Badie favours a third type of historical sociology where 'concepts are used to develop meaningful historical interpretation'.[2] This approach is not directed at hypothesis testing, but uses sociological concepts to make sense of historical trajectories. Through detailed case studies it also spells out the embeddedness of the concepts used. Comparative studies are especially pertinent in this process since they bring out embeddedness more clearly than single cases. 'The socio-historical identity of the modernity invented in the West...is only fully perceptible when opposed to another political order, constructed in another context, and facing other challenges, which engenders a practice of politics of a different nature' (1987a: 13). However, comparison can play this role only if cases are more than illustrations of preconceived theories. In other words, while Skočpol argues in favour of a 'variable-centred' approach, Badie defends a 'case-centred' approach.[3]

According to Badie, even this modest use of historical sociology is ridden with problems, which the researcher cannot resolve, but can reduce by critical awareness (1983: 97ff.). The main problem is that, as do all historical approaches, it tends to overrate continuities and underestimate ruptures. In making sense of history, one is unwittingly led to accentuate cumulative events and conditions while underestimating the role of the arbitrary. The researcher is led back to the domain of linear causalities and falls back on evolutionary arguments. Moreover, historical presentation tends to produce the impression that events are unified in a '*démarche totalisante*' (1983: 67). Badie follows Popper in warning about the risk inherent in summing up traits and events with possibly different causes and dynamics under a single heading and treating them as equivalent.

If introducing history appears problematic, introducing the second missing element, culture, is even more hazardous. Badie agrees with Weber that 'political order is above all the outcome of conflicts between individuals and groups with diverging material interests and values', and is therefore obliged to account for the divergence of values. But Weber himself, in Badie's reading, remained caught in an evolutionary vision and '*de facto* provides the criteria for a political modernization'. Weber classified all societies that do not follow the western pattern as non-rational and traditional (1985: 606–7). Badie underlines that such a classification is teleological, and that the binary categories rational-irrational, modern-traditional are inadequate tools for dealing with the empirical plurality of rationalities and political behaviour.

More sensitive concepts, defined in relation to the plurality of values, must be developed. Values are an essential aspect of culture, for which Badie uses Geertz's definition: culture is an 'intersubjective system of meaning' which informs action (1989a: 344). In other words, integrating culture in the study implies

> revealing the *cultural codes*, that is the integrated systems of meaning, formed in history, and filling the function of controlling the processes of social and political transformation. Accounting for these codes should then allow us to define the content and the orientations of the different social objects which specify each significant social space.
>
> (1983: 73)

This said, it is difficult to define a cultural code exactly and to propose how it should be revealed. The twofold tradition for treating culture in political science, as Badie sees it, has provided little to build on. The most common attitude by far is to ignore culture altogether. Authors who have incorporated 'culture' have usually done so 1) in a tautological way, or 2) as a residual category for explaining phenomena which cannot be accounted for by other means. The study of culture has been left to scholars in other disciplines, notably sociology and anthropology.[4]

To sum up, Badie argues that in order to introduce time and space in the analysis, it is necessary to develop a historical sociology of culture. However, there is little to build on. Authors in historical sociology offer a well-developed corpus regarding the use of history in sociology, yet contribute little to the study of culture. Those who have attempted to include culture – Skočpol, Barrington Moore and Wallerstein ignore it – have usually reduced it in different ways. Perry Anderson reduces it to the legal system and particularly to the regulation of property rights; Bendix reduces it to legitimacy and Stein Rokkan reduces it to religious institutions (Badie 1983: 61–7).

Towards a historical sociology of culture

Badie's own approach is not entirely clear-cut. He is more prone to point out the 'weakness' of the enterprise than to define it and specify how studies of 'the historical sociology of culture' should be pursued (1983: 133 ff. and 1989a: 344 ff). He makes the point that there is no *definition* of political culture or the elements that can be apprehended. Second, the *level of analysis*, viz. the limits of the community sharing a common political culture, is unclear. Should the limits be drawn according to nation, religion, language, tribe or clan? Third, political culture is *open and shifting*. Outside influences and interventions constantly modify it, making it virtually impossible to pin down its meaning. Fourth, *the status* of political culture as an operational concept is ambiguous. It cannot be more than a variable whose relative weight is always uncertain. Finally, Badie deplores that *falsification* of explanations in a historical sociology of culture is impossible (1983: 67).

However, when we examine Badie's project, these 'weak' points appear to be the consequence of a misconstrued attempt to evaluate the research with a set of criteria belonging to a theory based on precisely the universal assumptions Badie is rejecting. Rather than shortcomings, the points Badie makes logically follow from his project. How could there be a general definition of culture and method of approaching it, if the aim of the study is precisely to 'reveal the *cultural codes*, that is, the integrated systems of meaning, formed in history, and filling the function of control on the processes of social and political transformation'? How could there be a clear delimitation of the community appropriate to study, if concepts and categories (including community) are to be defined by the political culture of the object? Finally, how could such a project be termed in a Popperian way, allowing it to be tested?

Consider how Badie proposes to study modernity:

> political modernity, in what is its identity as well as in what has favoured or troubled its transfer [to areas outside the West], must be understood as a way of thinking politics, as a manner of accommodating relations of domination and hence of practising political development, and finally as a source of opposition mobilisation.
>
> (1987a: 15)

Does not a project couched in terms of 'thinking', 'accommodating relations of domination' and 'practising politics' sound like one suggested by those who refute methods which assume that a common exterior criterion can be used to test a theory?

It would seem that the major difficulty is the position on relativism and the related question of how it is possible from the perspective of one culture to understand a foreign culture, both left out of Badie's list of difficulties. How can claims to plurality of value-systems, of understandings of the self or the other, of modernities, and of rationalities coexist with the assumption of a single logic to account for them? In Badie's work there is a continuous tension between the particular, the non-transferable on the one hand, and the universal, the generalizable on the other. He emphasizes the need to develop universal concepts, to speak one language, and to study 'Reality', yet his studies are constructed around the claim that there are no generalizable explanations, that what has to be accounted for is the singular, that concepts change meaning in different contexts and cannot be transferred from one context to another, and that ultimately the rationalities change (1989a: 351). The ambiguity is well expressed in the statement: 'Rediscovering cultural plurality – and relativity – is a valuable acquisition in recent critical sociology; however, to fall into the most absolute culturalism and the most total relativism can only lead to paradox' (1987a: 10). Badie suggests no theoretical solution to this inherent problem which is after all not surprising. However, Badie's studies presuppose that it is possible to communicate between cultural codes. Through a process of studying and interacting with different cultural codes it is possible to understand them. This clearly requires applied studies.

POLITICAL CULTURE IN PRACTICE: THE STATE

Since the theoretical claims made by Badie are inseparable from the analysis of historical phenomena, a reference to it is important both to reflect its position in the work and to clarify theoretical points. This section will therefore concentrate on the applied study of 'historical sociology of culture'. We have seen that Badie defines culture as an intersubjective system of meaning (Geetz's definition). Political culture then becomes the intersubjective system of meaning underlying politics. It might further be recollected that modernity (a form of political culture) is defined 'as a way of thinking politics, as a manner of accommodating relations of domination and hence of practising a political development, and finally as source of opposition mobilisation' (1987a: 15). Three interwoven elements (thinking, practising and managing change), will be taken as the components of 'political culture'. We will show how Badie uses them to explain state-building in different contexts. First, 'practising politics' will be discussed mainly with regard to Europe through the work *La Sociologie de l'état* (Badie and Birnbaum 1979). The different European trajectories of state development underline that political culture is formed by practice and cannot be deduced from any single aspect (such as religion). Next, the aspect of political culture, 'thinking politics', will be discussed through Badie's comparison of state-building in the West (here treated as a unity) and in the Islamic world in *Les Deux Etats* (1987a). The difference in 'thinking politics' clarifies some fundamental differences in political culture. The 'management change', the last component of political culture, will be dealt with through *L'Etat importé* (1992a). This work shows that political culture is perpetuated *via* change. The generalization of the state outside western Europe masks diversities of political culture.[5] The problems caused by 'importing' state practices brought Badie to take a more active interest in IR.

The western state: practising politics

Badie and Birnbaum consider the *duality* of the secular and the religious common to western European political thinking. The Church and the Prince opposed each other 'precisely on the grounds of a duality of categories which all the actors accept, recognize *a priori*' (1983: 98). This, according to Badie, remains the case throughout the history of Christianity, including the absolutist period and the Reformation.[6] Since duality is a shared assumption, variations in political culture cannot be explained by religion alone. Instead political practice seems significant. For instance, the linking of feudalism with the establishment of a strong central state (absolutism) is supported by Badie and Birnbaum. But since feudalism took different forms across Europe, the states that emerged were correspondingly diverse. The initial trajectories become self-reinforcing and survive the cultural and historical context of their origin.

Some of Badie's arguments with regard to France and the UK can serve as illustrations. In France, national unification was slow and allegiance to the centre long remained weak. The state's reaction was centralization, which eventually perpetuated itself (Badie and Birnbaum 1979: 173–88). The first European army was French; from 1551 the king began to send out *fonctionnaires*, with powers overriding those of local officers; Richelieu systematically destroyed local fortifications; the revolutionary national assembly established eighty-three *départements* to undo regional communities; Napoleon definitely put the *administration* outside the realm of the common law; minds and education were increasingly controlled from the centre; and economic life was subjected to the control of the state through mercantilism and nationalization. The effect of centralization and extensive intervention was the formation of a bureaucracy and the creation of what Toqueville considered to be '*une classe particulière*' of '*fonctionnaires administratifs*'.

> The result is a particularly original relation between the categories of rulers. To the extent that the state, as organization, has made itself independent of the ruling class and of the entire civil society, it seems to monopolize the representative function of which Parliament is consequently deprived.
>
> (Badie and Birnbaum 1979: 187)

In Britain, on the contrary, the state developed through and reinforced relations of collaboration between the political centre and the periphery

(Badie and Birnbaum 1979: 196–203). Allegiance to the political centre was achieved early. The elites in Britain coexisted with the centre. The state did not centralize control. Instead of sending out emissaries to break up regional solidarities, it relied on locals. Moreover, the borders of Great Britain are more obvious than those of the continental countries. There was no reason to develop a strong army, and the navy was developed as much for conquering external markets as for military defence. 'In Great Britain, it is the market that dominates and not the state, whereas in France or in Prussia the state organizes the market.' The outcome was a weak state with a low level of institutionalization. The civil service developed late, and was kept apart from actual political power. In Britain the civil servants constitute an 'almost totally marginalized governing category'. The situation is one where, 'instead of a state, it is a social class that governs Great Britain, an establishment to which the middle classes and the local gentry are linked and which includes the aristocracy ... as well as the bourgeoisie' (Badie and Birnbaum 1979: 199).

In short, Badie argues that variation in historical practice in Europe has produced a range of political cultures. Consequently, in spite of a common religion, and a common way of understanding the world, European countries have developed different forms of states and diverging political cultures.

> Western political modernity derives its identity and its singularity from its relation to a historical context and shared stakes, and above all from a common culture.... Western political modernity ceases to be singular when it is analyzed in terms of concrete challenges represented by the construction of each of the European systems.
>
> (1987a: 13).

The state in the 'land of Islam': thinking politics

The second element of political culture, thinking about politics, comes to the fore in Badie's comparison of the Islamic world and the West. A radical difference between state-building in the Islamic world and in the West is that the contexts are marked by fundamentally different or even opposite ways of understanding politics. This does not presuppose an immutable 'Muslim' way of thinking politics. New practices and ideas are constantly integrated and old ones transformed. However, they are combined with the pre-existing political culture which persists, albeit in altered form.

According to Badie, politics in Islamic political 'thought' is diametrically opposed to western political thinking: the duality between temporal and spiritual is even more radically rejected than is commonly accepted. It is usually argued that early Islamic political thinking was tainted both by 'Islamic' and 'Hellenistic' traditions. According to Badie this thesis misinterprets the meaning of the Hellenistic imports and exaggerates the tensions they caused. Muslim political thinkers adjusted the Hellenistic concepts and theories to their own framework.

Arab thinkers used mainly Plato's monist and communitarian ideas, as distinct from the ideas of Aristotle, introduced in the West by Thomas Aquinas. Moreover, the parts of Plato which would have required a revision of the Islamic position on the unity of temporal and the spiritual were transformed. For instance, the Platonian concept of *nomos* (ideal), to which laws should conform to be just, was assimilated to the *Shari'a*.[7] Likewise, Fārābi justifies separating ideal and legitimate policies (revealed) from real and imperfect (human) ones with reference to Plato. Even in the Hellenistic version of Muslim political philosophy, Badie argues, human reason can be no more than instrumental in revealing the superiority of the divine law. The ignorant polity (ignorance not of reason but of divine revelation) – *djāhiliyya* – remains the rejectable polity. The search for revealed truth, not for rationality, explains the effort put into education and political persuasion by the *falāsifa* (e.g. Nāser ed-Din Tūsi). 'The Islamic scholastic of the *kalām* is founded on the double proposition that reason cannot be a substitute for the revealed truth and cannot consist in anything but a method of gaining access to this truth' (1987a: 49).[8]

The 'Hellenism' of the *falāsifa* remained essentially Islamic, in accepting the unity of the spiritual and the temporal. The unity of the religious and the political gives fundamental political concepts a new meaning. Unlike its western counterpart, Islamic political theory makes a sharp distinction between *power* as authority and power as *puissance*. Whereas the former is in the hands of God, the latter is the empirically observable human

Table 6.1 Modernity viewed by contemporary thinkers from the Muslim world

current	*vision of modernity*	*main exponents*
reformists	compatibility of Islam and modernity; only sign of rupture is in the acceptance of nation-state defined in terms of continuity	Rifà'a Ràfi' al-Tahtawi, Ibn Abi Diāf, Khayer-ad-Din, Husayn al-Marsafi, Mustafa Kāmil
revivalists	the need to return to the sources and to find the roots of an alternative modernity, and to discover alternative political forms; Islam accepted not only as religion but as civilization	Djamal-ad-Din al-Afghani, Muhamad 'Abduh, Rashid Ridā, Ahmad Khān Bahādur
Islamists	same as revivalists, but in addition there is the radical incompatibility between Islam and western modernity, and the responsibility for failed modernity is imputed to this incompatibility	Hasan al-Bannā, 'Abd al-Kādir 'Audah, Abū al-'Alā al-Mawdūdi, Sayyid Kutb
secular (mainly socialism, *ba'thism*)	secular modernity based on the nation-state to be imported from the West	Shibli Shumayyil, Farah Antūn, Michel Aflak, Salāmah Mūsa

power, necessary to maintain social order. The first is tied to legitimacy, the second to necessity. In this context *legitimacy* can never be constructed around human reason, but is religiously derived.

Political thinking in predominantly Muslim countries continues to reflect the unity of the temporal and the spiritual. First, the political debate around modernity and the effects of importing state and political practices from the West have continuously been posed in terms of their compatibility or incompatibility with the Muslim religion (Table 6.1). Second, the importance of religious movements in politics indicates continuity. They are often the origin of the political opposition since they, more than other movements, are able to challenge the legitimacy of the regime by claiming to know 'the right' interpretation of the revelation, but also because they are difficult to repress and can be controlled only at the risk of eroding legitimacy. Inversely, the limited role of non-religious radical political movements, notably Marxism, mirrors a lack of legitimacy sharpened by the role of minorities in these movements (Armenians, Jews and Christians).

Badie summarizes the continuity in political thinking in his idea of a *culture of riot* as opposed to a culture of citizens in the West. In the Muslim world, 'political dialogue' is inconceivable. Political opposition is directed against the political scene as such, whereas in the West demands for political change aim for specific policies. Opposition is expressed in riots, not in debate. Political opposition explodes as the community (not the individual) considers the political power-holder illegitimate. Badie would not claim that thinking about politics alone could explain the culture of riot. Differences in political practice are equally significant. The strong vertical solidarities (family, ethnicity, regions, etc.) in most Muslim countries weaken the role of horizontal solidarities, diminishing the potential role of trade unions and political parties in mediating and channelling political demands.

Governments live with the culture of riot by controlling the political periphery. Because of the radicalism of political opposition, they try to contain it by combining repression with neo-patrimonial and clientelistic practices. This only increases the radicalism of an opposition which sees that the path to negotiated political change is blocked (Table 6.2).

In short, making sense of politics in the Muslim world requires an understanding of Islamic political thought. Islamic political thought, notably the lack of separation between the religious and the temporal, leads to a specific perception of essential aspects of political life, including community, individuality, legitimacy, sovereignty and property. This informs political actors' understanding of themselves and others. Moreover, the political thinking prevalent in the Muslim world is one of the main factors creating a political culture of riot, as opposed to a European culture of citizenship. Because of this political culture, governments in Muslim countries are trapped in vicious circles: the culture of riot obliges rulers to control the political periphery. To do this they rely on clientelism and repression. Clientelism and repression block democratic change and radicalize an already radical

Table 6.2   Contemporary political regimes' handling of the culture of riot

	relations with social groups	legitimacy	central actor, power-holder	examples
conservative	relying on relations with traditional local leaders	traditional, absence of foreign influences	king, traditional leader	Ottoman Empire, Persia, Morocco, Gulf states
revolutionary	rejection of traditional elites, construction of new solidarities	modernization project, nationalism	army, bureaucracy, technocrats	Kemalist Turkey, Iran, Mossadegh's, Algeria, Nasser's Egypt
counter-modernization	rejection of traditional elites, alliance with the miserable	restoration project, religion	religious establishment	post-revolutionary Iran

opposition. This in turn reinforces the need to control the periphery, the reliance on clientelistic relations, and vertical solidarities.

The 'imported state': managing change

The vicious circle identified in the states of the Islamic world has a direct bearing on the third component of political culture: the management of change. The mode of change not only influences the prevailing political culture, but also sets the stage for possible future transformations. In *The Imported State*, Badie generalizes insights and conclusions from his studies of the state in the Muslim world to other non-western cultures which also imported political practice, imported ideologies, imported institutional roles for political parties and for the administration.[9] Their legal systems are expected to resolve conflicts in a society for which they were not designed, and over which the laws usually have little or no grip.

> The reality is that, interiorised as it may be by local elites, the state model does not function and merely reproduces itself formally in the societies of the third world[...] the state in Africa as in Asia remains a pure product of importation, a pale copy of the European political and social systems, a heavy, inefficient foreign body and a source of violence.
>
> (Badie and Birnbaum 1979: 163).

A threefold logic underlies the import of the western state model, as follows.

First, an interactive logic of *dependency* spurs import (1992a: 36). By dependency, Badie means a system where the leaders are dependent economically, but also technologically and symbolically, on interaction with 'patron states'. Even states defining their identity by refusing the 'West' (India, Libya) remain tributary to this same West for their political system as well as their negative identity. Dependency is expressed in 'sovereignty appro-priations' (1987a: 55 ff.). The diplomatic, socioeconomic and institutional activities of client states are taken over by the patrons to a certain extent. However, the clearest expression of dependency is the lack of (institutional, ideological, technological, symbolic or economic) alternatives.

Second, the western state is imported and maintained because of its *universalist pretensions.* In the western intellectual tradition, the state is the outcome of the spread of knowledge and reason. The warnings of classical thinkers, including Weber and Durkheim, that the state is rooted in a specific culture and might not be transferable have been constantly forgotten and ignored. Instead, political development is equated with the adoption of this model. The 'hegemony of western modernity' further spreads with the 'westernization of the international scene' through 1) the 'territorialization of the world' (1992a: 82 ff.); 2) the use of western international law (1992a: 102 ff.); and 3) the 'rules of the international game' (1992a: 110 ff.). Since the treaties of Westphalia, the state is expected to monopolize international violence. The international system rests on the 'fiction of sovereignty'.

Lastly, the western state is imported because a *'class of importers'*, a state elite (bureaucratic or intellectual), makes it part of its strategies. These strategies are partially a matter of choice. Rulers often adopt foreign techniques to strengthen themselves against external (Ottoman Empire, Turkish Republic) or internal (Meji Japan) threats. Likewise, revolutionary leaders use imported political practices and ideologies to distance them-selves from the West (Indonesia's or Zimbabwe's use of socialism). How-ever, imports are also involuntary. Policies pursued often have *unintended consequences.* The introduction of clocks in the Ottoman Empire was an (unintended) consequence of the army's modernization and it had the (unintended) consequence of challenging the ulema's authority. Moreover, policies may have *composition effects.* Atatürk's modernization policies implied measures that polarized the army against the religious establish-ment – initially allies – and eventually led to the abolition of the caliphate (1926).

The logic that leads to adopting the state also indicates major problems in managing the ensuing change. Dependency on the West, difficulties in escaping the universalistic pretensions of the state, and inclusion of imports in elite strategies hinder the development of real alternatives. As the political centre increasingly relies on and lives in an imported political culture, it cuts itself off from the more traditional sections of society. A vicious circle similar to that observed in the Muslim world is formed. Governments pay off various groups and end up in a neo-patrimonial logic which blocks democratic change. This vicious circle is most visible in the absence of civil societies based on a division of public/private spheres, an individualization of social relations, citizenship, horizontal solidarities, and the spread of associations (1992a: 116–18). The more or less authoritarian attempts to emulate a controllable civil society through corporatist strategies or personal 'father of the nation' incitements invariably fail. Political protests, conse-quently, direct themselves against the political system as such rather than against specific policies or individuals. 'Internal disorder' is the consequence of the failure to universalize the state. The problems of the Islamic state no longer appear isolated, related to a specific way of thinking about politics, but as the outcome of general difficulties in managing political change.

The difficulty of coming to terms with change influences the international order. Discontent is rarely contained in a national sphere. Movements of protest are typically rooted in solidarities rejecting the 'national community' as the adequate space of political dissent. Religious and ethnic movements have no reason to stop at national borders. On the contrary, media are formidable promoters of cross-border solidarities. The international 'order' becomes directly affected as radical movements oppose the legitimacy of the international order as such. Protests are directed against international borders (the Iran–Iraq war) or crystallized around international objects (oil in the Aegean) or issues (the Rushdie affair). The international order may spread state practice, but the difficulties of imported states in turn undermine the international order.

Badie's concept of the imported state underlines that the fate of nations and, more importantly, the destiny of the people within their boundaries, are inseparable from the international system. Globalization invalidates the original culture and the 'happy savage'. It will probably not give countries who need to solve their political problems the breathing-space necessary to do so. Since the difficulties intrinsic in the imported state cannot be considered or resolved on a national level, the international system is of immediate concern. Moreover, the international system is becoming increasingly affected by the legitimacy crises of states outside the West. Civil wars, disputes over state boundaries and increasingly militant rejection of the West appear as chief causes for international 'disorders' at present. This is where Badie's work is of relevance to the debates in International Relations.

BERTRAND BADIE AND THE DEBATES IN INTERNATIONAL RELATIONS

The opening lines in *Le Retournement du monde* (the reversal of the world) state that the international system is the most unstable of all political systems, and that the crisis of the nation-state, though not in itself sufficient to explain this instability, is a link connecting many issues (Badie and Smouts 1992: 11). From the outset the crisis of universalism at the level of the state is directly tied to the international level. Indeed, the reversal of both the conventional world order and of the tools for analysing it, is the conclusion of Badie's earlier work on the plurality of the state and on the non-transferability of concepts across cultural borders. In this section we will first examine the reasons for which Badie and Smouts argue that the plurality of actors and of frames of reference makes it impossible to retain conventional conceptions of national and international politics. Then we will place their arguments in the French IR tradition. Badie's work ties up with the work of Raymond Aron. However, unlike Aron, Badie rejects a higher level theory for the international system. This brings us to the debates in general IR theory, where Badie's work is best seen as a contribution to 'critical' or 'reflectivist' writing.

The reversal of International Relations

The present international system is the reverse of what it is commonly presented to be. This is Badie's and Marie-Claude Smouts's central claim. The international system cannot be seen as resting on the triad of sovereignty, territoriality and security which is said to organize politics, space and motives. It 'is more diffuse in terms of power and more dispersed in terms of action, it emancipates individuals and groups but restricts sovereignty, liberates particularism and impedes institutionalization' (Badie and Smouts 1992: 241). To account for this new order, or increased disorder, the authors argue that it is necessary to step outside the conventional boundaries of IR theory and to draw on the 'new horizons which the progress in sociology, in comparative politics and in the study of transnational flows offer' (Badie and Smouts 1992: 19). However, the work remains allusive as to what these contribute. The book's limited ambition is to be 'less than a work of theory but more than a simple introduction, [its ambition] is to be a guide through the labyrinth of events and approaches' in IR (Badie and Smouts 1992: 11). Three issues dominate the book: 1) the proliferation of international actors; 2) the impossibility of disregarding the effects of the interaction of a plurality of rationalities; and 3) the ensuing need for a revision of traditional IR concepts based on a single rationality.

A plurality of actors

The claim that the state is no longer the only, or even the central, actor in IR remains controversial. However, the idea that states have little in common but their denomination is likely to be even more contentious in a subject which has been based on the assumption that all states are equal, at least in principle.

Reversing the customary explanation of problems with sovereignty as being caused by transnationalism, Badie and Smouts point to the uncertainty of the nature of the state as one of the factors fuelling the development of *transnational flows*. The legitimacy deficit of imported states fuels alternative, often infra-national and supra-national, solidarities and legitimacy forms, which by definition disregard the limits of the state. Further, the uncertainty of the nature of the state, augmented by the transformation of states (the end of empire), gives free rein to new nationalist and particularist claims (as in the former USSR). The increase in internationally articulated religious and ethnic claims can be seen in this perspective. In a more conventional vein, Badie and Smouts also join the chorus of voices in IR and political science pointing to the effect of transnational flows on political order and the legitimacy of states. The identity of the state is directly affected by the large number of transnational flows. The central role of the state as provider of security, the sovereign and upholder of order on its territory, is constantly threatened as non-state actors take over part of these functions or contest the right of the state to keep them.

The plurality of non-state actors marks the 'revenge of the real and concrete societies on a rather abstract state order' (Badie and Smouts 1992: 70). New international actors emerge to challenge the artificially constituted state. This 'restricts' the state's ability to act. The state cannot master flows, more stable and more perennial, linked to 'long conjunctures, and to des *variables lourdes*'.[10] State policies and conventional diplomatic techniques are inept in dealing with conflictual relations which transcend the interstate realm such as international protests (non-governmental organizations) and violence (terrorism) (Badie and Smouts 1992: 110).

A plurality of rationalities

The plurality of actors leads to a plurality of rationalities interacting in the international system (Badie and Smouts 1992: 24). Each new actor, emerging on the international scene, has a political culture of its own, and its own perception of the identity of self and other, of past and present. To the extent that this perception motivates (international) action, it excludes the possibility that a universal system or theory could account for the international system.

This is not only significant for the *many new areas* of transnational interaction, as has been implied by many students of IR, but Badie and Smouts also argue that it fundamentally alters the outlook on *traditional issues* in IR. For instance, accepting the idea that states are not the same and that they follow differently defined rationalities, means that strategic thinking has to be revised. The effect of plural rationalities is strongest outside the conventional diplomatic sphere. Conflicts evade the control of the state. They take place between states with different political cultures, but also between entities which do not share the same state or even explicitly deny it. Armed conflict often involves movements that either defy the state (civil wars) or simply ignore it (organized crime). Diplomacy loses its effectiveness as it has to deal with movements outside the beaten path, that follow different rules or explicitly reject the diplomatic rules. 'Already largely utopian in the old inter-state system, the regulation of war and the pacific settlement of conflicts has disappeared with the privatization of violence' (Badie and Smouts 1992: 184).

Badie and Smouts recognize that there is a conventional sphere of interstate action managed by diplomats sharing a diplomatic culture. *A la* James Rosenau they therefore separate the sphere of statecraft from a sphere of transnational relations. While the state sphere is stable and functions according to an international diplomatic culture, non-state relations are unstable and follow no predetermined, or rather a myriad of, logic(s) and culture(s).

Thus, the sociology of IR is constantly confronted with a duality of codes: for the necessities of international exchanges, a universal code apparently constructed around the notion of sovereignty; for the deep forces, a multiplicity of repertoires, of which it is impossible to know which one will be used.

(Badie and Smouts 1992: 145–6)

In these conditions it is difficult to establish norms and rules for most international action. There can be no question of a rule arrived at by consensus of all the international actors. This does not exclude that rules and norms govern behaviour in certain spheres of international life. However, these cannot in any sense be conceived as permanent consensus or rationality-based. International rules and norms are reinterpreted and disputed at all times. There is a constant disregard of the 'rules of the game' by those who deny their validity.

The revenge of the actor on the system

The methodological consequence that Badie and Smouts draw from the increased complexity of the relations is that the actor has to be granted a more central place in the analysis. The actor takes revenge on the system (Badie and Smouts 1992: 240). It is necessary to find a way of accounting for the multiple rationalities, for the multiplicity of identities, cultures and motives interacting internationally. To ignore them would be disastrous both for understanding international phenomena and for any practical translation of this into political practice. 'In general, by reducing the other to the self, actors lose all rationality, yet believe themselves to be acting in the name of a universal rationality' (Badie and Smouts 1992: 28). However, integrating the multiplicity of rationalities present in the second 'code' of the '*forces profondes*', is more easily said than done. The authors hint at the need to revise the central concepts of IR, viz. Badie's exhortations to abandon universalizing approaches and introduce historically and culturally sensitive studies. However, IR has been particularly resistant to change:

Since it cannot function on all these levels, the theory of IR has a tendency to privilege that of universality, residing on ground cleared by European history and philosophy from which it draws its main arguments. The academic divide between internationalists and specialists of 'exotic' political systems reinforces this withdrawal [of IR] by impeding the necessary *fécondation mutuelle*.

(Badie and Smouts 1992: 146)

Badie and Smouts join other IR scholars in deploring the insufficiency of the instruments at the disposal of the analyst for studying an increasingly complex reality. The concept of power, for instance, is increasingly elusive and appears to vary with the perception one has of it (Badie and Smouts 1992: 146). Moreover, conventional systemic analysis appears unable to define the system, its functioning and the rules of change (Badie and Smouts 1992: 156).

However, and perhaps this is what could be expected, Badie and Smouts propose no alternative theory of IR. If any actor has multiple identities with reference to different, not necessarily compatible, and dynamic cultural contexts and if the choice of how to define the self, at any particular moment in time, is the outcome of a complex strategy, there can be no general theory.

> The extreme diversity of internal political orders makes the identification and the number of the actors of the international system very uncertain; *it also makes it impossible to reduce to any single paradigm the articulation between the internal and the external order.*
>
> (Badie and Smouts 1992: 29; my italics)

Badie also argues that, for understanding change in IR, the concept of structure is only an obstacle. There is no such thing as an international structure. A structure can be nothing more than the culturally embedded network of the actors.[11] Instead, the authors suggest accounting for diversity by taking the actor as point of departure. 'The "self" and the "other" is no longer a philosophical question or a problem of foreign relations taken on by the state. Foreign policy is made daily and implies each individual' (Badie and Smouts 1992: 243).

Français malgré lui?

How does this way of treating IR relate to a would-be French tradition? Unlike the British, who claim to have 'the only fully fledged non-American tradition of IR scholarship' (see Chapter 2 on Vincent in this book), the French are unconcerned with the independence of their IR. Debates take place cross-nationally if not transnationally. Most IR scholars have their intellectual training in other fields and the studies are frequently interdisciplinary.[12] Badie is typical in both respects.

First, Badie is a foreigner in the French IR community (in addition to being half Iranian by nationality). His work has drawn heavily on foreign debates and literature. The works on 'culture and politics' and on 'development' have their frames of reference within classical 'international' literature. Likewise, the discussion of the state in the Muslim world refers to and is based on 'Orientalist literature'. Badie has worked as a developer of debates and an introducer of ideas, rather than as a carrier of a national tradition. Moreover, Badie approached IR from political science and continues to refer mainly to debates in political science. This has the advantage of bringing a new perspective to the field but it also leads to stunning omissions of IR literature. The relative absence of the 'English School' of IR is striking, since the spread of the system of states and the effects of cultural plurality and multiple loyalties on the international system are central also to this tradition. Feminist IR (Peterson and Runyan 1993) is not even mentioned in the sociology of IR despite the focus on identities constituted outside the framework of the state and on cross-national soli-darities and movements. And the 'poststructuralists' are dismissed with an airy 'this picture is not a "deconstruction" of the world by authors caught in a fashionable post-structuralism' (Badie and Smouts 1992: 237).

Badie's work fits one of many French IR traditions well: the sociological one (Aron 1984, Merle 1982). Many issues raised by Badie and Smouts are present also in Aron's work. Aron discusses non-state actors and trans-national phenomena extensively. He deals with the multitude and diversity of states, recognizing the particular problems of the Muslim states with regard to a secular political order. Finally, Aron shares the view of IR as part and parcel of extended political science.

> A total science or philosophy of politics would include international relations as one of its chapters, but this chapter would keep its originality because it would *treat the relations between political units each of which claims the right of implementing its own justice and of being the sole master of the decision to fight or not to fight.*
>
> (Aron 1984: 20; original emphasis)

The point where Badie and Smouts differ from Aron and add a new perspective to French IR is on the status of theory. For Aron, the objective of the sociologist is to formulate general propositions, either in terms of the determinants of the elements constitutive of the international order, or in terms of their regularities in the succession of international orders (1984: 184). The sociologist's function is to contextualize an element of the theory. This presupposes that theory is not itself a matter of contextuality and history, as Badie would argue that it is. The heterogeneity of the system does not affect the theory describing it. Thus, Aron can observe civilizational clashes (1984: 325) and differences in the meaning of states (1984: 375–7), and can argue that the neutrality of the state is inconceivable for many people (1984: 375), or that development and institutions are not transfer-able (1984: 378), without considering that this influences the 'theoretical level'.

Badie and Smouts draw the opposite conclusion. They argue that the multiplicity of meaning changes the fundamental categories of IR and alters theory. Since the concepts of sovereignty or state – at the heart of IR – are not of universal validity, it is impossible to carry out an analysis of IR based on these concepts. No 'specificity of the international system' exists to make it possible to proceed at Aron's higher theoretical level (or at least the specificity has yet to be identified). The role of 'sociology of IR' is to make conceptual sense of the international realm and events within it, simultaneously redefining and improving the concepts used for this, rather than to find generalities or to contextualize a universally applicable logic.

In the camp of the challengers

At this point Badie enters the current debate in IR. International Relations, and especially the part of it usually dubbed realism, seems to suffer from an ongoing or never-ending crisis (Guzzini 1992: Chapter 16). The 'challenges to the discipline' are directed at the alleged incapacity of realism to deal with the study of 'the international', either in terms of raising relevant empirical questions or in terms of its theoretical baggage. One offspring of the debate has been the development of international political economy. To cover the entire debate is both impossible and unnecessary for the present purposes. Suffice it to say that Badie's work joins in the debate concerned with questioning the adequacy of the theoretical foundations of the discipline.

Mainstream IR has come under attack for its failure to question its own perception of the world. Authors of various intellectual traditions have questioned developments within the IR tradition and their arguments have piled up before a mainstream which seems both unwilling and unable to take a stand on them. Who and what are excluded from IR debates and why? What are the implications of these exclusions (Ashley)? What are the foundations of the discipline and what do they imply? What are the implications of a 'God's-eye view on the world' (Walker)?

By accepting the idea of a plurality of states, by challenging the notion of sovereignty and the adequacy of a universal logic to explain the international system and by denying it the specificity that realists would accord it, Badie finds himself in the camp of some of these critics. They are sometimes lumped together with Marxist, Gramscian and Frankfurt School critics, under the heading of reflectivists. They themselves prefer the more noble denomination 'dissidents' and see themselves as speaking from 'exile' (*International Studies Quarterly* – exile?!).[13] Like these self-proclaimed marginals, Badie is questioning the founding myths of theories, the binary construction of identities, the reification of specific categories and concepts such as sovereignty, and the a priori nature of the categories for apprehending policies and events (1985 and 1986d). As is rather natural, the categories and concepts questioned are the same: the concepts of state, sovereignty, individual and community. The outcome is also equivalent: through denial of the special status of the international as well as of an assumed universal logic Badie's position is close to Walker's (see Chapter 12 on Walker in this book). Walker prefers the notion of 'World Politics' to IR, as 'politics' indicates that the problems of the rest of political science are shared also by the IR community.

At the core of the methodology proposed by these 'dissidents', among whom we now include Badie, is the call for the introduction of history and space, i.e. historical and social context. The important point, though, is not the idea of space and time as such, but rather the way in which they are to be integrated in the analysis. Keohane's response to this call provides a clear example of how mainstream IR and dissidents talk at cross purposes. Keohane sees no need for abandoning the 'rationalist' approach to introduce time and space into the discussion. He retains only the need to contextualize both concepts and institutions and considers an individualistic, rational choice perspective well equipped to do this: 'In quite a short time research stimulated by rationalistic theory has proposed new hypotheses about why governments create and join international regimes, and the conditions under which these institutions wax or wane' (Keohane 1989: 173). In other words, a 'rationalist approach' can account for time and space alike.

Like Aron, Keohane infers nothing from the critique that could shake the foundations of the 'rationalist approach'. While accepting the fact that there are different rules and norms at work and that these have to be set in their historical context to be apprehended, he denies the concomitant claim that this alters the functioning of the theory. Yet this is precisely the point of Walker's critique: 'The epistemological claim to a universally applicable scientific method coexists quite uneasily with the contrary claim, articulated in ontological, ethical, and ideological forms, that human life is fragmented' (Walker 1991: 166).

To pose the issue in terms of a position on relativism might not be false, but is certainly not the way that the would-be dissidents (or Badie) would like to see their position. They prefer to avoid the seemingly endless debate to which there might be no answer. Consequently, the issue of relativism remains obscured or neglected. Instead, the authors in this tradition point to their contribution in terms of taking problems seriously and not shying away because there are no clear and easy answers.

> The key issue raised by most recent forms of critical theory, whatever their differences, is not some primordial divide between the modern and the postmodern – and thus between the objectivist and the relativist, the responsible and the irresponsible – but the erasure of critical scholarship in the name of an epistemologically legitimated social science that continues to treat ontological difficulties much as King Canute treated the incoming tide.
>
> (Walker 1992: 199)

CONCLUSION

Now, if all this is already there, why bring in Badie? The answer lies partly in his contribution of new elements to the debate, notably regarding the conception and practice of politics in the non-Western and particularly the Arab world. Badie examines the central concepts of the discipline in the light of his material and shows the plural meanings of notions such as community, individual, state. More importantly, Badie poses the problem of the implications of the multitude of worlds – raised by a large number of dissidents – with particular clarity. In a concrete way, at times absent from the more philosophical 'discourses' and 'texts' of other critics of mainstream IR, Badie confronts the issues of the left out, the culturally and socially determined. Walker questions the founding myths, the binary categories developed to understand the world by tracing the historical evolution of specific concepts through their philosophical treatment. A rereading of Machiavelli becomes one way of contesting the claims to universality of realism and its attachment to a 'fixed point' (Walker 1989: 41). Badie would arrive at a similar conclusion, but through the use of a comparative method allowing him to demonstrate the evolving meanings of one concept in different traditions and thereby to abolish the foundation of the universalizing claims attached to it. Both are ways of introducing time and space into the analysis 'seriously' enough to allow them real importance.

Badie does what many critics of orthodox IR call for. He focuses on the overlooked in concrete terms, acknowledges 'other worlds' and attempts to spell them out. He gives solid evidence for various perceptions of the world and the effects of these on the system as such. This applied way of raising theoretical issues may enhance the debate between applied and theoretical scholars. Badie's theoretical contributions should be welcomed by those who want applied research programmes, who object to an excessively abstract debate and who are impatient to get on with the job.

NOTES

I am grateful to the participants in this book-project for comments, encouragement and discussion. Particular thanks go to the editors and Stefano Guzzini. Moreover, Monica Berkman, Clifford Geertz, Knud-Erik Jørgensen, and Susan Strange have read and commented on earlier drafts. Last but not least, a meeting with Bertrand Badie and his comments on an earlier draft have been very helpful.

1 For an overview of the approaches see Skočpol (1982).
2 This tradition includes Geertz (1968), Thompson (1966), Starr (1982) and Bendix (1977).
3 The distinction is developed by Ragin (1987).
4 This is not the place to retrace the debate. Stenographically, Badie draws on the semiotic approach in anthropology, and on a reading of Weber, accentuating the role of structures in establishing culture and the articulation of culture, and other determinants of social and political action. See Badie 1983 (Chapter I for the anthropological heritage; Chapter II for treatment of Weber, Durkheim and Parsons; Chapter III for the failure of political science to integrate culture). See also 1986d: 119 ff. and 1985: 608–21.
5 All aspects of political culture could have been presented in any of the works. The following division is only a device for discussing Badie's key works.
6 See Badie and Birnbaum (1979: 145–8) and Badie (1983: 117) for the point on absolutism. See Badie (1983: 118–39) for a discussion of protestantism.
7 Since the *nomos* is equated with the *Shari'a*, the prevailing presentation of Ibn Rushd (Averroës) as the defender of the duality of truth is false according to Badie (1987a: 43–55).
8 There are different interpretations of what this method entails. According to the motazilist school of the eighth century, the Koran should be interpreted according to the circumstances, while the hanbalites rejected such distancing as heretic.
9 'Imported' refers to the 'transfer to a given society, of a social, political or economic model or a practice, generated and invented in a history and social order which are fundamentally different from its own' (1992a: 126).
10 These underlie the *forces profondes* that Smouts defines as 'basic evolutionary forces at the root of understanding world development' (Smouts 1987: 286). *Forces profondes* is a concept in French IR attached mainly to the work of Renouvin and Duroselle (1964) and of Duroselle writing alone (1978).
11 Interview, 30 June 1993.
12 This is no place to overview the wealth of IR studies in France. It might, however, be useful to give some examples of the wide variety of coexisting

traditions. There is a lively historical tradition (Renouvin and Duroselle 1964; Fontaine 1981; Moreau Defarges 1990; Milza 1982; Senarclens 1993); influential works on foreign policy analysis (Grosser 1961; Grosser 1978; Hassner 1971); a well-established strand of strategic studies (Beaufre 1966; Lellouche 1986; Boniface and Heisbourg 1986), wider security studies (Hassner 1993), and a rather unique version of 'geo-politics' (Lacoste 1976); and a distinctive sociologically and theoretically oriented IR (Aron 1984; Merle 1982). In addition to this, there are original works produced in IR-related fields (which would probably be classified as IR or IPE elsewhere), such as some fields of international economics, which in France has always been strongly linked with the political economy tradition (Grjebine 1985), development studies (Amin 1988) and the French School of Regulation (Boyer 1986), not to mention the abundance of excellent area studies.

13 See Keohane's defence of mainstream IR (1989). For the critique see *International Studies Quarterly* 1990.

REFERENCES

Works by Bertrand Badie

Badie, Bertrand (1977) 'La Philosophie Politique de l'Hellénisme Musulman: l'Oeuvre de Nàser-ed din Tusi', *Revue Française de Science Politique* (avril): 290–304.
——(1978) *Le Développement politique*, Paris: Economica.
——(1981a) 'Contrôle Culturel et Genèse de l'Etat', *Revue Française de Science Politique* (avril): 325–42.
——(1981b) 'Le Concept de Culture et son Utilisation en Sciences Sociales', in Marcel Merle (ed.) *Pour ou contre une interprétation culturaliste des relations internationales*, Paris: AFSP.
——(1983) *Culture et politique*, Paris: Economica.
——(1985) 'Formes et Transformations des Communautés Politiques', in M. Grawitz and Jean Leca (eds) *Traité de Science Politique*, Vol. I, Paris: PUF, pp. 599–663.
——(1986a) 'La Légitimité des Formes de Contestation en Culture Islamique', in A. Kazancigil (ed.) *L'Etat au pluriel*, Paris: Economica and UNESCO.
——(1986b) 'Les Ressorts Culturels du Totalitarisme', in Guy Hermet (ed.) *Totalitarismes*, Paris: Economica.
——(1986c) 'Culture et Politique', *Universalia*.
——(1986d) 'Communauté, Individualisme, et Culture', in Pierre Birnbaum and Jean Leca (eds) *Sur l'individualisme*, Paris: Presses de la Fondation Nationale des Sciences Politiques, pp. 109–31.
——(1987a) *Les Deux Etats. Pouvoir et Société en Occident et en Terre d'Islam*, Paris: Fayard.
——(1987b) 'Inventions et Réinventions de l'Etat', in *Mélanges Offerts à Maurice Duverger*, Paris: PUF.
——(1988a) 'Iran: Une Révolution Déconcertante', *Etudes* (janvier): 5–14.
——(1988b) 'Avenir Incertain pour le Zimbabwe (synthèse d'un rapport d'expertise sur le terrain commandé par le CCFD)', *Etudes*, (novembre): 437–48.
——(1988c) 'Le Transfert de Technologie Politique dans le Monde Arabe', *Bulletin du CEDEJ*: 109–24.
——(1988d) 'Etat et Légitimité en Monde Musulman', *Annuaire de l'Afrique du Nord*: 19–30.
——(1988e) preface to D. Apter, *Pour l'Etat/Contre l'Etat*, ed. B. Badie, Paris: Economica.
——(1989a) 'Comparative Analysis in Political Science: Requiem or Resurrection?', *Political Studies* (September): 340–51.

——(1989b) 'L'impact de la Révolution Française sur le Monde Musulman', *Revue Internationale des Sciences Sociales* (février): 7–18.

——(1989c) 'Terrorisme et Etat', *Etudes Polémologiques*: 7–20.

——(1989d) 'L'Analyse des Partis Politiques dans le Monde Musulman', in Yves Mény (ed.) *Etudes Offertes à Georges Lavau*, Paris: Presses de la Fondation Nationale des Sciences Politiques, pp. 271–87.

——(1991) 'Démocratie et Religion', *Revue Internationale des Sciences Sociales* (août): 545–56.

——(1992a) *L'Etat importé. Essai sur l'occidentalisation de l'ordre politique*, Paris: Fayard.

——(1992b) 'Analyse Comparative et Sociologie Historique', *Revue Internationale des Sciences Sociales* (août): 363–72.

——(1992c) 'L'Etat en Développement', *L'Année Sociologique*: 189–203.

——(1993) 'Flux Migratoires et Relations Transnationales', *Etudes Internationales* (mars): 7–16.

——(1995) *La Fin des territoires. Essai sur le désordre international et l'utilité sociale du respect*, Paris: Fayard.

Badie, Bertrand and Birnbaum, Pierre (1979) *Sociologie de l'état*, Paris: Grasset.

——(1994) 'Sociologie de l'Etat Revisitée', *Revue Internationale des Sciences Sociales* (juin): 189–203.

Badie, Bertrand, Coulon, Christian, Cubertafond, Bernard, Dumont, Paul and Santucci, Robert (eds) (1984) *Contestations en pays islamiques*, Vol. I, Paris: Centre des Hautes Etudes sur l'Afrique et l'Asie Modernes.

——(1987) *Contestations en pays islamiques*, Vol. II, Paris: Centre des Hautes Etudes sur l'Afrique et l'Asie Modernes.

Badie, Bertrand and Hermet, Guy (1990) *Politique Comparée*, Paris: PUF, Thémis.

Badie, Bertrand and Santucci, Robert (1984) 'Essai d'Analyse de la Contestation Fondamentaliste et Marxiste dans Plusieurs Pays Islamiques', in Bertrand Badie, Christian Coulon, Bernard Cubertafond, Paul Dumont and Robert Santucci (eds) *Contestations en pays islamiques*, Vol. I, Paris: Centre des Hautes Etudes sur l'Afrique et l'Asie Modernes, pp. 11–29.

——(1987) 'La Contestation Islamique: Offres et Attentes', in Bertrand Badie, Christian Coulon, Bernard Cubertafond, Paul Dumont and Robert Santucci (eds) *Contestations en pays islamiques*, Vol. II, Paris: Centre des Hautes Etudes sur l'Afrique et l'Asie Modernes, pp. 9–29.

Badie, Bertrand and Smouts, Marie-Claude (1992) *Le Retournement du monde. Sociologie de la scène internationale*, Paris: Presses de la Fondation Nationale des Sciences Politiques and Dalloz.

Works by other authors

Amin, Samir (1988) *L'Eurocentrisme. Critique d'une idéologie*, Paris: Anthropos.

Aron, Raymond (1984 [1961]) *Paix et guerre entre les nations*, Paris: Calmann-Lévy.

Beaufre, André (1966) *Stratégie de l'action*, Paris: Armand Colin.

Bendix, Reinhard (1977) *Nation-Building and Citizenship*, Berkeley, CA: University of California Press.

Boniface, Pascal and Heisbourg, François (1986) *La puce, les hommes et la bombe. L'Europe face aux nouveaux défis technologiques et militaires*, Paris: Hachette.

Boyer, Robert (ed.) (1986) *Capitalismes fin de siècle*, Paris: PUF.

Duroselle, Jean-Baptiste (1978) *Histoire diplomatique de 1919 à nos jours*, Paris: Dalloz.

Fontaine, André (1981) *Un seul lit pour deux rêves: Histoire de la détente, 1962–1981*, Paris: Fayard.

Geertz, Clifford (1968) *Islam Observed: Religious Development in Morocco and Indonesia*, New Haven, CT: Yale University Press.

George, Jim and Campbell, David (1990) 'Patterns of Dissent and the Celebration of Difference: Critical Social Theory and International Relations', *International Studies Quarterly* 34 (3): 269–94.

Grjebine, André (1985) *La nouvelle économie internationale. De la crise mondiale au développement autocentré*, Paris: Presses Universitaires de France.

Grosser, Alfred (1961) *La IVe République et sa politique extérieure*, Paris: Colin.

—— (1978) *Les occidentaux. Pays d'Europe et les Etats Unis depuis la guerre*, Paris: Fayard.

Guzzini, Stefano (1992) *The Continuing Story of Death Foretold: Realism in International Relations/International Political Economy*, Florence: European University Institute, Working Paper no. SPS 92/20.

Hassner, Pierre (1971) 'On Ne Badine Pas avec la Force', *Revue française de science politique* 21 (6).

—— (1993) 'Beyond Nationalism and Internationalism: Ethnicity and World Order', *Survival* 35 (2).

International Studies Quarterly (1990) special issue: 'Speaking the Language of Exile. Dissidence in International Relations', *International Studies Quarterly* 34 (3).

Keohane, Robert O. (1989) 'International Institutions: Two Approaches', in Robert O. Keohane (ed.) *International Institutions and State Power: Essays in International Relations Theory*, Boulder, CO: Westview Press.

Lacoste, Yves (1976) *La géographie, ça sert, d'abord, à faire la guerre*, Paris: Maspero.

Lellouche, Pierre (ed.) (1986) *L'Initiative de défense stratégique et la sécurité de l'Europe*, Paris: IFRI.

Merle, Marcel (1982) *Sociologie des relations internationales*, Paris: Dalloz.

Milza, Pierre (1982) *Le nouveau désordre mondial*, Paris: Flammarion.

Moreau Defarges, Philippe (1990) *La politique internationale*, Paris: Hachette.

—— (1992) 'Gender and Critique in the Theory of International Relations', in Peterson, V. Spike (ed.) *Gendered States: Feminist (Re)Visions of International Relations Theory*, Boulder, CO: Lynne Rienner Publishers.

—— and Runyan, Anne Sisson (eds) (1993) *Global Gender Issues*, Boulder, CO: Westview Press.

Ragin, Charles (1987) *The Comparative Method: Moving Beyond Qualitative and Quantitative Strategies*, Berkeley, CA: University of California Press.

Renouvin, Pierre and Duroselle, Jean-Baptiste (1964) *Introduction à l'histoire des relations internationale*, Paris: Armand Colin.

Senarclens, Pierre de (1993) *De Yalta au rideau de fer. Les grandes puissances et les origines de la guerre froide*, Paris: PFNSP and Berg.

Skočpol, Theda (1982) 'Emerging Agendas and Recurrent Strategies in Historical Sociology', in Theda Skočpol (ed.), *Vision and Methodology in Historical Sociology*, Cambridge, MA: Cambridge University Press.

Smouts, Marie-Claude (1987) 'The Study of International Relations in France', *Millennium* 16 (2): 281–6.

Starr, Paul (1982) *The Social Transformation of American Medicine*, New York: Basic Books.

Thompson, E. P. (1966) *The Making of the English Working Class*, New York: Vintage Books.

Walker, R. B. J. (1989) 'The Prince and the Pauper: Traditions, Modernity, and Practice in the Theory of International Relations', in James Der Derian and Michael J. Shapiro (eds) *International/Intertextual Relations: Postmodern Readings of World Politics*, Lexington, MA: Lexington Books.

—— (1991) 'History and Structure in the Theory of International Relations', *Millennium* 18(2): 163–82.

—— (1992) 'Gender and Critique in the Theory of International Relations', in Peterson, Spike V. (ed.) *Gendered States. Feminist (Re)Visions of International Relations Theory*, Boulder, CO: Lynne Rienner Publishers.

7 John G. Ruggie: transformation and institutionalization

Ole Wæver

John G. Ruggie, born in 1944 in Graz, Austria, emigrated to Canada in 1956 and to the United States in 1967. His BA (1967) is from McMaster University in Canada and his PhD (1974) from the University of California at Berkeley. Since 1991, Ruggie has been Dean of the School of International and Public Affairs at Columbia University, where he was Professor of Political Science from 1978 to 1987. In between, he served as director of the University of California's Institute on Global Conflict Co-operation while Professor of International Relations at the University of California, San Diego.

The task for students of international organization is to specify when, where, and how states seek to organize activities internationally.

(John Gerard Ruggie 1972a: 877)

INTRODUCTION

'Regimes', 'embedded liberalism', 'epistemic communities' and 'collective balancing': what unites these diverse concepts in IR theory? That they have all been launched by John Gerard Ruggie.[1] Not only by coining terms, but more importantly by pointing out theoretical directions and making sometimes small but decisive conceptual adjustments to unfolding research programmes, John Ruggie has significantly influenced the direction taken by major theoretical movements in recent IR theory. In 1990 Robert Keohane said about an article by John Ruggie from 1975 that it 'foreshadowed much of the conceptual work of the next decade' (Keohane 1990: 755).

A pure and simple explication of Ruggie's writings together with an attempt to present their inner logic would seem justified for two reasons. One is the argument given in Chapter 1 of this book, that the discipline considers authors as authors only if they are old (and preferably dead), or among the most 'boxable' of contemporaries, while authors who make idiosyncratic cross-linkages will be dealt with in the discipline's self-reflections mainly as addenda to the 'real' theoreticians (Ruggie as a comment on Waltz; Ruggie as a variation on regime theory; Ruggie as a variation on Keohane's multilateralism) or as contributors to specific fields of inquiry (Ruggie on the liberal world economy, Ruggie on human rights). Thus, first, Ruggie is a paradigmatic case of a non-paradigmatic and therefore potentially 'invisible' author. The other reason is the fact that Ruggie has so far not himself presented a unified, concentrated book joining together the diverse strands of his work. An ambitious work – mostly announced as *The Structure of Planetary Politics*[2] – was forthcoming for a period in the 1980s but seems now revoked. A collection of his greatest hits with connecting text is fortunately under preparation ('International Transformations: A Structurationist Account', to be published by Routledge). So far, Ruggie's work has been found in a number of articles on seemingly rather dispersed issues. To tie this together could almost be the justification for this chapter. It will, however, as do the other chapters of this book, have its own plot. It will read in parallel the moves made in three arenas and how they related: substantial argument on an issue; a contention in the context of IR theory; and an elaboration on the level of ontology.

PARADIGMS, QUESTIONS AND ORGANIZATION

To some Ruggie is a refined neo-realist, author of an influential article subtitled 'Towards a neo-realist synthesis' and often heralded as the first step towards a 'modified neo-realism' (Kelstrup *et al.* 1990) or important in the development of a 'structural realism' in contrast to Waltz's neo-realism (Buzan *et al.* 1993) or a central element in the emergence of the neo-neo synthesis of neo-realism and neo-liberalism (Wæver 1992, 1994, and see Chapter 1 of this book). To others, Ruggie is part of the reflectivist revolt in IR. When Robert Keohane defined this camp – and designated it as the official challenger to the dominant rationalist group – he listed Alker, Ashley, Kratochwil and Ruggie as the 'best-known' of 'several scholars with a distinctive and similar point of view, who have recently challenged the predominant rationalistic analysis of international politics' (Keohane 1988: 381; 1989: 161). Marlene Wind, among others, has with hesitation labelled Ruggie as a poststructuralist (Wind 1993: 100). Ruggie has contributed key elements of what became incredibly mainstream (regimes, especially). He has taken part in projects such as Krasner 1982 – almost the 1980s *definition* of the establishment in IR. Still, he is also the author of eloquent critiques of that same establishment (Ruggie 1980b, 1989, 1992b; and, in particular, the most quoted critique of regime theory, Kratochwil and Ruggie 1986). What do we make of this? Simply a confused character? I do not think so. Rather an author well versed in the literature debating 'schools' and 'paradigms', but disrespectful of this way of approaching the discipline. The paradigms fixation does not organize the work of John Ruggie – therefore a theme of the present chapter will be how to write *across paradigms* – but he is certainly not unaware of the debates and their periodic importance. I hope to show how Ruggie consciously operates in this field dominated by debates about and among 'paradigms' without playing the standard game of boxes. Exactly because Ruggie seldom defines himself by these positions there is a reason for *reading* how he anyway does relate to and manipulate them. The first focus is thus relational: how does Ruggie play the paradigms game?

The second layer of excavation is a search for the more general – permanent or evolving – more or less implicit apparatus which ties together so much diversity. What is the ontology, what the methodology employed in these studies? We will concentrate on ontology with a few remarks on epistemology and methodology.[3]

Each section will thus contain three parts: 1) the substantial argument: what are the articles in this case about, what do they argue, what positions are they opposing, why and how; 2) how does this relate to 'grand debates' in IR: how does Ruggie draw on and how does he modify the different paradigms; 3) ontology.

The sections are not organized chronologically only. Nor are there easy divisions into themes. International collaboration stands at the beginning and the 'end': from Ruggie 1972a to Ruggie 1992a and 1993e. And in some sense it is *the* guiding theme all the way. A second emerging concern is 'international transformations'. It has possibly been present all along, but only more recently as a possible object for scientific inquiry and theory formation. Thus, the chapter is organized in two main parts: the first four sections treat the central formulations on the issue of collaboration as such (each defined by a key text from respectively 1972, 1975, 1986 and 1992 but supplemented by elements from related texts). Then follows one indirectly (through neo-realism) and one directly on transformations. The conclusion is the final section.

COLLABORATION I: TECHNOLOGY AND TECHNIQUE

The substantial argument

'Collective Goods and Future International Collaboration' (1972a) opens with a reflection on the emerging consensus that a postmodern or post-industrial society is under way. Students of international organizations, Ruggie claims, are preoccupied with some of the same ideas.

More specifically, similarities stem from the fact that the 'post-' discussions in relation to highly industrialized societies are concerned with two fundamental changes: that services, information, education – all *publicly relevant goods* – are increasingly important; and that ours is a society in which these goods are produced and/or purchased communally, i.e. the raising role of public decisions and planning *vis-à-vis* the market. (Those were the days. . . .) These themes reappear in the literature on international organization: science and technology create possibilities that cannot be fully exploited by the states. Co-operation, information exchange and joint monitoring are said to be needed both in order to compete, grow and gain and in order to handle the hazards of these technologies. Just as in domestic society, in international society the states are forced to accept a higher degree of regulation and control. But how is that to be conceptualized? What does it mean to talk about this as to be 'required', John Ruggie asks. 'Are there technological imperatives to which states will respond? Are there human imperatives to which states will respond?'

Already in this the first published paper by John Ruggie, we find several themes that can be followed up to the most recent articles: reflections on postmodern international relations; the problematique of international responses to an increasing 'need' for co-operation; a suspicion against easy, functionalist conclusions as to automatic responses and rational solutions; a keen interest in the role of technology and information in driving changes; and – not least – the question of the logic of, preconditions for and forms of international collaboration.

After outlining the questions (as quoted above), Ruggie

> poses the basic problem of international organization as one of national *choice under constraints*: that is, given the structure of the contemporary interstate system, what are the general conditions under which states, with differing objectives and different capabilities, choose to collaborate with others?
>
> (1972a: 875)

Sceptical of technological or functional automatism, Ruggie sees the concern with 'integration' as only 'the limiting case of a more general phenomenon'. The more general set of questions is:

> given the structure of the contemporary interstate system, when, where, and how do states seek to organize activities internationally? And what particular mode of organization – co-ordination, collaboration, integration – is selected under what conditions? They are, then a subset of questions about *international organization* in general.

Scientific and technological developments might shape international co-operation but only when and to the extent that they influence 'a particular configuration of actor objectives and capabilities *vis-à-vis* a particular issue' (ibid.: 877). We need a model of the general dynamics of international organization.

Ruggie therefore presents *a model of state behaviour*. A state will co-operate in order to compensate for a lack of either of two resources: capabilities or techniques (knowledge of cause–effect relations in either problems or solutions). Against weighs a general desire to avoid dependency caused by co-operation. The model brings various – not enormously surprising – conclusions regarding the impact of specific variables, but concludes that there is an inbuilt self-limiting mechanism in international co-operation. Task expansion and spillover are certainly not to be expected unless some other factors change; co-operation does not automatically lead to more co-operation (ibid.: 881).

In terms of private versus public goods in a refined fourfold version, it is demonstrated that 'different kinds of activities will lead to different organizational forms, *not* because of a priori substantive differences, but because of the impact of the collective dimension that the behaviour of states may exhibit' (ibid.: 886). That is, the relational, political nature of the issue as it stands among the states is more important for the form of collaboration than its technical substance.

It is concluded that science and technology are not a unique field which automatically recasts international relations. It can create co-operation of different kinds but not in a way radically different from other issue areas. A further conclusion is the usefulness of studying international organization with one's point of departure in the existing forms of organization, i.e. in terms of devolution of existing structures rather than with a focus – as most research on international organization at the time – on 'the evolution of collective actors – how organizations come to be established, how they come to grow, to have important functions, and to acquire authority "above" the level of states'.

On his way towards presenting 'the model', Ruggie clarifies his assumptions about the nature of the international system, 'as a modified Westphalian system' (ibid.: 877), decentralized and based on sovereign equality. In practice, this system has become partially but progressively modified with spheres of influence, supranational actors, interconnectedness, and even the principle of decentralization is modified 'to the extent to which states subsequently "will" collective principles and forms of decision making' (ibid.: 877). In the terminology of later decades one would say that the system is anarchic in the technical sense but modified by institutionalization, but Ruggie here stresses in particular the possible *choice* of states to organize internationally in various different ways. The state is characterized as rational, utility-maximizing, and preferring to limit dependence on others.

IR paradigms

Ruggie is here dealing with questions rather similar to Ernst Haas, who has obviously been important to Ruggie's thought at many stages but not least the early ones. There is in the article a move towards a respect for the choice of states – to some extent paralleled by Haas's development (from Haas 1958 to Haas 1964). Ruggie, however, is much more consistent in taking *politics* seriously. Always sceptical of 'automatic', technological (functional) explanations, he insists on a political formulation with a decisive role for states making choices. This would in the standard approach throw him into the realist box. But at the same time the approach is essentially liberalist, utilitarian in the same way as much neo-liberalism in the 1980s is: it starts from the state and therefore feels on safe realist ground, but the motives are 'value-maximizing', not risk-driven, and therefore it can be said not to be realism but liberalism (cf. the relative gains debate: Grieco 1988, 1990; Keohane 1993; Ruggie 1992b). With our present standards, Ruggie's approach is typical neo-neo-ism (at the meeting-point of rationalist liberalism and rationalist realism), but we should remember that this was not the way the theory landscape looked in 1972. At the time, the impression would rather be of a liberalist theme but possibly signalling a change of emphasis within liberal thought.

The article is not very 'radical' (if we use 'radical' for the third corner of the IR triangle, covering Marxism, postmodernism and whatever is the extreme, conflictual attacker at the time). The kind of 'postmodernism' and 'post-industrialism' examined were of the rather evolutionary type and thus essentially liberal rather than radical. The most radical element which points beyond liberalism and realism was a vision of an international order so 'highly differentiated and exceedingly complex...that it will share nothing with typical visions of "supersystems" towards which the natural logic of events is said to be propelling us' (1975a: 893; with a footnote (self-)reference to 1972b on 'Contingency, Complexity, and Post-Modern Form' – a bridge from the present theme to the issues in section 6, Ruggie 1983a, 1989 and 1993a).

Ontology

As quoted, Ruggie is pleasantly explicit about the modified Westphalian system as well as the state, but some further ontological markings can be found. Functionalism is criticized for being 'essentially apolitical' (1972a: 876). His own restoration of 'politics' essentially means the rational choices of the dominant units: i.e. that states choose according to their aims and modus operandi, not in accordance with some supra-logic of 'integration' or 'functional co-operation'. Functions and functional contexts 'do not exist *apart from* a particular configuration of actor attributes in relation to any given issue: different actors' differing objectives, pursued with unequally distributed resources, define "functional" contexts' (1972a: 876).

Ontologically, not much else than states acting politically is given independent power. 'Technology and all that' exists as an important reality, but is not in and of itself deciding anything. A political filtering and phrasing is necessary. The source for *this* is not much touched upon. Ruggie 'sought explicitly to avoid evolutionary or functionalist assumptions' (1975a: 892), but the price was to give ontological primacy to rationalist states in a choice of theoretical perspective. The only other kind of factor that entered with an independent reality was the political nature of goods, i.e. the relational, political character of an issue area.

COLLABORATION II: REGIMES

The substantial argument

Ruggie's 'International Responses to Technology: Concepts and Trends' (1975a) takes as its starting-point, again, a widespread argument about a global challenge and its allegedly 'necessary' consequences.

> The necessity has emerged, this line of reasoning continues, to restructure our international institutional frameworks in keeping with the unhitching of nature's constants which science and technology have effected. But on what basis? According to what principles? Toward what ends?
> (Ruggie 1975a: 557; footnote deleted)

As an overall framework for studying this, Ruggie suggests a combination of on the one hand the 1972 model (the tension between the need to respond collectively and the desire to maintain national autonomy) and on the other hand

> the tension between science, heavily informed by consensual knowledge of cause/effect relations, and politics, heavily informed by normative purposes, negotiated priorities and available capabilities.
>
> (1975a: 558)

The latter tension defines the *situation*, the '1972 tension' defines the *response*. The article introduces an edited volume (Ruggie and Haas 1975) and continues mainly by setting up typologies and clarifying concepts.

The general framework is a perspective on international behaviour as *institutionalized*, in the sense that behaviour is co-ordinated and patterned, and therefore not completely unpredictable. This 'milieu or situation to which polities respond, as they construct international arrangements, is not a physical or natural or technological but a *social* milieu' (1975a: 559 f.). Therefore there is nothing inevitable about such a situation, it is negotiated by the parties concerned (ibid.: 567) and thus *inherently unstable*, subject to continued renegotiation (ibid.: 568). States then respond to this 'collective situation', and by 'collective response' is meant 'the international institutionalization of certain aspects of national behaviour which results from the responses of states' (ibid.: 568).

Here Ruggie makes a point out of what was in the 1972 article a remark: the theme is to be *international organization*, not international organiza*tions*, *institutionalization*, not institutions. The more common terminology has the disadvantage of excluding the study of collective behaviour not performed by international organizations. Paradoxically, it also has the effect of making it impossible to determine the role that organizations do play, because there is no conception of the broader collectivities in which they operate (cf. further Kratochwil and Ruggie 1986). And it has led to the false assumption that the game among organizations is a zero-sum one, that the new gain only at the cost of the old ones, and, for instance, that international organizations necessarily imply a weakening of the state.

> The alternative, that within international collectivities, international organizations, multinational corporations, states and sub-state actors may be becoming stronger, coexisting as allies as well as competitors as the domain of public as opposed to private choice increases, is ruled out.
>
> (1975a: 569)

This theme will recur in later writings too. The 1975 article is, however, first of all important for the next move it makes:

> In depicting the 'collective response' of states to collective situations occasioned by science and technology, I will differentiate among three levels of institutionalization: (1) the purely cognitive, which I will call

'epistemic communities;' (2) that consisting of sets of mutual expectations, generally agreed-to rules, regulations and plans, in accordance
with which organizational energies and financial commitments are
allocated, and which we are calling 'international regimes;' and (3) international organizations.

(1975a: 569)

This effective move – introducing epistemic communities, regimes and
organizations – meant a reconceptualization of the whole field of 'international organization', ensuring a focus on organization (not organizations)
and institutionalization. More generally, Ruggie argues against the ordinary
conception of 'authority' as formal super- and subordination relations where
supranationality is a precondition for international authority to emerge.
He, instead, emphasizes that authority ultimately refers to voluntary compliance, which has only (recently) been expressed most often in relations of
sub- and superordination. Acceptance of a regime can be institutionalized
nationally as part of national choice, and thus make for neither sub- nor
superordination, but rather a 'transordinate' structure. Jurisdiction is exercised collectively by states, not lifted to a higher authority.

A second – less emphasized – important step is the 'epistemic' side. It is a
continuous theme with Ruggie that situations are always socially constructed, inherently political. But more specifically he begins here to emphasize the role of the historical emergence of images and metaphors that
contribute to the shaping of social life (cf. 1975b: 139–44).

IR paradigms

It seems that we are here moving out of a realist state world. Institutionalization and internationalization of authority have their own reality. On the
other hand, there are no 'liberalist' assumptions about automatic progress,
functional spillover or anything like that. The building blocks *are* the states.
As in his 1972a, one of the most radical arguments is the vision of an
international order where Ruggie this time continues into proposing 'a
formulation of the structure of international authority which differs from
that we normally have in mind, and to suggest an international organizational strategy which runs counter to many now pursued' (1975a: 579). The
new formulations on 'internationalization of political authority' (1982: 380;
cf. 1975a: 579 ff.) point towards an approach where an essential category of
which the international system is made up becomes located at various levels,
and not basically derived from the states. This reinforces the power of the
basic argument of the article: for treating variations within institutionalization as an independent source of explanation.

Ontology

Ontologically, this article leans towards a liberalist or pluralist image where
the basic stuff of IR is a social quality (in this case 'authority') which is not

tied by definition to any specific political unit (e.g. the state) but to be studied empirically at various levels. In the paradigms of IR, this was at the time not a typical liberalist position, because liberal IR tended to make grand assumptions about processes like integration and formation of international organizations derived from technological or other imperatives. Ruggie's world is too political to allow for this.

COLLABORATION III: GOVERNANCE

The substantial argument

Without making a big methodological fuss about the fact that the next key text is co-authored with Friedrich Kratochwil, I will just notice how this text constitutes an interesting second-order reflection on developments which include the prior writings of amongst others John Ruggie, not least the *regimes* approach. The article is essentially a critical examination of the value and potentials of and the future foundations for the study of regimes. This is packed inside a larger examination of the study of 'international organization'. There has been a shift in recent years, the two authors argue, in the study of international organization 'away from international institutions, toward broader forms of international institutionalized behaviour' (Kratochwil and Ruggie 1986: 754), and

> this shift does not represent a haphazard sequence of theoretical or topical 'fads' but is rooted in a 'core concern' or a set of puzzles which gives coherence and identity to this field of study. The substantive core around which the various theoretical approaches have clustered is the problem of international governance. And the observable shifts in analytical foci can be understood as 'progressive problem shifts' in the sense of Imre Lakatos's criterion for the heuristic fruitfulness of a research program. This evolution has brought the field to its current focus on the concept of international regimes.
>
> (ibid.: 754; two footnotes deleted)

By examining the contents of the journal *International Organization* they find four (often overlapping) phases in the study of 'international governance': 1) first, articles that concentrated on formal organizations and assumed that 'international governance' was what international organizations did, and that their behaviour could be explained by their formal attributes such as charters and voting procedures; 2) in the second phase this largely legalistic approach was supplanted by an interest in the actual decision-making processes within international organizations; 3) the third phase abandoned the assumption that international governance is what international organizations do, and started studying the actual roles of international organizations in broader processes (of what can now be but then was not labelled international governance). Thereby, international organization and international relations were two separate fields to be related but not identical. Global governance is not coterminous with the activities of international organizations, but these anyhow still play some role in the broader process. From here follows logically the fourth phase: 4) regime theory. The third wave lacked a concept for that wider context for international organizations (international governance), but another cause for the regime problematique was to be found in developments in the international system: the relative US decline did not immediately cause an unravelling of those institutional arrangements set up after the Second World War with the USA as hegemon. Why did the states not turn to beggar-thy-neighbour behaviour as they 'should' according to dominant assumptions? Unless the explanation simply was that US hegemony actually was not declining (Strange 1982; Russett 1985), one would have a theoretical anomaly that regime theory could elegantly handle: the regimes were a product of the American power order but continued beyond this. They must have a kind of 'relative autonomy' in relation to underlying power structures (cf. Krasner 1982) and thus be worth studying.

Kratochwil and Ruggie have two main criticisms of regime theory. The first is that 'epistemology fundamentally contradicts ontology!' (1986: 764). Yes, regime theory has discovered interesting phenomena related to values, norms, etc., but since these are actually intersubjectively constituted they cannot be studied with the positivistic and utilitarian-instrumental tools to which the regime literature remains tied. A more interpretative or hermeneutic approach is demanded.

The second problem is that with this increasing grasp on the wider problem of governance, 'international institutions of a formal kind have been left behind' (1986: 771). This implies a danger that theory gets out of touch with practice, and it is a problem for theory too, since we ought to be able to study international organizations after all. It is therefore 'necessary to link up regimes in some fashion with the formal mechanisms through which real-world actors operate' (ibid.: 772).

IR paradigms

The evolutionary story shows that despite its in many ways 'realism-friendly' premises, regime theory should – due to its problematique – first of all be seen as an outgrowth of liberal (international organization) study. It is a phase in the self-transforming activities of liberalist IR. This interpretation is underlined by Kratochwil and Ruggie's argument that we are dealing with a discipline in search of its own dependent variable (1986: 755) – not as often assumed the same thing we as a discipline attempt to explain with different 'independent variables'. The field of study is displacing its own analytical focus in order to find the decisive point. Probably not an unrealistic description of how fields work: what holds a theory or a research programme together is neither dependent nor independent variable, but *the plot*, the idea about a kind of process, puzzle, or tension (and over time coherence can only be explained sociologically as a disciplinary process; Foucault 1972). This perspective makes it more clear that it is some kind of 'movement' that represents this continuity over time, not an object.

At another level the article is a sharp critique of approaches inspired by rational choice and an appeal for hermeneutic approaches. As in Ruggie 1983e and 1990b the article calls for *a theory* of international organization, not just writings on organizations using superficial inspiration from various theories in other social sciences. The Kratochwil and Ruggie article was central in signalling the arrival of a 'new institutionalism' in IR.

The position is more clearly 'reflectivist' and critical *vis-à-vis* established, rationalist approaches, and connects thereby to the third camp, the 'radical' one, but certainly the article is also and maybe primarily inscribed in – and articulating – the continuity of a *liberal* tradition.

Ontology

The article is extremely explicit on the intersubjective ontology of regimes, and the necessity to respect this. This is first of all used as a case for the correct and necessary epistemology. Seemingly a debate over epistemology and methodology, it is actually also a new step in regard to ontology. Institutions are not just emerging realities of the same character as states and old supra-state ambitions. They are first of all intersubjective in nature and this level of social reality has substance and is researchable.

Embedded liberalism

The approach advocated is more clearly seen through a specific, 'empirical' analysis, where, furthermore, arguments of principal importance to pp. 183–96 first appear. Ruggie deals with the international economy first of all in the two articles 1982 and 1991, but 1980a, 1981, 1983c, 1984 and 1994c are relevant too.

An important article from 1982 is about the regimes for money and trade and their relationship to the evolution of the international economic order in the postwar period. Along the lines of the Kratochwil and Ruggie article, Ruggie refers to the 'prevalent model of the formation and transformation of international economic regimes': on the basis of the Waltzian assumption that international authority follows capability rather closely, economic regimes – and especially 'open' and 'liberal' international economic orders – have been depicted as the result of a concentration of economic capabilities to the point where a 'hegemon' appears (Great Britain in the late nineteenth century and the USA after the Second World War). Such a liberal order is a strong regime since it has to restrain self-seeking states from meddling directly in domestic and international economic affairs as they would, given the competitive international political system, be disposed to do. A liberal order, however, constructs authority relations in a way where market forces are given maximum scope. This order will unravel, the theory of hegemonic stability predicts, if the concentration of economic capabilities erodes.

Ruggie claims that this model is insufficient 'because it does not encompass the phenomenological dimensions of international regimes' (1982:

382). Political authority represents always a fusion of power with legitimate social purpose. The purpose side is left out of the prevailing interpretation which focuses on power only, and 'power may predict the *form* of the international order, but not its *content*' (1982: 382). The Dutch hegemony of the seventeenth century had particular features that can be explained only if related to this specific society, just as an order based on a German Second World War victory would have been different from the American one, even if it had been equally 'hegemonic'. This can most persuasively be argued, if it is proven that the two favourite illustrations – the nineteenth century and post-Second World War liberal international economic orders – are different. This they are, because one represents laissez-faire liberalism, the other not.

With this approach to authority, the sources of regime change double too: to the changes in power distribution studied by hegemonic stability theory are added changes in social purpose. The two do not necessarily co-vary, and we can imagine situations of a hegemon (in power terms) whose programme differs fundamentally from that of its leading rivals, or one where there is a congruence of social purpose without a hegemon, the latter possibly being the case since 1971.

The analysis draws on Polanyi's *The Great Transformation* (1944), which introduced the terms 'embedded' and 'disembedded' economic orders, referring to situations where the economy is merely a function of the social in which it is contained, and situations where a separate economic system emerges with an idea of a distinctive economic motive and 'economic relations are taken to be autonomous and responsive only to their own endogenous laws of motion' (Ruggie 1983c: 433).[4] This latter model evolved in nineteenth-century Europe, and caused regimes of free trade and the gold standard. This 'singular departure' can be understood only if one includes the force of 'a captivating social metaphor', that of the market (1982: 386).

State–society relations were radically transformed, and the role of the state redefined. The ensuing laissez-faire system, however, broke down with the next transformation of state–society relations, that of the interwar period. Then 'land, labor, and capital had all seized upon the state in the attempt to reimpose broader and more direct social control over the market forces. Once this domestic transformation began, late in the nineteenth century, international liberalism of the orthodox kind was doomed' (Ruggie 1982: 387). In contrast to Polanyi's predictions, a kind of capitalist inter-nationalism was restored after the war, but it had to take into account that the relationship between market and authority had changed, and govern-ments assumed a much more direct responsibility for domestic social secur-ity and economic stability; Ruggie labels it 'embedded liberalism'. It was essentially a compromise:

> unlike the economic nationalism of the thirties, it would be multilateral in character; unlike the liberalism of the gold standard and free trade, its multilateralism would be predicated upon domestic interventionism.
>
> (Ruggie 1982: 393)

The victory of multilateralism reflected the extraordinary power of the USA, but the connection of multilateralism with the aim of domestic stability 'reflected the shared legitimacy of a set of social objectives to which the industrial world had moved, unevenly but "as a single entity"' (1982: 398).

The form that liberalization of trade and money eventually took was consistently related to the form of the regimes: governments did encourage a division of labour (as they would also have done in classical type liberalism) to realize comparative advantages and gains from trade, but since they were also committed to minimize socially disruptive domestic adjustment, they fostered trade mainly within continents and within sectors, not to speak of intra-firm; there was actually a decline of specialization in different sectors of manufacturing activity among the industrialized countries. Transactions are based on the narrow margins of cost differences relating to similar activities, but not the mutual benefits of divergent investment, production, and export structures. The economic gains from trade are smaller, but – since functional differentiation is lower – domestic stabilization is better shielded and adjustment costs are low. The vulnerabilities of far-reaching 'Ricardian' specialization among sectors would not be compatible with 'embedded liberalism'. Against dominant liberal, Marxist and realist explanations of this pattern of interactions (1982: 402), Ruggie suggests that since the pattern is a very nice correlate to what should be expected from the regimes, the possibility that the regimes actually played an important mediating role should be taken seriously. Regimes

> do not determine international economic transactions. For determinants we have to look deeper into basic structural features of the world political economy.... They play a mediating role, by providing a permissive environment for the emergence of certain kinds of transactions.
>
> (1982: 404)

On this basis, Ruggie addresses the changes of the 1970s. A pervasive interpretation in terms of discontinuity is countered by a Ruggian representation in terms of 'norm-governed change'. This reinterpretation follows from his insistence on the dual sources of regimes: power and purpose. If the power base erodes, the strength of the regime is also in some sense sapped, and the *instruments* (rules and procedures in the classical Krasner terminology) of the regime will have to change, but with the purpose unchanged, the *normative framework* (principles and norms) is likely to remain unaltered (1982: 384). Change within a normative framework towards instruments better suited to the new power situation would be norm-governed, not norm-transforming change (1982: 405). The article makes a strong case for interpreting the post-1971 changes as rule-governed, in contrast to widespread interpretations in terms of the defeat of free trade and the arrival of mercantilism.

A decisive factor is what ideal is compared with post-1971 practices. The conclusion is therefore dependent on Ruggie's prior critique that the common tendency to view the postwar regimes as liberal regimes, but with lots of cheating taking place on the domestic side, fails to capture the full complexity of the embedded liberalism compromise.

(1982: 398)

This follows from the intersubjective notion of regimes: what constitutes a deviation 'cannot be determined simply by "objective" examination of individual acts in reference to specific texts. Rather, deviation will be determined by the "intersubjective" evaluation of the intentionality and consequences of acts within the broader normative framework and prevailing circumstances' (1982: 405). Rationales and justifications even for deviation are critical in assessing the efficacy of regimes. 'Governments in the trenches, not analysts perched on Archimedean points, are the ultimate judges of what constitutes compatibility' (1991: 210). The 'new protectionism' is integral to postwar liberalization and has not significantly limited trade, but first of all served to slow down structural change and minimize the social costs of domestic adjustment.

Change has been 'rule-governed' and mainly consisted in inventing instruments better adapted to new circumstances and mostly compatible with the norms of the regimes, in some cases even closer to the original intentions of the regimes. Despite hegemonic decline, continuity is significant, because social purposes have remained constant. The hegemonic stability thesis focuses only on the power shift, but regime analysis has to pay equal attention to the configurations of state–society relations and ensuing 'social purposes'.

The real danger is not to the liberalism part of embedded liberalism, but to embeddedness. Both the denationalization of economies with ensuing loss of governmental instruments and a fraying of domestic social safety threaten the ability 'of governments at home to sustain their part of the social compact on which postwar international liberalization has hinged' (1994c: 2).

COLLABORATION IV: MULTILATERALISM

The substantial argument

'Multilateralism: the Anatomy of an Institution' can be seen as a delivery of what Kratochwil and Ruggie promised at the end of the 1986 article, linking 'back' to organizations themselves to enrich the study of regimes and governance. In 1992 Ruggie then sets out to show how 'the form that institutions assume affects vitally the role that institutions play on the world stage today' (1992a: 597).

The article is presented in a more policy-relevant mode as an attempt to explain why parts of the international institutional order appear surprisingly robust and adaptive. This cannot be handled just by pointing to 'institutions' and the enduring service these supply. Instead Ruggie claims that the explanation is to be found in a key feature of the institutional order: that it is multilateral in form. This form enhances (under given conditions) its adaptability and durability.

To focus on 'multilateralism' means that one has a lot of conceptual work to do, for this concept has been poorly defined and often mixed up with other features of institutionalization. The article has been 'written with two sets of protagonists in mind' (1992a: 597). First, neo-realists and similar structuralists for whom institutions matter little should be shown that institutions are important and not derivatory from deep structure. The second set of protagonists, more interestingly, is his 'fellow institutionalists' of whom most neglect the *form* that institutions take.

Nor is it enough (as done by Keohane, for instance) to define multi-lateralism nominally ('the practice of co-ordinating national policies in groups of three or more states'; Keohane 1990: 731), since practices that are essentially bilateralist such as the Bismarckian alliance system would fulfil this definition and thereby be multilateralist. There is a qualitative dimension of multilateralism that has to enter the definition. It co-ordinates

> on the basis of 'generalized' principles of conduct – that is, principles which specify appropriate conduct for a class of actions, without regard to the particularistic interests of the parties or the strategic exigencies that may exist in any specific occurrence.
>
> (1992a: 571)

This is in contrast to an arrangement – possibly among 'three or more states' – that is bilateralist in form and differentiates relations case-by-case on the basis of 'particularistic grounds or situational exigencies'. Institutions (for instance, defined by Keohane [1990: 732] as 'persistent and connected sets of rules, formal and informal, that prescribe behavioral roles, constrain activity, and shape expectations') can take three forms: multilateralism, bilateralism and imperialism. ' *"Multilateral" is thus an adjective that modifies the noun "institution"'* (Ruggie 1992a: 570) Thus, 'multilateralism is a generic institutional form of modern international life' (1992a: 567) not to be mixed up with formal multilateral institutions, which are more recent and so far, less important.

From the definition, one can directly deduce two traits of multilateralism. Generalized organizing principles entail *indivisibility* among the members with regard to the range of behaviour in question. This indivisibility, Ruggie emphasizes, 'is a *social construction*, not a technical condition: in a collective security scheme, states behave as if peace were indivisible and thereby make it so. Similarly, in the case of trade, it is the GATT members' adherence to the MFN norm which makes the system of trade an indivisible whole, not some inherent attribute of trade itself' (1992a: 571). Second, multilateralism generates among the members expectations of 'diffuse reci-procity' (Keohane 1986a). Both of these traits should make multilateralism highly demanding, and if it appears at some point to be common this is an interesting puzzle worth explaining.

Postwar multilateralism of course asks for an explanation somehow related to the USA, to US hegemony. Here Ruggie essentially argues that although explanation from US hegemony is correct, 'it was less the fact of American *hegemony* that accounts for the explosion of multilateral arrangements than it was the fact of *American* hegemony' (1992a: 568; cf. 593). All hegemonies are not alike, things would have been different had Nazi Germany or the Soviet Union or even the UK been the hegemon. Multilateralism served as 'a foundational architectural principle' on which American postwar planners attempted to reconstruct the postwar world, in the economic as well as the security realm. Why was this so? It can be deduced neither from structural system-level theories (neo-realism *à la* Gilpin or Waltz) nor from functional system-level theories that, given their logic of limiting institutional inefficiencies, would have expected the same outcome independent of the attributes of the state making the calculation. Ruggie wants us to take seriously this particular hegemon, i.e. delving into its domestic realm. Drawing on some of the insights from the embedded liberalism analysis, he shows the importance of a US attempt to project the experience of the New Deal regulatory state into the international arena, and the role of domestic bindings on the state actors in shaping the security strategy. Specificities related to the United States are needed in order to explain the particular multilateral shape given to 'it's' international order.

Will it then all disappear together with American hegemony? So far, not only are multilateral institutions hanging on defensively, as predicted by the new institutionalists – the famous 'relative autonomy' explaining a certain time-lag between power structure and regime (cf. Krasner 1982; Guzzini 1992: 161f; Guzzini 1993) – but there are actually 'numerous instances of active institutional adaptation and even creation' (Ruggie 1992a: 594). A possible explanation could be: multilateralism.

The two traits typical of multilateralism, which make it difficult to achieve in the first instance – diffuse reciprocity and the generalized organizing principles – render it more elastic and self-sustaining. Furthermore, the dependence on domestic environments helps to explain the durability of multilateral arrangements, for so far no stark domestic divergences undermine the post-Cold War order. Finally, the fact that multilateralism actually *works* relatively well in many cases plays a role. Partly by being *de facto* governed by smaller subsets of states, the institutions are less inefficient than expected, and furthermore, they are in some cases inventive themselves and play relative to the member states an increasing role in problem definition and plan suggestions. Thus, the very multilateral form seems to be an important element in explaining that the international institutional order today is quite robust and adaptive.

IR paradigms

Here we seem to be clearly within a traditional liberalist argument, seemingly in line with the dominant neo-neo approach: states are the central actors but institutions matter. But, it is explicitly stated, this cannot be grasped within the 'currently ascendant logic of instrumental rationality'. So it is *the neo-neo problematique within a non-rationalist framework*.

Ontology

It is still – as in the previous phases – clear that institutions are given a certain independent reality, and at the same time constantly kept in close contact with the states, never allowed to be analysed in any 'idealist' mode on their own. Functional needs are denied any ultimate explanatory power, but taken seriously. More clearly than previously the domestic side is upgraded in explaining the content of regimes; this parallels most sharply the analysis in the 'Embedded Liberalism' articles. It is necessary to look at the content of a regime, at the domestic order it is linked to.

Most interesting in the 1992a article is the status of this new differentiation inside the concept of institutions; the ontological status of an adjective. It is stressed that the adjective 'multilateral' has an independent explanatory power beyond that of the noun 'institution'. Simultaneously, the relationship of institutions to their political environment is generally not loosened up. This indicates that the question of institutional autonomy contains two different axes that are normally not kept separate. The institution has an independent importance, not because it is able to challenge the sway of the state, but because *its* attributes shape outcomes.

It sounds as if we have almost come full circle to Kratochwil and Ruggie's first phase of the study of international organizations. 'Within it, the assumption was made... that the formal attributes of international organizations, such as their charters, voting procedures, committee structures, and the like, account for what they do' (1986: 755). But we have not. We are not talking about the *formal* characteristics of the organization, but the generic subcategories of institutions. The conceptualization of multilateralism is rather a reply to their own call after the fourth phase: to get concrete mechanisms back in the study. The reason for the Kratochwil and Ruggie appeal was that

> in order for the research programme of international regimes *both* to contribute to ongoing policy concerns *and* better reflect the complex and sometimes ambiguous policy realm, it is necessary to link up regimes in some fashion with the formal mechanisms through which real-world actors operate.
>
> (Kratochwil and Ruggie 1986: 772)

These formal mechanisms are not only organizations, they include of course also that which is 'in' conventions and regimes. Multilateralism is such a mechanism.

What has happened ontologically with the multilateralism article is that institutionalization is taken seriously enough ontologically speaking for subcategories within it to be elevated to explanatory status without having this argument bogged down as a version of the one about the relative power of states and institutions. The institution can be highly state-controlled or not, and it can be an order, a regime, or an organization, the *form* it takes has importance. This is based on the prior premise that institutions matter. The argument is therefore placed within the new institutionalism. Only if the noun institution matters, does it make sense to start arguing that the adjective matters. But some of the 'institutions matter' argumentation in, for instance, Keohane (1989: Chapter 1) could have been greatly helped by the (implicit) distinction between the two axes of importance involved in Ruggie's article.

American foreign policy, the UN, peace-keeping and collective security

Ruggie's 'discovery' of multilateralism allows him to make a series of political interventions, which otherwise would not have been possible.

In several recent writings (1992c, 1992d; 1993b, 1993c, 1993d; 1994a, 1994b; 1995a, 1995b; forthcoming) he has returned to subjects he had dealt with previously: collective security in the UN (1974) and US policy towards the UN (1985, 1990a). In arguments about UN peacekeeping and US policy on, for example, Bosnia and Somalia, Ruggie argues that 'The chief defining attribute of multilateralism, including collective security arrangements, should be construed not as universality but as nondiscrimination' (1993d: 30). Thus one should work to avoid geographical or other bias, but not be disillusioned by the impossibility of securing universal coverage. As to the US role, Ruggie argues strongly for American leadership and that military force should remain with the member states (and be mobilized in multinational coalitions), not be acquired by the UN as such (1992c, 1992d, 1993c). Again we see, as with the liberal world economy, that naive acceptance of the liberal ideal as yardstick will lead to impossible demands and inevitable disillusion, whereas an understanding of the principles actually operated by the actors leads to the possibility of assisting in improving and strengthening a multilateralist approach to international security.

Especially in relation to American foreign policy it is important thus to overcome the apparent dilemma between full collective security and unilateralism. By stressing instead the specific type of organization – one based on generalized norms – it is possible to undermine a separation between institutions and realism, and thereby combat the 'ultra-realism' of a John Mearsheimer (1995). In the postwar period, the USA did pursue 'realist' alliance politics, but had to choose a *form* therefore; anti-institutionalist realists argued, for example, against NATO and UN peacekeeping, but such policies were pursued by American presidents who were in many ways still 'realist'. Hereby, Ruggie points to the importance of the forms chosen; for instance, for the way NATO and the EU have been able to continue beyond the end of the Cold War as they probably could not have done had they been more narrow bilateral systems of alliances. (Again, we see the importance of not discussing institutions in their relative power *vis-à-vis* states, but seeing how *any* order is institutionalized in some form, whether that be on the basis of unilateralist balance-of-power politics or generalized multilateralism.)

Finally, one could notice in these policy writings how Ruggie derives American strategy from America's geopolitical conditions, and thus again stresses the specificity of the domestic/international interface in the case of the USA. The price of this is a loss of general access to domestic variables in the case of non-US states, the gain is a powerful inroad into American debates about self-definition, purpose and policy at a crucial moment (see especially 1994a, 1995a and forthcoming). This is where a major part of Ruggie's work is located in the mid-1990s, but to understand fully these 'policy writings', one needs the theoretical basis in the theory of multi-lateralism, but thereby also the general approach to international collaboration (previous sections).

NEO-REALISM

The substantial argument

Ruggie 1983a is a review essay, 'Continuity and Transformation in the World Polity'. Waltz's *Theory of International Politics* has been presented above (Chapter 3), so here we will proceed directly to Ruggie's own moves. We will postpone the question of how to interpret this assenting essay on neo-realism. One can take it at face value as improving on neo-realism in a constructive spirit, and one can see it using neo-realism as a pretext for developing a theory of transformations.

First, Ruggie underscores that the methodology and social ontology of Waltz are actually Durkheimian: society is not just the summation of individuals but 'a specific reality which has its own characteristics', characteristics that stem from the system formed by the individuals, by their combination. Waltz emphasizes one specific level in the social totality: the structure made up of the positioning of units in the international system, anarchy and polarity.

Second, Ruggie clarifies the concept of structure employed by Waltz:

> Waltz strives for a 'generative' formulation of structure. He means for the three (or, internationally, two) components of structure to be thought of as successive causal depth levels. Ordering principles constitute the 'deep structure' of a system, shaping its fundamental social quality. They are not visible directly, only through their hypothesized effects. Differentiation, where it exists as a structural property, mediates the social effects of the deep structure, but within a context that has already been circumscribed by the deep structure. ... When all is said and done, however, this generative model eludes Waltz.
>
> (1983a: 266)

This implies that concepts such as sovereignty 'are not simply descriptive categories. Rather, they are components of generative structures: they shape, condition, and constrain social behaviour' (1983a: 280).

Third, this points towards the point where Ruggie adds a rectification of Waltz's implementation of his own scheme. A dimension of change is missing from Waltz's model. This is argued by way of a historical case: it is shown that Waltz's explanation 'provides no means by which to account for, or even to describe, the most important contextual change in international politics in this *millennium*: the shift from the medieval to the modern international system' (1983a: 273). This was a shift within anarchy. The medieval system was anarchic just as was the modern one – but it operated differently,[5] thus there must have been structural causes at play, and these were not level-3 differences (distribution of capabilities). But they can be seen as an instance of change exactly at that second level, which Waltz himself closed off. 'Differentiation of units', the second component of structure, was dropped by Waltz, Ruggie argues,

> as a result of giving an infelicitous interpretation to the sociological term 'differentiation' taking it to mean *differences* rather than that which denotes *separateness*. The modern system is distinguished from the medieval not by 'sameness' or 'differences' of units, but by *the principles on the basis of which the constituent units are separated* from one another. If anarchy tells us *that* the political system is a segmental realm, differentiation tells us *on what basis* the segmentation is determined. The second component of structure, therefore, does *not* drop out; it stays in, and serves as an exceedingly important source of structural variation.
>
> (Ruggie 1983a: 273 f.)

By this move he claims that *inside* the condition of anarchy, it is possible to have different orders that are distinguished as to the way the units are constituted. A medieval system based on conditional ownership and unconditional, personal authority, is very different from the modern system of sovereign states, but it is still anarchic since there is no overarching authority ('world government'). The medieval system took the form of a patchwork of overlapping authorities, while the modern one is based on the principle of sovereign statehood. Each of these structural arrangements can then at the third level be varied as multipolar, tripolar, or bipolar. In a medieval world one could also detect the major powers; however, they would not take our form of territorially delineated states, but would be strange units such as a British king with some odd authority over Calais, and influence over various other places on the continent secured by marriage and other personal arrangements; the Pope as another power centre; etc. This takes us some way towards overcoming the problem of 'change'. When more different 'systems' are possible due to the inclusion of level 2, a theory which first of all tells us what kind of politics and behaviour follows from what system, becomes much more interesting. The system changes more often.[6]

Sovereignty is discussed as 'a form of *legitimation* that pertains to a *system* of relations' (1983a: 276). With the advent of absolute private property and mutually exclusive territorial state formation ensued a major legitimation crisis, which lead to laborious philosophical work, known as our modern classics of political thought and international law. Ruggie shows here among other things the close correspondence between private property rights and the international role of the principle of sovereignty. Thereby, the structure opens up towards areas not normally covered by IR theory, certainly not by Waltzian neo-realism: when the character of units enters at the second level, issues like the hegemonic form of state–society relations that prevails internationally at a given time become an attribute of the international system (e.g. the range and depth of state intervention in domestic affairs). This is where the link to the Ruggie of sections 3 and 4 becomes most clear: the state/society-related regimes become tied to the second level of Waltzian structure.

The international political system becomes more closely linked to other dimensions of social life by the Ruggian reformulation of the second level. The definition of property rights and the organization of political space, and thereby more generally capitalist production relations and interstate political relations, are closely linked. Still, Ruggie states that he shares 'Waltz's view on the priority of the states system, so long as the deep structure of anarchy prevails' (1983a: 281), so it is not that he returns international relations to a derivative position *vis-à-vis* economy or technology, but that he insists on seeing 'a more comprehensive social formation' wherein international relations operate in close connection with other forms of sociality. This is handled through the opening of a dimension of differentiation between international systems: the second tier of structure as an important dimension of variation.

Not only does Ruggie show *that* a major form of change in the international system is missing from Waltz's model, he also begins an explanation of *why* such change happens. He here returns to Durkheim's stress on the volume and dynamic density of societies. 'Volume' is easy because that means the number of socially relevant units, i.e. the third level of structure according to Waltz. But 'dynamic density' is missing in Waltz.

> By this Durkheim understands the quantity, velocity, and diversity of transactions that go on within society. But Waltz, as we have seen, banishes such factors to the level of process, shaped by structure but not in turn affecting structure in any manner depicted by his model.
>
> (1983a: 281)

The pressure of dynamic density is most directly operative on prevailing property rights in a society. Thus, when this element is not tied into the theory, dynamic density does not seem to have much international effect. (And Waltz can restrict himself to refuting traditional interdependence arguments.) But with the opening of the second level of structure, dynamic density becomes highly relevant.

Several IR authors share a wish to introduce *a something* between structure and unit. Ruggie talks of dynamic density, Buzan of interaction capacity, and Keohane and Nye suggest 'process'. The missing issues can be said to be systemic but non-structural (in Waltz's sense of political, positional arrangement of units). A major move is therefore to devise and define such a category of the *non-structural systemic* (instead of expanding the structure). Less clear is how this links into the theory. Is it a general causal 'factor' competing with other variables for explaining specific instances, or is it a factor which should not be used to explain the outcome of singular events, but seen only as a subterranean movement, which – with an interval of centuries – causes changes to the structure? The latter seems to be closer to Ruggie's suggestion.

A final criticism of Waltz is that he overemphasizes systemic forces, and '*unit-level processes* become all product and are not at all productive' (Ruggie 1983a: 284). 'The problem with Waltz's posture is that, in any social system, structural change itself ultimately has no source *other than* unit-level processes. By banishing these from the domain of systemic theory, Waltz also exegenizes the ultimate source of systemic change. . . . As a result, Waltz's theory . . . contains only a reproductive logic, but no transformational logic' (1983a: 285).

IR paradigms

How has Ruggie then located himself among the paradigms? Did 'Continuity and Transformation' mark his conversion to neo-realism, or was this sympathetic review essay a Trojan horse by which the particular Ruggian mix of radical methodology and liberal problematique entered into the camp of neo-realism itself?

Does he basically buy into the Waltzian approach, or is his critique one of neo-realism as such? Despite what Ruggie might want to say today, the 1983 article is presented very much as 'constructive critique' meant to 'amend and augment the theory in a manner that is not incompatible with its basic realist precepts' (quoted from the summary). According to Ruggie, his critique is an assessment of 'whether Waltz succeeds on his own terms. I find that he does not do so fully. Part of the reason lies in errors of omission and commission, part is inherent to the enterprise as Waltz conceives of it' (1983a: 273). Thus, there *are* inherent errors, but this charge is more or less concentrated in the argument against Waltz's interpretation of 'differentiation' (and thereby the exclusion of the second analytical component of structure). 'Its defects can be compensated for in a suitably amended and augmented neo-realist formulation. Such a formulation would go some way toward subsuming the major competing systemic theories' (1983a: 285).

Less clear is Ruggie's position regarding the unit level. Is this to remain an undifferentiated field for empirical variation (as suggested by Waltz), or is it a space to be filled out by a theory of 'domestic sources of foreign policy' (as suggested by Keohane and Nye and in some places by Waltz)? Ruggie clearly upgrades domestic politics in articles like 'Embedded liberalism' (1982) and 'Multilateralism' (1992a), but systematically: how is it conceived and placed in relation to structure and dynamic density?

It seems that 'domestic' in Ruggie always refers to the state–society relationship in th(os)e state(s) able to shape the international order, central politico-economic regimes or the principle for separating units. There is not much about a multitude of domestic arenas in all their difference (and in their resulting cross-pressure *vis-à-vis* the international environment). Nor is there much interaction, political interplay between units. This might be an understandable perspective seen from the USA. When one lives in what could almost be called the 'systemic state', it is natural to focus on the close relationship between the domestic politics of this one state and how it relates to dominant structures internationally. It is just not very typical or representative. General domestic politics seems in this sense still to be left out.

Ontology

Ruggie does not – as do so many other critics of Waltz – make a big issue out of the analogies to micro-economy and what can be seen thereby as a paradoxical, implicit ontological atomism (Wendt 1987). Should this be taken to imply that he accepts or even supports this? No, he cannot be buying into the atomistic ontology since he has criticized the choice theoretical conception of regimes, for example, and in the Waltz article he stresses that the system is a social reality in its own right and therefore its structure has independent explanatory force, as has the systemic, unit-related force of dynamic density. Instead of criticizing Waltz, Ruggie reads atomism out of him, and replaces it by a Durkheimian Waltz.

His main critique is that it is a mistake of Waltz – and Durkheim – to turn a methodological principle into an ontological one (1983a: 285) and thereby exclude change by definition. The opening of the second tier makes it possible in principle that we could move towards a postmodern (or neo-medieval) system. Ruggie does not argue that this change is happening, but he constructs a theory which does not in advance shut off this option. Thus, ontologically his basic categories and units have a plasticity that is seldom seen in IR theory. The question of 'continuity and change' becomes a very gradual and localized one. Almost no statements can be made universally valid, and thereby no blockings imposed ontologically. But given Waltz's layered structure, one can take some things relatively more for granted than others and thereby on the basis of their regularities investigate change at other levels. There is, however, a price to be paid for such detailed differentiation, as follows.

A study of the metaphors used by different IR authors shows for Ruggie an exceptionally high presence of 'industry and machine metaphors' – mechanisms, forces, and matrix of constraints (Staun Poulsen 1995: 63 ff.). This stems less from Waltz than from the 'scientific realism' which Ruggie draws on as an antidote to positivism: the world contains more than simple events and correlations – there are equally real 'mechanisms', generative structures at various levels. A bit surprisingly, this has not been attacked by fellow 'reflectivists' (cf. Chapter 1 on the potential debate between deconstructivism and constructivism), but instead by Krasner, who in a revival of basic (pre-neo-)realism argues that state interests and power politics explain it all; meta-institutional forms (such as sovereignty or territoriality) stressed by the English School and Ruggians do not constrain and thus not shape (1993, 1994, 1995). Generative structure is unnecessary metaphysics. The ontological irritant of Ruggie 1983 is the status given to 'structure'. Despite the appeal for leaving more leeway for unit-level forces – and thus some basic structurationism – Ruggie's structures are powerful and partly self-sustaining *qua* generative. Krasner is right in picking Ruggie as his main target of attack, because Ruggie actually goes quite far in establishing powerful (generative) structures – in a sense more structure than Waltz since Ruggie reintroduces the second tier. Ruggie here differs markedly from poststructuralists, but in practice also from 'mainstream constructivists' such as Wendt who spend most of their time pointing to the malleability of structure. Ruggie seems to respect structure more, which shows in his constant emphasis on change from within orders rather than from without and in his scepticism towards too easy and too fast 'transformations'.[7]

AN EMERGING THEORY OF TRANSFORMATIONS

At the end of the 1983 article, Ruggie states that

> Waltz's posture...is a welcome antidote to the prevailing superficiality of the proliferating literature on international transformations, in which the sheer momentum of processes sweeps the international polity along toward its next encounter with destiny.
>
> (1983a: 285)

On the other hand, Waltz – even if he could be right about the future continuity in the international system – has excluded the *possibility* of change by the way his theory is constructed. Ruggie zooms in on the issue of a *theory of transformation*. How does one construct a theory which is neither 'swept away' nor in its defining doing away with change? How can one study the gradual and marginal changes and assess in some systematic way whether and when they make up a qualitative shift?

Earlier studies often concluded that change was 'rule-governed', i.e. not upsetting the underlying logic (1980a: 549 f.; 1983a: 283, n. 60; 1989). A 1993 article addresses directly the issue of transformations. 'Territoriality and Beyond: Problematizing Modernity in International Relations' begins with an argument for raising the issue of territoriality. It is a distinctive trait of modernity in international politics, and therefore a transformation here would define a major transformation of this system. Yet, the concept of territoriality has been little studied in IR.

Changes in the EU and in the global economy illustrate the issue whether developments somehow move beyond state sovereignty and territoriality towards overlapping authorities and non-territorial ('off-shore') markets and production. When noting these challenges, we should not hopelessly search for 'entities that are institutionally substitutable for the state', which would just leave the realists to conclude that nothing has fundamentally changed.

> The long and the short of it is, then, that we are not very good as a discipline at studying the possibility of fundamental discontinuity in the international system, at addressing the question of whether the modern

system of states may be yielding in some instances to postmodern forms
of configuring political space.

(1993a: 143 f.)

A major part of the article consists of an analysis of how territoriality came
about. This is partly a rerun of the medieval-to-modern argument from the
1983 article, but it makes more clear the mechanisms by which the change
happened and not least the logical and ontological status of the different
dimensions of change.

First it is argued how and why territoriality is a distinct form of politics. It is
characteristic of the modern system of rule 'that it has differentiated its subject
collectivity into territorially defined, fixed, and mutually exclusive enclaves of
legitimate dominion' (1993a: 151). 'Modes of differentiation are nothing less
than the focus of the epochal study of rule' (1993a: 152). This clearly points
towards a focus on the second tier of Waltzian structure, although Waltzian
terminology and the whole link to neo-realism are now downplayed.

Since the modern system of states is socially constructed, the way to
'account for' the modern principle of territoriality is to deal with 'the
"raw materials" that people used and drew upon in constructing it'. These
were developments in three dimensions, irreducible to one another: material
environments, strategic behaviour and social epistemology. 'Irreducible'
means that none of them caused the others, only their joint articulation
made for the transformation. Production, military technology and the
monetarization of economic relations are central elements in the material
part, and 'altered the matrix of constraints and opportunities for social
actors, giving rise to different situations of strategic action among them'
(1993a: 154). Society had *first to imagine itself in new forms*, conceive
appropriate orders of rule and exchange, symbolize identities, propagate
norms and doctrines, before the state order could come into place. Thus it
could not be directly materially determined or just a matter of instrumental
rationality. There is an important element of social construction, of social
epistemes. The change in concepts of ownership and sovereignty is linked to
cosmological changes in the concepts of time and space, not least the
change in the visual arts: the invention of single-point perspective.

Different strands of IR theory can explain parts of the story. Neo-
realism, the microeconomics of institutions and cultural theories: each takes
one of the three factors, all of which were essential but none of which was
individually able to cause the transformation. None of the theories is a
candidate for grand theory, nor can they just be added up, and therefore
one can only make contingent and limited generalizations.

Examining the social practice whereby the new unity was achieved, an
innovative element is 'the process of "unbundling" territoriality, which
made it possible for the new territorial states, who viewed their individual
subjectivity as constituting a self-sufficient moral and political field, to form
a society of states' (1993a: 160). This refers to a powerful paradox:

Having established territorially fixed state formations, having insisted
that these territorial domains were disjoint and mutually exclusive, and

having accepted these conditions as the constitutive basis of international society, what means were left to the new territorial rulers for dealing with problems of that society that could not be reduced to territorial solution?

(1993a: 164)

Common spaces (such as waterways) were one kind of problem. The solution to this was found through the handling of another problem which became in a sense paradigmatic : the problem of diplomatic representation led to the invention of a fictitious place, 'extraterritoriality'. In order to be able to communicate with each other these newly sovereign states had to tolerate islands of alien sovereignty within themselves. The general pattern, Ruggie describes as an 'unbundling of territoriality', which 'has become a generic contrivance used by states to attenuate the paradox of absolute individuation' (1993a: 165; cf. Kratochwil 1986). Functional regimes, common markets, political communities, are other forms of unbundling territoriality.

The unbundling of territoriality is a stabilizing mechanism that has been and is employed by the modern system to handle its anomalies, but it is at the same time the place where a rearticulation of international political space would occur, where the new, pressing elements are accumulating. For instance, the EC (now the EU) is possibly the first 'multiperspectival polity' that has emerged.

That is to say, it is increasingly difficult to visualize the conduct of international politics among Community members, and to a considerable measure even domestic politics, as though it took place from a starting point of twelve separate, single, fixed viewpoints. Nor can models of strategic interaction do justice to this particular feature of the EC. For the collectivity of members as a singularity, in addition to the central institutional apparatus of the EC, has become party to the strategic interaction game.

(1993a: 172)

In current debates on neo-medievalism in relation especially to developments in Europe (Luke 1991; Wæver 1991, 1995; Wind 1993), one could usefully register Ruggie's analysis of patterns of change. Ruggie suggests three (1993a: 166 f., emphasis added): '*Unanticipated consequences* played a major role in determining the ultimate outcomes of long-term changes... - fundamental transformation may have long-standing sources, but when it came it *came quickly* by historical standards' (punctuated equilibrium), and change is *never complete*. Several new forms compete, and history in this sense 'sorts itself out' much more slowly and less clearly than the dates and breaks that we in our aggregate judgements designate as turning points.

In the economic system we see the emergence of features that do not as such directly challenge the existing organizing format (the classical defence of sovereignty made by traditionalists) but rather play the role of embodying new logics, that could be – or not be – inventing principles that become central in an increasingly important postmodern system. This is a space-of-flows which operate in real time alongside the space-of-places ('national economies').

This non-territorial global economic region is a world, in short, that is premised on what Lattimore described as the 'sovereign importance of movement,' not of place. The long-term significance of this region, much like that of the medieval trade fairs, may reside in its novel behavioral and institutional forms, and in the novel space–time constructs that these forms embody, not in any direct challenge that it poses as a potential substitute for the existing system of rule.

(1993a: 172 f.)

This is an important argument. Where Ruggie had previously concluded that we did not witness radical change, but 'rule-governed change' shaped by existing structures, and thus no transformation, the 1993 article registers that radical novelty is a possibility, because it emerges in the paradoxical form of unbundling of territoriality, which is both a logical product of territorial sovereignty and also a potential transcendence hereof. Non-revolutionary transformation![8]

CONCLUSION: TRANSFORMING INSTITUTIONALIZED LIBERALISM IN IR

He has dressed up as neo-realist, he has been treated as a leading 'reflectivist', nevertheless his main effects seem consistently to be among the liberalists. Actually, the evolution of liberal IR in the last twenty years is difficult to describe without including Ruggie's contributions. Only among a few realists (Buzan, ego) are his contributions seen as essential, and in the radical corner he is mainly acknowledged for his critique of the 'enemy' and for suggestive ideas relating to neo-medievalism (e.g. Wind 1993).

His impact on liberalism is worth concentrating on. He has recurrently played a key role in moving the core concern of liberal IR.[9] First, liberal IR was marked by an interest in the semi-automatic, de-politicized role of science and technology in transforming international relations, and in the multiplication of international institutions. Ruggie here shifted the issue to that of collaboration (where technology and science is only one among many themes) and he insisted that it all inevitably operated in a political framework. This involved a shift from organizations to organization and through several steps to institutionalization and differentiations within this concept. Later Ruggie in a sense came full circle with an interest in the grand transformations that change radically the nature of IR, thus the classical 'liberal' interest in some break that will end realist repetition and recurrence. Ruggie studies here transformations that are closely related to technology (but never de-politicized, thus *not* coming full circle) – at the same time as he in 1992a and 1993e returns almost to formal institutions, to multilateralism. Kratochwil and Ruggie (1986) present their analysis explicitly in terms of the step-by-step evolution of the problematique of governance, *de facto* liberalism in IR.

At present the activities of Ruggie do not look very much like liberal IR. It is in a sense still neo-realism (second tier) – at least as much as in the

1983a article – but he does not want to dress it up like that any more (indicating that the tactical interpretation of the 1983 article was correct?). Such study of the force behind deep change is not what concerns either liberals or realists at the moment, but an interest of the radical corner (Ashley; Walker; Cox). Also Ruggie's methodology and his insistence on the central role of the epistemic/discursive in the medieval-to-modern transformation seem to locate him more clearly than ever in the radical box. Yet, there seems to be a pattern that might predict something else. Ruggie has systematically had a major impact on a specific corner of the triangle (liberal IR) without ever clearly locating himself there. In some sense he probably can identify with at least the ambitions of that corner (when it is not too rationalist) and this is in a sense his research community, but major impulses, inspirations and arguments have been drawn from realism and radical reflectivism. Is a postmodern liberalist emerging?

Of course, one cannot predict the future fate of Ruggie's theory of transformations on the basis of 'patterns' in the 'interparadigmatic' effects of an author. But *if* the pattern holds, Ruggie is rearticulating once again the liberal agenda. And it is logical because it would be back to (one of) the roots of IR liberalism: arguing (against the realists) for the possibility of radical change, for non-continuity in International Relations (cf. Wæver 1992: Chs 1–3).

The subsections on ontology have shown a rare plasticity of units and categories – history can transform even the most basic units, but it is always a process beginning from here, not from an alternative, an 'it could be different' (as with many deconstructivists or constructivists), or from the 'necessity' of some transformation (as with much liberalism). Ruggie's work is more like realism in taking the existing constellation as the necessary foundation, making a similar political choice for linking up to existing institutions: states as well as international organizations. With his conceptual adaptability, and especially the non-fixation of the modern, territorial state, Ruggie has become a leading exponent of what could be called post-sovereign realism (or rather not sovereignty-bound realism). In a period where realism has become stereotyped into being necessarily state-fixated (cf. Chapter 1 of this book), this no longer looks like realism, but rather like a forgotten kind of liberalism. Ruggie stands at the meeting-point of realism and liberalism – as the neo-neo synthesis – but decidedly not on a 'rationalist' (rational choice) basis.

As shown in section 5, when revising neo-realism, a 'third' factor encompassing technological development, norms, degree of institutionalization, and international society has to come in as the underlying, gradual, slowly emerging trend which causes from time to time systemic change; whether it is called 'dynamic density' (Ruggie), 'process' (Keohane and Nye) or 'interaction capacity' (Buzan), it is essentially *the liberal factor* – all that which liberal theory has always wanted to insert as giving hope for evolutionary but ultimately qualitative change based on progress. Logically these factors are systemic but non-structural (not part of the positional arrangement of units). Attempts to put these into the structure have therefore correctly been resisted by Waltz, but his own conclusion of dumping it all on the unit level is clearly unsatisfactory. Developments in technology, including the innovation and diffusion of nuclear weapons, are a question not only of who has them but also of the systemic effects of these factors entering the system. Possibly, as part of the emerging redistribution of roles in the attempts at synthesis and division of labour of the 1990s, the liberalist contribution might shift from theories of co-operation and learning (where liberalism is challenged by rationalist realism and constructivism respectively) to the systemic level – explore the liberal factor: how do these deep forces of technology and enlightenment actually alter the system structure, and how can this be studied? (Work like Moravcsik 1992 and Burley 1995 can be read as the beginnings hereof.)

Why label this 'liberal'? Because the recurring issue between realism and liberalism in IR has been the possibility of *progress*, of basic change away from IR as the realm of repetition and recurrence (Wight 1966 [1960]; Bull 1972: 34; Morgenthau 1946). The conceptualization of the liberal factor is in the present presentation oriented less towards the continuous, gradual impact directly from 'interaction capacity' to ongoing politics (which might be what a Keohane, for instance, is first of all interested in) but more towards the way 'interaction capacity' influences structure.[10] In the latter perspective it is emphasized how long-term (very rare) historic – epochal – change is driven by 'the liberal factor' (technology, progress, civilization). An order is shaken when the subterranean forces of change hit the political ordering, has not occurred for the last four hundred or so years. This is not technological determinism or a new version of historical materialism, for transformations – as argued in section 6 – need a discursive interpretation (Ruggie 1983a, 1993a) since the specific rearticulation of political time-space after the upheaval cannot be deduced from 'dynamic density'/interaction capacity, but nor should the change be seen as *triggered* by discursive processes. Thus, the liberalists are in the long run and in a few periods 'right': International Relations is not a field of repetition and recurrence alone, the qualitative change we know from society at large will ultimately reach IR too (although most likely remaining within the framework of anarchy). Thus also the liberalist agenda – so far confined to separate debates like foreign policy analysis (FPA) or integration theory, and only partly liberated through 'neo-liberal institutionalism' – might gain from a rearticulation of the lines of debate in accordance with the 'fourth' debate (cf. the introduction to this book and Wæver 1994).

Is this not a way to arrest Ruggie's thought, to box him as liberal? No, because, by now, paradigms are not viewed as static any more. Liberalism changes. In the changing constellations of theories, in the various debates, the one that represents (draws on) liberalism is, however, repeatedly influenced in a major way by Ruggie. Thus, while Ruggie rarely presents his own arguments in terms of debates over 'paradigms', he seems to have an excellent political nose (also) in the politics of the discipline; the moves he makes are neither fruitless one-man operations nor repetitions of well-established positions. He acts along the lines that are at the specific time (on their way to becoming) main lines of exchange in the discipline. To read Ruggie, thus – paradoxically – demands a solid grasp of the changing constellations of internal debate about discipline in IR. If we are now *after the fourth debate* (Chapter 1) in a mood of synthesis, where moderate reflectivists and thinking rationalists try to operate a division of labour among traditions, the liberal factor could be one of the key components. And there would be one statistical generalization not broken: that Ruggie has proved prophetic a remarkable number of times, and generally on behalf of liberal IR, whether he likes and wants it or not. The 1993 article on transformations and territoriality would hardly be read as typically 'liberal' IR, but maybe in five to ten years it will self-evidently be seen as quintessential liberalism. Here a 'statistical' inference regarding the relationship between Ruggian inventions and the evolution of liberal IR ties into a possible reinterpretation of the overall constellation of theories/paradigms in the 1990s, and this all points to what is after all an extremely classical, though forgotten, liberal problematique: transformation. Not revolution, but dispassionate transformation. Transformation through, not (only) against, institutionalization.

NOTES

I would like to thank my coeditor and all contributors to this book, as well as the project group in Copenhagen, Barry Buzan, Jaap de Wilde and Wojchiech Kostecki – and here Lene Hansen again – for commenting on several versions of the paper. Robert Keohane and John Ruggie gave most helpful written comments.

1 Other concepts like 'multilateralism' and 'international governance' have in their basic conceptualization been significantly influenced by Ruggie. The 'regime' concept was (re)launched in modern IR theory by Ruggie (1975a); 'multilateralism' was raised to a significant analytical concept by him (1992a) and its launch came through a project co-ordinated by him (Ruggie 1993e); 'embedded liberalism' was presented by him (1982); 'epistemic communities' draws on the Foucaldian use of the term 'episteme' but Ruggie first gave it the more sociological twist (1975a: 569 f.), which was later to be developed by Peter Haas and Emanuel Adler in particular; 'collective balancing' was suggested by Ruggie (1993b) (as a new type of UN 'peace keeping' operating in a suasion mode); and 'governance' was used as the unifying term for different approaches to the study of international organizations, regimes, etc., by Kratochwil and Ruggie (1986) (but was used in parallel by other writers such as James Rosenau).
2 Or in Kratochwil and Ruggie (1986: 766, n. 48): *Planetary Politics: Ecology and the Organization of Global Political Space*; nothing less.
3 Contrary to what often happens nowadays, 'ontology' as the issue of 'what is' should not become a fashionable label for that which was discussed in the third (interparadigm) debate: basic images of international relations, as, for instance, state-centric versus pluralist. Ontology should refer to more basic questions about what 'stuff' the world is made of: relations, processes, action, units (self-conscious, present to themselves and relating to other units each given in and of themselves), consciousness, the march of the world-spirit, or power? Cf. Patomäki (1992) and Erik Ringmar's argument on pp. 276–7 of the present book.
4 Polanyi's work was already centrally placed in Ruggie (1975b: 145 f).

5 The crucial empirical task is to demonstrate that the modus operandi followed by the medieval system differed from the modern one. It was therefore an excellent idea for Markus Fischer (1992) to attempt to check whether the Middle Ages actually necessitates the second tier in an explanation, or whether it accords to 'normal' behaviour as expected from the first and third tiers. Unfortunately this, the major critical discussion of Ruggie's argument, takes the form of a misguided refusal of three non-arguments; that ideal norms guide practice; that medieval Europe was a departure from an anarchic balance of power behaviour; and that communitarian logic dominates over egoistic behaviour. These are not Ruggie's claims. Evolving work by Stephen Krasner could promise a more perceptive investigation (1993, 1995).

6 Difficult questions remain regarding how exactly to define the second tier of structure. Buzan *et al.* 1993 contains another attempt. In section one Buzan opts for a tighter approach than Ruggie's in that he retains Waltz's dichotomy (different or same units), whereas in section two Little leans towards variations in type of unit. In their continued work (1994, 1995), Buzan and Little attempt to develop each of these questions conceptually (functional differentiation, structural differentiation). Ruggie's concept is probably located between the two and does not include all variations in form of unit, only those that change the principle of separation among units; on the other hand, these exist in more than two forms: medieval is different from modern is different from postmodern. Cf. Wæver 1994.

7 The problem is how to reconcile this structuralism with Ruggie's constant emphasis on the political, discursive and intersubjective construction of political orders. How deep are the structures, and deep into what? When Ruggie stresses how 'generative structures' differ from 'descriptive structures' in referring to 'the underlying principles that govern the patterning of interactions' (1983a: 266, n. 16), there seem to be 'real' structures that mercilessly produce their effects, while in other texts the central social facts are negotiated among actors and are rules constituted intersubjectively and dependent on what actors think. The status of structure is an ambiguity somewhere between ontology and epistemology. Not until 1995b does Ruggie offer a clarification of his basic epistemology, and there it is in terms of 'narrative knowledge' – which seems to point to a status of structures as 'emplotment', an arrangement of elements that produce convincing stories. But still: are the stories convincing because the structures are so, or are there structures because of the way we tell our stories? The compatibility of narrative epistemology and 'generative structure' is not immediately obvious, but could possibly be established (Wæver in preparation).

8 The discussion of IR paradigms and ontology of this last article will be taken as part of the conclusion.

9 One could almost phrase this in terms of Gaston Bachelard's idea of scientific progress through the 'no' to seemingly convincing, easy, nice theories (1940). Ruggie's contribution constantly takes the form of an epistemic rupture: he questions the dominant *way of formulating a question* within liberalist IR, but by enabling a new and different formulation does not prevent the project, but, on the contrary, gives it a more promising foundation.

10 A certain structuralism might be a precondition for studying epochal transformation. A more Wendtian constructivism leads rather to an image of constant, gradual change. To be able to put down markers and say that this is one system, this is another, demands – unless these markers are simply arbitrary points on a scale – that orders are endowed with some self-reproducing capacities, and change therefore becomes stepwise. With a concept of generative structure, Ruggie gets less change than some very voluntarist theories do, but he can make strong statements about it when it happens – because change has a name when orders have attributes.

REFERENCES

Works by John Gerard Ruggie

Ruggie, John Gerard (1972a) 'Collective Goods and Future International Collaboration', *American Political Science Review* 66(3): 874–93.

——(1972b) 'The Structure of International Organization: Contingency, Complexity, and Post-Modern Form', in *Peace Research Society (International) Papers*, Vol. XVIII, n.p.: the London Conference, 1971, pp. 73–91.

——(1974) 'Contingencies, Constraints, and Collective Security: Perspectives on UN Involvement in International Disputes', *International Organization* 28(3): 493–520.

——(1975a) 'International Responses to Technology: Concepts and Trends', in John Gerard Ruggie and Ernst B. Haas (eds) 'International Responses to Technology', a special issue of *International Organization* 29(3): 557–83.

——(1975b) 'Complexity, Planning and Public Order', in Todd R. La Porte (ed.) *Organized Social Complexity: Challenge to Politics and Policy*, Princeton, NJ: Princeton University Press, pp. 119–51.

——(1978) 'Changing Frameworks of International Collective Behavior: On the Complementarity of Contradictory Tendencies', in Nazli Choucri and Thomas W. Robinson (eds) *Forecasting in International Relations: Theory, Methods, Problems, Prospects*, San Francisco: W. H. Freeman pp. 384–406.

——(1980a) 'On the Problem of "the Global Problematique": what Roles for International Organizations?', *Alternatives* 5(4) (January): 517–50.

——(1980b) review of Stephen D. Krasner, 'Defending the National Interest: Raw Materials Investments and U.S. Foreign Policy', *American Political Science Review* 74(1): 296–9.

——(1981) 'The Politics of Money', *Foreign Policy* 43: 139–54.

——(1982) 'International Regimes, Transactions, and Change: Embedded Liberalism in the Postwar Economic Order', *International Organization*, 36(2): 379–415; reprinted in S. D. Krasner (ed.) *International Regimes*, New York: Columbia University Press, 1983.

——(1983a) 'Continuity and Transformation in the World Polity: Toward a Neorealist Synthesis', *World Politics* 35(2): 261–85; reprinted in R. O. Keohane, *Neorealism and Its Critics*, New York: Columbia University Press, 1986.

——(ed.) (1983b) *The Antinomies of Interdependence: National Welfare and the International Division of Labor*, New York: Columbia University Press.

——(1983c) 'International Interdependence and National Welfare' and 'Political Structure and Change in the International Economic Order: the North–South Dimension', in J. G. Ruggie (ed.) *The Antinomies of Interdependence: National Welfare and the International Division of Labor*, New York: Columbia University Press, pp. 1–39 and 423–87.

——(1983d) 'Human Rights and the Future International Community', *DÆDALUS: Journal of the American Academy of Arts and Sciences* 112(4): 93–110.

——(1983e) review of Rüdiger Jütte and Annemarie Grosse-Jütte (eds) *The Future of International Organization* (1981) in *American Journal of International Law* 77(10): 172 f.

——(1984) 'Another Round, Another Requiem? Prospects for the Global Negotiations', in Jagdish N. Bhagwati and John G. Ruggie (eds) *Power, Passions, and Purpose: Prospects for North–South Negotiations*, Cambridge, MA: the MIT Press, pp. 33–48.

——(1985) 'The United States and the United Nations: toward a New Realism', *International Organization* 39(2): 343–55.

——(1989) 'International Structure and International Transformation: Space, Time and Method', in James N. Rosenau and Ernst-Otto Czempiel (eds) *Global Changes and Theoretical Challenges: Approaches to World Politics for the 1990s*, Lexington, MA: Lexington Books, pp. 21–36.

——(1990a) 'United States Strategy in a Changing World', *Disarmament: a periodic review by the United Nations* 13(4): 16–31.

——(1990b) review of Oran R. Young, 'International Co-operation: Building Regimes for Natural Resources and the Environment' (1989), *Political Science Quarterly* 105(2): 352 f.

——(1991) 'Embedded Liberalism Revisited: Institutions and Progress in International Economic Relations', in Emanuel Adler and Beverly Crawford (eds) *Progress in Postwar International Relations*, New York: Columbia University Press, pp. 201–34.

——(1992a) 'Multilateralism: the Anatomy of an Institution', *International Organization* 46(3): 561–98.

——(1992b) intervention as discussant in the Keohane/Grieco panel on absolute and relative gains at the annual meeting of the American Political Science Association, Chicago, in September.

——(1992c) 'No, the World Doesn't Need a United Nations Army', *International Herald Tribune*, 26–7 September.

——(1992d) 'When America Talks, Thugs Listen', *Los Angeles Times*, 1 December.

——(1993a) 'Territoriality and Beyond: Problematizing Modernity in International Relations', *International Organization* 47(1) (Winter): 139–74.

——(1993b) 'The United Nations between Peacekeeping and Enforcement', paper presented at the Symposium on Collective Responses to Common Threats, Royal, Ministry of Foreign Affairs, Oslo, 22–3 June.

——(1993c) 'Is there a Real Bill Clinton Who'll Stand Up?', *New York Newsday*, 6 June.

——(1993d) 'Wandering in the Void: Charting the UN's New Strategic Role', *Foreign Affairs* 72(5): 26–31.

——(ed.) (1993e) *Multilateralism Matters: The Theory and Praxis of an Institutional Form*, New York: Columbia University Press.

——(1994a) 'Third Try at World Order: American and Multilateralism after the Cold War', *Political Science Quarterly* 109(4) (Fall): 553–70.

——(1994b) 'Peacekeeping and U.S. Interests', *Washington Quarterly* 17(4) (Autumn): 175–84.

——(1994c) 'Trade, Protectionism and the Future of Welfare Capitalism', *Journal of International Affairs* 48(1) (Summer): 1–12.

——(1995a) 'The False Premise of Realism', *International Security* 20(1) (Summer): 62–70.

——(1995b) 'Peace in Our Time? Causality, Social Facts, and Narrative Knowing', in American Society of International Law, *Proceedings, 89th Annual Meeting, 1995*.

——(forthcoming) *Winning the Peace: America and World Order in the New Era*, New York: Columbia University Press for the Twentieth Century Fund.

——(in preparation) 'International Transformations: A Structurationist Account'.

——and Bhagwati, Jagdish N. (eds) (1984) *Power, Passions, and Purpose: Prospects for North–South Negotiations*, Cambridge, MA: MIT Press.

——and Gosovic, Bronislav (1976) 'On the Creation of a New International Economic Order: Issue Linkage and the Seventh Special Session of the UN General Assembly', *International Organization* 30(2): 309–46.

——and Haas, Ernst B. (eds) (1975) 'International Responses to Technology', a special issue of *International Organization* 29(3).

——(1981) 'Information Exchange and International Change: the Case of Infoterra', *International Relations* 7: 979–97.

——(1982) 'What Message in the Medium of Information Systems?', *International Studies Quarterly* 26(2): 190–219.

——and Kratochwil, Friedrich (1986) 'International Organization: a State of the Art on an Art of the State', *International Organization* 40(4): 753–75.

——and Leyton-Brown, David (1986–7) 'The North American Political Economy in the Global Context: an Analytical Framework', *International Journal* 42(1) (Winter): 3–24.

Works by other authors

Bachelard, Gaston (1940) *La Philosophie du non*, Paris: Gallimard.

Bull, Hedley (1972) 'The Theory of International Politics, 1919–1969', in Brian Porter (ed.) *The Aberystwyth Papers*, Oxford: Oxford University Press, pp. 30–55.

Buzan, Barry and Little, Richard (1994) 'The Idea of "International System": Theory Meets History', *International Political Science Review* 15(3): 231–55.

——(1995) 'Reconceptualising Anarchic Structure: Accommodating Structural and Functional Differentiation of Units' (April).

——and Jones, Charles (1993) *The Logic of Anarchy: From Neo-realism to Structural Realism*, New York: Columbia University Press.

Fischer, Markus (1992) 'Feudal Europe, 800–1300: Communal Discourse and Conflictual Practices', *International Organization* 46(2): 427–67.

Foucault, Michel (1972) *The Archeology of Knowledge*, New York: Pantheon Books.

Grieco, Joseph M. (1988) 'Anarchy and the Limits of Co-operation: a Realist Critique of the Newest Liberal Institutionalism', *International Organization* 42(3): 485–508.

——(1990) *Co-operation among Nations: Europe, America, and Non-tariff Barriers to Trade*, Ithaca, NY and London: Cornell University Press.

Guzzini, Stefano (1992) 'The Continuing Story of a Death Foretold: Realism in International Relations/International Political Economy', Florence: European University Institute, Social and Political Sciences, working paper.

——(1993) 'Structural Power: the Limits of Neo-realist Power Analysis', *International Organization* 47(3): 443–78.

Haas, Ernst B. (1958) *The Uniting of Europe: Political, Social and Economic Forces 1950–1957*, Stanford, CA: Stanford University Press.

——(1964) *Beyond the Nation-State: Functionalism and International Organization*, Stanford, CA: Stanford University Press.

Kelstrup, Morten, Petersen, Ib Damgaard and Schou, Tove Lise (1990) 'Om International Politiks Teori: Neo-realisme og Interdependens-analyse', in M. Kelstrup (ed.) *Bidrag til Studiet af International Politik og den ny europæiske udvikling*, Vol. III of Nyere Tendenser i Politologien, Copenhagen: Politiske Studier, pp. 13–57.

Keohane, Robert O. (1986a) 'Reciprocity in International Relations', *International Organization* 40(1) (Winter): 1–27; reprinted (1989) in his *International Institutions and State Power: Essays in International Relations Theory*, Boulder, CO: Westview Press, pp. 132–57.

——(ed.) (1986b) *Neo-realism and Its Critics*, New York: Columbia University Press.

——(1988) 'International Institutions: Two Approaches', ISA presidential address, reprinted in *International Studies Quarterly* 32(4): 379–96 and (1989) in his *International Institutions and State Power: Essays in International Relations Theory*, Boulder, CO: Westview Press, pp. 158–79.

——(1989) *International Institutions and State Power: Essays in International Relations Theory*, Boulder, CO: Westview Press.

——(1990) 'Multilateralism: an Agenda for Research', *International Journal* 45(4): 731–64.

——(1993) 'Institutionalist Theory and the Realist Challenge: After the Cold War', in David Baldwin (ed.) *Neo-realism and Neo-liberalism: The Contemporary Debate*, New York: Columbia University Press, pp. 269–300.

——and Nye, Joseph S., Jr (1977) *Power and Interdependence*, Boston, MA: Little, Brown.

——(1987) '*Power and Interdependence* Revisited', *International Organization* 41(4): 725–53.

Krasner, Stephen D. (ed.) (1982) 'International Regimes', a special issue of *International Organizations* 36(2) (Spring); reprinted (1986) as his *International Regimes*, Ithaca, NY: Cornell University Press.

——(1993) 'Westphalia and All That', in Judith Goldstein and Robert O. Keohane (eds) *Ideas and Foreign Policy: Beliefs, Institutions, and Political Change*, Ithaca, NY: Cornell University Press, pp. 235–64.

—— (1994) 'International Political Economy: Abiding Discord', *Review of International Political Economy* 1(1): 13–19.

—— (1995) 'Compromising Westphalia', *International Security* 20(3): 115–51.

Kratochwil, Friedrich (1986) 'Of Systems, Boundaries, and Territoriality: an inquiry into the Formation of the State System', *World Politics* 39(1) (October): 27–52.

—— (1989) *Rules, Norms and Decisions: On the Conditions of Practical and Legal Reasoning in International Relations and Domestic Affairs*, Cambridge: Cambridge University Press.

Luke, Timothy (1991) 'The Discipline of Security Studies and the Codes of Containment: Learning from Kuwait', *Alternatives* 16(3) (Summer): 315–44.

Mearsheimer, John (1995) 'The False Promise of International Institutions', *International Security* 19(3) (Winter): 5–49.

Moravcsik, Andrew (1992) 'Liberalism and International Relations Theory', Working Paper 92–6, Cambridge, MA: Harvard University, Center for International Affairs.

Morgenthau, Hans J. (1946) *Scientific Man vs. Power Politics*, Chicago: University of Chicago Press.

Patomäki, Heikki (1992) *Critical Realism and World Politics. An Explication of a Critical Theoretical and Possibilistic Methodology for the Study of World Politics*, Studies on Political Science no. 12, Turku: University of Turku, Department of Political Science.

Polanyi, Karl (1944) *The Great Transformation*, Boston, MA: Beacon Press.

Russett, Bruce (1985) 'The Mysterious Case of Vanishing Hegemony; or, Is Mark Twain Really Dead?', *International Organization* 39(2) (Spring): 207–31.

Slaughter, Anne-Marie (formerly Burley) (1995) 'International Law in a World of Liberal States', *European Journal of International Law* 6.

Snyder, Glenn (1984) 'The Security Dilemma in Alliance Politics', *World Politics* 36: 461–95.

Staun Poulsen, Jørgen (1995) 'Postsuveraenitet: et Semiotisk og Metaforteoretisk Studie af det Post-Moderne Internationale System' [Post-sovereignty: a Semiotic and Metaphor-Theoretical Study of the Postmodern International System], MA thesis, University of Copenhagen, Institute of Political Science.

Strange, Susan (1982) '*Cave! hic dragones*: a Critique of Regime Analysis', *International Organization* 36(2): 479–96; reprinted in S. D. Krasner (ed.) (1986 [1982]) *International Regimes*, Ithaca, NY: Cornell University Press.

Wæver, Ole (1991) 'Territory, Authority and Identity: the Late Twentieth-Century Emergence of Neo-medieval Political Structures in Europe', paper presented at the first EUPRA conference in Florence (November).

—— (1992) *Introduktion til Studiet af International Politik*, Copenhagen: Politiske Studier.

—— (1994) 'After the Fourth Debate: Patterns of IR Theory in the 1990s', unpublished mimeo.

—— (1995) 'Identity, Integration and Security: Solving the Sovereignty Puzzle in E.U. Studies', *Journal of International Affairs* 48(2) (Winter): 389–431.

—— (in preparation) 'The Politics of International Structure', book manuscript.

Waltz, Kenneth (1979) *Theory of International Politics*, New York: Random House.

Wendt, Alexander (1987) 'The Agent–Structure Problem in International Relations Theory', *International Organization* 41(3): 335–70.

Wight, Martin (1966[1960]) 'Why Is There No International Theory?', in Herbert Butterfield and Martin Wight (eds) *Diplomatic Investigations*, London: Allen and Unwin, pp. 17–34.

Wind, Marlene (1993) 'Poststrukturalisme og International Politik: en Diskussion af den Metateoretiske og Disciplinudviklingsmæssige Baggrund for 1980ernes Kritiske International Politik Teori', MA thesis, University of Aarhus, Institute of Political Science.

8　Hayward Alker: an exemplary voyage from quantitative peace research to humanistic, late-modern globalism

Heikki Patomäki

Hayward R. Alker, Jr (b. 1937 in the USA) received his doctoral degree from Yale University in 1963, where he also did his MA in 1960. However, he did his B.Sc in mathematics at the MIT. Although Herbert Marcuse was the exemplary teacher of his first political science course, his early work was heavily influenced by the pluralism of Robert Dahl, who was also his teacher at Yale, and Karl Deutsch, who not only was his teacher but also hired him as a research assistant. Alker was a Professor of Political Science at the MIT from 1968 to 1994, while he was also spending some periods of time in Michigan, Santiago (Chile), Geneva (Switzerland) and Uppsala and Stockholm (Sweden) as a visiting professor. Since 1995 he has been a professor at the University of Southern California.

> Simple learning is goal-seeking feedback, as in a homing torpedo. It consists in adjusting responses, so as to reach a goal situation of a type that is given once and for all by certain internal arrangements of the [neural] net; these arrangements remain fixed throughout its life. A more complex type of learning is the self-modifying or *goal-changing* feedback. It allows for feedback readjustments of those internal arrangements that implied its original goal, so that the net will change its goal, or set for itself new goals...
>
> (Deutsch 1963: 92)

Quite a few International Relations scholars agree that one of the most exciting recent developments in the field has been the rise of what Robert Keohane has termed 'reflectivism' (Keohane 1988).[1] However, only few have recognized[2] the major role that Hayward R. Alker, Jr has played in the rise of that movement.[3] This fact alone would suffice for writing a chapter on Alker. What is even more noteworthy, however, is the emancipatory potential inherent in Alker's development story: by showing how one can learn, and also develop, radically new approaches, Alker should be able to make us see the false necessity of the rigidities of a given academic character and goal. As scholars in the field, we could learn from Alker's learning, not only from the innovative paths of his long voyage. In other words, we should be interested in both what and how he has learned.

Alker's scientific career began with measuring politics and analysing the United Nations. In the early 1960s, the behaviouralist movement was about to reach its climax in the social sciences, particularly in the United States, while IR as a discipline was still dominated by the classical 'political realism' of Kennan, Morgenthau and Kissinger. Like many other peace researchers in the behaviouralist movement, Alker believed in the possibility that an improvement in political conditions might be stimulated with the help of knowledge produced with the Scientific Method. He also attacked the loose, journalistic style of writing IR that was common in the early 1960s.

The 'angry idealism' of Alker's first phase had three major pillars: the advocacy of modern, rigorous social sciences; a partially quasi-Kantian, partially Grotian, pluralist theory of conflicts; and the belief in the potentialities of the United Nations. Alker's advocacy of rigorous social sciences notwithstanding, even during this phase he always tried to take seriously the claims of those who did not share his fundamental assumptions and concerns. Alker saw open, critical discussions among representatives of different approaches as a prerequisite for scientific progress. Reliance on a given Scientific Method – whatever it may be assumed to be – was not enough for him.

The second pillar was his theory of conflicts – and particularly the Cold War conflict – that relied partially on the notion of misperception, partially on his pluralistic account of social reality. Alker, together with Russett, asserted for instance that 'numerous uncertainties and misperceptions continue regarding the nature of the distinct issues before the UN'. There are many different political opinions, but they are often misperceived and their native misunderstood. Alker and Russett go on to ask whether 'we can find a way of naturally and objectively summarizing the issues before the General Assembly without losing their specific content?' (Alker and Russett 1965: 9). Noteworthily, they indicated that the moral-political aim of their study was the reduction of international tension.[4] In arguing for this possibility, they also built on an underlying Grotian – although positivist and utilitarian – account of the nature of international society, according to which rules and institutions matter:

> Rules of order are often followed, in both local and international society, because of various kinds of expected gains or losses. A reputation for morality and law-abidingness can be useful, and the contrary reputation damaging.
>
> (Alker and Russett 1965: 146)

The third pillar of Alker's first phase is related to the United Nations. The direct (even if qualified) analogy between domestic party politics and world politics in the General Assembly gives support to his trust in the positive potentialities of the UN. 'The world could be thought of as a political system in which the major blocs are analogous to two parties that compete for the favor of the uncommitted voters' (ibid.: 147). Further, Alker claims, with Russett (ibid.: 148), that 'by providing a forum where the parties must participate in a continuing electoral competition for the allegiance of the neutrals, the United Nations performs a major function in preserving the system's stability'. To summarize, the moral-political idea behind Alker's behaviouralist phase was to try to overcome – or at least to ease – the tension between the blocs of the Cold War with the help of a more adequately functioning United Nations and by utilizing the increased scientific understanding provided by empirically oriented modern social sciences.

The problems of the post-colonial world come more deeply into this picture only gradually. It was while teaching methodology as a visiting professor in Santiago, Chile in the early 1970s that Alker most fully opened his mind to radically different epistemological perspectives which he found to cut across different geo-political locations. In Allende's Chile, Alker had many discussions on the techno-rational domination aspects of rigorous and expensive standards of scientific practice. Eventually, he made the observation 'that mathematical social science... distorts social relations to the extent that it participates in and mirrors our alienation under "capitalism"' (Alker 1977a: 3).

At least in his later rationalization, Alker refers to his lengthy 1974(a) article 'Are There Structural Models of Voluntaristic Social Action' as summarizing a major turning-point (but see also Alker and Christennsen 1972). Nonetheless he, like Herbert Simon, still used, even if not exclusively, the criteria of validity of the statistical tradition. In that 1974 article, which he says 'evoked considerable resistance' among the causal modelling logical empiricists of the time and which did not find a publisher in the United States,[5] Alker argued that

> humanistic scholars are often right (sometimes for the wrong reasons) in objecting to statistical models of complex social behavior; but [I claim] also that a faith in positivist approaches to explaining voluntaristic social action is sustainable if an appropriate transformation of those approaches takes place?
>
> (Alker 1974a: 199–200)

In other words, he argued that the faith in positivist social sciences has to be reconciled with the social theories of more 'humanistic', 'voluntaristic social action' scholars, otherwise the faith in positivism was not justified.

In his second phase, culminating in the Chile years and lasting till 1976, Alker was gradually moving towards thoroughly informational – and also hermeneutico-dialectical – ontologies as well as towards his new, more late-modern (or postmodern) mode of globalism. All the time, he was trying to account carefully for all his epistemological, methodological and substantial moves. In methodology, he was mostly interested in artificial intelligence, qualitative-mathematical analysis of the Prisoner's Dilemma game play, and global socioeconomic and ecological modelling. After having taken one more step towards a full-scale critical reflectivism, he explained his position – in 1977, in the context of discussing quantitative dependencia theories – of the mid-1970s as follows:

> I usually argued that quantitative Marxian mathematical political economy and qualitative, nonanalytic computer simulations like those by Abelson, Boudon, and Brunner struck me as avoiding at least some of these problems [of positivism].
>
> (Alker 1977a: 28, n. 4)

When doing more concrete research, he still wrote about the evolutionary possibilities of the United Nations' conflict management system, but was also increasingly concerned about ecological problems and large-scale violent conflicts such as the War of the Pacific. By 1977, he had developed the basics of a new dialectical approach to the study of world politics, an approach that was not only reflective but also very original, even idiosyncratic. An extraordinary paper from 1977, in which he outlines many of his new ideas, is called 'Can the End of "Power Politics" Be Part of the Concepts with which its Story Is Told?' Even though it is merely an unpublished APSA paper,[6] it is the first time he made public the most radical results of his long rethinking process (which, of course, still continues as an open-ended process).

Alker's third phase can be termed as 'humanistic, late-modern globalism'. He summarizes his position by asking whether we can combine 'the evident ability of the greatest historical writers to catch our moral and political imaginations, and comment profoundly on the choices before us', with the 'hard-won professional commitment to falsifiable scientific theorizing' (Alker 1987: 4). Indeed, this is what he is now doing, trying to combine history-based, moral-political visions with falsifiable scientific theorizing. In explicating his innovative position further, he also comments on Wallerstein's challenging point that given its heavily narrative accounts most historical research seems not to lend itself to quantification:

> I do not think quitting is the right response to Wallerstein's challenge. ... Nor do I think that 'quantification' is the only mode of formalization necessary or appropriate for the logical and empirical rigor and tractability that mathematical representations have given to so many of the natural and social sciences. We must broaden and deepen the universe of scientifically relevant modelling approaches appropriate for the formal analysis of interpretative and theoretical world histories. Historical evidence, much of it textual, should not *a priori* be reduced to quantitative time series, or otherwise ignored.
>
> (Alker 1987: 4–5)

This passage should give a good starting-point for analysing Alker's humanistic, late-modern, globalist approach to the study of world politics. In the following, I shall discuss Alker's approach by suggesting *lessons* from his development. This indicates two things. First, it reveals that, at the general level, I sympathize with many of the ideas of the third-phase Alker. Second, that I find what Alker has written – even if my interpretation of his ideas and development should be seen as a fusion of horizons in a Gadamerian sense[7] – very relevant to the topical methodological and political challenges of IR and peace research.

There will be four 'lessons', and after them a more critical section on the limitations and problems of Alker's approach. The four lessons are not easily expressible in one short sentence, and thus I have simply categorized them in accordance with their topics. These topics are: 1) how to collect and analyse data; 2) how to analyse and help to solve collective dilemmas; 3) how to broaden, pluralize and deepen scientifically relevant epistemologies and their corresponding modelling approaches; and 4) how to theorize history. These lessons can and should be read both as interpretative guidelines to Alker's works and as methodological arguments that are based on Alker's works.

THE FIRST LESSON: HOW TO COLLECT AND ANALYSE 'DATA'

As Alker began his career as a mainstream empiricist it is appropriate to begin from what is often assumed to be the basic operation of social sciences: empirical data collection and analysis. It was Alker's conviction in the 1960s that 'statistics in particular is an appropriate, reality-oriented, quantitative discipline for dealing with many of the key international relations theory-building problems'. Many considered Alker's early studies to be among the most rigorous exemplars of the scientific approach to the study of international relations. Thus the research designs of those early studies of Alker were often also replicated. A few years later this 'self-critical methodologist interested in what was "really" going on' (see Alker 1976a: 46) found himself dissatisfied about the practice of being replicated. Why? The replicators seemed to lack any awareness of the vulnerability of simplistic data theoretic or modelling assumptions. 'The more I have learned about the limitations of my early work, the more attracted others became to it', Alker (ibid.: 50) commented ironically. Should this kind of development be called scientific progress?[8]

What was wrong with his early work? In his PhD thesis dealing with voting behaviour in the General Assembly, Alker used multiple regression analysis and factor analysis. Soon this approach turned out to be flawed, for it could not answer such simple questions as did aid buy votes or was aid a result of favourable voting behaviour? Furthermore, Alker realized that 'separate regression equations might not add up causally'. His first response was to develop more complex ways of analysing data, the core of which was constructed simply from the roll-call of votes of countries in the General Assembly and from the (subjectively interpreted) situational characteristics of these countries. As Alker learned that factor analysis, too, can have a causal interpretation, he worked for a while on the assumption that empirical phenomena are structured by some underlying causal models. Yet there seemed to be something wrong with this approach, too, for the world political reality was, at least apparently, able to transcend all attempts to specify a definite causal model, with unchanging, lawlike coefficients, of its causal interrelations. And this was the case despite the fact that the studies were focused intensively only on one functional area, the collective security practices.

Perhaps there was something wrong with the most fundamental assumptions concerning the nature of reality and data? Indeed, in Alker's tenacious, self-critical attempts to improve upon his past modelling exercises, there finally occurred an explicit ontological shift from quasi-mechanical causality, first towards an ontology of information-processing, characteristic to cybernetics and artificial intelligence, and then, eventually, towards an ontology of conversational or discourse analysis (see Alker 1986a: 2).

Most clearly, the ontological shift was evident in Alker's new modes of understanding *what data are*. For one thing, he began to rely on *precedent logics* 'that are used like psychologics to interpret historical successes and failures' (1976a: 51). The testing of hypotheses about precedent logics – what are the relevant precedent cases and how do actors learn from them? – required a new kind of data, namely *verbal data*. As a consequence of this and other similar methodological shiftings, data were not seen any more merely in terms of behaviour and (subjectively interpreted) situational characteristics. Eventually, Alker generalized from his experiences – which made it rational for him to broaden and deepen the notion of 'data' – and concluded that ultimately *our understanding of the nature of data depends on our social ontology*. According to the ontology of intersubjectively constituted social entities, we have to have multi-perspective descriptions of social events and characteristics:

> Whether an *act* should be described as a threatening, promising, or mocking *action* is determined by the perceptions, interpretations, judgments, commitments and shared meaning conventions of the parties involved. The correct *description* of a social action is thus more than a reliable *convergence* of coder and/or diplomatic judgments; its *meaning and identity* is *constituted* by the *multiple* interpretative perspectives of the principal actors in such events. Such interpretative complexities, I believe, are an appropriate emphasis for an increasingly historical, practical, institutionally-aware and internationally constituted political science.
>
> (1991: 5–6)

A related ontological and data-theoretical point is expressed already in Alker's (1977a: 3) complaint that 'mathematical social science...distorts social relations to the extent that it participates in and mirrors our alienation under "capitalism"'. Alker refers here to the fact that the standard North American statistical practices were – and still are – much too individualistic and mechanistic to account for *internal relations* between entities. As Ollman puts it, positivist practices presuppose that any social factor is always

> logically independent of other social factors to which it is related. The ties between them are contingent, rather than necessary; they could be something very different without affecting the vital character of the factors involved, a character which adheres to that part which is thought to be independent of the rest. [However,] in Marx's view, such relations are internal to each factor (they are ontological relations), so that when an important one alters, the factor itself alters; it becomes something else.
>
> (Ollman 1971: 15)

Alker himself is not arguing that there are merely internal relations (as some Hegelians – and even Ollman – might do). Rather, his point is that the identities of social entities, such as rules, actors, institutions, are relational, that social entities are interconnected at the ontological level. For one thing, this view makes it possible to claim, as Bhaskar (1986: 307–8) does, that 'positivism at once naturalises and normalises things and reflects in an endless hall of mirrors the [individualistic and atemporal] self-image of Bourgeois Man'. Methodo-logically, the dialectical view evokes the claims that quantitative, composi-tional statistical knowledge is no more objective than the essentially qualitative, relational knowledge and that, rather, one should accept that the standard statistical knowledge is conceptually and ontologically secondary to the much richer relational knowledge (see also Patomäki 1992a: 57–8). But let us hear how Alker himself explains and clarifies his position:

> When both internal and external relations affect case relationships, case-matching or precedent-seeking efforts become more complicated and historically more interesting. Similarity matching and dissimilarity con-trasting of procedurally specified data stories are external comparisons unless the attributes used in such efforts are in some sense essential, characteristic, and case-identifying ones. Obviously one wants to relate essential characteristics. The analytical problem, for which statistics can only be moderately helpful, is to develop ontologically cogent distinc-tions between essential and inessential properties of the case descriptions.
>
> (1988a: 235)

The second major change in Alker's understanding of the nature of ade-quate data was more epistemological than ontological. Alker began to emphasize that data – collected in accordance with a particular procedure – are always interpreted by somebody from some particular perspective, and that typically the perspectives of scholars are analogical with the perspectives of the involved political actors (with whom they more or less share some but not all formative perspectives). Quite obviously, with the adoption of this kind of understanding, data lose their seemingly innocent and neutral status. Consequently, one should get rid of the reifying effects of the positivist social scientific practices. In line with Alker's new episte-mological perspectivism and his lasting aim at constructing falsifiable scien-tific theories, Alker advised, in 1977, scholars to follow the rule that

> the findings of scientific experts with different doctrinal/value emphases must be examined, checked, and compared at least to the extent likely regime participants differ in their environmental assessments.
>
> (1977b: 48)

Later on, he generalized and radicalized his position, without ever advocat-ing incommensurabilism or an absolutely relativistic 'anything goes' atti-tude. All of us who are advocating modest relativism know that the incommensurability thesis is vulnerable, for instance, to the problems of self-reference.[9] Alker's point has always been to enable *better scientific practices*. In 1988, he stated his own 'first lesson' for empiricists as follows:

> Data-coding procedures should be considered key dependent variables in an emancipatory peace research because they often (sometimes uncon-sciously) reflect just those social and political forces affecting war and peace that are supposed to be the objectives of investigation.
>
> (1988a: 224)

He illustrates this thesis with a 'true story'. In a pioneering North American study on the quantification of levels of co-operation and conflicts in international events data, out of the five student coders one was a citizen of a Third World country and a woman (the others were white men from the USA). Her codings did not 'reliably' agree with those of the others and were discarded for most purposes. She then went on to co-found a new important paradigm of conflict research, lateral pressure theorizing. The name of this woman is, of course, Nazli Choucri (cf. Choucri and North 1975). This example illustrates how the apparently 'unreliable' ways of seeing may simply stem from different interpretative perspectives which, moreover, typically correspond to the perspectives of particular actors (and thus reflect different 'social forces'). Moreover, to the extent that the 'unreliable' ways of seeing are novel, they can also become scientifically significant. Thus, lateral pressure theory which was co-developed by Choucri 'redefined the meaning and significance of imperialism as it had been experienced by domestic populations within great powers, their unequal allies, and Third World countries' (Alker 1988a: 225).

According to Alker's third-phase theory of data, relatively objective data collection is possible if and only if the collectors are explicit and reflective about the case inclusion and exclusion rules for a data set. They should also be explicit about the normative bases, procedural preferences and political allegiances that inform coding practices. To emphasize: this kind of normative and methodological explicitness is a prerequisite for adequate data construction.

An ontological parallel is that in the construction of a data set, one should include the reasons actors give for the actions they take (or avoid) and the precedents they cite (or avoid) *for justifying their (in)actions*. Moreover, one should also include different narrative accounts of the relevant episodes, as presented by the actors. The reasons, precedents and narratives of actors can then be analysed both hermeneutically by searching for a justified, sense-making account of the whole and critically by assessing the validity claims of the actors.

Finally, there is the question of deviant cases. Johan Galtung (1977: 72–95) has argued that the study of the deviant cases should teach us the crucial variables of an invariance and thereby help to break that invariance. Trying to go beyond this formulation, Alker also demands that one should take the best and the worst cases and use them to uncover the practical 'grammars' of action and habit making such outcomes possible. These 'grammars' should then be seen as in part changeable, that is, as both potentially negotiable or debatable and therefore political.

THE SECOND LESSON: HOW TO ANALYSE AND HELP TO SOLVE COLLECTIVE DILEMMAS

The Prisoner's Dilemma (PD) is a game-theoretical model in which individual utility maximization appears to be self-defeating, or at least contradictory to, or in conflict with, overall or longer-term public or collective rationality.[10] Many major problems of political science have been scrutinized in terms of this model. These include market 'imperfections', the 'tragedy of global commons', interstate insecurity, arms races, crisis bargaining, and also systems of subordination, which can be seen as artificial and consciously structured systems of Prisoner's Dilemmas of the subordinates.

Alker, who entitled his 1976a autobiographical essay 'Individual Achievements Rarely Sum to Collective Progress', analysed the Prisoner's Dilemma model for the first time in his path-opening 1974 essay 'Are There Structural Models of Voluntaristic Social Action?' In this 'Structural Models' essay, Alker tried to find less reductionistic models than the linear or non-linear behaviouristic models, i.e. he tried to find 'multilevel models of voluntaristic social action systems' which could nevertheless be interpreted to be causally or 'structurally' deterministic.

The Prisoner's Dilemma is so well known, at least in the context of mainstream political science and IR, that there should be no reason to (re)present its general two-person or no-person game matrixes, game-trees, or mathematical formulas. In his 1974 article, Alker's main point was that it is possible to develop and partially to corroborate more empirically adequate models of voluntaristic social action, in line with the 'nearly pervasive concern of leading non-Marxian Anglo-American social science theorists and philosophers', but very much 'unlike most social scientific statistical work that has emphasised simple specifications and often interpreted them positivistically or behaviouristically' (1974a: 236). He argued, however, that these 'empirically more adequate' models of iterated or repeated games are necessarily more complex than their predecessors. For instance, the Artificial Intelligence-looking Emshoff model – in which a game has both a history and a future, and in which actors are learning from the outcomes of their previous choices in a probabilistic manner, according to a certain algorithm – is empirically more adequate and a possible solution to the problematic of infinite reflective regress back to mutual calculations. It is also a very different and much more complex solution than the standard – but in most cases misleading – simple prescription of minimax (guaranteed loss minimizing) and maximin (secure-gain maximizing) strategies.

In many real-world cases of collective goods, the assumption that PD games have a history and a future, too, is adequate, but not in all cases. If the stakes in a 'game' are extremely high, such as loss of one's job, years in prison, death of a subordinate by the masters (perhaps in a concentration camp), or a nuclear war, would not a single-choice 'game' be a more adequate model than an iterated one? In his 1975 analysis of the descriptive foundations of polimetrics, Alker turned, following Baumgartner and Burns, and Burns and Buckley, to developing a new PD model by redefining it as a three-actor domination system and *not* viewing it as an iterated game. In this way he was able to analyse the logic as well as moral and causal limitations of 'divide and conquer' or 'divide and rule' strategies of various rulers/masters of the world history, including those of the modern totalitarian nation-states.[11]

In contrast to the standard practice of presenting the PD in an abstract form, Alker (1975: 180–8) takes a three-party model in the context of the narrative; it was probably developed after the original model with its numerical payoffs. In a typical variant of the Prisoner's Dilemma narrative, the position and power of the District Attorney (DA) is not taken into account at all, although (s)he has the capability to get the prisoners to do something they would not otherwise do. This capability is based on the DA's position in the system of legal and penalty practices, which enables him or her to control communication. That control is crucial in this context in at least two respects. First, the DA can use it (plus the absence of counsel) to decrease the trust that Prisoner A has in Prisoner B. Second, (s)he can use it to paint an uncorrected and rather black picture of Prisoner B, thus causing Prisoner A to feel less loyalty (which pre-exists contingently), solidarity and sympathy for his or her partner (see Alker 1975: 180–8[12]). Seen in this way, the modality or technique of power on which the PD is based is *panopticism*, described, modelled and explained by Foucault:

> Each individual, in his place, is securely confined to a cell from which he is seen from the front by the supervisor; but the side walls prevent him from coming into contact with his companions. He is seen, but he does not see; he is the object of information, never a subject of communication. The arrangement of his room, opposite the central tower, imposes on him an axial visibility; but the divisions of the ring, those separated cells, imply a lateral invisibility. And this invisibility is a guarantee of order.
>
> (Foucault 1979: 200)

This socially produced invisibility of individual actors is also the crucial facility for the power of the DA. This asymmetrical power would be diminished if there were regulative rules such as 'Prisoners should be allowed to talk with their attorney before interrogation', or if the prisoners nevertheless considered each other as loyal partners instead of strategic calculators. Indeed, even the associated PD narrative is an extremely abstract interpretation, for it abstracts this 'game' from the more contextual rules as well as from such questions as the following. Are the prisoners really guilty? Why are they committed to egoist means-ends rationality? Why are they not allowed to talk to their lawyers before interrogation (a talk with an attorney would provide the possibility of indirect communication)? And, consequently, can it be said that the legal system in question is democratic or authoritarian, just or unjust? On the basis of these considerations, Alker developed a complex model for estimating the power of the DA and the factors giving rise to that power.

Alker's approach to resolving PDs did not stop developing with this still somewhat positivist model of a three-party system of domination (his criticisms of positivism notwithstanding, he was still looking for a model of 'rational' incentives and, indirectly, for mathematically definable and analysable structural invariances of social action). In Alker and Hurwitz's 1980 'student manual' called *Resolving Prisoner's Dilemmas*, there is an explication of some of the substantial and edificatory (cf. Rorty 1980: 359) reasons for moving towards thoroughly conversational and dramaturgical social ontologies. It is not only that empirical and theoretical reasons seemed to be pointing towards more complex models of intentional and voluntaristic – although in a sense also structurally determined – social action. It is also the case that there are close connections between the world understandings of different research paradigms – with their parallels in the actors' world understandings – and of actors' abilities to resolve PDs.[13] These connections include the following (Alker and Hurwitz 1980: 80–2):

1 Communication of co-operative intention increases an actor's commitment to it in ambiguous circumstances.
2 Players develop co-operative goals in the iterated PD as a result of a recognition of each other's behaviour as communication of motives, intention, and expectations.
3 PDs are more often resolved when the game is redefined as a problem for moral discourse; and even more in the line of Habermas: 'PD becomes problematic due to distorted, constrained, or suppressed communication.'

As these observations can be seen to indicate, making it clear that there is a form of consciousness that is beyond 'strategic rationality' means that the reasons for moving towards more humanistic and late-modern, interpretative social ontologies can be explicated also in terms of Hegelian dialectical development of consciousness. The basic idea has been formulated by Olafson in one of Alker's favourite references:

> The difficulty which mankind experiences and which it is able to solve only very gradually and very slowly is one of achieving a conceptualisation of the self that will permit that reciprocity to emerge as something more than a kind of appendage to an already fully constituted self. The crucial insight on which Hegel's position rests has to do with interdependence of our concept of the self and our concept of the other and it involves the claim that these conceptions move forward pari passu until they reach a point at which an underlying identity of the one with the other is grasped.
>
> (Olafson 1979: 241)

Olafson is very careful in pointing out that the underlying identity is not the Hegelian absolute one, nor should it be seen as a deterministic outcome of an evolutionary history, but rather it involves the constitutive reciprocity and potentialities of change inherent in the Habermasian undistorted and unconstrained communicative interaction.[14] With these points as a background, one should be able to understand Alker and Hurwitz's concluding lines in 1980 on Prisoner's Dilemmas:

> *As a formal non-co-operative game or psychological experiment, the Prisoner's Dilemma was misdefined and/or underspecified.* Surely this thesis follows from our own view of PD experiments as moral dramas on scientific stages.... It [also] accepts at least one implication of Plon's critique as well: that formal PD games underspecify or mispresent socially relevant class/domination relations. PD avoidance and promotion

are part of liberal capitalism's self-justificatory efforts, but they also transcend the politics of the contemporary era. One should really study the interaction of rules of play, rules of the game and rules of the different social orders in which the game is embedded. Our dramaturgical perspective accepts the view that real life PD dilemmas need actively to be recreated. Essentially they involve three or more unequally powerful actors following incomplete scripts about their own moral choices, scripts whose lines are at least partially revisable in the actual context of their recurrence.

(Alker and Hurwitz 1980: 118)

In his 1980 article with Mefford, which fuses Alker's interests in the United Nations' collective security system and PD modelling, he goes on to analyse security as a contradiction between individually reasonable security-seeking practices and collective security. That is, Alker scrutinizes problems of traditional state security in terms of a PD situation. By building upon an organizational model based on the Emshoff model, in which actors are learning from their previous choices, and by ending up with something that is quite reminiscent of Deutsch's well-known cybernetic model of foreign policy-making,[15] Alker, Bennett and Mefford try to analyse not only the practical intentionality of means–ends calculation but also the processes which define and redefine political goals themselves.

By focusing their analysis on the cognitive processing within organizations, Alker, Bennett and Mefford emphasize the importance of studying how precedents or lessons from the past are initially acquired and then subsequently applied in the practical activity of problem-solving during the day-to-day conduct of foreign policy. Their point is that an individual actor's course of action is principally determined by the prior construction of the set of possible initiatives and consequences attributable to the parties involved. This is a cognitive process which involves defining new situations on the basis of comparison with previously experienced situations which exist as richly described incidents in individual and collective memory. These incidents are typically structured as sequences of action, as *narratives*, the elements of which are selected and linked together by causal and intentional connectives to yield a plausible ordering or configuring. From this perspective, it can be argued that there are two 'orders of constraint' which shape and select policy:

1 The first comprises factors that *set a bound on the scope and diversity of the narratives* (or scenarios) the policy-making apparatus is capable of generating. In the Foucauldian terminology, discourses are bound by the way they define the field of possible objects, the position and role occupied by the speaking and acting subject, and the mode of functioning of the language with respect to objects. Narratives, in turn, are bound by the available set of abstract narrative structures.

2 The second involves *the mechanisms of choice which select and amalgamate the narratives under consideration*. In the Foucauldian terminology, this is a matter of the form and way of localization and circulation of

discourse(s) within the foreign policy making organisations; power, also in the more traditional Weberian sense – as the capability of an actor positioned within a social relationship to carry out his own will despite resistance – and organizational structures come into the picture here.

In this way, Alker is approaching the Foucaldian (Foucault 1991a: 56–7; Foucault 1991b) and also Ricoeurian (1984 and 1988) way of studying changes and continuity of discursive formations, even though the original point of departure had been, a decade earlier, the rather conventional, at least semi-positivist study of collective security practices and iterated PDs.

Also of great interest for an IR theorist is the result of Alker's (together with Hurwitz and Rothkin) latest 'game-theoretical' study entitled 'Fairy Tales Can Come True: Narrative Constructions of Prisoner's Dilemma Game Play'. The main claim of that study is that the mechanisms generating reciprocity are *not* the simplistic 'tit-for-tat' strategies discussed by Rapoport and Chammah and, in an evolutionary fashion, by Axelrod.

> Rather, the players reflectively explore their historically developing situations, and frequently (re)construct their social relationships and (eventually multi-move) strategies as the game proceeds, until a stable pattern of play, based on mutually supporting interpretations, has developed.
> (Alker, Hurwitz and Rothkin 1993: 19)

On the basis of Alker's innovative studies on PD games, what should be concluded about how to analyse and help to solve collective dilemmas? Acknowledging also that there are many drastically different variations of situations of collective dilemmas, Alker's methodological point is twofold: (1) we should really study the interaction of rules of play, rules of the game and rules of the different social orders in which the game is embedded, rather than abstract and reductionistic models of it; and (2) we should focus our analytical skills on studying the (logics of the) scripts about actors' moral choices, scripts whose precedential, narrative-embedded, and dramaturgical lines are at least partially revisable in the actual context of their recurrence – and thus also potentially political.

LESSON THREE: HOW TO BROADEN AND DEEPEN SCIENTIFICALLY RELEVANT MODELLING APPROACHES

Recall now the response of Alker to Wallerstein's challenge, to the critical claim that given its heavily narrative accounts most historical research seems not to lend itself to quantification. Alker argued, in accordance with the main results of his studies of the late 1970s and early 1980s, that 'we must broaden and deepen the universe of scientifically relevant modelling approaches appropriate for the formal analysis of interpretative and theoretical world histories'. It is clear that from the early 1980s onwards, Alker has very rigorously followed his own suggestions and instructions. Nevertheless, for many of those who have stayed in the mainstream of political science, IR and peace research, Alker's two hermeneutical-structuralist studies of this period may seem utterly incomprehensible, or at least irrelevant to the concerns of 'serious' political science.[16] In contrast to this view, I would like to argue that these two studies are among the most interesting published works of the 1980s in the whole field. In 'Two Reinterpretations of Toynbee's Jesus', the basic research questions are posed as follows:

> In the light of both traditional and more recent scholarly approaches, what are the appropriate, scientific ways to ascertain the meanings within the Jesus story? What motivating power or charisma does this story, or 'myth', contain? What basic structure or structures, what infectious, self-replicating, 'viral' qualities account for this power? Can we discover some of the ways in which its deepest structure has been rewritten into different 'surface' texts? Or do the 'rewrites' that are discussed by many traditional scholars themselves differ in their fundamentals? Which versions of the Jesus story, thought of as an imitable hero story, have had more or less appeal in which personal, cultural, economic, or political contexts, thought of in contemporary or historical terms?
>
> (Alker, Lehnert and Schneider 1985: 52)

Alker, Lehnert and Schneider are looking for 'analytically reproducible, motivationally suggestive plot structures implicit in story texts', with the help of computer-assisted hermeneutical analysis. In other words, Alker, Lehnert and Schneider ask: What are the cultural and/or universal factors that limit the scope and diversity of the narratives that actors are capable of generating? The fundamental aim is thus to find very general, widely spread, emotion-generating 'logics' of narrative construction, implicit in the way in which elements of narratives are selected and linked together by causal and intentional connectives to yield a plausible ordering or configuring, a story.

How should, and could, one answer the questions posed by Alker and his colleagues? Assuming that motivationally productive, mimetic, plot-like structures help to give meaning to children's stories, religious and political myths, narrative histories, as well as to the precedents constitutive of the problem-solving of the day-to-day conduct of foreign policy, the first scientific goal must be an adequate and operational identification of these structures through careful textual analysis. Once identified, their connections to the reflective monitoring of conduct and, indeed, to the lives of actors must be investigated. It is obvious that one needs systematic coding procedures for the identification of elements of narratives and their structures. It is stated in the 'Two Reinterpretations' paper that 'reasonably explicit and reliable heuristic and grammatical coding rules exist for most of this process, but no completely programmed and validated coding algorithms are available' (ibid.: 65). Note also that although Alker, Lehnert and Schneider use computers both in their coding and their analysis of the textual material, they make it very clear that 'computers can help focus, clarify, criticize, explicate; they do not supplant the human interpreter' (ibid.: 90).

Model-building endeavours in computational hermeneutics can be quite complicated. Lehnert found 199 molecule-like structures, Alker and Schneider many more, of which computer search algorithm further identified about half as undominated, 'top-level units'. Most of these were found to be connected with each other. On the basis of this finding, central and transitional undominated plot units were organized as episodical clusterings of the Jesus narrative. From this clusterings schema, Alker, Lehnert and Schneider attempted to formulate generalizations about narrative structures. There are also some suggestions about how these allegedly (culturally) general structures are connected to the reflective monitoring of conduct and to the lives of different actors. However, in spite of the fascinating and captivating character of these suggestions and tentative generalizations, there are only a few concrete, precise statements that an IR scholar or a peace researcher could utilize in her or his own field. In my judgement, one should view this rather lengthly essay as another path-opening analysis of the research possibilities open for those who are willing to give up their positivist prejudices.

For a peace researcher or an IR scholar, 'Fairy Tales, Tragedies and World Histories' is more concretely suggestive. This 1987 article, the idea of which goes back to mid-1970s, begins with the observation that despite their obvious differences, very similar configurative elements connect fictional stories and traditional histories. Now, remember the claims (1) that 'conflict and crisis, as well as the steady state in which violence remains latent, can be partially explicated in terms of dynamics which are approximated by the interactions of artificial systems equipped with the story-building and story-appraising characteristics', and (2) that the stories constituting foreign policies – as well the actions of political movements – are often world histories. From this perspective, the importance of Alker's attempt to analyse and explain the appeal of great world histories should be obvious.

To delimit his area of study, Alker chose three schools of writing world histories (and futures) as his object of analysis. The first one is the global modelling studies evoked by the Club of Rome's amplification of debates occasioned by Jay Forester's *World Dynamics*. The second one is the *Annales* studies of modern world systems stimulated by Ferdinand Braudel's exemplary writings. Finally, he also examines Marxist analysis of the long waves of capitalist development, as exemplified by Ernest Mandel's theories. Alker is *not* treating these studies 'merely' as – potentially policy-constituting – fairy tales, but, rather, he is trying to leave space for finding out the relative sense-making (and truthfulness) of these three different styles of history writing. Perhaps this also explains the choice of the textual objects of his study, the fact that he did not take the neo-realist world historical fairy tale of the 'hegemonic cycles' up for a textual analysis?[17] At least he writes that

> I take it to be one of the reasons for the relative 'success' of such studies is the extent to which the authors or their fellow workers have combined drama-like readability with an impression of historical and/or scientific

trustworthiness and the quasi-metaphysical, almost inevitable grandeur to which seekers after total truths (including myself) are especially susceptible.

(1987: 3)

Alker is also perfectly aware that the determinism – and, yes, positivism – of the studies of Forrester, Braudel and Mandel does not 'leave much room for individual or group responses to the enormous moral, economic and political issues raised by their accounts' (1987: 3):

> Life is not a myth or a fairy tale with a guaranteed happy ending; neither is it an inevitable tragedy, one that encompasses all of Western civilization or the human species. Nor are most political or cultural leaders successfully heroic. Should one then refrain from attempting to give meaningful interpretations to world history? Or should one try to refrain from being 'ideological' in making such efforts, if it is indeed possible to do so? Can we indeed refrain from mythical, poetic or moralistic and ideological elements in writing scientific histories of the challenges, the limits and the potentialities of our times? ... If [the impossibility of this] is accepted, then we may ask these question in another way: Is there some improvement possible in the way scientific historical accounts approach value questions, structural constraints and human choice possibilities that seem to give all great world histories the reflective character and dramatic force of a tragic morality play or the ironic happiness of a Russian fairy tale?

(1987: 4)

The bulk of the paper is devoted to the analysis of narrative structures *per se*. The point of departure is the way Propp, in his analysis of Russian fairy tales, reduces all of his analysed tales to a single structure, or schema, with two variations of the middle-of-the-story events. First, the setting, or the preparatory aspect of a story, is defined. Then the story develops from villainy or some kind of lack: through the completion of some difficult tasks, either the villain must be overcome or the lack must be resolved, or both. In the middle of the story, there are two possibilities: either (1) a 'struggle, then victory' sequence of episodes: the branding of the hero, a struggle between hero and villain, the defeat of the villain (this is the peak of the narrative, perhaps with some initial misfortune), the pursuit of the hero, as well as unfounded claims by false heroes; or (2) a 'solution to a difficult task' sequence of episodes: unfounded claims by false heroes (hero still at home), difficult task, hero branded (often in and/or before battle by princess), preliminary or almost final solution may occur (this is the peak of the narrative, perhaps with some initial misfortune), hero is pursued, hero is rescued from pursuit. Finally, the hero is recognized, he is given a new appearance or new possessions, and any false heroes, as well as any still unpunished villains, are dealt with. The end scene is that the hero is married (to the princess) and/or ascends the throne, etc. This narrative structure can be generalized as a set of rewrite rules for a simple story grammar, in terms of STATES and EVENTS, and THEN connectives, and CAUSE connective.

Even though this more abstract and formal way of expressing the generative structure of narratives is better at conveying text composition syntax than the semantic and pragmatic dependencies among story elements that are still present in Propp's formalization, basically Alker sticks to the formal rewrite rules when he illustratively analyses the structure of Mandel's *Long Waves of Capitalist Development*. The constructive point of this illustration is the derived general instruction that we should measure 'actual historical sequences' and 'think of possible world historical developments in terms of alternative story grammars' because this kind of thinking and analysis 'can enlighten and orient us toward a better future of constrained, but multiple possibilities' (ibid.: 28). In other words, the analysis of narrative structures should be brought back to the analysis of world historical episodes, tendencies and structures, in order to improve models of these, to make them more imaginative and more sensitive to different world historical possibilities.

What else has Alker to say about how to broaden and deepen scientifically relevant modelling approaches in the post-positivist era? In a paper from 1981, when commenting more generally on the global modelling studies evoked by the Club of Rome's amplification of debates occasioned by Jay Forrester's *World Dynamics*, Alker (1981a: 353) says that 'too many people identify political/administrative cybernetics with Forrester–Meadows world modelling'. They may also identify it with sophisticated econometric modelling that includes, for example, error feedbacks, or with the more complicated models of systems theories. But this perspective on global modelling is very narrow and problematic for a number of reasons:

> I want to correct such false impressions. Relevant contributions include communications-oriented redefinitions of the essence of politics; the reintroduction into logico-empirical inquiry of teleological ontology and epistemology; emancipatory cybernetic hierarchies of knowledge; linguistic understanding and action; scientific modeling of systemic reproductive and self-productive processes, as well as pathological and healthy, even innovative and creative transformations therein; and a non-economic vocabulary for evaluating political successes and failures.
> (1981b: 353)

Alker not only points to the relevant social theoretical contributions for enriching the potentialities of global modelling, admitting that the relevant literature is often 'heavily historical and not easily formalizable' (ibid.: 370), but also outlines a new set of problems for those global modellers whose background is in the cybernetic tradition. He terms this *the dialectics of state formation in centre–periphery systems*. It is dialectical because the works within this problematic should also deal with identity-involving or constitutive relations between centres and peripheries, and between national parts and systemic wholes. The emphasis on state formation comes already from Deutsch's cybernetic and communication-centred studies on nation-building. The idea that all this occurs in larger centre–periphery structures came, naturally, from the Dependencia School and World System Analysis, and it was supported by the (in 1981 still quite popular) studies of dependency relations and autocentric strategies for their reversal. But Alker wanted to include other themes as well, and to show how all these could be systematically modelled:

> Bruno Fritsch's concern with the increased capital formation requirements of modernizing nation-states exploitatively interdependent with their environments adds an important ecological moment to state formation problematique as previously formulated.... The inner-relations of imperialistic powers and their self-reconstituting, power-balancing systems also seem a particularly recalcitrant problem for the would-be narratively oriented global modeler.... If nations, classes, or global systems can be identified in terms of their innermost, constitutive production modes or organising principles, a fair approximation to such identities can be obtained using incompletely prespecified metaprograms, frames, demons, scripts, or production systems, as these procedural entities are currently conceived in artificial intelligence research.
>
> (1981a: 372–3)

Despite his inspiring suggestions, Alker has never systematically shown, by doing an exemplary study, how one could and should conduct more appropriate global modelling. Perhaps Ashley's 1980 book *The Political Economy of War and Peace*, which is a brilliant work in the lateral pressure paradigm, comes closest to what Alker has in mind.[18] Nevertheless, his methodological works from 1977 onwards offer many valuable hints, concrete suggestions, and even detailed, although only partial, modelling exercises for anyone interested in improving the past global modelling approaches. In addition to the models of narrative structures, one can find among his works a refined, artificial-intelligence-based analysis of the inner relations of imperialistic powers and their self-reconstituting, power-balancing systems (1977a); a case for a 'neo-classical polimetrics', which is grounded in political argumentation about practical choices in particular contexts, argued itself in the context of analysing and quasi-formal modelling of the 'dialectical logic of Thucydides' Melian dialogue' (1988b; see also 1984a); and exercises in linguistic, computer-assisted political discourse analysis (for instance, Alker, Duffy *et al.* 1990; Alker, Lebedeva *et al.* 1991). These and other related works do not amount to an articulation of a full-scale approach to rigorous post-positivist global modelling, but they are certainly arguments about how to broaden and deepen scientifically relevant modelling approaches.

THE FOURTH LESSON: HOW TO THEORIZE HISTORY

Many of the points made in the previous three lessons are immediately relevant from the point of view of the question 'How to theorize history?' I will now finally scrutinize Alker's approach to theorizing world history by exposing the 'Dialectics of World Order' project, initiated by Alker and developed in transnational co-operation with Tahir Amin, Thomas Biersteker and Takashi Inoguchi.[19] The 'Dialectics of World Order' project is an attempt to theorize recent world history and possible futures in the dialectical and post-positivist terms of Alker's third phase.

The first outcome of this project, an article called 'Dialectical Foundations of Global Disparities', was published in 1981. In that article, four contending, interpenetrating systems of global order are proposed as appropriate units for an inquiry: capitalist power-balancing, Soviet socialism, corporatist-authoritarianism, and collective self-reliance. The fact that one cannot any more be straightforwardly content with some of Alker's hypotheses does not invalidate his approach. On the contrary, the far-reaching and unexpected transformations of the 1980s and early 1990s seem to confirm his fundamental – and well-grounded – assumption that world history should be analysed (interpretatively) as an open process, in which choices of actors do make a difference, sometimes also to the intended direction. Furthermore, even though one should try to reidentify the relevant world orders, many of Alker's 'hypotheses' are still fruitful in investigating their interrelations. These include the following:

1 every region of the world unequally reflects the mutually interpenetrating and (sometimes) opposed world orders
2 besides revolutionary class conflicts, two major determinants of the birth of newer state types have been the world wars (the Cold War included) and the intense pressures for modernization associated with relatively late development in a world of more technically advanced, predatory and powerful actors.

'From Imperial Power Balancing to People's Wars: Searching for Order in the Twentieth Century', a 1989 article written by Alker, Biersteker and Inoguchi, continues Alker's interest in collective security practices, and applies the same kind of thinking to analysing the development and relative (in)validity of different modern models of peace and order. Alker, Biersteker and Inoguchi (1989: 135) limit themselves to an emphasis on three 'partially implemented, globally oriented security-seeking programs of the past century: the Eurocentric balance of power, Wilsonian collective security, and international socialist transformation through people's wars'. The difference between the analysis of 'world orders' and this analysis is that while the former was concerned with the production modes that are also constitutive, in the latter case only the organizing principles are analysed.

The organizational principles of the Eurocentric power-balancing model of the nineteenth century – and in a heavily modified form, of the Cold War (cf. Patomäki 1992b: 212–14) – included the idea that states were considered and treated as unitary actors, reciprocally recognizing, interacting with and differentiating among themselves. The system maintained itself by a mixture of force, the threat of the use of force, dynasty-supporting marriages, alliances and diplomatic means. Further, unrestrained power was seen as a threat to all other system members, hence the prescriptive principles of action that collective power, through the use of alliances, should be used against any state or bloc that became inordinately powerful ('balancing' policies, in accordance with the central principle of astronomy, mechanics and economics of the time). Both hegemonical aspirants and their equilibrating antagonists were expected to stop fighting rather than eliminate a core-state actor.

Alker, Biersteker and Inoguchi (1989) treat collective security simply as a power-balancing alternative. They argue, quite provocatively, that 'Wilsonian collective security was not diametrically opposed to power-balancing, but rather redefined and globalized an older Eurocentric power-balancing system' (ibid.: 145). The only difference was/is that any threat to peace was/is assumed to be of basic concern to all members of the international society. Consequently, aggression was/is outlawed by a 'balance' of 'all against one'. However,

> Wilson [also] called for a world of nationally homogeneous, self-determining, market-oriented, trade-fostering, democratic states whose public opinion would support the condemnation of future aggressors. This liberal image of a co-operative world of rational, predictable people and states represents a major change from the balance-of-power era.
>
> (ibid.: 146)

However, this call for making the world homogeneous meant in practice that war-avoiding doctrines and theories of collective security became *coupled to war-fighting practices and doctrines* such as Wilson's total war designed to end all wars. And Wilson was not the only one who offered progressive, total alternatives to traditional diplomatic practices: proletarian internationalism of Lenin, Kautsky, Luxemburg and other Marxists was at that time Wilson's major world political rival. While for Wilson 'peace' meant also status quo, Lenin was advocating a major, world-wide socioeconomic change. Consequently, Leninism formed the background for those from Mao and Lin Biao in China in the 1930s to the Sandinistas of the 1980s who have developed and propagated the conception of 'people's wars'. This conception usually includes the belief that a future classless society will eventually guarantee an eternal peace. Mobilizing the whole society to a – violent, if necessary – revolutionary struggle for socialism would/should thus create the basis for a lasting peace and order.

The analysis of Alker, Biersteker and Inoguchi has practical-political implications. They demand more contextually sensitive and historically reflective doctrines of collective security, 'some less total, more realistic alternatives' (ibid.: 159). I would like to go further along these lines and suggest that we should also seek alternatives that do not define or presuppose an eternal order, whether Wilsonian, Leninist or whatever, that would amount, in particular circumstances, to function as the status quo. Any status quo that would be preserved with the help of Wilsonian 'all against one' power-balancing policies – even though this is perhaps possible only as long as somebody is able to orchestrate and legitimate the actions of 'all' – will eventually work against the basic underlying principle, that is, peace.

Hence, contextual peaceful *changes* should be made an institutionally guaranteed, always open-possibility.[20]

In any case, to the extent that one is willing to accept at least some of the methodological notions that Alker has developed during his third phase, the summary of these studies should have been able to illustrate how to theorize history in an interpretative and heuristic manner. This concludes the fourth and final lesson from Alker's development. It is finally time to consider some limitations and problems of Alker's approach.

SOME PROBLEMS AND LIMITATIONS OF ALKER'S APPROACH

Up to this point, my story about Alker could have been read as a simple fairy tale. However, as Alker has argued, life is not a myth or a fairy tale with a guaranteed happy ending, nor is it an inevitable tragedy. We need more complex, more interesting stories. On the one hand, Alker has already been recognized, even if his arguments have been rarely followed: he was the President of the ISA in 1992–3. On the other hand, although it certainly may still be plausible to envisage Alker as a lonely, courageous and insightful figure, heroic in his attempts to rethink the methodological foundations of IR and peace research, his constructive solutions to the lack of convincing scientific, moral and political results are far from the final ones. Of course, there cannot be any final solutions, but there are some problems in Alker's approach that can already be discerned.

An obvious limitation of Alker's approach is the fact that he has been, after all, mostly concerned with the problems of peace, war and (in)security, the only major exception being ecological concerns (see Alker 1989c and Alker and Haas 1993). Those doing international/global political economy or normative political theory may not be able to find as many interesting things in Alker's texts. Furthermore, in his third phase Alker has also strongly emphasized communication, discourses and narratives, which for some may indicate that Alker is not able to analyse hard, 'material facts' of life. This emphasis of Alker's – and some contrary evidence[21] – notwithstanding, I think it is misleading to presume that Alker has taken the side of the 'idealists' in the (outmoded) debate between 'idealists' and 'materialists'. Yet, this is precisely the interpretation of Chase-Dunn (1989: 31). Chase-Dunn claims that Alker has 'a cybernetic conception of systemic structure in which social information becomes coded in cultural and symbolic systems'. This, he claims, presupposes that Alker has adopted an idealist philosophy. Alker qualifies his metaphor or analogy in a manner that should make it clear that he is not an ontological reductionist ('idealist'):

'Moments' of social totalities might be thought of as aspects of societal life-worlds that are unified or 'reciprocally' and 'internally' related in historical life-contexts by their essential (capitalistic?) generative modes of work, speech, and control. These are not the 'repetitive' or non-reflecting, lifeless systems for which cogent empirical science is possible.

(1982: 83, referring to the ideas of Habermas)

Moreover, I think it is fairer to set him alongside the 'critical scientific realists' such as Rom Harré and Roy Bhaskar than the 'idealists'. Attempts to overcome the dualism between agents and structures, ideas and 'materia', and superstructure and basestructure, are at the core of the critical realist social ontology. Consider, for instance, the following quotation from Alker, which is an explicit commitment to this kind of thinking:

> One can take from Roy Bhaskar's brilliant book, *Scientific Realism and Human Emancipation*, a very clear statement of the guiding motivation of such a newer conception [of the reality of things]: Emancipatory peace research epistemologically directs its 'learning from the data' toward the emancipatory 'uncoupling (of) the present from the causality of the past', replacing 'depotentialising (disempowering, oppressive)' psychological, social, and ecological structures by 'potentialising (empowering, enhancing)' ones. Conceiving of emancipation as a 'special qualitative kind of becoming free' that consists in the self-directed '*transformation...from an unwanted and unneeded to a wanted and needed source of determination*', Bhaskar argues that it 'is both causally presaged and logically entailed by explanatory theory, but that it can only be effected in *practice*'.
>
> (1988a: 237)

If Alker cannot be adequately criticized because of his alleged ontological 'idealism' (there will always be 'determination' and 'structures'), one could certainly criticize him for having never really gone through all the implications of his different methodological propositions and game openings. Alker has worked like Foucault, who has happily admitted: 'My books aren't treatises in philosophy or studies of history: at most, they are philosophical fragments put to work in a historical field of problems' (Foucault 1991b: 74). Alker's papers and articles, too, are philosophical fragments put to work in a historical field of problems. Although there is clearly a family resemblance between all of his post-1977 papers, articles, essays and books, nevertheless there *may be* too much room for ambivalences, ambiguities and contradictory interpretations. But note the relativity of this criticism: those comprehensive views that are able to admit that there are holes, silences, contingent incommensurabilities, ambivalences, and ambiguities are more open to change and learning than those which resist admitting this much (cf. Bhaskar 1989: 155; Patomäki 1992a: 231).

From a wider perspective, perhaps the main problem with Alker's approach – to the extent that it is intended to be a full-scale 'approach' – is that he has tied himself to such an extent to developing formalizable ways of modelling social worlds. One may interpret this as a lasting trace of his early belief in Modern Science, or one may see it as a fruitful commitment to thorough and systematic analysis. In either case the problem remains: as Alker (1981a: 370) himself admits, the relevant literature on world politics and history is often 'heavily historical and not easily formalizable'.

To be sure, Alker is sensitive to this problem. Indeed, in one place he (1977a: 15) even defines himself as a 'radical traditionalist' to indicate that he attempts a synthesis between the 'traditional', epistemologically sceptical and the progressive, epistemologically optimistic (liberal, Marxist) approaches. In addition to the 'Dialectics of World Order' papers, he has also written a non-formalistic, sympathethic paper on Hedley Bull's world society problematic – a nice contrast to his 1966 article on the non-additivity problem – arguing that Bull's criticism of quantitative 'co-operation under anarchy' problematique has considerable force (1986b: 4).

In his 1992 presidential address called 'The Humanistic Moment in International Studies: Reflections on Machiavelli and Las Casas', Alker (1992a: 347) also argues for recovering 'the humanist ideals and approaches which sometimes get lost in our modern strivings for scientific rigor'. What does Alker mean by 'humanist ideals and approaches'? He (ibid.: 347) characterizes them as the 'critical, interpretative, lesson-drawing disciplines centered around grammar, rhetoric, history, and moral philosophy'. Furthermore, he connects the recovery of these ideals and approaches to the beginning of the end of modernity and is willing to anticipate subsequent eras of history. He should thus be seen as a late-modern humanist who is nevertheless interested in developing rigorous methods.

But the problem remains: there is a gap between what one can analyse with the help of computer-assisted methods, (quasi-) formalities and rigorous models, however humanistic these methods, formalities and models might be, and what is 'heavily historical and not easily formalizable'. Alker's partial answer to this problem is his 'Dialectics of World Order' project, which shows a possible way of theorizing history in an interpretative and heuristic manner. In my view, this is not enough. One should be able to go beyond this, to find a more general but pluralistic, diversity-encouraging research methodology for historical social sciences (as Wallerstein or Giddens would call it). There are many hints at this kind of methodology, like the following:

> As Rescher puts it: 'Reasoning can proceed not just inferentially' (ampliatively from axioms) 'but also dialectically' (reductively, argumentatively) from a complex, contradictory set of plausible initial positions. 'There are two different sorts of cognitive disciplines – the hard (*e.g.* physics), for which the mathematical (ampliative model [of reasoning]) is doubtless optimal, and the soft (*e.g.* history) for which the dialectical/reductive model is optimal'.
>
> (1990: 181, n. 5)

This might open a path towards an abstractly defined, 'soft' notion of *iconic modelling*. Iconic models are based on the dialectical/reductive way of reasoning; concerned with the explicit reflection on the metaphors and analogies used in formal and non-formal social scientific explanations alike; able to incorporate the temporal, narratively structured dimension of social worlds in them; and leave room for both explanatory emancipation and imaginary edification. Although all evidence-based interpretations of texts and explanations of social reality, when understood in terms of iconic modelling, can only be transsubjective and periodic, they must put forward more general truth-claims in order to be truly open to critical dialogues with Others.[22]

A BRIEF SUMMARY AND A FEW CONCLUDING REMARKS

As Alker's development has been an intertextual journey through different philosophical and social scientific texts, so we all are in the midst of such a journey, at least in principle. But far too many of us seem to be afraid or incapable of travelling very far: 'It is safer to stay at home and in the neighbourhood.' Therefore, I think that it is not an overstatement to call Alker's voyage 'exemplary'.

Alker's development may be divided into three different phases. The 'behaviouralist idealism' of the first phase had three pillars: belief in science; a particular theory of conflicts; and cautious belief in the potentialities of the United Nations. Even at the risk of a teleological reading, Alker's second phase is largely understood here as a transitional one. Of course, at that time Alker could not foresee his further development; yet he argued that the faith in positivist social sciences has to be reconciled with the social theories of more 'humanistic' scholars, otherwise the faith in positivism is not justified. Finally, Alker's mature third phase may be called 'late-modern, humanistic globalism'.

Alker's long voyage shows how one can learn and develop new approaches. Scholars should not see themselves as condemned to stick to doing research within the approach they have once learned. There is no reason to think that we are forced to stay where we already are, without long-term movement, without direction and occasional revisions of direction, without turns and sometimes re-turns. Indeed, the story of Alker's voyage should be able to reveal the false necessity of building an academic home and then staying in the neighbourhood for ever. Thereby this developmental story could even contribute to inducing emancipatory changes in the field, to help to empower others to start their own voyages, perhaps from where Alker has guided us.

In trying to construct a sense-making narrative out of Alker's writings, I classified them in four groupings, each dealing with a question. 1) How to collect and analyse data? 2) How to analyse and help to solve collective dilemmas? 3) How to broaden and deepen scientifically relevant modelling approaches? 4) How to theorize history? After having shown the way Alker developed, step by step, new, humanistic, late-modern research methods and modelling possibilities, I also discussed some of the weaknesses and limitations of Alker's approach. Even though it is of course true that Alker has not resolved all major methodological problems of historical social sciences, he has been in the avant-garde of IR and peace research. As the need for reconstructive critical-theoretical approaches is now widely accepted, I confidently expect his path-breaking writings to be read and discussed much more often in the future than in the past.

NOTES

1 Perhaps a better term would be 'critical and reflective approaches' or just 'critical reflectivism'.
2 In the analyses of the position(s) of Richard K. Ashley (Spegele 1992; Wæver 1989), Alker is not even mentioned, although Ashley was Alker's student and research assistant, and certainly was both encouraged and influenced by him. Alker has been overlooked by others, too. For instance, Mark Neufeld's (1993a, 1993b) two review articles on reflectivism and interpretativism, respectively, lack any analysis of Alker's position. In Neufeld's first article, Alker gets cited only once (1993a: 69). As an introduction to the citation there is: 'Thus, in a manner similar to Smith [Alker and Biersteker (1984)] affirm...'. In fact, however, it is Steve Smith (1987: 202) who partially relies on Alker's and Biersteker's article, not the other way round. In the latter of Neufeld's review articles, Alker is mentioned (1993b: 53, n. 56) but not even cited.
3 Of course, Alker is not the only founding father of this movement. Scholars such as Friedrich Kratochwil, John Ruggie and R. B. J. Walker had already started to develop somewhat similar ideas in the 1970s and early 1980s quite independently of Alker.
4 Alker wrote (1976a: 45): 'My first "way of seeing" the UN political process was heavily influenced by Dahl–Lipset–Haas type pluralism. And it was grounded in my personal commitments. World cleavages might not be so cumulatively destructive if they did not reinforce each other.'
5 It was published in the European journal *Quality and Quantity* in September 1974.
6 *Journal of Peace Research* rejected it when Alker submitted it there! Eventually it ended up as Alker 1996.
7 In the words of Gadamer (1977: 94) the truth of hermeneutics is that it 'allows what is foreign and what is one's own to merge in a new form by defending the point of the other even if it be opposed to one's own point of view'. It should be noted that in the case of me interpreting Alker there are no really opposing viewpoints, rather just differences of opinion and emphasis within a broadly defined perspective.
8 In a later paper Alker (1984a: 165) even points out that the technical advance in the statistical programs of computers has been a *disservice* to the scientific development: 'it has left many with the false impression that experimentally oriented analyses of variance, sample-based cross-tabulations, and regression analyses of non-experimental data are – or should be – the analytical logics at the core of "polimetrics".'
9 Neufeld (1993a: 69) is thus simply wrong in his claim that Alker and Biersteker (1984) 'accept that contending paradigms in International Relations are incommensurable'.
10 In the more technical terminology of the game theory, one says that in the Prisoner's Dilemma game the outcome of the individually rational choices is Pareto inferior (or is not Pareto optimal), that is, there is an outcome in which both (or all) players simultaneously could do better (for moving towards a Pareto optimal state, it would be enough for there to be one player who could do better while all others would do as well).
11 Note that for Alker totalitarianism is not an unique feature of Soviet or Chinese socialism or of the Nazisms and Fascisms of Continental Europe (or of Latin America, Africa and Asia, for that matter). Rather, Alker (1981b: 91) is very explicit in saying that 'more or less recessive variants of totalitarianism can be found in the state forms of contemporary China, the Soviet Union, Germany, Japan, and the United States'.
12 Note that the loyalty of prisoners might also be due to the fact that they belong to the same community, movement, or organization, which has particular normatively binding regulative rules of its own.

13 Note also that any way of defining the problem and its 'solutions' is based on a value-judgement, on an adoption of a perspective. Who defines what is the problem of this kind of situation in a particular context?

14 Furthermore, the contextual *Lebenswelt* is in any communication-situation as the ever-present and taken-for-granted background that is 'always already' there when we act; hence the attributes 'undistorted' and 'unconstrained' should be viewed as hermeneutically relative ideals, not absolute principles.

15 The 'crude' – although rather complex – model of information flows in the foreign policy decision-making can be found in the appendix of the *Nerves of Government* (Deutsch 1963: 258–61); the basic assumptions of this model are discussed sympathetically but reconstructively (from a more reflectivist position) in Alker 1981a; the model itself is critically and reconstructively scrutinized, in an attempt at tentatively opening more fruitful paths of iconic modelling to those analysing foreign policies, in Patomäki (1992a: 198–204).

16 Perhaps the bottom line for those not understanding Alker's methodological, political and moral development would be the following: 'Our research activity has also been, in a way, a Faustian romance: our entertaining commitment has been to unify a Promethean science (Artificial Intelligence or computational text analysis) and the ineffabilities of self-serving and self-transcending love' (Alker, Lehnert and Schneider 1985: 94). For a more thorough articulation of a somewhat similar, (late-)modernist moral vision which recasts the relation between our ultimate ideals of love and empowerment, see Unger (1984).

17 Fortunately, this has been done by Grunberg (1990). She argues, after having tried to show that 'the theory of hegemonic stability fails to meet reasonable criteria of empirical accuracy and analytic consistency', that there are 'mechanisms of mythic interference with theory-building' and that this interference can explain the rhetorical appeal of the neo-realist hegemonic stability theory.

18 Ashley (1980). On the cover of the book, there is a brief introductory and evaluative note by Alker: 'If Choucri and North's *Nations in Conflict* was arguably the best book in the 1970's produced by what Zinnes calls the Scientific Study of International Politics (SSIP), Ashley's major work may well secure that position in the 1980's. At the same time that it fulfills the promise of that school, it transcends its unreflective epistemological narrowness, confronting and redefining the major political issues of the day. Thus it confirms the frightening prospect that Choucri and North's lateral pressure perspective, developed in their analysis of the roots of World War I, also applies to the current USA–USSR–PRC superpower competition. Changing modes of power-balancing are accounted for at the same time that Soviet "social imperialism" is shown to be both imitative of earlier Western expansionism and contagiously infecting the Chinese. Ecologically sensitive redefinitions of democraphic-technological-bureaucratic "growth", not just clever power balancing realignments, are shown to be prerequisities for a peaceful future.'

19 This is the name of the planned book or 'an advanced text on theories of international relations', which, however, will probably never come out. Be that as it may, most of the intended chapters have been published somewhere. In addition to Alker (1981b), Alker and Biersteker (1984), and Alker, Biersteker and Inoguchi (1989), one should mention at least Amin (1991). The unpublished but nonetheless excellent Alker, Biersteker and Inoguchi (1985) – although it is perhaps in need of updating – should be noted, too.

20 In an outcome of a project that includes authors (Guzzini, Wæver) and a 'figure'/'master' (R. B. J. Walker) from this volume, the theme of peaceful changes in world politics is discussed and sometimes also debated extensively; see Patomäki (1995).

21 In Alker (1986a: 2) it is stated that he shares 'the ontological commitments of both Plato and Leibniz'. There Alker also talks about the 'ideal reality of linguistic and conceptual transformations and the ideal-material reality of social

talk'. Talk is real also in the critical realist understanding, as are linguistic and conceptual transformations, but the ontological commitments of Plato and Leibniz are much less easily reconcilable with realism.
22 I have discussed some of these ideas in Patomäki (1992a: particularly chapters 4 and 7).

REFERENCES

Works by Hayward R. Alker, Jr

Alker, Hayward R., Jr
(1964) 'Dimensions of Conflict in the General Assembly', *American Political Science Review* 58(3) (September): 642–57.
——(1965) *Mathematics and Politics*, New York: Macmillan.
——(1966a) *World Handbook of Political and Social Indicators* with Bruce Russett, Karl Deutsch, and Harold Lasswell, New Haven, CT: Yale University Press.
——(1966b) 'Causal Inference and Political Analysis', in J. Bernd (ed.) *Mathematical Approaches in Political Science*, Vol. II Dallas, TX: Southern Methodist University Press.
——(1966c) 'The Long Road to International Relations Theory: Problems of Statistical Nonadditivity', *World Politics* 18(4) (July): 623–55.
——(1968a) 'Decision Makers' Environments in the Inter-Nation Simulation', in William S. Coplin (ed.) *Simulation in the Study of Politics*, Chicago: Markham Press.
——(1968b) 'A Typology of Ecological Fallacies: Problems of Spurious Associations in Cross-level Inferences', in Mattei Dogan and Stein Rokkan (eds) *Quantitative Ecological Advances*, Cambridge, MA: MIT Press.
——(1968c) 'Research Possibilities Using Aggregate Political and Social Data', in Stein Rokkan (ed.) *Comparative Research across Cultures and Nations*, Paris: Mouton.
——(1968d) 'Supranationalism in the United Nations', in Louis Kriesberg (ed.) *Social Processes in International Relations: a Reader*, New York: Wiley, and in James Rosenau (ed.) *International Politics and Foreign Policy: a Reader in Research and Theory*, New York: Free Press.
——(1970a) 'Computer Simulation, Conceptual Frameworks and Coalition Behaviour', in Sven Groennings, Michel Leiserson and E. W. Kelley (eds) *The Study of Coalition Behavior*, New York: Holt, Rinehart and Winston.
——(1970b) 'Integration Logics', *International Organization* 24(4): 869–914.
——(1970c) 'Statistics and Politics: The Need for Causal Data Analysis', in S. M. Lipset (ed.) *Politics and Social Science*, Oxford: Oxford University Press; reprinted (1971) *Proceedings of the American Society of International Law* 65: 33–9.
——(1970–1) 'Le Comportement Directeur (Directive Behavior)', special issue of *Revue française de sociologie* XI–XII. An English version was published (1972) in the Proceedings of the Australian UNRSCO seminar, *Mathematics in the Social Sciences in Australia*, Canberra: Australian Government Publishing Service.
——(1973) 'Political Capabilities in a Schedule Sense', in Hayward R. Alker, Karl W. Deutsch and Antoine H. Stoetzel (eds) *Mathematical Approaches to Politics*, Amsterdam: Elsevier, pp. 307–73.
——(1974a) 'Are There Structural Models of Voluntaristic Social Action?' *Quality and Quantity* 8: 199–246.
——(1974b) 'Computer Simulations: Inelegant Mathematics and Worse Social Science?', *International Journal of Mathematical Education in Science and Technology* 5(2) (April–June): 139–55.
——(1975) 'Polimetrics: Its Descriptive Foundations', in Nelson W. Polsby and Fred I. Greenstein (eds) *Handbook of Political Science*, Reading, MA: Addison-Wesley.

—— (1976a) 'Individual Achievements Rarely Sum to Collective Progress' (autobiographical reflections), in J. Rosenau (ed.) *In Search of Global Patterns*, New York: Free Press, pp. 38–58.

—— (1976b) 'Research Paradigms and Mathematical Politics', in *Social Science Yearbook for Politics* 5, Munich: Olzog Verlag, pp. 13–50.

—— (1976c) 'Boudon's Educational Thesis about the Replication of Social Inequality', *Information* 15(1): 33– 46.

—— (1977a) 'Can the End of "Power Politics" be Part of the Concepts with which its Story Is Told?', a paper presented at the 1977 APSA Conference, Panel 2–5.

—— (1977b) 'A Methodology for Design Research on Interdependence Alternatives', *International Organization* 31(1) (Winter): 29–63.

—— (1977c) 'Global Modeling Alternatives', working paper distributed by the Wissenschaft-Zentrum, Berlin; later published (1985) as 'Global Modeling Alternatives: the First Twenty Years', in Michael Don Ward (ed.) *Theories, Models, and Simulations in International Relations: Essays in Honor of Harold Guetzkow*, Boulder, CO: Westview Press, pp. 9–37.

—— (1979a) 'From Information Processing Research to the Sciences of Human Communication', *Informatique et Sciences Humaines* 40–1 (mars–juin): 407–20.

—— (1979b) review of Johan Galtung, *Methodology and Ideology: Theory and Methods of Social Research*, Vol. 1, *American Political Science Review* 73(1) (March): 205–6.

—— (1981a) 'From Political Cybernetics to Global Modeling', in R. L. Merritt and B. M. Russett (eds) *From National Development to Global Community*, London: Allen and Unwin, pp. 353–78.

—— (1981b) 'Dialectical Foundations of Global Disparities', *International Studies Quarterly* 25(1): 69– 98.

—— (1981c) 'On Critical Compassion in the Historical Judgment of Stalin', *Soviet Union* 8 (Part I): 25–8.

—— (1982) 'Logic, Dialectics, Politics: Some Recent Controversies', in Hayward R. Alker, Jr (ed.) *Dialectical Logics for the Political Sciences*, Amsterdam: Rodopi.

—— (1983) 'Comment on Schubert's View of Paradigmatic Evolution: from the Ridiculous to the Sublime, and back?', *Politics and the Life Sciences* 1(2) (February): 110–12.

—— (1984a) 'Historical Argumentation and Statistical Inference: Towards More Appropriate Logics for Historical Research', *Historical Methods* 17(3) (Summer): 164–73; errata published in 17(4): 270.

—— (1984b) review of Vladimir Lefebvre, 'Algebra of Conscience: a Comparative Analysis of western and Soviet Ethical Systems', *Ethics* 94(3) (April): 520–3.

—— (1986a) 'Bit Flows, Rewrites, Social Talk: Towards More Adequate Informational Ontologies', a paper presented at the University of Tokyo, later published (1988) in M. Campanella (ed.) *Between Rationality and Cognition*, Turin: Meynier.

—— (1986b) 'The Presumption of Anarchy in World Politics', a revised version of a Griffith lecture at American University, Washington, DC, 10 March 1986.

—— (1987) 'Fairy Tales, Tragedies and World Histories: Towards Interpretive Story Grammars of Possibilist World Models', *Behaviormetrika* 21: 1–28; this has been translated into Russian and was reprinted (1988) Moscow: Progress Publishers.

—— (1988a) 'Emancipatory Empiricism: Towards the Renewal of Empirical Peace Research', in Peter Wallenstein (ed.) *Peace Research: Achievements and Challenges*, Boulder, CO: Westview Press.

—— (1988b) 'The Dialectical Logic of Thucydides' Melian Dialogue', *American Political Science Review* 82(3) (September): 805–20. An earlier draft was published in Russian (1988) Moscow: Progress Publishers.

—— (1988c) 'Toward Globalized Event-Data Research on Avoidable War', in Marcia K. Chicoine (ed.) *Data Development for International Research Update* 3(2) (October): 2–5, University of Illinois at Urbana-Champaign.

—— (1989a) 'Uppsala Fireworks: Data-Based Thoughts on the Origins and Possible Obsolescence of the European State System', in Peter Wallensteen (ed.) *States in Armed Conflict 1988*, Report No. 30, July, DPCR, Uppsala: Uppsala University.

—— (1989b) 'An Orwellian Lasswell for Today', in L. Savage, J. Combs and D. Nimmo (eds) *The Orwellian Moment: Hindsight and Foresight in the Post-1984 World*, Fayetteville, AR: University of Arkansas Press.

—— (1989c) 'World Politics as Ecopolitics: a Framework for the Comparative Analysis of Recent Political Writings on World Geography, the Global Environment and Planetary Ecology', prepared for delivery at APSA, Atlanta, 1 September.

—— (1990) 'Rescuing "Reason" from the "Rationalists": Reading Vico, Marx and Weber as Reflective Institutionalists', *Millennium* 19(2) (Summer): 161–84.

—— (1991) 'Making Peaceful Sense of the News: Institutionalizing International Conflict Management Events Reporting Using Frame-Based Interpretative Routines', a paper prepared for the panel of DDIR project at ISA, Vancouver, BC, 19–23 March 1991.

—— (1992a) 'The Humanistic Moment in International Studies: Reflections on Machiavelli and Las Casas', International Studies Association, 1992 presidential address, *International Studies Quarterly* 36: 347–71.

—— (1992b) 'Historicity for Beginners: Can It Be Rightly Taught?', prepared for the Karl Deutsch issue of the Wissenschaft-Zentrum publication, *WZB-Mitteilungen 56* (June): 45–7.

—— (1994) 'If Not Huntington's "Civilizations," Then Whose', a paper prepared for the 1994 ISA Convention in Washington DC, 25 March 1994.

—— (1996) *Rediscoveries and Reformulations: Humanistic Methodologies for International Relations*, Cambridge: Cambridge University Press.

—— with Amin, Tahir, Biersteker, Tom and Inoguchi, Takashi (in preparation) 'The Dialectics of World Order'.

—— and Barnard, J. J. (1978) 'Procedural and Social Biases in the Jury Selection Process', *The Justice System Journal* 3(3) (Spring): 220–40.

—— and Bennett, James (1977) 'When National Security Policies Bred Collective Insecurity: the War of the Pacific in a World Politics Simulation', in K. W. Deutsch, B. Fritsch, H. Jaguaribe and A. S. Markovitz (eds) *Problems of World Modeling: Political and Social Implications*, Cambridge, MA: Ballinger.

—— and Mefford, D. (1980) 'Generalized Precedent Logics for Resolving Insecurity Dilemmas', *International Interactions* 7(2): 165–206.

—— and Biersteker, T. J. (1984) 'The Dialectics of World Order: Notes for a Future Archeologist of International Savoir Faire', *International Studies Quarterly* 28: 121–42.

—— and Biersteker, T. J. and Inoguchi, T. (1989) 'From Imperial Power Balancing to People's Wars: Searching for Order in the Twentieth Century', in J. Der Derian and M. Shapiro, *International/Intertextual Relations*, Lexington, MA: Lexington Books.

—— and Bock, Peter G. (1972) 'Propositions about International Relations', *Political Science Annual*, 3: 385–495.

—— and Brunner, Ronald D. (1969) 'Simulating International Conflict: a Comparison of Three Approaches', *International Studies Quarterly* 13(1) (Spring): 70–110.

—— Buckley, W. and Burns, T. R. (1976) 'Introduction and Overview', in T. R. Burns and W. Buckley (eds) *Power and Control: Social Structures and their Transformation*, London: Sage Publications.

—— and Christensen, Cheryl (1972) 'From Causal Modelling to Artificial Intelligence: The Evolution of a UN Peace-Making Simulation', in J. A. LaPonce and Paul Smoker (eds) *Experimentation and Simulation in Political Science*: Toronto: University of Toronto Press.

—— Deutsch, K. W. and Markovits, A. S. (1976) 'Global Opportunities and Constraints for Regional Development: a Review of Interdisciplinary Simulation

Research Toward a World Model as a Framework of Studies of Regional Development', *Social Science Information* 16(1): 83–102.

—— and Stoetzel, A. (coedited and co-authored) (1973) *Mathematical Approaches to Politics*, San Francisco: Jossey-Bass.

—— with Duffy, G., Hurwitz, R. and Mallory, J. (1990) 'Text Modeling for International Politics: Tourist's Guide to RELATUS', in V. M. Hudson (ed.) *Artificial Intelligence and International Politics*, Boulder, CO: Westview Press.

—— and Haas, P. M. (1993) 'The Rise of Global Ecopolitics', in N. Choucri (ed.) *Global Accord: Environmental Challenges and International Responses*, Cambridge, MA: MIT Press.

—— Hostika, C. and Mitchell, M. (1976) 'Jury Selection as a Biased Social Process', *Law and Society Review* 11(1) (Fall): 9–41.

—— and Hurwitz, R. (1980) *Resolving Prisoner's Dilemmas*, Cambridge, MA: APSA.

—— and Inoguchi, T. (1985) 'The Decline of the Superstates: the Rise of a New World Order', a paper prepared for delivery at the World Congress of Political Science, IPSA, Paris (15–20 July).

—— Hurwitz, R. and Rothkin, K. (1993) 'Fairy Tales Can Come True: Narrative Constructions of Prisoner's Dilemma Game Play, 2', paper presented at annual meeting of American Economic Association, Anaheim, California.

—— with Lebedeva, M., O'Donnell, S. and Polanyi, L. (1993) 'Retelling Cold War Stories: Uncovering Cultural Meanings with Linguistic Discourse Analysis', prepared for IVth US–Soviet workshop on models and concepts of interdependence between nations, Moscow (26–8 June).

—— with Lehnert, W. and Schneider, D. (1985) 'Two Reinterpretations of Toynbee's Jesus: Explorations in Computational Hermeneutics', in G. Tonfoni (ed.) *Artificial Intelligence and Text Understanding, Guaderne de Ricerca Linguistica #6*, Parma: Edizione Zora, pp. 49–94.

—— and Puchala, Donald (1968) 'Trends in Economic Partnership: The North Atlantic Area, 1928–1963', in J. David Singer (ed.) *Quantitative International Politics: Insights and Evidence*, New York: Free Press.

—— and Russett, B. (1964), 'On Measuring Inequality', *Behavioral Science* 9(3): 207–18.

—— (1965) *World Politics in the General Assembly*, New Haven, CT: Yale University Press.

—— with Sherman, F. L. (1982) 'Collective Security-Seeking Practices since 1945', in Daniel Frei (ed.) *Managing International Crises*, London: Sage Publications.

—— and Tickner, J. A. (1977) 'Some Issues Raised by Previous World Models', in K. W. Deutsch, B. Fritsch, H. Jaguaribe and A. S. Markovitz (eds) *Problems of World Modeling: Political and Social Implications*, Cambridge, MA: Ballinger.

Works by other authors

Amin, Tahir (1985) *Nationalism and Internationalism in Liberalism, Marxism and Islam*, Islamabad: International Institute of Islamic Thought.

Ashley, R. (1980) *The Political Economy of War and Peace. The Sino-Soviet-American Triangle and the Modern Security Problematique*, New York and London: Nichols and Pinter.

Bhaskar, R. (1986) *Scientific Realism and Human Emancipation*, London: Verso.

—— (1989) *Reclaiming Reality. A Critical Introduction to Contemporary Philosophy*, London: Verso.

Chase-Dunn, C. (1989) *Global Formation. Structures of the World-Economy*, Cambridge, MA and Oxford: Blackwell.

Choucri, N. and North, R. C. (1975) *Nations in Conflict. National Growth and International Violence*, San Francisco: W. H. Freeman.

Der Derian, J. (1992) *Antidiplomacy. Spies, Terror, Speed, and War*, Cambridge, MA and Oxford: Blackwell.

Deutsch, K. W. (1963) *The Nerves of Government. Models of Political Communication and Control*, London: Free Press of Glencoe (Macmillan).

Foucault, M. (1979 [1975]) *Discipline and Punish. The Birth of the Prison*, trans. A. Sheridan, Harmondsworth: Penguin Books.

—— (1991a [1972]) 'Politics and the Study of Discourse', in G. Burchell *et al.* (eds) *The Foucault Effect. Studies in Governmentality*, London: Harvester Wheatsheaf.

—— (1991b [1981]) 'Questions of Method', in G. Burchell *et al.* (eds) *The Foucault Effect. Studies in Governmentality*, London: Harvester Wheatsheaf.

Gadamer, H.-G. (1977) *Philosophical Hermeneutics*, ed. and trans. D. Linge (texts originally published in German in 1960–72), Berkeley, CA: University of California Press.

Galtung, J. (1977) 'Science as Invariance-Seeking and Invariance-Breaking Activity', in J. Galtung, *Methodology and Ideology. Theory and Methods of Social Research*, Vol. 1, Copenhagen: Christian Ejlers.

Grunberg, I. (1990) 'Exploring the "Myth" of Hegemonic Stability', *International Organization* 44(4): 431–77.

Hoffmann, S. (1959) 'International Relations: The Long Road to Theory', *World Politics* XI: 346–77.

Keohane, Robert (1988) 'International Institutions: Two Approaches', *International Studies Quarterly* 32(3): 379–96.

Neufeld, M. (1993a) 'Reflexivity and International Relations', *Millennium: Journal of International Studies* 22(1): 53–76.

—— (1993b) 'Interpretation and the "Science" of International Relations', *Review of International Studies* 19(1): 39–61.

Olafson, F. A. (1979) *The Dialectic of Action. A Philosophical Interpretation of History and the Humanities*, Chicago and London: University of Chicago Press.

Ollman, B. (1971) *Alienation. Marx's Conception of Man in Capitalist Society*, Cambridge: Cambridge University Press.

Patomäki, H. (1992a) *Critical Realism and World Politics. An Explication of a Critical Theoretical and Possibilistic Methodology for the Study of World Politics*, Studies on Political Science No. 12, Turku: University of Turku, Department of Political Science.

—— (1992b) 'What Is It That Changed with the End of the Cold War? An Analysis of the Problem of Identifying and Explaining Change', in P. Allan and K. Goldmann (eds) *The End of the Cold War. Evaluating Theories of International Relations*, Dordrecht: Martinus Nijhoff.

—— (ed.) (1995) *Peaceful Changes in World Politics*, TAPRI Research Reports, Tampere: Tapri.

Ricoeur, P. (1984) *Time and Narrative*, Vol. 1, trans. K. McLaughlin and D. Pellauer, Chicago and London: University of Chicago Press.

—— (1988) *Time and Narrative*, Vol. 3, trans. K. Blamey and D. Pellauer, Chicago and London: University of Chicago Press.

Rorty, R. (1980) *Philosophy and the Mirror of Nature*, Oxford: Blackwell.

Smith, Steve (1987) 'The Paradigm Dominance in International Relations: The Development of International Relation as a Social Science', *Millennium: Journal of International Studies* 16(2): 189–206.

Spegele, Roger D. (1992) 'Richard Ashley's Discourse for International Relations', *Millennium: Journal of International Studies* 21(2): 147–82.

Unger, R. M. (1984) *Passion. An Essay on Personality*, New York: Free Press (Macmillan).

Wæver, Ole (1989) 'Tradition and Transgression in International Relations: a Post-Ashleyan Position', Working Papers 24, Copenhagen: Centre for Peace and Conflict Research.

9   Nicholas G. Onuf: the rules of anarchy

Marlene Wind

Nicholas Greenwood Onuf (b. 1941 in the USA) received his doctoral degree from Johns Hopkins University in 1967, where he also did his undergraduate work with Robert Tucker and George Liska. Originally he had planned to finish his PhD studies at Yale under Karl Deutch, but returned to Johns Hopkins on completion of his Masters degree in 1965. As an undergraduate, Onuf had caught an interest in international law through Robert Tucker. His interest was stimulated further at Yale through contact with Myres McDougal and his associates, and resulted in 1967 in his PhD thesis entitled 'The Conscious Development of International Law.'[1] From 1970 to 1994, inter-rupted only by visiting professorships at other universities in the USA and abroad, Onuf was a professor of International Relations at the School of International Service, the American University, Washington DC. After twenty-eight years in Washington, Onuf moved in 1994 to the Department of International Relations at Florida International University.

> The reconstruction of International Relations requires that the discipline be stripped of its current pretensions. If this is taken as abandonment of International Relations (the discipline as it is) and the possibility of inter-national theory (theory peculiar to International Relations), then I agree. I do not agree that it means giving up on international relations as well.
>
> (Onuf 1989b: 27)

Few scholars like to be called mainstream. Nicholas Onuf is not, however, in any strong danger of being classified in such a way – on the contrary. He can, in at least two respects, be positioned safely on the margins of the contemporary International Relations field. First, although a political scientist and IR scholar by training, Onuf has during his studies and in most of his professional career been preoccupied with international law, and legal and social theory. A short glance at his list of publications gives the impression that the person with whom we are dealing in this chapter cannot be characterized as a classical IR scholar. Thus, it was not until the publication in 1989 of his book *World of Our Making: Rules and Rule in Social Theory and International Relations* (hereafter referred to as WOOM) that his name started appearing in contemporary writings on IR theory – at least among so-called 'reflectivists'.[2]

Another important reason for placing Onuf on the margins of the IR field is perhaps more controversial but, it seems to me, also more interesting. It has to do with his refusal to grant the study of relations between states (IR) any disciplinary independence. This is not meant to imply that we should stop studying world politics. Rather, that we should cease to regard IR as a self-contained enterprise different from other social practices (Onuf 1989b: 14; Goodman 1978: 6 ff.). What makes it worth paying an extended visit to Onuf is thus first that he, as opposed to many contemporary IR scholars, in almost all of his academic work stresses the IR discipline's link to its historical roots: international law and legal theory. Second, that he, with the point of departure in the most recent social theory in his book *World of Our Making* from 1989, has launched a cross-disciplinary and agent–structure-integrated approach to the study of world politics. He labels this approach or theory 'constructivism' – drawing heavily on Anthony Giddens's theory of structuration (Giddens 1979; 1984). At its most basic (and radical) level a constructivist position holds that there is no such thing as a pre-social anarchical order. In order for social agents to act meaningfully – whether within or outside the state border – they have to draw on practice-based rules of the game including past experience, habits and more or less mechanical routines. Any action – no matter how calculated *or* how trivial – will be fundamentally and thereby ontologically dependent on these. In promoting such a position Onuf clearly joins those poststructural and critical IR scholars of the 1980s who have refused to buy into the vision of interstate relations as intrinsically ruleless. As opposed to other critical theorists, however, Onuf is not satisfied with a mere deconstruction of the IR discipline's basic building blocks. As will become clearer in the following, rather than a *deconstruction* Onuf's constructivism represents an ambitious attempt to *re*construct not only IR, but the entire social sciences.

Because Onuf's work is so densely written (some might even say impenetrable) and touches on so many different legal, social and IR topics, the main focus in this chapter will be on two main tenets: 1) the IR discipline's legal roots and here especially Onuf's demonstration of IR realism's liberal origins (the first and second sections); and 2) a presentation and critical discussion of Onuf's constructivist position (the third and fourth sections). The first section goes back in time and seeks to explore Onuf's early interest in the origins of social order. Onuf traces our conventional idea of international anarchy to writing by international lawyers and legal theorists of the nineteenth century. Building on these insights the section focuses on Onuf's critique of the classical Hobbesian link between order and physical sanctions. The section also gives a preliminary idea of the distinction between what Onuf names a 'liberal' paradigm and a 'constructivist' one pertaining to the overall social sciences. The second section goes more into detail with Onuf's genealogy anarchy. Onuf argues that the idea of interstate anarchy as we conceive of it today originates in writing by 'liberal' legal positivists at the beginning of the nineteenth century. The close affinity between positivist legal theory and modern regime theory is also addressed. The third section emphasizes the specificities of Onuf's version of constructivism; the two 'operative paradigms' of the social sciences (liberalism and constructivism) are discussed in more detail, constructivism's origins in linguistics and sociology are explicated, and finally the fruitfulness of constructivism for the study of international transformation is addressed. The fourth section seeks to evaluate constructivism's possible contribution to IR as a field of study and gives some suggestions for future research.

FROM LEVIATHAN ON A WORLD SCALE TO THE QUESTION OF SOCIAL ORDER

> International legal order is doubly ignored because its existence is inexplicable in the languages of both law and order. Political theory ignores the problem of international order by denying it empirical credibility. Legal theory is less cavalier. International law exists, most theorists agree, but efforts to explain how it works fail the test of credibility.
>
> (Onuf 1979: 244)

After the Second World War, when the study of world politics emerged decisively as an independent discipline within the social sciences, the image of relations between states as a Leviathanless state of nature was cultivated as what Onuf has called 'an objective reality setting it apart from other human practices' (Onuf 1989b: 14). At the time the image of IR as a war of all against all not only was utilized to demarcate IR from political science more generally, but also contributed to structure 'the scientific puzzle' to which the discipline was expected to respond: how and why would otherwise self-regarding states co-operate in such an environment? This picture no longer quite holds, however. In the past decades given the rising popularity of theories of social choice especially as cultivated in organizational economics, the image of society as something ontologically pre-social, with egoistic actors struggling for survival and/or maximization of individual utility, has penetrated into the overall political and social sciences (see, for instance, Keohane and Ostrom 1994: 403–28).[3] IR has, in other words, come to share openly what Onuf names a 'liberal paradigm', with several other social science disciplines:

> After World War II, scholars versed in microeconomic theory sought to extend its range of application, in the first instance to cover a new slice of social reality brought into being by public welfare policies. In so doing, these scholars poached on the disciplinary domain of Political Science most successfully – they produced elegant and satisfying solutions to a number of puzzles that had either defied Political Scientists or had eluded their attention. This move beyond the market came at no cost to microeconomic theory's formal specificity and explanatory power.... Adherents argue that all relations of authority should be considered in this light. This of course is a claim to constitute a new, far-reaching discipline, now dubbed Political Economy, for which the theory of social choice is said to be a proper paradigm theory.

Social choice theorists recognized the applicability of their theory whenever a discipline assigned paradigmatic significance to terms like 'rational actor' or 'interest', whether the context was marketing, voting, or fighting.

(Onuf 1989b: 1

Only three distinct 'operative-paradigms', as Onuf calls them, can be tified within the social sciences, and they are – as he sees it – not e convincing. While endorsing a Kuhnian idea of paradigms as social structions, Onuf's operative paradigms part company with Kuhn's in more embracing – cutting across (instead of demarcating) individua ciplines. Apart from a Marxist perspective, which has become less fas able in recent years and accordingly plays only a limited role in O discussion, two remaining positions can be said to compete for promir within today's social sciences. The leading one is a *liberal paradigm*, he be understood in philosophical (that is, utilitarian) and *not* IR terms. other is the one that Onuf himself endorses, a so-called '*construct paradigm* of political society. It is in the ongoing tension between t two perspectives that Onuf's scholarship can be situated.

While sociologists reaching back to Durkheim and Weber for long questioned the image of society as an atomist pre-social order, things very different in IR. Reflectivists like Onuf were in other words among the first to problematize more generally the image of interstate relations as a Hobbesian war of all against all.[4] A meta-theoretical critique of the conscious and perhaps also unconscious reproduction of the anarchy presumption[5] in mainstream theorizing about world politics is thus one of the main tenets in Onuf's so far most important book from 1989. Although the anarchy debate in IR is of a relatively recent date, one of the main concerns of WOOM was to show that to those international lawyers and legal philosophers, who have been engaged in the ongoing problematization of positivist legal theory, a theoretical critique of the anarchy assumption in interstate relations is far from new. What Onuf has in mind here is *not* the sometimes rather tedious literature occupied with world order modelling that engaged many idealist legal philosophers in the nineteenth century and forms such a strong interest in the so-called WOMP (World Order Models Project), but rather more philosophically, sociologically and anthropologically inspired work concerned with questions of relations between rules, norms and sanctions systems in all types of social orders (see, for instance, Barkun 1967; Onuf 1982b; Frank 1988; Snyder 1993; Alexander 1982).[6]

WOMP was initiated in the USA by among others Richard Falk. The scholars involved in the project objected to the formalistic legal training they had received and argued that international law was in need of a 'paradigm shift' towards normative theory. The project set out to define how four essential values for mankind could be realized: the minimization of large-scale collective violence, the maximization of social and economic well-being, the realization of fundamental human rights and of conditions of political justice, and the maintenance and rehabilitation of ecological quality (Suganami 1989: 148).[7]

While working as a visiting research fellow at Princeton University from 1973 to 1976, under the auspices of Richard Falk, Onuf was, however, rather ambivalent towards these world modelling projects. What he was interested in then and what has been central to most of his later work (and in fact to all those more philosophically informed legal critiques of the Leviathan model) was, as noted above, investigations into the status and practical working of those rules and norms encountered both in so-called hierarchical legal systems and in decentralized orders such as the states system and, for instance, primitive societies.

Onuf's introductory essay to the book he edited at Princeton was called 'Global Law-Making and Legal Thought' and it touched on precisely these issues. Both this essay and one published three years earlier in the *American Journal of International Law* contained a fundamental critique of the so-called 'domestic analogy',[8] implying that order will depend on physical sanction systems. Introducing his 'Law-Making' essay, he notes that

> If the present essay slights a major intellectual tradition devoted to the problem of social order, it is that associated with Western political thought. This essay... may thus be taken as a complementary attack on one of the greatest of all intellectual puzzles – the nature and origins of social order.
>
> (Onuf 1982c: 1)

Bearing in mind the above comment about the still increasing popularity of social choice theories within the overall social sciences, we may certainly find that the existence of social order constitutes an intellectual puzzle. Or to put it slightly differently, if one's point of departure for theorizing is a Hobbesian state of nature – a lot of anomalies (read: order) are left to be explained.

Onuf's early reluctance towards the numerous legal theorists who saw the 'solution' to the anarchy problem among states as one of working for a supranational sanctioning arrangement also included the work of his former teacher and colleague Richard Falk.[9] In his *A Study of Future Worlds* from 1975, Falk argued for the need to establish a 'world-government-like machinery' including assemblies, secretariats, councils, world security forces, a world grievance system and a world disarmament service (see also Koskenniemi 1990; Burley 1993: 209–14).

As Onuf argues, the scholarly call for formal 'authority above the state' is far too simplistic and fundamentally neglects the more profound philosophical discussion of the idea of social order:

> The relations of sovereigns are indisputably conflictual. They are not, however, merely anarchical. They display order even in the midst of conflict. Such order as this cannot be political, as we have been using the term, because authority [here meaning backed by physical power: M.W.] explains nothing about the order. *Only if political theory reaches*

beyond the causal sequence of authority, law, and order, which is at its heart, and searches for the origins, supports, and limits of each, do we have a chance of explaining international order. The sequence may be reversed, after all, just asking, Where does authority come from?

(Onuf 1979: 244; emphasis added)

Although the query about where authority and order come from (if not primarily from a Leviathan with sanctioning powers) was given a central position on Onuf's agenda in most of his writings during the 1970s and 1980s, it was only gradually that he began to emphasize the close link between the critique of classical legal theory and the post-positivist concern for how society is constituted through language and social practice. His 1989 book was clearly the culmination of this surge beyond causal inferences. Before we go into this work in a little more depth, however, we need to take a closer look at his critique of the Hobbesian paradigm as explicated in positivist legalism. The demonstration of the intimate – but in the IR literature completely discarded – link between *liberal* legal theory of the nineteenth century and IR *realism* of today, is one of Onuf's most significant contributions (see Onuf 1989b; 1994b).[10] To put it in another way, when we as IR scholars have talked about law, and of course especially about international law, we have linked it to liberalism understood as Kantian idealism – to utilize Martin Wight's distinction between Realism, Grotianism and Kantianism (Bull 1977; for a recent example see Suganami 1989). This image fits nicely for the Kantian world order modelling projects referred to above. However, as will become clearer in the following section, the affinity between positivist international-law theorists and IR *realism* is in fact much more prevalent than the one conventionally drawn between international law and IR *liberalism*.

POSITIVIST LEGALISM, THE HOBBESIAN PARADIGM AND THE QUESTION OF ANARCHY – OR THE LIBERAL ORIGINS OF IR REALISM

Historically and conceptually [legal: M.W.] positivism, more than any other system of legal thought, is identified with the Western state system. The central positivist tenet, developed presently, that law is made by men and, by extension, human collectivities called states, is the dominant jurisprudential stance of our time. As with the state system itself, we can decry positivism in specifics without affecting the way it colors our vision of social reality.

(Onuf 1982c: 1–2)

In International Relations, the assumption that a Hobbesian Leviathan is a prerequisite for order inside the state and, consequently, that order cannot exist in the world-political sphere, is not just a well-known realist doctrine. It is, as also indicated above, the most fundamental theoretical building block of the entire IR discipline. But where does this metaphor originate from conceptually? In IR, we normally attribute this idea to the realists of this century, perhaps H. J. Morgenthau and E. H. Carr in particular (see Morgenthau 1985: 295; Carr 1981; see also Aron 1966). Still, most realist writers go further back in history than Hobbes when the elusive recurring patterns of world political life are pictured (see, for instance, Waltz 1979; Gilpin 1981). However, as Onuf makes explicit both in his earlier and in more recent work, the radical distinction that characterizes life inside, as opposed to outside, the state border was most forcefully articulated and promoted in our by now well-known IR version by *liberal* legal theorists of the nineteenth century.[11] Clearly, such a point collides not only with conventional presentations of the development of the discipline but equally with several critical theorists who have sought to trace the anarchy presumption back to the birth of the European states system (see, for instance, Chapter 12 on R. B. J. Walker in this volume).

Drawing on J. G. A. Pocock, Onuf argues that it was not until the late eighteenth and early nineteenth centuries that the understanding of order as dependent on one single authority possessing power came to be accepted by most European statesmen and scholars (Onuf 1979: 252; 1982c: 4–13 ff.; 1989b: Ch. 5, 425–46; see also Pocock 1957). As Onuf points out, in the centuries after the Peace of Westphalia 'state and anarchy were limiting conditions for political society, rules and rulers the norm' (Onuf 1989b: 168; see also Nardin 1983: 65 n.). The conceptual idea of relations of states has thus not changed markedly through the centuries or, as Onuf points out in an essay on the genealogy of the idea of international legal order:

> In the Middle Ages the order–authority problem simply did not exist. The affairs of man obtained their order from a higher, authoritative order. Authority attested to the fact of higher order and assured mundane order. That order was imperfectly realized in human affairs cast no doubt on the perfection of its source or even the legitimacy of its less than perfect agents. It is this openly antiempirical quality of medieval thought that lent itself to secular challenges and in due course invited the scientific revolution.
>
> (Onuf 1979: 252)

That we do not find the order–authority distinction of the Middle Ages in our by now common-sense understanding, is of course due to the fact that the state as a unitary and territorially demarcated actor was not invented at that point in time (see Onuf 1991: 429 ff.; see also Ruggie 1986; Ruggie 1993; Wæver 1991; see also Wæver on Ruggie in Chapter 7 of this volume).

Onuf's point here is significant. He draws to our attention that it was the quest for internal legal legitimacy emerging among the developing democracies around the turn of the nineteenth century that – in itself – gradually led to the adoption of what he and Klink have together referred to as a 'substantial', as opposed to a formal, anarchy conception (Onuf and Klink 1989: 149–50). Substantial anarchy implies not just the formal absence of a head of state but, as indicated above, a much more far-reaching understanding: 'the absence of guidance provided by virtue, rights and manners' (Onuf 1989b: 164 ff.). One can thus say that it was not until the aspiring democratization of western European states that the image of relations among sovereigns came to be conceived of as fundamentally pre-social. Or to put it slightly differently, with the need for political legitimacy inside the state deduced from one secular, effective sovereign, there followed an almost entirely negative conception of interstate relations. It was *the difference* between the ordered inside and the wilderness outside the state border that set the stage for our now conventional image of IR as a pre-social order. One problematic result of this conceptual development is, however, as another constructivist and former student of Onuf, has put it:

> By making social order dependent upon law and law, in turn, upon the existence of certain institutions – be they the existence of a sovereign or central sanctioning mechanisms – we understand the international arena largely negatively, i.e. in terms of a 'lack' of binding norms, of central institutions, of a sovereign will, etc.
>
> (Kratochwil 1989: 2)[12]

As opposed to the natural law system which dominated Europe in the Middle Ages and in which individuals were regarded as legal subjects in a cosmic order, the rise of the states system in Europe came to mean that territorial sovereigns were the only source of legal obligation: 'Positivist doctrine interprets the fact that the order is international to mean that the subjects are and can only be independent and fully sovereign nation-states' (Onuf 1982c: 7). While such ideas clearly resemble realism more than what is conventionally promoted as liberal IR theory, what should be stressed here is not just that those positivist legal theorists who promoted the clear distinction between the domestic and the international sphere were liberal thinkers with strong democratic sentiments, but also that they were liberals in the true sense of the word. As I will show, the affinity between the utilitarian thrust of these legal theorists and our own IR realists inclined to choice-theory is hard to discard.

Some of the authors to whom one ought to pay much more attention when trying to make sociological sense of the life-span of IR as a social science discipline, and especially of the dominance of realism therein, are people like Jeremy Bentham and John Austin. They lived at the turn of the eighteenth/nineteenth centuries and contributed strongly to a radicalization of the Hobbesian contention that 'without the terror of some Power, to cause them [the rules: M. W.] to be observed, are contrary to our natural passions. . . . Covenants without the Sword, are but *Words*, and of no strength to secure man at all' (Hobbes 1988: 223; Onuf 1989b: 164 ff.). As will be later illustrated in my sketch of Onuf's constructivist approach to IR in section 3, the contention that language and culture in themselves constitute no regulative (and constitutive) effect on human action is perhaps one of the most focal points of disagreement among Hobbesian (liberal) realists and constructivists.

The idea of linking order to the fear of punishment in strict causal terms originates from Galileo and classical physics, and later was reinforced by Newton's theory of gravity (Pocock 1957; Taylor 1985), where the mechanistic prediction of movement was related directly to the invocation of force (see also Little 1977). Consequently, in reasoning along such lines, customary law and those international conventions that had been regarded as essential to the working of international society in Europe for centuries, were rejected as having any effect when it came to regulating *and* theorizing about interstate behaviour. J. G. A. Pocock has made the same point in his reading of the Hobbesian tradition, the understanding being that

> law may be custom, but custom alone has no binding force; for custom to become law requires that there should already exist an authority capable of making law by his injunctions. Therefore, no law can be immemorial; before there can be law there must be a sovereign; and every law must have been made at a particular time.
>
> (Pocock 1957: 163)[13]

In his emphasis of the link between nineteenth-century liberalism and those parts of modern IR realism inspired by the choice-theory (also referred to as 'rationalist'), Onuf thus stressed how the legal positivists of the time came to draw a sharp line between state actions that originated in 'choice' and actions based on habit or custom. One of the most influential legal thinkers of the early nineteenth century, John Austin, utilized the distinction between positive law that was backed by the command of a sovereign *and* positive morality that was not, to draw up the fundamental difference between the national and international spheres:

> international law, or the law obtaining between nations, regards the conduct of sovereigns considered as related to one another. And hence it inevitably follows, that the law obtaining between nations is *not* positive law: for every *positive law* is set by a given sovereign to a person or persons in a state of subjection to its author. As I have already intimated, the law obtaining between nations is (improperly so called) set by general opinion. The duties which it imposes are enforced by *moral* sanctions.
>
> (Austin 1954: 201)[14]

The idea that states are the sole sources of law in the international system and, accordingly, that everything at any time (in conflict as in co-operation) depends on the rather arbitrary 'goodwill' of the particular sovereign is often referred to as 'the concept of consent' (Nardin 1983: 211; Frank 1988: 753–9). Not very surprisingly, the concept is even today highly disputed among legal scholars. As Onuf notes in his 1982 essay, if read along positivist lines, the concept is, however, voluntaristic – and thereby entirely contradictory. In other words, how can international obligations be binding in the first place if they cease to be so when/if a particular sovereign no longer considers himself bound by them? (see Onuf 1982c: 4 ff., 28, see also p. 253 in this book.)[15]

For any contemporary student of International Relations, the description of states as purely unconstrained and as a calculative power/utility maximizer, will be familiar. It is the core of realism and what Onuf refers to as 'the liberal paradigm'. The parallels between legal positivists and today's choice-theoretically inclined realists or regime theorists is, in other words, hard to overlook (see also Burley 1993: 217–22). What unites them is that they both see the international system as made up of anomic self-regarding state-actors where 'self-help' – as Waltz has put it – is the only thing that counts at the end of the day. It is assumed not only that the state has an unalterable will and interest that have stayed the same over the centuries, but also that state-actors will perceive themselves as fundamentally uninfluenced by the norms that they implicitly or explicitly might have committed themselves to at earlier stages (see, for instance, Keohane 1984; Axelrod 1984; for a critique see Frank 1988; Onuf and Klink 1989; see also Kratochwil 1989; Wendt 1992 and 1994; Milner 1993). This is exactly how contemporary regime theorists analyse international institutions – informed by neo-classical economics. The primary purpose of and reason for international co-operation in this literature is the reduction of transaction costs and the increase in states' regulatory efficiency. No fundamental normative underpinnings are necessary as long as the sanctioning mechanisms are in place (Keohane 1984; Garrett 1992; Moravscik 1991 and 1993). What we are facing here, in other words, is not just what we above referred to as an emergent synthesis among the study of institutions in industrial economics and international relations but also between IR-regime theory and international law. Or as a contemporary international lawyer puts it in an essay celebrating this development:

> The early regime theorists' insistence on deriving a theory of international institutions from realist premises was a clever strategic move within political science. Reinventing international law in rational-choice language stopped the traditional 'Realist–idealist' debate cold. 'Efficiency' and 'transparency' are hardly legalist-moralist sentiments. They are the language of rational calculation, effective not only with political science Realists but also with a large and growing number of international lawyers' domestic colleagues.
>
> (Burley 1993: 220)

Rational choice and institutional economics, in other words, have not only replaced old realist–idealist tensions in IR but have also stripped out old classical normative questions of 'life and death' in international law and world politics. Burley is clearly quite happy with this development. For her the great advantage of the rapprochement between regime theory and international law is not only that we 'finally' get rid of all legalist (and WOMP) talk of the possibility of progress in the international system and replace it by investigations into how regimes actually work. But, she argues, knowledge about these issues might also aid future governments and international organizations in setting up more efficient arrangements for solving international collective action problems. It certainly seems as if Onuf's liberal paradigm is turning into something resembling a 'supra-paradigm' for the entire social sciences – just as predicted by hard-core rationalists like Keohane and Ostrom in their special issue of *Theoretical Politics* from 1993 (see Keohane and Ostrom 1993).

To some students of IR, it may of course appear slightly provocative to hold that rationalist regime theory has close links to the social atomism and voluntarism of positivist legal theory. In other words, have we not always been taught that theorists of regimes – as opposed to more hard-headed realists – stress the importance of rules, norms, principles and decision-making procedures in interstate co-operation? Is it not closer to collective commitment on the international scale than to social atomism and thereby to liberalism rather than realism, one could ask. True enough; this is certainly the conventional textbook version of the story. However, that the conventional textbook story goes like this does not necessarily make it correct. As argued, among others, by Kratochwil and Ruggie in their still impressive 'deconstruction' of the regime literature from 1986, the rational-choice epistemology of most regime theory fundamentally contradicts the intersubjective ontology of regimes as normatively layered institutional orders (Kratochwil and Ruggie 1986; Kratochwil 1989; Kratochwil 1993: 443–72; see also Frank 1988; Nardin 1983: 171; Wind 1996b). In an article co-written with Frank Klink, Onuf has illustrated how Kenneth Oye *et al.*'s work on 'co-operation under anarchy' from the mid-1980s can be seen as one of the most obvious examples of such a contradiction (Onuf and Klink 1989: 149–50, 167). 'Nations dwell in perpetual anarchy, for no central authority puts limits on the pursuit of sovereign interests', as Kenneth Oye states in his opening remark (Oye 1985: 1; see also Rittenberger and Mayer 1993: 408).[16] However, as Onuf and Klink have argued, 'Wherever there are politics, there are limits' (Onuf and Klink 1989: 149–50). Yes, limits, but also always choices, it should be added.[17] From a constructivist point of view, limits or normative restraints are not and should not be understood merely as freely installed or deliberately set up sanction systems. Nor are they simply regulative, static or independent of actual practice. Rules and norms also make action possible and very often perceived constraints are ideational and closely linked to discourse and questions of legitimacy.

To sum up: international law positivists theorize about the treaty-making process among states in exactly the same manner as IR rationalists study international institutions. Because treaties, as positivist lawyers regard them, are the artefacts of sovereign states, they exist only as obligation-imposing structures, as long as they serve the long- or short-term purpose of the individual sovereign. Such a position clearly stresses a fundamental difference between the expected possibility of order inside and outside the state border.

With the constructivist point of departure that Onuf endorses in his latest book, however, treaty-making as well as international relations more generally is much more complex and with implications going far beyond the consent and immediate control of the individual sovereign. This is especially so when a time-dimension and a transformational 'logic' are introduced. As also David Dessler has argued, the macro-level reproduction of sovereignty as a fundamental and constitutive aspect of international society can best be regarded as an unintended result of day-to-day interaction at the micro-level (Dessler 1989: 469; Kratochwil 1989: 61; Ruggie 1993: 166; see also Onuf 1994b).[18] A constructivist would agree with the rationalists that the rules that actors set up and consent to deliberately do probably produce some intended results; that is at least what we expect them to do. But sanctioning or regulating action is not the only function of rules in day-to-day life. As Onuf points out, for instance, in his essay from 1994 on 'The Constitution of International Society', following rules (or not) also produces the largely unintended result of strengthening (or weakening or even supplanting) those rules (Onuf 1994b). Over time these will become constitutive for that particular social sphere in the sense that the rules will be the often unproblematized or legitimate point of departure for future acts. Such a stance is important because it suggests what to look for when analysing gradual change – for instance, in a basic institution like sovereign state-hood. The analytical and theoretical implications of such a distinction between 'rule-types' will become clearer in the following section where we will go into the specificities of Onuf's constructivist alternative.

In any case, it should be unnecessary at this point to stress Onuf's general scepticism towards theories that hold that practice-produced rules and norms in world politics are of little or no importance or that only self-imposed rules, norms and procedures as known from transaction-cost-analysis and neo-classical economics will be important when trying to grasp interstate relations (see Onuf 1994c).

From his constructivist corner, Onuf has noted: 'If legal order [backed by enforcement: M. W.] is not defined as the root source of a social order, then we may ask without prejudice (or at least that prejudice) how particular social orders actually work. We become sociologists' (Onuf 1982c: 33). However, these points indicate not only that we should perhaps all become sociologists, but also a clear weakness in Onuf's attempt to create social theory. As we have already seen, and as I will attempt to show more explicitly below, he is clearly more interested in explaining how rules and social orders *work* than in how they *change*. Indeed, one could argue that it is necessary to understand how social orders work and are reproduced before any changes can be detected. But such a point fundamentally contradicts constructivism – at least as I understand it – as a theory of social transformation. Thus an attempt to conceptualize change in the international system must be at the core of a constructivist research programme. In his most recent work, Onuf in fact indicates this himself, albeit without discussing it in any detail (Onuf 1994b: 18–19).

Before we discuss, in the concluding section, how and whether constructivism might contribute to a better analytical conception of social change, we need a more detailed understanding of some of the core elements of the theory. Also here it will become apparent that the question of how to conceptualize system-transformation will be crucial.

CONSTRUCTIVISM: ON WORLD-MAKING THROUGH DAILY PRACTICE

> Sovereignty, directive-rules and the state – each necessitates the other in a tight unbroken circle.... The legal positivist penchant for directive-rules is partly a cultural bias, given the large proportion of directive-rules in Western practice, and partly an appreciation of the problem of securing a legal order from external threats to its independence.
>
> (Onuf 1989b: 142)

It was not until the publication of WOOM in 1989 that Onuf presented a full-fledged theory, building on the insights about rules and social order that he had been concerned with in many of his earlier writings. In the following attempt to explicate Onuf's constructivist approach to IR and social life more generally, we will have to focus on a few central bearings. To repeat very briefly, Onuf distinguishes only two[19] competing positions, ontologies – or, as he calls them, following Kuhn, paradigms – as pertaining to the social sciences in general: 'liberalism' and 'constructivism'. There is nothing really exceptional in this, however. Most sociologists and what we these days in political science refer to as 'New Institutionalists' identify this analytical distinction as cutting through most, if not all, social science disciplines (see March and Olsen 1989; Powell and DiMaggio 1991; Wind 1996b).[20] For the purpose of analytical clarity, a short rehearsal of what Onuf sees as the core of the so-called 'liberal paradigm' will be appropriate.

As an operative paradigm, 'liberalism' nowadays materializes in theories of social choice and microeconomic theorizing throughout the social sciences.[21] However, in its vision of man and human action in general, it has been dominant in western philosophy at least since the seventeenth and eighteenth centuries and the scientific revolution (Taylor 1985: 24 ff.). In IR, the rational actors are not individuals but states. Once defined as striving for a maximization of self-interest, the actions of states, so the conventional story goes, become predictable, like the laws in physics (see Waltz 1979). Only external forces constrain the intentions, goals and desires of individual actors and it is on this basis alone that the regularities of world politics can be estimated, as Onuf puts it: 'there is no surprise to renewed assertions, influenced by the theory of social choice, that international relations are purely anarchic, for anarchy is liberalism carried to its logical extreme: The only limits on rational conduct are those imposed by material conditions. If international relations are purely anarchic, then Political Economy is their perfected description' (Onuf 1989b: 18–19).

In spite of liberalism's ongoing popularity, several IR reflectivists and other critical social theorists have in recent years directed our attention to the inconsistency and problematic character of this paradigm for understanding social relations more generally. Nicholas Onuf belongs to this group of dissidents. However, Onuf is not just a disbeliever, he is also in a very distinct sense a 'believer' with his own all-embracing theoretical alternative. To put it in slightly different terms, while drawing on insights from several different social theories and philosophical perspectives, constructivism, as represented by Onuf, is just as ambitious in its explanatory aspirations as its liberal competitor. But what does a constructivist position entail and how exactly does it build on and extend Onuf's earlier insights about rules and social order?

As opposed to the social atomism of liberalism, constructivism sees agents and structures – man and society – as fundamentally co-constituted (Onuf 1989b: 58; Giddens 1984: 2 ff.). This implies that agents – always – in their action will be fundamentally dependent on the structures in which they are embedded, no matter whether the theorist conceives these as material or purely ideational. However, the reproduction and persistence of these structures will depend fundamentally on the ongoing day-to-day 'deeds' or practices undertaken by the actors. As Onuf argues:

> Constructivism holds that individuals and societies make, construct or constitute each other. . . . Individuals make societies through their deeds, and societies constitute individuals, as they understand themselves and each other, through those same deeds. Some of these deeds are deliberate attempts to make, or make over, society; most are not.
>
> (Onuf 1994c: 4)

In WOOM he puts it in this way:

> the constructivist position I defend . . . emphasizes the continuous co-constitution of micro- and macro-level phenomena . . . I develop a micro-level understanding of what rules are . . . but go on to the macro-level by considering what they do . . . how [does] competence with rules constitute culture, which is indeed a macro-level concern(?).
>
> (Onuf 1989b: 29)

In examining this ongoing co-constitution between agents and structures, any analysis should therefore set out by looking at 'deeds' or practices performed by social actors. 'Deeds done, acts taken, words spoken – these are all the facts there are', as Onuf puts it (Onuf 1989b: 36). One implication of such a position will be that the question of whether a society is anarchical, hierarchical, or, for instance, heteronomously organized, as in the Middle Ages, will be *the* object of analysis – and not something given by assumption as in neo-realism or in rational choice theory – whether applied to the domestic or international scene. The stress on the co-constitution between agents and structures thus emphasizes the importance of rules and norms for all aspects of human action. As Onuf puts it:

> . . . people need rules for all but their most transient exchanges. When they confront the necessity of dealing with each other without knowing if they follow the same rules, they learn what they commonly know and make what other rules they need. In other words competence with rules is a defining feature of human cognition and the presence of rules is a defining feature of human condition.
>
> (Onuf 1994c: 8)

Constructivism in Onuf's version is thus closely affiliated to Anthony Giddens's theory of structuration, even though the latter's main aim was to rebut classical functionalist sociology and, not like Onuf, mainly theories of social choice.[22]

In arguing that rules make society meaningful, and that meaning is a prerequisite for action, sense-making precedes 'sensing', to put it in strictly anti-empiricist terms. In other words, we do not have an unmediated access to the world: 'the ongoing (re)construction of reality is rarely distinguishable from the known, felt, lived-in world we "really" inhabit' (Onuf 1989b: 157). Clearly, 'matter also matters' – but as Onuf argues: 'never without rules being implied' (Onuf 1989b: 22). This can of course also be seen as a point against the more radical poststructuralists who argue that no stable rules in social life can be said to exist. It might be true – as Onuf argues – that postmodernists replace rules by texts although I find this claim somewhat misleading. However, as Onuf rightly stresses also, texts, intertextuality and indeed any discursive critique of what is seen as 'modern' will in itself not only be deeply imbedded in, but also fundamentally dependent on, rules (Onuf 1994b: 6).

To sum up: these almost symbolic interactionist points[23] stress that no human action takes place in a pre-social space – not even in Hobbes' state of nature. The rules make it possible to 'go on' in life as Wittgenstein would say. Thus, 'The world *becomes* of our making' through our knowledgeable application of practice-based rules. Consequently, constructivism does not take the same view of social actors as Harold Garfinkel, who has referred to them as 'structural dopes' following rules blindly (Garfinkel 1967: 66–8). Actors make choices all the time, but the *perception* of possible routes of action will always be conditioned by past experience and the overall social setting. Parallel points were made by Wittgenstein in his *Philosophical Investigations*, when he described language games as 'a form of life' giving rise to social institutions (Wittgenstein 1968).

One preliminary way into grasping the dispute between the liberal and the constructivist positions within the overall social science picture is to spell out the difference between 'regulative' and 'constitutive' rules – though for Onuf this is only a first and very early step. Anthony Giddens stresses the distinction between the two rule-types in the following way:

> Rules have two aspects to them, and it is essential to distinguish these conceptually.... Rules relate on the one hand to the constitution of meaning, and on the other to the sanctioning of modes of social conduct.
>
> (Giddens 1984: 18)

Regulative rules thus represent what the language philosopher John Searle has called our common sense or 'paradigm' understanding of rules. We usually refer to them when we talk about the 'laws of nature', 'scientific laws' and causal 'if-then' propositions found, for instance, in criminal law: 'if you steal from others you will get punished' (Searle 1969: 34). We employ regulative rules all the time in our daily practice, i.e. by commanding someone to do something or by explicitly forbidding a certain action.

Very often a command or prohibition will be backed by a sanction but a 'threat' can easily be implicit or culturally conditioned and consequently not as direct as in criminal law. If regulative rules are implicit or culturally bound they overlap with the second type, constitutive rules – even though the latter deal primarily with the constitution of meaning. As Michel Foucault has shown so convincingly, the *definition* of what 'makes sense' in any social setting at any given point in time is never completely arbitrary and can certainly – by its mere accentuation – contain strong regulative elements (Foucault 1990: 92). The important distinction between regulative and constitutive rules might become a little clearer if we follow Searle's example in his reference to games like football:

> The rules of football or chess, for example, do not merely regulate playing football or chess, but as it were they create the very possibility of playing such games. The activities of playing football or chess are constituted by acting in accordance with the appropriate rules ... constitutive rules constitute (and also regulate) an activity the existence of which is logically dependent on the rules.... Regulative rules characteristically take the form of imperatives ... constitutive rules take quite a different form, e.g. 'A check-mate is made when the king is attacked in such a way that no move leaves it unattacked.'
> (Searle 1969: 33–4; Rawls 1955: 25).

Rules in games are of course too static to be compared directly to the constitutive rules of social life. Furthermore, as noted above and as Onuf stresses over and over again, all social rules are both regulative and constitutive though some, at least by first impression, can be identified as almost purely regulative. However, the importance of constitutive rules for social action is exactly what is missed out in those parts of the social sciences that like to see themselves as 'would-be' natural sciences. Here the observation of behavioural regularities suffices. If we return to Searle's football game above, this would mean that we would stick to an observation of the moves the players made on a grass field without having any idea of what they were running for or what small signs, signals and informal rules of the game implied. When applied to the study of world politics, leaving out investigations into constitutive rules inevitably means that we stay on the surface of things instead of trying to get an idea of what Kratochwil and Ruggie in their study of international regimes have referred to as 'the intersubjective aspects' of interstate co-operation (Kratochwil and Ruggie 1986).

In outlining his constructivist theory, Onuf is, however, unhappy with the regulative/constitutive distinction of rules. Building on Searle's speech act theory, he argues that not two but three aspects of rules can be said to influence all human relations. He calls these 'instruction-rules', 'commitment-rules' and 'directives'. In emphasizing these, Onuf challenges the traditional focus on regulative – or as he calls them 'directive' – rules in western culture: 'In the culture of the West, the prominence of directive-rules has inspired in political and legal theory a preoccupation with enforcement as the external dimension of support for rules' (Onuf 1989b: 127). In identifying his three rule categories Onuf could have taken a Foucaldian track, but he is, it seems, much less interested in institutional power and knowledge as power than Foucault. Instead, Onuf follows Searle, though rather eclectically, in the latter's differentiation of rules as applied to speech acts.

In his theory, Searle (inspired by John L. Austin and Wittgenstein) demonstrates how we, when we speak, apply distinct speech acts based on very specific rules (Searle 1969). Altogether Searle identifies five types of speech acts pertaining to different social situations. The first is that of 'assertives', which are claims about a certain state of affairs – for instance, 'X counts as Y' – and which thereby perform a constitutive function. Assertives are thus often never questioned by the actors employing them but will be important for any socializing process. One can also say that any body of assertive statements represents 'a form of life'. The second speech act, that of 'directives', is close to what we earlier referred to as regulative rules, or to what H. L. A. Hart has called 'standing orders' (Hart 1961: 73): 'Do this or that'. The third speech act is 'commissives' through which we bind ourselves to performing actions by creating obligations: 'I promise to do this or that'. The fourth speech act that Searle mentions, the expressive; has the explicit purpose of convincing a counterpart of something. Finally, we have 'declaratives', which quite clearly perform a declarative action through stating something: 'The meeting is opened' or, in a wedding ceremony, 'I hereby declare you a married couple'.

Now, what Onuf does is to deduce the rules of social life directly from Searle's speech act categories. However, for some reason which seems unspecified, he selects only the first three speech act rules, which he argues can subsume the last two (declarative and expressive).[24] This means that Onuf, as indicated above, ends up with three – instruction-rules, directives and commitment-rules – which, as he sees it, pertain to all human actions, independently of history and culture. But where does all this take us? One could indeed have expected that Onuf's overall purpose for moving to speech acts, while at the same time stressing the prominence of 'deeds' in his constructivist theory, was to develop a tool for analysing practice-based discourse in international life. Considering the behavioural action analysis that we still find in 90 per cent of all IR studies, such a project would have been welcomed. However, this is not at all the case. Onuf is in fact not interested in speech acts as such. What he *is* interested in, at least in WOOM, and what he uses the distinction between instruction-rules, directives and commitment-rules for, is to build Grand Theory (Onuf's own choice of words). He puts it in this way: ' . . . humanity has devised *only three* durable solutions to the problem of using rule to advantage. I also claim that there are only three durable solutions to the problem of rule [in world politics: M. W.]' (Onuf 1989b: 23). Accordingly, only these three types 'bear', as he argues, 'on the full range of human practices' (ibid.):

> 'great theories' of the Western political tradition are responses to the operative reality of political society. Yet none of them suffice as a

paradigm theory.... Although it is immodest to say, I see my work here as a tentative first step toward that paradigm.

(Onuf 1989b: 22)

A little later he develops this point:

> I believe I have identified three categories of rules.... These categories derive from a consideration of language as enabling people to perform social acts and achieve ends by making statements of assertion, direction, and commitment. Once aware of these categories, I encountered various formulations of them in many texts, classic and contemporary, to engage my attention. They are discernible in great theories from which International Relations scholars have adduced the centrality of anarchy for international relations.... Because these categories apply equally to rules and rule, I see them significantly supporting the rules–rule coupling as decisive for political society. Because they bear on the full range of human practices for which political society is the operative term, they are indispensable for sorting out the materials that close reading provides for the disciplinary construction project.

(Onuf 1989b: 23)

With the instruction, directive and commitment-rules in mind, Onuf then goes through different texts (historical, theoretical, philosophical, political) where he argues that the three rule categories can be found. One example of this is the cognitive universal of man where he finds 'abductive, deductive, inductive' types of reasoning. The human character is constituted by 'shame, dread and guilt' and by three senses, 'touching, seeing, hearing'. The same trilogy can be found in world politics, where Onuf detects exactly three different types of regimes relating to instruction, directive and commitment-rules in 'monitory, executive and administrative' regimes. And three types of rule: 'hegemony, hierarchy and heteromony'; and so on. Such a division of everything into three appears rather arbitrary, however, and it never becomes quite clear what the overall purpose of this manoeuvre is. Is Onuf like the liberalists searching for an Archimedean point on which to base his theory? If yes, could he not have gained more directly from the insights of that whole body of micro-sociological theory that has specialized in rebutting rational choice theory and thereby the liberalist paradigm? (See, for instance, Helle and Eisenstadt 1985.) I will get back to this last point briefly in the conclusion below. Furthermore, considering the anarchy/order discussion that was the focus of attention in the preceding sections, there is nothing really new or controversial in Onuf's demonstration of different rule-relations in world politics. Nor in his points that these result in inequalities in the state system. I am quite convinced that neither mainstream hegemony theorists nor specialists in dependency studies would have any argument with this. They would simply see – for instance – 'hegemony as rule' as an expression of power which would not collide with their overall view of world politics as substantially anarchical. To put it differently, mainstream IR theorists have never disputed that states have unequal status in terms of power and that this results in an uneven distribution in the international system; quite the contrary. Clearly, new insight into these issues is not what Onuf seeks to come up with. Rather, as the quote above shows and as I have just indicated, what he *is* trying to do is to create transcendental rules–rule categories that reflect, as it were, a 'truer' reality and that transcend time and space. I must admit that I, personally, find it very difficult to reconcile such a position with constructivism, which, as also Onuf himself suggests, has strong nominalist aspects. It is equally symptomatic that neither this metaphysical quest nor the rules–rule dichotomy and the division of everything into three is touched upon in Onuf's following constructivist writings in the 1990s.

An immediately important implication of Onuf's constructivism for the study of world politics is nevertheless a fundamental scepticism towards the idea that International Relations constitutes a ruleless anarchy in the Hobbesian sense.[25] Constructivism can, in other words, best – or at least at this stage – be seen as a meta-theoretical critique of the classical opposition between anarchy and order found in – and, indeed, demarcating – the entire IR field. It questions the lifeline of IR realism as *the* core theory of world politics. It also enables us, I will argue, to see constructivism as a possible and indeed highly called-for theoretical development and revival of the (otherwise dying?)[26] British international society tradition.

WOOM and most of Onuf's later writings are first and foremost engaged in ontological claims about how agents and structures are constituted in the world. However, it is, I would hold, just as important to stress the epistemological implications of a constructivist point of departure when studying world politics. The problem with the dominance of liberalism as an operative paradigm is not only its hard core: the fundamental voluntaristic/ atomistic ontology that already at the outset makes it impossible to conceive of the influence of rules and normative constraints in world politics. But also that it will be unable to conceive of, for instance, changes in power *as legitimacy* between different actors in the system. As indicated above, IR theories adopting a neo-realist or a rational choice point of departure will necessarily be static and unable to perceive anything new happening 'out there' (Onuf 1991; Strange 1994; Ruggie 1989 and 1993). In their eagerness to build general theory going across time and space, rationalists simply have to stick to the assumption that states as territorially demarcated and power-maximizing actors have always existed – even before the 'invention' of the European states system (see Waltz 1979; Gilpin 1981). To put it differently, the claim that it has been and always will be possible to locate power and authority in a territorial state is a 'necessary' starting-point for the IR rationalists of today. How would one be able to model the world, to predict the outcome of strategic interaction through advanced game theory, if one could demonstrate that legitimacy – and thereby power – had shifted or was in the process of shifting towards other social actors in the system? What about the European Community in these years? It does indeed become increasingly difficult for many mainstream IR scholars to continue to support the idea that the integration process can be reduced to a bargain between autonomous power-maximizing states. However, the static vision is still promoted and, I would argue, is even the most dominant in contemporary European Community studies (see Moravscik 1991 and 1993; Garrett 1992; Grieco 1992; Taylor 1991; for a critique see Wind 1994 and 1996b).

The points just made, in other words, explicate the intimate link between a theory's ontological claims and its epistemology. Only if the international system is perceived as *substantially* anarchic (and if it makes any sense to conceive of states as unitary rational actors) will it be meaningful to make theories of social choice the basis for studying European and world politics.

As Onuf argues following Giddens, social theorists should avoid making either actors or structures primitive: 'neither individuals nor society can have come first, for neither can be said to exist without the other' (Onuf 1994c: 4; see also Alexander 1982: 67; Alexander 1987). This is of course easier said than done. Several critiques have argued that no matter how sensible and logical this sounds – especially for our day-to-day experience – it none the less conflates agents and structures and makes empirical research along constructivist lines extremely difficult (Held and Thompson 1988; M. Taylor 1989; Archer 1985; Carlsnaes 1992). Whether Onuf succeeds in his endeavour to synthesize an agential and a structural perspective in a way that enhances our understanding of social and interstate relations will be touched upon in the following concluding section.

CONCLUSION: FROM STATIC TO DYNAMIC CONSTRUCTIVISM?

> Among peoples, political theorists favour the alternative premise that anarchy, not order, reigns. By not existing, international order needs no explaining. Evidence to the contrary can be explained away as anomalous or ephemeral, and therefore not of theoretical interest. From this follows the dominance of concern for conflict and disorder and the paucity of theory in the study of international politics.
>
> (Onuf 1979: 244)

A 'reconstruction' of the IR field along constructivist lines involves, first of all, an emphasis on the importance of rules and norms in all social relations. This is what makes constructivism cross-disciplinary. The stress on rules is, furthermore, what connects micro- and macro-levels of analysis to each other and, thereby, as Onuf points out with reference to Wittgenstein, a position that directs our attention from epistemology to ontology.

In this concluding section I will focus on three (though not Onuf's 'magic three') central points of criticism and suggestions for future constructivist investigations. The first is concerned on the one hand with Onuf's quest for an all-embracing and cross-disciplinary approach to world politics and social analysis and on the other with his curious neglect of an entire bulk of writings in recent post-positivist social theory that explicitly attempts to integrate actor and structure perspectives. What the theorists that I am thinking of here build on is neo-Parsonian systems theory, ethnomethodology and symbolic interactionism – in themselves complete and consistent theoretical frameworks that, quite clearly, could have supported any constructivist argument (for an overview see Alexander, Giesen, Munch and Smelser 1987; Knorr-Cetina and Cicourel 1981; see also Powell and Di-Maggio 1991; March and Olsen 1989). Like Giddens, these theoretical perspectives reject both methodological individualism and collectivism in favour of what Knorr-Cetina calls 'methodological situationalism' (Knorr-Cetina and Cicourel 1981: 2). This implies among other things an acknowledgement of the knowledgeability of social actors parallel to a stress on the influence of macro-structures when the depth of societal transitions is to be assessed. Thus, even though the sociologists for long have emphasized the need to move from a 'normative' to a more 'cognitive' conception of rules in social theory, Onuf does not in any systematic way draw on this body of work in launching his version of constructivism.[27]

A second point of criticism that could be raised against Onuf's constructivist alternative has already been touched upon above and has to do with the statism of his theory. This might indeed be due to the abstract character of Onuf's constructivist alternative – especially as launched in WOOM – and thereby the absence of any concrete specification. However, as Buzan, Little and Jones, among many others, have emphasized, there are important lessons to be drawn – also for substantive theorizing about world politics – from a constructivist perspective (Buzan, Little and Jones 1993: 102 ff.). One of the most crucial of these is exactly the question of how to study international transformation. Because recent IR theory and of course neo-realism in particular 'was *designed* to explain why the anarchical structure of the international system has persisted throughout world history', the question of how to conceive of changes in the international structure has become one of the most crucial inroads into critical IR theory in recent years (Buzan, Little and Jones 1993: 102; my emphasis; see also Ruggie 1993 and Wæver's Chapter 7 on Ruggie in this volume).

This once again takes us back to Giddens. Even though Giddens, as noted in passing in section 3 above, has been heavily criticized for conflating agents and structures in his attempt to explain the reproduction of social systems, the missing dynamic in Onuf's constructivism could have gained, I would argue, from Giddens's thesis of how 'unintended consequences of micro-level practices' create macro-level structures (Giddens 1984: 17). The idea is also emphasized by many of the social theorists referred to above and implies that the macro-level 'results' of practice-based rules employed by knowledgeable agents over time come to represent the conditions on which new actions are taken and so on. The thesis is, in fact, quite simple and equates the reproduction of language, which can be seen as an unintended result of reasoning actors (most often unaware), and the application of grammatical rules in meaningful communication. But what would be the implications of this for world politics and for the study of international transformation?

The need for a theory of international transformation that takes into account both agential and structural properties has, as I mentioned briefly above, been well made by John Ruggie, initially in his critique of the statism of neo-realism from 1983, though without endorsing a constructivist perspective. Later, Ruggie explicitly invoked constructivism, arguing that any theory of international politics 'worth its salt' should at least attempt to trace changes in power and legitimacy over time (Ruggie 1989 and 1993). World politics is not an ahistorical realm governed by predictable laws – as Waltz and Gilpin have argued – but a product of social practice. As Ruggie has noted, the changes in property rights (the constitutive rules of the international system) from the medieval order to the modern state system, can be seen as a result of the employment of new rules, but also as a shift in power and legitimacy: 'Once a property right is socially recognized... the institutional context of the exercise of power is transformed' (Ruggie 1989: 24). It does indeed seem absurd that power analysis in IR has been so focused on military capacity and that scholars have spent so little time (if any) on the link between the reproduction of international rules of the game and power as legitimacy.

Onuf has also, in some of his more recent writings, opened up towards a more dynamic constructivist approach, both in his article on 'Sovereignty: An Outline of Conceptual History' from 1991 and in his 'Intervention for a Common Good' from 1994. Both articles implicitly and explicitly criticize the lack of historical and conceptual sensitivity in rationalist theories of world politics. The article on sovereignty digs into the historical archives in order to show how the concept originated and how it may now be changing – after two hundred years of stasis. Such investigations into the link between ideas and the world we inhabit are no doubt highly called for. The same can be said of Onuf's article on our changed perceptions of humanitarian intervention (Onuf 1994b). Here Onuf convincingly demonstrates how the changed ideas of human rights in the international community in recent years have increased the legitimacy of intervention into the internal affairs of other states. Not only is sovereign statehood itself undergoing rapid transformation as a consequence of this development, but it is no longer only states that interfere with other states' internal affairs, but more often non-state actors, i.e. NGOs. There might not be much new in this increased reference to 'the common good' when intervention is on the international agenda, but as Onuf argues, 'What is new is this: governments once were solely responsible for the common good; now they share this responsibility, and all sorts and degrees of affiliation, with other institutions operating within and across state frontiers' (Onuf 1994c: 3). This shift makes a clear difference because it indicates a change in legitimacy which might have severe consequences for the practice of sovereignty in the post-Cold War world.

Because concepts, sentences, utterances (deeds done, acts taken, words spoken, as Onuf puts it) invoked by human agents/state officials at a given point in time depend upon the context in which they are employed, conceptual analysis can contribute to a better understanding of how and why certain legitimate orders are reproduced while others are not. As Onuf puts it: 'concepts ought not be detached from the political discourse with which they are embedded...concepts *constitute*...discourse. They do so through the conduct of arguments, which, although responsive to events, we can see as having been *about* concepts' (Onuf 1991: 427; original emphasis).

Here Onuf's classification of rules into instruction, directive and commitment categories could be of some help. It could tell us something about what to look for when analysing transformations of the international rules of the game. Changes in rules and the innovation of new concepts can thus be seen as an often unintended result of reasoning actors' fights over – and public disagreements about – the 'correct' interpretation of, especially, instruction and commitment rules.

Constructivism does, it seems, launch a different but just as forceful a micro-foundation for the social sciences as rational choice theory. However, although Onuf several times underlines his late-modern rather than postmodern allegiances, it is hard to see why he needs abstract universal rule-categories to make such an argument convincing (see Onuf 1994b: 11–12).

The third and final point of criticism against Onuf's constructivism that I have chosen to emphasize here is his neglect of the so-called 'English School' in IR. As Nick Rengger among others has noted, there is a rather obvious link between constructivism and the concerns of the English IR tradition (Rengger 1992: 354).[28] The classical international society tradition in IR – as it is also often called – is represented by scholars like Hedley Bull, Martin Wight, Adam Watson, James Mayall and Alan James. Unfortunately, but like many American IR theorists, Onuf completely neglects this body of work.[29] The fact that Onuf omits the English School might indeed be due to the fact that the classical international society tradition has been unable to fulfil our theoretical expectations, as Ole Wæver has recently argued (Wæver 1992). Although I agree with Wæver that a strong theoretical core, or, as I would prefer to call it, a micro-foundation, is lacking and needs to be developed if the School is to have any chance of revival, this hardly legitimates Onuf's neglect. Nor do I agree with Wæver in his attempt to 'save' the School by linking it up with American regime theory, as it was launched in the 1980s.[30] Rationalist regime theory is and remains – as Onuf and many other reflectivists have shown – a dead-end with severe and up until now unresolved ontological and epistemological inconsistencies (cf. Kratochwil & Ruggie 1986; Kratochwil 1993; Behnke 1995). In fact, Wæver is well aware of this.[31] Another route to take is the one tentatively suggested by Rengger, which establishes a connection between the society tradition and constructivism.

The problem with the English School in this respect has been that in defining themselves against the American quantitative mainstream in the 1960s, they (and of course especially Hedley Bull) relied on a purely epistemological and methodological critique (see Bull 1969). In other words, Bull never really engaged in any through *ontological* discussion of how and whether to conceive of international politics as a society or a system. Or, to sum it up briefly: the English School never developed or invoked a micro-theory of the relationship between rules and human (state) action. In reading and rereading Bull and not least the sources for his work, I believe it can be shown that his leaving out any such discussion is due to the fact that he was heavily inspired by the positivist legal theorist H. L. A. Hart (Hart 1961).[32] It seems in other words as if, once again, we will have to turn to law and legal theory in order to grasp the essence of central theoretical issues concerning rules, order and change in social life. Thus, Hart (and to a certain extent also Bull) has claimed that the existence of rules and norms in decentralized legal orders such as international relations, is an empirical question, about which, because of the absence of hierarchical authority, one cannot theorize explicitly (see Hart 1961: 89–95, 100–2, 106–7). In other words, in an attempt to moderate positivist legal theory, Hart argued that imperative (or what he called primary) rules might and often do exist in non-hierarchical legal orders, but that there will be no constitutive (secondary) rules in this sphere; that is, rules empowering and defining the validity of primary rules. In Onuf's language, there would be no instruction and commitment rules (Onuf 1994b: 13–15). One important consequence of such a stance is that one will not be able to *theorize* about the institutionalization of the international system with some rules and norms being more fundamental than others. Bull *et al.* would, as we know, never agree to such a claim, bearing in mind their consistent emphasis on the constitutive structures in international society such as diplomacy, sovereignty, the balance of power and international law. However, the international society theorists have never engaged in a discussion of these issues and here IR constructivists like Onuf with a strong micro-theory of social action might be of assistance:

> A[n] ... option [in developing the 'International' society tradition: M. W.] is to continue and deepen the investigation of the nature of the rules and norms that govern world politics and, as a result, reformulate the understanding of international society and what helps to constitute it. Such an option would very often incorporate much of the traditional view of international society, but its diagnosis would be different. ... Normative projects of this kind are visible in the writings of, among others, Terry Nardin, Friedrich Kratochwil [and] Nicholas Onuf.
>
> (Rengger 1992: 367)

Is Onuf then a Master in the Making? It is difficult to judge because up until now only very few scholars have embraced constructivism as an approach to the study of world politics; and even fewer Onuf's version of it. The fact that almost no one has been tempted by constructivism *à la* Onuf, however, has more to do with the unnecessary obscurity of his argument (especially as launched in WOOM) than with the overall soundness of constructivism as an approach to the study of social transformation. In several other parts of the social sciences – especially comparative politics, public administration, law and sociology – constructivism (or some version of it) has already for decades proved extremely fruitful. The mere idea that students of social phenomena should strive to incorporate both agential and structural properties into their analysis and consequently that actors are both enabled and constrained by historical paths and institutions is an almost trivial point invoked by sociologists more than a hundred years ago. In spite of its triviality, however, it seems that IR scholars in particular have paid very little attention to this insight. For this reason alone constructivism in its different versions deserves a place – not just a small corner – in the study of world politics.

NOTES

For helpful comments and criticisms to this chapter I am especially indebted to the editors of this volume. I would also like to thank Bernhard Giesen and Nicholas Onuf for constructive suggestions.

1 The dissertation was never published but sections of it came out subsequently in Falk, Kratochwil and Mendlovitz 1985.
2 The labels 'reflectivism' versus 'rationalism' are adopted from Robert Keohane 1988. Whereas reflectivism covers all types of critical IR theorists, from Gramscians to poststructuralists, rationalism refers to the mainstream of today's IR. In my (and I think also Keohane's) reading, this means mainly regime theory and neo-realism. For a more indepth elaboration see Ole Wæver's introduction in this volume.
3 In a recent joint project between Robert Keohane and Elinor Ostrom, this development is celebrated (R. Keohane and E. Ostrom (1994) 'Introduction' to a special issue of *Journal of Theoretical Politics* 6(4): 403–29). The authors argue that the insights from organizational economics (transaction cost-analysis and principal agent theory) represent a theoretical inroad into issues pertaining to most parts of the social sciences. The authors furthermore see these microeconomic-based theories of collective action as the most promising way of accumulating knowledge about human behaviour within all social science disciplines (p. 404). Representatives of this strand of theory would include D. North; G. Hardin; K. Shepsle; O. Williamson; and others.
4 One can argue that this neglects earlier, less successful attempts; for instance, the English School of International Relations. It also leaves out important writings of a more Marxist flavour. However, I do not consider that IR idealism represents a theoretical critique of Realism. Both realists and idealists employ the domestic analogy. Furthermore, idealists seek to transcend the state system and to create a world community of some sort, while constructivists do not. As will become clearer later in this chapter, constructivists are not propagating grand plans for a new world order.
5 This term has of course been stolen from Hayward Alker's impressive tour de force from 1986. The manuscript remains unpublished. See also Chapter 8 in this volume.
6 For a comprehensive discussion of the question of social order among sociological and political theory classics see Alexander 1982.
7 In his *The Domestic Analogy and World Order Proposals* from 1989, Hidemi Suganami outlines the debate between, on the one hand, those who believe that the transfer of the domestic legal order to the international scene is the only solution to the problem of international order; and, on the other, those who argue that the international system should not at all be compared to the domestic order. The latter hold that the international system, in spite of the fact that it is composed of sovereign states, should not be regarded as an atomistic state of nature. Rather it should be analysed as a society with its own informal institutions and rules of the game. Where Onuf is concerned, he supports the latter, rather than the former. For an elaboration on another critical theorist's very different experiences with the WOMP see Lene Hansen's Chapter 12 in this volume.
8 Onuf never used this phrase himself. It is of course adopted from Hedley Bull.

9 Onuf characterized idealistic world order studies as produced by 'vanguard intellectuals', or more generally: 'recent rhetoric about the global village, spaceship earth, and global interdependence is at best evidence of communitarian sentiments among vanguard intellectuals' (Onuf 1979: 248). For another extremely critical analysis of the projection of a government-like rule of law on to the international system, see Martti Koskenniemi 1990. As he put it: 'The fight for an international Rule of Law is a fight against politics' (op. cit., p. 5).

10 Compare Ole Wæver's discussion of the positioning of realism and liberalism in IR theory in the introduction to this volume. See also Wæver 1994a.

11 The close connection between liberalist political thinking in the nineteenth century and neo-realism has also been emphasized by Keith L. Shimko. In pointing this out Shimko holds that it is possible to draw a sharp distinction between classical Realism and neo-realism. Shimko argues that only neo-realism is influenced by utilitarianism and thereby liberal philosophy. This is entirely false. Classical theorists like Carr and Morgenthau were both influenced by utilitarianism especially as it was presented among nineteenth century international legal-theorists such as John Austin. See Shimko 1992; Morgenthau 1946: Ch. 19.

12 A parallel argument can be found in Ashley 1988: 230.

13 'When long use obtain the authority of Law, it is not the Length of Time that maketh the Authority, but the will of the Sovereign' (Hobbes 1988: 313).

14 Emphasis in the original.

15 For an indepth problematization of this entire body of thinking in international law, see Frank 1988: 755–9. See also Nardin 1983: 171 ff. and d'Amato's 'What counts as law' in Onuf 1982b.

16 In a recent publication on the status of regime theory in international relations, Oye's book is still hailed as one of the most significant. See Rittenberger and Mayer 1993; for a critical review of the position taken there, see Behnke 1995; see also Kratochwil 1993.

17 As Onuf puts it: 'I hold that rules do not "govern" all that is social. People always have a choice, which is to follow rules or not. Instead rules govern the construction of the situation within which choices are made intelligible' (Onuf 1989b: 261).

18 As noted by D. Dessler: 'some rules underpin not only action but also other rules or rule-structures. For example, when two nations sign an arms control treaty, they not only adopt a set of operative arms control regulations, but they also reproduce the rules associated with the underlying practice of sovereignty (rules that give the nations the very identity required to make treaties possible)' (Dessler 1989: 469).

19 As noted in section 1, Onuf does originally work with a third paradigm, Marxism, but this is not taken at all seriously as an independent position in his book. To be fair to Marx it has in fact been argued that he was the first 'true' constructivist. As Onuf notes, it was Marx who stated that 'Men make their own history, but they do not make it just as they please; they do not make it under circumstances directly encountered, given and transmitted from the past' (quoted in Onuf 1994b: 5).

20 It is important to stress that those who go under the label new or neo-institutionalists in IR differ radically from those scholars within political science who identify themselves as 'New Institutionalists'. It certainly seems confusing but the labels are turned upside-down. Those political scientists marketing themselves as 'New Institutionalists' (for instance, March and Olsen 1989; Powell and DiMaggio 1991; and others), could be almost 100 per cent identified with reflectivist/constructivist scholars in IR. At the same time, the new or neo-instutionalists we meet in IR are all committed to a rational-choice point of departure (see Wendt and Duvall 1989).

21 A good example is Mancur Olson's theory of explaining collective action from the aggregation of individual interests and preferences (Olson 1968).

22 For a more philosophical discussion of constructivism see Erik Ringmar's Chapter 10 in this volume.

23 Onuf himself never refers to symbolic-interactionism in his work. Nor does he in any serious way draw on the ethnomethodological tradition of Harold Garfinkel. However, I, for one, find several affiliations with these bodies of thought – also with Goffman's frame-analysis – in Onuf's description of the linkage between social situations and the function of rules. For instance, Jef Verhoeven notes: 'individuals construct reality in a process of symbolic interaction and...individuals form interpretations and acts in relation to others....There are social roles, positions, rank order, bureaucratic organizations, social codes, norms, etc. Their function is to help the interpretation and definition of the situations that are at the base of social "joint actions". If people do not take into account these structures, then the ongoing activity has no meaning at all. But even these social structures have no life apart from the definition given by the individuals, even in joint actions' (Verhoeven 1985: 84).

24 Several things are curious in Onuf's selection. Not only is there his neglect of declarations and expressives in social communication and therefore also inter-state affairs, but also his reliance on Searle and thereby speech as the *only* way of expressing rule-following behaviour. What about those signals that are not expressed through speech but through symbolic behaviour and rituals? As David Dessler has convincingly argued, many of the following expressions are stated in purely gesticulative terms: 'signals of support, opposition, hostility, friendship, condemnation, indifference, commitment, resignation' (Dessler 1989; see also Bull 1977: 316). The same point emerges in Raymond Cohen's almost ethno-methodological description of the diplomatic discourse: 'Conscious of the very close attention paid by diplomatic observers to actions and articulations of all kinds and of the paramount importance of being able to say no more and no less than is intended, the diplomatic profession has evolved, over many years, a very subtle and variegated stock of words, phrases, euphemisms, gestures and man-oeuvres, each item having its own wit and shade of meaning' (Cohen 1981: 31). Put differently, where would such a body of practices fit into Onuf's model?

25 Onuf puts it in the following manner: 'In constructivist terms, the international system must be a society insofar as it is constituted by the deeds of many individuals, themselves constituted as agents. This process of constitution depends on rules, without which deeds have no social meaning' (Onuf 1994b: 8). Onuf is pigeon-holing many postmodernists – or at least what I have referred to as poststructural IR theorists – when he argues that they see 'Stories about international legal theory, like most legal and political talk in the modern world, [relating] to a single, controlling argument' (ibid.: 6). It would indeed be interesting to learn whom Onuf has in mind here.

26 I am thinking of Wæver's discussion of the (not too bright) future of the 'International Society tradition' in Britain – or 'The English School' as it is also called. See Wæver 1992; see also note 31 p. 261.

27 In sociological theory one talks about the move from 'hot' to 'cool' theories of rules and norms in social integration. This represents first and foremost a rejection of functionalist system theory where what one was interested in was consensus (normative integration) rather than conflict. This has been referred to as 'hot' theories of norms whereas the so-called 'cognitive turn' in sociology in the 1960s implied a move to microsociological perspectives that were much more open towards conflict – for instance, through studies of 'negotiated' orders (ethnomethodology). This move from a 'hot' to a 'cool' conception of norms and rules resembles, I would argue, Onuf's critique of the WOMP's and idealist IR positions.

28 Agreeing with Onuf in his critique of liberalism Rengger notes that they are 'insensitive to' and 'more seriously, hugely' underrate 'the importance of our membership in a community and a culture for social theory...the liberals

exaggerate our capacity for, and the value of, individual choice, and even if liberals have the right account of individuals' capacity for choice, they ignore the fact that this capacity can only be developed and exercised in a certain kind of social and cultural context...these assumptions give rise to the view that, in important senses, community creates no values' and that values 'exist independently of communal identification' (Rengger 1992: 354).

29 For a more profound discussion of the main tenets of the English School, see I. B. Neumann's Chapter 2 in this volume.

30 Similar and, in my view, just as unconvincing 'synthesis-proposals' have been promoted by Barry Buzan (1993) and Tony Evans and Peter Wilson (1992). The authors here referred to seem to be especially unaware of the ontological inconsistencies in mainstream regime theory and the way these problems have been stressed in recent years by reflectivist IR scholars.

31 O. Wæver actually shows three possible ways of relaunching the 'international society tradition'; one is, as noted above, the regime approach. Another is towards historically focused studies in classical political theory and international law. A final approach is that of semiotic analysis; this comes closest to the one I have put forward here. See Wæver 1992: 157 ff.

32 Interestingly enough, Hart's legal theory (as it pervades domestic society) was in fact inspired by prominent contemporary figures such as Wittgenstein and Winch. Hedley Bull's own influence on these theorists, however, was only indirect – through Hart. See the discussion in MacCormick 1981: 10–19.

REFERENCES

Works by Nicholas G. Onuf

Onuf, N. G. (1969) 'Do Books of Readings Contribute to Scholarship?', *International Organization* 23(1): 98–118.

—— (1970a) 'Professor Falk and the Quasi-Legislative Competence of the General Assembly', *American Journal of International Law* 64(2): 149–355.

—— (1970b) 'International Law-in-Action and the Numbers Game', *International Studies Quarterly* 14(3): 325–33.

—— (1971a) 'The Principle of Non-intervention, the United Nations and the International System', *International Organization* 25(2): 209–27.

—— (1971b) 'Further Thoughts on a New Source of International Law: Professor d'Amato's "Manifest Intent"', *American Journal of International Law* 65(5): 784–91.

—— (1974) *Reprisals: Rituals, Rules, Rationales*, Research Monograph no. 42, Princeton, NJ: Centre of International Studies, Princeton University.

—— (1975a) 'Peace Research Parochialism', *Journal of Peace Research* 12(1): 71–8.

—— (1975b) 'Law and Lawyers in International Crises', *International Organization* 29(4): 1035–54.

—— (1979) 'International Legal Order as an Idea', *American Journal of International Law* 73(2): 246–66.

—— (1982a) 'Comparative International Politics', *Yearbook of World Affairs*, 36: 197–212.

—— (1982b) (ed.) *Law-Making in the Global Community*, Durham, NC: Carolina Academic Press for the Centre of International Studies, Princeton University.

—— (1982c) 'Global Law-Making and Legal Thought', introduction to his (ed.) *Law-making in the Global Community*, Durham, NC: Carolina Academic Press and Princeton University.

—— (1983) Reports to the Club of Rome, *World Politics* 36(1): 121–46.

—— (1984) 'Prometheus Prostrate', *Futures* 16(1): 47–59.

Onuf, N. G. (1985a) 'Do Rules Say What They Do? From Ordinary Language to International Law', *Harvard International Law Journal* 26(2): 385–410.

—— (1985b) 'International Codification: Interpreting the last Half-Century', in Richard Falk, Friedrick Kratochwil and Saul Mendlovitz (eds) *International Law: a Contemporary Perspective*, Vol. 2, *Studies on a Just World Order*, Boulder, CO: Westview Press.

—— (1987a) 'The Paradox of Nonalignment', in William C. Olson (ed.) *The Theory and Practice of International Relations*, 7th edn, New York: Prentice-Hall.

—— (1987b) 'Rules in Moral Development', *Human Development* 30(5): 257–67.

—— (1989a) (in Arabic) 'After International Relations: The Constitution of Disciplines and Their Worlds', *Arab Journal of International Studies* 2(1): 4–24.

—— (1989b) *World of Our Making: Rules and Rule in Social Theory and International Relations*, Columbia, SC: University of South Carolina Press.

—— (1991) 'Sovereignty: an Outline of Conceptual History', *Alternatives* 16(4): 425–46.

—— (1992) (in Japanese) 'Sovereignty and Modernity', in Hiroharu Seki, Louis Goodman, Shiro Okubo and Masaru Tamamoto (eds) *U.S.–Japanese Relations in the Age of Globalization*, Tokyo: Nihon Hyoronsha.

—— (1994a) 'Civitas Maxima: Wolff, Vattel and the Fate of Republicanism', *American Journal of International Law* 88(2): 280–303.

—— (1994b) 'The Constitution of International Society', *European Journal of International Law* 5(1): 1–19.

—— (1994c) 'Intervention for a Common Good', in Michael Mastanduno and Gene Lyons (eds) *Beyond Westphalia? National Sovereignty and International Intervention*, Baltimore, MD: Johns Hopkins University Press.

—— (1994d) 'Imagined Republics', *Alternatives* 19(3): 315–37.

—— (1995) 'Levels', *European Journal of International Relations* 1(1): 35–58.

—— and Birney, Richard K. (1974) 'Peremptory Norms of International Law: Their Source, Function and Future', *Denver Journal of International Law and Policy* 4(2): 187–98.

—— and Johnson, Thomas J. (1994) 'Peace in a Liberal World: Does Democracy Matter?', in Charles W. Kegley, Jr (ed.) *Controversies in International Relations Theory: Realism and the Neo-liberal Challenge*, New York: St Martin's Press.

—— and Klink, Frank (1989) 'Anarchy, Authority, Rules', *International Studies Quarterly* 33(2): 149–73.

—— and Olson, William (1985) 'The Growth of a Discipline: Review', in Steve Smith (ed.) *International Relations: British and American Perspectives*, Oxford: Blackwell.

—— and Onuf, Peter (1990) 'American Constitutionalism and the Emergence of a Liberal World Order', in George Athan Billias (ed.) *American Constitutionalism Abroad: Selected Essays in Comparative Constitutional History*, Westport, CT: Greenwood Press.

—— (1993) *Federal Union, Modern World: The Law of Nations in an Age of Revolutions*, Westport, CT: Greenwood.

—— and Peterson, Spike (1984) 'Human Rights from an International Regimes Perspective', *Journal of International Affairs* 37(2): 329–92.

—— and Seabold Walter G. (1981) 'Late Capitalism, Uneven Development and Foreign Policy Postures', in Charles W. Kegley, Jr and Pat McGowan (eds) 'The Political Economy of Foreign Policy', in *International Yearbook of Foreign Policy Studies*, Vol. 6, n.p.: Sage, pp. 23–37.

Works by other authors

Alexander, J. C. (1982) *Theoretical Logic in Sociology*, Vol. 1, *Positivism, Prepositions, and Current Controversies*, Berkeley, CA: University of California Press.

——, Giesen, B., Munch, R. and Smelser, N. J. (eds) (1987) *The Micro-Macro Link*, Berkeley, CA: University of California Press.

Archer, M. (1985) 'Structuration versus Morphogenesis', in H. J. Helle and S. N. Eisenstadt (eds) *Macro-Sociological Theory: Perspectives on Social Theory*, Vol. 1, Beverley Hills, CA: Sage.

Aron, R. (1966) *Peace and War. A Theory of World Politics*, New York: Anchor Press.

Ashley, A. (1988) 'Untying the Sovereign State: a Double Reading of the Anarchy Problematique', *Millennium: Journal of International Studies* 17(2): 227–62.

Ashley, R. (1986 [1984]) 'The Poverty of Neo-realism', in R. Keohane (ed.) *Neo-realism and Its Critics*, New York: Columbia University Press.

Austin, J. (1954 [1832]) *The Province of Jurisprudence Determined*, London: Weidenfeld & Nicolson.

Axelrod, R. (1984) *The Evolution of Co-operation*, New York: Basic Books.

Barkun, M. (1967) *Law Without Sanction*, New Haven, CT: Yale University Press.

Behnke, A. (1995) 'Ten Years after – the State of the Art of Regime Theory: A Review of Rittenberger & Mayer (eds) 1993', *Co-operation and Conflict* 30(2): 179–97.

Bernstein, R. J. (1983) *Beyond Objectivism and Relativism: Science, Hermeneutics, and Practice*, Philadelphia, PA: University of Pennsylvania Press.

Bull, H. (1969) 'International Theory. The Case for a Classical Approach', in K. Knorr and J. Rosenau (eds) *Contending Approaches to International Politics*, Princeton, NJ: Princeton University Press.

—— (1977) *The Anarchical Society. A Study of Order in World Politics*, London: Macmillan.

Buzan, B. (1993) 'From International System to International Society: Structural Realism and Regime Theory meet the English School', *International Organization* 14(3): 327–52.

—— Little, R. and Jones, C. (1993) *The Logic of Anarchy: Neo-realism to Structural Realism*, New York: Columbia University Press.

Carlsnaes, W. (1992) 'The Agency–Structure Problem in Foreign Policy Analysis', *International Studies Quarterly* 36(3): 245–70.

Carr, E. H. (1981 [1939]) *The Twenty Years' Crisis 1919–1939*, London: Macmillan.

Cohen, R. (1981) *International Politics. The Rules of the Game*, London: Longman.

Cox, R. W. (1986[1981]) 'Social Forces, States and World Orders: beyond International Relations Theory', in R. Keohane (ed.) *Neo-realism and Its Critics*, New York: Columbia University Press.

Dessler, D. (1989) 'What's at Stake in the Agent–Structure Debate?', *International Organization* 43: 441–73.

Evans, T. and Wilson, P. (1992) 'Regime Theory and the English School of International Relations: A Comparison', *Millennium: Journal of International Studies* 21(3): 329–51.

Falk, R. A. (1975) *A Study of Future Worlds*, New York: Free Press.

—— Kratochwil, F. and Mendlovitz, S. (1985) *International Law: a Contemporary Perspective*, Boulder, CO: Westview Press.

Farr, J., Ball, T. and Hanson, R. L. (eds) (1989) *Political Innovation and Conceptual Change*, Cambridge: Cambridge University Press.

Foucault, M. (1977) *Power/Knowledge. Selected Interviews and Other Writings*, New York: Pantheon Books.

—— (1990 [1976]) *The History of Sexuality, An Introduction*, Vol. 1, New York: Vintage Books.

Frank, T. M. (1988) 'Legitimacy in the International System', *American Journal of International Law* 82: 705–59.

Garfinkel, H. (1967) *Studies in Ethnomethodology*, Englewood Cliffs, NJ: Prentice-Hall.

Garrett, G. (1992) 'International Co-operation and Institutional Choice: the European Community's Internal Market', *International Organization* 42: 533–60.

Giddens, A. (1979) *Central Problems in Social Theory*, London: Macmillan.
—— (1984) *The Constitution of Society*, Cambridge: Polity Press.
Gilpin, R. (1981) *War and Change in World Politics*, Cambridge: Cambridge University Press.
Goodman, N. (1978) *Ways of World-Making*, Indianapolis, IN: Hackett Publishing Co.
Grieco, J. (1992) *The Renaissance of the EC and the Crisis of Realist International Theory*, Working Paper no. 151, Durham, NC: Duke University.
Hart, H. L. A. (1961) *The Concept of Law*, Oxford: Oxford University Press.
Held, D. and Thompson, J. (eds) (1988) *Social Theory of Modern Societies: Anthony Giddens and his Critics*, Cambridge: Cambridge University Press.
Helle, H. J. and Eisenstadt, S. N. (eds) (1985) *Microsociological Theory: Perspectives on Sociological Theory*, Vol. 2, London: Sage.
Hobbes, T. (1988[1651]) *Leviathan*, Harmondsworth: Penguin Books.
Hollis, M. and Smith, S. (1991) *Explaining and Understanding International Relations*, Oxford: Clarendon Press.
Keohane, R. (1984) *After Hegemony: Co-operation and Discord in the World Political Economy*, Princeton, NJ: Princeton University Press.
—— (1988) 'International Institutions: Two Approaches', *International Studies Quarterly* 32: 379–96.
—— and Ostrom, E. (1994) 'Introduction', *Journal of Theoretical Politics* 6(4): 403–29.
Knorr-Cetina, K. and Cicourel, A. (eds) (1981) *Advances in Social Theory and Methodology*, New York: Methuen.
Koskenniemi, M. (1990) 'The Politics of International Law', *European Journal of International Law* 1(4): 4–32.
Kratochwil, F. (1989) *Rules, Norms and Decisions: On the Conditions of Practical and Legal Reasoning in International Relations and Domestic Affairs*, Cambridge: Cambridge University Press.
—— (1993) 'Norms versus Numbers: Multilateralism and the Rationalist and Reflectivist Approaches to Institutions – a Unilateral Plea for Communicative Rationality', in J. G. Ruggie (ed.) *Multilateralism Matters: The Theory and Praxis of an Institutional Form*, New York: Columbia University Press.
—— and Ruggie, J. G. (1986) 'International Organization: a State of the Art on an Art of the State', *International Organization* 40(4): 753–76.
Little, R. (1977) 'Three Approaches to the International System: Some Ontological and Epistemological Considerations', *British Journal of International Studies* 3: 269–85.
MacCormick, N. (1981) *H. L. A. Hart. Jurists: Profiles in Legal Theory*, London: Edward Arnold.
March, J. and Olsen, J. P. (1989) *Rediscovering Institutions: The Organizational Base of Politics*, New York: Free Press.
Milner, H. (1993) 'The Assumption of Anarchy in International Relations Theory: a Critique', in R. Baldwin (ed.) *Neo-realism and Neo-liberalism: The Contemporary Debate*, Columbia, NY: Columbia University Press.
Moravcsik, A. (1991) 'Negotiating the Single European Act: National Interests and Conventional Statecraft in the European Community', *International Organization* 45(1): 19–56.
—— (1993) 'Preferences and Power in the European Community: a Liberal Intergovernmentalist Approach', *Journal of Common Market Studies* 31(4): 473–524.
Morgenthau, H. J. (1985 [1946]) *Politics among Nations: The Struggle for Power and Peace*, 6th edn, New York: Knopf.
Nardin, T. (1983) *Law, Morality and the Relations of State*, Princeton, NJ: Princeton University Press.
Olson, M. (1968) *The Logic of Collective Action*, New York: Schocken.
Oye, K. (1985) 'Explaining Co-operation under Anarchy', *World Politics* 38: 1–25.

Pocock, J. G. A. (1957) *The Ancient Constitution and the Federal Law: A Study of English Historical Thought in the Seventeenth Century*, Cambridge: Cambridge University Press.

Powell, W. and DiMaggio, P. (eds) (1991) *The New Institutionalism in Organizational Analysis*, Chicago and London: University of Chicago Press.

Rawls, J. (1955) 'Two Concepts of Rules', *Philosophical Review*, 64(1).

Rengger, N. (1992) 'A City Which Sustains All Things? Communitarianism and International Society', *Millennium: Journal of International Studies* 21(3): 353–69.

Rittenberger, V. (ed.), with the assistance of Peter Mayer (1993) *Regime Theory and International Relations*, Oxford: Clarendon.

Ruggie, J. G. (1986) 'Continuity and Transformation in the World Polity: towards a Neo-realist Synthesis', in R. Keohane (ed.) *Neo-realism and Its Critics*, New York: Columbia University Press.

——(1989) 'International Structure and International Transformation', in J. Rosenau and E. O. Czempiel (eds) *Global Challenges and Theoretical Challenges*, Lexington: Lexington Books.

——(1993) 'Territoriality and beyond: Problematizing Modernity in International Relations', *International Organization* 47(1): 139–74.

Searle, J. R. (1969) *Speech Acts: An Essay in the Philosophy of Language*, Cambridge: Cambridge University Press.

Shimko, K. L. (1992) 'Realism, Neo-realism, and American Liberalism', *Review of Politics* 54: 281–301.

Skinner, Q. (1966) 'The Limits of Historical Explanations', *Philosophy 41*: 199–215.

Slaughter, A.M. (formely Burley) (1993) 'International Law and International Relations Theory: a Dual Agenda', *American Journal of International Law* 87: 205–39.

Snyder, F. (1993) 'Law and Anthropology: a Review', *EUI Working Paper Law*, no. 93/4.

Strange, S. (1994) 'Wake up Krasner! The World Has Changed', *Review of International Political Economy* 1(2): 209–19.

Suganami, H. (1989) *The Domestic Analogy and World Order Proposals*, Cambridge: Cambridge University Press.

Taylor, C. (1985) 'Language and Human Nature', in *Human Agency and Language: Philosophical Papers 1*, Cambridge: Cambridge University Press.

Taylor, M. (1989) 'Structure Culture and Action in the Explanation of Social Change', *Politics and Society* 17(2): 115–62.

Taylor, P. (1991) 'British Sovereignty and the European Community: What's at Risk?', *Millennium: Journal of International Studies* 20(1): 73–81.

Tully, J. (1988) *Meaning and Context: Quentin Skinner and his Critics*, Cambridge: Polity Press.

Verhoeven, J. (1985) 'Goffman's Frame Analysis and Modern Micro-sociological Paradigms', in H. J. Helle and S. N. Eisenstadt (eds) *Microsociological Theory: Perspectives on Sociological Theory*, Vol. 2, London: Sage.

Wæver, O. (1991) 'Territory, Authority and Identity. The Late Twentieth-Century Emergence of Neo-Medieval Political Structures', conference paper, Copenhagen: Centre for Peace and Conflict Research, pp. 1–36.

——(1992) 'International Society – Theoretical Promises Unfulfilled?', review article, *Co-operation and Conflict* 27(1): 147–78.

——(1994) 'After the Fourth Debate', unpublished draft.

Waltz, K. (1979) *Theory of International Politics*, Reading, MA: Addison-Wesley.

Wendt, A. (1991) 'Bridging the Theory/Meta-theory Gap in International Relations', *Review of International Studies* 17(4): 383–92.

——(1992) 'Levels of Analysis v. Agents and Structures: Part III', *Review of International Studies* 18: 181–5.

——(1994) 'Collective Identity Formation and the International State', *American Political Science Review* 88(2): 384–96.

Wendt, A. and Duvall, R. (1989) 'Institutions and International Order', in E. O. Czempiel and J. Rosenau (eds) *Global Challenges and Theoretical Challenges*, Lexington, MA: Lexington Books.

Wind, M. (1994) (in Danish) 'Europe towards a Post-Hobbesian Order? Or – How to Explain European Integration as an Unintended Consequence of Rational State-action', *Dansk Sociologi* 4 (Copenhagen).

——(1996a) 'The Rediscovery of Institutions in IR Theory and European Community Studies: a Reflectivist Critique of Rational-Institutionalist Approaches to the Study of Institutions and European Integration', in K. E. Jorgensen (ed.) *Reflective Approaches to European Governance*, London: Macmillan.

——(1996b) 'Europe: towards a Post-Hobbesian Order. A Constructivist Theory of European Integration – or How to Explain European Integration as an Unintended Consequence of Rational State Action', European University Institute, Working Paper.

Wittgenstein, L. (1968) *Philosophical Investigations*, Oxford: Blackwell.

10 Alexander Wendt: a social scientist struggling with history

Erik Ringmar

Alexander Wendt was born in 1958 in Mainz, West Germany. Since 1989 he has been at the Department of Political Science, Yale University; currently as Associate Professor. He took his BA in Political Science from Macalester College, in 1982 and his PhD in Political Science from the University of Minnesota, with a dissertation on 'The States System and Global Militarization'.

INTRODUCTION

Alexander Wendt was my dissertation adviser and I was his teaching assistant during my last semester in graduate school. Naturally this connection makes it difficult for me to evaluate his work in a fully objective manner. Former students are expected to say nice things about their former teachers, especially when they still depend on them for letters of recommendation. Yet, while it may be true that the ties that bind mentees to their mentors are nothing short of feudal – universities are medieval institutions after all! – the contemporary academic culture is not only feudal, but also thoroughly *modern*. As a result, any given field of scholarship will not only be characterized by various medieval residues, but also by the same paradoxes as all other features of modernity. The modern tradition, as Octavio Paz has pointed out, is fundamentally polemical and unstable since it is held together by unfaithfulness to tradition itself. To be modern is to revolt against authorities and established ways; it is not to search for 'the truth', but instead constantly to suggest new ways in which the world may be interpreted. '[M]odernity is a sort of creative self-destruction' (Paz 1974: 3).[1]

The degree to which contemporary International Relations scholars have been faithful to this modern code of infidelity is clearly demonstrated by the 'great debates' which regularly break out in their journals. The format and the ritual of these debates are always the same. First, an older – and invariably tenured – generation of scholars is brandished as methodologically and theoretically passé and as inattentive to what 'really is going on' in world politics. Second, a new method, theory, or perspective, is launched which, according to its young – and invariably untenured – proponents, provides the only means of breathing new life into the sclerotic *corps académique*. To make straw men out of the scholars of the earlier generation and to beat them as hard as possible is thought to be the only way to make a career for yourself. Incidentally it is also supposed to be the way in which science makes progress.

Caught between these contradictory imperatives, an ex-advisee may easily feel at a loss. Are you supposed to fulfil the feudal obligation regarding filial piety or attempt a modern intellectual patricide? And how am *I* to assess *my* ex-adviser's work? The only solution here is probably an ambiguous one. While I remain convinced that Alexander Wendt's writings constitute a seminal contribution to International Relations scholarship, I must express my reservations regarding many of the conclusions he reaches. Ex-advisees, after all, must not only express their gratitude and their admiration, but also – and perhaps unfortunately – make sure that science makes progress, *and* that they make careers for themselves.

A sociology of world politics

From the time of his first published work, Wendt's favourite whetstone has been the 'neo-realist' school of international politics, and in particular Kenneth Waltz and his *Theory of International Politics* published in 1979.[2] In this book Waltz reformulated the realist doctrine of the Cold War era in more up-to-date, and explicitly scientistic, terms. It is the 'structure' of the international system, Waltz argued, which limits the potential for co-operation between states, and which brings about insecurity, arms races and war. Given the impact of this structure, a study of the intentions of statesmen, or the size, character and attributes of individual states, will never be sufficient. 'Reductionist' factors like these cannot explain the recurring patterns of world politics whenever structural forces are at play. A theory of international politics must thus necessarily be a theory of the international system (Waltz 1979: 70–2).[3]

Like Waltz's, Wendt's principal aim has been to come up with a structural theory of international politics which takes the state as its basic unit, yet Wendt faults Waltz for the materialism, the individualism and the simplistic rationalism which the neo-realist approach implies. As Wendt powerfully has argued, material factors cannot be analysed apart from the social structures through which they are given meaning; individuals cannot be taken as the atomic units of our theories as long as they can be defined only socially; and while states and statesmen often can be said to act rationally, we need a theory of how not only interests, but also identities, are shaped. Very much in the intellectual tradition of Karl Deutsch and Ernst Haas, Wendt presents world politics as a *social* realm whose features ultimately are determined through the communication and the interaction of its units.

Yet, as we are about to see, Wendt has developed not one, but two, research agendas, and as I will try to show, there is considerable tension between them. While he began by making a case for the so-called 'structurationist' solution to the 'agent–structure problem', he has of late abandoned many of these earlier concerns in favour of a focus on 'representational structures' and the 'construction of state identities'. With apologies to Karl Marx, Martin Heidegger and Ludwig Wittgenstein, we could perhaps make a polemical distinction between an 'early' and a 'late' Wendt.

THE EARLY WENDT: STRUCTURATION ON A REALIST BASIS

Some articles are famous less for the answers they provide than for the questions they raise; articles that are quoted not primarily for their insights, but rather for the way in which they manage to point the attention of the scholarly community in new directions. Wendt's 1987 piece on 'The Agent–Structure Problem in International Relations Theory' was indeed precisely such an article. Although few traditional IR scholars may have fully understood its argument at the time, there was an almost universal agreement that Wendt had made an important contribution to the field.[4] Wendt made two basic claims: 1) existing theories of the international system need a way to combine a focus on structures with a focus on agents, and 'structuration theory' can provide such a way; 2) a 'scientific realist' view of structures allows us to study many of the social phenomena which traditional empirical social scientists have been forced to ignore.

The agent–structure problem

Wendt begins by introducing what he, following Anthony Giddens, calls the 'agent–structure problem'.[5] As he tells us, this problem arises from two truisms of social life. First, our belief that human beings are purposeful actors whose actions reproduce and transform society, and second, our conviction that society is made up of social relationships which structure the interaction between these human beings (Wendt 1987: 337–8). We are born into a world which is pre-organized – pre-structured – and which shapes us and moulds us in a number of different ways, but we are also intentional agents who act in this world and who re-create or transform the structures it contains.

If we accept these two pictures of social life, the problem becomes how to combine them. How should we conceptualize 'agents' and 'structures', and how should we conceive of their interrelationship? Wendt's answer to this question begins with a review of two attempts to deal with the problem as it pertains to international politics: Waltz's neo-realism and the world-system theory developed by Immanuel Wallerstein (Wendt 1987: 340–9).

While both Waltz and Wallerstein theorize about the international system, they conceptualize its structure in very different terms. The international system which Waltz describes is decentralized and anarchical and its only relevant actor is the state. Anarchy is reproduced as each state seeks to protect itself against the threats posed by other states. In international politics, as Waltz tells us, '[w]ith each country constrained to take care of itself, no one can take care of the system' (Waltz 1979: 106).[6] The position which one state occupies in relation to another will depend on its capabilities, and as a result the most important feature of the structure of the international system is its distribution of power. In the absence of a central organizer, balances of power between competing alliances and blocs assure at least a modicum of peace and stability.

The international system which Wallerstein describes, however, is not anarchic and its structure consists not of states and the distribution of power between them, but instead of the *principles* through which states and other agents are *produced*.[7] Wallerstein attaches particular importance to the principles which organize the world economy, that is, in our era, to global capitalism. It is global capitalism, and in particular the international division of labour, which constitutes certain groups of people as 'classes' and certain political units as 'states'.

In his review of these two accounts, Wendt acknowledges that each of them may have its uses, yet he strongly argues that they are insufficient if taken alone. The reason is that they focus on only one of the two sides of the agent–structure equation. Although Waltz talks about structural forces and effects, he takes states as given and defines the structure of the international system in terms of the distribution of power between them. As a result, his structure will be fundamentally 'agent-centric' and reducible to the properties of the units that comprise it. Waltz's structure appears to the scholar as it appears to each state – as a given, external constraint on action – but it has nothing to say regarding how action is possible in the first place, or regarding how the state itself was constituted (Wendt 1987: 342).

Wallerstein's fault is the opposite one. His structure accounts for the principles through which states are formed, but he is unable to view states in their capacity as agents. If the state is seen as the product of the organizing principles of the capitalist world economy, we cannot at the same time see how these organizing principles are reproduced.

In other words: the problem with each theory is that whatever it takes as given it cannot at the same time question. The neo-realists cannot theorize about the emergence and evolution of the state, and the world-system theorists cannot theorize about the emergence and evolution of the capitalist world system. Although very different at first appearance, the two theories – in their one-eyedness – come to resemble each other. Making either agents or structural principles the primitive unit of the analysis means that the view of world politics will inevitably be limited (Wendt 1987: 349).

What we need is consequently a way to theorize about *both* structures and agents. We have to open both of our eyes in order to see how the state and the international system are interacting. This is precisely what 'structuration theory' aims to do. As Wendt explains, structuration theory

> conceptualizes agents and structures as mutually constitutive yet onto-logically distinct entities. Each is in some sense an effect of the other; they are 'co-determined.' Social structures are the result of the intended and unintended consequences of human action, just as those actions presuppose or are mediated by an irreducible structural context.
>
> (Wendt 1987: 360)

When we explain the phenomena of world politics we should consequently do it with the help of both a structural and an agentistic approach. While a structural analysis deals with the conditions of possibility of state action –

with *how* something was possible – an agentistic analysis deals with the whos, whats, wheres and whys of actual world events. If we keep the two modes of explanation distinct, we can investigate how the one influences the other: how the international structure re-creates or transforms the state and how the state re-creates or transforms the international structure. As Wendt points out, a 'complete explanation of state action' must combine both methodologies (Wendt 1987: 364).[8]

Scientific realism

Imagine what a traditional social scientist, brought up on a 1960s fare of behaviourism and empiricism, would say about the argument developed thus far. 'Very interesting,' we can hear him or her say, 'but in all my years as a scientist I have yet to come across a "structure". Only that which can be observed is real and only the observable can be taken as a legitimate object of scientific analysis. "Structures" simply do not belong in this category.'

How are we to defend ourselves against this kind of empirical dogmatism? Wendt's answer is that the mere fact that generative structures cannot be observed does not count as a conclusive argument against their existence. It all depends on what our ontological commitments are – on what we take to be real. To an empiricist only that which can be observed exists, but nothing forces us to accept this conclusion. In fact, as Wendt points out, it is very common among contemporary natural scientists to posit the existence of a number of entities that are just as unobservable as social structures. Apart from the fact that social structures need human beings to create and re-create them, there is no essential ontological difference between, say, a molecular structure in physics and a generative structure in international politics. Both can be said to be 'real' since their effects can be observed (Wendt 1987: 352).

The same thing goes for causes. A traditional empiricist, following a Humean line of argument, would deny that causes exist, and argue that all that science can do is to come up with empirical generalizations through which observable events can be related in temporal sequences. While we legitimately may talk about the existence of a 'lawlike regularity', we can never talk about the existence of a 'cause'.[9] Against this Humean scepticism, however, Wendt argues that causes – although unobservable – are also real features of the world. Just as the existence of a structure may be imputed from its observable effects, the existence of a cause may be imputed from observable regularities. The natural sciences would have made no progress if they had not attempted to identify the underlying causal mechanisms that generate the phenomena which constitute the natural world (Wendt 1987: 353).

It is customary to call the view which Wendt defends here 'realism'. That is, a position which in its most commonsensical version holds that the world of everyday objects exists independently of the mind.[10] More precisely, we could call Wendt a 'scientific', or a 'transcendental', realist. That is, while he does believe that the world of everyday objects exists independently of the mind, he also holds that the unobservable entities and causal mechanisms posited by scientific theories exist independently of the scholars' perception of them (Shapiro and Wendt 1992: 210).[11]

Although scientific realism is a position in a philosophical debate, and although it as such carries no implications whatsoever in terms of our choice of a substantive theory of international politics, this does not mean that it is irrelevant to the practising social scientist. In an article co-written with Ian Shapiro, Wendt seeks to explain precisely what difference a realist view of the social world makes for concrete research. Shapiro and Wendt turn to one of the perennial questions of political theory for an illustration: why is it that people often given their consent to societal orders which from an outside observer's point of view are far less than perfectly fair, equal and just? How, in other words, is *consent* to be explained? As the authors make clear, empirical social scientists have had great difficulties answering this question. Since they have studied only the observable, empiricists have been forced to ignore latent and underlying conflicts, as well as all cases where structural power is at play. Empiricists can study neither how political agendas are manipulated nor the processes through which people's preferences and identities are shaped (Shapiro and Wendt 1992: 200–6).[12] As Shapiro and Wendt argue, it is simply not enough to ask an underpaid worker – in an opinion poll fashion – why she does not go on strike, since it is possible that her understanding of herself and her interests may be based on a distorted view of the world.

Once we take unobservable entities to be real, however, these kinds of cases also become amenable to study. Since the effects of structural power can be observed, we are safe to assume that structural power exists. Yet it may still not be immediately obvious what this realization means in terms of a concrete research agenda: how, after all, are we to study an *absence* – the absence of strikes, revolts and rebellions? While Wendt and Shapiro do acknowledge that this may be a tall order, they believe that we can make some headway by means of a counter-factual argument. We need to make a hypothesis regarding what things *would have been like* if only structural power had not been present, and then measure the difference between this condition and the one presently at hand.[13] The degree of genuine consent which people give to a societal order can thus be understood as the difference between the consent given under present conditions and what a person would choose to do, or to be, under conditions where structural power was not at play. In this way we may make an estimate of 'real' interests and 'real' identities.[14]

Critical assessment

Let us stop here for a moment and inject some critical remarks. Beginning with the structurationist research programme, the first thing to note is how inherently plausible it sounds. Structuration theory catches a simple, commonsensical insight: the dual facts that we are acted upon by our environment, but that we in turn also act upon it. From this truism it seems to follow that we should not choose actors at the expense of structures, or structures at the expense of actors, since we can, and must, choose both. The question is only whether Wendt is correct in arguing that traditional theories of International Relations can be assigned to either of these two poles, and whether a structurationist research programme which integrates them indeed is feasible.

While I am not aware of any scholars who have rushed to Wallerstein's defence, a number of writers have argued that Wendt's account of Waltz's structuralism is unfair. It is simply not true, they have said, that Waltz's theory is agentistic. Waltz does not only, as Wendt claims, define his structure in terms of the distribution of properties of the units it comprises, but he also provides it with 'a life of its own', as it were (Hollis and Smith 1991: 401–3).[15] Through the twin processes of socialization and competition, the structure has an independent and *causal* impact over states: while socialization reduces variety, competition forces one state to emulate the successful practices of other states. The structure is hence not only a constraint on action, but it also 'limits and molds' agents and 'points them in ways that tend toward a common quality of outcomes' (Waltz 1979: 63).[16]

Who is right? Is Waltz's structure agentistic or is it not? Or put into more analytical terms: what is it that Waltz's structure purports to explain? Is it, as Wendt claims, a rationalistic theory which explains how states act in order to attain their interests given certain constraints, or is it a sociological theory which explains also the *formation* of states? How we answer this question will, I believe, ultimately depend on how we decide to regard the relationship between actions, on the one hand, and identities, on the other. Put somewhat cryptically: if we decide that 'we are what we do', then – to the extent that Waltz's structure indeed explains state actions – it may also be thought of as a theory of identity formation. And, conversely, to the extent that it does not explain state action, it is not. And, similarly it is not a theory of identity formation if we decide that what we 'are' instead is to be accounted for in some other way than as a consequence of our actions.

Instead of involving ourselves in philosophical queries like these, however, we could view the same problem in *historical* terms. Doing this we might accept that the structure of the international system has (some degree of) causal impact over states once it has come into existence, but that it cannot account for the constitution of states *in the first place*. Although Waltz's theory may (or may not) work as a synchronic explanation, it decidedly fails as a diachronic account. Or as John Gerard Ruggie puts it, Waltz's theory 'contains only a reproductive logic, but no transformational logic' (Ruggie 1986: 152). What it lacks is a temporal account of the relationship between agents and structures; a *story* of how the one came to produce the other.

This is of course not surprising. All theories framed in terms of the causal powers of structures have problems dealing with questions of change.[17] Something which changes cannot be explained by something else which remains constant, and structures must remain constant if they are to remain structures (Taylor 1989: 121–22).[18] What we need is simply some other kind of theory. Wendt's suggestion here, as we saw, is to combine a theory of structures with a theory of agents. By bracketing first the actual and then its conditions of possibility, he hopes to derive a 'complete theory' of the 'mutual co-determination' of the two.

Yet, even if we agree that Wendt's critique of Waltz hits the mark, we may well wonder whether the alternative he himself proposes is an improvement. Can structuration theory really explain social change? The answer to this question must, I think, be given in the negative, and the reason is that the relationship which Wendt posits between agents and structures is still far too mechanistic. Wendt's structures produce agents which produce structures which produce agents, but nowhere in this ever-continuing oscillation is there space for anything *new* and *unexpected* to appear. As long as agents and structures are seen as 'mutually co-determined' it does not help to bracket the one side or the other since the *sources* of change still are left unaccounted for.[19]

What is missing from this framework is quite simply a convincing theory of action. Such a theory, I believe, would first of all have to find a way of conceptualizing the processes through which *meaning* is created in social life. The world is given meaning by human actors, the argument should go, and on the basis of these meanings human beings act. The emergence of the new can only be explained once we can account for how that which is interpreted in one set of terms comes to be reinterpreted in some other set of terms.[20] Chickens and eggs could perhaps be analysed with the help of Wendt's structurationist approach, but not human beings, and the reason is that human beings, but not chickens and eggs, have *consciousness*, a *culture*, and a *history*.

Yet our scepticism might go deeper. We may not only fault Wendt for the mechanical – indeed still structuralist – nature of the 'complete explanation of state action' which he advocates, but we may also suspect that such an account is impossible *in principle*. In order to address this issue we need to turn our attention to the conditions of possibility of structuration theory itself. What must the world be like for structuration theory to be possible? By virtue of what features of the world can we designate one thing as a 'structure' and another thing as an 'actor'?[21]

Social scientists who discuss this issue generally claim that they are engaging in a debate about 'ontology'. A debate, that is, concerning 'what there is'. Yet the social scientists' use of this term differs from the philosophers' use of it. While an ontological debate among philosophers might discuss what kind of 'stuff' constitutes the world – is it all 'spirit' or all 'matter'? – social scientists never talk about ontology as such, but always instead about *an* ontology, or *the* ontology which a certain theory presupposes.[22] They talk, in other words, about how the social world should be *regarded*. In this way 'ontology' comes to mean precisely what a natural scientist would call a 'model'.[23] The ontology *models* the world in a certain fashion – it makes us see something in terms of *some thing* – and on the basis of these models, theories are constructed and hypotheses deduced. It is through a process like this that world politics comes to be seen as a 'system' or a 'society', and states as 'persons', 'agents', 'poles', or 'billiard balls'.

What, then, is the status of these models? What is the relationship between our visions of the world and the world itself? As we saw, Wendt settles for a 'realist' answer to these questions, and in doing so he is once again defending an inherently plausible view. Common sense certainly agrees that the world exists independently of our minds, and if the physical world may contain structures that generate events, surely the social world might as well. Yet common sense is a shaky ground on which to build philosophy, and if we want to make a case for the 'real existence' of structures, agents, or causes, we need a better foundation. As Wendt correctly points out, however, empirical evidence alone cannot help us here. The world is not reducible to the observable except in the empiricists' version of it. In fact *none* of the positions in a debate regarding 'the real' can ever be conclusively proven either false or true. The reason is that the evidence which one position takes as a refutation easily can be redescribed in terms of another position as a confirmation.[24]

This fact, however, inevitably throws doubts also on Wendt's own conclusions and it would not be difficult to argue that the entities he identifies lack the 'real existence' he ascribes to them. In a way this conclusion follows already from the fashion in which the social scientists have framed their ontological debates. To 'model' some thing means to model some thing *in terms of* something else; to *see* some thing *as* some other kind of thing. But to see something as some other thing is emphatically *not* to talk about 'real existence', but instead to talk about one's own version of it. Ontological discussions among social scientists do not concern 'being', but instead what being *resembles*.[25] Think about it for a moment: could anything like a 'structure' – an architectural term – have a 'real existence' in world politics independently of the social researcher's description of it! 'Structures' are not things that we find in world politics, but instead things that we *apply* to world politics, and the same conclusion holds also for 'actors' or 'causes'.

THE LATE WENDT: SOCIAL INTERACTIONISM ON A CONSTRUCTIVIST BASIS

While nothing that Wendt recently has written indicates that he has begun to have doubts regarding the structurationist programme and its transcendental foundations, it is still a fact that his research agenda has changed. The late Wendt is quite different from the earlier scholar and writer by the same name. Perhaps he belatedly has come to realize that scientific realism is little more than an empty metaphysical belief, or perhaps it is world politics itself that suddenly has intervened and wreaked havoc with his scholarly pursuits: as the events of the early 1990s – the period of Wendt's *Kehre* – clearly demonstrated, history is more than just the mechanical interplay of agents and structures. Regardless of how the shift should be explained, however, it is still the case that today's Wendt prefers to talk about 'social interaction' rather than 'structuration', and about 'constructivism' instead of 'scientific realism'.

Constructivism and the international system

In making the case for a constructivist view of international politics, Wendt is once again using Kenneth Waltz as his foil. As Waltz had argued, it is anarchy which turns the world into a 'self-help system' where power politics is perpetuated and states are insecure. But if anarchy always produces these results, and if the structure of the post-1991 world was just as anarchic as the pre-1991 world, how was Waltz to account for the new international climate of *reduced* tensions and *increasing* co-operation? As the late Wendt concluded, Waltz's deduction of power politics from the fact of anarchy was flawed. Anarchy *may* certainly result in self-help and insecurity, but then again it may not. 'Anarchy', as Wendt's slogan went, 'is what states make of it' (Wendt 1992).[26]

Wendt begins this argument by classifying various International Relations theories according to the extent to which they regard knowledge as important in social life (Wendt forthcoming: 8).[27] To what extent, that is, does a certain theory take our representations of the world as crucial and what role does it attribute to brute material facts? A theorist who takes representations to be everything, Wendt calls an 'idealist', and a person who believes that material facts determine the world is a 'materialist'. When measuring political realism – in both its classical and its neo-versions – with the help of this yardstick, Wendt locates it at the materialist end of the continuum. According to political realism, the power of a state is determined by its material bases, and the structure of the international system is given by the distribution of these bases.

Yet as Wendt strongly argues, a materialist view of social life and of international politics is untenable. What matters in the end is not matter, but instead how matter is *represented*. It follows that, for example, balances of power must be understood not as balances between material means of destruction, but instead – in representational terms – as 'balances of threats' (Wendt 1992: 396 and Wendt 1994).[28] It is not what actually exists which deters statesmen from going to war, but instead what statesmen actually take to be existing.

Although Wendt defends an unabashedly idealistic position here, his idealism implies neither subjectivism nor arbitrariness. Knowledge, after all, is not a private business, and what we know we always know together with others.[29] Knowledge is a fact about *society* and not primarily a fact about individual human beings. Knowledge, furthermore, is always organized and always structured. There are, we could say, 'structures of social meaning' which we share with the other members of our societies, or which states share with other states who participate in international interactions. These structures give meaning to international politics and with their help statesmen and citizens make sense of the world. Focusing on these systemic features, Wendt is also able to make a case for a systemic theory of international politics, but unlike Waltz and the neo-realists, Wendt's structures are *representational* and *intersubjective* and not materialistic and individualistic (Wendt forthcoming: 1).[30]

Returning to Waltz's discussion of anarchy equipped with these analytical tools, Wendt is able to detect the flaw in his reasoning. The consequences of anarchy have nothing to do with the distribution of the material bases of power, but instead everything to do with the intersubjectively constructed meanings given to these bases. It all depends on how anarchy is interpreted and on how states regard each other's postures and intentions. Power politics is the result of *one* such interpretation, but it is not the only one possible. Anarchy has no 'essence' or 'meaning' apart from the essences and meanings which states attribute to it (Wendt 1992: 395; Wendt forthcoming: 15).[31]

If this indeed is the case, the question becomes how we are to account for power politics as a fact of world affairs. Why in fact do states constantly seek power? Here Wendt engages in a piece of state of nature theorizing which strongly reminds us of Jean-Jacques Rousseau's critique of Thomas Hobbes.[32] Just as Rousseau had argued that anti-social tendencies can arise only in a society and consequently are not a feature of the state of nature, Wendt argues that states under anarchical conditions have no reason either to be hostile to each other or to feel threatened. Hostility and threats are instead the results of how states interpret each other's signals and how they respond to them. Power politics was constructed as the threats of one state were mirrored by another state, and as threats and counter-threats came to be taken for granted as natural features of their interaction. As a naturalized and entrenched institution, power politics may of course be difficult to change, but since it is not a constitutive feature of anarchy as such, transformations are not ruled out in principle (Wendt 1992: 407).[33]

In theoretical terms, this emphasis on social interaction means that Waltz's narrowly rationalistic view of the international system must be expanded, but also that social 'practices' must receive more attention than they did in Wendt's earlier account. As he now realizes, there are not only structures on the one hand, and actors on the other, but also processes going on *between* them. In fact, social practice has come to take causal priority in the new model: '[i]n the last analysis', Wendt now tells us, 'agents and structures are produced or reproduced by practice, by what actors *do*' (Wendt 1994: 23–4).

Social interaction and the state

An issue that became particularly salient in the early 1990s concerned the nature of the many new political entities that emerged as a result of the end of the Cold War. As national boundaries suddenly were redrawn it became obvious that IR scholars lacked a way to explain the breakdown of old identities and the formation of new ones. Also Alexander Wendt turned to this issue and, as we might expect, he did it in the form of a critique of Kenneth Waltz.

How is a state's identity created? How do the members of a state know who they are? Although he did not phrase the question in quite these terms, Waltz's theory of international politics did hint at an answer to it. The structure of the international system, Waltz argued, makes all states similar in their functions: socialization and competition force them all to develop institutions through which their sovereignty can be guaranteed. The only difference between one state and another is given by differences in power between them; while states are alike in the tasks they face, they differ widely in their abilities to perform them (Waltz 1979: 90–1).

Yet, as Wendt argues, this proto-theory of identity formation is far too materialistic and radically undersocialized. If to have an identity is to be *different* from others, then a theory which makes everyone the same cannot be a theory of how identities are created. And even if we take into account what Waltz says regarding differences in capabilities, it is still an empirical fact that states differ from each other in more ways than the distribution of power can explain. Waltz's theory tells us nothing, for example, about whether states will be friends or foes, or whether they will be revisionists or status quo powers (Wendt 1992: 396). Similarly – and perhaps more importantly given the context of the 1990s – Waltz is unable to account for *changes* in identities. Since the material bases of power cannot explain why a state becomes a state of a particular kind, a projection of the future development of material bases cannot allow us to draw conclusions regarding future identities. Waltz cannot – to cite the example which seemed to be on everyone's mind in the early 1990s – tell us what kind of a state a future Russia will become.

What we must do, in Wendt's opinion, is to replace Waltz's emphasis on the causal powers of anarchy with a theory of the causal powers of social interaction, and his materialistic account of identity formation with a constructivistic one (Wendt forthcoming: 2). Once we do this, we will see that identities are not given by material factors, but instead are always *socially* constructed.[34] Just as a person is no one when alone and someone only when recognized by persons around her, a state has an identity only to the extent that it is recognized by other states.[35] Consequently also sovereignty must be thought of as a social and not as an individualistic concept. Sovereignty is not a property which 'belongs' to the state, but instead a status which is *conferred upon it* by other states.

Once we start talking about identities in this fashion, it is easy to add a discussion regarding interests. Identities and interests must be intimately connected for the simple reason that what we take our selves to be determines which interests we take our selves to have. It is only *as someone* that we can have, or not have, an interest in a particular thing. It follows that to the extent that identities are socially constructed, so are interests, and hence neither identities nor interests can be thought of as things that people 'have'. Just as we can be a 'someone' only in relation to others who recognize us, we can never want a 'something' all alone.[36]

Putting this point into a sociologist's vocabulary, Wendt analyses the relationship between interests and identities through the concept of a 'role' (Wendt forthcoming: 20). The roles that states assume, and the scripts of actions that go with these roles, are given by intersubjective structures of meaning operating at the level of the international system (Wendt forthcoming: 12).[37]

Once we come to see identities and interests as socially constructed, we have also obtained a new angle on the perennial question of how to achieve peace and co-operation between states. In traditional liberal discourse, matters of peace and co-operation have invariably been discussed either in terms of an idealistic project concerning how states are to be convinced not to make war on each other, or alternatively in terms of a rationalistic project concerning how to achieve co-operation between states who all look to their own self-interests. In both versions, however, the liberal project has run into difficulties. While liberal idealists have been criticized – indeed ridiculed – for their pollyannic prescriptions, liberal rationalists have themselves drawn the conclusion that co-operation between states is something very fragile and thus possible only given certain, rather favourable, conditions.[38]

The mistake which both versions of the liberal project have made, according to Wendt, is that they uncritically have accepted the political realists' starting-point: viz. that the state and state interests are given. If we, however, see both identities and interests not as determined prior to social interaction, but instead as *constituted through it*, then new analytical perspectives are immediately opened up. If social interaction determines both what we are and what we want to do, then new forms of interactions may create new forms of states with interests that are less likely to be in conflict with each other (Wendt and Friedheim forthcoming: 2). Although Wendt wavers a bit on exactly how this is to be achieved, he believes that increased interdependence, the convergence of domestic values, and the spread of global consumerism, may alter the way in which states identify with one another, and in this way create new, less conflict-prone, relations between states.[39]

Critical assessment

Above I made two points in criticism of the early Wendt: 1) a structurationist solution to the agent–structure problem cannot explain social change unless it is equipped with a credible theory of action; 2) to say that agents and structures have 'real' existence is to embrace a metaphysical position which cannot be refuted and which has no more plausibility than the alternative positions that contradict it. If we accept some version of these two arguments, it should be obvious that the late Wendt is an improvement on his earlier self. The late Wendt's focus on the constructedness of world politics and on the emergence of meaning through social interaction, constitutes an important contribution to the new research agenda which has emerged as a result of the end of the Cold War. Yet at least two problems remain unresolved: 1) there is a fundamental tension between the position of the early and the late Wendt; 2) there are a number of crucial factors that also the late Wendt fails to take seriously.

If the late Wendt is a constructivist, he is a highly reluctant one, and curiously enough the constructivism which he defends takes the form of a *substantive* theory of international politics and not the form of a philosophical argument. What matters to *states*, he says, are representations and not material facts. Yet it is surely a mistake to try to contain constructivism in this manner: the nature of the relationship between the world and our representations of it is surely a matter of *philosophical* concern and not a matter of IR theory. And as any philosophical constructivist will inform us, we can say nothing whatsoever about the world as it 'really is' since our only access to it passes through our representations, and these representations are not 'given' by the world, but instead *created by us*. The external world is not discovered, but constructed, and there is no 'real existence' apart from the real existences that we impute to it.[40] Unfortunately for Wendt, however, constructivism, thus understood, is radically opposed to scientific realism, and it is also likely to be highly sceptical of the structurationist solution to the agent–structure problem.

The contradiction between constructivism and scientific realism is immediately visible if we apply the constructivist conclusions not only to world politics, but also to ourselves as observers of world politics. If constructivism cannot be limited to substantive issues, then not only statesmen but also the social scientists themselves will come to live in the worlds they construct. Yet a social scientist who lives in a constructed world cannot consistently claim to be a scientific realist. The positions are contradictory: according to scientific realism, the *world* creates the representations we have of it; according to constructivism, *we* create the representations we have of the world.

Since the two positions cannot be combined, Wendt has to choose between them, and if he wants to be a consistent constructivist, he must reject scientific realism. If he does this, however, he will soon find that constructivism also is very difficult to combine with a structurationist research agenda. As a constructivist is likely to point out, no theory can be conceived of which covers more than a certain *aspect* of social life. Theorizing is possible within, but generally not *between*, perspectives. With the help of our models we can construct a certain world, but the different worlds which we construct are not cumulative and not necessarily even compatible (Goodman 1984: 24–44).[41] Each model makes us see some things rather than some others, but our different visions can never be added together since there is no point of view from which *everything* can be seen.

It follows that it is quite impossible to come up with anything even remotely resembling what Wendt referred to as a 'complete explanation of state action'. While the early Wendt of course was correct to point out that states may be seen both as products of their environment and as producers of their environment, a constructivist is likely to point out that states cannot be seen in both capacities *at once*. We can certainly 'bracket' the one perspective at the expense of the other, but there is no knowledge outside of brackets and the two visions of the state can never merge. This conclusion, I believe, explains why so few scholars have used structurationism as an actual research programme, and it explains why those who have have reached such banal results.[42]

Yet even if Wendt did renounce the fundamentalist inclinations of his past, theoretical lacunas would still remain. Consider, for example, his discussion of social practices. In the last instance, we are told, it is what states *do* that drives the theory. Social practices create/re-create structures which create/re-create agents which create/re-create practices, and so on. While this formulation perhaps may sound attractive, it does not explain how the causality of the model is supposed to operate. The emphasis on practices conflates agents and structures into something which cannot be distinguished and which consequently can be neither causally related nor properly understood.[43] All that will be left to us, it seems, are actions and their consequences, and from a structurationist perspective that can hardly be satisfactory.

Another way to put this is to point out that Wendt still provides no convincing theory of action. To the extent that practices are taken as the theoretical starting-point, these practices themselves cannot be explained, since that which is taken for granted by a theoretical framework cannot be analysed within the terms set by that same framework. Yet why, then, do states do what they do? The only thing which Wendt offers by means of clarification here is the concept of 'roles'. It is the socially recognized role which a state adopts that gives it a certain script to follow. But what, in that case, determines the choice of one particular role rather than another? One may have hoped that Wendt's discussions of identity formation would elucidate this latter matter, yet also here his focus remains fundamentally one-sided: the problem of identity formation is constantly seen from the perspective of the system and never as a problem each state and each statesman has to grapple with. He can tell us why a certain identity is recognized, but not *what that identity is*.

In a way this problem is an exact counterpart to the problem of agency which Wendt never properly addressed. His structural bias constantly sets limits to his investigation: just as the structure of the international system cannot make a state act, it cannot make someone have a particular identity. Just as the structure cannot explain historical changes, it cannot by itself explain changes in identities. What Wendt needs, but cannot provide with the help of the theoretical perspective he has made his, is an account of how states *interpret* the structures of international politics and how they *use* them in interaction with others.

CONCLUSION: TWO MODES OF THOUGHT

Let us in conclusion bring out a subtheme of our discussion: the relationship between a scientific investigation of world politics and a historical one. While these two approaches no doubt often are mixed in the actual work of actual researchers, they are nevertheless fundamentally different in spirit. Perhaps we could talk – in an ideal-type fashion – about two different modes of thought.[44]

The aim of the social sciences, first of all, is to systematize and formalize our knowledge of the world. The social scientist explains things by establishing lawlike generalizations between variables and by explaining these with the help of theories. 'Given the conditions x, y, or z,' the scientist concludes, 'event a will occur', or 'occur with .8 probability'. As a result of this way of proceeding, scientific theories will necessarily come to take on a *trans*-temporal quality; they become applicable regardless of different historical and cultural settings, and 'independent variables' explain contemporary events in the same way as they explain the events of the past or of the future. A successful scientific argument is conclusive – it establishes what we may take as true and what we may take as false.

History, on the other hand, is fundamentally narrative in character: it is *about* a something or a someone.[45] The aim of the historian is not primarily to explain, but instead to give an account of what happened; to tell a good, convincing, plausible story. All stories need plots, and the plot which the historian constructs unfolds through the actions undertaken by the characters that belong to it – 'plot', as already Aristotle suggested, 'is the *mimesis* of action.'[46] Since history deals with actions, it deals also with human consciousness, with interpretations, beliefs, intentions and hopes. The essence of history is change rather than stability: the story requires new developments, and it requires uncertainty since it is only by being open to the new and the unexpected that the story can catch, and hold, the attention of its audience. A successful story tells us something about the human condition; it has a happy, tragic, comic or absurd ending.

The extent to which these two modes of thought indeed are incompatible is perhaps best brought out by the fact that they correspond to two radically different ways of gaining knowledge about the world: by seeing and by listening (Arendt 1977: 110–25). While science presents a picture of the world, history can be known only by being told and listened to. While a picture is static and 'there' for everyone to look at, the story is sequential – unfolding word by word – and hidden until its very end. While the picture shows us what *is*, the story tells us what is in the process of *becoming*. While vision is the very touchstone of truth – 'I saw it with my own eyes!' – listening always puts us at the mercy of the authority of the story-teller.

The study of international politics was for a long time thought of as a historical, and not as a scientific, enterprise. The scholars of the discipline told stories about what the statesmen of the past had done and the statesmen of the present listened attentively. Classical political realism *à la* Morgenthau, Carr and Kennan was historical in this sense. It derived wisdom and guidelines, not theories and facts; it was concerned with the human condition rather than with scientific validity; with the whims of Ms *Fortuna* rather than with statistical probabilities. World politics, classical political realism affirmed, was something to be *done* rather than to be explained. In contrast, neo-realism is scientific through and through. It takes the fact of anarchy as a transhistorically given and concerns itself with its equally transhistorical effects. The structure of the international system is a picture and not a story.

Alexander Wendt is, as we have seen, very critical of the entire neo-realist project. He faults Waltz for the built-in materialism and rationalism of his theory, for its inability to explain social change, and for its lack of attention to the processes through which identities and interests are formed. As Wendt has made perfectly clear, while Waltz's book may provide *a* theory of international politics, it is not *the* theory. As a way to improve on the neo-realist framework Wendt introduces a number of radical reformulations: he focuses not on structures and not on agents, but on the interrelationship between them; he theorizes not about material facts and eternal imperatives, but about practices and processes and about the social creation of meaning. He tries, in a word, to put the neo-realist picture *into motion*, to historicize it, to move it closer to actions and thought and to human life as we know it.

Yet, in the final analysis, Wendt is also a social scientist and *not* a historian, and while he may try to historicize neo-realism, there are inevitably limits to any such enterprise. Even as a critic of neo-realism Wendt is trapped within the theoretical universe which neo-realism has constructed. He can, and does, improve on Waltz in several respects, but he cannot present a picture of that which only can be narrated. The mutual co-determination of agents and structures cannot explain historical transformations since it cannot account for human actions and for the emergence of the new. Scientific realism cannot make agents, structures and causes any more 'real' than other, rival, accounts. A theory of the construction of identities and interests is radically incomplete as long as it views individuals and collective entities only from the perspective of the system. Alexander Wendt is a social scientist struggling with history and in the end the success of his intellectual enterprise will depend on the extent to which international politics indeed allows itself to be caught within the grids constructed by science.

NOTES

I am grateful to Jens Bartelson, Andreas Behnke, Walter Carlsnaes, Diane Pranzo, Alexander Wendt and the co-authors of this volume for their comments and criticisms.

1 See also Lyotard (1988: 9–28).
2 Kenneth Waltz, *Theory of International Politics* (1979). In what follows I will quote from Waltz's chapters reprinted in *Neo-realism and Its Critics*, edited by Robert Keohane (1986).
3 For a critical discussion, see the articles in *Neo-realism and Its Critics* (1986).
4 For elaborations on Wendt's framework, see, for example, Dessler (1989); Carlsnaes (1992).
5 See, for example, Giddens (1984).
6 See Waltz, *Theory*, p. 106.
7 For Immanuel Wallerstein's work see, for example, (1974) and (1984).
8 Compare Wendt and Duvall (1989: 59–60).
9 For Hume's famous discussion, see Hume (1969: 121–42).

10 It is important to remember that 'realism' in this sense is a position in a *philosophical* debate and that as such it has no necessary relationship whatsoever with the *political* realism.

11 On 'transcendental realism', see Bhaskar (1979: 1–30).

12 This oversight is shared by scholars who advocate an 'interpretive approach' to social phenomena. As Wendt and Shapiro point out, it is not enough to study people's self-understandings since people often are unaware of the effects of the social structures which influence them. See Wendt and Shapiro (1992: 206–10).

13 Wendt refers us to Connolly's use of this method, see Connolly (1974: 46–83). Compare Lukes (1982: 47).

14 In this way we can also make a distinction between the 'real' and the 'subjective' interests of states. 'Real interests', as Wendt argues, are given by a state's structurally defined position; they are 'social structural or objective imperatives for competent state practice'. Any difference between these interests and what states in fact perceive to be their interests can be explained by reference to the 'individual and organizational decision-making pathologies in the state' (Wendt, 1987: 359–60, n. 65).

15 Compare Buzan, Little and Jones (1993: 110–18).

16 Waltz, *Theory*, p. 63.

17 Compare, for example, Ricoeur's critique of structuralism (1988a: 155–6).

18 There are, of course, structural theories, Marxist and other, which purport to explain change, but they invariably do so only by reconstituting stability at some 'deeper', more fundamental, structural level.

19 Compare Dessler's critique: 'Wendt tilts toward a structural determinism in his analysis of the relation between state and system, conceptualizing the state as an *effect* of the internally related elements comprising structure' (Dessler, 1989: 452, n. 45).

20 Compare Taylor (1989: 121–2).

21 For a radical critique of Giddensonian solutions, see Bartelson (1993: 39–42).

22 On philosophical discussions regarding 'ontology', see Hamlyn (1984: 34–59).

23 'In this article', as Dessler (1989: 445) puts it, 'I use "model" interchangeably with "ontology".' What are called 'ontologies' or 'models' could just as well be called 'metaphors'. See Black (1962); Hesse (1966).

24 As Danto (1989: 192) puts it: 'The world as we live it and know it is consistent with all possible philosophies of knowledge.'

25 I develop this argument in Ringmar (1996).

26 Compare Behnke (1993: 1).

27 Alexander Wendt, 'Chapter 1: Four Sociologies of International Politics', draft, October, 1993 (Cambridge, Cambridge University Press, forthcoming), p. 8.

28 Wendt (1992: 396); Wendt (1994). Compare Walt (1987).

29 Most famously argued by Wittgenstein. See Wittgenstein (1988: 262–75).

30 Wendt (1994: 4); Wendt (forthcoming: 1).

31 Wendt (1992: 395); Wendt (forthcoming: 15).

32 Compare Rousseau (1967: 204–63). Wendt himself notes this similarity (1992: n. 39, 402).

33 Wendt (1994: 19); Wendt (1992: 407).

34 Compare Mead (1964: 135–226).

35 Compare Ringmar (1996).

36 Alessandro Pizzorno (1986) makes this case very convincingly.

37 Wendt (forthcoming: 12); Wendt (1994: 6).

38 See, for example, the articles in *Co-operation under Anarchy* (1986).

39 Although he also recognizes that these processes under certain circumstances may have different, indeed contradictory, effects (Wendt and Friedheim 1995: 23).

40 Compare, for example, Goodman (1978); Bruner (1986a: 95–6).

41 Compare Masterman (1970: 83).

42 I am thinking in particular of Giddens's own attempts to write on international politics. See Giddens (1987).
43 Compare Archer (1982).
44 Compare Bruner (1986b: 11–43).
45 Compare Danto (1985).
46 Discussed in Ricoeur (1988b: 31–7).

REFERENCES

Works by Alexander Wendt

Wendt, Alexander (1987) 'The Agent–Structure Problem in International Relations Theory', *International Organization* 41(3): 335–70.
—— (1991) 'Bridging the Theory/Meta-Theory Gap in International Relations', review essay in *Review of International Studies* 17(4): 383–92; reply from Martin Hollis and Steve Smith followed by Wendt's 'Level of Analysis v. Agents and Structures: Part III', *Review of International Studies* 18: 181–5, and another reply.
—— (1992) 'Anarchy Is What States Make of It: The Social Construction of Power Politics', *International Organization* 46(2): 391–425.
—— (1994) 'Collective Identity Formation and the International State', *American Political Science Review* 88(2): 84–96, revised and published as 'Identity and Structural Change in International Politics', in Yosef Lapid and Friedrich Kratochwil, (eds) *The Return of Culture and Identity to International Theory*, Boulder, Co: Lynne Rienner, pp. 47–64.
—— (1995) 'Constructing International Politics', *International Security* 19: 71–81.
—— (forthcoming) 'Chapter 1: Four Sociologies of International Politics', in *Social Theory of International Politics*, Cambridge: Cambridge University Press.
—— and Barnett, Michael (1992) 'The International System and Dependent Militarization', in Michael Job (ed.) *The Insecurity Dilemma: National Security of Third World States*, Boulder, Co: Lynne Rienner, pp. 97–119.
—— (1993) 'Dependent State Formation and Third World Militarization', *Review of International Studies* 19(3): 321–47.
—— and Duvall, Raymond (1989) 'Institutions and International Order', in *Global Changes and Theoretical Challenges*, ed. James Rosenau and E. O. Czempiel, Lexington, MA: Lexington Books.
—— and Friedheim, Daniel (1995) 'Hierarchy under Anarchy: Informal Empire and the East German State', *International Organization* 49(3): 689–721: earlier version published in Thomas Biersteker and Cynthia Weber (eds) (forthcoming) *State Sovereignty as Social Construct*, Cambridge: Cambridge University Press.
—— Jepperson, Ronald and Katzenstein, Peter (1996) 'Norms, Identity and Culture in National Security', in Peter Katzenstein (ed.) *The Culture of National Security*, New York: Columbia University Press.
—— and Shapiro, Ian (1992) 'The Differences that Realism Makes: Social Science and the Politics of Consent', *Politics & Society* 20(2): 197–223.

Works by other authors

Archer, Margaret (1982) 'Morphogenesis versus Structuration: On Combining Structure and Action', *British Journal of Sociology* 33(4): 455–83.
Arendt, Hannah (1977) *Life of the Mind: Thinking*, San Diego, CA: Harcourt Brace Jovanovich.
Bartelson, Jens (1993) *A Genealogy of Sovereignty*, Stockholm: Stockholm University Press.
Behnke, Andreas (1993) *Structuration, Institutions and Regimes: The Case of CSBM*, Stockholm: Stockholm International Studies 93(1).

Bhaskar, Roy (1979) *The Possibility of Naturalism: A Philosophical Critique of the Contemporary Human Sciences*, Brighton, Sx: Harvester.

Black, Max (1962) 'Models and Archetypes' and 'Metaphor', in his *Models and Metaphors*, Ithaca, NY: Cornell University Press.

Bruner, Jerome (1986a) 'Nelson Goodman's Worlds', in *Actual Minds, Possible Worlds*, Cambridge, MA: Harvard University Press.

——(1986b) 'Two Modes of Thought', in *Actual Minds, Possible Worlds*, Cambridge, MA: Harvard University Press.

Buzan, Barry, Little, Richard and Jones, Charles (1993) *The Logic of Anarchy: Neorealism to Structural Realism*, New York: Columbia University Press.

Carlsnaes, Walter (1992) 'The Agency–Structure Problem in Foreign Policy Analysis', *International Studies Quarterly* 36(3): 245–70.

Connolly, William E. (1974) 'The Import of Contests over "Interests"', in *The Terms of Political Discourse*, Princeton, NJ: Princeton University Press.

Danto, Arthur (1985[1965]) *Narration and Knowledge: Including the Integral Text of Analytical Philosophy of History*, New York: Columbia University Press.

——(1989) *Connections to the World*, New York: Harper & Row.

Dessler, David (1989) 'What's at Stake in the Agent–Structure Debate?', *International Organization* 43(3): 441–73.

Giddens, Anthony (1984) *The Constitution of Society*, Cambridge: Polity Press.

——(1987) *The Nation-State and Violence*, Vol. 2 of *A Contemporary Critique of Historical Materialism*, Berkeley, CA: University of California Press.

Gilpin, Robert (1986) 'The Richness of the Tradition of Realism', in Robert Keohane (ed.) *Neo-realism and Its Critics*, New York: Columbia University Press.

Goodman, Nelson (1978) *Ways of Worldmaking*, Hassocks, Sx: Harvester Press.

——(1984) *Of Mind and Other Matters*, Cambridge, MA: Harvard University Press.

Hamlyn, D. W. (1984) *Metaphysics*, Cambridge: Cambridge University Press.

Hesse, Mary (1966) *Models and Analogies in Science*, Notre Dame, IN: University of Notre Dame Press.

Hollis, Martin and Smith, Steve (1991) 'Beware of Gurus: Structure and Action in International Relations', *Review of International Studies* 17: 393–410.

Hume, David (1969[1739–40]), *A Treatise of Human Nature*, Harmondsworth, Mx: Penguin.

Keohane, Robert (ed.) (1986) *Neo-realism and Its Critics*, New York: Columbia University Press.

Lukes, Steven (1982[1974]) *Power: A Radical View*, London and Basingstoke, Hants: Macmillan.

Lyotard, Jean-François (1988) 'Réponse à la question: qu'est-ce que le postmoderne?' in *Le Postmodern expliqué aux enfants: correspondance 1982–1985*, Paris: Galilée.

Masterman, Margaret (1970) 'The Nature of a Paradigm', in *Criticism and the Growth of Knowledge*, ed. Imre Lakatos and Alan Musgrave, Cambridge: Cambridge University Press.

Mead, George Herbert (1964[1932]), *Mind, Self, and Society: From the Standpoint of a Social Behaviorist*, Chicago: University of Chicago Press.

Oye, Kenneth A. (ed.) (1986) *Co-operation under Anarchy*, Princeton, NJ: Princeton University Press.

Paz, Octavio (1974) 'A Tradition against Itself', in *The Children of Mire: The Charles Eliot Norton Lectures, 1971–1972*, trans. Rachel Phillips, Cambridge, MA: Harvard University Press.

Pizzorno, Alessandro (1986) 'Some Other Kinds of Otherness: a Critique of "Rational Choice" Theories', in *Development, Democracy and the Art of Trespassing: Essays in Honor of Albert O. Hirschman*, ed. Alejandro Foxley, Notre Dame, IN: Notre Dame University Press.

Ricoeur, Paul (1988a) 'What is a Text? Explanation and Understanding', in *Hermeneutics and the Human Sciences*, Cambridge: Cambridge University Press.

——(1988b) *Time and Narrative*, Vol. 1, trans. Kathleen McLaughlin and David Pellauer, Chicago: University of Chicago Press.

Ringmar, Erik (1996) *Identity, Interest and Action: a Cultural Explanation of Sweden's Intervention in the Thirty Years War*, Cambridge: Cambridge University Press.

Rousseau, Jean-Jacques (1967[1755]) 'Discours sur l'origine et les fondements de l'inégalité parmi les hommes', in *Oeuvres complètes*, Vol. II, Paris: Seuil.

Ruggie, John G. (1986) 'Continuity and Transformation in the World Polity: Toward a Neo-realist Synthesis', in *Neo-realism and Its Critics*, ed. Robert Keohane, New York: Columbia University Press.

Taylor, Michael (1989) 'Structure, Culture and Action in the Explanation of Social Change', *Politics & Society* 17(2): 115–62.

Wallerstein, Immanuel (1984a [1974]) *The Modern World-System*, Vol. 1, New York: Academic Press.

——(1984b) *The Politics of the World Economy, the States, the Movements and the Civilizations: Essays by Immanuel Wallerstein*, Cambridge: Cambridge University Press.

Walt, Stephen (1987) *The Origin of Alliances*, Ithaca, NY: Cornell University Press.

Waltz, Kenneth N. (1979) *Theory of International Politics*, New York: Random House Addison-Wesley.

Wittgenstein, Ludwig (1988[1958]) *Philosophical Investigations*, ed. G. E. M. Anscombe, Oxford: Blackwell.

11 Jean Bethke Elshtain: traversing the terrain between

Jenny Edkins and Véronique Pin-Fat

Jean Bethke Elshtain is Laura Spelman Rockefeller Professor of Social and Political Ethics at the University of Chicago. A graduate of Colorado State University in 1963, she took a Masters in history before studying politics. She received her PhD from Brandeis University in 1973 with a dissertation entitled 'Women and Politics: a Theoretical Analysis'. She joined the faculty of the University of Massachusetts/Amherst, becoming a full professor in 1981, and moved to Vanderbilt University in 1988. Her books include Public Man, Private Woman: Women in Social and Political Thought, *named as one of the top academic books of 1981–2, and* Women and War, *published in 1987. She is also the author of over a hundred essays in academic journals, as well as book reviews and contributions to social debate.*

Jean Bethke Elshtain maintains an open and explicit connection between her personal and intellectual concerns throughout her vast work on the history of political thought, political and international theory, social theory, moral philosophy and women's studies. Her journey involves a search

> for a voice through which to traverse the terrain between particular loves and loyalties and public duties. The stakes are terrifyingly high. . . . This struggle is not war . . . but it is a fight, a fight that pits the moral voice against the insistencies of statecraft.
>
> (1987: 42)

She has become a leading figure and a 'public intellectual', contributing widely to contemporary debate, and her two major books, *Public Man, Private Woman* (1981b) and *Women and War* (1987), have been published in second editions with a new afterword and epilogue respectively. In 1995 her book *Democracy on Trial* (1995a) was reviewed on the front page of the *New York Times Book Review* – widely regarded as a considerable mark of achievement. Her impact on the discourse of political and international theory has not been straightforward. Why is her work of particular significance? What were the reasons for including her as one of the theorists discussed in this book?

One too obvious answer would be to see her inclusion as the only woman 'master' to be indicative of her status as a feminist. We have two objections to simply labelling her work in this way. Our first objection is that her status as a feminist is itself controversial. 'Radical' feminists have labelled her as too 'conservative'; namely, pro-family and critical of sexual politics as anti-male and diversionary.[1] To enter the debate of whether Elshtain is or is not a feminist would miss the point and undermine our purpose in discussing the impact and significance of her work. Our second objection relates to the status of feminism within International Relations theory. To categorize Elshtain as simply a 'feminist' is to accept the assumption that the only voice women have within the discipline is one that speaks from the margins as feminist. As a discursive strategy, the simplification and marginalization of Elshtain's position allows the discipline to ignore the wider and more radical implications of her work.

What we propose to do in this chapter is to explore the more significant aspects of her enterprise, not holding her captive to privileged understandings of what 'International Relations' should be, but allowing her work to take part in producing and reconstructing the discipline. Indeed, this is one of her explicit aims. By her own design, Elshtain is difficult to pigeonhole into a category that singularly describes her project. Arguably, this would please her since much of her work is to show the overlaps and points of meeting between disciplines and categories that have been traditionally separated. We will try to show how Elshtain's engagement with the discipline of International Relations is, in the main, a deconstruction of the way in which the discipline has traditionally created categories for itself. For example, 'International Relations' theory has been set against political theory, ethics against politics and war against peace.

Elshtain's work engages with these three examples of the self-definition of International Relations, exploring the international/domestic, war/peace and ethics/politics oppositions. The form of her engagement can be seen as a major contribution to developing a new approach to analysis within the study of world politics. In common with others in contemporary social and political theory, she is seeking to use the analysis of ideology, discourse or language games[2] to explore, deconstruct and reveal the workings of 'language' in politics and social life. Within International Relations theory, it is widely accepted that such social constructivism deserves attention. What Elshtain is attempting, we will argue, is to develop approaches based on giving a certain autonomy and reality to discourse. We will argue strongly for extending these further.

Her first engagement is with International Relations' concern with the public/private debate. She came to these concerns arguably as a political theorist, but her work speaks directly to the debates within International Relations theory concerning the existence of a separate 'international' sphere. The public/private distinction is a pivotal point in the common sense of politics, in the language game of power. There are a series of parallel distinctions: between man and woman, between public and private, and between international and domestic. In each case the distinction allocates power and prestige to the first category – man, public, international –

over the second – woman, private, domestic. This is pivotal in the gender argument. It is also pivotal in International Relations, which R. B. J. Walker has described as the crucial site of the debate over the relation between the universal and the particular (Walker 1993; see also Chapter 12 in this book).

Her second engagement with International Relations is her work on the discourse of war. As we shall discuss below, this work arose from her interest in the tension between 'private loyalties and public duty'. It also reflects an interest in the role of collective violence *per se*, and here Elshtain's concerns parallel those of other International Relations theorists. Her contribution is one which undermines standard conceptions of the role of war in political life. In particular, of course, it tackles the resonance of myths of men's and women's roles in conflict. *Women and War* is now a central text within the discipline, and widely read outside it.

Finally, the contribution of Elshtain's work provides us with a way of thinking about the place and possibility of ethics in International Relations theory and world politics. The importance of Elshtain's refusal to separate morals and politics cannot be underestimated. We hope to show how the intersection of ethics and politics is constructed as a complex site of conceptions of philosophical anthropology (what it means to be human), language and epistemology pointing towards an ethic that 'bears witness' to different voices – an ethic illustrated by her own work as a public intellectual.

PERSONAL CONCERNS: TRAVERSING THE BETWEEN OF PUBLIC AND PRIVATE

In this section we use some of Elshtain's methods to examine her own thought – to trace her 'desires and fears' as they appear in her work. As she says:

> Theorists must be understood and critiqued as theorists, first and foremost, for political theory is an activity of a particular kind to particular ends.... On the other hand, to ignore the thinker in the thought, as some advocate, is to perpetuate another kind of distortion.
>
> (1981b: xv)

As already remarked, Elshtain, like many other feminist writers, is explicit about her personal concerns: the initial chapter of *Women and War*, for example, is an autobiographical account. One of the most intriguing questions which this opens about Elshtain, and one which provides an insight into the originality of her contribution, is how she reconciles her upbringing within a Christian tradition with her work as a political theorist – how these elements are articulated[3] in her discourse. In the preface to *Public Man, Private Woman*, she draws a parallel between the task of the political imagination and that of 'bearing witness' within the Christian tradition. For Elshtain:

the task of the political imagination in our time [is] that of attesting as honestly as possible to the truth of the human tradition, to its perils and possibilities

(1981b: xii)

whereas in the Christian tradition

one who bears witness voices the discontents of society's silenced, ignored, abused or invisible members. The witness proffers reasons for that suffering in order that the silenced may find a voice, cry out for justice, demand to be seen.

(1981b: xii)

The process of bearing witness seems to be a basic motivation that appears in her work. In the first chapter of *Women and War* she describes her first encounter with war as a child and 'the witness I have borne myself, since my teens, as student, mother, and political theorist' (1987: 14). We learn of her fascination with war, her encounter with Joan of Arc, and her concern to be 'an American' when her family and others suffered for their German background during the Second World War. Her interest in war is related to a fascination with courage, testing, martyrdom, sacrifice and the patriotic cause. It is closely bound up with issues of identity and morality. However, it is not solely concerned with violence: she records her admiration for Gandhi, a 'martyr and fighting man of peace' (1987: 28), for two new exemplars of 'moral courage and a politics of hope' (1987: 32) – Martin Luther King and Albert Camus – and later for Vaclav Havel.

In part it seems to have been her fascination with war that led her to engage in the study of politics. What she found when she embarked on this was a split between her personal concerns and her academic study. The study of politics through the works of 'realists'[4] was divorced from *any* private understandings: 'There was no place for . . . political dreaming in the scientific study of politics as who gets what where when and how' (1987: 31). For Elshtain 'a politics stripped of moral consideration made no sense' (1987: 32). She wanted to reunite the two: 'the dominant image of the public man and the shaky vision of the private woman'. 'I hoped . . . I might one day put together mothering and political thinking rather than have to put one aside in order to engage in the other' (1987: 33).

Elshtain's own war is, in the end, a war of words. The role of the theorist is to unite the personal and public spheres again. This is a disruptive activity:

The witness is a disturber of the peace just as political discourse, if critique is its aim, must disturbingly shatter the artificial calm of official know-nothingness.

(1981b: 6)

The theorist expresses 'private vexations' in the public sphere. This can become the source of public change. Elshtain sees herself as a 'conceptual rebel' (1981b: 6), pushing the boundaries of a language game in new directions. This is, she thinks, potentially a dangerous exercise. It can unhinge the 'web of intermeshed meanings' (1981b: 6) upon which any given society relies. A criticism of her work to which we shall return later is that she underestimates the power of existing orthodoxies and their resistance to change, and overemphasizes the voluntarism of political theorists such as herself. But now we move on to explore how Elshtain stalks 'the elusive trail of meaning' (1981b: xiv).

THEORETICAL APPROACH: THE ELUSIVE TRAIL OF MEANING

In this section we look at Elshtain's theoretical approach and examine how she makes use of a particular view of language. As she describes it, the job of the theorist is in part to differentiate the 'immutable givens' from elements which can be transformed:

> Faced with an intricate mosaic within which relatively immutable givens are...thoroughly fused with social forms that are, in principle, transformable, the theorist must attempt to tease apart the interstices of these 'givens' within their institutional loci, explore the tissue of social relationships, and reflect on the fabric of personal identity.
>
> (1981b: 150)

Elshtain's method of approach, or more precisely her account of it, shifts during the course of her work. First, the terms in which she describes her enterprise vary, as the range of generally accepted methods within the enterprise of social science changes. Second, her choice of method changes according to her aims in any particular work, or indeed at different points within the same piece. Initially, she tends to describe her methods as interpretivist, in the manner of much work in the social sciences in the 1980s. Later, she uses approaches which seem to draw loosely on the work of people such as Foucault, and describes what she is doing in terms of discursive practices and genealogy. By the 1990s, her work is being spoken of as 'postmodern', and she is using terminology appropriate to this (1993; Sylvester 1994: 55–7). Within any particular work, she combines what could be regarded as a fairly traditional critical method of approach to thinkers within the accepted canon with a much broader technique of looking at the wider discourses.

According to her own earlier account, Elshtain is engaged on a search for hidden meanings. For Elshtain, focusing attention on meaning requires insight into 'meaning *to* the subjects of their own actions and life-worlds as well as meaning *for* the analyst or observer, from a necessarily removed vantage point, of those self-understandings, those meanings-to' (1981b: xiv). We are, among other things, meaning-bearing and meaning-creating agents. As such, theorizing requires, in Elshtain's view, an understanding of the relationship between language with its latent grammar of bedrock notions and rules, and our self-understanding as subjects. Basic notions contained and perpetuated in language 'comprise a society's intersubjectively shared realm': a realm comprising ideas, symbols and concepts that constitute a way of life (1981b: 5). Indeed, a subject cut off 'from human society and language...could neither identify objects, nor establish categories, nor engage in social relations' (1981b: 325). There is, for Elshtain, a symbiotic relationship between language(s) and intersubjectively constructed self-understandings and ways of life. The learning of basic notions is not the learning of discrete propositions. Rather, Elshtain accepts Wittgenstein's view that when 'we begin to believe anything, what we believe is not a single proposition, it is a whole system of propositions' (Wittgenstein 1969: §141). What she calls 'ordinary language', then, serves as a resource for the theorist to understand which basic rules and notions shape our self-understandings thereby providing the possibility of critique.

For Elshtain the move towards 'ordinary language' serves a number of purposes. Most importantly, it allows for the *inclusion* of 'meaning *to* the subjects of their own actions and life-worlds'.[5] 'Ordinary language' expresses a richness of experience and practice much greater, more complex and diverse than the languages solely created around objective, rationalist understandings of politics and international politics. The abstract descriptions and analyses sometimes employed by theorists 'bleach out the texture of historic experience' (1992b: 329). Elshtain's focus on and use of 'ordinary language' is a significant attempt to bring subjects' multifarious experiences, particularly women's experiences, into the domain of political and international theorizing. It is also an approach that tries to reveal 'the constitutive role of symbols, myths, metaphors, and rhetorical strategies' which Elshtain claims are often ignored by social science (1987: xi).

It should be stressed that Elshtain is very resistant to any notion of theory which acts as a totalizing explanatory framework.[6] Rather, she insists that 'the reasons why women and men, public and private, personal and political, have been variously conceived are *many*' (1981b: xv; italics added). Significantly, Elshtain's commitment to a form of theorizing that incorporates multiplicities of explanations and understandings is deeply linked to her view of language. As mentioned above, the belief in one proposition is the belief in a whole system of propositions. Therefore, a viable framework of analysis must take into account the system, or context, in which certain beliefs appear. Conceptions of women, for example, differ significantly according to the context in which they appear historically, socially and politically (Dietz 1987). Indeed, much of *Public Man, Private Woman* is devoted to tracing these differences. Thus, the reasons why certain conceptions of women, war, etc., prevail at any one moment cannot be reduced to a single cause, whether it be misogyny or human nature. For much the same reasons, she states that 'there can be no *grand, formalizable, universal theory* of international politics' (1995b: 271). Vitally, this allows for 'complexity, irony and paradox' to enter into theorizing (1993: 100). The use of irony, in particular, allows Elshtain to challenge notions of a fixed 'reality' through redescription.[7] Peace, ironically, belongs to the discourse of war. In the early to mid-1980s her concern with language, meaning and understanding led Elshtain to place herself within the interpretative *verstehen* approach expounded in the social sciences most notably by Max Weber

(Weber 1968) and often associated with the philosophy of the later Wittgenstein in Anglo-American human science (Wittgenstein 1953 and 1958; Hollis and Smith 1990).

This understanding of language directs us towards showing *how* certain discourses, often implicitly rather than explicitly, privilege unreflectively assumed notions of men and women, war and peace, public and private, international and domestic. For example, the privileging of one conception of international politics often requires the silencing or marginalization of another.[8]

This is achieved through Elshtain's method of critique which seeks to 'unpack... latent meanings, nuances, and shades of interpretation others may have missed or ignored' (1981b: xiv). Looking at the ways in which language structures our self-understandings and shared, intersubjectively constructed ways of life opens up the possibility of revealing the structures which silence, exclude and marginalize some groups of people from politics and international politics. Critique as an interpretative activity allows her

> [to] put together, like the pieces of a puzzle, what it is a man celebrates and what he condemns, what he desires and what he fears, what he looks towards and what he looks away from, which voices he listens to and which voices he silences.
>
> (1981b: 19)

It can also reveal how certain language games perpetuate and reinforce particular conceptions of women, war, politics, etc. Elshtain's own stated 'explicit intent is to push the boundaries of a historically constituted language game towards alternatives she sees though others may not' (1981b: 6). One of Elshtain's strategies of critique is to show how some discourses that make claim to the desirability of peace, for example, still rely on a grammar that undermines such a project. Again, this strategy relies on a holistic understanding of discourse. The claim here is that it is not enough to reconstruct one proposition, or conception, in a language game or discourse if the grammar remains the same. In other words, if the grammar (the ordering of whole systems of propositions) of a particular discourse remains in place, the reconstructive impact of a single proposition is severely limited.

An example of this strategy, which draws upon irony and paradox, would be Elshtain's analysis of the problem with peace:

> The problem is this: peace is... an ontologically suspicious concept. Peace never appears without its violent *doppelgänger*, war, lurking in the shadows. Peace is inside, not outside a frame of war – most especially in the most powerful and absolute (utopian, if you will) expressions of its desirability and realisability. War is threatening disorder; peace is healing order. War is human bestiality ('male' and 'male' alone argue many feminists); peace is human benevolence ('female' and 'female' alone argue many feminists). War is discordance; peace is harmony. The antinomies

may be proliferated almost endlessly with peace on one side of the ontological ledger.

(1988: 442)

Just as war has constructed various gendered identities embodied in notions of civic virtue and nationhood, so too has peace.

There is, then, a complex relationship between language and politics (1985b). Basic notions contained and perpetuated in language inform our self-understandings and 'comprise a society's intersubjectively shared realm', a realm comprising ideas, symbols and concepts that constitute a way of life (1981b: 5). Politics and international politics are such realms and, indeed, one may go further and argue that their separation as academic disciplines (as two different ways of life) is also deeply related to language. Elshtain sometimes describes herself as a 'political theory interloper in the world of international relations' (1991b: 340). As such, she challenges the orthodox separation of both disciplines, by showing how they became severed and, more importantly, 'the damage this split has done to the political acumen and explanatory powers of each' (1995b: 263). Elshtain believes that students of international politics can learn much from the study of political theory, including classical writings that constitute the tradition. A poignant example is to look back to the ancient Greeks in order to understand, in part, how it is that politics and international politics became severed. The traditional story begins with the Greeks who 'created the *polis and the world-beyond-the-polis*' (1995b: 263).

The traditional realist construction of this story heralds the beginning of a number of bifurcations: 'them/us, citizen/foreigner and limits to the discourse of justice *internally* with precious few limits to the reign of force *externally*' (1995b: 264; emphases added). This bifurcation is reflected in contemporary 'realist' discourse as idealists versus realists, the idealists being those who want to extend the range of *polis*-type justice throughout the world and the realists who 'know' that no such possibility exists. These dichotomous splits 'secure... the domain of domestic politics (the reign of justice) as the world of, and for, political theorists, saving international politics for specialists in what "states" do given the "system" in which they must operate' (1995b: 265). Such is the usual story told that justifies and, indeed, perpetuates the separation of the two enterprises.

However, for Elshtain there are always other stories to tell. As pointed out above, one of Elshtain's methods of critique is to 'unpack... latent meanings, nuances, and shades of interpretation others may have missed or ignored' (1981b: xiv). Political texts, as much as any other areas of discourse, can be approached in this way. Texts are contested terrain (1991b: 345). The claim here is that realism is constructed by a *particular* reading of a 'canonized' set of texts – Thucydides, Machiavelli, Hobbes, Clausewitz, etc.[9] The realist reading of Thucydides' *The Peloponnesian War*, for example, takes it as an account of the behaviour of states given a particular distribution of power. However, it can also be read, as Elshtain does, as an account of 'the way in which speech and action constitute particular civic identities'. On this reading what is 'inside' 'spills over and determines, or helps importantly to constitute, the context within which political bodies vie' (1995b: 267). As such the tasks of both political theorists and practitioners of international politics 'flow freely back and forth'.

What the student of international politics has to learn from rereading the classical texts is an understanding of how the discipline, entrenched in realist orthodoxy, constituted a tradition which defined international politics as *sui generis*. If one accepts Elshtain's point that such texts do not uphold the separation of politics and international politics, then it follows that as students of IR we do, indeed, have much to learn from political theory. Elshtain's contribution to IR and, in part, the reason for her inclusion in this volume, is that as a 'political theory interloper' she demonstrates the richness and complexity of understanding that can be gained by reconstructing the links and overlap between politics and international politics.

It is the method we have discussed in this section that she uses in her first book, *Public Man, Private Woman*, and it is to this that we now turn to begin our account of her work. We will use the discussion to continue our own examination of Elshtain's view of the public/private and her interest in it as a subject of study.

PUBLIC MAN, PRIVATE WOMAN

In *Public Man, Private Woman* Elshtain looks through what she calls the 'public/private prism' to shed light on the meaning of the political sphere. She examines a variety of thinkers from the canon, giving an outline of their general thought and an analysis of how they conceive the public/private split. She then moves to a different level to look for the aim or hidden purpose of their work. At this point her examination relies on psychoanalysis rather than on social or political theory of ideology, discourse, or language.

Elshtain suggests (1981b: 142) that we should not just ask the question What is politics for? but also What is politics a defence against? This is an interesting insight arising from her psychoanalytical approach. Her most explicit use of Freud's work is in a discussion of the relation of inner and outer 'realities', where she elaborates on ideas of 'projection':

> Men fear the sexual and reproductive power of women. This is reflected in the lengths to which they have gone to protect themselves by projecting that fear outward into social forms, by imbedding the need to defend themselves against women in institutions and activities, including those called 'political,' historically inseparable from war-making.... On the other hand, operating on a level both conscious and unconscious, is the conviction that women are weak and soft. Men define themselves by that which is 'not-woman,' therefore not vulnerable.... Men have, over the years, created hard, external institutions of enormous power both as a match for the vision of the powerful Mother within and as a protection, a hedge against their own 'weak, female' self.

(1981b: 142–3)

Politics is posited as a defence against 'the tug of the private', which Elshtain links with the female, characterized as unclean, sexual, bodily, and hence omitted from political (or public) speech. Because of 'shame', bodily functions are seen as 'private'. Women are linked with bodily functions and therefore with the private realm.

Elshtain traces the public/private dichotomy to the Greeks with their basic differentiation between the *polis* and the *oikos* (or household). Her task is to examine how thinkers within western political theory have treated the relation between the two spheres from the Greeks onwards, using this and an exploration of changing views of the roles of men and women in society to shed light on the meaning and ideology of the 'political'. In her view, for example, Plato extends the public sphere to cover all areas of life in the interest of 'order' and rationalization so that the private sphere becomes a buttress of the state. Women are allowed a voice in the public sphere in certain conditions only: the public is defined as inhospitable to all traditional emotional ties of affection and sentiment. By contrast, Aristotle regards women as debarred by their very nature from the political.

She sees Christianity as 'an alternative to the "Greek way"' (1981b: 54). In a chapter significantly entitled 'The Christian challenge, politics' response', she launches a robust defence of the Christian revolution 'which dramatically, and for the better, transformed the prevailing images of male and female, public and private' (1981b: 56).[10] It upended the Greek vision, which praised the public and regarded the private with shame and contempt. Instead, as the antithesis of the Greek view

Christianity redeemed and sanctified both *each individual life* as well as *everyday life*, especially the lives of society's victims, and granted each a new-found dignity – a *dignitas* – previously reserved only to the high born, the rich or the powerful. At the same time, the private sphere, that 'lesser' realm of necessity in Greek thought, was lifted from Greek contempt and elevated to an importance and honour once reserved exclusively for the sphere of 'freedom', that public space within which male citizens debated important things and were heroes together. Making the last first in this case meant that the first became, if not exactly the last, then lower than the angels and no higher than the body of the faithful. Suddenly the public realm, politics, found itself (though not uniformly) condemned as the work of the devil (at worst) or an unfortunate, if not particularly ennobling, necessity (at best).

(1981b: 58)

This reversal is seen as impacting on women in two ways: first, as all individuals are of importance and have a role, women are for the first time included; second, the values of compassion, caring and responsibility associated with women and the private are accepted in themselves (1981b: 61–2).

Luther marks a break with this Catholic vision and the arrival of a totally new concept of the human subject. By introducing the idea of piety and freedom as internal to the subject – a matter of inner beliefs, not external practices – his work was important in producing the possibility of the separation of personal faith from public obedience. This is followed by Machiavelli's 'amoral consequentialism' which Elshtain sees as making 'all social ties and relations suffer as the split between public and private widens into a gap and then a chasm' (1981b: 99). The theme of public and private is followed through two later schools of thought: the liberals 'bristling with promises of progress and a future of unending human improvement and rationality' anc the patriarchalists 'heavy with notions threaded back through a tradition of centuries h ved among lordly fathers and fatherly lords under the omniscient eye of God the Father' (1981b: 147). We return to Elshtain's interesting discussion of patriarchal theory below.

With the arrival of liberalism, the dichotomy established by the Greeks is reproduced, and scientism, rationality and instrumentalism pervade the public sphere. For Locke, for example, it is rationalism that separates public minds from private desires. This enables him to break with the past, with tradition as represented, for example, by patriarchy, and also to break with the passions. It is knowledge and the rationalization of human life that are seen as the way forward. The senses and the passions are irrational, personal and arbitrary, whereas knowledge, arrived at through reason, is shared. For Elshtain, this is upside down: for her, it is passions and desires that are shared, knowledge that divides. We all desire and need much the same – love, recognition and intimacy, for example – whereas what we come to *know* depends on particular social situations (1981b: 120). She sees dangers in the liberal language of contract and exchange permeating from the public political discourse of liberalism to the private sphere. Ironically, it was later in this liberal language, the 'language of rights', that women were forced to press their claims. They were unable to express a particular voice. There was no language available to enable 'women's experience to "speak to" the public realm' (1981b: 127).[11] Instead, they were forced to comply with the underlying assumptions of liberal, utilitarian thought with its stress on rationalization and calculability. In this way liberalism, far from being a radical departure from patriarchy, simply 'replaces older patriarchal perspectives...with another distortion' (1981b: 126). Although patriarchy's emphasis on traditional (male) authority had apparently been removed, in practice it remained enshrined in the 'rationality' of liberalism.

In Rousseau, Elshtain finds someone whose view of the role and importance of the human passions she shares. For Rousseau it is the pre-civilization human being, with passions and emotions undistorted by social structures, that is to be admired. Society is the realm of relations of domination, the family, that of love and duty. For Rousseau, 'private spheres [exist] as enclaves of respect for persons, autonomy, decency, and caring despite their being surrounded by an impoverished world' (1981b: 166). Rousseau's work is central to Elshtain's thought, as is that of Hegel. The notion of clarity of discourse as an ideal 'helps one to listen for silences, for breakdowns in human discourse, and to go on to ask why these silences occur....Hegel remains vital in any move towards social transformation that pivots on the morally autonomous, speaking human subject' (1981b: 183).

Elshtain's aim in the first half of *Public Man, Private Woman* was to bring to bear questions 'of one attuned to feminist issues' (1981b: 202) on thinkers in the canon of western political thought. In the second half of the book the tables are turned and feminist discourse becomes the subject of the inquiry, and its nature and meaning are examined through the eyes of the political theorist. She defends her approach against the argument of some feminist theorists that this way of looking at their work is an inappropriate one and adopts the by now conventional division into radical, liberal, Marxist and psychoanalytical feminisms. As we have noted elsewhere, her key argument in this section is that feminist thought shares the grammar of the discourse it purports to challenge.

Shared grammars: patriarchy and feminism

Elshtain's discussion of the influence of patriarchalism is an example of this argument. In an intriguing section of *Public Man, Private Woman* (1981b: 125–31), she argues that both patriarchy and feminism, two opposing positions, share the same grammar. She takes Robert Filmer, with his emphasis on the 'natural' and traditional authority of the patriarch deriving from Creation and the garden of Eden, as an example of patriarchalism. Filmer argues for the absolute power of the patriarch, whether god, king, or father. He sees no public/private split, and indeed no political sphere at all, and no private sphere demarcated from politics. As Elshtain puts it, the family is politicized and the commonwealth is made familial, leaving no room for individuals with diverse roles.

According to Elshtain, feminist thinkers still operate within Filmer's categories. It is at this point that we get our clearest clue yet as to Elshtain's own view on the public/private divide: her concern is to maintain the distinction. It is worth quoting this passage at length, as it explains her position so well:

if a thinker incorporates the private realm of the family into a total politicised structure of explanation, and flattens out all distinctions between what is public and what is private, the following dilemma necessarily emerges: if all relationships and activities, including our most intimate ones, are political in their essence, if politics is everything and everywhere, then no genuine political action and purpose is possible, as we can never distinguish the political from anything else. This imperative is at work in the writings of feminist analysts who urge that 'the personal is political' totally and *simpliciter*. [There is] a free flow between public and private, politics and family. All spheres and activities are characterised in a *single, 'privatised' public language*. [Radical feminists] preserve, with the dictum that the personal is political and the political personal, one of the basic notions of patriarchal theory.

(1981b: 104)

This is a powerful argument, though perhaps not as surprising as Elshtain portrays it. Both feminists and patriarchalists such as Filmer recognize the importance of gender in the political, though with opposite conclusions. Both are operating within an ideology that 'sees' gender. It is inevitable that opposing views share a great deal – opposition is possible only if this is so. In contrast, for liberals and realists the political is gender-neutral. They regard the issue of gender as irrelevant – something that is not on the agenda, not part of the grammar of their language games.

However, for Elshtain it is remarkable that despite the fact that patriarchal ideas had been shown to be 'irrational', they persisted. She draws attention to the fact that 'public and private vocabularies' do not reflect political theory in a simple way. 'Language, meaning and knowledge are social activities' (1981b: 125): they alter slowly, and terms from patriarchalism, for example, continue to resonate, even though patriarchalism has lost its credibility as a theory of politics. Patriarchy remains embedded in social thought: in metaphors, analogies, symbols within what Elshtain calls 'ordinary language'. The relation between 'self-conscious political theory and everyday life' is indirect:

> Changes in theory seep slowly into the political consciousness and vocabulary of an age and when they do they do not transplant totally what is there; instead new concepts, terms, and the meanings they convey enter the dense and diverse stream of human language, shaped and moulded by history, tradition and homely truths.
>
> (1981b: 126)

The relation between philosophy and everyday vocabulary has been explored by Gramsci (1971). In his memorable phrase '[a]ll previous philosophy...has left stratified deposits in popular philosophy...[it] has deposited...an infinity of traces, without leaving an inventory' (Gramsci 1971: 324).

What Elshtain does not explore, here at least, is how and why this should be so. What resonances do these ideas from philosophical systems find? How do they link with other aspects of what Gramsci would call 'common sense'? Is their impact ideological? If the role of political thought is crucial only in so far as it is effective in everyday language, is this not an important area to explore? For Gramsci, for example:

> what must next be explained is how it happens that in all periods there co-exist many systems and currents of political thought, how these currents are born, how they are diffused and why in the process of diffusion they fracture along certain lines and in certain directions.
>
> (Gramsci 1971: 327)

In a tantalizing section of *Public Man, Private Woman* (1981b: 126–31), Elshtain does look briefly at this very question and relates the survival of patriarchal terms to resonances with family life. This shows some indication of why these ideas may have been seductive, but the larger question, interesting to feminists and others, is whose interests were served? How is a particular discursive practice such as the 'traditional family' produced and reproduced? Where does power come into it? Elshtain sees the family as 'the locus of our most intense, highly charged and important human relationships' (1981b: 131), but she does not engage with questions of power and interests. We pursue the question of the family in Elshtain's thought below.

WOMEN AND WAR

In *Women and War*, Elshtain continues her exploration of the meaning of the political in the West as it has historically come to be understood, this time through an examination of the discourse of war. In this respect her work shares something with that of theorists such as Foucault, who uses, for example, a study of the discourse of madness to explore understandings of subjectivity and processes of purification and exclusion in the West. She explores the diverse discourses and identifies elements shared, with the aim of disrupting the powerful and resonant categories which give the discourses much of their power.

By the time we get to *Women and War*, Elshtain is using a method of discursive analysis more explicitly. She remedies a major criticism that can be levelled at *Public Man, Private Woman* – the focus on the thought of a few individuals – by exploring a wide area of discourse: films, texts, images and practices. Her 'method' involves 'interweaving past tales and remembrances, offering narrative space to many voices, bringing forward abstractions and details, commentaries and quotes' (1987: 195). She uses what she calls 'prototypical' characters to group her account around particular discursive positions. Terms such as 'narration', 'voice', 'constitutive' and 'discourse' abound.

Elshtain's concern remains with the construction of an opposition between everyday domesticity and the political sphere, in this case the sphere of communal violence in war, and how this can throw light on conceptions of the political. In *Women and War* women are seen as part of a domesticity which is 'at odds with war's destructiveness...representing home and hearth and the humble verities of everyday life' (1987: xiii). She begins by introducing us to two 'prototypical' constructions – the 'Just Warrior' and the 'Beautiful Soul' – which represent the dominant symbols of male fighters and female non-combatants. She makes the important point that these images are shared by different political positions. Both those feminists who argue that the public world is in dire need of more input from women *and* those anti-feminists who wish to keep women secure in the private realm use these constructions of the Beautiful Soul. It is these durable images that she proceeds to explore. She stresses the reality of such symbolic identities – how they have real effects – while at the same time attempting to undermine their impact by showing them to be constructions.

In *Women and War* Elshtain launches a thorough-going challenge to the realist dominance of the discipline of International Relations as she was taught it. The aim of her challenge is to reunite politics and moral discourse. She chooses to engage in battle on the ground which realism, above all, takes as its own: the nature of war. She questions its seduction, and traces its link with politics through the discourse of the Greeks to the International Relations academics of the present day. In a largely familiar trail, covering some of the same theorists as *Public Man, Private Woman*, Elshtain succeeds in showing how elements of earlier political thought remain with us in our discourse of war today. She undermines the notion of war as an absolute part of reality, something we must deal with in a realist fashion if we are not to be caught off guard. She demonstrates the way the discourse of war and that of the nation-state (the 'warfare state' (1987: 73) in Hegel) are intertwined through the discursive practices surrounding conscription, uniforms and the defeat of local identities by the imposition of a standard language and the removal of origins. The triumph of the state ideal is produced through this discourse. She draws our attention to the way Hegel sees 'forging identity through conflict and combat with and against the Other' as necessary (1987: 275, n. 67). This is a powerful critique of the realist view which sees the state as produced through the coming together of individuals, Hobbesian-style, and conflict between states as being due to conflicts of national interest. For Elshtain, forging national interest is forging the nation:

> We still have trouble accounting for modern state worship. The mounds of bodies of combatants and non-combatants alike sacrificed to the conflicts of nation states compel us to take seriously Hegel's story of identity, personal and collective, through conflict.
>
> (1987: 75)

In her examination of the formation of the nation-state through the appropriation of local identities, we see again that concern that arose in her discussions of public/private: the domain of the local is a domain of direct and immediate social interaction. This is not possible on the level of the nation-state, because of its size. The distinction is familiar to social theorists through the ideas of *Gemeinschaft* (community) and *Gesellschaft* (society or association) (Tönnies 1955).

When she turns to International Relations itself, she admits that she 'intends to have a bit of fun with this topic' (1987: 87 n.) – and she does. For example:

> Realist thinkers and partisans exude the confidence of those whose point of view long ago won the war. Realism's hegemony means that alternatives are evaluated *from the standpoint of realism* – hence the bin labelled 'idealism' which, for the realist, is more or less synonymous with dangerous if well-intentioned innocence with the world's ways.
>
> (1987: 87–8)

She launches a stinging attack on what she calls a 'professionalised war discourse' and its dangers. With their abstract scenarios constructed under the mantle of scientific study the realists are 'living out a perilous delusion. . . . No children are ever born, and nobody ever dies, in this constructed world. There are states, and they are what is' (1987: 90–1). She sees International Relations discourse as one of the 'dubious sciences that present truth claims that mask the power plays embedded in the discourse and the practices it legitimates' (1987: 91). Her work is a major challenge to realism. She historicizes war, and argues that morals are not just domestic: she fights against the politicizing of the domestic because she sees the family as the remaining arena of moral discourse, the public realm having become dominated by instrumental reason. She contrasts the scientism of realism with the subtleties of understandings which acknowledge and conjure with the complexities of the world. The alternative narratives which she discusses include pacifism, the 'just war' doctrine and strands of liberalism in their genealogy.

Following her 'exemplary tales' of the role of 'armed civic virtue' in the production of American unity and nationalism during the American Civil War and the First World War, she turns to what she portrays as the discourse which attempts to 'disarm' civic virtue. This alternative discourse has its roots in Christianity. Christianity provided for the first time for a 'principled resistance to public power' (1987: 126) and the possibility of freedom from politics. In this discourse, martyrdom (self-sacrifice for one's religious beliefs) has parallels with and, Elshtain suggests, functions (discursively or psychoanalytically perhaps) in analogous ways to sacrifice in war (1987: 127). The Christian response to war has two streams: pacifism and the just war discourse. Both 'evaluate social life *from the standpoint of the suffering, potential or actual victims*' (1987: 123). In Christianity, an early pacifism shifted to 'conditional acceptance of collective violence' (1987: 127). Elshtain is heavily critical of both discourses, seeing pacifism as absolutist and just war discourse as abstract and unhelpful. The professionalization of just war discourse and its abstract view of ethical systems can be as dangerous as the bloodless discourse of nuclear war strategists. And the 'crusading impulse lurking in the interstices' of just war talk also causes problems. Just war discourse when fused with this impulse leads to 'justified' and destructive 'holy wars'. Just war theory, Elshtain argues, can be treated as a canonical alternative to realism. Its sacred texts are Augustine, Luther, theorists of natural law and international law, and, in contemporary times, just war theorists in International Relations such as Walzer.

Both wings of just war discourse – the theological, mainly Catholic wing and Walzer's just war theory – require and presume a universal, non-relativistic ethic, moral judgements, and the efficacy of moral appeals. This is a vision of civic virtue that demands 'deep reflection' and 'presupposes a "self"' (1987: 152). In other words 'a morally formed civic character is a precondition for just war thinking as a civic virtue' (1987: 152). It is through the just war discourse that Elshtain's two 'prototypical' characters emerge: the Just Warrior and his counterpart the Beautiful Soul. In the same way as feminists and anti-feminists, both the discourse of pacifism and that of war share the Beautiful Soul. Pacifist discourse invariably reinforces – and hence props up – war discourse. Protests condemning war are expressed in 'terms that mirror that which they oppose: peace to war...

harmony to disorder... and so on. Peace cannot exist without war [and both] help structure Western civil society's view of itself' (1987: 253). Both assume the same gendered identity.

Elshtain proceeds to deconstruct this traditional division between men's and women's roles in war. In chapters on 'Women: The Ferocious Few/The Non-combatant Many' and 'Men: The Militant Many/The Pacific Few', Elshtain weaves together 'tales from the past, fragments of remembered or forgotten words' with the aim of loosening the hold of the assumptions 'that locate women in an auxiliary and pacific role... leaving the war, fighting and dying to the men' (1987: 164). She ends with an account which draws parallels between the 'Good Soldier' and the 'Good Mother': both experience terror, but 'the shelling over, the baby born, the terror is quickly shoved into the dark background as if it had never happened' (1987: 222). She argues that the inability to speak of such things is related to a 'particular structure of experience discontinuous with the expectations of everyday life', the fact that 'both are boundary experiences that forever alter the identities' (1987: 223) of those they touch. They are experiences that cannot be spoken of, or understood, by others.

Finally, following an account of liberal pursuit of a 'rational, peaceful, international society' (1987: 227) brought about by the removal of misunderstandings, the increasing interdependence of commerce and burgeoning international institutions, Elshtain again argues that 'feminism reproduces many assumptions that structure the discourses of realism and just war' (1987: 237). She proposes a *way of being* in the world that brings private conscience to bear on public decisions, that draws on irony and that recognizes complexities – a 'chastened patriot' (1987: 252) who seeks alternatives to 'the traditional, and dangerous, narrative of war and peace' (1987: 258; 1990: 163–80).

THE PUBLIC INTELLECTUAL

Elshtain is one of the very few International Relations theorists who have become public figures. She speaks to an audience wider than that of professional academics and has taken part widely in public debate, writing on issues such as abortion and the Gulf War, for example. In her latest book, *Democracy on Trial*, she argues that democracy is about 'permanent contestation between conservation and change, between tradition and transformation' (1995a: 136). Her own work has been criticized, often vehemently, by opponents of conservatism *and* opponents of progressive change. She responds robustly and from a firm moral standpoint. In this section we explore her position on the relation between moral thinking and politics, and ask how she views ethics.

In the preface to *Public Man, Private Woman*, Elshtain says that '[t]he angle of vision from which I began my journey into public and private, past and present, owes much to Rousseau's insistence that the thinker who wishes to separate politics from morals will never understand either. By refusing to separate politics from morals I hope I have understood both'

(1981b: xii). In this section we will try to elucidate Elshtain's understanding of politics and morals.

Elshtain puts 'debates on what it is to be a human being at the forefront of moral vision' (1981b: 3). There are a number of reasons for an inquiry into conceptions of the subject, or philosophical anthropology. Perhaps the most important in Elshtain's work is the link she makes between our conceptions of what it is to be human and the way in which they shape differing principles of social justice and public policy (1981a: 206). She says:

> A theorist's commitments to a particular view of human nature may remain at the level of implicit and unstated presumptions. Because tacit commitments to a theory of human nature are required and presumed by the manner in which a theorist structures the relations between, and the purposes of, persons within his political discourse, they can be teased out of the structure of his argument and linked explicitly to his theory. In this way all those elements which cohere to form an explanatory theory are opened to public debate and critical scrutiny.
>
> (1981a: 206)

Explorations into conceptions of the subject therefore open up critical space. Indeed, as pointed out above, much of Elshtain's work concentrates on precisely this and looks at the way in which it impacts on our understandings of politics, war and citizenship.[12] What, then, is Elshtain's understanding of the subject?

We are already familiar with her view that human beings are meaning-bearing and meaning-creating agents and that therefore our linguistic practices inform our understandings not only of ourselves, but of others. '[O]ur use of language ... is the basis of ... humanness' (1981b: 327). This presents us with a number of features of what it is to be human on Elshtain's view. First, it suggests that no human being, whether male or female, has a privileged epistemological standpoint. Knowledge and understanding will always be partial. As such we should resist the temptation of universalizing, and thereby privileging, our own contextually bound understandings of humanity.[13]

The multifarious cultural, political and social contexts in which subjects learn a variety of discourses, shape manifold self-understandings and spheres of activity. For Elshtain subjects do not possess asocial, fundamental characteristics. Here she is in disagreement with, for example, the liberal notion of human beings as 'atomistic, rational agents whose existence and interests are ontologically prior to society' (Dietz 1987: 2). Nor does Elshtain accept that subjects can be reduced to a single identity marker. For example, she criticizes some advocates of a 'politics of difference' who, on her view, reduce identity to race, ethnicity, gender, or sexual preference (1994). She points out that '[a]lthough gender may be determinative to some ends and purposes, it also matters where one is American or Russian, an urban Catholic or a rural Baptist', for example (1986b: 18). Again, Elshtain refutes any kind of reductionist interpretation of what it is to be human.

Her approach is a plea to allow for complexity of understanding(s) that acknowledges differences and refuses to be seduced by totalizing, simplistic frameworks of analysis which mark a narration of closure.[14] This introduces an important ethical stance for Elshtain. Refusing notions of 'neutrality' and 'objectivity' not only opens up the space for difference and variation, but more importantly 'makes exigent... the need for critical perspicuity and strong argument that invites counter argument' (1993: 106). In other words, 'accounting' for differences (rather than just remarking them) requires understanding one's own society, culture and self-understandings better, leaving both one's own society and that of the other open to criticism. The view that other ways of life are 'incorrigible' (i.e. cannot be criticized ethically or otherwise) is, therefore, firmly rejected. There can be some truth to the matter but not an ultimate Truth grounded in some Archimedean point. This implies that some truths of the matter do not exclusively depend on the context of a *particular* form of life but rely on the context within which forms of life meet and overlap (1993: 106). Recognition of difference turns on some shared elements – the 'other' is

> in the world with me: she, too, is a citizen. We both bear responsibilities to, and for, our society. We both, I hope, operate from a stance of good will... and an energetic desire to forge at least provisional agreements on highly controversial issues and, if we cannot, to remain committed nonetheless to the centrality of dialogue and debate.
>
> (1994: 197)

So, far from believing that the importance of difference requires a placid acceptance that 'anything goes', for Elshtain it is a critical stance directed towards ourselves and others leading to 'robust... dialogue' (1993: 106). In short, an ethic that *engages* with difference rather than simply remarking upon it (1994: 201).

Another important aspect of resisting singular notions of the subject is Elshtain's concern with the family.[15] She introduces the family, in part, to argue against 'one-dimensional' views that consider human beings as images of the market (Marxists), or in need of liberation from organic communities and family (Enlightenment rationalists) (1982a: 442). There are two interrelated elements to Elshtain's stress on the family. The first supplements her view of the subject outlined above. A recognition of the importance of the family to human life 'acknowledge[s]... the legitimate human needs for intimacy and security embedded and answered, however imperfectly, within the traditional family' (1982a: 444). One cannot think of human subjects in purely instrumental or functional ways. For Elshtain, we are also passionate, empathic creatures who need love and trusting, intimate relationships with specific others – either parents or their permanent surrogates, siblings, etc. Here Elshtain draws upon Rousseau's insights. Most vitally, the internalization of *specific* others (e.g. parents) provides 'the template of conscience that makes possible adult empathy, the qualities of pity and compassion' (1981b: 329). In short, moral sensibility as the capacity for human identification is learnt via specific loving relationships within the intimacy of a family. Without the context of the family and the moral grounding that it provides, morality in the wider social network would not be possible. Elshtain agrees with Hauerwas that 'the family is morally crucial to our existence' (quoted in 1981b: 329). Given Elshtain's aim of a 'reconstructive ideal of the private sphere', the needs of children for basic, long-term ties with specific others must be affirmed (1981b: 331). This is the second element Elshtain draws from her understanding of the subject and its relation to social justice and public policy.

Second, just as the acknowledgement of difference offers the possibility of political and social critique, so too does the affirmation of 'family life as the locus of humanisation' (1981b: 333). As an ideal, the family, along with the moral sensibility which it embodies and nurtures, actually '*challenges* social structures and arrangements' (1981b: 333).[16] What this challenge involves reveals Elshtain's commitment to the relationship between politics and ethics. In discussing her personal concerns above, we remarked her discontent with the study of politics as divorced from any private understandings. Her epistemological insistence that subjects' self-understandings be included in our methods of theorizing is one way in which private understandings find a place in her work. The other way in which she brings private understandings into politics is by looking towards the family and the role of mothering. For Elshtain, mothering is 'the humanising imperative' (1981b: 333). Drawing upon the work of Carol Gilligan, Elshtain holds that women have a distinct moral language that emphasizes responsibility, care, concern for others and obligation (1981b: 336). Crucially, not only is moral responsibility grounded in familial life what is necessary for us to be 'fully human' but its affirmation in the ideal of an ethical polity is an important aspect of active citizenship (1981b: 351). Thus,

> Rather than an ideal of citizenship and civic virtue that features a citizenry grimly going about their collective duty, or an elite band of citizens in their 'public space' cut off from a world that includes most of the rest of us, within the ethical polity the active citizen would be one who had affirmed as part of what it meant to be fully human a devotion to public, moral responsibilities and ends.
>
> (1981b: 351)

The family and the ethic that is nurtured within it, then, *challenges* social structures and arrangements. On Elshtain's understanding of the subject, what makes us human has within it the potential to challenge our historically created and sustained notions of citizenship, which in turn challenges our received notions of public and private. Furthermore, the social structures and arrangements that have underprivileged the role of women 'at home' are confronted. She says:

> The pity is not that women reflect an ethic of social responsibility but that the public world has, for the most part, repudiated such an ethic. Rather than denying women the meaning their traditional world provided, even under conditions of male domination, feminists should move

to challenge a society that downgrades female-created and -sustained values.

(1982a: 447)

This enlarged and complex view of the subject has important reverberations on thinking about ethics and politics. Elshtain insists that political morality is not simply a question of detached, abstracted, rational calculation. Here she fundamentally rejects much of realism's separation of ethics and politics embodied by accepted interpretations of the realist canon.

For her, morality must include understandings of the subject, and that requires remembering what ends ethical thinking is for. It is not for an abstract notion of 'nation-state autonomy' or 'national interest' *contra* the 'experts', i.e. the realists – it is for subjects who have passions, emotional needs, commitments to others, family and community ties, multiple identities, etc. (1985a; 1992a; 1992b). An appreciation of this, therefore, requires an ethic that refuses to drive a wedge between politics and ethics, the domestic and the international, the rational and the emotional, and ultimately the public and the private. Elshtain's approach is more holistic, seeking to show us how, historically, we have come to accept such brutal divisions and how they impoverish our endeavours as political and international theorists alike. Although Elshtain would not argue for abolishing distinctions completely, believing it to lead to philosophical absurdity,[17] she presses upon us the moral responsibility to accept and act upon an ethic which takes complexity and difference as its starting-point rather than reductionist, abstract frameworks of calculating 'utility' or 'lesser evil' – an ethic that 'bears witness' to global voices.

CONCLUSIONS

Given the complexity of her theorizing, Elshtain attempts to articulate a number of positions. First, she combines a commitment to social constructivism with one to psychoanalysis; second, a desire to reconstruct the social with an appreciation of the intractability of discursive formations. We will now explore some of the tensions this produces.

The primary starting-point of Elshtain's journey is her belief that 'social forms... are, in principle, transformable' (1981b: 150). She is concerned to show that unreflectively assumed categories such as women/men, peace/war, public/private, etc., are not transsocial, timeless givens. The questioning of their status as eternal, unchanging 'natural' elements to reality opens up the possibility of social transformation. Rather than accepting the social ordering of reality as immutable, Elshtain presses upon us the idea that social reality is, in part, constructed and mediated via symbols, myths, metaphors, etc., through language. However, a tension arises because of Elshtain's construction of the subject.

Elshtain, drawing on psychoanalysis, sees the family as the crucial site for the construction of the subject as 'fully human'. The implication is that this is where the primary formation of subjectivity takes place. It is within the family that a person's inner core is formed in relationships with a small number of unchanging and 'significant' others who mediate through language cultural values, meanings and symbols. In this conception, identity is *formed* in contrast to the Enlightenment subject, which is seen as born with an inner self that unfolds while remaining essentially the same.

However, there are, arguably, two risks inherent in the use of psychoanalytical theory. One is the tendency to posit the psychoanalytical processes of subject formation as transhistorical. The other is that the processes through which the subject is constituted are seen as universal and therefore, transsocial.[18] For Elshtain, the family as the site of subject formation is both of these. She says: 'the family's status as a moral imperative derives from its universal, pan-cultural existence in all known past and present societies. We are not dealing with a tangential, episodic cultural form but a trans-historical one' (1981b: 327).

Psychoanalysis is a universal form of argument which rests uneasily with Elshtain's sensitivity towards the multifarious social and linguistic contexts in which we develop understandings of self. This presents a tension in her work between the universal and the particular. Furthermore, Elshtain also impresses upon us the need to understand the historicity of some constructions of identity. Much of *Public Man, Private Woman* and *Women and War* does precisely this. Yet her use of psychoanalysis with regard to the importance of family insists upon transhistoricity.

A theory of discourse that relies on this vision of the subject finds it difficult to envisage certain forms of social change and transformation. One cannot insist upon both the historic and social processes of our self-understandings as subjects *and* the transhistorical and transsocial understanding of the self according to psychoanalysis. With regard to the possibility of change this presents an ambiguity. If the subject is already primarily formed within the family this mitigates against Elshtain's aim of critique. Her method of critique is meant to disrupt our self-understandings and, therefore, reconstruct them. If our self-understandings are already primarily formed within the family, it makes it difficult to envisage how they can be reconstructed later through critique.

However, if we were to accept that in principle social reality *could* be reconstructed, then we would need to examine the conditions under which change, for Elshtain, could be produced. The first condition requires the wholesale change of discourses, because of the structure of their grammar. Elshtain stresses the complex interrelations between concepts within discourse. Peace, for example, is not a concept that stands alone like an island. Rather, within it are a number of other assumptions about, for example, women as Beautiful Souls. Furthermore, the discourses of war and peace are constitutive of each other. Such interrelationships are powerful in the sense that, for Elshtain, changing one aspect of the discourse does not change the way in which the whole is ordered.[19] The implication of this for social transformation is that unless the grammar (the whole system of propositions) changes, the possibility of social change is limited. Here, her stress is on the autonomy of discourse. This undermines her more voluntaristic view that critique can challenge discourse by making us feel uneasy about the fixity and certainty of our conceptions, disturbing what discourses lead us to take for granted.

The second condition is contained in her notion of robust dialogue. The assumption seems to be that others can meet and engage with their differences, unhindered by relations of domination or power. Indeed, this seems to be why she has been attracted by Habermas's idea of the ideal speech situation (1981b: 311; 1982b). The ultimate aim is to construct *transformative* meanings through understanding and agreement (Tully 1989). And here Elshtain's stress seems to be on the autonomy of the subject.

The two conditions for social change we have discussed demonstrate a tension in Elshtain's work between giving autonomy to discourse and giving autonomy to subjects. When autonomy is given to subjects, change is seen as relatively straightforward. Issues of power and domination are treated as surmountable. If autonomy is given to discourse, change becomes problematic. It is difficult to conceive of whole discourses changing, as Elshtain requires. Her requirement that grammars be entirely replaced for substantive change to occur is too stringent. We would argue that change may take place gradually, within the discourse, regardless of whether some elements of the hegemonic discourse that is being challenged are still accepted. Discourses are not homogenous, uniform and grounded but shifting, mobile and continually contested. Change can then be seen as taking place by the rearticulation and repositioning of fragments of one discourse with another (Staten 1985: 88; Hall 1982 and 1986). This transforms the hegemonic elements into something other: they are no longer playing their original role, as Elshtain assumes.

Elshtain's contribution to International Relations opens up rich and complex thinking about broader issues such as those discussed here, thereby engaging us as 'IR' thinkers with wider discourses in social and political theory. Her strong commitment to the raising of moral dilemmas within the civic and international arena and her openness to personal concerns and loyalties provide a refreshing and politically crucial foil to other approaches within the discipline.

NOTES

We wish to thank the Economic and Social Research Council (ESRC) for financial support and colleagues in the Department of International Politics at the University of Wales, Aberystwyth for useful comments and suggestions.

1 See Stacey (1983) for an example of this view.
2 These terms derive from different theoretical traditions. The term 'language games' (together with 'grammar' and 'forms of life') comes from Wittgenstein (see below). Broadly speaking 'ideology' and 'discourse' resonate with Marxist and linguistic approaches respectively. All three terms will be used in this chapter.
3 Using the term 'articulated' here in Laclau's sense (Laclau 1977; Laclau and Mouffe 1985) to describe how a particular discourse links disparate elements.
4 Although we use the term 'realist' we recognize that it is a multifarious tradition that embodies significant differences. We therefore do not take the view that 'realism' must refer to a set of common assumptions to be meaningful.

5 Although she describes her approach as uncovering meanings *to* the subject, she is also concerned to reveal unconscious meanings that lie at the very root of the constitution of the psyche itself. She uses psychoanalysis as the basis of this.

6 This is where she is sympathetic to some postmodern work in IR which warns against grand narratives. See Elshtain (1993).

7 See also Rorty (1988).

8 See Mervyn Frost (1986) and Chris Brown (1992) on the impact of realism as the marginalization of normative IR theory, for example.

9 See Elshtain (1985a) for a detailed discussion of how the founding texts of realism suppress and deny female images and female-linked imperatives. For additional alternative readings of Thucydides see Garst (1989) and for Machiavelli, see Walker (1993: 26–49).

10 She acknowledges that this puts her at odds with much feminist thought and in particular with the political theorist Hannah Arendt (1958), who sees Christianity, in contrast, as a destructive life philosophy, which 'cheapened politics by pronouncing the sacredness of all life' (1981b: 56).

11 Current feminist work pursues a similar line on women and the human rights discourse and makes a similar point. Elshtain herself returns to this in her critique of rights discourse in *Democracy on Trial* (1995a).

12 For other elaborations of this theme see Elshtain (1986a).

13 One upshot of this is Elshtain's insistence on theoretical modesty (1995b: 271).

14 For Elshtain the markers of a narration of closure are: '(1) a search for some "original position" from which history has proceeded, with its beginning determining its forward movement, (2) a clearly identified, universally construed object of critique (for example: patriarchal culture [or anarchy]) that gives the political agenda supported by the narrative its form and meaning, (3) an explicit or implied universal subject, (4) a de-historicising sweep that deflects from cultural particularities in a search for the "root" of all ways of life, (5) a defined end-point ... (6) finally, an Archimedean point that offers the ... analyst claims of epistemological privilege' (1986b: 17).

15 Elshtain's definition of the family is 'the widely accepted, popular understanding of the term as having its basis in marriage and kinship, involving links between particular persons that cannot be reduced to instrumental terms' (1982a: 447). Her view of the family has created a considerable amount of controversy. See, for example, the critical reaction of Stacey (1983).

16 This is where she is in disagreement with some feminists who believe the family to be the affirmation of oppressive social arrangements and structures; in other words, with those who see the family as part of the problem and not as the solution.

17 See her comments about the 'personal is political' (1981b: 217–18).

18 For a discussion of the debate around the relationship between language, ideology and 'the subject', which examines in particular whether approaches using psychoanalytical theory imply a universal subject, see Hall (1980).

19 An example of this point would be her analysis of liberal feminism's nineteenth-century suffragists (1981b: 228–39). She claims that they failed to bring about any significant structural change because they 'accepted, implicitly if not explicitly, the already dominant presumptions of a particular split between the public-political, and a private-apolitical realm of sentiment and feeling; they simply placed a different interpretation on the relative value of these features of the dominant ideology' (1981b: 230).

REFERENCES

Works by Jean Bethke Elshtain

Elshtain, J. B. (1981a) 'Kant, Politics, and Persons – The Implications of his Moral Philosophy', *Polity* 14(2): 205–21.

——(1981b) *Public Man, Private Woman: Women in Social and Political Thought*, Oxford: Martin Robertson; 2nd edn with afterword, Princeton, NJ: Princeton University Press, 1993.

——(1982a) 'Feminism, Family and Community', *Dissent* 29(4): 442–9.

——(1982b) 'Feminist Discourse and its Discontents – Language, Power, and Meaning', *Signs* 7(3): 603–21.

——(1982c) 'Women as Mirror and Other – toward a Theory of Women, War, and Feminism', *Humanities in Society* 5(1–2): 29–44.

——(1985a) 'Realism, Just War, and Feminism in a Nuclear Age', *Political Theory* 13(1): 39–57.

——(1985b) 'The Relationship between Political Language and Political Reality', *PS* 18(1): 20–6.

——(1986a) *Meditations on Modern Political Thought: Masculine/Feminine Themes from Luther to Arendt*, London: Praeger.

——(1986b) 'The New Feminist Scholarship', *Salmagundi – A Quarterly of the Humanities and Social Sciences* 70(1): 3–26.

——(1987) *Women and War*, New York: Basic Books; 2nd edn with a new epilogue, Chicago: University of Chicago Press, 1995.

——(1988) 'The Problem with Peace', *Millennium* 17(3): 441–9.

——(1989) 'Hannah Arendt's French Revolution', *Salmagundi – A Quarterly of the Humanities and Social Sciences* 84: 203–13.

——(1990) *Power Trips and Other Journeys: Essays in Feminism as Civic Discourse*, Madison, WI: University of Wisconsin Press.

——(1991a) 'Ethics in the Women's Movement', *Annals of the American Academy of Political and Social Science* 515 (May): 126–39.

——(1991b) 'Feminist Themes and International Relations', in J. Der Derian (ed.) *International Theory: Critical Investigations*, London: Macmillan.

——(1991c) 'Sovereignty, Identity, Sacrifice', *Millennium* 20(3): 395–406.

——(1992a) 'Just War as Politics: What the Gulf War Told Us about Contemporary American Life', in D. E. DeCosse and J. B. Elshtain (eds) *But Was It Just?: Reflections on the Morality of the Persian Gulf War*, New York: Doubleday.

——(1992b) 'Epilogue: Continuing Implications of the Just War Tradition', in J. B. Elshtain (ed.) *Just War Theory*, Oxford: Blackwell.

——(1993) 'Bringing It All back Home, Again', in J. N. Rosenau (ed.) *Global Voices: Dialogues in International Relations*, London: Westview Press.

——(1994) 'Multiculturalism and Political Responsibility', in W. L. Taitte (ed.) *Individualism and Social Responsibility*, Dallas: University of Texas at Dallas, pp. 187–212.

——(1995a) *Democracy on Trial*, New York: Basic Books.

——(1995b) 'International Politics and Political Theory', in K. Booth and S. Smith (eds) *International Relations Theory Today*, Oxford: Polity Press, pp. 263–78.

Works by other authors

Arendt, Hannah (1958) *The Human Condition*, Chicago: University of Chicago Press.

Bottomore, T. B. (1962) *Sociology: A Guide to Problems and Literature*, London: Unwin Unibooks.

Brown, C. (1992) *International Relations Theory: New Normative Approaches*, London: Harvester Wheatsheaf.

Dietz, M. (1987) 'Context is All – Feminism and Theories of Citizenship', *Daedalus* 116(4): 1–24.

Frost, M. (1986) *Towards a Normative Theory of International Relations*, Cambridge: Cambridge University Press.

Garst, D. (1989) 'Thucydides and Neo-realism', *International Studies Quarterly* 33(1): 3–28.

Gramsci, Antonio (1971) *Selections from Prison Notebooks*, London: Lawrence & Wishart.

Hall, Stuart (1980) 'Recent Developments in Theories of Language and Ideology: a Critical Note', in Stuart Hall, Dorothy Hobson, Andrew Lowe and Paul Willis (eds) *Culture, Media, Language: Working Papers in Cultural Studies, 1972–79*, London: Routledge, pp. 157–62.

——(1982) 'The Rediscovery of "Ideology": Return of the Repressed in Media Studies', in Michael Gurevitch, Tony Bennett, James Curran and Janet Woollacott (eds) *Culture, Society and the Media*, London: Methuen, pp. 56–90.

Hall, Stuart (1986) 'Variants of Liberalism', in James Donald and Stuart Hall (eds) *Politics and Ideology*, Milton Keynes Bucks: Open University Press, pp. 34–69.

Hollis, M. and Smith, S. (1990) *Explaining and Understanding International Relations*, Oxford: Clarendon Press.

Laclau, Ernesto (1977) *Politics and Ideology*, London: Verso.

——and Mouffe, Chantal (1985) *Hegemony and Socialist Strategy*, London: Verso.

Rorty, Richard (1988) *Contingency, Irony and Solidarity*, Cambridge: Cambridge University Press.

Stacey, J. (1983) 'The New Conservative Feminism', *Feminist Studies* 9(3): 559–83.

Staten, Henry (1985) *Wittgenstein and Derrida*, Oxford: Blackwell.

Sylvester, C. (1994) *Feminist Theory and International Relations in a Postmodern Era*, Cambridge: Cambridge University Press.

Tönnies, Ferdinand (1955) *Community and Association [Gemeinschaft und Gesellschaft]*, trans. and supplemented C. P. Loomis, London: Routledge & Kegan Paul; reprinted 1974.

Tully, James (1989) 'Wittgenstein and Political Philosophy – Understanding Practices of Critical Reflection', *Political Theory* 17(2): 172–204.

Walker, R. B. J. (1993) *Inside/Outside: International Relations as Political Theory*, Cambridge: Cambridge University Press.

Weber, Max (1968 [1922]) *Economy and Society: an Outline of Interpretative Sociology*, ed. G. Roth and C. Wittich, New York: Bedminster Press.

Wittgenstein, L. (1953) *Philosophical Investigations*, Oxford: Blackwell.

——(1958) *Zettel*, Oxford: Blackwell.

——(1969) *On Certainty*, Oxford: Blackwell.

12 R. B. J. Walker and International Relations: deconstructing a discipline

Lene Hansen

R. B. J. Walker was born in 1947 in Reading, England. He received his BA degree from the University of Wales, Swansea in 1968, and both his MA and PhD degrees (1977) from Queen's University, Ontario, Canada. Since 1981 he has been at the University of Victoria, British Columbia, from 1986 as an associate professor with tenure and from 1992 as a professor. He has also been a visiting fellow at the Australian National University and at Princeton University, and since 1989 the editor of Alternatives. *Walker's main fields are early-modern political thought, contemporary social and political thought, international political theory, and theories of discourse, ideology and culture.*

The last half of the 1980s witnessed a growth in a new kind of literature in International Relations theory, a literature variously labelled as 'post-modernist', 'deconstructivist', or 'poststructuralist', and associated especially with authors like Richard Ashley, James Der Derian, Michael Shapiro and R. B. J. Walker (see also Chapter 13 on Der Derian in this book). Even though 'the establishment' might have harboured considerable suspicion towards these attacks on the traditional conceptions of International Relations (IR), poststructuralism is now often seen as an alternative establishment of its own.[1]

This is not to say that poststructuralism 'won' against the prevailing wisdom of neo-realism or neo-liberalism (see Ashley, Cox, Keohane and Waltz in Keohane 1986), but it attracted attention, and succeeded in opening up considerable room in debates about International Relations. Evidence of acceptance is, for instance, the publishing of a special issue of *International Studies Quarterly* in 1990, edited by Ashley and Walker (Walker and Ashley 1990a), and the ISA presidential address by Robert Keohane in 1988. The address has become famous for Keohane's distinction between a 'rationalist' and a 'reflectivist' approach to the study of international institutions; poststructuralism was framed as a variety of reflectivism, although not as the only perspective in that category (Keohane 1989, see also Chapter 4 on Keohane in this book; other non-poststructuralist reflectivists dealt with in this book are Nicholas G. Onuf and Alexander Wendt).

What is poststructural International Relations theory? It would probably be an overestimation of its coherence to call it *a* theory or school, but many common themes can be identified. Poststructural IR has been inspired by

French philosophy, especially Michel Foucault and Jacques Derrida, and particularly by the method of *deconstruction*. Deconstruction involves two steps, or a 'double gesture', in the words of Derrida. First, it attempts to show how every text depends on a dichotomy, which is always – even if implicitly – a hierarchy. The hierarchy is then reversed. Second, the dichotomy is undermined without transcending it in a Hegelian *Aufhebung*. 'Deconstruction is a form of "criticism" that aims at thinking through, reasoning out, in contrast to rejecting. Deconstruction is done not to get rid of a theory but in order to re-inscribe it in a new way' (Wæver 1989: 63–4).

In several articles Walker and Ashley have presented a deconstruction of the discipline IR. They have in short shown how IR is part of an extensive dichotomization of international relations–domestic politics. The picture of international relations as a domain of violence, repetition and anarchy depends on a picture of the national political community as characterized by order, progress and peaceful resolution of conflicts. The international and the national are oppositions, and thus dependent on each other. The use of the strategy of deconstruction means that poststructural IR has, to a large extent, been written up against realism, especially neo-realism, and 'the discipline as such' (not always distinguishing between the two).[2] Walker has, together with Ashley, given the most full-fledged presentation of a poststructural analysis on the meta-theoretical level, which is one reason for including a chapter on Walker in a book about 'Figures of International Thought'.

A second reason is Walker's analysis of the principle of state sovereignty. The idea of state sovereignty has long been contested. From outside the realist camp, liberals have often claimed that the state is losing its sovereignty due to interdependence and transactions above and below the state level, and Marxists have seen the forces of capital taking over on an international scale. In the post-Cold War era, however, the questioning of state sovereignty seems to have gained force beyond the liberal and the Marxist approaches. The integration process in western Europe has been characterized as 'the first truly postmodern international political form' (Ruggie 1993: 140), and the metaphor of neo-medievalism, hinting at a situation in which there is no single sovereign authority, has appeared in order to describe the political organization of western Europe (Wæver 1991). Internationally organized humanitarian interventions in Iraq to protect the Kurds, and in Somalia and Bosnia to protect the civilian population, have also been interpreted as a blow to the idea of state sovereignty. At the moment it is difficult to say whether West European integration and/ or humanitarian intervention will be lasting phenomena; both have certainly become increasingly questioned. But there are other challenges to state sovereignty, which are likely to be more permanent, connected with the internationalization of the world economy and the development of information technology.

A third reason for reading Walker is that he has a strong theoretical orientation, as well as a political concern for the way entities like 'community', 'state' and 'international system' structure our opportunities. The emphasis in Walker's works on theory as well as political practice offers a fascinating account of how one can have a theoretically informed analysis of politics and, the other way round, how a political stand relates to a certain theoretical interest. Walker's awareness of politics is also worth noting because poststructuralism is often construed by its critics to have no moral foundation, and therefore no possibility of setting moral or political standards. In the case of Walker this is certainly wrong.

This chapter has three sections: one showing how the principle of state sovereignty can be taken as the focus of Walker's theoretical project (here the main source will be Walker's book *Inside/Outside: International Relations as Political Theory* [hereafter *Inside/Outside*], 1993); one on how the discipline of IR is being constructed, and the way Walker locates himself with regard to it; and one on the more political side of Walker with a special focus on Walker's treatment of the concept of security. In the conclusion some questions are raised regarding where Walker's account of sovereignty and IR takes us.

Walker himself would probably disagree with this division of his works into theory and politics:

> my suspicions are always raised when it is suggested that the alternatives before us can be reduced to only two, even if they are said to be complementary...I would not frame it as a duality of practice and critique but simply of unity and diversity.
>
> (Walker, Guzzini, and Patomäki 1995: 428)

A justification for making the division despite Walker's likely disagreement, is that even if his theory and political standpoint are inextricably linked, the emphasis given to one of the aspects is more profound in some texts than in others, and it changes to some extent over time as well. A highly theoretical article from 1980 is followed by a period of more political articles and the book *One World, Many Worlds: Struggles for a Just World Peace* from 1988. From then on the focus shifted to more theoretical articles, collected in *Inside/Outside*, whose preface, however, promises a subsequent volume, which should be more focused on questions of contemporary world politics and political identity. So perhaps if Walker's authorship can be portrayed like a pendulum shifting between theory and politics, the pendulum in the future might be about to make a swing to politics.

Three sources of social influence on Walker have been, first, the World Order Model Project (among its members, Saul Mendlovitz and Richard Falk), which Walker participated in from about 1980; second, the group of scholars introducing poststructuralism or critical theory into IR from the mid-1980s (amongst others Ashley, Shapiro and Der Derian; see Chapter 13 on Der Derian in this volume; see p. 316), and, finally, the importance of place: Walker has lived and taught in Victoria, British Columbia, what he calls a 'place on the edge of many worlds', for more than a decade (Walker 1993a: xi). The two former sources, which will be dealt with in more detail in sections 2 and 3, can be seen to have had an impact on the political and the theoretical aspects of Walker's writings respectively. Intellectually

Walker started out as a student of political theory and philosophy, which then became the basis for his critique of the discipline of International Relations.

THE THEORETICAL PROJECT: DECONSTRUCTING THE PRINCIPLE OF STATE SOVEREIGNTY

The principle of state sovereignty has a special status both in International Relations theory and in political theory as well as in Walker's writings. His overall concern is to bring out the basic, ontological principles constituting International Relations as a theoretical and political realm. The principle of state sovereignty is seen as the key to understanding international relations as a specific modern resolution of questions of political identity, and in *Inside/Outside*, the principle of state sovereignty is explicitly the focus of analysis and the starting-point for discussion of issues such as ethics and democracy; the more recent concrete articles on security and gender treat the principle of state sovereignty as the central constitutive principle of modern political life (Walker 1990b and 1992a). The emphasis on state sovereignty has become more explicit over the years; in the three chapters in *Culture, Ideology and World Order* (Walker 1984a), for instance, the principle of state sovereignty is mentioned less than in the later works.

The principle of state sovereignty 'expresses the claim by states to exercise legitimate power within strictly delimited territorial boundaries' (Walker 1993a: 165). In this short description of state sovereignty, the territorial dimension is underlined: there are two political spaces in the modern world of sovereign states; one within states and another between states. These two spaces produce different conceptions of time: inside states there is justice, law, freedom and social progress made possible by the sovereign authority governing the state. Time then becomes one of progress and history in the form of cumulative positive achievements. In the international space time is framed differently: here the idea of progress is replaced by repetition or the deferment of the progressive project into eternity. The self-interested states and/or the lack of overarching authority lead to a (potential) state of conflict, power politics and war.

The different accounts of life inside states and relations between them depend upon each other: they are constituted as oppositions. Descriptions of international relations are produced as the negation of politics which takes place inside states. In fact, the concept of international 'relations' implies the lack of politics between states: politics needs an arena with order, freedom and authority, which is missing in the international realm. Ashley makes the same argument using the concept 'political community' about the inside, and he argues that the lack of community is what allegedly characterizes the outside (Ashley 1987). The world is divided into international relations and domestic politics, or International Relations theory and political theory as the equivalent academic disciplines have been named.

Walker's account of how state sovereignty constitutes a division between inside the state and outside the state is based on a deconstruction of IR texts presenting the 'classical portrait' of IR, which is close to realism. Realism emphasizes the fundamentally different character of inside and outside and criticizes idealism for its belief that the political community inside states can be extended to encompass the outside as well. Walker, however, does not view idealism as any better than realism and its insistence on the absolute impossibility of transgressing the border between the national and the international. Realism and idealism have essentially the same conception of political life; they both argue that political community exists within states, and that if there is to be a community among states, it has to take the same form as life inside states. The two approaches then disagree whether or not it is possible to reach political community internationally. What both realism and idealism fail to do is to break the dichotomous conception of inside and outside, and to present an account of the international which is *different* from, but not a negation of, the national.[3]

The status of dichotomies

In order to move beyond the principle of state sovereignty, Walker argues, we need to understand why it has been such a powerful idea. Its power derives from the fact that it is an extremely elegant answer to the fundamental question of political identity: it tells us 'who we are' and 'where we are' by drawing a number of borders between inside and outside, between 'us' and 'the others'. In *Inside/Outside* Walker wants to make the reader aware of how the classical IR texts, and thereby the conventional understanding of international relations, repeat binary oppositions over and over again. At the end of the book he notices that since his own text keeps returning to the key themes identity–difference, inside–outside and time–space, he ends up parodying the familiar IR opposition. This, however, shows what a powerful and elegant answer state sovereignty has been (Walker 1993a: 160).

The principle of the sovereign state makes a distinction between inside and outside possible. However, the distinction is not only one between inside and outside, it is also one between identity and difference, self/other, inclusion/exclusion, unity/diversity and universality/particularity. There is in other words a long list of binary oppositions which follows and constitutes the distinction between inside the state and outside the state, so that identity, self, inclusion, unity and universality are to be found on the inside, and the other halves of the pairs on the outside. The oppositions are connected to one another in a long chain of equivalence (Laclau and Mouffe 1985). Inside is bound to universality, unity, presence, identity and self whereas outside is bound to particularity, diversity, absence, difference and other. 'Inside' is not just a neutral spatial concept which tells us what the state is, 'inside' has in addition all the connotations stemming from the other elements or concepts in the chain: 'identity' and 'self' give 'inside', which demarcates 'outside' ('difference' and 'other') as threatening. In principle it is possible that the chain can be broken and the opposition rearticulated in a new relationship, a potential positive movement, but it is not yet determined whether or not there are some fundamental, universal dichotomies which will 'always' be here. The question of the status of binary oppositions is important when assessing the possibility of changing the principle of state sovereignty: the more universal the questions, the more difficult to change.

Three dichotomies stand out as the central ones in Walker's writings even if they have a different expression over time. They are: inside–outside, self–other and particularity–universality although the exact wording may differ slightly: inside–outside may be called internal–external, self–other called us–them or identity–difference, and universality–particularity phrased as unity–diversity or general–particular. Two dichotomies are more visible than the others in *Inside/Outside*: inside–outside and universality–particularity.

The inside–outside distinction has a prominent place, as shown by the title *Inside/Outside*. It is not explicitly stated if the distinction has relevance for the modern period only or if it is of a more lasting kind, but certain factors indicate that inside–outside is primarily a feature of the modern period and the sovereign state. When Walker describes the political organization of the Middle Ages, no distinction is drawn between what is inside and what is outside, and in one of his latest articles the main focus is on universality–particularity and self–other (Walker, Guzzini and Patomäki 1995). In short, Walker apparently invests a kind of 'geographic' character in inside–outside, one that is connected to territoriality.

Universality–particularity by contrast is obviously present in other periods than the modern one: 'the principle of state sovereignty expresses an historically specific articulation of the relationship between universality and particularity in space and time' (Walker 1993a: 176). The principle of the sovereign state is only one solution to the question of universality–particularity, the Middle Ages was characterized by a different resolution: the principle of hierarchical subordination, that is, a hierarchical incorporation of particularity into an overarching universalism.

> The advantage of principles of hierarchical subordination, of course, is that they provide a plausible account of the relationship between particular individuals and the world in which they participate. They permit an understanding of the world as a continuum from low to high, from the many to the few, from God's creatures to God, from the temporal to the eternal.
>
> (Walker 1990b: 10)

In Walker's earlier articles universality–particularity was the central opposition (1984a–d). Therefore it would be reasonable to expect universality–particularity to be rearticulated in a post-sovereign period: we could not just sidestep the question of universality–particularity in a new political order, and the solution usually argued by the radical writers in favour of some kind of global community is *not* a viable alternative, since that proposal claims that universalism without particularism is possible.

The third dichotomy central in Walker's writings is self–other, or identity–difference. The question of political identity will pose itself also in an alternative political order – and it is not an easy question to answer (Walker 1993a: 160). The principle of state sovereignty has been so resistant precisely because it has offered such a powerful answer to this problem. Although the self–other dichotomy has a relevance beyond the modern period, there is nevertheless some room within it: there is a distinction between seeing the other as a stranger or as an enemy, and a distinction between seeing the other as the negation of oneself, and thus threatening, or as something/somebody different from oneself (Walker 1988a: 166). Walker wishes that we could move beyond the binary oppositions, something which is extremely difficult to do. The direction to work in, despite the difficulties, is probably to try to move the binary oppositions from being negations coming in pairs, to being relations of difference between more than two entities.

If one is to insert a critical comment on Walker's reading of the dichotomous constitution of state sovereignty one could argue that he sometimes ties the oppositions so closely together that it is very difficult to distinguish the oppositions of a universal kind from the non-universal ones. It is especially difficult to determine which ones are tied into the big, modern, sovereignty knot, and which ones are independent of this (Is us–them typical of the sovereign state? Do nation and state have a necessary correlation? Will there always be inside/outside just differently constituted without the sovereign state?). It thus becomes harder to suggest a rearticulation in a post-sovereign situation. The difficulty of opening up the principle of state sovereignty within a Walkerian framework also has to do with his choice of historical perspective. Despite a short description of the political organization in the Middle Ages, and numerous references to Machiavelli and Hobbes, Walker writes an account of the modern period when the clear division between national and international was institutionalized. As a consequence the different forms of sovereignty in other historical periods are not dealt with at length. In earlier periods the dichotomies were articulated in ways different from the modern ones, and some entered the stage at a later point than others (Bartelson 1995). The advantage of a longer historical perspective, or a genealogy of sovereignty, is that the modern political organizing principle of state sovereignty becomes easier to rearticulate; it does not appear to be the only and unshakeable solution.

The end of state sovereignty?

Having deconstructed the principle of state sovereignty and exposed the dichotomous thinking behind the principle one might assume that it would be fairly easy to come up with alternatives to the sovereign state. This is not the case. Walker says that sovereignty is losing its capability as a convincing answer, but there is no alternative at hand because the spatio-temporal resolution, which is the core dimension of the principle of state sovereignty, is almost as firmly rooted in the radical critique of state sovereignty as it is in the conservative defence of the principle (Walker 1993a: 17). The radical critique much too often argues in favour of world government and a global universalism following then in the footsteps of idealism, simply replacing the international with a global state.

When Walker argues that the principle of state sovereignty is losing its credibility, because of the processes of temporal acceleration, for instance, he makes clear that

> What is at stake in the interpretation of contemporary transformations is not the eternal presence or imminent absence of states. It is the degree to which the modernist resolution of space–time relations expressed by the principle of state sovereignty offers a plausible account of contemporary political practices, including the practices of states.
>
> (Walker 1993a: 14)

The question of state sovereignty or not is not a question one can simply test empirically by looking at, for instance, multinational firms, the flow of capital and goods across borders, interdependence or international regimes. The disappearance or preservation of the sovereign state is not a methodological or epistemological question, but first of all an ontological one. The distinction between methodology/epistemology and ontology is emphasized by Walker, who argues that we cannot meaningfully deal with the questions of 'how to study the state' as long as we have not paid enough attention to the question 'what is a state'.

An analysis of the disappearance of state sovereignty necessitates a look at the categories of time and space. The principle of state sovereignty is first of all a *spatial* resolution to the relation between universality and particularity (Walker 1993a: 11, 78, 177), and the spatial resolution makes a temporal resolution possible as well. Inside is an account of time as linear progress, which makes it possible for the universalist aspirations to come true. Outside the state time is one of repetition and clashes between particular wills, and there is 'a *deferment* of domestic community's essential project for a universal and timeless rational unity' (Ashley 1987: 414). The spatial and the temporal together give what Walker calls 'the spatio-temporal resolution' of questions of political community or political identity.

The modern conception of state sovereignty has *space* as the most important dimension. Walker's basic argument showing that state sovereignty is under attack affirms the increasing significance of *temporality*: 'the experience of temporality, of speed, velocity and acceleration' (Walker 1993a: 5). A change in time conception is what first of all makes the principle of state sovereignty tremble, and the question is then whether a changing time conception leads to a changed conception of space as well. Walker says that it does, because 'the hope that temporality may be tamed within the territorial spaces of sovereign states alone is visibly evaporating' (Walker 1993a: 155).

In Walker's description of the changing time conception, acceleration and speed have caused the distinction between time inside the state and outside the state to collapse – and thereby opened up a rearticulation of the whole inside–outside construction – but Walker does not expand on what this means in more detail. In 'the sovereign state spatio-temporal resolution' time is one of progress on the inside and one of recurrence or deferment on the outside. When Walker writes that temporality can no longer be tamed within the territorial spaces of sovereign states, he is not suggesting a 'time of linear progress' being copied 'outside' as well. The time conception must be changing much more radically than that, it must change both inside and outside, probably breaking the rigid division constituted by the principle of state sovereignty. If Walker indicates in what direction the time conception might change, all he says about the space conception is that the territorial spaces of the sovereign state will be challenged by the change in temporality. It is obvious that space and territory are connected in the sovereign state resolution. It is less obvious, however, if Walker thinks that space and territory are always tied together in a 'spatio-temporal solution', if a change in the category of either time or space will eventually lead to a change in the other category, or if it is possible, for instance, to rethink the modern conception of space which is so closely tied to the idea of territory; in other words to conceive of a de-territorialized conception of space.

EXPLAINING THE DISCIPLINE

In one of his first publications, *Political Theory and the Transformation of World Politics* (1980), Walker addressed the question 'What constitutes IR as a discipline?' Discussing the great debates, the first one between the utopians and the realists, the second one between the scientists (behaviouralists) and the traditionalists, he linked the division between inside (the national) and outside (the international) to the participants in the debates. The traditionalists insisted on keeping the division between domestic and international politics, as the realists did in the first debate, whereas the behavioralists, as the utopians had argued before them, spoke in favour of making no division between the domestic and the international realm: both realms could be analysed by domestic liberal theory (Walker 1980: 33). So even if Walker's analysis of the principle of state sovereignty is not fully developed in 1980, the essence of the analysis laid out in *Inside/Outside* is already visible.

In *Inside/Outside* IR is characterized as a discursive space or horizon which both defines and limits the legitimate responses to a problem (Walker 1993a: 43). The idea of a specific discipline called IR then is both a consequence of the division between inside and outside, and at the same time reinforces and upholds that division. IR is in short both cause and effect, and depends on the principle of state sovereignty. This also leads Walker to see IR theories not as explanations but as something to be explained: 'Theories of international relations are more interesting as aspects of contemporary world politics that need to be explained than as explanations of contemporary world politics' (Walker 1993a: 6). Since Walker is quite sceptical towards the possibilities for solving the problems of humanity inside the prevailing division between inside and outside, domestic politics and international relations, he is also highly critical towards IR as a discipline.

Political realism is usually presented as *the* tradition of IR, a tradition which includes Machiavelli, Hobbes and Thucydides. Walker argues, however, that the notion of a coherent body of literature stretching from classical Greece until present time is a myth rather than a fact. The tradition functions – besides offering clues about 'the historically constituted nature of both the theory and practice of international relations' – as a legitimating device. It sets the limits for what is considered acceptable IR theory (Walker 1993a: 29).

Realism and idealism can be seen as mutually constituting IR, because each depends on the other in making its arguments. Idealism is what realism warns about because it does not recognize the difference between inside and outside. Realism's account of the outside points at what idealism wants to eradicate by extending universality and reason to the outside. At a deeper level, however, Walker challenges the common assumption that realism has the status as *the* tradition of IR: 'the dominant theoretical tradition in international relations theory is not political realism but idealism, for it is the possibility of universality proclaimed by idealism that makes possible the discursive linkage between difference, relativism, anarchy, tragedy and violence' (Walker 1993a: 74–5). Realism idealizes a certain conception of politics inside the state and then uses this ideal definition of 'the political' to declare everything which fails to meet its standards non-political. Despite realism's declared distance to idealism, it is in other words a form of idealism itself.

Still the notion of realism as *a* and *the* tradition has been so dominant that even poststructuralists have spent most of their time arguing against realism, not idealism. Another reason for concern is the fact that neo-realism has attracted 'a profound and in some places even hegemonic influence on the analysis of contemporary world politics' (Walker 1993a: 104), something poststructuralism is highly critical of given neo-realism's inclination to dichotomize inside–outside, lack ontological reflection, neglect history, and rely solely on structural explanations (for examples of other critical assessments of the epistemological, ontological and methodological choices of neo-realist Figures of International Thought see Chapter 3 on Waltz and Chapter 5 on Gilpin in this book).

On the basis of Walker's deconstruction of the principle of state sovereignty, the consequences of a shift to a postmodern period and a rearticulation of the spatio-temporal resolution must be that IR as a discipline becomes undermined. The rationale for its existence is shattered with the breakdown of the sharp inside–outside division. A new theory and better explanations are needed, Walker says, but it has to be a theory taking fundamental theoretical and philosophical issues into consideration, it has to be a political theory.

'Political theory' tends, however, to have a double meaning in Walker's writings. On the one hand, political theory is the theory about domestic politics; it does not describe the different kind of politics which goes on between states – which is in fact not politics but *relations*. Political theory and international relations theory divide the world between them. Political theory deals with state affairs while IR theory is concerned with affairs between states. On the other hand, 'political theory' is used as a concept on a higher level, encompassing theory about life both in the state and between the states. A general assumption is that political theory analyses the fundamental questions about how to define and organize political communities, and that international relations theory is in need of the kind of reflection which political theory provides, especially on ontological questions. Walker seems to locate himself as 'doing political theory' in this second meaning of the term, and it is this kind of political theory IR needs.

The discipline has, however, sadly enough, lived a happy life in isolation, and

> To the philosophically inclined outsider, the discipline often presents itself as a realm of barbarians, besmirched with the woad of neo-Machiavellian policy analysis, or as entirely given up to the altars of crude empiricism. The wider implications of various modes of knowledge appear to be foreign to it; normative and ethical issues seem to be raised in only a peripheral manner; and it tends to demonstrate a crippling stagnation of the imaginative and critical resources required to confront an increasingly complex world.
>
> (Walker 1980: 49)

Taking a stand on philosophical issues is not, however, Walker emphasizes, the same as simply extending the domestic to the international system, as done by idealists and most radical critics.

Walker holds himself at a distance from IR as a discipline: seeing IR as depending on the principle of state sovereignty which needs to be re-articulated, and as something to be explained rather than an explanation. Although he is more positive towards poststructural IR than towards the rationalist perspective, he does not want to inscribe himself in the gallery of IR theorists:

> I have sought to interrogate the assumptions, reifications and textual strategies of international relations theory not because I hope to contribute to a better explanatory theory, *at least not one about international relations*, but in order to problematise theoretical and practical horizons that continue to be taken for granted.
>
> (Walker 1993a: 159; emphasis added)

But even if Walker distances himself from IR he is to a large extent treated as an IR theorist: editing a special issue of *International Studies Quarterly* on 'Speaking the Language of Exile: Dissidence in International Studies' together with Ashley, having *Inside/Outside* published in the book series 'Cambridge Studies in International Relations', being an important figure in university courses on poststructural IR and, now, a theorist assessed in a book on IR figures of thought. Clearly Walker is writing on the border of IR, but being on the border is still not being outside. As laid down in the beginning of this chapter poststructuralism is not a critique from the outside, it works with the concepts already given, but shows how binary oppositions construct meaning – it does not throw the concepts away. Walker has, at least to some extent, to be inside IR to work his way through it in order to move towards the discipline or approach he calls 'world politics' which does not share IR's ontological privileging of the state as *the* political community or *the* actor on the international arena.

AVOIDING TRADITIONAL RADICALISM

Walker's theoretical analysis of state sovereignty and IR has been coupled with a concern for alternative ways of structuring political life, for a change from international relations to world politics, or, expressed in a richer rhetoric, 'struggles for a just world peace', as the subtitle of his book *One World, Many Worlds* (1988) goes. The political commitment is formulated in accordance with the theoretical principles, an alternative to the existing state-based system has to avoid taking the form of universalism: a global state is not a real alternative, it is only a repetition. Unfortunately the radical critique has not always kept its distance from the idea of a global community, not seeing that claims to universality involve principles of exclusion (Walker 1988a: 102). Therefore, Walker has warned about what could be called 'traditional radicalism', which 'has perhaps been overdetermined in its embrace of universalism as the obvious solution to the fragmentation and particularisms of the modern states system' (Walker 1994b: 237).

Critical social movements: the quest for alternatives

The World Order Models Project (WOMP) was an, or even the, example of trying to find a third path between the state system in its present form and a global universalism, Walker argues. WOMP had started in the mid-1960s, and Walker joined from the beginning of the 1980s. In 1988 *One World, Many Worlds* was published as part of Walker's task as rapporteur of the Committee for a Just World Peace, associated with WOMP. Writing on behalf of the committee Walker had to bring together a number of different positions, and the book might therefore present a less definitive statement of Walker's own position than, for instance, *Inside/Outside*. He has noted, however, 'that these claims [about social movements] still stand up fairly well' (Walker, Guzzini and Patomäki 1995: 407).

A 'double exclusion' prevents an understanding of the importance of social movements for world politics, argues Walker; first, social movements are located on the inside, international relations constitute per definition a realm which does not lend itself to political or social processes; second, social movements are perceived as social, that is, as removed from the sphere of politics. 'To make contact, social movements and world politics require some kind of mediating agent. First, the social has to find some expression within the explicitly political practices of the state. Then the state has to mediate with other states' (Walker 1994a: 670). Despite these attempts to allocate social movements to a non-political space inside the state, they nevertheless challenge the conventional account of political identity provided by the sovereign state and the 'constitutive modern articulation of spatiotemporal relations, both as the way things are and as the way things must and should be' (Walker 1994a: 673).

One World, Many Worlds wanted to 'examine our contemporary trajectories from the point of view of critical social movements' (Walker 1988a: 2). Despite passages where the use of 'inside–outside' and 'particularity–universality' shows that Walker is definitely at play, the major part of the book reads like a *Festschrift* for critical social movements. These movements have the capacity of getting beyond the dilemma of choosing between the state (system) or a global community:

> They present a sober assessment of specific challenges that have to be met. They offer some idea of how the grand visions and aspirations of the past need to be reworked and of how to respond more coherently to the conditions of the present. Critical social movements raise crucial questions about the nature of political life in a world of rapid change, both in terms of where political action ought to take place and in what form it ought to occur.
>
> (Walker 1988a: 31)

Walker distinguishes between critical social movements and conventional or reactionary ones. Critical movements have a consciousness of the way means and ends are dialectically related, they are not (only) concerned with state power as are conventional movements, are not closed, inward, or backward-looking, nor annihilating histories as do the reactionary movements. Finally they explicitly reject violence (Walker 1988a: 78–9, 91). One has to wait until p. 111 in the celebration of critical social movements before the temptations for these movements are listed. They might, first, romanticize the will of the people (a trap that *One World, Many Worlds* itself is not wholly successful in avoiding); second, mistake the interests of particular groups for universal interests; and third, ignore the conflicts of interest that can arise between social movements.

One World, Many Worlds tends to oppose people to states, and critical social movements to elites. Critical social movements can potentially re-articulate political identity in ways which question the identity provided by state sovereignty, and they appear therefore as a or sometimes even *the* positive actor. But making a dichotomization of state versus people goes against Walker's own theoretical account of the principle of state sovereignty which argues that the major reason why the principle of state sovereignty is so powerful is because it answers the question of political identity, it 'tells us who we are', 'tells the people who they are', and it ties state, people and political identity together. When 'the state' is restricted to a purely institutional, governmental definition, and people and political identity are located outside the state, it becomes difficult to understand why the sovereign state has been such a long-lasting principle, as it is no longer answering the decisive question of political identity.

The account of critical movements can be criticized on several points. First, despite the attempt to define them as 'distinguishable in part by their capacity to recognize and act creatively upon connections among structures, processes, and peoples that do not enter significantly into the calculations of conventional political actors or that are denied by movements of a more reactionary character' (Walker 1988a: 3), there is in the end no way to decide whether a movement is critical or not, except by Walker's declaration of its status. Equally, who 'the people' are seems to have little status outside Walker's own choice. It is also difficult to see why critical movements should have a higher knowledge about the world, and their own action in it, than, for instance, nationalistic movements? And why is it necessary that a critical movement should have a knowledge about the whole, know 'that to challenge a specific dam is to challenge the economic, political, social, and cultural assumptions of a whole society' (Walker 1988a: 67)? In Walker's defence it should be added, however, that he recently warned against 'a romantic strategy of "listening to the movements"'; he seems in other words to be moving towards a more critical perspective on the critical movements (Walker 1994a: 674).

From national to world security

One of the substantial issues *One World, Many Worlds* deals with is security, an issue Walker has discussed in other writings as well. His security analysis is linked to a deconstruction of the principle of state sovereignty (Walker 1993a). IR has traditionally positioned the national and the international as each other's mutually constituting oppositions. But, poststructuralists argue, the border between the domestic and the international is constituted through practice, it is porous and moveable, not given and impermeable as realism claims (Ashley 1987). Security politics is located right on the border between inside and outside and is therefore involved in keeping the distinction between politics inside the state and mere relations on the outside (Walker 1990a: 11–12). Because the principle of state sovereignty has made the state the only thinkable political community the security of states has gained a monopoly on what security can be, and who it can be for, and attempts to challenge the conventional understanding of security as 'state security' are therefore met by great resistance (Walker 1990a: 6). The problem is that the principle of state sovereignty is such a powerful answer to the questions of political identity, it 'tells us who we are'. An alternative conception of security has to come up with an alternative to the sovereign state as *the* political community, and a global community based on universalism must be excluded as an alternative since it is false to believe that universalism without particularism is possible (Walker 1990a: 10).

Walker's attempt to formulate an alternative concept of security without falling into the trap of universalism is called 'world security'. 'World security' relates itself to the security of states because of the continuing dominance of the principle of state sovereignty, but it also attempts to question the definition of security as state security, challenge the prevalent account of political identity building on state sovereignty and reflect on forms of insecurity such as ethnic conflict, terrorism, human rights, mal-development, famine, and environmental degradation which 'have now become integral themes in contemporary debates about security' and now 'all stimulate far-reaching debates about who we are' (Walker 1990b: 23–4). The concept of security is in other words broadened to include a variety of threats normally excluded from a strategic studies analysis.

Strategic studies and realists have often argued against traditional radic-alism that its broadening of the concept of security emptied the concept by making everything potentially bad a security problem, and that the concept thereby became analytically useless. The same question could be posed to Walker: does the concept of 'world security' identify an infinite list of security problems or are there limits as to what qualifies as a security problem? The answer is that Walker's writings are slightly ambiguous on this point. He states on the one hand that the forms of insecurity listed above are voiced in contemporary debates, that social movements in parti-cular have rearticulated the meaning of security (1988a: 117–28). The redefinition of security is then based on observations of people's and move-ments' struggles to redefine security, and Walker's analysis has therefore an empirical foundation, at the same time as it involves political and ontolo-gical choices. In this reading of Walker's call for 'world security' it is possible to argue that there is a limit on what threats are, a limit depending on what find their way into the contemporary debates and the agendas of new social movements, a limit located in the security discourses found at a given point in time.

The writings on 'world security' can, however, be read as leaning in a different direction as well. There seems to be a tendency to characterize these threats as threats to world security even if they were not articulated as such or if they are no longer on the security agenda of, for instance, the so-called new social movements. The 'many contemporary forms of insecurity' are then identified as real threats independently of the security discourses, and one (here the researcher) can distinguish between real and unreal or perceived threats. The limit on what qualifies as security problems is in this case depen-dent on the sovereign researcher, not on the actors or the security discourses.

One of the main analytical institutions in IR, the 'levels of analysis' schema, is vigorously criticized by Walker:

> As an expression of the inbred common sense of modern political dis-course, this schema hides most of its ontological significance under a chaste appeal for analytical clarity and explanatory parsimony. Yet categories that manage to frame an account of the horizontal territori-alities of the modern state as a hierarchical arrangement of inclusions and exclusions are neither modest nor simply analytical in their accom-plishments, and parsimony often comes at the high cost of conceptual oversimplification and ideological conceit.
>
> (Walker 1994b: 671)

The scheme's three levels identify three possible referent objects for security: individual security, state security (usually labelled national security), and global security (the world is seen as composed by individuals) or international security (the world is made up by states). Realism privileges the state, whereas traditional radicalism privileges the individual/the global. Although Walker is keen not to establish any grand alternative to the 'levels of analysis' scheme, some categories are still important in his conceptualization of security; they are: people, social movements, state, and elites. In a critique of conventional thinking about national security Walker writes: 'Security is then often casually identified with the interests of elites and governments (the "national interest") rather than with society as a whole. More significant, security is identified with the citizens of states and not with people in general' (Walker 1988a: 119). And 'The primary subject of security is people – not states, nor elites, nor the affluent, nor the stronger' (Walker 1988a: 124–8).

The category of 'people' plays a central role, in particular in the book *One World, Many Worlds* (1988), but it is not explicitly discussed. One can, however, read out three different meanings: first, Walker speaks about *the* people, the entire humanity, or the global. When people and global are set equal to each other it seems as if Walker's conception comes rather close to the universalism he himself warns against. Second, Walker writes about peoples. What distinguishes peoples from nations, nations which are organized in nation-states (at least as the guiding ideal)? *If* peoples take the form of nations then it is not necessarily the case that we are led back to the sovereign state and national security, but nations are also potentially conflicting particulars, as are states, which means that the realist model might in the end not be fully avoided. Third, people can mean individuals. Walker never explicitly uses the term 'individual security', although he argues that central to an understanding of security is the question of 'who it is who is to be made secure' (Walker 1993a: 140). These three different interpretations of 'people/peoples' all give different conceptualizations of security; they all point at different referent objects for security: the global, the nation/state (or a similar undefined collective entity), and the individual (the global and the individual conceptions are interrelated in the sense that *the* people consists of all individuals on earth).

CONCLUSION

An analysis of state sovereignty is not a novel idea introduced by Walker. Portraying the domestic and the international as two distinct realms was not invented by Walker either, as Martin Wight's famous 'Why Is There No International Theory?' testifies (Wight 1966). New, however, is Walker's clear account of how the national and the international are *conditional on* one another, and how all 'universal' questions about who and where we are, are systematically embedded in and answered by the principle of state sovereignty.

One might well ask now where Walker's exposition takes us with regard to the question of sovereignty in the mid-1990s. What questions are raised, what issues come into focus?

First, are we rapidly approaching 'the end of sovereignty'? No, says Walker. Even if we agree with Walker that state sovereignty is being seriously contested, we are still at the most at the beginning of a post-sovereign period – a period with traces of sovereignty where some forces are pulling towards dissolving state sovereignty and other forces are upholding it. If Walker, on the one hand, predicts the weakening of state sovereignty, he, on the other hand, also emphasizes over and over again that the principle has been so persistent because it is such a convincing answer to the question of political identity. State sovereignty will not give in without a fight.

Second, what about democracy, which we have become used to associating or even identifying with the sovereign state? Walker shows that democracy, as we know it, depends on the sovereign state, and a revision of the definition of democracy therefore has to involve a rearticulation of state sovereignty as well. And the other way round: breaking up state sovereignty as the political organizing principle must lead to a reconsideration of democracy. An example of a coinciding struggle between reformulating sovereignty and democracy is the debate over the 'democratic deficit' of the European Union (EU) (Wæver and Kelstrup 1993). How is democratic accountability to be established inside a union consisting of strong nation-states unwilling to simply lift the nation-states to the level of (western) Europe? Should the national affiliation between voters and elected be dissolved with regard to the European Parliament? These are only a few of the many questions raised in the debate about democracy in the EU.

Third, does the question of sovereignty have particular importance in specific geographic areas? Western Europe has already been suggested as a site where integration has gone beyond traditional interstate co-operation, but Walker, somewhat surprisingly, at least to a western European, does not seriously discuss the European case. Surely Europe is not the world, but given that the principle of state sovereignty was born in Europe, and given Walker's assumption that sovereignty is being threatened, it is still surprising that Walker does not devote some energy to western Europe, or 'the first truly postmodern international political form', as John Gerard Ruggie calls it (Ruggie 1993).

Parts of what has been termed as the Third World could also experience an increasing challenging of the concept of state sovereignty. In the era of decolonialization all states were equally sovereign. This era is now being replaced by an era of post-decolonialization where all states are not automatically equally sovereign. Weak states with low degrees of internal cohesion might be considered less sovereign and therefore possible 'recipients' of foreign intervention in various forms (Buzan 1994).

Fourth, is there anything missing in Walker's account of state sovereignty? The most important omission seems to be his neglect of nation as a concept distinct from the state even if the stories of the state and the nation have to include one another. The concept of nation is mentioned in passing in *Inside/Outside*, and Walker seems to make some kind of distinction between national and critical movements in *One World, Many Worlds*, but a thorough account does not appear.

A fifth point, where does this leave IR as a discipline? Since IR depends on state sovereignty, the disappearance of sovereign states would be a life-threatening attack on IR. But if it is difficult to move away from state sovereignty it is equally difficult to bury IR. One could also add the persistence of the discipline's institutions: journals, conferences and positions, and even a critic like Walker uses these institutions, because they are the only way to engage in the debate. And 'IR' is never a static substance – the content of the journals, the workshops, the conferences and the professors appointed will always change.

Finally, is a political attitude involved? Definitely! Walker sees sovereignty as a question of *political* identity. One has to set political standards and come up with alternatives to the present organization of political life, which is sharply divided between inside and outside. It is definitely false to claim – as so many critics do – that poststructuralism is apolitical.

NOTES

1 I would like to thank those who have contributed to this chapter and this book, especially Ole Wæver, Barry Buzan, Richard Little, R. B. J. Walker, Jaap de Wilde and Michael C. Williams.
2 The deconstruction of the discipline IR has been followed by more concrete deconstructions, or readings, of IR-related phenomena, such as deterrence, spy novels, or the front page of a treaty (Tunander 1989; Der Derian 1992; Dillon and Everard 1992). See also Chapter 13 on Der Derian in this book.
3 The search for an account of the international which is different from the negation of the national has been central for Hedley Bull. Walker argues that Bull does not really succeed in this because he locates himself between realism and idealism, and therefore 'his analysis seems to be drawn in both directions at once' (Walker 1993a: 69). On the English School see Chapter 2 on Vincent in this book.

REFERENCES

Works by R. B. J. Walker

Walker, R. B. J. (1979) 'Holistic Knowledge and the Politics of Fragmentation', in William Higgison (ed.) *An Image of the Whole: Knowledge and Curriculum in an Age of Fragmentation*, Kingston, Ontario: Queen's University Faculty of Education.
——(1980) *Political Theory and the Transformation of World Politics*, World Order Studies Program, Occasional Paper no. 8, Princeton, NJ: Princeton University, Center of International Studies.
——(ed.) (1984a) *Culture, Ideology and World Order*, Boulder, CO: Westview Press.
——(1984b) 'East Wind, West Wind: Civilizations, Hegemonies, and World Order', in his *Culture, Ideology and World Order*, Boulder, CO: Westview Press, pp. 2–22.
——(1984c) 'World Politics and Western Reason: Universalism, Pluralism, Hegemony', in his *Culture, Ideology and World Order*, Boulder, CO: Westview Press, pp. 182–216; also (1981) in *Alternatives* 7(2): 195–227.
——(1984d) 'Contemporary Militarism and the Discourse of Dissent', in his *Culture, Ideology and World Order*, Boulder, CO: Westview Press, pp. 302–22; also (1983) in *Alternatives* 9(3): 303–22.

Walker, R. B. J. (1986) 'Politics, Ideology and Everyday Life', in W. Magnusson and R. B. J. Walker *et al.* (eds) *After Bennett: The New Politics of British Columbia*, Vancouver: New Star Books, pp. 325–35.

——(1987) 'Culture, Discourse, Insecurity', *Current Research on Peace and Violence* 10(1): 50–64; also (1986) in *Alternatives* 11(4): 455–74.

——(1988a) *One World, Many Worlds: Struggles for a Just World Peace*, Boulder, CO: Lynne Rienner and London: Zed Books.

——(1988b) 'Genealogy, Geopolitics and Political Community: Richard K. Ashley and the Critical Social Theory of International Politics', *Alternatives* 13(1): 84–8.

——(1990a) 'The Concept of Culture in the Theory of International Relations', in John Chay (ed.) *Culture and International Relations*, New York: Praeger, pp. 3–17.

——(1990b) 'Security, Sovereignty, and the Challenge of World Politics', *Alternatives* 15(1): 3–27.

——(1990c) 'Sovereignty, Identity, Community: Reflections on the Horizons of Contemporary Political Practice', in R. B. J. Walker and S. H. Mendlovitz, *Contending Sovereignties: Redefining Political Community*, Boulder, CO and London: Lynne Rienner, pp. 159–85.

——(1991) 'State Sovereignty and the Articulation of Political Space/Time', *Millennium: Journal of International Studies* 20(3): 445–61.

——(1992a) 'Gender and Critique in the Theory of International Relations', in V. Spike Peterson (ed.) *Gendered States*, Boulder, CO: Lynne Rienner, pp. 179–202.

——(1992b) 'Pedagogies on the Edge: World Politics without "International Relations Theory"', in Lev Gonick and Edward Weisband (eds) *Teaching World Politics: Contending Pedagogies in World Politics*, Boulder, CO: Westview Press.

——(1993a) *Inside/Outside: International Relations as Political Theory*, Cambridge: Cambridge University Press. Includes the following earlier works (some in updated versions):

• 'The Prince and the Pauper: Tradition, Modernity and Practice in the Theory of International Relations', from *International/Intertextual Relations: Postmodern Readings of World Politics*, ed. James Der Derian and Michael Shapiro, Lexington, MA: Lexington Books, 1989, pp. 25–48.

• 'Ethics, Modernity and the Theory of International Relations', from *International Relations: Global and Australian Perspectives on an Evolving Discipline*, ed. Richard Higgott and Jim L. Richardson, Canberra: Australian National University, Department of International Relations, 1992, pp. 128–62.

• 'History and Structure in the Theory of International Relations', from *Millennium: Journal of International Studies* 18(2) (1989): 163–83.

• 'Realism, Change and International Political Theory', from *International Studies Quarterly* 31(1) (1987): 65–86.

• 'The Territorial State and the Theme of Gulliver', from *International Journal* 39(3) (1984): 529–52.

• 'On the Spatiotemporal Conditions of Democratic Practice', from *Alternatives* 16(2) (1991): 243–62.

• *State Sovereignty, Global Civilization and the Rearticulation of Political Space*, World Order Studies Program, Occasional Paper no. 18, Princeton, NJ: Princeton University Center of International Studies, 1988.

——(1993b) 'Violence, Modernity, Silence: from Max Weber to International Relations', in David Campbell and Michael Dillon (eds) *The Political Subject of Violence*, Manchester: Manchester University Press, pp. 137–60.

——(1993c) 'World Order and the Reconstitution of Political Life', in R. Falk, R. Johansen and S. Kim (eds) *The Constitutional Foundations of World Peace*, Albany, NY: State University of New York Press.

——(1994a) 'Social Movements/World Politics', *Millennium: Journal of International Studies* 23(3): 237–46, University of New York Press.

——(1994b) 'On the Possibility of World Order Discourse', *Alternatives* 19(2): 237–46.

——(1994c) 'On Pedagogical Responsibility: a Response to Roy Jones', *Review of International Studies* 20(3): 313–22.

——(1994d) 'Norms in a Teacup; Surveying the New Normative Approaches', review article, *Mershon International Studies Review* 38, supplement 2: 265–70.

——(1994e) 'The More Things Change: Sovereignty, Quebec and the New World', *Constitutional Forum* 23(3): 237–46.

——(1995a) 'International Relations and the Possibility of the Political', in Ken Booth and Steve Smith (eds.) *International Political Theory Today*, Cambridge: Polity, pp. 306–27.

——(1995b) 'From International Relations to World Politics', in Joseph Camilleri *et al.* (eds) *The State in Transition*, Boulder, CO: Lynne Rienner, pp. 21–38.

——(1995c) 'After Modern Utopia: Reflections on the Possibilities of World Order Discourse', in H. Patomäki (ed.) *Peaceful Changes in World Politics*, research report no. 71, Tampere: Tampere Research Institute, pp. 380–403.

——and Ashley, R. K. (eds) (1990a) 'Speaking the Language of Exile: Dissidence in International Studies', special issue of *International Studies Quarterly* 34(3).

——(1990b) 'Speaking the Language of Exile: Dissident Thought in International Studies', in the special issue of *International Studies Quarterly* 34(3): 259–68.

——(1990c) 'Reading Dissidence/Writing the Discipline: Crisis and the Question of Sovereignty in International Studies', in the special issue of *International Studies Quarterly* 34(3): 367–416.

——Guzzini, Stefano and Patomäki, Heikki (1995) 'Possibilities and Limits of Republican World Politics: Concluding Trialogy', in H. Patomäki (ed.) *Peaceful Changes in World Politics*, research report no. 71, Tampere: Tampere Peace Research Institute, pp. 404–30.

——and Magnusson, Warren *et al.* (eds) (1984) *The New Reality: The Politics of Restraint in British Columbia*, Vancouver: New Star Books.

——(1986) *After Bennett: The New Politics of British Columbia*, Vancouver: New Star Books.

——(1988) 'Decentring the State: Political Theory and Canadian Political Economy', *Studies in Political Economy: A Socialist Review* 26: 37–71.

——(1991) 'Socialism and Monotheism: a Response to Jenson and Keyman', *Studies in Political Economy* 34: 235–9.

——and Mendlovitz, Saul H. (eds) (1987a) *Towards a Just World Peace: Perspectives from Social Movements*, London: Butterworth.

——(1987b) 'Peace, Politics and Contemporary Social Movements', in their *Towards a Just World Peace*, London: Butterworth, pp. 3–12.

——(eds) (1990a) *Contending Sovereignties: Redefining Political Community*, Boulder, CO and London: Lynne Rienner.

——(1990b) 'Interrogating State Sovereignty', in their *Contending Sovereignties: Redefining Political Community*, Boulder, CO and London: Lynne Rienner, pp. 1–12.

Works by other authors

Ashley, Richard K. (1987) 'The Geopolitics of Geopolitical Space: Toward a Critical Social Theory of International Politics', *Alternatives* 12(4): 403–34.

Bartelson, Jens (1995) *A Genealogy of Sovereignty*, Cambridge: Cambridge University Press.

Bull, Hedley (1977) *The Anarchical Society: A Study of Order in World Politics*, London: Macmillan.

Buzan, Barry (1994) 'National Security in the Post-Cold War Third World', *Strategic Review for Southern Africa* 16(1): 1–34.

——Kelstrup, Morten, Lemaitre, Pierre, Tromer, Elzbieta and Wæver, Ole (1990) *The European Security Order Recast: Scenarios for the Post-Cold War Era*, London: Pinter.

Der Derian, James (1987) *On Diplomacy: A Genealogy of Western Estrangement*, Oxford: Blackwell.

——(1992) *Antidiplomacy: Spies, Terror, Speed, and War*, Oxford: Blackwell.

Dillon, G. M. and Everard, Jerry (1992) 'Stat(e)ing Australia: Squid Jigging and the Masque of State', *Alternatives* 17(3): 281–312.

Keohane, Robert O. (ed.) (1986) *Neo-realism and Its Critics*, New York: Columbia University Press.

——(1989) *International Institutions and State Power: Essays in International Relations Theory*, Boulder, CO: Westview Press.

Laclau, Ernesto and Mouffe, Chantal (1985) *Hegemony and Socialist Strategy: Towards a Radical Democratic Politics*, London: Verso.

Ruggie, John Gerard (1993) 'Territoriality and Beyond: Problematizing Modernity in International Relations', *International Organization* 47(1): 139–74.

Tunander, Ola (1989) *Cold Water Politics: The Maritime Strategy and Geopolitics of the Northern Front*, London: Sage.

Wæver, Ole (1989) 'Beyond the "beyond" of Critical International Theory', Working Papers, no. 1/1989, Copenhagen: Centre for Peace and Conflict Research.

——(1991) 'Territory, Authority and Identity. The Late 20th-Century Emergence of Neo-Medieval Political Structures in Europe', paper presented at the European Peace Research Association's conference in Florence (November).

——Buzan, Barry, Kelstrup, Morten and Lemaitre, Pierre with Carlton, David *et al.* (1993) *Identity, Migration and the New Security Agenda in Europe*, London: Pinter.

——and Kelstrup, Morten (1993) 'Europe and its Nations: Political and Cultural Identities', in Ole Wæver, Barry Buzan, Morten Kelstrup and Pierre Lemaitre with David Carlton *et al.* (1993) *Identity, Migration and the New Security Agenda in Europe*, London: Pinter, pp. 61–92.

Wight, Martin (1966) 'Why Is There No International Theory?', in H. Butterfield and M. Wight (eds) *Diplomatic Investigations. Essays in the Theory of International Politics*, London: Allen & Unwin, pp. 17–34.

13 James Der Derian: the unbearable lightness of theory

Jef Huysmans

James Der Derian studied at McGill University, Canada and Balliol College, Oxford (1979–83) (UK) where he received an MPhil and a DPhil under the supervision of Hedley Bull. Since 1984 he has been teaching at the University of Massachusetts at Amherst.

Reading Der Derian's writings is often a bit of a rough ride. Many of his texts suck the reader into a magic world, a pastiche of science fiction, cartoons, Disneyland, CIA reports, spy novels, IR theory, movies and so on. She is pulled from one image into another and finally gets out, just because that full stop appears to be the last one (e.g. Der Derian 1993a). His writings thus embody a highly aesthetic dimension: they do not only relate particulars and wholes, but also draw enumerations of particulars. In this aesthetics the reader is moved from figure to figure in an almost photographic experience (Lash 1988, 1993). In this essay I cannot 'reproduce' this 'light' aspect of his writings. It might be attempted by constructing an essay as a compilation of semi-arbitrarily chosen pieces of his writings. However, such an essay would not fit the design of this work. Here, I shall rather introduce Der Derian's reflexive contributions to IR, i.e. how he relates particulars and wholes, 'facts' and theories, theories and meta-theories, etc. Hence, this essay (re)tells how Der Derian reflects upon conditions and changes of order/disorder (reality) and how he uses particular 'instruments' in his attempts to apprentice some fragments of the master 'Life-world'.[1] It is this 'heavy', more 'scholarly' Der Derian who is (re)written below.

In this essay, however, I will not construct Der Derian into a continuously unfolding identity (a unity): 'author in theories of international relations'. Rather, 'Der Derian' is understood to be a space-body which offers a home for particular intersections of many (inter)texts. This essay thus (re)writes pieces of a space and not the struggle of a master – hero within the archives of international relations. Der Derian will be cut as a poststructural interventionist in IR-ir[2] fed by a desire for disclosing IR-ir to make a life with-in difference possible. A first part will outline what a poststructural approach consists of. In that part, I will also indicate where Der Derian locates himself in the IR debates. A second part of the essay will draw his 'empirical' research project as an analysis of mediations of estrangements. In a last part, some normative 'claims' which feed Der Derian's narrative will be hinted at.

POST-CLASSICAL POSTSTRUCTURALISM

Der Derian's interventions in debates in IR are highly informed by what one might call a post-classical poststructuralism (to contribute to the hyperinflation of 'posts') which draws heavily upon classical realist authors, especially those referred to as masters of the English School (Wight, Bull; cf. Chapter 2 on Vincent in this book), French poststructural social theory (Foucault, Barthes, Derrida) and the master-thinker Nietzsche. Because of this post-classical poststructuralism Der Derian might be positioned in IR as a reflectivist (Keohane 1988), an optimistic postmodern skeptic (Rengger 1992), a late-modernist (Constantinou 1993), a reinscriber (Hoffman 1991), a dissident (Ashley and Walker 1990), a danger (Walt 1991), depending on the authors who attempt to categorize IR texts. Whatever the label, they all indicate that Der Derian is part of the meta-debate in IR often referred to as the 'third debate' (Lapid 1989). It would, however, probably be better labelled the 'fourth debate' (with the third debate being the paradigm one of the 1970s and the fourth the debate between neo-realist, neo-liberal synthesis versus reflectivism; e.g. Wæver 1995: 257 and Chapter 1 of the present volume). In this debate Der Derian ploughs interpretative furrows which churn up well-ordered and hyper-preserved behaviourist and positivist gardens in fanciful post-classical poststructural cuts.

Post-classicalism

In the preface to *On Diplomacy*, Der Derian identifies his work as 'a tentative step toward a post-classical theory of international relations' (1987a: vi). The traditional approach stresses interpretation above verification. It attempts to judge international relations by building upon philosophy, history, and to a certain extent law. Great texts in political and international theory are interpreted within their historical context. But history is largely understood as a continuous development toward the present, which thus turns into the 'up until now most developed state of affairs'. In *On Diplomacy* the *post*-classical dimension is largely introduced as a distancing from this understanding of history. A post-classical theory will interpret history not in a teleological sense, but rather as a discontinuous play of many forces and formations, often antithetical to the continuous reading of historical happenings (1987a: 2–3).

However, the following year finds Der Derian defining himself out of post-classical thought. In 'Philosophical Traditions in International Relations' the post-classical category – a subcategory of post-rationalist thought – shares the teleological view of history with the classical one. It differs in as much as its investigations reveal 'the degree to which the classical discourse in its canonical selection and interpretation imparts...a conservative, rationalist order to a reluctant reality' (1988: 191). Whatever defines the 'post' of 'post-classical', it remains that Der Derian's writings often gain body in a respectful handling of classical theories of IR (this is most explicitly the case in *On Diplomacy*, but his later works also contain traces of the classical approach; see, for example, his argument for a Ulyssesian realism in 1995: 26) in an attempt to move beyond this 'classicism'. Both the dimensions that define the 'post' of 'post-classical' above are aspects of this 'going beyond'. The main sources which feed his post-classicism are poststructural texts and Nietzsche's writings, which have been heavily used by poststructural authors also (Descombes 1979: 13, 93; Sarup 1988: 4–5; Harland 1987: 170).

Poststructuralism

For Der Derian, a poststructural approach is one which acknowledges the constitutive nature of language but which breaks with semiotic analyses of decoding meaning and identity into binary oppositions (1988: 192). It assumes that subjects have no immediate access to the world; their relation to objects is always mediated by scripts (discourses, texts, intertexts). In this mediation language is not a transparent tool which communicates the reality of the object to the subject. Language is rather understood as opaque; it adds something crucial (Shapiro 1989: 14). Linguistic practices produce meaning and value in the sense that they constitute what the object means to the subject.[3] This third dimension of the relationship between subjects and objects – mediating, meaning-constitutive scripts – is the subject of research in poststructuralism. For example, in his analysis of intelligence Der Derian writes:

> What I suggest, then, is that for this textual moment we leave causation to the political scientists and the promulgation of monologic truths to the national security state courtiers, in favor of an intertextual approach which investigates how these two discourses – the fictive literature of international intrigue and the 'factive' literature of national security and espionage – produce meaning and legitimate particular forms of *power* and espionage.
>
> (1992: 46)

This none the less does not imply that poststructuralism is a psychological approach to international relations. The script is not produced by individual subjects, but rather largely inherited by them. It is something upon which they must draw to speak sensibly – it is an institution (Shapiro 1989: 14–15). Does this mean that a script is something objective, external to interaction? No, a script is intersubjectively constituted, or, in other words, it is embedded and constructed in the inner logic of interaction.

A script is always open to change; it is as contextual as the interaction in which it is embedded. This leads to the problem of social order: how is meaning stabilized if there is no final arbiter because the object cannot decide and interaction is spatio-temporally specific? The answer is by *forgetting* (Shapiro 1989: 15). Many scripts are socially silenced, subjugated, or simply forgotten while others are privileged and thus become or remain dominant. Poststructural analysis of international relations uncovers how international social orders rely on such forgetting: 'our organizing strategy is to deconstruct or denaturalize through detailed interpretation the inherited language, concepts, and texts that have constituted privileged discourses in international relations' (1989a: 4). It follows that this kind of analysis is highly political: it undermines strategies of forgetting which are used to impose particular scripts. Power is thus involved, and can actually not be separated from the analysis of impositions of scripts. In that sense one might characterize poststructural analysis as 'insurrectional textuality' (Shapiro 1989: 13).

Often, critics of poststructuralism state that it is something to be postponed until further notice. This 'further notice' then refers to an assumed lack of an empirical and/or theoretical research project. Der Derian's writings explicitly turn down this kind of critique. First, his texts comprise a well-outlined empirical research project. Second, they also contain theorizations of world politics, e.g. his theorization of diplomacy by theories of alienation or of the present condition of anti-diplomacy by using Virilio's theorization of speed (cf. below). Moreover, in *Antidiplomacy* and elsewhere he explicitly states that poststructuralism does 'not destroy or deny the existence of the ground for a constructive theory' (1992: 7–8). It only argues against particular forms of theory: those which are totalizing and monological (1989a: 4).

A poststructural analysis of scripts can take two forms (Shapiro 1989: 14). First, it might analyse scripts and their relationship to power in a historical way, interpreting the origins and displacements of discourses-texts. This approach appears in Der Derian's genealogical analyses. However, poststructural analysis may also approach discourses-texts in a more structural way. Here the analysis stresses how particular scripts draw boundaries and create identities and binary differences. Der Derian labels this dimension of his analyses 'symptomology' – or, in a more contemporary terminology 'semiology'. Although most of his texts comprise a mixture of the two approaches, *On Diplomacy* is explicitly a genealogical work while *Antidiplomacy* is a more outspokenly symptomologic one.

But what does genealogy actually refer to? And does Der Derian use specific techniques of semiological analysis? Below I will sketch what genealogy as a method stands for. Because of its numerous uses and because it gives Der Derian's texts a specifically light and sometimes weird and fascinating look, it is also worth explaining intertext as a semiological technique of analysis.

Genealogy

How can post-classical poststructuralism study history without falling into the trap of historicism? The answer is genealogy. A genealogy draws a history of the present. This does not mean that it projects present needs and statuses on to history or that it considers the present as the final stage of a continuously developing history. It is called a history of the present because it discloses present discursive practices. It helps us understand our present condition by breaking its artificially conserved unity and normality. The layered character and heterogeneity of life are exposed in great detail. Three methodological principles guide the genealogist.

First, a genealogical analysis does not look for continuities or a movement of history to a single goal – to an end of history. It rather emphasizes the accidental character of historical events; 'It must record the singularity of events outside of any monotonous finality' (Foucault 1977: 139). A genealogist thus interprets history by means of discontinuities and accidental events rather than understanding it as a continuous unfolding of a particular *telos*.

Second, a genealogy does not look for an origin which would embody the essence of things. It rather starts from the assumption that the secret behind things is that they do not have an essence. 'At the origin one does not find an inviolable identity but disparities' (Foucault 1977: 142). A genealogy is based on the assumption 'that reality is not simply a uniform surface but is built of manifold interconnected layers, building upon each other' (Szakolczai 1993b: 42). In a genealogy, authors do not look for foundations, they rather distrust what is presented as an essence. Rather, gaps, dislocations, distances absorb their attention.

Third, genealogy is a method that does not focus on the thing itself. It concentrates on both the conditions which surround it and its effects. Thus, it zooms in on the two end-points rather than on the 'object' itself (Szakolczai 1993b: 41). In this sense a Nietzschean genealogy differs from other genealogies. A genealogy usually traces the origins of an institution. In this process references to surrounding conditions are rather accidental. In a Nietzschean genealogy, however, 'the real question of "origins" is about the conditions in which an institution, a character, or an evaluation is established' (Szakolczai 1993b: 21). In the chapter on proto-diplomacy in his genealogy of western estrangement, Der Derian states it as follows:

> the question central to this chapter is not how the works of Augustine influenced the policies of Charlemagne, but how together they generated a 'regime of truth', meaning an ensemble of sacralized texts, rules, and political power, from which it was possible for the earliest institutions of proto-diplomacy to emerge.
>
> (1987a: 70)

A genealogy consists of an interpretative history of interpretations, in the sense that it records series of interpretations (Foucault 1977: 151–2). Hence the centrality of discourse (the locus of meaning). In *On Diplomacy* Der Derian records series of paradigms, which he might as well have called discourses. In this study of series of interpretations, relations of power are central because one does not simply study series but rather how they involve games of forgetting (cf. above), of establishing normality, of creating order in conditions of disorder. The analysis desires to lay bare how each domination establishes a system of rules which is not a finality but only a temporal expression of a particular domination (Foucault 1977: 148). For example, Der Derian's genealogy of realism (1995) helps us to make sense of contemporary realism as an orthodoxy and indicates how it camouflages a heterogeneous space of plurality. A history of the present also hints at new possibilities for scripts; for example, the opening up of the closure of realism pictures different scripts and different forces. See among other Der Derian's formulation of a Ulyssesian realism (1995) or his argument for a Nietzschean understanding of security (1993c).

Der Derian uses genealogy heavily in his writings. *On Diplomacy* comprises his most detailed and extensive genealogy. Although it contains a tendency to universalize the concept of alienation and at particular places suggests a theorization of alienation which raises the interesting question whether genealogy and theorization can be combined, it is one of the very rare works in IR that come close to a Nietzschean (Foucaldian?) genealogy. Also his later work formulates genealogical fragments, but it never resembles the way genealogy takes shape in *On Diplomacy*. Moreover, in these later works genealogy is often more or less reduced to a contextualized history of the meanings of a particular concept.

Intertext

Intertextualism is sometimes used as a synonym for poststructuralism or postmodernism (see Der Derian and Shapiro 1989). It then refers to a particular characteristic of the textuality of the social world, namely, that in a space of a given text, several utterances, taken from other texts, intersect and thus constitute new meaning[4] (Kristeva 1980: 36). Here a text is interpreted as the result of a redistribution of several different texts (Kristeva 1986: 111). In other words, intertextuality refers to the phenomenon that texts are constituted in an intersection of other texts. Consequently, one might state that a text always refers beyond itself to other texts.

Without really taking part in this debate about the constitution of meaning, one might turn this idea into a particular, deconstructive/constructive technique of analysis. That is what Der Derian has done. He interweaves sources belonging to different genres in an attempt to interpret a particular issue: fragments of movies, cartoons, computer programmes, simulation exercises, novels, academic papers, speeches by decision-makers, TV images, statistics, etc. This technique presents the reader with a text in which fragments of texts that are considered to belong to different genres, to disciplines that are normally kept separate from one another, are glued together into a pastiche. The meaning that this writing comprises is embodied by the pastiche, and not by the fragments taken separately. The fragments are thus more than illustrations or separate pieces of information; they are interrelated to constitute a new text.

One of the most intriguing aspects of his use of the technique is that he draws together popular culture and academic and political sources. Sources belonging to the 'genre of novels', 'genre of video games', 'genre of movies' are in IR normally, if present at all, used as illustrations to mitigate – to lighten – an analysis. Their alienness to the discipline is always articulated.

The differentiation between 'serious' and popular sources is meticulously guarded. Der Derian's writings, however, often 'work' precisely by the opposite strategy: a de-differentiation between the genres. It is exactly in this de-differentiation, the explicit creation of an intertext, that the analysis is performed – it is not something supplementary to the 'real' analysis.

Another interesting dimension of Der Derian's intertextual analysis is that he does not limit his sources to written ones but also pays attention to images. Text then refers to any system of signs and not to writing only. His work is full of references to TV images, to noise, to simulations, to movies, etc.

Traces of the technique can be found in *On Diplomacy*, but it is actually only fully developed in his analyses of the late- or postmodern condition of anti-diplomacy (good examples are: 1993a, 1991, 1989b and the chapter on the Gulf War in 1992). In 'The C.I.A., Hollywood, and Sovereign Conspiracies' (1993a) the reader bumps into a lecture at the American Academy of Political Science, Machiavelli, Hitchcock, Robert Redford and surrounding noise in *Three Days of the Condor*, the film *JFK*, Nietzsche, a *New York Times* editorial, a cartoon. A large section of 'S/N: International Theory, Balkanisation, and the New World Order' (1991) consists of a diary he kept during his participation in the Baltic Peace and Freedom cruise in 1985, while the article ends with a Billy Bragg gig in Prague and a quote from the Soviet linguistic and literary theorist Mikhail Bakhtin.

This comment on pastiches ends the first part in which I have tried to show where Der Derian ploughs his furrows in IR-ir and how he does this – his epistemological and methodological position. But what images does the ploughing show? What do the pastiches tell us about world politics? In other words, what world political problems is Der Derian interested in, and what does he say about them?

THE MEDIATION OF WESTERN ESTRANGEMENT[5]

Besides his interventions in (meta-)theoretical debates in IR, Der Derian has also produced a considerable amount of writings in which he analyses the problematic of estrangement and its mediation. If one had to reduce this 'empirical–theoretical' research to one label, 'mediation of Western estrangement' would be a possibility. While *On Diplomacy* largely explores mediations of estrangements by means of the concept 'alienation' and Hegel's, Feuerbach's, Marx's and Sartre's theories of alienation, *Antidiplomacy* builds more on Baudrillard's analysis of simulations and hyperreality, Foucault's concept of surveillance, and above all on Virilio's theorizations of speed and chronopolitics. In an attempt to sketch some fragments of Der Derian's analyses of this vast problematic, I will first roughly indicate what the concepts 'alienation', 'mediation' and 'diplomatic culture' refer to in his writings. Then I will draw some fragments of his genealogy of western estrangement and argue the importance of the analysis for a wider debate in IR-ir. Finally, I will outline how he analyses the late- or postmodern condition in international relations.

Alienation, mediation and diplomatic culture

The interest in alienation rests on a belief that 'the neglected terrain of diplomacy's origins and transformations [cannot] be fully illuminated without the rich history, conceptual variations, and theories of alienation' (1987a: 28–9). Alienation has a double meaning, but the connotations got intermingled only after the contract writers had turned their thought to the concept. In its economical and juridical meaning it refers to transfers of rights and property. But alienation also refers to a separation, e.g. of man from God or of sovereign state from sovereign state.

But a concept is not yet a theory. For a theory of alienation, Der Derian turns to Hegel's philosophy, Feuerbach's and Marx's secularization of Hegel's theory and Sartre's extension of it to spheres beyond the workplace and capitalism. In these theories, alienation as transfer-estrangement becomes a driving force of history (1987a: Chapter 2; 1987b). Der Derian uses these theories at particular places in *On Diplomacy* to explain forms of estrangements and their mediation.

Man's condition of alienation, which is one of a separation accompanied by feelings ranging from indifference to hostility, requires mediation. Der Derian's *On Diplomacy* analyses the interestices of alienation from which diplomacy emerges as a mediation (1987a: 70). Mediation refers to a connecting link for the purpose of reconciliation or intervention (1987a: 6). In this process of mediation, (diplomatic) culture plays an important role. Culture refers here to a system of symbols and social constraints which provides a mediation by which alienated individuals (re)possess some kind of universality (1987a: e.g. 38, 42).

The subject of Der Derian's genealogy of western estrangement is how different forms of estrangements and their mediation are displaced in particular contexts.

A genealogy of western estrangement and diplomatic theory

It is difficult to give an overview of the content of *On Diplomacy*. First, because it is a genealogy: it looks for discontinuities, for events and accidental happenings rather than for regularities, laws, causal relations, etc. In that sense the book resembles a tapestry with a very complex design which is constantly remade. The book does not offer any clearly separated, finished carpets which can be compared while they hang on a wall. Second, *On Diplomacy* is a very dense book. In 200 pages only it traces a genealogy of western estrangement from its biblical origins to the present condition of techno-diplomacy.

The genealogy develops in six chapters, each covering a particular paradigm of estrangements and its mediations; see Figure 13.1.

	ESTRANGEMENT horizontal	MEDIATION vertical	
mytho-diplomacy	• between tribes • between Christianity and Islam	man from God	one-sided sacral mythical
proto-diplomacy (Machiavellian paradigm)	• between city-states • between city-states and hegemonic empires		one-sided secular (*raison d'état*)
diplomacy	between states		reciprocal secular (*raison d'état*)
anti-diplomacy (theory) neo-diplomacy (reification)	intra- and extra-national between strata	strata from universal brotherhood	one-sided secularized mythical (utopia)
techno-diplomacy	between states and peoples		one-sided technical

Figure 13.1 Paradigms of diplomacy

In Figure 13.1 I have treated anti-diplomacy and neo-diplomacy as two sides of the same paradigm. In the genealogical logic of Der Derian's work it does not really make sense to separate paradigms on a theory/practice distinction, i.e. the one referring to the theory and the other to its reification in international practice. This figure is an overview which might be of help for the readers of *On Diplomacy* but which actually violates the genealogical – anti-essentialist – and complex content of Der Derian's work.

The genealogy starts with mytho-diplomacy. This refers to a mediation between man and God and between peoples (Jews/other tribes; Christians/Muslims) through sacred symbols. The mediation thus uses normative and not observable knowledge. Priests play an important role because they manipulate the knowledge and rituals through which estrangement is mediated. The analysis deals with the Jewish mytho-diplomacy, the Christian one (Augustinian paradigm), and the institutionalization of the latter by the papacy.

A second paradigm focuses on the mediation of estrangement of the newly articulated city-states, especially in Italy, at the end of the Middle Ages and in the early Renaissance. Proto-diplomacy, as expressed in the Machiavellian paradigm, mediates an estrangement of city-states from hegemonic empires in an extreme state of anarchy.[6] Like the Augustinian paradigm, which mediates the estrangement between a myth of unity and an atomized reality and between two mythical units (Islam/Christianity), it formulates a one-sided mediation of a one-sided estrangement. Proto-diplomacy differs from the early mytho-diplomacy among others because it desacralizes the mediation – *raison d'état* plays a central role – and because it introduces a form of mediation based on permanent residence.

Contrary to the Augustinian and Machiavellian paradigm, diplomacy – the third paradigm – consists of a mediation of *mutual* estrangement of states. The problem which new states confronted was a disintegration of antiquated mediations (papacy and emperor): each state had its own king. A new mediation was required 'to reconcile relations among states *mutually* estranged from a mythical and temporal unity, but still tenuously connected by the integral values and practices inherited from that very unity' (1987a: 109). Secular and reciprocal diplomacy based on permanent residence was an answer to these problems. In the chapter on diplomacy, Der Derian argues how the emergence of the diplomatic system and the state system are interrelated, how it is at least partly based on the development of a mutual estrangement, and how the diplomatic system requires a structure of balance of power to operate.

While diplomacy mediates the mutual estrangement of states, anti-diplomacy mediates estrangement between strata within a state or across states (e.g. between classes, between nation and monarchy). The former formulates a mediation of the particular alienation of states, the latter develops a mediation of the universal alienation of mankind from a utopian state of universal brotherhood. Here the problem is not that particular entities (states) are estranged from universal entities (e.g. church, emperor) but rather that new forces of universalism are estranged from the particularism of diplomacy. While diplomacy stresses a horizontal, reciprocal mediation between states, anti-diplomacy formulates a vertical one of the estrangement of man from a universal utopia. Der Derian develops these ideas in an analysis of utopianism, the utopia of terror and the micro-utopias of the *philosophes*.

The fifth paradigm, neo-diplomacy, relates directly to anti-diplomacy; it is the international manifestation – reification – of anti-diplomatic theory. Neo-diplomacy refers to a revolutionary mediation which claims a unity between peoples or class over state borders. It is a continuation of revolutionary war by other means (e.g. propaganda, negotiating with diplomats without complying with the diplomatic rules of engagement) to liberate peoples or class. The two experiences of neo-diplomacy Der Derian analyses, the French Revolution (end of the eighteenth century) and the Russian Revolution (beginning of the twentieth century), both failed because the military extension of neo-diplomacy failed.

Finally, the genealogy ends with a short outline of the challenges recent technological innovations pose to diplomacy. Communication and weapon technologies are inscribed by alienation and set a new problem of estrangement and mediation. 'The immediate question is how technology, in the sense of technical invention applied to social relations, has transformed the relevant mediation of estrangement' (1987a: 203). In *On Diplomacy* Der Derian gives only some indications of how technology challenges diplomacy, largely by an analysis of the case of nuclear weapons. For a profound analysis of this new condition one has to turn to later writings.

On Diplomacy includes several contributions to IR theory. First, by studying diplomacy in a genealogical way and from the angle of alienation, the analysis introduces new tools for the study of diplomacy. It moves the theory beyond the rich, classical analysis of the phenomenon, without breaking with the classical furrows. It develops rather in a dialogue with the classical approach than in a confrontation (after all the work builds on a doctorate supervised by Hedley Bull). The theories of alienation and the genealogical method make it possible for Der Derian to avoid a state-centric approach of diplomacy without giving up the centrality of power politics for understanding developments in world politics. This extends the set of problems of diplomacy from one of communication of messages between communities, exchanged by official agents (Bull 1977: Chapter 7) to one of problems of estrangement and its mediation which focuses on the (inter)relation between universalism and particularism and between inside and outside. The analysis fully appreciates differences between diplomacy and other paradigms of estrangement and its mediation. It also makes it possible to locate the displacements of paradigms within the specificity of a spatio-temporal context – the then traced battle-lines between forces and strategies. In that sense, contrary to stories which focus on repetitions of the same or on a progressive development of a *telos*, Der Derian's tale interprets the history of diplomacy as always open to new displacements.

But his work does not only offer ideas and a method for the study of diplomacy. Via his analysis of diplomacy and other systems of mediation of estrangement, he participates in one of the important debates in present IR-ir; namely the debate on the crisis of state sovereignty which feeds a general discussion of identity, inside/outside, universalism/particularism, and political community (cf. Chapter 7 on Ruggie, 9 on Onuf, 10 on Wendt and 12 on Walker in this volume.)

However, while Walker (1993) and Onuf (1989, 1991) mainly analyse major classical works in political and social theory (Machiavelli, Hobbes, Bodin, etc.) – masters of political philosophy – Der Derian much more explicitly interprets both practices (as conserved in the archives) and the major philosophical works. He actually does not draw a strict distinction between them: both are important to form the battle-lines from which dominant and subjugated forms of mediation arise (cf. Chapter 2 on Vincent in this volume).

The debate on inside/outside and universalism/particularism focuses mainly on the crisis of sovereignty. In approaching the issue in terms of estrangement and its mediation, Der Derian widens the scope. The crisis of sovereignty is shaped as one particular problem of alienation and its mediation. He does not, moreover, limit the disclosure of sovereignty to the late Middle Ages and the early Renaissance, the crucial period for analysing the battle-lines out of which the sovereign state system arose as the dominant organization of European politics. In his chapters on anti- and neo-diplomacy, Der Derian argues how that dominant system has been challenged by subjugated scripts in later periods. By outlining the play of subjugated scripts against a relatively well-established dominant one, his disclosure of the dominant system opens up the debate. The disclosure does not work by showing how a dominant order has arisen as one particular order out of an historically specific situation of disorder, but rather inversely, by focusing on moments of disorder in a situation of relative order.

Finally, Der Derian's genealogy complicates the inside/outside problematic by showing that identity and alienation have not only a horizontal dimension but also a vertical one. On the one hand, states are separated from other states, which mutually estranges people inside a state from those outside this state and inside another state. On the other hand, inside states particular strata may be estranged from one another – inside one stratum (e.g. the proletariat) and outside another (e.g. the bourgeoisie). Der Derian shows how this internal inside/outside problematic may gain a global dimension when the strata unify with similar strata in other states – Proletarians of all countries, unite! – thus turning the double inside/outside problematic into an inside/inside one: to be simultaneously inside the state and inside the brotherhood of mankind. In the analysis of anti- and neo-diplomacy Der Derian indicates how this latter differentiation, which embodies the tension between two estrangements, i.e. the cross-cutting of a horizontal estrangement between particulars (particular alienation between states) and a vertical one of particulars from a universal utopia (universal alienation of mankind), contains seeds of challenges to the state system. The scheme could be put to good use for understanding actual challenges to the state system, of which particularly the environmental problematic and population flows strike the eye.

Symptomology of late- or postmodern conditions of estrangement and its mediation

Since *On Diplomacy*, Der Derian's texts mainly formulate a symptomology of the late- or postmodern condition in (western) world politics. This condition is characterized as a legitimation crisis of the domination of western international society. Modern international society gained its identity from a diplomatic culture and collective estrangements from the Antichrist, the colonial native, the Soviet threat, the international terrorist (Campbell 1992). In the new condition of world politics, sometimes referred to as one of growing neo-medievalism (Ruggie 1993), these sources of identity have been undermined. Sources of collective estrangement are fading, especially since the end of the Cold War. This has led to a more fragmented and less monotonous estrangement. Also national sovereignty has been considerably undermined by new technologies, a multiplication of non-state actors, and external regional combinations (e.g. the European Union) and internal disintegrations (e.g. nationalism). Finally, western power is declining. The present crisis of legitimacy combines a crisis of political legitimacy, national identity (traditional forms of identity creation no longer hold) and traditional forms of practical knowledge.

In this condition of crisis, a new anti-diplomacy has arisen which attempts to mediate, but also constitutes new estrangements. It differs from previous anti-diplomacy because of the new techniques of power and the new representation of dangers which constitute and mediate estrangement in the present condition. At issue are the technique of surveillance, the politicization of speed, and simulation (1990). In his analysis of three forces (surveillance, speed and terror) and one war (the Gulf War of 1990–1) Der Derian shows that these new techniques are more transparent and pervasive than previous ones, are more real in time than in place, and are, furthermore, produced and sustained rather through an exchange of signs than through goods. As we will see, the three elements are closely interrelated. Below, the three new techniques of power will be dealt with separately.

Surveillance

Surveillance is a technostrategic force (a force which uses and is used by technology for the purpose of war, 1992: 3) of normalization and, according to Der Derian, the most powerful response to the new condition of estrangement and accelerated pace. 'To watch without being watched to control' might well be its slogan. Bentham's panopticon is often used to explain how surveillance works. The panopticon is an architectural construction, i.e. a prison, where the guards populate a tower which is located in the middle of the building, while the prisoners populate the cells which are placed in the buildings surrounding the tower and with 'windows' which give out on the tower. The building is constructed in such a way that the guards can always watch any individual prisoner without the prisoner ever knowing whether he/she is being watched or not.

Surveillance thus works via a distribution of certainty and uncertainty (Lyon 1993: 657–8): the guards are certain they can always accumulate information and perform direct supervision (the two related phenomena that surveillance connects, according to Giddens 1984: 127) while the prisoners are completely uncertain about the actual exercise of this control. Thus, surveillance embodies a form of power which is pervasive in its effects but discontinuous in its action.

This distribution of certainty and uncertainty is used as a force of normalization. Normalization involves two processes. First, it defines the normal (us) and the abnormal (other); it thus estranges through a creation or separation of the abnormal. Second, it attempts to control the abnormal and the normal and thus the relationship between the two. In other words, it mediates the estranged relationship between us (watchers) and others (those watched). This mediation has an anti-diplomatic quality because the other (the potential enemy) is watched in order to prepare us better for countering possible subversive actions. It thus is not a form of voyeurism just for pleasure but rather a continuation of war by other technical means; in other words, it is a technostrategic voyeurism.[7]

Der Derian's analysis mainly indicates how new technologies compared to human intelligence (HUMINT) increase the potential for surveillance in such a way that one might speak of a qualitative jump in the production of pervasiveness and transparency.[8] HUMINT differs from technical intelligence (TECHINT) in that 'it lacks the ubiquity, resolution, and pantoscopic power of the technical intelligence system, as well as its apparent capability to provide value-free detailed information about the object of surveillance: "the picture does not lie"' (1992: 31). Beside the ubiquity of TECHINT and the detail of the image, it also comprises an increase in speed by which the information is circulated. One of the consequences of TECHINT is that surveillance has invaded the sphere of everyday life: surveillance is everywhere – in shopping centres, in the airport, etc. – looking for terrorists, for spies, in short, for 'dangerous elements'. The most intriguing consequence is that the technologically innovated surveillance by great powers has created a cybernetic system of advanced paranoia. In the cyberspace of surveillance we can see and hear the other, but we might always expect to hear and see her or him still better, i.e. to develop more pervasive technology. This might create paranoia because the cyberspace is rooted in and feeds the dangerous quality of the other: we watch him/her because he/she may be dangerous, and the closer we watch, the more we get infatuated with the danger the other possibly embodies. In other words, the means that are used to mediate our estrangement from the other (TECHINT), also produce estrangement.

Thus, technologically innovated surveillance has increased transparency and pervasiveness, it has driven the realness of the data to hyperreality[9] and has considerably speeded up the pace with which the data are circulated. This has made it possible to mediate a fragmented estrangement in an anti-diplomatic way, but it is also characterized by a feedback loop in which estrangement is increased.

The politicization of speed

Where the politicization of speed is concerned, Der Derian starts from the observation that in IR speed has been largely ignored as a significant political factor. Der Derian's main source is Paul Virilio's work (1992: Chapter 6). According to the latter, the great revolution in the industrial age has been the democratic one – one of acceleration. The incredible increase in speed (in transport, weapons, media) has resulted in a collapse of distance: the faster one can travel to the other side of the world and/or the faster information can be transmitted from sender to receiver, the less territorial distance counts. This collapse of territorial distance has a political quality. It influences relations between people; it changes A's work and war relations with B because what counts more and more in their strategic relation is the speed of travel, of weapons, of information, in other words, speed, speed and again speed (Shapiro and Neubauer 1989: 302). Consequently, in strategic relations the control and distribution of time (chronopolitics) become more important factors than the control and distribution of territory (geopolitics). In other words, pace becomes more important than space. This is what Der Derian refers to as the (s)pace problem in international relations: 'international relations is shifting from a realm defined by sovereign places, impermeable borders and rigid geopolitics, to a site of accelerating flows, contested borders, and fluid chronopolitics' (1992: 129–30).

This unambiguously suggests that the politicization of speed considerably affects the state/diplomatic system. If the importance of exchanges or flows which are not controllable by territorially defined borders increases, then that implies an erosion of sovereignty. The politicization of speed (chrono-politics) thus questions dominant forms of political community. Where is sovereignty to be located in a world of chronopolitics (Walker 1993; Shapiro 1991; Luke 1991 and 1993)? It also affects estrangement and its mediation. The collapse of territorial distance into chrono-closeness has brought the other into our living rooms. TV screens daily transmit an incredible amount of (virtual) others from all over the world within visual reach. The separation between us and the other is currently among others mediated by speed (Virilio 1989: 147). This mediation appears in Der Derian's cases (terrorism, Gulf War, spies) as an anti-diplomatic one: mediation of a one-sided alienation as a continuation of war by other means. Speed also changes the representation of dangers. In a situation of chrono-closeness dangers produced by state practice cannot be postponed to an indefinite future. They are immediately and unambiguously experienced here and now (Shapiro 1991: 468). The fact that dangers cannot be postponed any more does not imply that we will experience an accumulation of dangers. Why? The speed by which new dangers are produced increases too, and this may reduce the impact of any particular danger on our estrangement since in our hyperreal, accelerated reality we easily forget past dangers when new arrive. We begin to resemble nomads moving through dangers. (On the concept of nomad see Bauman 1992a: 693–4 and 1992b: 164–7, 193–5; see Der Derian's analysis of the failure to re-create a new arch-foe for the West in the Gulf War: Der Derian 1994b: 24). Finally, it does not need much imagination to see that the diplomatic system which is based on residential mediation is undermined in a world where information is transmitted from one side of the globe to the other in less than seconds, and in which technical intelligence tends to produce more detailed data than on-site inspection.

Simulation

The third technique of power which shapes the late- or postmodern condition according to Der Derian is simulation.

'Simuler est feindre d'avoir ce qu'on n'a pas' (Baudrillard 1981: 12). It differs from pretending, i.e. to feign you do not have something you actually have, in that there is no object. In other words, simulation breaks the principle of reality. It questions the difference between real and imaginary, between true and false. In simulations, e.g. a computer simulation of a battlefield, the model becomes more real than the real. It becomes hyperreal. It no longer produces images but simulacra which have no referent, or have lost their relationship to it. That means that the exchange of signs which simulation produces is not a matter of favouring the sign over the real. It is not an inversion of the sign-referent relation but rather an implosion. When the model becomes more real than reality, the relationship between sign and referent implodes. The main task of the production of such simulacra is to mask the absence of reality and thus to save the reality principle.

In this hyperreal world war turns into cyberwar: a war which does not (only) take place in a territorial space but above all in a virtual space, a cyberspace. This is 'a globally net-worked, computer-sustained, computer-accessed, and computer-generated, multidimensional, artificial, or "virtual" reality' (M. Benedikt quoted in Der Derian 1992: 199–200 n. 4). In this space geographical distance does not really matter since reality is produced on a screen, an object is not physical or necessarily a representation of a physical object but is made of pure data, pure information, and the information is derived from the exchange of symbols. In this virtual reality spectacle becomes central. When war turns into cyberwar, the spectacle of war (the battlefield) turns into a war of spectacle – i.e. a war of simulations, of data. (Here Der Derian is once again drawing on Virilio.) In the Gulf War this virtual reality was present in the preparations for the war, especially in the many computer simulations used by the military. (Note that simulations here precede reality, that the map comes before the territory.) Virtual reality was also present in the execution of the war because decision-making depended on the data transmitted via satellites to the national command authority. And finally, it was also present in the reproduction of the war in the living room (on TV screens) (1992: 114–16).

Simulations function in Der Derian's story as an anti-diplomatic force: they are a continuation of war by means of verisimilitude (1992: 186). A cyberwar feigns to be true and real in a play in which the distinction between image and real has imploded. Second, simulation also affects estrangement. The 'other' – the foreigner, the enemy – becomes more real than real, i.e. hyperreal in a world of simulations. The more the 'other' becomes hyperreal – e.g. more 'enemy' than the real enemy – the less we see of ourselves in the other and thus the more 'other' she or he becomes. In that sense simulation can increase estrangement. Finally, simulation is used to mediate estrangement. We try to find lost certainty and truth – security and confidence – in a cyberspatial world to settle our estrangement from the empty world we are faced with after the collapse of the Cold War.

To conclude, the three techniques of power embody a reformulation of the problematic of space. Space is no longer primarily territorial in the late- or postmodern condition. Geographical space has been considerably challenged by the triad chrono-cyber-hypertransparent space.[10] The latter provokes geospace by understanding distance in terms of time rather than geography, by substituting hyperreal, simulated space for real space, and by radically disclosing a well-shaded space. The forces of production – speed, simulation and surveillance – of the challenge create new forms of estrangement while simultaneously mediating these estrangements. This circle contains a tendency to explode into a spiral (cf. the feedback loop above, and see also Virilio 1993: 262 ff.). But there is another effect too. In this chrono-cyber-hypertransparent space we are driven closer and closer to a hyperreal other, which might make it more difficult for us to see parts of ourselves in the other, which means a radicalization of estrangement, a considerable increase in the gap between us and others. As Der Derian suggests in *Antidiplomacy*, in this world diplomacy, a peaceful, reciprocal mediation of estrangement has an important role to play. It 'must negotiate the meaning and values that constitute identity out of difference' in order to make it possible to live in difference (1992: 165).

DISCLOSING IR-ir: OR, ABOUT DESIRE AND ETHOS

Der Derian's interventions – the intertexts he produces – embody a double desire. On the one hand, they express a longing for defamiliarizing, opening up, breaking through established orthodoxies, taken-for-granted practices, closedness. The other side hopes for a life in difference, in ambiguity, in heteroglossia, in polyphony, in dialogue without a need to reduce it to monologue. In short, the intertexts embody both an ethos of critique and an ethos of living with-in difference. This position is heavily informed by, among others, Bakhtin, Nietzsche and Foucault.

An ethos of critique is characterized first by a rhetoric of disruption.[11] Der Derian's writings comprise a rhetoric which attempts to defamiliarize familiar understandings of world politics. As an example one might refer to his extensive use of genealogy as a way of arguing that what is taken to be the highest development or the logical outcome of historical developments is nothing more, but nothing less either, than an accident. This rhetoric of disruption is not fed by a faddish desire for innovation but by 'a suspicion that there are high moral costs attached to the kinds of inertial systems of thought that become institutionalized in high politics and higher learning' (1995: 4–5). Or, as he states in *Antidiplomacy*: 'A defamiliarizing theory can liberate the practitioner and thinker from the kind of political stasis and intellectual staleness that serve to defend against the effects of rapid historical change – at possibly great future costs' (1992: 22).

This brings us close to a second characteristic of Der Derian's ethos of critique: its exposition of dangers (e.g. 1994b). His writings are not looking for alternatives, for new orthodoxies, but rather formulate genealogies and/ or semiologies of sets of problems to lay open the changing constellations of dangers. This exposition is not constructed from some external point of view but rather from the inside, as a participant in IR-ir, and it does not narrate big stories but rather small, local ones – no essentialist myths of origin but retrojections from unsteady positions in the present (Pels 1992: 52).

As Bernstein remarks, this ethos can work only when it presupposes and challenges an ethical-political horizon, which is mostly kept implicit. But the more one talks about disclosing intertexts in favour of alternative possibilities, the more radical a positive affirmation (and not just a negative characterization of the kind 'it is not...') is required for the rhetoric to work (Bernstein 1991: 156–7). Der Derian's intertext contains general traces of this affirmative side in its many arguments for building a life with-in difference: 'it is not in synthesis, but by learning to live with irreconcilable differences and multiple identities – in high theory and in everyday practices – that we might find our best hope for international relations' (1992: 9).[12]

The ethos of living with-in difference relates a desire for 'embracing' difference, ambiguity and uncertainty to the problem of identity. Identity requires difference in order to be; self-identity is created through alienation with-in which difference is turned into otherness. The paradox is that alienation is required for the constitution of self-identity, yet it also has potentiality to become repressive upon the other and the self – among others by turning others into scapegoats to ascertain self-identity (see also Connolly 1991: 64 ff). Diplomacy is potentially a paradoxical mediation which should make it possible to construct identity inside a world of differences. Its main tool is a Bakhtinean dialogue; a dialogue not in the sense of two voices speaking but as a process in which understanding involves mutual responsive acts towards the other – communicative acts in which identity is not fixed but constantly develops through the communicative process.

THE UNBEARABLE LIGHTNESS OF DER DERIAN'S WRITINGS

As it has been (re)constructed in this article the core theme that runs through Der Derian's intertexts is a complex problematics of disorder. His intertexts perform an action of disordering. They defamiliarize the familiar and turn orthodoxy into heterodoxy. In that sense they attempt to create chaos in IR-ir. Further, the intertexts demonstrate how order is made out of disorder, how order is again followed by disorder, etc. Moreover, both his more recent genealogies and symptomologies of fragments of the present condition are reflections within and upon a condition of high disorder – one in which the old order is dead and a new not yet born (the firstborn – New World Order – is actually already dead (1994b: 24)).

> The dissolution of order is an event that nobody can escape; and an event that has no internal, in-built, natural solution. The only 'natural' solution would be a return to the previous order, but this is by definition impossible, as it is exactly its dissolution that is the problem. The result is an increased self-awareness, necessary reflexive activity.... The point is that the problem itself involves reflexivity. It is there that the true novelty of the situation lies: reflexivity emerges, enters the stage as any other activity of thinking, in the sense of problem-solving.
>
> (Szakolczai 1993a: 19)

In such a condition, reflections on disorder and order, on problematizations, are an important ordering activity. In that sense one might say that Der Derian's intertexts perform a disordering activity which paradoxically is ordering. Der Derian's disclosing of IR-ir is not easy criticism but a demanding ordering activity, informed by an ethos of living with-in difference.

The intertexts interweave these dimensions of the problematic of disorder into a playful game/style which gives Der Derian's ordering/disordering writings their late- or postmodern lightness; a lightness which may sound somewhat unbearable for much of the scholarly seriousness in IR but which succeeds well in (en)lightening the international heaviness in a carnivalesque *fin de siècle*.

NOTES

I would like to thank James Der Derian, Sam de Smedt, Arpad Szakolczai and the other contributors to this book for helpful comments.

1 A Nietzschean humbleness toward the contingencies of the world leads Der Derian to identify himself as a perpetual apprentice rather than a master in the making: 'I must say I found the title a strange one: I see myself more as a perpetual apprentice (think of Mickey as the Sorcerer's Apprentice in *Fantasia*) than a "master in the making". Besides, the only "Master" in IR that I have spotted recently is the contingency of world politics, which is constantly at work to "unmake" those who think they can tame it with the latest theory' (personal correspondence, 3 February 1994).

2 'IR' refers to the discipline International Relations while 'ir' refers to the practice of international relations. A hyphen is used to indicate a close but not oppositional relationship between two terms while a slash is mostly used for indicating the mutual constitutive relationship of oppositional terms.

3 The mediation is not a question of causal determination. The script does not determine what the object is but only constitutes what it means.

4 The term 'text' is used in a metaphorical sense: it refers to the manifestation or materialization of meaning in different forms.

5 Estrangement is preferred to diplomacy because the latter refers only to a specific kind of mediation: one which mediates the mutual estrangement between sovereign states (see also 1995: 244).

6 The situation in which proto-diplomacy gained ground was a very complex one: horizontal estrangement between new states, vertical estrangement between man and God, as articulated and mediated by Christianity (the papacy), horizontal estrangement between Islam and Christianity, and estrangement from the breakdown of hegemonic empires were all present. To complicate it even more, besides warriors and the Church, the market also gained in importance.

7 It might be remarked that Der Derian sheds insufficient light on the link between the panopticon as a particular technique and the process of normalization. As stated above, normalization involves not simply a technique of control (panopticism) but also the definition of what is to be controlled. It should be remembered that Michel Foucault's analysis of the panopticon and panopticism, which was largely responsible for the introduction of the term in present social theory, is an integral part of his analysis of discipline as a technique of power (Foucault 1975: 137–229). It is this double dimension of discipline and panopticism which constitutes the horizontal play of power, to which normalization refers: the internalization of normality in the interaction.

8 Communications intelligence, electronic intelligence, radar intelligence, telemetry intelligence and photointelligence constitute a new regime of power in international relations (1992: 31).

9 The consequence for the panopticon of the production of a hyperreal surveillance, in which discipline itself becomes virtual (Lyon 1993: 669), is not further researched by Der Derian, although it would not be a big step for him to take. Baudrillard's piece 'La fin du panoptique' in *Simulacres et simulation*, a work Der Derian is familiar with, might be used as a starting-point (Baudrillard 1981: 48–56). He has signalled an intention to deal with this question in the forthcoming work *Virtual Security*, however.

10 A focus of criticism in the literature that analyses these challenges to the existing international order is that they often theorize the forces challenging the existing order and the consequences of the challenge for that order, but do not really

focus on the inner working or the interplay of two different kinds of order, which embody radically different organizing principles.

11 In this part on the ethos of critique I lean heavily on Bernstein's (1991: 143–71) analysis of Foucault's philosophical ethos.

12 Because Der Derian's work does not comprise indications of how this living with-in difference might look more concretely, his texts leave the political-ethical horizon somewhat vague and run the risk that readers understand such statements as another unquestioned affirmation of western-centric liberal pluralism. This raises the interesting question of the politics and ethics of post-structuralism; a question which unfortunately is often debated in a too pamphleteerish way (e.g. Norris 1992; Krishna 1993). For a positive view of the politics of so-called poststructural authors see Keenan's (1987: 19 ff.) analysis of Foucault and Der Derian's response (1994a) to Krishna's criticism (1993) of his work.

REFERENCES

Works by James Der Derian

Der Derian, James (1987a) *On Diplomacy: A Genealogy of Western Estrangement*, Oxford: Blackwell.

—— (1987b) 'Mediating estrangement: a Theory for Diplomacy', *Review of International Studies* 13(2): 91–110.

—— (1988) 'Philosophical Traditions in International Relations', *Millennium* 17(2): 189–93.

—— (1989a) 'The Boundaries of Knowledge and Practice in International Relations', in J. Der Derian and M. Shapiro (eds) *International/Intertextual Relations. Postmodern Readings of World Politics*, Toronto: Lexington.

—— (1989b) 'Spy vs. Spy: The Intertextual Power of International Intrigue', in J. Der Derian and M. Shapiro (eds) *International/Intertextual Relations. Postmodern Readings of World Politics*, Toronto: Lexington.

—— (1990) 'The (S)pace of International Relations: Simulation, Surveillance and Speed', *International Studies Quarterly* 34(3): 295–310.

—— (1991) 'S/N: International Theory, Balkanisation, and the New World Order', *Millennium* 20(3): 485–506.

—— (1992) *Antidiplomacy: Spies, Speed, Terror, and War*, Oxford: Blackwell.

—— (1993a) 'The CIA, Hollywood, and Sovereign Conspiracies', *Queens Quarterly* (Summer): 1–100.

—— (1993b) 'Fathers (and Sons), Mother Courage (and her Children), and the Dog (and the Beef)', in J. Rosenau (ed.) *Global Voices. Dialogues in International Relations*, Boulder, CO: Westview Press.

—— (1993c) 'The Value of Security: Hobbes, Marx, Nietzsche and Baudrillard', in G. Dillon and D. Campbell (eds) *The Political Subject of Violence*, Manchester: Manchester University Press.

—— (1993d) 'Diplomacy', entry in *Oxford Companion to Politics of the World*, Oxford: Oxford University Press.

—— (1994a) 'The Pen, the Sword, and the Smart Bomb: Criticism in the Age of Video', *Alternatives* 19(1): 133–40.

—— (1994b) 'Simulation: The Highest Stage of Capitalism?', in D. Kellner (ed.) *Baudrillard: A Critical Reader*, Oxford: Blackwell.

—— (1995) 'A Reinterpretation of Realism: Genealogy, Semiology, Dromology', paper for a seminar on New Thinking in International History, University of Chicago, 6 November 1993, in James Der Derian (ed.) *International Theory: Critical Investigations*, New York: SUNY Press, pp. 363–76.

—— (forthcoming) *Virtual Security*, New York: Free Press.

—— and Shapiro, Michael (eds) (1989) *International/Intertextual Relations. Postmodern Readings of World Politics*, Toronto: Lexington.

Works by other authors

Ashley, Richard and Walker, Rob (1990) 'Speaking the Language of Exile: Dissident Thought in International Studies', *International Studies Quarterly* 34(3): 259–68.

Baudrillard, Jean (1981) *Simulacres et simulation*, Paris: Galilée.

Bauman, Zygmunt (1992a) 'Soil, Blood and Identity', *Sociological Review* 40(4): 675–701.

——(1992b) *Mortality, Immortality & Other Life Strategies*, Cambridge: Polity.

Bernstein, Richard (1991) *The New Constellation*, Cambridge: Polity.

Bull, Hedley (1977) *The Anarchical Society*, London: Macmillan.

Campbell, David (1992) *Writing Security. United States Foreign Policy and the Politics of Identity*, Minneapolis, MN: University of Minnesota Press.

Connolly, William (1991) *Identity/Difference. Democratic Negotiations of Political Paradox*, London: Cornell University Press.

Constantinou, Costas (1993) 'Late Modern Diplomacies', *Millennium* 22(1): 89–96.

Descombes, Vincent (1979) *Le même et l'autre*, Paris: Les Editions de Minuit.

Foucault, Michel (1975) *Surveiller et punir*, Paris: Gallimard.

——(1977) 'Nietzsche, Genealogy, History', in M. Foucault, *Language, Counter-memory, Practice. Selected Essays and Interviews*, Oxford: Blackwell.

Giddens, Anthony (1984) *The Constitution of Society*, Cambridge: Polity.

Harland, Richard (1987) *Superstructuralism*, London: Methuen.

Hoffman, Mark (1991) 'Restructuring, Reconstruction, Reinscription, Rearticulation. Four Voices in Critical International Theory', *Millennium* 20(2): 169–85.

Keenan, Tom (1987) 'The "Paradox" of Knowledge and Power: Reading Foucault on a Bias', *Political Theory* 15(1): 5–37.

Keohane, Robert (1988) 'International Institutions: Two Approaches', *International Studies Quarterly* 32(4): 379–96.

Krishna, Sankaran (1993) 'The Importance of Being Ironic: a Postcolonial View on Critical International Relations Theory', *Alternatives* 18(3): 385–417.

Kristeva, Julia (1980) *Desire in Language*, Oxford: Blackwell.

——(1986) 'Revolution in Poetic Language', in T. Moi (ed.) *The Kristeva Reader*, Oxford: Blackwell.

Lapid, Yosef (1989) 'The Third Debate: On the Prospects of International Theory in a Post-Positivist Era', *International Studies Quarterly* 33(3): 235–54.

Lash, Scott (1988) 'Discourse or Figure? Postmodernism as a "Regime of Signification"', *Theory, Culture & Society* 5(2–3): 311–36.

——(1993) 'Reflexive Modernization: The Aesthetic Dimension', *Theory, Culture & Society* 10(1): 1–23.

Luke, Timothy (1991) 'The Discipline of Security Studies and the Codes of Containment: Learning from Kuwait', *Alternatives* 16(3): 315–44.

——(1993) 'Discourses of Disintegration, Texts of Transformation: Re-Reading Realism in the New World Order', *Alternatives* 18(2): 229–58.

Lyon, David (1993) 'An Electronic Panopticon? A Sociological Critique of Surveillance Theory', *Sociological Review* 41(4): 653–78.

Norris, Christopher (1992) *Uncritical Theory. Postmodernism, Intellectuals and the Gulf War*, London: Lawrence & Wishart.

Onuf, Nicholas (1989) *World of Our Making. Rules and Rule in Social Theory and International Relations*, Columbia, SC: University of South Carolina Press.

——(1991) 'Sovereignty: Outline of a Conceptual History', *Alternatives* 16(4): 425–46.

Pels, Dick (1992) 'Kennispolitiek. Een gebruiksaanwijzing voor Foucault', *Kennis en Methode* 16(2): 39–62.

Rengger, Nick (1992) 'No Time like the Present? Postmodernism and Political Theory', *Political Studies* 40(3): 561–70.

Ruggie, John (1993) 'Territoriality and Beyond: Problematizing Modernity in International Relations', *International Organization* 47(1): 139–74.

Sarup, Madan (1988) *An Introductory Guide to Post-structuralism and Postmodernism*, London: Harvester Wheatsheaf.

Shapiro, Michael (1989) 'Textualizing Global Politics', in James Der Derian and Michael Shapiro (eds) *International/Intertextual Relations. Postmodern Readings of World Politics*, Lexington, MA: Lexington Books.

——(1991) 'Sovereignty and Exchange in the Orders of Modernity', *Alternatives* 16(4): 447–77.

——and Neubauer, Deane (1989) 'Spatiality and Policy Discourse: Reading the Global City', *Alternatives* 14(3): 301–25.

Szakolczai, Arpad (1993a) 'From Governmentality to the Genealogy of Subjectivity: On Foucault's Path in the 1980's', *EUI Working Papers in Political and Social Sciences, 93/4*, Florence: European University Institute.

——(1993b) 'Nietzsche's Genealogical Method: Presentation and Application', *EUI Working Papers in Political and Social Sciences, 93/7*, Florence: European University Institute.

Virilio, Paul (1989) (in Dutch) *Het Horizon-Negatief*, trans. A. Mulder and P. Riemens, Amsterdam: Duizend & Een; from his *L'horizon négatif* (1984).

——(1993) *L'insécurité du territoire*, Paris: Galilée; first published in 1976 by Edition Stock.

Wæver, Ole (1995) 'Resisting the Temptation of Post Foreign Policy Analysis', in Walter Carlsnaes and Steve Smith (eds) *European Foreign Policy: The EC and Changing Perspectives in Europe*, London: Sage, pp. 238–73.

Walker, Rob (1993) *Inside/Outside: International Relations as Political Theory*, Cambridge: Cambridge University Press.

Walt, Stephen (1991) 'The Renaissance of Security Studies', *International Studies Quarterly* 35(2): 211–39.

14 Conclusion

Iver B. Neumann

> Me: two million words.
> (Jean Paul Sartre)
>
> I am one thing, my writings are another.
> (Friedrich Nietzsche)

'The so-called "I" is merely a unique combination of partially conflicting "corporate we's"', Kenneth Burke (1959: 263) remarked around the time when most of the contributors to this volume were born. The discipline of International Relations (IR) has, by treating its own history as a series of debates or a set of paradigms or traditions or schools, come to honour this epigram. It tends to see its practitioners as nothing more than incidental sets of views and specialities. Perhaps one could think of the weave of this volume as an attempt to reverse Burke's epigram. We started with the 'corporate we' of the discipline of International Relations, identified twelve threads of authorships, and scrutinized them in their own right. The time has come to step back and have a look at the weave once again, and to comment on the stuff of our masters' theorizing, on how they have taken care of their IR selves in charting their trajectories, and finally on what kind of weave the discipline of IR may be said to be when judged on the strength of those trajectories taken together. Before all that, however, it may be meet to honour all the calls for reflection which rise from these chapters by reflecting a little on what has been gained by our exercise.

Contrary to IR, other social disciplines such as anthropology, sociology and for that matter history tend to represent themselves in terms of genealogies of their own great and good. We have apparently followed their example, and reinstated the Author as the central figure of the discipline. Inasmuch as this is a move which brings IR further into line with other social inquiry, it could be argued that what is going on here is the 'normalization' of a discipline, in the sense that its self-representation edges closer to that of its cousins.

That such a disciplining thrust makes its presence felt in these pages, seems to me undeniable. Whereas what is seen here is definitely a return to authorships, however, the status conferred on the Author seems to be rather different from what is still traditional and therefore 'normal' in the social sciences. The point becomes obvious if one compares the way authors are treated here and in the only previous book on IR masters, Kenneth

Thompson's *Masters of International Thought* from 1980. This work, which was among the main sources of inspiration for the present volume, examined a previous generation of IR scholars. In doing so, Thompson found it wholly unproblematic to treat his masters as bounded individuals who each had a sovereign voice.

This is hardly the way we have treated our masters in the making. We have not seen the authorial signature as the mark of foundation on the texts in question, and we have not attempted to put a Sartrean equation mark between texts and person. As Jef Huysmans writes about 'his' author, ' "Der Derian" is understood to be a space-body which offers a home for particular intersections of many (inter)texts'. The above chapters all seem to go about their work in this way. When Roland Barthes (1977) hailed the death of the Author in a celebrated essay, he also made a point of stressing how what he called the 'scriptor' remains as one thread in the weave that is his or her authorship. If the chapters in this volume have chosen to unweave these intersections of texts by the thread that is the trace of the author, it does not mean that that trace will lead back to a *Sovereign* Author. After the death of the Sovereign Author, we found the author to be alive and well as a focus for our treatment.

What kind of treatment have we meted out to those authors? There is always an element of uneasiness in striking up a dialogue with one's masters. Derrida reported on one such moment of uneasiness when he reflected on the experience of lecturing about his former master Foucault in the following manner:

> Now, the disciple's consciousness, when he starts, I would not say to dispute, but to engage in dialogue with the master or, better, to articulate the indeterminable and silent dialogue which made him into a disciple – this disciple's consciousness is an unhappy consciousness.
>
> (Derrida 1978: 31)

Since there cannot be a discipline without a steady consecration of new disciples, however, such uneasiness seems to be part of the hard-wiring of intellectual life, and therefore inescapable. The more pressing challenge is perhaps to avoid letting this uneasiness turn into an unnecessarily violent treatment, so that master-making evolves into master-bashing. As pointed out by Erik Ringmar, this temptation springs not only from the tensions inherent in the relationship itself, but also from the political economy of academia. As he puts it, 'To make straw men out of the scholars of the earlier generation and to beat them as hard as possible is thought to be the only way to make a career for yourself'. One hopes the readings presented here have stuck to the straight and narrow in this procedural regard, and turn to the fruits of those readings.

THE STUFF OF IR THEORIZING

The introduction to this volume conceptualizes the present polyphony of IR voices as the tail-end of a 'fourth debate' between rationalists and reflectivists. Rationalists are presented as a tightly knit group of neo-realists and neo-liberalists who agree on about 90 per cent, while keeping up a very private battle about how to settle the remaining 10 per cent by means of empirical tests. Reflectivists, on the other hand, are presented as starting from the premise that the discipline is basically 'just one more expression of the dominant attitudes of modernity, a hunt for objectivity, control and security'. Indeed, my co-editor goes so far as to see the mode of the debate as one of war. As he also acknowledges, however, this volume has done nothing if it has not shown that such generalizations about the state of the discipline are fast approaching, or have indeed already passed, their due dates. Large IR departments seem to want a reflectivist on board these days, and even the home of the rationalist neo-neo synthesis, *International Organization*, is no longer as staunchly rationalist in its publishing profile as it was only a few years ago.

What is happening is definitely not some kind of dialectical move towards consensus. Rather, a new dialogue is being forged out of a dying shouting-match. The characteristic lack of *rapport* reported by Stefano Guzzini, as Richard Gilpin failed to engage Richard Ashley's meta-critique of neo-realism in 1986, is already a decade away. In 1995, on the contrary, James Der Derian was able to put together a reader on international theory which featured a number of articles written by masters treated in Thompson's book (Morgenthau, Wight), as well as by our masters in the making (Alker, Elshtain, Keohane, Walker, Wendt), and to have a card-carrying member of the English School (Watson) write an introduction for it into the bargain. The success of such confidence-building measures as this one suggests that the blunt English word 'war' no longer covers the discipline's *modus operandi*. Instead, the Greek 'polemics' – which has war as a root meaning but nevertheless may be used to cover a whole range of other relations also – is once again a more appropriate term.

The difference over what stuff to theorize is still very much with us, however. Among our masters in the making, Waltz and Gilpin unabashedly stick to the state as the Archimedes point from which to theorize, and avail themselves of what are referred to as the microeconomic theory of the firm and the economic approach respectively. A quote from Onuf may be used by way of comment: 'If international relations are purely anarchic, then Political Economy is their perfected description.' Yet, as Onuf is quick to add, if the international relations of states are subsumed in a world politics of a heteronomy of actors, then that description is less than perfect, indeed downright misleading. So, in contradistinction to a concept like 'economy', which privileges a certain kind of already fixed and rational actor, Walker offers the concept of 'culture', and he does so exactly because it may open up the field:

> Thus the significance of the concept of culture in the analysis of contemporary international relations is not that it offers a convenient category of socio-scientific explanations, or a convincing account of human nature, or a helpful classification of the difficult forms of human

practices there have been. Rather it hints at all the uncertainties of modernities, and at a multitude of struggles – on the grounds of tradition or postmodernity, of gender, race, religion and ethnicity, of socialism and capitalism, of the Other, of the future, of the local community, of the state and of the planet – to reconstitute the conditions of human existence in the face of tremendous structural transformation.

(Walker 1991: 12–13)

Waltz's parsimonious approach and Walker's thick description throw up rather different snapshots of world politics. Furthermore, differences as to what constitutes proper raw material for theorizing lead to different views of what qualifies as a theory. As Mouritzen reminds us in his Popperian analysis of Waltz, Popper insists that the spatio-temporal surroundings of a theory's conception belong to the sphere of gossip. Onuf and other constructivists must, however, insist not only on the advantage of rooting theorizing firmly in time and space, but on the inevitability of doing so, and on the inevitability of letting go of the idea of theoretical parsimony. By the token of double hermeneutics, the theorists and the theorized are both historically situated, and since this predicament cannot be avoided, it should be made explicit and reflected upon.

The tension between what may be referred to as the nomothetic and ideational imperatives upon the IR scholar – whether he or she is out to capture a generalized insight afloat in time or space or the logic of a historically lodged sequence – is a theme in all these chapters. Two examples will suffice. What separates Ringmar's early and late Wendts from one another seems to be that the latter is more receptive to Nietzsche's claim that only that which has no history can be defined. Again, Anna Leander writes that

In Badie's work there is a continuous tension between the particular, the non-transferable on the one hand, and the universal, the generalizable on the other. He emphasizes the need to develop universal concepts, to speak one language, and to study 'Reality', yet his studies are constructed around the claim that there are no generalizable explanations, that what has to be accounted for is the singular, that concepts change meaning in different contexts and cannot be transferred from one context to another, and that ultimately the rationalities change.

Most of this volume's masters in the making, and all the master-makers, see the nomothetic theoretical ideal as at least problematic and at most violent. And yet, there is little by way of explicit theorizing of how the allegedly ideational studies of the discipline relate to one another. Here we have a topic which is sorely in need of more theorizing. Just as the author remains after the death of the Sovereign Author, there is at least a possibility that a universalism, however razor-thin, will remain after the death of Universalism. By the same token, one of the key concepts of world politics, 'humanity', seems to be ripe for theorizing as the space for dialogue inside the fourth debate widens, or develops into a fifth debate.

It is fast becoming a cliché that, whereas in a former epoch the overriding political question was 'What is to be done?', the question which rules the roost now is 'Who are we?' At least this generalization seems to hold when the stuff which is theorized by the masters in the making under discussion here is compared with the stuff theorized by the masters of the former generation treated in Thompson's book. Thompson offered his readings under headings such as normative foundations, power, conflict, order. His opening sentence went like this: 'It is not surprising that theologians and religious historians are in the forefront of those who search for a normative foundation for politics' (Thompson 1980: 1). Although his book was published only sixteen years ago, it is already hard to imagine a similar opening to a book on the discipine. Some theorists will still be preoccupied with foundations and ethics (but they will not even necessarily be the same theorists these days), but not a single one of our masters in the making comes even close to being a theologian or a religious historian. The discipline may seem to have been thoroughly secularized.

If one compares the stuff theorized by Thompson's masters with that theorized by ours, the major new 'abouts' are political economy and identity. While it is hardly fruitful to see the preoccupation with identity as a substitute for the one with religion, it is none the less tantalizing that they both make a concern out of the importance of meaning in political life. In a Durkheimian perspective, religion is society's celebration of itself. Celebration of the self is also at the core of much identity politics. There does seem, therefore, to be a certain logic whereby identity studies have been substituted for religious speculation.

THE CARE OF THE IR SELF

If collective identities may be counted among the stuff which our masters are particularly eager to theorize, then it is by their very theorizing that they shape personal identities for themselves as IR theorists. 'A reflexively ordered narrative of self-identity provides the means of giving coherence to the finite lifespan, given changing external circumstances' (Giddens 1991: 215). How have our masters taken care of their IR selves in responding to the linguistic and non-linguistic elements of IR discourse and of world politics at large?

It may in principle be possible to become a master of certain crafts without consecrating disciples; from the realm of painting, van Gogh comes to mind as one example. Yet, in IR and probably throughout academia, it is at least a great help and probably necessary to acquire a number of master-makers who will read, apply, expand and comment on one's work. This is not simply a question of self-aggrandizement, but rather a case of the widespread urge felt by most people who think they do something important to let others know about it. In a word, good students have their uses. It comes as no surprise, therefore, that most of our masters in the making have put a lot of energy into supervising doctoral students. Teaching remains part and parcel of the master's craft.

Yet, by the same token, the demands that teaching and research make on one's time must often come into conflict. One may think about this in terms of the two general master scripts which Charles Taylor (1989) sees hovering over contemporary western society. On the one hand, there is an anti-hero script which affirms everyday life. In our case, everyday life may be taken to mean supervision, committee work, lecturing, etc. On the other hand, there is the hero script – one is supposed to open new horizons, come up with new insights, conquer some turf, name a research programme. This is the script of choice in this volume, as it is in so many other circumstances. Those who seek a narrative other than the affirmation of everyday academic life will ask what the trajectories of our masters may tell us about the pros and cons of caring for the IR self in this or that way.

Theory is always theory for, and so one way of answering this question may be to ponder whom, except for their own doctoral students and immediate colleagues, our masters actually choose to address. Gilpin invokes a realist tradition from Machiavelli to Morgenthau, where the task is one of providing counsel to princes. Walker responds to this commitment to serve the state in a fashion recalling the early members of the Frankfurt critical school, and goes looking for an acting and critical subject in world politics to which he may serve as counsel. He finds it in a category of 'critical social movements'. Whereas Walker's practice is also similar to the modern ideal of the '*intellectuel engagé*', Wendt is presented as a specimen of another modern ideal of the intellectual – 'a person who studies reality only indirectly – by studying the processes through which reality is made'.

Der Derian seems to renounce the counsel bit favoured by Walker, but signals a similar interest in marginalized groups by teaching in prisons, and by using his work to foreground the 'muffled cries' from voices traditionally understood to reside at the margins of world politics. He also responds to the fragmentation of the public sphere by publishing in a non-academic but thematically specialized magazine like *Wired*. Elshtain stands out as the only full-blooded public intellectual of the lot, the only one who finds it worth-while to publish copiously for a general public. Her loneliness among our masters in this regard is an important fact to which I will return below.

With the possible exception of Elshtain, then, our masters prefer to make themselves inside the confines of the discipline. It may be no coincidence that the two masters on the make who probably define today's mainstream more than anybody else, are also the two who seem to follow the tightest career scripts. Waltz seems to have made it a speciality to publish only works whose epistemological and ontological presuppositions are all mainstream, but whose conclusions are all *contre-courant*. The crowning example must be his thesis that more widely dispersed nuclear powers may lead to a safer world (Waltz 1981). Since, as Hans Mouritzen puts it, Waltz makes a point of being the Muhammed Ali of IR, always seemingly fighting with his guard down, not to take him on has perhaps become the nearest thing in international relations theory to refusing a dare. (Mouritzen also holds that the reason why Waltz can afford this pose is that, given the way he sets it all up, the only one who can falsify his claims and knock him out is himself. Anyone who would like to follow Waltz's example in this regard may like to treat this rejoinder as more than by the way.)

It seems to be no coincidence either that perhaps the major upshoot of the Waltzian debates is a book edited by the other tightly scripted master, Keohane (1986). Keohane has persistently chosen to theorize the stuff which has at any one time been the major theoretical concern of the mainstream, be that the interface of politics and economics, intergovernmentalism, hegemonic stability theory, neo-realism, neo-liberalism, post-Cold War European integration, and who better than Keohane himself would know what is next, perhaps constructivism? His contributions have, furthermore, consistently held the same temperature as the ongoing international relations which he has set out to theorize. They were warm when the case in point was transgovernmental ties in the optimistic early 1970s, tepid when it was the interdependence of 'the West' as that optimism began to fade, cold when it was the hegemonic stability of the USA during what has been called the Second Cold War, and once again warmer after the fall of the Wall. If Waltz has made a point of being *contre-courant*, Keohane has definitely been or perhaps even defined what it means to be *au courant*. Michael Suhr makes a similar point above when he writes about Keohane that 'When one reads his advice to the reflectivists – that they are too marginal, are invisible – one can get the impression of a writer who is very much aware of how pragmatic one needs to be in order to be heard by mainstream scholars of International Relations'.

At the other extreme from Waltz and Keohane, there is Onuf, who has consistently ploughed his own furrow without seeming to care too much about what has been going down in the rest of the discipline. Between these two extremes, Walker and Der Derian have both declared themselves as following Julia Kristeva (1986) in taking up a self-imposed exile on the margins of the discipline. The margin, however, is still very much part of the discipline (and, as a sometime Russianist, it strikes me as a rather cosy place to be an exile). Both Walker and Der Derian have surely seen to it that their voices have not been so far removed from the mainstream as to be altogether inaudible and illegible. They have, as it were, consistently engaged the mainstream by addressing the concerns which it has done its best to occlude. As argued in the introduction and echoed in this conclusion, the mainstream does indeed seem to have changed somewhat as a result of their efforts.

Ole Wæver's Ruggie also excels in the art of nudging the course of the mainstream in some new direction. He is made out to have done it, however, not by placing himself on the margins, but rather by making his moves so close to the mainstream that he has often been considered as being either part of it or something like its official dissident. Since the jury of mastermakers is always out, one of the things to which one may look forward to is the comparisons which future master-makers will make of Keohane's and Ruggie's respective roles in shaping and defining mainstream thought over the past fifteen years.

The chapters above also suggest other master paths. Vincent is the team player who self-consciously takes up his stance inside a certain school and puts all his efforts into propelling forward what he sees as not only his own but the entire English School's research programme. If Vincent insisted on swimming in one school, Alker, on the contrary, has roamed from one school to the other and spawned incontinently in all of them. And then there is Wendt, that epitome of a bridge-builder.

THE WEAVE OF IR

The ways in which our masters in the making have severally cared for their IR selves do not seem to be all that different from the way Thompson's previous generation of masters went about it. If we step back from the individual threads of authorships to survey once again the weave of IR in its entirety, however, one difference stands out. The isclation of the discipline from the larger non-specialized conversation on world politics seems to be growing. If theory is always theory for, so scientific disciplines are also always there for something and somebody. In most cases, a discipline may not be seen as a goal in itself – those who want self-referential reflection tend to congregate in the discipline of philosophy. The previous generation of IR masters counted a Butterfield and a Morgenthau in its ranks. Theirs would be immediately recognizable names in most English-speaking intellectual households of the 1950s. Where Britain is concerned, one could probably add E. H. Carr's name as well. How many of our masters in the making may count on a readership or even on name recognition beyond the rather tightly drawn confines of the discipline itself? Probably not a single one. The discipline's voices speak, but they seem increasingly to speak to one another.

The previous generation's masters often made a point of being organic intellectuals in the sense that they contributed to the running policy debates of their day by writing book-length essays and the occasional newspaper article. With the already mentioned exception of Elshtain, to which one may add Ruggie, our masters simply do not seem to take an interest in the print media which uphold an international public sphere. It may be argued that this is not a result of their own specialization, but of their having been crowded out of the newspapers by a group of columnists which is itself becoming ever more specialized. One may also plead the case that the public sphere has itself narrowed, particularly in the USA. Perhaps so, but as long as publications such as the *New York Review of Books*, the *New Left Review*, the *New Statesman* and for that matter the *International Herald Tribune* and the *Financial Times* sport articles by the masters of history, economics and anthropology, this predicament must still at least in some degree be a result of their own choices about where and what to publish. The seemingly growing intellectual isolation of IR in this regard is in no small measure a result of the rather narrow publishing practices of its masters. By the same token, IR masters no longer seem to be in the running for becoming masters of social inquiry at large. Philosophy can afford to be a self-referentiating pursuit, and even to celebrate itself as such. It would be surprising if the discipline of International Relations should be able to afford the same.

At first glance, there is a paradox here, since the growing specialization of scholarship in the discipline should make it easier for each and every master to peddle his or her special expertise in the public realm. This paradox is only apparent, however. The reason why a Butterfield or a Morgenthau was asked to address a wider audience and was then listened to was of course not because of their specialized research agenda, but for the very opposite reason: they were thought of as being able to offer a general view. Contemporary IR masters should be expected to be able to do the same. A Derrida can publish on stuff which has been widely theorized by IR scholars such as nuclear deterrence, European identity, the collapse of the Soviet Union, and racism, and his publications reach a world audience. There is no principle reason why an IR scholar should not at least try to do the same.

Perhaps there lies buried a general warning to the discipline here. The present division of labour in the social sciences is a result of developments which stretch some 80 to 120 years back in time, to the heyday of a previous epoch when the production of knowledge was related to other societal processes in a way rather different from what is the case now. All around us, the weaves of social disciplines are unravelling. Economists become geographers, anthropologists become historians, philosophers become political scientists, and on and on in an accelerating swirl. New subdisciplines emerge – in IR there is international theory, critical strategic studies, comparative foreign policy, international ethics, diplomatic studies, geopolitics, international political economy, area specializations of all kinds. When a good doctoral thesis is deemed to have veered too far from the IR mainstream, it may crop up in a publisher's catalogue under Cultural Studies. This growing eclecticism is part of the present condition, and it has its advantages. However, it certainly increases the pressure on IR scholars to set aside chunks of their time to address not only their research specialities, but also the big picture. Interestingly, it may be that the mainstream of the discipline is in more need of responding to this challenge than its margins. What is at issue, in other words, is not a call to homogenize, streamline, or silence writing practices. On the contrary, it is a call to open up the increasing number of little pockets which are forming inside and on the borderlines of the discipline so that the larger conversation on the stuff of interest to the discipline will not simply move elsewhere.

Two very different charges may be levelled in this regard. One is Henri Lefebvre's (1991: 24), that ' "theoretical space" is already nothing more than the egocentric thinking of specialized western intellectuals – and indeed may soon be nothing more than an entirely separated, schizoid consciousness'. The other is R. B. J. Walker's, that 'Theories of international relations are more interesting as aspects of contemporary world politics that need to be explained than as explanations of contemporary world politics' (Walker 1993: 6). Well yes, on the one hand social disciplines are hemmed in, and on the other they are part of the seamless web that is contemporary world politics. A partial answer to these charges of isolation and of lacking a project different from the mainstream may be to lodge publications elsewhere, in publications which are not 'IR'.

So what about the cohesion of the discipline? Will the weave be unravelled all the way down? Hardly. A subterranean theme of the reinscription of the discipline which is going on in this volume and elsewhere, perhaps even the warp to the weft of the authorships, is the importance of one particular kind of social space – that of the university. The masters shuttle from one university to the other – to lecture, to participate in a conference or a workshop, to sit on a doctoral or tenure committee. If their texts meet inside the covers of books or as entries in some bibliography, their 'space-bodies' also meet, and the meetings add to the integration of the discipline. The institution of the university is the non-linguistic discursive element which holds the discipline together in lieu of shared epistemological and ontological presuppositions. For it cannot be denied that the readings presented here have done nothing if they have not demonstrated the extent to which epistemological and also ontological questions are contested in present-day IR. So apart from a shared interest in emerging world politics, which is not exclusive to IR scholars, what keeps the discipline together is the spatiality of universities and the activities they frequently host.

That is not to say that the discipine is not 'about' something. The stuff to be theorized is definitely still there for the asking. Indeed, disciplines *must* in one sense or another be 'about' something, and these 'abouts' lend them a certain cohesion. It was pointed out in the introduction how the institutionalized academic discipline of IR owes its existence to the perceived need to strike up a conversation about how to avoid a repetition of the First World War. As may be seen in a number of the chapters above, the role of violence in human conflict is still among the stuff of IR theorizing. One should, for example, expect a discipline of IR to be able to say a number of interesting things about what has happened in the former Yugoslavia. It is evident from the uncertainty with which we have tried to relate to these wars and the often bland comments we have had to offer, however, that our theorizing of this aspect of world politics is wanting. If it is not exactly a blank spot, we definitely have not worked it into the weave of the discipline in as thorough a manner as we could and should have done.

Of course, the wider 'about' involved here is order. Nicholas Onuf has been quoted above to the effect that 'Only if political theory reaches beyond the causal sequence of authority, law, and order, which is at its heart, and searches for the origins, supports, and limit of each, do we have a chance of explaining international order'. It is a long time since the human sciences started to treat societal integration as not something which explains other things, but something which is itself in need of explanation. Order in world society is an 'about' which must remain constitutive of a discipline of IR. One notes that the success of Wendt's constructivist article 'Anarchy Is what States Make of It' (as well as his inclusion here as a master in the making) seems to be mainly due to a widespread feeling in the discipline that the order/anarchy nexus still remains a, or even the, key question, and that a dialogue among rationalists and reflectivists may go some way towards deepening our understanding of it.

Another 'about' which is sorely in need of more theorizing may be found at the interstice of the interests and identities of human collectives. For example, the national interest remains an often invoked but seldom defined entity that could do with some more theorizing. Those in the discipline who hold it dear have still not picked up the gauntlet thrown down by Clifford Geertz over thirty years ago, when he wrote that

> The main defects of the interest theory are that its psychology is too anemic and its sociology too muscular. Lacking a developed analysis of motivation, it has been constantly forced to oscillate between a narrow and superficial utilitarianism that sees men as impelled by rational calculation of their consciously recognized personal advantage and a broader, but no less superficial, heroism that speaks with a studied vagueness of men's ideas as somehow 'reflecting', 'expressing', 'corresponding to', 'emerging from', or 'conditioned by' their social commitments.
>
> (Geertz 1964: 64)

The growing number of people in the field who focus on identities, and particularly state identities, have still to spell out just how identities translate into interests. As Erik Ringmar puts it above, 'Just as we can only be a someone in relation to others who recognize us, we can never want a something all by ourselves'.

So, how to capture the stuff of the discipline of IR, the trajectories of its masters in the making and its place in the world in one image to stand at the end of this volume? Perhaps one may think of the sum of relations between human collectives as a world society, and draw on Yuriy Lotman's image of the semiosphere to depict it:

> imagine a museum hall where exhibits from different periods are on display, along with inscriptions in known and unknown languages, and instructions for decoding them; besides there are the explanations composed by the museum staff, plans for tours and rules for the behaviour of the visitors. Imagine also in this hall tour-leaders and the visitors and imagine all this as a single mechanism (which *in a certain sense* it is). This is an image of the semiosphere. ... In fact, everything continued in the actual memory of culture is directly or indirectly part of that culture's synchrony.
>
> (Lotman 1990: 126–7)

The discipline may not agree upon the status which should be given to the different human collectives which make up world society, or on the basic mode or modes of relations between them. And yet, perhaps one may think of all our masters in the making as particularly agile hall tour-leaders to a world society which is always coming into its own.

NOTE

I should like to thank Barry Buzan, Lene Hansen and Ole Wæver for comments on earlier drafts.

REFERENCES

Barthes, Roland (1977) 'The Death of the Author', in Roland Barthes, *Image Music Text*, London: Fontana, pp. 142–8; essay first published in 1968.
Burke, Kenneth (1959) *Attitudes toward History*, Los Altos, CA: Hermes.
Der Derian, James (1995) *International Theory: Critical Investigations*, New York: SUNY Press.
Derrida, Jacques (1978) 'Cogito and the History of Madness', in Jacques Derrida, *Writing and Difference*, London: Routledge, pp. 31–63.
Geertz, Clifford (1964) 'Ideology as a Cultural System', in David E. Apter (ed.) *Ideology and Discontent*, New York: Free Press, pp. 47–76.
Giddens, Anthony (1991) *Modernity and Self-Identity: Self and Society in the Late Modern Age*, Cambridge: Polity.
Keohane, Robert O. (ed.) (1986) *Neo-realism and Its Critics*, New York: Columbia University Press.
Kristeva, Julia (1986) 'A New Type of Intellectual: The Dissident', in Julia Kristeva, *The Kristeva Reader*, ed. Toril Moi, Oxford: Blackwell, pp. 292–300; essay first published in 1977.
Lefebvre, Henri (1991[1974]) *The Production of Space*, Oxford: Blackwell.
Lotman, Yuriy (1990) *Universe of the Mind: a Semiotic Theory of Culture*, London: I. B. Tauris.
Taylor, Charles (1989) *Sources of the Self: The Making of Modern Identity*, Cambridge: Cambridge University Press.
Thompson, Kenneth W. (1980) *Masters of International Thought: Major Twentieth-Century Theorists and the World Crisis*, Baton Rouge, LA: Louisiana State University Press.
Walker, R. B. J. (1991) 'The Concept of Culture in the Theory of International Relations', in Jongsuk Chay (ed.) *Culture and International Relations*, New York: Praeger, pp. 3–17.
——(1993) *Inside/Outside: International Relations as Political Theory*, Cambridge: Cambridge University Press.
Waltz, Kenneth N. (1981) *The Spread of Nuclear Weapons: More May Be Better*, Adelphi Papers no. 171, London: International Institute for Strategic Studies.

Index